Revolutionary Patriots

of

Frederick County

Maryland

1775-1783

Henry C. Peden, Jr.

HERITAGE BOOKS
2006

HERITAGE BOOKS
AN IMPRINT OF HERITAGE BOOKS, INC.

Books, CDs, and more—Worldwide

For our listing of thousands of titles see our website at
www.HeritageBooks.com

Published 2006 by
HERITAGE BOOKS, INC.
Publishing Division
65 East Main Street
Westminster, Maryland 21157-5026

Copyright © 1995 Henry C. Peden, Jr.

All rights reserved. No part of this book may be reproduced or transmitted in any form or by any means, electronic or mechanical, including photocopying, recording or by any information storage and retrieval system without written permission from the author, except for the inclusion of brief quotations in a review.

International Standard Book Number: 978-1-58549-307-4

INTRODUCTION

This book has been compiled for the purpose of serving as a research tool for locating Marylanders from Frederick County who served in the military during the Revolutionary War, 1775-1783 (soldiers), pledged their service (associators), rendered material aid to the army, took the Oath of Fidelity (jurors), served in an office or on a committee at the town, county or state levels, or otherwise contributed in some fashion as patriots to support the freedom of the American colonies from the rule of Great Britain.

This volume is the sixth in a series on patriots of Maryland. Many of the entries give dates of birth, death, marriage and other genealogical data. This work is offered with the hope that it will encourage interest and membership in such patriotic organizations as The Sons of the American Revolution, The Daughters of the American Revolution, and The Society of the Cincinnati.

Each entry in this book has been documented from primary and secondary record sources, and a key to that documentation has been implemented within the text. A letter followed by a number is the code used for a source and the page within the source. For example, "[Ref: A-55]" indicates that the reference is "Archives of Maryland, Volume 18, page 55." The following sources were consulted in the preparation of this book:

A = *Archives of Maryland, Volume 18*. "Muster Rolls and Other Records of Service of Maryland Troops in the American Revolution, 1775-1783" (Baltimore: The Maryland Historical Society, 1900)

B = Clements, S. Eugene and Wright, F. Edward. *The Maryland Militia in the Revolutionary War* (Silver Spring, Maryland: Family Line Publications, 1987)

C = Carothers, Bettie. *9000 Men Who Took the Oath of Allegiance and Fidelity to Maryland During the Revolution, Volume I* (Lutherville, Maryland: Privately Compiled by the Author, 1978)

D = *Maryland Historical Society Manuscript MS.1814: Revolutionary War Collection* (Maryland Historical Society Manuscripts Division)

E = *Maryland Historical Magazine*. "Journal of the Committee of Observation of the Middle District of Frederick County, September 12, 1775 - October 24, 1776." Volume XI, pp. 50-66, 158-175, 237-260, Volume XII, pp. 10-21, 302-321 (Baltimore: Maryland Historical Society, 1917)

F = Scharf, J. Thomas. *History of Western Maryland, Volume I* (Baltimore: Regional Publishing Company, 1968, reprint)

G = Brumbaugh, Gaius M. *Maryland Records: Colonial, Revolutionary, County and Church From Original Sources, Volume II.* (Baltimore: Genealogical Publishing Company, 1985, reprint)

H = Hodges, Margaret. *Unpublished Revolutionary Records of Maryland Volume 1* (Baltimore: Privately Compiled by the Author, circa 1941)

I = Williams, T. J. C. and McKinsey, Folger. *History of Frederick County, Maryland* (Baltimore: Regional Publishing Company, 1979, reprint), 2 volumes.

J = McGhee, Mrs. Carl W. *Maryland Revolutionary War Pensioners, War of 1812, and Indian Wars* (Washington, DC: Privately Compiled, 1952)

K = McGhee, Lucy K. *Maryland Pension Abstracts: Revolution, War of 1812, and Indian Wars* (Washington, D.C.: Privately Compiled, 1966)

L = Miller, Richard B. "Some Little-Known Data Regarding Maryland Signers of the Oath of Fidelity." *Maryland Genealogical Society Bulletin*, Vol. 27, No. 1 (Baltimore: MD Genealogical Society, 1986)

M = *Western Maryland Genealogy* (New Market, Maryland: Catoctin Press, January, 1985 - July, 1995), 11 volumes.

N = *National Genealogical Society Quarterly*, Volume 30, No. 3 (1942), pp. 111-112, and Volume 25, No. 2 (1937), pp. 56-59

O = Schildknecht, Calvin E. *Monocacy and Catoctin, Volume III*

(Westminster, Maryland: Family Line Publications, 1994)

P = Papenfuse, Edward. *A Biographical Dictionary of the Maryland Legislature, 1635-1789* (Baltimore: Johns Hopkins Press, 1979)

Q = *Frederick County Court Minutes, 1779* (Original Record Books at the Maryland State Archives in Annapolis, Accession No. MdHR 6835)

R = Papenfuse, Edward et al. *An Inventory of Maryland State Papers, Vol. I, "The Era of the American Revolution, 1775-1789"* (Annapolis: Hall of Records Commission, 1977)

S = *Frederick County Court Minutes, 1778* (Original Record Books at the Maryland State Archives in Annapolis, Accession No. MdHR 6833)

T = White, Virgil D. *Genealogical Abstracts of Revolutionary War Pension Files* (Waynesboro, TN: National Historical Publishing Company, 1990), 4 volumes.

U = *Sons of the American Revolution, Maryland Society, Membership Applications (Approved Originals), 1889-1993* (Baltimore: University of Baltimore, Langsdale Library), Filed by Maryland State Numbers.

V = *Archives of Maryland, Volume 43.* "Journal and Correspondence of the State Council of Maryland, 1779-1780" (Baltimore: The Maryland Historical Society, 1924)

W = *Archives of Maryland, Volume 11.* "Journal of the Maryland Convention, July 26, 1775 - August 14, 1775," and "Journal and Correspondence of the Maryland Council of Safety, August 29, 1775-July 6, 1776" (Baltimore: The Maryland Historical Society, 1892)

X = *Archives of Maryland, Volume 12.* "Journal and Correspondence of the Maryland Council of Safety, July 7, 1776 - December 31, 1776" (Baltimore: The Maryland Historical Society, 1893)

Y = *Archives of Maryland, Volume 16.* "Journal and Correspondence of the Council of Safety, January 1, 1777 - March 20, 1777," and the "Journal and Correspondence of the State Council, March 20, 1777 - March 28, 1778" (Baltimore: The Maryland Historical Society, 1897)

Z = *Archives of Maryland, Volume 21.* "Journal and Corresponsondence of the Council of Maryland, April 1, 1778 - October 26, 1779" (Baltimore: The Maryland Historical Society, 1901)

It should also be noted that an entry indicating that someone had deserted or was missing should not necessarily reflect in an adverse light. The rather lax military discipline of the day did allow individuals to leave the service unannounced, return home to handle personal business, and oftentimes the individual returned to service in a short time. Naturally, many did desert, but seeing this entry on the muster role does not necessarily mean the individual absconded or went over to the other side.

Likewise, the taking of the Oath of Fidelity and Allegiance in 1777-1778 did not always mean that the person who took the oath was all that patriotic. Many men (who were age 18 and over) took the oath out of fear for their lives, to avoid a treble tax, to avoid losing their land, or perhaps to avoid the social stigma of being labelled a coward. Many Frederick Countians were true and unfailing patriots and should be recognized for it. Some lists of persons who took the oath in Frederick County are available at the Maryland Historical Society (Manuscript MS.1814), or in the Frederick County Court Minutes maintained at the Maryland State Archives. However, not all of these signers were included in the book by Bettie Carothers [see above]. These missing signers have been included in this work.

It was not possible to know exactly who all of the "patriots" of Frederick County were since many lists of soldiers in the militia and continental regiments are not extant. Further, many of these men could have served in any of the eight regiments in Maryland (including the German Regiment) or perhaps in another state. If a name should appear in this book and you know the soldier was not a Frederick County native or resident, please understand that it was thought best to include them when in doubt, rather than omit them altogether. Naturally, there will be unintentional omissions and errors in a book such as this. Corrected information is welcomed.

Henry C. Peden, Jr.
August 1, 1995

REVOLUTIONARY PATRIOTS OF
FREDERICK COUNTY, MARYLAND, 1775-1783

AARON, Levy. Private who enlisted in the German Regiment and served at the Battle of White Plains on September 5, 1778, under Lt. Col. Ludwick Weltner [Ref: A-267].

ABEL, Elizabeth. See "Godfrey Haller," q.v.

ABELL, John. Paid for the services he rendered to the military in December, 1779 (nature of the services not stated). [Ref: V-44].

ABLE, Cuthbert. Sergeant in the 1st Maryland Regiment who enlisted on February 1, 1780, and served in the Southern Army of the United States under Lt. William Lamar in the late Capt. Beatty's company. He was also a sergeant in the 7th Maryland Regiment in 1780-1781 [Ref: A-184], and served in the capacity of an A. F. M. [Assistant Forage Master] from January through July, 1781 [Ref: A-184, A-389].

ABLE, John. Private in the German Regiment in 1776 in Capt. Henry Fister's company under the command of Col. Hussecker [Ref: A-261].

ACK, Adam. See "Adam Occ," q.v.

ACK, Matthias. Associator in December, 1775 [Ref: E-163]. Juror to the Oath of Allegiance in 1778 [Ref: C-21, and S-264, which latter source listed the name as "Mats. Eck."].

ACKERMAN, Jacob. See "Jacob Ockerman," q.v.

ACORD, Joseph. Juror to the Oath of Allegiance in March, 1778 [Ref: S-263, but not listed in Ref: C-22].

ACRE, Conomus. Private who enlisted on July 19, 1776 [Ref: A-51].

ADAIN, Francis Grand. See "Francis Granadam," q.v.

ADAMS, Alexander. Private who enlisted July 22, 1776 [Ref: A-49].

ADAMS, Eva Margaret. See "William Albaugh," q.v.

ADAMS, Jacob. Private in Capt. John Kershner's company who guarded prisoners at Fort Frederick, 1777-1778, and was discharged June 6, 1778 [Ref: A-328].

ADAMS, James. Private who enlisted on July 1, 1776, in Capt. Peter Mantz's company, marched from Frederick Town to Leonardtown, and from there to Philadelphia, arriving August 23, 1776 [Ref: A-47].

ADAMS, Martin. Ensign in Capt. Normand Bruce's company of militia in 1775 [Ref: E-54].

ADAMS, Nathaniel. Private, enlisted February 23, 1778 [Ref: A-314].

ADAMS, Peter. 2nd lieutenant in Capt. Peter Mantz's company of militia in 1775 [Ref: E-50, B-47]. Commissioned 2nd lieutenant in the Middle District Militia on March 26, 1776 [Ref: A-44, W-287]. Juror to the Oath of Allegiance in 1778 [Ref: C-21]. One "Peter Adam" was an Associator in December, 1775 [Ref: E-163].

ADAMS, Peter. Private at Fort Frederick on June 27, 1778, in Capt. John Kershner's company, and guarded prisoners of war [Ref: A-328].

ADAMS, Thomas. Private who was enlisted on July 20, 1776, by Capt. Jacob Good [Ref: A-46]. Drafted on June 13, 1781, but provided a substitute. [Ref: D-1814].

ADAMS [ADAM], Valentine. "Valentine Adams" was a Juror to the Oath of Allegiance in 1778 [Ref: C-21]. "Valentine Adam" was an Associator in December, 1775 [Ref: E-163]. "Valentine Adam" provided wheat for the military in July, 1782 [Ref: R-535].

ADAMSON, Jeremiah. Associator in December, 1775 [Ref: E-163]. Juror to the Oath of Allegiance in 1778 [Ref: C-21].

ADLUM, John. 2nd lieutenant in Capt. Charles Beatty's company of militia in 1775 [Ref: E-51]. Associator in December, 1775 [Ref: E-163]. Captain from 1776 to at least 1779 [Ref: B-47, W-199]. Chosen to serve on the Committee of Observation in the Middle District of Frederick County in 1775 [Ref: E-302, I-85]. Juror to the Oath of Allegiance in 1778 [Ref: C-21]. "John Adhun" was an election judge on November 25, 1776 [Ref: F-476]. Loaned $1,000 for the use of the State of Maryland in June, 1780 [Ref: V-520].

AGHERN, John. Private in the 7th Maryland Regiment who enlisted in Frederick Town between January and April, 1780, and subsequently was reported as "deserted" (no date given). [Ref: A-334].

AGNEW, James. Associator in December, 1775 [Ref: E-163]. Juror to the Oath of Allegiance in 1778 [Ref: C-21].

AHALT, Ann Mary. See "James Cochran," q.v.

AHERN [AHEARN], William. Private who enlisted on May 16, 1778, and served in the 6th Maryland Regiment until August 16, 1780, when he was reported missing (after the Battle of Camden). [Ref: A-322].

AIM, John. Private who enlisted on July 19, 1776 [Ref: A-51].

AIRES, James. Militia substitute on June 13, 1778 [Ref: A-326].

AKERMAN, Jacob. Petitioned the General Assembly under the Act of May 12, 1780, stating that he had been a non-juror to the Oath of Allegiance and Fidelity in 1778 due to "ignorance" and now desired relief under the Act and to take the Oath [Ref: L-101].

AKINBRODE, John Yost. Associator in December, 1775 [Ref: E-163]. Juror to the Oath of Allegiance in 1778 [Ref: C-21].

ALBAUGH, Christian. Associator in December, 1775 [Ref: E-163]. Juror to the Oath of Allegiance in 1778 [Ref: C-21].

ALBAUGH, Jacob. See "Jacob Erbaugh," q.v.

ALBAUGH, Lawrence. See "Lawrence Aubock," q.v.

ALBAUGH, Peter. "Peter Allbaugh" was a non-enroller who was fined by the Committee of Observation in April, 1776 [Ref: E-248].

ALBAUGH, Philip. Fifer in Capt. Valentine Creager's company of militia in 1775 [Ref: E-53]. Associator in December, 1775 [Ref: E-163]. Juror to the Oath of Allegiance in 1778 [Ref: C-21]. Also, see "Philip Aulpaugh," q.v.

ALBAUGH, William [Johan William] (March 8, 1723, Bavaria - January 13, 1794). He served on the Committee of Observation in 1775 [Ref: I-85] and enrolled as an Associator in December, 1775 [Ref: E-163]. He signed as a Juror to the Oath of Allegiance, 1778 [Ref: C-21]. "William Albaugh (blacksmith) died testate in 1794, leaving children Abraham, John, Zachariah, Christian, Margaret Prodbeck, Macbelena [sic] Etsler, and "my son by marriage Peter Stimmel." [Ref: M-9:36]. His wife Magdalene had died in 1793, and a son Abraham (July 27, 1762 - July 13, 1830) had married Eva Margaret Adams (1771-1848) in 1791 [Ref: U-1989A].

ALBAUGH, William Jr. Associator in December, 1775 [Ref: E-163]. Juror to the Oath of Allegiance in 1778 [Ref: C-21].

ALBAUGH, Zachariah. Associator in December, 1775 [Ref: E-163]. "Zachariah Allbaugh" was a non-enroller fined by the Committee of Observation in April, 1776 [Ref: E-248]. "Zachariah Albaugh" was a juror to the Oath of Allegiance in 1778 [Ref: C-21]. "Zacharian Allbaugh, Sr." died testate in 1782, leaving wife Susannah and children Zachariah and David (plus others unnamed). [Ref: M-6:29]. "Zachariah Allbaugh applied for a pension (S2902) on October 29, 1832, Licking County, Ohio, aged 74, stating after the war he lived 8 years in Maryland and 36 years in Pennsylvania." He was born on October 31, 1758, in Frederick County, and died on November 8, 1857."[Ref: T-32].

ALBEN, Archibald. Associator in December, 1775 [Ref: E-163]. Juror to the Oath of Allegiance in 1778 [Ref: C-21].

ALBRECHT, Margaret. See "Philip Fisher," q.v.

ALBRIGHT, Stephen Miller. Associator in December, 1775 [Ref: E-163]. Juror to the Oath of Allegiance in 1778 [Ref: C-21].

ALDRIDGE, John Simpson. Private who enlisted on August 8, 1776 [Ref: A-49].

ALDRIDGE, William. Associator in December, 1775 [Ref: E-163]. Juror to the Oath of Allegiance in 1778 [Ref: C-21].

ALDRIDGE, Zachariah. Private in militia in July, 1776 [Ref: A-42].

ALEXANDER, Jacob. Private who enlisted March 3, 1778 [Ref: A-315]. Served in the German Regiment at White Plains on September 5, 1778, under Lt. Col. Ludwick Weltner [Ref: A-267]. "Jacob Alexander, aged 59, and old Revolutionary soldier who served in Capt. Stricker's Company of Infantry, recruited at Middletown and saw duty down in the Peninsula at Annapolis, Monmouth, and in the German Legion, died Friday, May 1, 1814, at Middletown. He was appointed sergeant after the Battle of Monmouth; was also in Sullivan's Army on the frontier and in expeditions; served 3 years." [Ref: N-58, N-59].

ALEXANDER, John. Militia substitute from May to December 10, 1781, and "marched to Annapolis." [Ref: A-653].

ALEXANDER, Mary Ann. See "David Stottlemeyer," q.v.

ALEXANDER, Samuel. Associator in December, 1775 [Ref: E-163]. Juror to the Oath of Allegiance in 1778 [Ref: C-21].

ALEXANDER, Thomas. Associator in December, 1775 [Ref: E-163]. Juror to the Oath of Allegiance in 1778 [Ref: C-21].

ALEXANDER, Valentine. Associator in December, 1775 [Ref: E-163]. Juror to the Oath of Allegiance in 1778 [Ref: C-21].

ALINGER, Chr. Private who enlisted on July 19, 1776 [Ref: A-51].

ALLAR, Philip. Associator in December, 1775 [Ref: E-163]. Juror to the Oath of Allegiance in 1778 [Ref: C-22].

ALLEN, Bennett. Associator in December, 1775 [Ref: E-163]. Juror to the Oath of Allegiance, 1778 [Ref: C-22]. One "Bennett, or Benedict Allen, was one of the most extraordinary figures in the colonial history of Maryland. He was a graduate and Fellow of Wadham College, Oxford, was ordained deacon of the Church of England by the Bishop of Oxford on the 23rd of September, 1759, and priest by the same diocesan 2 years later. He was licensed for Maryland on the 3rd of September, 1766, by the Bishop of London, and came over to the province in 1768, with letters to Governor Sharpe from Frederick, last Lord Baltimore, who commended him to the Governor's special consideration as one of his most particular friends, desiring that he might have the first good living or parish of the Established Church that offered itself, or if one good living good not be had, then two indifferent ones. The Governor finally inducted Mr. Allen into the rectorship of St. Ann's at Annapolis... He [subsequently] became rector of All Saints in Frederick County and served there until 1777. In that year the Church of England in Maryland was deprived of its livings and Mr. Allen forced to return to England." [Ref: F-464, F-465]. (Ed. Note: It cannot be said with certainty that this Rev. Bennett Allen was the patriot who was the associator in 1775, and he certainly was not the juror in 1778 since he had returned to England in 1777.)

ALLEN, Jacob. Defective from the Maryland Line on March 15, 1781 [Ref: A-416].

ALLEN, James. Private in the militia, March 9, 1776 [Ref: B-166]. Private in the 7th Maryland Regiment in 1780 who had enlisted in Frederick Town between January and April, 1780 [Ref: A-334].

ALLEN, Jeremiah. Private in the Skipton District Militia under Capt. Thomas Waring on April 16, 1776 [Ref: B-167, D-1814].

ALLEN, Michael. Loaned $400 for the use of the State of Maryland in June, 1780 [Ref: V-520].

ALLENDER [ALINDER], William. Private who enlisted on May 20, 1778, and served in the 2nd Maryland Regiment [Ref: A-294, A-323].

ALLER, George. Drafted on June 13, 1781, but subsequently reported as "deserted" (no date given). [Ref: D-1814].

ALLER, Joseph. Drafted on June 2, 1783; "agreed to pay an equal part of the expense - paid 6 pounds." [Ref: B-169].

ALLGUIRE, Joseph. Petitioned the General Assembly under the Act of July 3, 1780, stating that he had been a non-juror to the Oath of Allegiance and Fidelity in 1778 due to "ignorance" and now desired relief under the Act and to take the Oath [Ref: L-101].

ALLIN, William. Private stationed at Fort Frederick in June, 1778 [Ref: A-328].

ALLISON, Blaney. Corporal in Capt. Normand Bruce's company of militia in 1775 [Ref: E-55].

ALLISON, Henry. Private who enlisted on July 13, 1776 or July 22, 1776 [Ref: A-43, A-49].

ALLISON, William. Paid by the Committee of Observation "for carriage of 5 chests of provisional arms" in 1775 [Ref: E-65].

ALLSOP [ALSOP], John. Associator in December, 1775 [Ref: E-163]. Militia substitute from May to December 10, 1781, and marched to Annapolis [Ref: A-653]. Juror to the Oath of Allegiance in 1778 [Ref: C-22]. Private in Capt. William Beatty's company in the 7th Maryland Regiment,in 1779, having enlisted September 4, 1777, for 3 years [Ref: N-30:112, A-45, and A-310, which latter source stated he had enlisted August 5, 1776]. Disabled at the Battle of the Barges, and invalid pension commenced on November 29, 1783, and ceased November 1, 1789 [Ref: A-630, A-631]. John Alsop, a soldier in the Second Maryland Regiment, was wounded at Battle of Cowpens [Ref: F-475].

ALLSOP [ALSOP], Joseph. Drummer in the Middle District Militia in 1776 [Ref: A-72]. Substitute on June 8, 1778, who served in the 7th Maryland Regiment as a private until discharged on March 30, 1779 [Ref: A-184, A-325]. Also, a substitute from May to December 10, 1781, and "marched to Annapolis." [Ref: A-653].

AMBROSE, Henry. Juror to the Oath of Allegiance in March, 1778 [Ref: S-263, but not listed in Ref: C-22].

AMBROSE [AMBROSY], Jacob. "Jacob Ambrose" was captain of a company of militia in 1775 [Ref: E-54, B-48, O-92]. "Jacob Ambrosy" was an Associator in December, 1775 [Ref: E-163]. "Jacob Ambrosy" took the Oath of Allegiance in 1778 [Ref: C-22]. "Jacob Ambrose" served on the Committee of Observation in 1775 [Ref: I-85].

AMERICK, Peter. Private in the German Regiment in 1776, with Capt. Henry Fister's company under the command of Col. Nicholas Hussecker [Ref: A-261].

AMMERSLEY, John. See "John Hammersly," q.v.

ANDERSON, Captain. See "Bazel Norman," q.v.

ANDERSON, Elizabeth. See "Richard Davis," q.v.

ANDERSON, Richard. 2nd lieutenant in Lower District Militia [now Montgomery County] under Capt. Edward Burgess on August 7, 1776 [Ref: A-42, although Ref: X-187 states he was commissioned on August 5, 1776, and served under Capt. Benjamin Spyker]. Richard "applied for a pension (S10059) in Washington, D. C., on October 13, 1819, stating he had been a captain in the Maryland Line. He lived in Frederick County, Maryland, at the time of his application for pension. He also received bounty land warrant no. 51-300-11 in June, 1790. In 1828 he lived in Sumter District, South Carolina, and died on June 22, 1835, leaving these children: William W., Franklin, Richard, Alfred, Juliet, and Anne." [Ref: T-58, J-8].

ANDERSON, Thomas. Associator in December, 1775 [Ref: E-163]. Private who was enlisted on July 20, 1776, by Capt. Jacob Good [Ref: A-46]. Juror to the Oath of Allegiance in 1778 [Ref: C-22].

ANDESS, Matthias. Private in the Middle District Militia in 1776 [Ref: A-72].

ANDESS, William. Associator in December, 1775 [Ref: E-163]. Juror to the Oath of Allegiance in 1778 [Ref: C-22]. He died testate in 1783, leaving these twelve children: Mary Catherine, Andrew, Matthias, Christiana, Peter, John, Catherine, Adam, Elizabeth, Margaret, Frederick, and Charity [Ref: M-6:33].

ANDRE, Major. See "John Stricker," q.v.

ANDREWS, Peter. Juror to the Oath of Allegiance in 1778 [Ref: C-22]. "Peter Andrew" was an Associator in December, 1775 [Ref: E-163].

ANGLE, Jacob. Juror to the Oath of Allegiance in March, 1778 [Ref: S-263, but not listed in Ref: C-22].

ANGLE, John. Associator in December, 1775 [Ref: E-163]. Juror to the Oath of Allegiance in 1778 [Ref: S-263, and C-22, which spelled his name "Angel."].

ANGLE, Charles. Provided wheat for the military in June, 1782 [Ref: R-526].

ANGLEBERRG [sic], Philip. Drafted on June 2, 1783 [Ref: B-169].

ANGLER, Philip. Non-Enroller who was fined by the Committee of Observation in May, 1776 [Ref: E-248]. "Philip Englar (1736-1817) and brother Jacob came from Switzerland, perhaps from Appenzell. Philip married Margaret Holverstot (1742-1819); both are buried at Wolfe's Cemetery south of Union Bridge. Philip was a minister of Pipe Creek Brethren Church. Their fourth child was Elder David Englar (1773-1839) who married Elizabeth Stem (1777-1849) and also preached at Pipe Creek. Both are buried at Pipe Creek Cemetery." [Ref: O-153].

ANKRIM, Jacob. Associator in December, 1775 [Ref: E-163]. Juror to the Oath of Allegiance in 1778 [Ref: C-22, and S-263, which latter source spelled the name as "Jacob Ancrum, Jr."]. Also, see "Richard Ankrim, Sr.," q.v.

ANKRIM, Richard Jr. Associator in December, 1775 [Ref: E-163]. Juror to the Oath of Allegiance in 1778 [Ref: C-22, and S-263, which latter source spelled the name as "Ancrum."].

ANKRIM, Richard Sr. Associator in December, 1775 [Ref: E-163]. Juror to the Oath of Allegiance in 1778 [Ref: C-22, and S-263, which latter source spelled the name "Ancrum."]. "Richard Ankrom" died testate in 1794, leaving wife a Elizabeth and three children Richard, Jacob, Aron, and a grandson Richard ("son of my deceased son Richard"), and two granddaughters Nancy and Sarah Delashmutt [Ref: M-9:35, M-9:36].

APPLE, Peter. Associator in December, 1775 [Ref: E-163]. Juror to the Oath of Allegiance in 1778 [Ref: C-22, S-263]. One "Johan Peter Apfel, or Apple, arrived in Philadelphia in 1732. In 1740 he married Maria Catherine Henckel (1711-1785)... They first lived south of Frederick, but later moved to a farm adjoining Apple's Church near Thurmont. They had the following children: Eva Rosina (b. 1742), Johan Peter Jr. (1744-1775), Maria Charlotta (1746-1820), Maria Catherine (1747-1829), Anna Magdalena (b. 1750) and Johan Martin (b. 1751)." [Ref: O-130]. "Peter Aple, yeoman," died testate in 1779 [Ref: M-5:134].

APPLEBY, John. Associator in December, 1775 [Ref: E-163]. Juror to the Oath of Allegiance in 1778 [Ref: C-22].

ARCHLEY, Thomas. Served on the Committee of Observation in 1775 [Ref: I-85].

ARMER, Patrick. Enlisted on June 2, 1781 for 3 years, but was later reported as "deserted" (no date given). [Ref: D-1814].

ARMSE, Robert. Juror to the Oath of Allegiance in March, 1778 [Ref: S-263, but not listed in Ref: C-22].

ARMSTRONG, James (Reverend). Served in the 2nd Maryland Brigade from November, 1778, to April, 1780 [Ref: A-294].

ARMSTRONG, John. Private in the German Regiment; roll dated October 23, 1776 [Ref: A-264]. Discharged on July 26, 1779 [Ref: A-265].

ARNOLD, Abraham. Drafted on June 2, 1783; "hath not appeared, gone to Redstone" (Pennsylvania). [Ref: B-168].

ARNOLD, Andrew. Non-Enroller who was fined by the Committee of Observation in April, 1776 [Ref: E-248]. One Andrew Arnold (1740-1821) was a son of John George and Catherine Arnold [Ref: O-181].

ARNOLD, Anthony Jr. Associator in December, 1775 [Ref: E-163]. Juror to the Oath of Allegiance in 1778 [Ref: C-22].

ARNOLD, Anthony Sr. Associator in December, 1775 [Ref: E-163]. Juror to the Oath of Allegiance in 1778 [Ref: C-22]. "Antony Arnold, farmer" died testate in 1792, leaving wife Margaret and children Samuel, Archibald, Antony [sic], John, Ann (married), Caterine [sic], William, and Joseph [Ref: M-8:178].

ARNOLD, Archibald. Associator in December, 1775 [Ref: E-163]. Juror to the Oath of Allegiance in 1778 [Ref: C-22].

ARNOLD, Daniel. Non-Enroller who was fined by the Committee of Observation in April, 1776 [Ref: E-248].

ARNOLD, David. Petitioned the General Assembly under the Act of May 12, 1780, stating he had been a non-juror to the Oath of Allegiance and Fidelity in 1778 due to "ignorance" and now desired relief under the Act and to take the Oath [Ref: L-101]. One David Arnold (1759-1844) was a minister in the Middletown Valley [Ref: O-181].

ARNOLD, George. Juror to the Oath of Allegiance in March, 1778 [Ref: S-263, but not listed in Ref: C-22]. Militia substitute on June 2, 1778 [Ref: A-324]. Private in the German Regiment who served at the Battle of White Plains on September 5, 1778, under Lt. Col. Ludwick Weltner [Ref: A-266]. "George Arnold applied for a pension on December 16, 1818, in Somerset County, Pennsylvania, aged 67, stating he had been a soldier in the Maryland Line during the Revolutionary War, and had resided in Somerset County for 30 years. In 1820 his wife (not named) was aged 65 and they had 2 daughters (not named) one of whom was blind. On June 20 or July 2, 1831, he married Eve Plumb, widow of Jacob Plumb (died December, 1817), in Millersburg, Ohio. George Arnold died on December 23, 1836, in Holmes County, Ohio (or June 22, 1836, per his stepson Jacob Plumb, who was aged 70 in August, 1856). Eve Arnold applied for a pension (W25356) in Medina County, Ohio, on March 3, 1856. They had lived in Pennsylvania until 1816 when they moved to Wayne County, Ohio." [Ref: T-79].

ARNOLD, John. Non-Enroller who was fined by the Committee of Observation in April, 1776, but when it was determined that he was "over age" the fine was later remitted [Ref: E-248]. Petitioned the General Assembly under the Act of May 12, 1780, stating he had been a non-juror to the Oath of Allegiance and Fidelity in 1778 due to "ignorance" and now desired relief under the Act and to take the Oath [Ref: L-101]. One John Arnold died testate in 1790, leaving wife Catharine and children John Jr., Samuel, Zachariah, Daniel, Mary, Susanna, Margaret, and Cathrine [sic]. [Ref: M-8:35]. One John Arnold was paid for hauling wheat and flour for the military in June, 1782 [Ref: R-520].

ARNOLD, John (of John). Non-Enroller who was fined by the Committee of Observation in April, 1776 [Ref: E-248].

ARNOLD, Joseph. Juror to the Oath of Allegiance in March, 1778 [Ref: S-263, but not listed in Ref: C-22].

ARNOLD, Peter. Petitioned the General Assembly under the Act of May 12, 1780, stating he had been a non-juror to the Oath of Allegiance and Fidelity in 1778 due to "ignorance" and now desired relief under the Act and to take the Oath [Ref: L-101].

ARNOLD, Samuel. Associator in December, 1775 [Ref: E-163]. Juror to the Oath of Allegiance in 1778 [Ref: C-22].

ARRAN, Michael. Private who enlisted on August 5, 1776, in the Flying Camp under Capt. Philip Meroney [Ref: A-45, N-30:112].

ARTER, Daniel. Associator in December, 1775 [Ref: E-163]. Juror to the Oath of Allegiance in 1778 [Ref: C-22].

ARTHUR, Michael. Non-Enroller who was fined by the Committee of Observation in April, 1776 [Ref: E-248]. Drafted on June 2, 1783 [Ref: B-168].

ARTIS, James. Private who enlisted on July 29, 1776 [Ref: A-44].

ASHBURNER, John. Non-Enroller who was fined by the Committee of Observation in May, 1776 [Ref: E-248].

ASHLEY, James. Private who enlisted on April 25, 1778 [Ref: A-321]. Private in the German Regiment who fought at the Battle of White Plains on September 5, 1778, under Lt. Col. Ludwick Weltner. He was still in the military service in 1779 [Ref: A-264, A-267].

ASHMORE, John. Private in the 1st Maryland Regiment in 1780 who served in the Southern Army of the United States under Lt. William Lamar in the late Capt. Beatty's company until transferred to the light infantry on March 12, 1781 [Ref: A-390].

ASKEY, Zachariah. Private who enlisted on July 13, 1776 [Ref: A-43]. Defective from Maryland Line on September 21, 1780 [Ref: A-414]. Enlisted on January 24, 1781, for the duration of the war, and was reported as "deserted" (no date given). [Ref: D-1814].

ASTIN [AISTON], John. "John Aiston" was a fifer in Capt. John Stoner's company of militia in 1775 [Ref: E-56]. "John Astin" was an Associator in December, 1775 [Ref: E-163]. Juror to the Oath of Allegiance, 1778 [Ref: C-22].

ATCHISON, Henry. Private who enlisted August 5, 1776 [Ref: A-44].

ATKINSON, William. Private who enlisted March 5, 1778 [Ref: A-315].

ATTIGE, John. Non-Enroller who was fined by the Committee of Observation in April, 1776 [Ref: E-248].

AUBER, John. Sergeant, 2nd Maryland Regiment. Disabled at the Battle of Eutaw Springs; invalid pension commenced November 29, 1783, and ceased on March 6, 1788, with the cause of pension ceasing as "dead." [Ref: A-630, A-631, F-475, which latter source also listed a "John Ober" who was also wounded. Same person?].

AUBOCK, Lawrence. Ensign in Capt. Michael McGuire's company of militia in 1775 [Ref: E-56, B-49].

AUGHE, Hannah. See "Matthias Young," q.v.

AUGUSTEEN, John. Private in Capt. John Kershner's company; guarded prisoners at Fort Frederick, 1777-1778; and, subsequently reported as "deserted" on May 26, 1778 [Ref: A-328].

AULPAUGH, Philip. Private who enlisted on July 1, 1776 in Capt. Peter Mantz's company; marched from Frederick Town to Leonardtown, and from there to Philadelphia, arriving August 23, 1776 [Ref: A-47]. Also, see "Philip Albaugh," q.v.

AULT, Henry. Private in the militia, March 9, 1776 [Ref: B-166].

AULT, John. Private in the militia, March 9, 1776 [Ref: B-166].

AULT, William. Private in the militia, March 9, 1776 [Ref: B-166].

AUSTIN, James. Private in the militia, March 9, 1776 [Ref: B-166].

AUSTIN, Thomas. Private in the militia, March 9, 1776 [Ref: B-166].

AWBLE, John. Associator in December, 1775 [Ref: E-163]. Juror to the Oath of Allegiance in 1778 [Ref: C-22].

AYEGHAM, Andrew. Associator in December, 1775 [Ref: E-163]. Juror to the Oath of Allegiance in 1778 [Ref: C-22].

AYSELL, Peter. Associator in December, 1775 [Ref: E-163]. Juror to the Oath of Allegiance in 1778 [Ref: C-22].

AZELIP, Richard. See "Richard Hazlip," q.v.

BABBS, John. Private who enlisted in Frederick on August 5, 1780, and subsequently marched to Annapolis under Capt. Beatty. Record noted that he "followed the 1st Troops." [Ref: A-344].

BABS, William. Non-Enroller who was fined by the Committee of Observation in April, 1776 [Ref: E-248].

BACESER [?], Daniel. Juror to the Oath of Allegiance in March, 1778 [Ref: S-263, but not listed in Ref: C-22].

BACH, Adam. Associator in December, 1775 [Ref: E-164]. Juror to the Oath of Allegiance in 1778 [Ref: C-22].

BACH, Michael. Associator in December, 1775 [Ref: E-164]. Juror to the Oath of Allegiance in 1778 [Ref: C-22].

BACHER, John. Associator in December, 1775 [Ref: E-163]. Juror to the Oath of Allegiance in 1778 [Ref: C-22].

BACHLEY, James. Associator in December, 1775 [Ref: E-163]. Juror to the Oath of Allegiance in 1778 [Ref: C-22].

BACKER, Peter. Lieutenant at Fort Frederick, 1778, in Capt. John Kershner's company, guarding prisoners of war [Ref: A-328].

BAER, Henry. See "Henry Bear," q.v.

BAER, Jacob. See "Samuel Beall White," q.v.

BAGER [BAUGHER], Susannah Catherine. See "Andrew Fogel," q.v.

BAIL, Peter. Drafted on June 13, 1781, and provided a substitute [Ref: D-1814].

BAILE, Nicholas. Corporal in Capt. Michael McGuire's company of militia in 1775 [Ref: E-57].

BAILEY, Matthew. Associator in December, 1775 [Ref: E-163]. Juror to the Oath of Allegiance in 1778 [Ref: C-22].

BAILEY, Mountjoy (1755-1836). Served as adjutant in Col. Murdock's Battalion in 1776 [Ref: X-113]. On June 28, 1782, he wrote to the Governor about the lack of prisoner guards in Frederick Town [Ref: R-525]. He was a captain in the 7th Maryland Regiment, a charter member of the Society of the Cincinnati, and married Elizabeth Edelin, daughter of Christopher, by 1784. Their children were Benjamin, Richard, Eleanor, and Elizabeth [Ref: P-119].

BAILEY, Thomas. Soldier in the Maryland Line. Enlisted in Baltimore and "applied for a pension (S34634) in Washington County, Maryland on March 27, 1818, aged 72. He lived in Frederick County in 1820 and stated he had no family. Thomas Bailey died August 20, 1824." [Ref: T-117, J-25, F-472].

BAILEY, William. Captain in the 29th Battalion in 1777 [Ref: B-49]. "William Baley" gave money in the amount of 5 lbs. 5 sh. 11 p. and then 26 lbs. 7 sh. 2 p. for arms and ammunition for the militia in 1775 [Ref: E-62, E-63].

BAILY, Susan. See "Frederick Henep," q.v.

BAINBRIDGE, Peter (Upper Catoctin). Appointed by the Committee of Correspondence to solicit subscriptions in 1775 to purchase arms and ammunition [Ref: I-85]. Associator in December, 1775 [Ref: E-163]. Juror to the Oath of Allegiance in 1778 [Ref: C-22]. "Peter Bambridge" gave money in the amount of 10 lbs. 10 sh. for arms and ammunition for the militia in 1775 [Ref: E-63]. "According to apparently reliable statements recorded in his son Absalom's family Bible, Peter Bainbridge was born near Princeton, New Jersey, March 20, 1721, and died February 9, 1806... He was married twice. His first wife was Joanna Oake, by whom he had one child... His second wife was Ruth White, to whom he was married in January, 1760, and by whom Peter had seven sons and three daughters... Peter Bainbridge held several civil and military offices and was active in local government. As a Justice of the Frederick County Court beginning in June, 1758, he was present at every session except the November 1762 Term, and was one of the 12 justices who, at the November 1765 session, refused to enforce and thereby repudiated the British Stamp Act... During the French and Indian War, he was commissioned a captain in the Maryland Militia and raised a company which served 41 days in 1767. His patriotic service resumed during the Revolutionary War, when on January 24, 1775, he was appointed to promote subscriptions for arms, etc., in the Upper Catoctin District. His name was on the Middle District List of Associators on December 27, 1775... The children of Peter and Ruth were Edmund (c1760-c1789, Kentucky), Peter W. (1762-1842, Kentucky), Julia (unmarried), Dr. Absalom (1766-1826, Missouri), Dr. Abner (Romulus, New York), Mahlon (1771-1814, New York), John (1773-1846, New York), Joanna (died in Baldwin Co., Georgia)..." plus an unidentified daughter and son. [Ref: M-5:146-150]. Also, see "Yost Blickenstiffe," q.v.

BAIRD, Elizabeth. See "Mathias Firestone," q.v.

BAIRD, Jacob. Associator in December, 1775 [Ref: E-164]. Juror to the Oath of Allegiance in 1778 [Ref: C-22].

BAIRD, Nicholas. Private in the German Regiment, muster roll dated October 23, 1776 [Ref: A-264].

BAIRD, Paul. Associator in December, 1775 [Ref: E-164]. Juror to the Oath of Allegiance in 1778 [Ref: C-22].

BAIRD, Peter. Corporal in Capt. Joseph Wood, Jr.'s company of militia in 1775 [Ref: E-53]. Associator in December, 1775 [Ref: E-164]. Juror to the Oath of Allegiance in 1778 [Ref: C-22].

BAIRD, William. Served on the Committee of Observation in 1775 [Ref: I-85]. Served in the House of Delegates from the Upper District of Frederick County in 1775 [Ref: F-479].

BAIRFORD, Edward. Private who enlisted on June 19, 1780, for three years, in Capt. Michael Bayer's company, and "joined the regiment at Northumberland." [Ref: A-268].

BAKER, Abraham. 1st lieutenant in the Upper District Militia in the 36th Battalion on April 20, 1776 [Ref: W-356].

BAKER, Catharine. See "Adam Froshour," q.v.

BAKER, Ernst. Associator in December, 1775 [Ref: E-164]. Juror to the Oath of Allegiance in 1778 [Ref: C-22].

BAKER, Frederick. Provided wheat for the military in May, 1782 [Ref: R-515].

BAKER, Henry. Captain of a militia company in 1775 [Ref: E-54, B-49], and captain in Col. Johnson's battalion in 1776 [Ref: X-555]. Captain in the Linganore Battalion on January 17, 1777 [Ref: Y-54].

BAKER, Isaac (Conococheague). Appointed by the Committee of Correspondence to solicit subscriptions in 1775 to purchase arms and ammunition [Ref: I-86].

BAKER, Isaac. Soldier in the Maryland Line who "applied for pension (R414) on September 29, 1834, in Sangamon County, Illinois, aged 78, stating he was born in Baltimore County, Maryland, on August 6, 1758, and moved to Frederick County in 1781. In the spring of Harmar's defeat he moved to Nicholas County, Kentucky, for 5 years and then moved to Sangamon County, Illinois." [Ref: T-122].

BAKER, Joel. Corporal, enlisted December 19, 1776, in Capt. William Beatty's company, 7th Maryland Regiment [Ref: A-310].

BAKER, John. Associator in December, 1775 [Ref: E-163]. Private who enlisted on July 1, 1776 in Capt. Peter Mantz's company; marched from Frederick Town to Leonardtown, and from there to Philadelphia, arriving on August 23, 1776 [Ref: A-47].

BAKER, John. Associator in December, 1775 [Ref: E-163]. Juror to the Oath of Allegiance in 1778 [Ref: C-22].

BAKER, John. Associator in December, 1775 [Ref: E-163]. Private in the Skipton District Militia under Capt. Thomas Waring on April 16, 1776 [Ref: B-167, D-1814].

BAKER, John D. Served in the Pennsylvania Line and applied for a pension on April 4, 1818, aged 79, in Frederick County, Maryland. Died in 1823. [Ref: J-25].

BAKER, Joseph. Associator in December, 1775 [Ref: E-163]. Juror to the Oath of Allegiance in 1778 [Ref: C-22].

BAKER, Maurice. Private who enlisted on July 19, 1776 [Ref: A-51].

BAKER, Rowland. Private who enlisted in Frederick on August 9, 1780, and subsequently reported "deserted" (no date). [Ref: A-344].

BAKER, Samuel. Associator in December, 1775 [Ref: E-164]. Juror to the Oath of Allegiance in 1778 [Ref: C-22].

BAKER, W. (Rock Creek Hundred). Appointed by the Committee of Correspondence to solicit subscriptions in 1775 to purchase arms and ammunition [Ref: I-86]. William Baker served on the Committee of Observation in 1775 [Ref: I-85].

BAKER, Teter. Militia substitute on June 6, 1778 [Ref: A-325].

BAKMER, Adam. Associator in December, 1775 [Ref: E-164]. Juror to the Oath of Allegiance in 1778 [Ref: C-22].

BALDWIN, Elijah. Ensign in Capt. Abraham Hayter's company of militia in 1775 [Ref: E-52, B-49].

BALDWIN, John. Private who enlisted on April 18, 1778, and served in the 2nd Maryland Regiment [Ref: A-294, A-320].

BALDWIN, Thomas. Drafted on June 2, 1783 [Ref: B-169].

BALEY, John (Burnt House Woods Hundred). Non-Enroller who was fined by the Committee of Observation in June, 1776 [Ref: E-248].

BALL, James. Corporal in Capt. Samuel Plummer's company of militia in 1775 [Ref: E-54].

BALL, John. Paid 36 shillings by the Treasurer of the Western Shore "for the use of his house for barracks" in July, 1776 [Ref: X-89].

BALLARD, Jonathan. Soldier in the Maryland Line who enlisted in Bladensburg, Prince George's County, and "applied for a pension (S34639) in Frederick County on April 29, 1818, aged 63. In 1820 his wife Catharine was aged 52 and a grandson John was aged 9." [Ref: T-137. However, Ref: J-25 states he was age 76 in 1818].

BALLINGER, William. Non-Enroller who was fined by the Committee of Observation in April, 1776 [Ref: E-248]. See "Thomas Plummer," q.v.

BALSEL [BALZEL], Charles. "Charles Balsell" was a 1st lieutenant in Capt. James Johnson's company of militia in 1775 [Ref: E-52, B-50]. "Charles Balzel" was an Associator in December, 1775 [Ref: E-163]. "Charles Balzel" was 1st lieutenant in the German Regiment in 1776 in Capt. Henry Fister's company under the command of Col. Hussecker [Ref: A-261, X-48]. "Charles Baltzel" was a captain from May 10, 1777, until declared a supernumerary on January 1, 1781 [Ref: A-365]. "Charles Balsel" took the Oath of Allegiance in 1778 [Ref: C-22]. "Major Charles Baltzell, died at his farm near Woodbrough on December 31, 1813, aged 77. He was a native of Germany and in his youth served several campaigns in the Seven Years' War. He subsequently emigrated to this country and settled in Maryland. He was a soldier in the Revolutionary War from the beginning until the army was disbanded, when he became a member of the Society of the Cincinnati." [Ref: F-471]. "Charles Baltzell" was a captain in the Maryland Line and received bounty land warrant no. 238-330-4 in March, 1800; papers were burned in the fire of 1800 [Ref: T-139].

BALSEL, Jacob. "Jacob Balsell" was a sergeant in Capt. Philip Rodenbieler's company of militia in 1775 [Ref: E-51]. "Jacob Balsel" was an Associator in December, 1775 [Ref: E-164]. Juror to the Oath of Allegiance in 1778 [Ref: C-22, S-263]. Also, see "Jacob Balzel," q.v.

BALSELL, Peter. Juror to the Oath of Allegiance in March, 1778 [Ref: S-263, but not listed in Ref: C-22].

BALSELL, Richard. Captain in the 37th Battalion of militia on May 15, 1776 [Ref: B-50, W-427].

BALSER, John. Associator in December, 1775 [Ref: E-163]. Juror to the Oath of Allegiance in 1778 [Ref: C-22]. "John Baltzer," an innkeeper, died February 27, 1811 [Ref: F-471].

BALZEL, Jacob. Associator in December, 1775 [Ref: E-163]. Juror to the Oath of Allegiance in 1778 [Ref: C-22]. One "Jacob Baltzell" died on October 25, 1802, and "John Jacob Baltzell" died May 31, 1838, aged 87 [Ref: F-470, F-473]. Also, see "Jacob Balsel," q.v.

BALZEL, John. Sergeant in the German Regiment, 1776, in Capt. Henry Fister's company under the command of Col. Nicholas Hussecker [Ref: A-261]. "John Balsel" was an Associator in December, 1775 [Ref: E-163]. "John Balsel" took the Oath of Allegiance in 1778 [Ref: C-22].

BALZEL, Michael. Associator in December, 1775 [Ref: E-163]. Juror to the Oath of Allegiance in 1778 [Ref: C-22]. "Michael Baltzell, Sr." died on September 12, 1821 [Ref: F-472].

BANFIELD, James. Private in the Skipton District Militia under Capt. Thomas Waring on April 16, 1776 [Ref: B-167, D-1814].

BANTZ, Adam. Associator in December, 1775 [Ref: E-164]. Juror to the Oath of Allegiance in 1778 [Ref: C-22].

BANTZ, George. Private in the German Regiment. Served at White Plains on September 5, 1778, under Lt. Col. Ludwick Weltner [Ref: A-267].

BANTZ, Valentine. Associator in December, 1775 [Ref: E-163]. Juror to the Oath of Allegiance in 1778 [Ref: C-22].

BARGER, Philip. Juror to the Oath of Allegiance in March, 1778 [Ref: S-267, but not listed in Ref: C-30].

BARKER, James. Associator in December, 1775 [Ref: E-163]. Juror to the Oath of Allegiance in 1778 [Ref: C-22].

BARKER [BARCKER], John. Corporal in Capt. Valentine Creager's company of militia in 1775 [Ref: E-53].

BARKSHIRE [BERKSHIRE], Henry. Private who enlisted on August 5, 1776, in the Flying Camp under Capt. Meroney, and was subsequently reported as "deserted" (no date given). [Ref: A-45, N-30:112]. One "Henry Barshire" took the Oath of Allegiance in March, 1778 [Ref: S-263].

BARLOW, John. Private who enlisted on March 4, 1778 [Ref: A-315]. On June 8, 1780, "pardon [was] granted to John Barlow, convicted at Frederick County Court for the murder of Thomas Cooper." Enlisted in the 7th Maryland Regiment on July 20, 1780 [Ref: V-191, V-224].

BARLOW, Richard. Enlisted in the 7th Maryland Regiment on July 20, 1780 [Ref: V-224].

BARNES, Richard Weaver (or Richard Barnes, weaver?). Private in the militia in July, 1776 [Ref: A-42].

BARNES, Robert W. See "Ralph Briscoe," q.v.

BARNET, Daniel. Private in the 1st Maryland Regiment in 1781 wjo served in the Southern Army of the United States under Lt. William Lamar in the late Capt. Beatty's company. Record indicates he had "deserted" in January, 1781 [Ref: A-391]. "Daniel Barnett" enlisted on May 11, 1778 [Ref: A-322].

BARNET, Isaac. Private who enlisted on July 19, 1776 [Ref: A-51].

BARNET, Jessey. Private in the 7th Maryland Regiment who enlisted in Frederick Town between January and April, 1780 [Ref: A-334]. "Jesse Barnett" was a drummer (or fifer), 1st Maryland Regiment, 1781, and served in the Southern Army of the United States under Lt. William Lamar in the late Capt. Beatty's company [Ref: A-389].

BARNET, Luke. Associator in December, 1775 [Ref: E-163]. Private who enlisted August 5, 1776 in the Flying Camp under Capt. Philip Meroney [Ref: A-45, N-30:112]. Juror to the Oath of Allegiance in 1778 [Ref: C-22]. "Luke Barnett" took the Oath of Allegiance in 1778 [Ref: C-22]. "Luke Barnett" was an Associator in December, 1775 [Ref: E-163].

BARNET, Nathaniel. Associator in December, 1775 [Ref: E-163]. Juror to the Oath of Allegiance in 1778 [Ref: C-22].

BARNET, William. Associator in December, 1775 [Ref: E-163]. Juror to the Oath of Allegiance in 1778 [Ref: C-22]. One "William Barnitt" enlisted on August 5, 1776, in the Flying Camp under Capt. Meroney [Ref: A-45, N-30:112].

BARNET [BARNETT], Robert. Private who enlisted May 7, 1778 [Ref: A-322]. Pensioned at $40 per annum on October 30, 1819, under Act of June 7, 1785 and dating from March 4, 1789 [Ref: J-8, G-318, citing the U. S. Pension Rolls of 1835, but was not found in Ref: T-160].

BARNET [BARNT], Jacob. Corporal at Fort Frederick, 1778, in Capt. John Kershner's company, guarding prisoners of war [Ref: A-328].

BARNEY, Commodore and Ann. See "John Stricker," q.v.

BARNEY, Moses. Sergeant, 1st Maryland Regiment, 1781, and served in the Southern Army of the United States under Lt. William Lamar in the late Capt. Beatty's company, but was "recruiting in Maryland from January to July, 1781." [Ref: A-389].

BARNOVER, George. Juror to the Oath of Allegiance in March, 1778 [Ref: S-263, but not listed in Ref: C-22].

BARR, Henry. Associator in December, 1775 [Ref: E-163]. Juror to the Oath of Allegiance in 1778 [Ref: C-22].

BARR, Isaac. Captain in the militia, 1778-1779 [Ref: H-17].

BARR, John. Signed as Juror to the Oath of Allegiance in March, 1778 [Ref: S-263, but not listed in Ref: C-22].

BARRETT [BARRATT], Alexander. Private in the militia in July, 1776 [Ref: A-42].

BARRETT, Jesse. Enlisted in the 7th Maryland Regiment on May 15, 1780 [Ref: V-175].

BARRETT [BARRET], Lemuel (Esquire). Appointed captain of a rifle company in July, 1776, but was replaced by Thomas Beall because "he (Lemuel) never acted agreeable to his warrant." [Ref: X-54, X-113].

BARRETT, Samuel. Captain in the militia in 1776 [Ref: B-50].

BARRETT, Thomas (D. S. T.). Private who enlisted on July 24, 1776 [Ref: A-50].

BARRETT, Thomas. Private who enlisted on July 25, 1776 [Ref: A-50].

BARRETT [BARET], Tobias. Associator in December, 1775 [Ref: E-164], and a Juror to the Oath of Allegiance in 1778 [Ref: C-22].

BARRICK, Catherine. See "George and Adam Devilbiss," q.v.

BARRICK, Christian. Provided wheat for the military in May, 1782 [Ref: R-516].

BARRICK, Frederick. Associator in December, 1775 [Ref: E-163]. Juror to the Oath of Allegiance in 1778 [Ref: C-22].

BARRICK, George. Associator in December, 1775 [Ref: E-163]. Juror to the Oath of Allegiance in 1778 [Ref: C-22].

BARRICK, Henry. Drummer in Capt. Valentine Creager's company of militia in 1775 [Ref: E-53]. Associator in December, 1775 [Ref: E-163]. Juror to the Oath of Allegiance in 1778 [Ref: C-22]. "Henry Berreck" was a private who enlisted on July 1, 1776, in Capt. Peter Mantz's company; marched from Frederick Town to Leonardtown, and from there to Philadelphia, arriving on August 23, 1776 [Ref: A-47]. He "applied for a pension (S8054) in Frederick County on October 30, 1833, aged 75, stating that he volunteered under Capt. Peter Mantz and was attached to Col. Griffith's Battalion of the Flying Camp. Subsequently, marched to Annapolis, Leonard Town, Annapolis, Philadelphia, and New York. Engaged the enemy at Harlem Heights around September 20, 1776. Marched to White Plains and engaged the enemy. Then marched to Crotans Bridge, Peckskill, Fort Lee, Fort Washington, Hackinsack, New Jersey, New York, Brunswick, and Princeton. After December 1, 1776, he marched to Philadelphia and then back to Frederick County, as his six months enlistment had expired. He died May 8, 1834, and three or four of his children received the final payment due him (but no names were given at time of payment on April 11, 1842)." [Ref: K-6, T-168].

BARRICK [BARRACK], Jacob. Corporal in Capt. Valentine Creager's company of militia in 1775 [Ref: E-53]. Associator in December, 1775 [Ref: E-163]. Private in the Middle District Militia in 1776 [Ref: A-72]. Juror to the Oath of Allegiance in 1778 [Ref: C-22]. One "Jacob Barrack, or Barrock" was a private on August 5, 1776, in the Flying Camp under Capt. Philip Meroney [Ref: A-45, N-30:112]. One "Jacob Barrick" provided wheat for the military in May, 1782 [Ref: R-516].

BARRICK, Jacob (of Jna.). Corporal in Capt Valentine Creager's company of militia in 1775 [Ref: E-53].

BARRICK, Jacob (of William). Associator in December, 1775 [Ref: E-164]. Juror to the Oath of Allegiance in 1778 [Ref: C-22].

BARRICK, John (of Peter). Associator in December, 1775 [Ref: E-163]. Juror to the Oath of Allegiance in 1778 [Ref: C-22].
BARRICK, John (of Handel). Associator in December, 1775 [Ref: E-163]. Juror to the Oath of Allegiance in 1778 [Ref: C-22]. Ensign in the militia on April 28, 1779 [Ref: Z-369, and H-16, which latter source had misspelled his name as "John Banick, of Handl."]. 1st lieutenant in 1782 [Ref: O-182, and H-50, which latter source had spelled his name "John Barrick, of Handiel"]. A "Handeal Barrick" died testate in 1787 [Ref: M-7:89].
BARRICK, John Jr. Sergeant in Capt. Valentine Creager's company of militia in 1775 [Ref: E-53]. Associator in December, 1775 [Ref: E-163]. Juror to the Oath of Allegiance in 1778 [Ref: C-22].
BARRICK [BARRACK], John Sr. Associator in December, 1775 [Ref: E-163]. "John Barrack" was appointed "to hand about the Association paper" in Manor Hundred in 1775 [Ref: E-305]. "John Barrick, Sr." subscribed to the Oath of Allegiance in 1778 [Ref: C-22].
BARRICK, John Crist. See "John Cristbarrick," q.v.
BARRICK, Mary Ann. See "William Crom," q.v.
BARRICK [BARRACK], Peter. Associator in December, 1775 [Ref: E-163]. 1st lieutenant in Capt. Valentine Creager's company of militia in 1775 [Ref: E-53]. Juror to the Oath of Allegiance in 1778 [Ref: C-22]. "Peter Barrack" was paid for recruiting services on January 11, 1780 [Ref: R-260]. "Peter Barrick" was a captain in the militia in 1782 [Ref: K-7, B-50, O-182].
BARRICK, Peter. Nephew of Capt. Peter Barrick. Born in Frederick County and enlisted there "in the year last before Cornwallace the British General was taken by the troops of the United States." He had volunteered under Major Philip Smith to drive a team to haul provisions for the American Army and continued in that service for 3 months. A short time afterwards he was drafted under Capt. Peter Barrick [Barrack] for 9 months and was engaged in guarding the magazine at Frederickstown and provisions at Fort Frederick. He was given a discharge, but it was destroyed by fire which consumed his house and all his household property. After the war he lived in Virginia, Ohio, and Illinois. He "applied for a pension (R555) on September 1, 1834, aged 72, Champaign [Crawford?] County, Illinois. One Alexander M. Barrick of Crawford County, Illinois, filed as an heir at law of Peter Barrick on November 19, 1852. William Barrick, of Coles County, Illinois, also filed as an heir on October 31, 1855. No relationships were stated." [Ref: T-168, K-7].

BARRICK, Philip. 2nd lieutenant in Capt. Valentine Creager's company of militia in 1775 [Ref: E-53, O-182]. Associator in December, 1775 [Ref: E-164]. Juror to the Oath of Allegiance in 1778 [Ref: C-22]. "Philip Barrack" was paid for recruiting services for the 7th Maryland Regiment on January 11, 1780 [Ref: V-54].

BARRICK, William. Associator in December, 1775 [Ref: E-163]. (Name appeared twice on the Associators list). Subscribed to the Oath of Allegiance in 1778 [Ref: C-22]. William Barrick died testate in 1791, leaving a wife Catharine and children Jacob, George, William Jr., Catharine Devilbiss, Mary, Susannah, Michael, and Sarah [Ref: M-8:86].

BARRIER, Philip. See "Philip Burrier," q.v.

BARRINGER, David. Private in the Middle District Militia in 1776 [Ref: A-72].

BARROW, John. Non-Enroller who was fined by the Committee of Observation in May, 1776 [Ref: E-248].

BARRY, John. Private who enlisted on July 19, 1776 [Ref: A-51].

BARTH, Susanna Catherine. See "Andrew Fogel (Vogler)," q.v.

BARTON, Henry. Associator in December, 1775 [Ref: E-163]. Juror to the Oath of Allegiance in 1778 [Ref: C-22].

BARTON, Martha. See "Adrian Hoblitzell," q.v.

BARTS, Samuel. Private in the German Regiment who served at White Plains on September 5, 1778, under Lt. Col. Weltner [Ref: A-266].

BARTTOMEW, Peter. Private who enlisted May 20, 1778 [Ref: A-323]. "Peter Batolomey" served in the German Regiment at White Plains on September 5, 1778, under Lt. Col. Ludwick Weltner [Ref: A-266].

BARWICK, Handle [Handel]. Loaned $1,000 for the use of the State of Maryland in June, 1780 [Ref: V-520].

BARWICK, John. Loaned $600 for the use of the State of Maryland in June, 1780 [Ref: V-520].

BARWICK, William. Loaned $500 for the use of the State of Maryland in June, 1780 [Ref: V-520].

BASHT, William. Private in Capt. Bayer's company, served 3 years and was discharged July 17, 1779 at Camp Wyoming [Ref: A-271].

BATES, John. See "Peter Fine," q.v.

BATES, Philip. Private in the German Regiment who served at White Plains on September 5, 1778, under Lt. Col. Weltner [Ref: A-266].

BATESON, William. Private who enlisted July 29, 1776 [Ref: A-44].

BAUD, Francis. Corporal in Capt. William Shields' company of militia in 1775 [Ref: E-56].

BAUER, Susanna. See "Jacob Bireley," q.v.

BAUGH, Michael. Private who enlisted on July 1, 1776 in Capt. Peter Mantz's company, marched from Frederick Town to Leonardtown, and from there to Philadelphia, arriving August 23, 1776 [Ref: A-47].

BAUM, Jacob. Signed as Juror to the Oath of Allegiance in March, 1778 [Ref: S-263, but not listed in Ref: C-22].

BAUM, John. Militia substitute from May to December 10, 1781, and "marched to Annapolis." [Ref: A-653]. He "applied for a pension on October 2, 1832, aged 74, in Clearfield Township, Cambria County, Pennsylvania, stating he enlisted in Frederick County, Maryland, and served in the Maryland Line. The children by his first wife (not named) were: Catharine (born January 13, 1782); Martha (born December 12, 1789, and married Richard Nagle); John (born December 12, 1790); and, Barbara (born September 12, 1801). John married secondly to Mary Forshey in 1830, and died on August 2, 1836. His widow applied for a pension (W8109) on October 4, 1851, in Blair County, Pennsylvania." [Ref: T-189].

BAUMGARDNER, Barbara. See "George Lemmon (Layman)," q.v.

BAUMGARDNER, Henry. Soldier in the Pennsylvania Line who "applied for a pension (S22098) on August 8, 1832, aged 74, in York County, Pennsylvania, a resident of Frederick County, Maryland, near the Pennsylvania line. He stated that he was born in 1758 in Frederick County and enlisted in York County (part that is now Adams County) and was living with George Kitzmiller at the time." [Ref: T-189].

BAUMGARDNER, John. See "John Burngardener," q.v.

BAUMGARDNER, Michael. See "Michael Bumgardner," q.v.

BAUMGARTNER, George. Private, enlisted July 24, 1776 [Ref: A-50].

BAUMGARTNER, William. Private, enlisted July 24, 1776 [Ref: A-50].

BAWL, John. Non-Enroller who was fined by the Committee of Observation in April, 1776 [Ref: E-248].

BAXTER, Benjamin. Associator in December, 1775 [Ref: E-164]. Juror to the Oath of Allegiance in 1778 [Ref: C-22].

BAYER, Adam. Associator in December, 1775 [Ref: E-164]. Juror to the Oath of Allegiance in 1778 [Ref: C-22].

BAYER, Jacob. Private who enlisted on July 1, 1776 in Capt. Peter Mantz's company; marched from Frederick Town to Leonardtown, and from there to Philadelphia, arriving on August 23, 1776 [Ref: A-47]. Juror to the Oath of Allegiance in 1778 [Ref: C-22, S-263].

BAYER, John Adam. Associator in December, 1775 [Ref: E-163]. Juror to the Oath of Allegiance in 1778 [Ref: C-22].

BAYER [BOYER], Michael. Associator in December, 1775 [Ref: E-163]. 2nd lieutenant in the German Regiment in July, 1776, in Capt. Henry Fister's company under the command of Col. Nicholas Hussecker [Ref: A-261, X-48]. Juror to the Oath of Allegiance in 1778 [Ref: C-22]. Captain from May 25, 1778, served at Camp Wyoming in 1779, and declared a supernumerary on January 1, 1781 [Ref: A-270, A-365]. "In December, 1816, the Treasurer of the Western Shore was directed to pay Michael Boyer [sic], late a captain in the Revolutionary War, quarterly, during his life, a sum of money equal to the half pay of a captain, as further compensation to him for his services during the Revolutionary War." [Ref: G-322]. "Major Michael Buyer [sic] was a lieutenant in the Revolutionary War and at the Battle of Brandywine was ordered by Col. Parker, of Virginia, to station a picket guard of fourteen men on the top of the hill between the American and British lines, and not to abandon it on point of death. Accordingly, he took the station and threw up a small breastwork. After remaining at his post for some time, he saw the regiment of grenadiers called the Queen's Regiment advancing up the hill to attack him. He thought of his orders and the folly of opposing a whole regiment with fourteen men, but he determined to have one fire. He ordered his men to wait until the British advanced to point blank shot, to take good aim, and then retreat to the main body at the bottom of the hill. His orders were obeyed, and he drew his men off in safety. Some time afterwards a number of British officers who were in the Battle of Brandywine were made prisoners and were quartered at the house of Col. William Beatty, about four miles from Frederick, the native place of Col. Buyer [sic]. He met with one of them, and asked him what had become of the regiment which advanced up the hill to a breastwork and received the fire of the picket guard at the top. The British officer replied he remembered the circumstance well, and that the fire from the picket guard killed the captain and eleven men, and that when they marched up to the breastwork they found it so slight that they kicked it over with their feet." [Ref: F-460, F-467].

BAYER, Philip. Associator in December, 1775 [Ref: E-164]. Juror to the Oath of Allegiance in 1778 [Ref: C-22].

BAYLER, Joseph (Unity Hundred). Non-Enroller who was fined by the Committee of Observation in June, 1776 [Ref: E-248].

BAYLEY, William (lower part of Potomac Hundred). Appointed by the Committee of Correspondence to solicit subscriptions in 1775 to purchase arms and ammunition [Ref: I-86]. "William Bayley, Jr." served on the Committee of Observation in 1775 [Ref: I-85]. He also served in the House of Delegates and attended the Provincial Convention on August 14, 1776 [Ref: F-476, F-479].

BAYLIE, William and Margaret. See "Jacob Brunner," q.v.

BAYMAN, Thomas. Private who enlisted August 5, 1776, in the Flying Camp under Capt. Philip Meroney [Ref: A-45; not in Ref: N-30:112].

BAZALER, Henry. Petitioned the General Assembly under the Act of May 12, 1780, stating that he had been a non-juror to the Oath of Allegiance and Fidelity in 1778 due to "ignorance" and now desired relief under the Act and to take the Oath [Ref: L-101].

BAZALER, Michael. Petitioned the General Assembly under the Act of May 12, 1780, stating that he had been a non-juror to the Oath of Allegiance and Fidelity in 1778 due to "ignorance" and now desired relief under the Act and to take the Oath [Ref: L-101].

BEADEN, John. Private in the militia in July, 1776 [Ref: A-42].

BEAKLEY, Israel. Non-Enroller who was fined by the Committee of Observation in April, 1776 [Ref: E-248].

BEALE, Harriet. See "Elisha Williams," q.v.

BEALE, Samuel (Colonel). See "Peter Sholly," q.v.

BEALL, Alexander Edmonston. Private in militia in 1776 [Ref: A-42].

BEALL, Alexander Robert. Private in militia in 1776 [Ref: A-42].

BEALL, Basil. 2nd lieutenant in Capt. William Luckett, Jr.'s company of militia in 1775 [Ref: E-55]. Associator in December, 1775; name appeared twice in the list [Ref: E-163, E-164]. 1st lieutenant in Capt. Thomas Frazer's company in the 34th Battalion on June 11, 1776 [Ref: B-51, W-476]. Juror to the Oath of Allegiance in 1778 [Ref: C-22].

BEALL, Brooke (upper part of Potomac Hundred). Appointed by the Committee of Correspondence to solicit subscriptions in 1775 to purchase arms and ammunition [Ref: I-86]. Served on the Committee of Observation in 1775 [Ref: I-85].

BEALL, Charles. Served on the Committee of Observation in 1775 [Ref: I-85]. Non-Enroller who was fined by the Committee of Observation in April, 1776, but he apparently enrolled and the fine was discharged in May, 1776 [Ref: E-248]. Provided wheat for the military in June, 1782 [Ref: R-522].

BEALL, Eleanor Ogle. See "Guy Elder," q.v.

BEALL, Elisha. 2nd lieutenant in Capt. Samuel Plummer's company of militia in 1775 [Ref: E-54, B-51]. 1st lieutenant in the Middle District Militia in 1776 [Ref: A-44]. Loaned $250 for the use of the State of Maryland in June, 1780 [Ref: V-520].

BEALL, George (Captain). Appointed an Inspector of George Town Warehouses in the Lower District of Frederick County on September 21, 1776 [Ref: X-293]. Paid for services rendered to the military (nature of the services not stated) in December, 1779 [Ref: V-44].

BEALL, James (of William). Associator in December, 1775 [Ref: E-164]. Juror to the Oath of Allegiance in 1778 [Ref: C-22].

BEALL, James. Associator in December, 1775 [Ref: E-164]. Juror to the Oath of Allegiance in 1778 [Ref: C-22]. One James Beall was a private who enlisted on August 5, 1776, in the Flying Camp under Capt. Philip Meroney [Ref: A-45, N-30:112]. One James Beall was a corporal in Capt. Robert Wood's company in 1775 [Ref: E-53].

BEALL, James McCormack. Private who enlisted on August 5, 1776, in the Flying Camp under Capt. Philip Meroney, and was reported as "deserted" (no date). [Ref: A-45]. However, Ref: N-30:112 listed his name as just "James McCormack," not "James McCormack Beall."].

BEALL, James (of Roger). Private in the militia in July, 1776 [Ref: A-42].

BEALL, Jeremiah. Private in the militia in July, 1776 [Ref: A-42].

BEALL, John (Linganore Hundred). Appointed by the Committee of Correspondence to solicit subscriptions in 1775 to purchase arms and ammunition [Ref: I-86]. Served on the Committee of Observation in 1775 [Ref: I-85]. One John Beall served as a private in the 6th Maryland Regiment from July 1, 1778, until discharged on April 1, 1779 [Ref: A-187].

BEALL, Leaven. Private in the militia in July, 1776 [Ref: A-42].

BEALL, Lloyd. Private who enlisted on July 13, 1776 [Ref: A-43].

BEALL, Mordecai. 1st lieutenant in Capt. Robert Wood's company of militia in the 2nd Battalion on November 29, 1775 [Ref: E-53, B-51]. Associator in December, 1775 [Ref: E-164]. Captain in the 37th Battalion of militia on May 15, 1776 [Ref: B-51, W-427]. Juror to Oath of Allegiance in 1778 [Ref: C-22].

BEALL, Ninian. Juror to the Oath of Allegiance in March, 1778 [Ref: S-263, but not listed in Ref: C-22]. He "applied for a pension on May 5, 1818, aged 57, Frederick County, Maryland, and in 1820 he was living in Butler County, Ohio, a resident of St. Clair Township, with a wife, aged 47, and children: John, aged 15; Joseph, aged 12; Margaret, aged 10; James, aged 8; and, Sarah, aged 5. Ninian Beall married Christiana Stull in August, 1780, in Frederick County, where he enlisted during the Revolutionary War. He died on June 13, 1836. His widow applied for a pension (W9722) on November 12, 1839, aged 66, in Ripley County, Indiana. A son Ninian Beall was aged 50, born October 27, 1792, in

Frederick County, and a son Zephaniah Beal [sic] was born April 10, 1795. Also mentioned was one "Zeremiah Beal" who lived in Dearborn County, Indiana in 1835, and a "Mrs. Elizabeth Beal" who lived in Montgomery County, Indiana, in 1842 (no relationships were stated)." [Ref: T-197].

BEALL, Ninian Magruder. See "Guy Elder," q.v.

BEALL, Rezin (General). See "Lawrence Everhart," q.v.

BEALL, Richard, of Samuel (Northwest Hundred). Appointed by the Committee of Correspondence to solicit subscriptions in 1775 to purchase arms and ammunition [Ref: I-86].

BEALL, Samuel. Colonel of the 36th Battalion in 1776 [Ref: B-51, W-356]. Served in the House of Delegates from the Upper District on August 14, 1776 [Ref: F-476, F-479]. Also, see "Samuel Bell," q.v.

BEALL, Samuel Jr. Served on the Committee of Observation in 1775 [Ref: I-85]. Associator in December, 1775 [Ref: E-163]. Juror to the Oath of Allegiance in 1778 [Ref: C-22].

BEALL, Thaddeus. 2nd lieutenant in the Lower District Militia [now Montgomery County] under Capt. Edward Burgess on August 7, 1776 [Ref: A-42].

BEALL, Thomas. Private in the militia in July, 1776 [Ref: A-42]. One Thomas Beall, "a soldier in the Maryland Line, applied for a pension (S45270) on June 28, 1818, in Preble County, Ohio, stating he was born in July, 1761." [Ref: T-197].

BEALL, Thomas (of George). Served on the Committee of Observation in 1775 [Ref: I-85]. Appointed captain of a rifle company in July, 1776 [Ref: X-113]. Reviewed and passed troops in 1781 [Ref: B-168].

BEALL, Walter. Associator in December, 1775 [Ref: E-163]. Juror to the Oath of Allegiance in 1778 [Ref: C-22].

BEALL, William Jr. Associator in December, 1775 [Ref: E-164]. Juror to the Oath of Allegiance in 1778 [Ref: C-22].

BEALL, William Murdock (c1742-1823). Served on the Committee of Observation in 1775 [Ref: I-85]. Associator in December, 1775 [Ref: E-163]. Juror to the Oath of Allegiance in 1778 [Ref: C-22]. Justice of the Peace in 1777. Loaned $1,000 for the use of the State of Maryland in June, 1780 [Ref: V-520]. Judge of the Court of Appeals for Frederick County on May 23, 1778 [Ref: Z-109]. Judge of the Orphans Court in 1781 [Ref: F-476, F-480]. Mrs. Beall, wife of William, postmaster, died on April 26, 1810, and William M. Beall died on November 5, 1823, aged 81 [Ref: F-471, F-472, P-125].

BEALL, Zephaniah. Ensign in the 16th Battalion of Militia on June 25, 1776, and ensign in the Lower District Militia [now Montgomery County] under Capt. E. Burgess in August, 1776 [Ref: A-42, W-515].

BEAMER, George. See "Jacob Gilbert," q.v.

BEAMER, Henry. Juror to the Oath of Allegiance in March, 1778 [Ref: S-263, but not listed in Ref: C-22].

BEANY, Jacob. Associator in December, 1775 [Ref: E-164]. Juror to the Oath of Allegiance in 1778 [Ref: C-22].

BEAR [BARE], George. Served on the Committee of Observation in 1775 [Ref: I-85]. Associator in December, 1775 [Ref: E-164]. Juror to the Oath of Allegiance in 1778 [Ref: C-22]. Paid for services rendered to the military in 1779 (nature of the services not stated) [Ref: V-44].

BEAR, Henry (1758-1848). Associator in December, 1775 [Ref: E-164]. Private who enlisted on July 1, 1776 in Capt. Peter Mantz's company; marched from Frederick Town to Leonardtown, and then to Philadelphia, arriving August 23, 1776 [Ref: A-47]. Juror to the Oath of Allegiance in 1778 [Ref: C-22]. "Henry Baer" was pensioned in 1831, age 76 [according to Ref: J-33; however, Ref: T-111 stated he applied for a pension (S8051) on December 27, 1832, aged 74, in Frederick County]. "Henry Bear, aged 91, the last of the Revolutionary survivors of Frederick County, died on February 17, 1848. He entered the service in 1776 as a volunteer. He was one of the company that marched from Frederick under the command of Capt. Peter Mantz, and which formed part of the old Maryland line." [Ref: F-474]. Henry Bear married Elizabeth Shellman in 1779 and daughter Susanna Bear (1790-1862) married John Feister (1787-1869) in 1812 [Ref: U-1012]. Also, see "William Blair (Captain)," q.v.

BEAR, Mary. See "Samuel Brandenburgh," q.v.

BEARAE [sic], Jacob. Private who was enlisted on July 20, 1776, by Capt. Jacob Good [Ref: A-46].

BEARD, Frederick. Private who enlisted August 5, 1776 in the Flying Camp under Capt. Philip Meroney [Ref: A-45, N-30:112]. Militia substitute from May to December 10, 1781; "marched to Annapolis." [Ref: A-653]. He "applied for a pension (W3379) on November 26, 1833, in Adams County, Pennsylvania, aged 76 on November 1, 1833, stating he was born in Frederick County, Maryland, lived in Adams County, but enlisted in Frederick County (Frederick Town) on June 1, 1776, as a private in Capt. Philip Maroney's Company of the Maryland Flying Camp. He fought in the battles of White Plains and Fort Washington, and served 6 months. In 1777 he served again for 2 months. In the spring of 1781 he enlisted and served under Capt. Valentine Creager, remaining in service until the surrender of Cornwallis [at Yorktown in October, 1781]. His widow Magdalin Beard applied for his pension on February 14, 1846, in Adams County, aged about 85, stating she had married the soldier on December 2, 1783. He had died on March 9, 1842, aged 83 years, 5 months, and 9 days, and was buried at Emmittsburg, Maryland. Their children were: Jacob Beard, born September 24, 1784; John Beard, born June 2, 1786; Elizabeth Beard, born August 10, 1788; Frederick Beard, Jr., born January 15, 1790; Anna Maria Beard, born September 20, 1792; George Beard, born December 8, 1794; Samuel Beard, born November 4, 1796; Ann Catharine Beard, born October 7, 1798; Ann Margaret Beard, born January 14, 1801; Maria Magdalin Beard, born December 8, 1802; and, Joshua Beard, born March 9, 1805." [Ref: T-201, K-9].

BEARD, Jonathan. Private in the Middle District Militia in 1776 [Ref: A-72]. One Peter Beard died testate in 1794, naming wife Catharine and son Jonathan Beard (among others). [Ref: M-9:36].

BEARD, Nicholas. "An Anglo-Irish original settler, he settled at Beard's Church where he held extensive grants of land and was a member of Capt. William Heyser's Company in the Revolutionary War. Private Nicholas Beard (Baird) enlisted on May 22, 1777. The mason work on Old Fort Frederick, Washington County, Maryland, built in 1756, was superintended by Nicholas Beard, the southwest corner having been built by his own hands." [Ref: U-1990].

BEARD, William. "Applied for a pension (S2370) in Ross County, Ohio on October 11, 1832, aged 72 on December last, stating he was born in Washington County [then Frederick County], Maryland on December 27, 1760 or 1761, and moved to North Carolina in May, 1779. He was drafted in Rhoanne [Rowan] County and in 1780 returned to Lincoln County, North Carolina. He enlisted there and in December, 1780, returned to Washington County, Maryland. He enlisted there also, and later moved to Virginia and then to Ohio in 1810. [Ref: T-201, T-202]. It should be noted that there was another William Beard who was from York County, Pennsylvania, and served in Frederick County, Maryland during the Revolutionary War, after which he moved to Belmont County, Ohio." For more information, see Revolutionary War Pension R671 [Ref: T-202, K-10].

BEATTY, Charles (c1736-1804). Surveyor, formerly of Georgetown, and member of the General Assembly in 1773. Active patriot throughout the Revolution. Chosen to serve on the Committee of Observation of the

Middle District of Frederick County in 1775 [Ref: E-302, I-85]. Captain of a militia company in 1775 [Ref: E-51]. Associator in December, 1775, and was appointed "to hand about the Association paper" in Frederick Town [Ref: E-163, E-305]. Juror to the Oath of Allegiance in 1778 [Ref: C-22]. Colonel of the 1st Battalion in 1776 [Ref: E-57, B-52], and Colonel in the Flying Camp in 1776 [Ref: A-46]. Lieutenant of Frederick County, 1777 and 1778 [Ref: A-314]. Commander of the militia with the rank of lieutenant colonel in the Continental Army, and Deputy Quartermaster General in 1778 [Ref: E-302]. "This patriot acted a conspicuous part in the Revolutionary War. At the darkest period of those troubled times, when Washington was retreating through New Jersey, and every man's heart sunk within him, the call to arms was heard to resound through the generally quiet and peaceable town of Frederick, and the people sprang to the rescue of their country. The troops were marshaled on the beautiful green inclosures now occupied by the Catholic institutions. There was a whole battalion present, consisting of eight companies. Col. Charles Beatty addressed them, and invited those who were willing to aid 'to step forward,' whereupon the whole battalion advanced except three men, who afterwards, amid the jeers of their comrades, also volunteered. The soldiers marched under Col. Beatty, and saw some service at the Battle of Brunswick, where three men were killed out of one company. Among them was Lieutenant Grosch. The colonel was a wealthy, public-spirited man." [Ref: F-457, F-448]. Served in the House of Delegates and attended the Provincial Convention in 1775 [Ref: F-479, P-127].

BEATTY, Elijah. Associator in December, 1775 [Ref: E-164]. Juror to the Oath of Allegiance in 1778 [Ref: C-22].

BEATTY, James. 2nd lieutenant in Capt. William Beatty's company of militia in 1775 [Ref: E-55]. Loaned $1,000 for the use of the State of Maryland in June, 1780 [Ref: V-520].

BEATTY, John. Associator who was appointed "to hand about the Association paper" in Israel Creek Hundred in 1775 [Ref: E-305]. Served in the House of Delegates in 1779 [Ref: F-479].

BEATTY, Robert. Captain of a militia company in 1775 [Ref: E-55].

BEATTY, Thomas (Middle Monocacy). Appointed by the Committee of Correspondence to solicit subscriptions in 1775 to purchase arms and ammunition [Ref: I-86]. Served on the Committee of Observation in 1775 [Ref: I-85]. Associator in December, 1775 [Ref: E-164]. Juror to the Oath of Allegiance in 1778 [Ref: C-22]. Commissioned an ensign in Middle District Militia on March 26, 1776 [Ref: W-199, W-287]. Captain in the militia from May 12, 1779, to 1781 [Ref: H-15, B-52]. Served in the House of Delegates in 1781 [Ref: F-479]. Mrs. Thomas Beatty died on April 30, 1805 [Ref: F-470, N-57].

BEATTY, William (1739 - May 1, 1803). Son of William Beatty (1693-1757) and Elizabeth Carmack (died 1756). Served in the French and Indian War in 1756. Captain of a militia company in 1775 [Ref: E-55]. Resident of Manor Hundred. Appointed by the Committee of Correspondence to solicit subscriptions in 1775 to purchase arms and ammunition [Ref: I-86]. Associator in December, 1775 [Ref: E-163]. Chosen to serve on the Committee of Observation on September 12, 1775 [Ref: E-302]. Lieutenant Colonel of the 1st Battalion in 1776 [Ref: E-57, B-52]. Colonel of militia [Ref: H-15]. Sheriff of Frederick County in 1776 and Judge of the Orphans' Court from 1777 to at least 1783 [Ref: F-476, F-480, E-302]. Agent for the Purchase of Provisions for the Army on March 25, 1778, Justice of the Peace in 1777, and Court Justice on November 21, 1778 [Ref: E-302, F-476]. Juror to the Oath of Allegiance in 1778 [Ref: C-22, S-263]. Lieutenant of Frederick County in 1780 [Ref: A-345]. "Col. William Beatty died at his plantation on May 1, 1803, aged 64." [Ref: F-470, but Ref: M-6:98 states he died on April 25, 1801, aged 62]. He married Mary Dorathy Grosh and had children William, Henry, Elizabeth, John C., Cornelius, Sophia, Mary, George, Otho, Eleanor, Elie, Adam, John Michael, Daniel, William Affordby, and Lewis Augustus. [Ref: M-6:98-102]. Also, see "Michael Bayer," q.v.

BEATTY, William Jr. (June 19, 1758 - April 25, 1781). Born in Frederick County, the oldest child of Col. William Beatty (1739-1803) and Mary Dorathy [sic] Grosh (1739-1810). He was appointed to the rank of an ensign in the Middle District Militia in July, 1776 [Ref: A-44, F-458]. "In a short time he was appointed a lieutenant in the Maryland Line of Continental Troops, and spent the winter in raising recruits for the regiment to which he belonged. In the discharge of this unpleasant, difficult duty he acquitted himself with much credit, and in the following spring joined the army at Middlebrook, New Jersey. William's merit as an officer was soon discovered by the commander-in-chief and he was promoted to a captaincy in the 1st Maryland Regiment [September 14, 1778]. "At the Battle of Hobkirk's Hill, near Camden [South Carolina], which was fought on the 25th day of April, 1781, Capt. Beatty, while gallantly leading on the right company of the First Maryland Regiment, received a mortal wound. Thus fell, in the twenty-third year of his age, this brave and promising young officer." [Ref: A-310, E-302, F-458, F-459]. Bounty land warrant application 644-300 mentioned his oldest brother Henry Beatty of Winchester, Virginia, formerly of Maryland, and a Charles A. Beatty of Montgomery County, Maryland (no relationship stated). A Cathrina Kimball stated that William Beatty married Mary Dorothy (no last name given) and died without issue [Ref: T-205]. Capt. William Beatty was also paid for recruiting services for the 7th Maryland Regiment on January 11, 1780 [Ref: V-54].

BEATTYS, Philip. Militia substitute on June 3, 1778 [Ref: A-325].

BEAVEN, William. Drafted on June 2, 1783; "discharged, is poor and had a wife and three children." [Ref: B-169].

BEAVER (BEIBER), Mary Ann. See "Mathias Firestone," q.v.

BECK, Andrew. Associator in December, 1775 [Ref: E-164]. Juror to the Oath of Allegiance in 1778 [Ref: C-22].

BECK, James. Associator in December, 1775 [Ref: E-164]. Juror to the Oath of Allegiance in 1778 [Ref: C-22].

BECK, Margarethe. See "(Johann) Ulrich Reever (Rieber)," q.v.

BECKENBAUGH, Adam. Associator in December, 1775 [Ref: E-164]. Juror to the Oath of Allegiance in 1778 [Ref: C-22].

BECKENBAUGH, Anne Mary and Casper. See "Lawrence Everhart," q.v.

BECKENBAUGH, Leonard. See "Leonard Peckenpaugh," q.v.

BECKER, George. Militia substitute from May to December 10, 1781, and "marched to Annapolis." [Ref: A-653].

BECKERSON, John. Private in the German Regiment in 1776, with Capt. Henry Fister's company under the command of Col. Nicholas Hussecker [Ref: A-261].

BECKETT, Humphrey. Private, 1st Maryland Regiment, 1780, and served in the Southern Army of the United States under Lt. William Lamar in the late Capt. Beatty's company until transferred to the light infantry on March 12, 1781 [Ref: A-390]. He "applied for a pension on June 5, 1818, in Pickaway County, Ohio, stating he had received a pension under the Act of April 25, 1808. In 1825 he moved to Warren County, Indiana and died there April 2, 1830, and was also called Dr. Becket. He had married February 22, 1786, to Mary or Polly (no last name given) who was born May 15, 1762. His widow applied for a pension (W9726) September 14, 1833, in Warren County, Indiana, and died December 25, 1839. Family records in 1820 show Elizabeth Beckett was aged 33 and had married James Becket on June 7, 1812, and was a widow with three small children in 1820 and in Warren County, Indiana; Benjamin or Benjamin H. Becket was aged 27, Maria Becket, aged 13, and later married a man named Raney; Egbert Becket, aged 11; Alfred Becket, aged 9; Polly Becket, aged 7; also, children shown were Ann or Anna, born April 21, 1796; William, born November 23, 1798; Carle, born April 24, 1801; Eliza, born October 11, 1803; also shown were: Lucy, daughter of James and Elizabeth Becket, married Sylvester Stone on December 11, 1817. In 1852 the only surviving children were Benjamin H., Elizabeth, and Alfred Becket, and Mariah or Maria Raney, were living in Iroquois County, Illinois." [Ref: T-208].

BECKETT, James. Private who enlisted on August 5, 1776, in the Flying Camp under Capt. Philip Meroney [Ref: A-45, N-30:112]. Juror to the Oath of Allegiance in 1778 [Ref: S-263, but not in Ref: C-22].

BECKETT, William. Associator in December, 1775 [Ref: E-164]. Juror to the Oath of Allegiance in 1778 [Ref: C-22, and S-263, which source listed this name twice].

BECKWITH, Benjamin. Associator in December, 1775 [Ref: E-163], and a Juror to the Oath of Allegiance in 1778 [Ref: C-22]. Drafted on June 13, 1781; provided a substitute [Ref: D-1814]. He "applied for a pension (S2063) on July 21, 1832, in Morgan Township, Morgan County, Ohio, aged 72, stating he had served in the Maryland Line. He was born about 12 miles from Washington, D. C. in Frederick County, Maryland, and enlisted there and later moved to Cumberland County [sic], Maryland for 10 years. He then moved to Frankfort in Hampshire County, Virginia, then to Newton Township in Muskingum County, Ohio, for 10 or 12 years, and then to Morgan Township, Morgan County, Ohio." [Ref: T-209].

BECKWITH, George. Ensign in Capt. David Moore's company of militia in 1775 [Ref: E-56]. Associator in December, 1775 [Ref: E-164]. Captain in the militia on June 22, 1778 [Ref: H-17, B-52, Z-145]. George "applied for a pension on March 25, 1833, in Montgomery County, Maryland, stating he served in the Maryland Line and was born on November 16, 1760, near Frederick Town, Maryland, and enlisted there. After the war he lived in Montgomery County except for a short time in Prince George's County, Maryland. His widow Ann or Leanah applied for a pension (W9355) on September 17, 1850, aged 77 or 78, in Montgomery County, Maryland, stating they had married in October, 1781, and George had died on December 13, 1849. She also applied for bounty land warrant no. 91507-160-55 on May 16, 1855, in Washington, D. C., aged about 80." [Ref: T-209].

BECKWITH [BECKETH], Nicholas. Private who enlisted on July 1, 1776 in Capt. Peter Mantz's company, and marched from Frederick Town to Leonardtown, and from there to Philadelphia, arriving on August 23, 1776 [Ref: A-47].

BECKWITH, William. Soldier in the Maryland Line who "applied for a pension (S2071) on July 21, 1832, in Morgan County, Ohio, aged 74, a resident of Morgan Township. He had lived in Frederick County, Maryland, about 12 miles from Washington, D.C. William's daughter Rebecca Beckwith, of New York City, in 1836 stated he had died on October 27, 1836, and stated that he had three children: herself, Richard, and Tobias Beckwith. Richard had left home in 1819 and was presumed dead, and Tobias died in Morgan County, Ohio, on January 16, 1823, leaving her the only surviving child." [Ref: T-210].

BECRAFT, Benjamin. Associator in December, 1775 [Ref: E-164]. Juror to the Oath of Allegiance in 1778 [Ref: C-22].

BECRAFT, George. Associator in December, 1775 [Ref: E-164]. Juror to the Oath of Allegiance in 1778 [Ref: C-22].

BECRAFT, Peter (Northwest Hundred). Appointed by the Committee of Correspondence to solicit subscriptions in 1775 to purchase arms and ammunition [Ref: I-86]. Associator in December, 1775 [Ref: E-164]. Juror to the Oath of Allegiance in 1778 [Ref: C-22]. "Peter Becraft, planter" died testate in 1780, leaving a wife Mary and children Elizabeth, James, Peter, and Joice, and grandchildren Mary, Rebecca, Peter, William, and Joshua Mockbee [Ref: M-5:164].

BEDFORD, Gunning. See "John Stricker," q.v.

BEEDING, Henry. Private who enlisted on July 18, 1776 [Ref: A-49].

BEEDING, Joseph. Private who enlisted on July 25, 1776 [Ref: A-49].

BEELER, Elizabeth. See "John Cronise (Kronise)," q.v.

BEEN, John. Private who enlisted on July 18, 1776 [Ref: A-50].

BEFFINGTON, Thomas. Associator in December, 1775 [Ref: E-164]. Juror to the Oath of Allegiance in 1778 [Ref: C-22].

BEGOLE, William. Corporal in Capt. Basil Dorsey's company of militia in 1775 [Ref: E-52].

BEIKER, Michael. Private in the German Regiment in 1776, with Capt. Henry Fister's company under the command of Col. Nicholas Hussecker [Ref: A-261].

BELL, John. Private in the Skipton District Militia under Capt. Thomas Waring on April 16, 1776 [Ref: B-167, D-1814]. Militia substitute on June 6, 1778 [Ref: A-325].

BELL, Peter. Private who enlisted on July 1, 1776, in Capt. Peter Mantz's company; marched from Frederick Town to Leonardtown, and from there to Philadelphia, arriving August 23, 1776 [Ref: A-47].

BELL, Samuel. Colonel, 36th Battalion, January 3, 1776 [Ref: H-3].

BELLOWS, Isaac. Private who enlisted on May 14, 1778 [Ref: A-324].

BELSER, Peter. Juror to the Oath of Allegiance in March, 1778 [Ref: S-263, but not listed in Ref: C-22].

BELSOOVER, Jacob. Private in German Regiment, on muster roll dated October 23, 1776 [Ref: A-264]. "Jacob Beltzhoover" was a private in the German Regiment; discharged on July 26, 1779 [Ref: A-265].

BELT, Jeremiah. "Jeremiah Belt 3rd" petitioned to form the horse troops in 1781 [Ref: B-167]. "Jeremiah Belt" provided wheat for the military in May, 1782 [Ref: R-515].

BELTZER, Christopher. Corporal in Capt. Philip Rodenbieler's company of militia in 1775 [Ref: E-51].

BEMER, Henry. Associator in December, 1775 [Ref: E-163]. Juror to the Oath of Allegiance in 1778 [Ref: C-22].

BEMHART, John. Private who enlisted on July 19, 1776 [Ref: A-51].

BENGER, John. Associator in December, 1775 [Ref: E-163]. Juror to the Oath of Allegiance in 1778 [Ref: C-22].

BENIER, Philip. Non-Enroller who was fined by the Committee of Observation in April, 1776, but he apparently enrolled because the fine was remitted in June, 1776 [Ref: E-248].

BENNETT, John. Private who enlisted on May 18, 1778 [Ref: A-323]. "John Bennet" was a private in the German Regiment at White Plains on September 5, 1778 [Ref: A-266]. This or perhaps another John Bennett was a private who enlisted on July 1, 1776, in Capt. Peter Mantz's company, and marched from Frederick Town to Leonardtown, and then to Philadelphia, arriving on August 23, 1776 [Ref: A-47].

BENNETT, John. Associator in December, 1775 [Ref: E-163]. Captain in the Upper District Militia, 31st Battalion, on May 15, 1776 [Ref: B-52, W-426]. Juror to the Oath of Allegiance in 1778 [Ref: C-22].

BENNETT, Rinear. Private who enlisted on July 24, 1776 [Ref: A-50].

BENNING, Daniel. Private who was enlisted on July 20, 1776 by Capt. Jacob Good [Ref: A-46]. Private, 1st Maryland Regiment, 1781, and served in the Southern Army of the United States under Lt. William Lamar in the late Capt. Beatty's company. Record indicates he had "deserted" in January, 1781 [Ref: A-391].

BENT, George. Served on the Committee of Observation in 1775 [Ref: I-85].

BENTER, George. Private who was enlisted on July 20, 1776, by Capt. Jacob Good [Ref: A-46].

BENTER, Henry. Private in the German Regiment, muster roll dated October 23, 1776 [Ref: A-264]. Discharged on October 12, 1779 [Ref: A-265].

BENTER, Melcher. "Melcher Benter" was a private in German Regiment, muster roll dated October 23, 1776. "Melcher Benner" was a private in German Regiment until discharged on July 17, 1779 [Ref: A-264].

BENTFIELD, William. Associator in December, 1775 [Ref: E-164]. Juror to the Oath of Allegiance in 1778 [Ref: C-22].

BENTLEY, Rebecca and Ruth. See "Joseph Wood," q.v.

BENTLEY, Solomon. Sergeant in Capt. Joseph Wood, Jr.'s company of militia in 1775 [Ref: E-53]. Associator in December, 1775 [Ref: E-163]. Juror to the Oath of Allegiance in 1778 [Ref: C-22]. 1st sergeant in the Middle District Militia in 1776 [Ref: A-72]. 2nd lieutenant in the militia on April 27, 1779, and 1st Lieutenant on August 16, 1781 [Ref: H-16, B-53, Z-368].

BENTLEY, William. Associator in December, 1775 [Ref: E-164]. Juror to the Oath of Allegiance in 1778 [Ref: C-22]. Loaned $2,000 for the use of the State of Maryland in June, 1780 [Ref: V-520].

BENTZ, Martin. Sergeant in Capt. Jacob Ambrose's company of militia in 1775 [Ref: E-54].

BENY, John. Associator in December, 1775 [Ref: E-163]. Juror to the Oath of Allegiance in 1778 [Ref: C-22].

BERGER, John. Juror to the Oath of Allegiance in March, 1778 [Ref: S-263, but not listed in Ref: C-22]. Substitute on June 13, 1781, for 3 years, and was later reported "deserted" (no date given). [Ref: D-1814].

BERGER, Philip. Loaned $400 for the use of the State of Maryland in June, 1780 [Ref: V-520].

BERKSHIRE, Henry. See "Henry Barkshire," q.v.

BERNHART, Rachel. See "Joseph Wood," q.v.

BERRINGER, Chn. Private who enlisted on July 19, 1776 [Ref: A-51].

BERRY, John. Private who enlisted on July 24, 1776 [Ref: A-50].

BETES, Jacob. Associator in December, 1775 [Ref: E-163]. Juror to the Oath of Allegiance in 1778 [Ref: C-22].

BETSWORTH, John. Militia substitute from May to December 10, 1781, and "marched to Annapolis." [Ref: A-653].

BETTS, Richard (Linganore Hundred). Non-Enroller who was fined by the Committee of Observation in June, 1776 [Ref: E-248].

BEVINS, Thomas. Associator in December, 1775 [Ref: E-163]. Juror to the Oath of Allegiance in 1778 [Ref: C-22].

BEYER, Catharine. See "John Smith," q.v.

BEYER [BEUYER], John. "John Beuyer" was a sergeant in Capt. John Carmack's company of militia in 1775 [Ref: E-56]. "John Beyer" was an

Associator in December, 1775 [Ref: E-164]. Juror to the Oath of Allegiance, 1778 [Ref: C-22].

BEYRLEY, Ludwick and George. See "Lodwick and George Bireley," q.v.

BIDDLE, Andrew. 1st lieutenant in the Linganore Battalion of militia on June 22, 1778 [Ref: H-17, B-53, Z-144].

BIER, Philip. Associator in December, 1775 [Ref: E-163]. Juror to the Oath of Allegiance in 1778 [Ref: C-22].

BIERLY, Michael. See "Michael Bireley," q.v.

BILINGER, Martin. Paid by the Committee of Observation "for carriage of three chests of provisional arms" in 1775 [Ref: E-64].

BILINGER [BILGINGR], Adam. Corporal in Capt. Jacob Snowdenberger's company of militia in 1775 [Ref: E-56].

BILLOW, John. Corporal in Capt. Henry Baker's company of militia in 1775 [Ref: E-54]. Private who was enlisted on July 20, 1776, by Capt. Jacob Good [Ref: A-46].

BILSEL, Henry. 2nd lieutenant in Capt. Jacob Ambrose's company of militia in 1775 [Ref: E-54].

BINKLER, Jacob. Private stationed at Fort Frederick on June 27, 1778, in Capt. John Kershner's company, and guarding prisoners of war [Ref: A-328].

BIRD, John. Private in the German Regiment, 1776, in Capt. Henry Fister's company under the command of Col. Hussecker [Ref: A-261].

BIRELEY, George. Associator in December, 1775 [Ref: E-163]. Juror to the Oath of Allegiance in 1778 [Ref: C-22, and S-263, which latter source spelled the name "George Beyrley."].

BIRELEY, Jacob. "Jacob Bireley" was enrolled as an Associator in December, 1775 [Ref: E-164]. "Jacob Bierley" was a Non-Enroller who was fined by the Committee of Observation in April, 1776 [Ref: E-248]. Juror to the Oath of Allegiance in 1778 [Ref: C-22]. He married Maria Dorothea ---- and a son, John George Birely (c1773 - August 16, 1834) married Susanna Bauer (1778-1837) and lived near Thurmont, Maryland [Ref: U-2668].

BIRELEY, Lodwick. Associator in December, 1775 [Ref: E-164]. Juror to the Oath of Allegiance in 1778 [Ref: C-22, and S-263, which source spelled the name "Ludwick Beyrley."]. "Ludwig Beyerle married Eva Maria Heffner, daughter of Michael. He migrated with father John Michael to Lancaster County, then to Monocacy about 1762." [Ref: O-198]. "Lodowick Birely" provided wheat for the military in May, 1782 [Ref: R-517].

BIRELEY, Michael. Associator in December, 1775 [Ref: E-164]. (This name appeared twice on the list of Associators). One subscribed to the Oath of Allegiance in 1778 [Ref: C-22]. "Michael Bierly" was 2nd lieutenant in 37th Battalion of militia on April 15, 1778 [Ref: B-53, Z-35].

BIRGISS, Jacob. Non-Enroller who was fined by the Committee of Observation in April, 1776 [Ref: E-248].

BIRGISS, John. Non-Enroller who was fined by the Committee of Observation in April, 1776 [Ref: E-248].

BISER, Daniel. Corporal in Capt. Herman Yost's company of militia in 1775 [Ref: E-52].

BISHOP, Jacob. Private in the German Regiment, muster roll dated October 23, 1776 [Ref: A-264]. Discharged on July 26, 1779 [Ref: A-265].

BISHOP, Jeremy. Corporal in Capt. Robert Beatty's company of militia in 1775 [Ref: E-55].

BISHOP, Thomas. Private who enlisted on March 4, 1778 [Ref: A-315]. Private in the 2nd Maryland Regiment. Disabled at the Battle of Guilford Court House, his invalid's pension commenced on November 29, 1783, and ceased on November 1, 1789 [Ref: A-630, A-631].

BISSEL, Adam. Associator in December, 1775 [Ref: E-163]. Juror to the Oath of Allegiance in 1778 [Ref: C-22].

BISSETT, Thomas. Private who enlisted on July 18, 1776 [Ref: A-50].

BITZELL, Henry. Associator in December, 1775 [Ref: E-164]. Juror to the Oath of Allegiance in 1778 [Ref: C-22]. "Henry Bitesele" was a 1st lieutenant in the Catoctin Battalion of militia (no date given). [Ref: B-53].

BLACK, Francis. Private in the 7th Maryland Regiment who enlisted in Frederick Town between January and April, 1780, and reported as "gone to Camp" [Ref: A-334].

BLACK, Frederick. Corporal in Capt. Robert Beatty's company of militia in 1775 [Ref: E-55].

BLACK, Valentine. Furnished powder and lead for use of the militia in Frederick Town in 1775 [Ref: E-60, E-61]. Loaned $1,000 for the use of the State of Maryland in June, 1780 [Ref: V-520].

BLACKBURN, Alexander. Associator in December, 1775 [Ref: E-163]. Juror to the Oath of Allegiance in 1778 [Ref: C-22].

BLACKBURN, William. Private in the militia, July, 1776 [Ref: A-42].

BLACKMORE, George D. Soldier in the Maryland Line who "applied for a pension (S45898) on May 11, 1830, in Sumner County, Tennessee, aged 70 on February 20 last, stating he had enlisted at Frederick Town,

Maryland in 1777, when he ran away from his stepfather, and where his mother died about 1792. He left Maryland in 1783 and went to Kentucky and then to French Lick, Tennessee. He also served in the Indian Wars of 1785-1794. In 1830 he had a wife, daughter, and son (no names given) and he died September 27, 1833." [Ref: T-281].

BLAIR, Jon. Private in the 1st Maryland Regiment, 1781, and served in the Southern Army of the United States under Lt. William Lamar in the late Capt. Beatty's company. Record indicates he was wounded March, 1781, and in the hospital in July, 1781 [Ref: A-392].

BLAIR, William (1730 - November 26, 1778). Appointed by the Committee of Correspondence to solicit subscriptions in 1775 to purchase arms and ammunition [Ref: I-86]. Associator in 1775 and appointed "to hand about the Association paper" in Tom's Creek Hundred [Ref: E-163, E-305]. Gave money in the amount of 4 lbs. 18 sh. 9 p. for arms and ammunition for the militia in 1775 [Ref: E-63]. Lieutenant colonel in the 3rd Battalion in 1776 [Ref: E-58. However, Ref: H-3 indicates Blair was commissioned a lieutenant colonel in the 25th Battalion on January 3, 1776, while Ref: B-53 indicates it was the 35th Battalion]. Chosen to serve on the Committee of Observation on September 12, 1775. Judge of the Orphans' Court on June 4, 1777, and Court Justice on November 21, 1778 [Ref: E-302]. Justice of the Peace in 1777 [Ref: F-476, F-480]. Juror to the Oath of Allegiance in 1778 [Ref: C-22]. He died on November 26, 1778, testate, leaving a wife Hannah, daughters Elizabeth, Mary, Naomi, and Hannah Susanna Francisca, and sons Samuel and John [Ref: M-5:132, F-470].

BLAIR, William. Captain of a militia company in 1775 [Ref: E-55]. "It was in the hottest of the fight at Brooklyn Heights, Long Island, New York, where its gallant Captain Blair fell mortally wounded. Captain Blair was of Scotch-Irish extraction, and was noted for his gallantry and indomitable pluck. A grandson of old Grandmother Hoover, who died near Emmittsburg, an aged lady who lived over one hundred years, and personally witnessed some Indian forays on Tom's Creek and the upper Monocacy, she personally knew nearly all the men in Capt. Blair's company and was present when they left the Tom's Creek settlement for the Revolutionary campaign. She and the neighbors gave them a good shake of the hand and, like the mother of the Gracchi, bid them return with their swords or muskets or be transfixed to them. After the Battle of Long Island [August, 1776], a meeting was held at the old tavern of Henry Bear, at the sign of John Wilkes, Patrick Street, Frederick Town, and measures were taken to fill up the ranks decimated by DeHeister's and Knyphausen's Hessians." [Ref: F-461]. Also, see "William Elder, of Guy," q.v.

BLAIR, William. Private in the militia, March 9, 1776 [Ref: B-166].

BLANE, David. Petitioned the General Assembly under the Act of May 12, 1780, stating he had been a non-juror to the Oath of Allegiance and Fidelity in 1778 due to "ignorance" and now desired relief under the Act and to take the Oath [Ref: L-101].

BLANEY, Adam. Petitioned the General Assembly under the Act of May 12, 1780, stating he had been a non-juror to the Oath of Allegiance and Fidelity in 1778 due to "ignorance" and now desired relief under the Act and to take the Oath [Ref: L-101].

BLESSING, Jacob. Non-Enroller who was fined by the Committee of Observation in May, 1776, but he apparently enrolled because the fine was discharged in June, 1776 [Ref: E-248]. "Jacob Blussing" was an Associator in December, 1775 [Ref: E-164], and a Juror to the Oath of Allegiance in 1778 [Ref: C-22]. "Jacob Blessing, Sr." was the head of household (over age 45) in Middletown Valley in the 1800 census [Ref: O-89].

BLEVER, James. "James Blever" was a private in the Revolutionary Army, of Frederick County, who pensioned October 30, 1819, at $40 per annum, under Act of June 7, 1785, dating from March 4, 1789 [Ref: G-321, citing the U. S. Pension Rolls of 1835]. "James Blewer or Blever," a soldier in the Maryland Line, applied for a pension (S10093) on June 2, 1820. A child (unnamed) of his received the final payment on July 17, 1844; "it appeared the soldier had died on December 7, 1833." [Ref: T-299].

BLICKENSTIFFE, Yost. Non-Enroller who was fined by the Committee of Observation in April, 1776 [Ref: E-248]. "Ulrich and Jost [Yost] Blickensdoerfer whose family originated at Hedinger, Canton Zurich, first fled to Germany. They emigrated from Speyer in the Rhine Valley in 1749. Yost bought land in Middletown Valley in 1762 and 1772. Yost wrote to Annapolis complaining against treatment by Magistrate Capt. Peter Bainbridge. In the Middletown Valley of the census of 1800 were three Blickenstaff families. Joseph and Yost and their wives were over 45 years old. Yost with a child under 10 years was probably Yost Jr... Another source records immigrant Hans Jakob Blickensdoerfer whose wife was Veronica Magdalena Burkholder. Their son Joseph or Yose Blickenstaff (1735-1826) married in 1799 secondly to Margaret Faller (1778-1830)... Numerous Blickenstaff descendants are buried at Grossnickle Meetinghouse of the Church of the Brethren and at the United

Brethren Church at Wolfsville, both in northern Middletown Valley." [Ref: O-90].

BLIZZARD [BLIZARD], James. Associator in December, 1775 [Ref: E-164]. Juror to the Oath of Allegiance in 1778 [Ref: C-22].

BLOTTEN, Peter. Associator in December, 1775 [Ref: E-164]. Juror to the Oath of Allegiance in 1778 [Ref: C-22].

BLUEBAUGH, Jacob. Juror to the Oath of Allegiance in March, 1778 [Ref: S-263, but not listed in Ref: C-22].

BLUBOCK, Jacob Jr. Associator in December, 1775 [Ref: E-164]. (Name appeared twice on list of Associators). Took the Oath of Allegiance in 1778 [Ref: C-22]. The other could have been "Jacob Bluebaugh," q.v.

BLUER, James. "On March 10, 1832, Treasurer of the Western Shore was directed to pay James Bluer, of Frederick County, during life, quarterly, half pay of a private, in consideration of the services rendered by him during the Revolutionary War." [Ref: G-321].

BLUSSING, Jacob. See "Jacob Blessing," q.v.

BLYTH, Jacob. Private who enlisted in Frederick on August 16, 1780, and marched to Annapolis under Capt. William Beatty [Ref: A-344].

BOARDY, Peter. Private who enlisted on July 18, 1776 [Ref: A-49].

BOCKES, John. See "John Bokius," q.v.

BOCKIAS, Erasmus. See "John Bokius," q.v.

BODENHAMER, John. Associator in December, 1775 [Ref: E-163]. Juror to the Oath of Allegiance in 1778 [Ref: C-22].

BOE, William. Private who enlisted on July 20, 1776, by Capt. Jacob Good [Ref: A-46].

BOGGASS, Samuel. Commissioned a 1st lieutenant on October 13, 1777 [Ref: H-4; however, Ref: B-54 indicates it was on January 3, 1776].

BOHRES, Peter. Associator in December, 1775 [Ref: E-163]. Juror to the Oath of Allegiance in 1778 [Ref: C-22].

BOKEY, Matthias. Provided wheat for the military in July, 1782 [Ref: R-534].

BOKIUS, John. Corporal in Capt. Charles Beatty's company of militia in 1775 [Ref: E-51]. "John Bockes" took the Oath of Allegiance in March, 1778 [Ref: S-263]. One "Erasmus Bockias" died testate in 1783, naming his eldest son John (among others). [Ref: M-6:83].

BOLSET, Henry. Associator in December, 1775 [Ref: E-164]. Juror to the Oath of Allegiance in 1778 [Ref: C-22].

BOLSINGER, George. Associator in December, 1775 [Ref: E-163]. Juror to the Oath of Allegiance in 1778 [Ref: C-22].

BOLSON [POLSON?], Andrew (Burnt House Woods Hundred). Non-Enroller fined by the Committee of Observation in August, 1776 [Ref: E-248].

BOLSON [POLSON?], James (Burnt House Woods Hundred). Non-Enroller fined by the Committee of Observation in August, 1776 [Ref: E-248].

BOLTON, James. Ensign in the militia, 1778-1779 [Ref: H-17].

BOLY, Charles. 2nd Corporal in Capt. Philip Thomas' company of militia in 1775 [Ref: E-50].

BONAGAL, George. Private who was enlisted on July 20, 1776, by Capt. Jacob Good [Ref: A-46].

BONE, Nicholas. Associator in December, 1775 [Ref: E-164]. Juror to the Oath of Allegiance in 1778 [Ref: C-22].

BONETRAYER, Christopher. Non-Enroller who was fined by the Committee of Observation in May, 1776 [Ref: E-248].

BONNAL, George. Associator in December, 1775 [Ref: E-164]. Juror to the Oath of Allegiance in 1778 [Ref: C-22].

BONTZ, George. Militia substitute on June 2, 1778 [Ref: A-324].

BOOGHER, Andrew. Juror to the Oath of Allegiance in March, 1778 [Ref: S-263, but not listed in Ref: C-22].

BOOGHER, Bartholomew. Provided wheat for the military in June, 1782 [Ref: R-521].

BOOGHER, George. Private who enlisted on May 4, 1778 [Ref: A-321].

BOOKER, Abraham. Private who enlisted on July 29, 1776 [Ref: A-43].

BOOME, Bartle. Defective from the Maryland Line on July 1, 1780 [Ref: A-414].

BOONE [BOON], Abrm. Juror to the Oath of Allegiance in March, 1778 [Ref: S-263, but not listed in Ref: C-22].

BOONE, Adam. Soldier in the Maryland Line who "applied for pension (S8075) on November 13, 1832, in Montgomery County, Maryland, aged 71, stating that he first served as a substitute for his father, Nicholas Boone, who lived on Pipe Creek, in Frederick County, Maryland. After the war he married (no name given) and lived with Gov. Thomas Johnson, of Maryland, for 7 years as manager of his mill. He later moved to Buckeystown in Frederick County, Maryland, and then to Montgomery County, Maryland. Soldier died on August 26, 1837." [Ref: T-323].

BOONE [BOON], Jacob. Associator in December, 1775 [Ref: E-164]. Non-Enroller who was fined by the Committee of Observation in May, 1776 [Ref: E-248]. Juror to the Oath of Allegiance in 1778 [Ref: C-22].

BOONE, John. Non-Enroller who was fined by the Committee of Observation in May, 1776 [Ref: E-248].

BOONE, Richard. Private in the 1st Maryland Regiment, 1781, who served in the Southern Army of the United States under Lt. William Lamar in the late Capt. Beatty's company. Record indicates he was killed on March 15, 1781 [Ref: A-391].

BOONE, Samuel. Petitioned to form the horse troops in 1781 [Ref: B-167].

BOOT, Adam. Private in the militia on March 9, 1776 [Ref: B-166].

BOOTH, Bartholomew. Served on the Committee of Observation in 1775 [Ref: I-85]. Associator in December, 1775 [Ref: E-164]. Juror to the Oath of Allegiance in 1778 [Ref: C-22].

BOOTH, R. Associator in December, 1775 [Ref: E-164]. Juror to the Oath of Allegiance in 1778 [Ref: C-22].

BOOTH, Robert. Private in the militia, March 9, 1776 [Ref: B-167].

BOOTH, W. Associator in December, 1775 [Ref: E-164]. Juror to the Oath of Allegiance in 1778 [Ref: C-22].

BOOTH, William. Private in the militia, March 9, 1776 [Ref: B-167].

BORDERS, Elizabeth. See "Jacob Yoast (Yeast)," q.v.

BORRANCE, William. Non-Enroller who was fined by the Committee of Observation in May, 1776 [Ref: E-248].

BORTH, John. Associator in December, 1775 [Ref: E-164]. Juror to the Oath of Allegiance in 1778 [Ref: C-22].

BOSLEY, Mary Ann. See "Archibald Roberts," q.v.

BOST, Peter. Associator in December, 1775 [Ref: E-164]. Juror to the Oath of Allegiance in 1778 [Ref: C-22].

BOSTION, Jacob. Private in the Middle District Militia in 1776 [Ref: A-72]. Andrew "Bostian" died testate in 1789 and named wife Maria Alberdina and a son Jacob (among others) [Ref: M-7:137].

BOSTION [BASTIAN], Michael. Juror to the Oath of Allegiance in March, 1778 [Ref: S-263, but not listed in Ref: C-22].

BOSWELL, Alexander. Associator in December, 1775 [Ref: E-164]. Juror to the Oath of Allegiance in 1778 [Ref: C-22].

BOTELER, Edward. Associator in December, 1775 [Ref: E-164]. Juror to the Oath of Allegiance in 1778 [Ref: C-22].

BOTELER, Henry. Captain in the Upper District Militia in Frederick County on March 9, 1776. Captain of a militia company in Washington County in 1777 [Ref: B-166, B-237, and W-546, which latter source mistakenly spelled the name "Hy Bateler."].

BOTELER, Henry Edward. Sergeant in the militia of Frederick County on March 9, 1776. Sergeant in Capt. Henry Boteler's militia company of Washington County in 1777 [Ref: B-166, B-237].

BOTTOMS, Catharine. See "Peter Shull," q.v.

BOTTS, Joseph. Private in the 1st Maryland Regiment, 1781, who served in the Southern Army of the United States under Lt. William Lamar in the late Capt. Beatty's company. Record indicates he was in the hospital in July, 1781 [Ref: A-392].

BOUCHER [BUCHER], Abraham. Private who enlisted on July 1, 1776 in Capt. Peter Mantz's company, and marched from Frederick Town to Leonardtown, and from there to Philadelphia, arriving on August 23, 1776 [Ref: A-47].

BOUGH, Baltis. Associator in December, 1775 [Ref: E-163]. Juror to the Oath of Allegiance in 1778 [Ref: C-22].

BOUGHERS, Daniel. Non-Enroller who was fined by the Committee of Observation in April, 1776 [Ref: E-248].

BOUKER, John. Associator in December, 1775 [Ref: E-164]. Juror to the Oath of Allegiance in 1778 [Ref: C-22].

BOULONGER [BOULANGER], John. Private, 7th Maryland Regiment, who enlisted in Frederick Town on February 11, 1780, and subsequently reported as "deserted" (no date given). [Ref: A-312, A-334].

BOULTON, David. Militia substitute on June 6, 1778 [Ref: A-325].

BOULTON, James. Ensign in the Linganore Battalion of militia on June 22, 1778 [Ref: B-55, Z-145]. Also, see "James Bolton," q.v.

BOUN, Nicholas. Associator in December, 1775 [Ref: E-164]. Juror to the Oath of Allegiance in 1778 [Ref: C-22].

BOUNDS, Thomas. Juror to the Oath of Allegiance in March, 1778 [Ref: S-263, but not listed in Ref: C-22].

BOUSER, Henry. Private in the militia, March 9, 1776 [Ref: B-166].

BOWARD, Michael. Private in the German Regiment, muster roll dated October 23, 1776, and discharged July 16, 1779 [Ref: A-191, A-264].

BOWDEN, John. Drafted on June 2, 1783 [Ref: B-168].

BOWDEN, Thomas. Private in the 7th Maryland Regiment from February 16, 1777, until discharged on February 16, 1780 [Ref: A-188].

BOWDEN, William. Associator in December, 1775 [Ref: E-164]. Juror to the Oath of Allegiance in 1778 [Ref: C-22].

BOWEN, James. Militia substitute from May to December 10, 1781, and "marched to Annapolis." [Ref: A-653].

BOWER, Abraham. Private stationed at Fort Frederick on June 27, 1778, in Capt. John Kershner's company, and guarding prisoners of war [Ref: A-328].
BOWER, Boston. Private in the 7th Maryland Regiment from June 2, 1778, until discharged on April 1, 1779 [Ref: A-190].
BOWER, Christopher [Christian?]. Associator in December, 1775 [Ref: E-163]. Juror to the Oath of Allegiance in 1778 [Ref: C-22]. "Christian Bower, miller," died testate in 1790 [Ref: M-7:186].
BOWER, John. Corporal in Capt. Robert Beatty's company of militia in 1775 [Ref: E-55].
BOWER, Stephen. Non-Enroller who was fined by the Committee of Observation in May, 1776 [Ref: E-248].
BOWER, Tuter. Associator in December, 1775 [Ref: E-164]. Juror to the Oath of Allegiance in 1778 [Ref: C-22].
BOWERSMITH, George. Private who enlisted July 20, 1776 [Ref: A-50].
BOWIE, Alexander Jr. Served on the Committee of Observation in 1775 [Ref: I-85].
BOWIE, Allen (Rock Creek Hundred). Appointed by the Committee of Correspondence to solicit subscriptions in 1775 to purchase arms and ammunition [Ref: I-86]. Gave money in the amount of 1 lb. for arms and ammunition for the militia in 1775 [Ref: E-63].
BOWIE, Allen Jr. Commissioned 1st lieutenant in Capt. E. Harden's Company in the 29th Battalion of militia on May 14, 1776. [Ref: W-424, D-1814]. Also, see "Samuel Swearingen," q.v.
BOWLES, Thomas. Served on the Committee of Observation in 1775 [Ref: I-85]. Associator in December, 1775 [Ref: E-163]. Juror to the Oath of Allegiance in 1778 [Ref: C-22].
BOWMAN, Baltis. Corporal in Capt. John Stoner's company of militia in 1775 [Ref: E-56].
BOWMAN, Daniel. Private, enlisted on January 21, 1778 [Ref: A-314].
BOWMAN, Jacob. Private who enlisted on July 1, 1776 in Capt. Peter Mantz's company; marched from Frederick Town to Leonardtown, and from there to Philadelphia, arriving August 23, 1776 [Ref: A-47].
BOWMAN, John. Private in the Skipton District Militia under Capt. Thomas Waring on April 16, 1776 [Ref: B-167, D-1814]. Juror to the Oath of Allegiance in March, 1778 [Ref: S-263, but not listed in Ref: C-22].
BOWMAN, Philip. Associator in December, 1775 [Ref: E-163]. Private who enlisted on July 1, 1776 in Capt. Peter Mantz's company; marched from Frederick Town to Leonardtown, and from there to Philadelphia,

arriving August 23, 1776 [Ref: A-47]. Juror to Oath of Allegiance in 1778 [Ref: C-22].

BOWNS, Thomas (Manor Hundred). Non-Enroller who was fined by the Committee of Observation in June, 1776 [Ref: E-248].

BOWYER, Christian. Petitioned the General Assembly under the Act of May 12, 1780, stating that he had been a non-juror to the Oath of Allegiance and Fidelity in 1778 due to "ignorance" and now desired relief under the Act and to take the Oath [Ref: L-101].

BOYD, Andrew. Associator in December, 1775 [Ref: E-163]. Juror to the Oath of Allegiance in 1778 [Ref: C-22].

BOYD, Archibald. Associator in December, 1775 [Ref: E-163]. Furnished lead for use of the militia in Frederick Town in 1775 [Ref: E-61]. Clerk for the Committee of Observation in 1775 [Ref: E-303, I-85]. Juror to the Oath of Allegiance in 1778 [Ref: C-22].

BOYER, Casper. Petitioned the General Assembly under the Act of May 12, 1780, stating he had been a non-juror to the Oath of Allegiance and Fidelity in 1778 due to "ignorance" and now desired relief under the Act and to take the Oath [Ref: L-101].

BOYER, George. Associator in December, 1775 [Ref: E-164]. Juror to the Oath of Allegiance in 1778 [Ref: C-22]. Private who enlisted on July 1, 1776 in Capt. Peter Mantz's company; marched from Frederick Town to Leonardtown, and from there to Philadelphia, arriving on August 23, 1776 [Ref: A-47].

BOYER, Jacob. Served on the Committee of Observation in 1775 [Ref: I-85]. Associator in December, 1775 [Ref: E-164]. Juror to the Oath of Allegiance, 1778 [Ref: C-22]. "Jacob Boyer, Sr." died February 1, 1809 [Ref: F-471].

BOYER, John Godlieb. Soldier in the Maryland Line who "applied for a pension on March 11, 1833, in Fayette County, Kentucky, aged 70, stating he was drafted in Fredericktown, Maryland, and volunteered there and at Richmond, Virginia. He was born on August 4, 1762, married Anna Mary Zealor on April 10, 1786, and died on June 5, 1833. His widow applied for a pension (W8376) on April 5, 1839, in Fayette County. She was born February 17, 1769, and their children were: Mary, born February 28, 1787; Margret, born October 12, 1788; Ezra, born April 4, 1790; Henry, born December 5, 1791; Jacob, born March 10, 1793; William, born December 9, 1794; also shown was an Alfred Boyer who married Elizabeth Jane Lawman on December 16, 1829 and Alfred Boyer married Zerelda McCoy on September 24, 1834, but no relationship was stated to soldier or widow." [Ref: T-350].

BOYER, Joseph. Associator in December, 1775 [Ref: E-164]. Juror to the Oath of Allegiance in 1778 [Ref: C-22].

BOYER, Lambert. Lieutenant in the 6th Maryland Regiment from April 7, 1777, until he resigned on October 12, 1777 [Ref: A-186].

BOYER, Mathias. Private in the German Regiment, 1776 [Ref: A-266].

BOYER, Melchier. Petitioned the General Assembly under the Act of July 3, 1780, stating that he had been a non-juror to the Oath of Allegiance and Fidelity in 1778 due to "ignorance" and now desired relief under the Act and to take the Oath [Ref: L-101].

BOYER, Michael. See "Michael Bayer," q.v.

BOYER, Paul. Private who enlisted on August 5, 1776, in the Flying Camp under Capt. Philip Meroney [Ref: A-45, N-30:112].

BOYER, Peter. Captain and paymaster for the German Regiment on February 7, 1780 [Ref: V-81].

BOYLE, Robert. Private who enlisted on May 19, 1778 [Ref: A-323].

BOYNE, Jacob. Associator in December, 1775 [Ref: E-164]. Juror to the Oath of Allegiance in 1778 [Ref: C-22].

BRADDOCK, Nicholas. Non-Enroller who was fined by the Committee of Observation in May, 1776 [Ref: E-248].

BRADFORD, William. Volunteer, enlisted July 18, 1776 [Ref: A-50].

BRADLEY, Dominick. Corporal in Capt. Jacob Ambrose's company of militia in 1775 [Ref: E-54]. Associator in December, 1775 [Ref: E-163]. Juror to the Oath of Allegiance in 1778 [Ref: C-22].

BRAITHWAITE [BRAITHWAIT], William. Private who enlisted on May 1, 1778, and served in the 2nd Maryland Regiment [Ref: A-294, A-321].

BRANDENBURG [BRANDENBURGH], Samuel (1756-1833). Associator in December, 1775 [Ref: E-164]. Juror to the Oath of Allegiance in 1778 [Ref: C-22, S-263]. Drafted on June 2, 1783, but "never appeared." [Ref: B-168]. "Samuel Brandenburg, a soldier in the Revolution, married Mary Bear (1760-1817), and a son Henry Brandenburg (1792-1869) married Mary Kemp (1801-1859). Buried in the Brandenburg graveyard near Wolfsville, Maryland." [Ref: O-91].

BRANDENBURG, William. Soldier in the Maryland Line who "applied for a pension (S2405) on October 2, 1832, in Clarke County, Ohio, aged 73 on October 8, 1831, and a resident of Bethel Township, stating he lived three miles from Middletown in Frederick County, Maryland, at enlistment. He was born October 8, 1758, in Middlesex Township, New Jersey, and in 1812 moved to Fayette County, Pennsylvania. In 1816 he moved to Montgomery County, Ohio, and then the following fall moved to Bethel Township, Ohio." [Ref: T-366].

BRANGLE, George. Associator in December, 1775 [Ref: E-164]. Juror to the Oath of Allegiance in 1778 [Ref: C-22].

BRANNER, Joseph. Private who enlisted on May 18, 1778 [Ref: A-323].

BRANWOOD, James. Private in the Middle District Militia in 1776 [Ref: A-72].

BRASELTON, Isaac. Sergeant in Capt. Henry Baker's company of militia in 1775 [Ref: E-54]. Associator in December, 1775 [Ref: E-164]. Juror to the Oath of Allegiance in 1778 [Ref: C-22].

BRASELTON, Jacob. Associator in December, 1775 [Ref: E-164]. Juror to the Oath of Allegiance in 1778 [Ref: C-22].

BRASELTON, John. Associator in December, 1775 [Ref: E-164]. Juror to the Oath of Allegiance in 1778 [Ref: C-22]. "John Brazleton, yeoman," died testate in 1788, leaving sons William, John (his heirs), Jacob, and Isaac, and daughters Esther, Elizabeth, and Ann [Ref: M-7:134].

BRASHEARS, Morris. Private in the militia, July, 1776 [Ref: A-42].

BRASHEARS, Rezin. 2nd lieutenant in Linganore Battalion of militia, 1776-1777, under Capt. William Brashears [Ref: B-55, X-555, Y-55].

BRASHEARS, William Jr. Captain in Col. James Johnson's battalion on December 28, 1776, captain in the Linganore militia on January 17, 1777, and resigned on June 10, 1778 [Ref: H-5, B-55, X-555, Y-55].

BRATTLE, John. 1st corporal in the Middle District Militia in 1776 [Ref: A-72].

BRATTON, James and Rachel. See "John Wood," q.v.

BRAWN, Henry, Petitioned the General Assembly under the Act of May 12, 1780, stating he had been a non-juror to the Oath of Allegiance and Fidelity in 1778 due to "ignorance" and now desired relief under the Act and to take the Oath [Ref: L-101].

BRAWNER, Henry. Associator in December, 1775 [Ref: E-163]. Juror to the Oath of Allegiance in 1778 [Ref: C-22]. Private who was enlisted on July 20, 1776 by Capt. Jacob Good [Ref: A-46].

BRAWNER, Richard. Associator in December, 1775 [Ref: E-163]. Juror to the Oath of Allegiance in 1778 [Ref: C-22]. He died testate in 1783, leaving wife Elizabeth and children Ignatius (oldest son), Edward, William, Jeremiah (youngest son), Lucy, Teresa, Mary, Monica, and Elizabeth [Ref: M-6:85, M-6:86].

BRAWNER, Thomas. Associator in December, 1775 [Ref: E-164]. Juror to the Oath of Allegiance in 1778 [Ref: C-22].

BREECHER, John. Private in the German Regiment, muster roll dated October 23, 1776 [Ref: A-264].

47

BREEZE [BREASE], John. "John Brease" was a private who enlisted on August 5, 1776, in the Flying Camp under Capt. Philip Meroney [Ref: A-45, N-30:112]. "John Breeze was a soldier in the Maryland and Pennsylvania Lines who applied for a pension (S36429) on May 28, 1818, in Mason County, Kentucky, aged 63, in 1821, and was referred to as 'John Breeze, Sr.' He lived in Frederick County, Maryland, at enlistment in 1776, and also enlisted in Lancaster, Pennsylvania, in 1777. Thomas Kirk, Sr., aged 93, and Thomas Kirk, Jr., aged 60, in 1819 signed affidavits for the soldier." [Ref: T-373].

BREIN, Harriet and John. See "John McPherson," q.v.

BRENER, Philip. Private who enlisted on July 19, 1776 [Ref: A-51].

BRENGEL, Elizabeth. See "John Steiner (Stoner)," q.v.

BRENT, George. Delegate to the Maryland Convention "for that district of Frederick County, which lies west of Locking Creek, appeared and took his seat on May 16, 1776." [Ref: F-476].

BRERDAH, Peter. Ensign (or 3rd lieutenant) in the Upper District Militia, 31st Battalion, on May 15, 1776 [Ref: B-56, W-426].

BREWER, Emanuel. Petitioned the General Assembly under the Act of May 12, 1780, stating that he had been a non-juror to the Oath of Allegiance and Fidelity in 1778 due to "ignorance" and now desired relief under the Act and to take the Oath [Ref: L-101].

BRIAN, Isabella. See "John Montgomery," q.v.

BRICKER, Lodowick. Petitioned the General Assembly under the Act of May 12, 1780, stating that he had been a non-juror to the Oath of Allegiance and Fidelity in 1778 due to "ignorance" and now desired relief under the Act and to take the Oath [Ref: L-101].

BRIDENBAUGH, Valentine. Associator in December, 1775 [Ref: E-164]. Juror to the Oath of Allegiance in 1778 [Ref: C-22].

BRIGGS, William. Private who enlisted on July 25, 1776 [Ref: A-50].

BRIGHT, William. A soldier from Frederick County who died in the service during the Revolutionary War [Ref: F-475].

BRIGHTWELL, John. Associator in December, 1775 [Ref: E-164]. Juror to the Oath of Allegiance in 1778 [Ref: C-22]. One John Brightwell died testate in 1791, leaving wife Sarah and children (names not given in will). [Ref: M-8:89].

BRIGHTWELL, William. Corporal in Capt. David Moore's company of militia in 1775 [Ref: E-56]. Associator in December, 1775 [Ref: E-164]. Juror to the Oath of Allegiance in 1778 [Ref: C-22].

BRIMBOCK, John. Associator in December, 1775 [Ref: E-164]. Juror to the Oath of Allegiance in 1778 [Ref: C-22].

BRINE, Daniel. Associator in December, 1775 [Ref: E-164]. Juror to the Oath of Allegiance in 1778 [Ref: C-22].

BRINGLE, John. Associator in December, 1775 [Ref: E-164]. Juror to the Oath of Allegiance in 1778 [Ref: C-22].

BRINGLE, Laurence. Together with Jacob Gomber he loaned $4,000 for the use of the State of Maryland in June, 1780 [Ref: V-520].

BRINGLE, Christian. See "Christian Pringle," q.v.

BRINSFORD, William. Private who was enlisted on July 20, 1776, by Capt. Jacob Good [Ref: A-46].

BRISCOE, Gerard (Seneca). Appointed by the Committee of Correspondence to solicit subscriptions in 1775 to purchase arms and ammunition [Ref: I-86].

BRISCOE, John and Ann. See "Lindsey Delashmutt," q.v.

BRISCOE, Ralph. "Ralph Busco" was a 1st lieutenant in Capt. James Mackall's company of militia in the 34th Battalion on June 11, 1776 [Ref: B-58, W-476, which sources both mistakenly spelled the name as "Busco," and E-65, which mistakenly spelled the name as "Buseo." The name is actually "Briscoe." Ralph Briscoe (1747-1831), a son of John Briscoe and Anne Wood, of Charles County, married first to Ann Mackall and second to Sarah Trammell Delashmutt, widow of Lindsey, in 1792. Also, see "Lindsey Delashmutt," q.v., and Henry C. Peden, Jr.'s *Marylanders to Kentucky, 1775-1825*, for additional Briscoe family information, plus "Briscoe Notes" compiled by Robert W. Barnes at the Maryland Historical Society Library in Baltimore.]

BRISCOE, Sarah. See "Lindsey Delashmutt," q.v.

BRISON, John. Associator in December, 1775 [Ref: E-163]. Juror to the Oath of Allegiance in 1778 [Ref: C-22].

BROADBECK, Henry. Juror to the Oath of Allegiance in March, 1778 [Ref: S-263, but not listed in Ref: C-22].

BROMCORD, Adam. Associator in December, 1775 [Ref: E-164]. Juror to the Oath of Allegiance in 1778 [Ref: C-22].

BROOK, Raphael. Petitioned to form the horse troops in 1781 [Ref: B-167].

BROOK, Roger. Juror to the Oath of Allegiance in March, 1778 [Ref: S-263, but not listed in Ref: C-22].

BROOKE, James. Private in the 1st Maryland Regiment, 1781, who served in the Southern Army of the United States under Lt. William Lamar in the late Capt. Beatty's company. Record indicates he "deserted" in January, 1781 [Ref: A-391]. One James Brooke died testate in 1784, leaving his property to his brothers and sister; however,

James had died without executing the will "because of the violant rage of his sickness." [Ref: M-6:124].

BROOKE, Richard (upper part of New Foundland). Appointed by the Committee of Correspondence to solicit subscriptions in 1775 to purchase arms and ammunition [Ref: I-86]. Major in the militia on August 15, 1776 [Ref: B-56].

BROOKE, Thomas. Served on the Committee of Observation in 1775 [Ref: I-85].

BROOKOVER, John. Soldier in the Maryland and Virginia Lines who "applied for a pension (S5300) on October 4, 1832, in Wood County, Virginia, aged 72, stating he was an apprentice at Three Springs in Maryland when he enlisted and his father lived at Carroll's Manor, Maryland; later moved to Muddy Creek near Uniontown, Pennsylvania; then about 1812 moved to Wood County, Ohio [sic]. Soldier stated he believed he was born near Bladensburg, Maryland." [Ref: T-399].

BROOKS, Charles. Private in the 7th Maryland Regiment from May 29, 1780, until reported missing on August 16, 1780 (after the Battle of Camden, South Carolina). [Ref: A-190].

BROOKS, James (schoolmaster). Non-Enroller who was fined by the Committee of Observation in April, 1776 [Ref: E-248].

BROOKS, James. Private in the 7th Maryland Regiment who enlisted in Frederick Town between January and April, 1780, and subsequently reported as "deserted" on July 1, 1780. [Ref: A-190, A-334].

BROOKS, John. Private in the 7th Maryland Regiment who enlisted in Frederick Town between January and April, 1780 [Ref: A-334, V-175].

BROONER, Henry, Peter, and Stephen. See "Henry, Peter, and Stephen Brunner," q.v.

BROOYAN, John. Associator in December, 1775 [Ref: E-163]. Juror to the Oath of Allegiance in 1778 [Ref: C-22].

BROSSLEDAY, ----. Captain in militia, December, 1776 [Ref: B-56].

BROTHER, Valentine. Sheriff of Frederick County, 1779 [Ref: F-480]. Henry Brother died testate in 1791, leaving wife Eleanor and sons Henry and Valentine [Ref: M-8:87]. See "Valentine Brunner," q.v.

BROUGHTON, Adam. Private in the 7th Maryland Regiment from July 20, 1778, until discharged on April 9, 1778 [Ref: A-190].

BROUGHTON, William. Private, enlisted April 20, 1778 [Ref: A-324].

BROWN, Edward. Associator in December, 1775 [Ref: E-164]. Private who enlisted on July 18, 1776 [Ref: A-50]. Juror to the Oath of Allegiance in 1778 [Ref: C-22].

BROWN, Frederick and Jane. See "James Ervin (Irvine)," q.v.

BROWN, George. Associator in December, 1775 [Ref: E-163]. Ensign in the 37th Battalion of militia who was recommended in the stead of Joshua Delaplaine on June 29, 1776, and served in Col. James Johnson's Battalion of Militia on December 28, 1776 [Ref: X-503, X-555]. 2nd lieutenant in the Catoctin Battalion on August 16, 1781 [Ref: B-57].

BROWN, George. Private who enlisted on April 21, 1778 [Ref: A-320]. Juror to the Oath of Allegiance in 1778 [Ref: C-23, S-263].

BROWN, Godfrey. Associator in December, 1775 [Ref: E-164]. Juror to the Oath of Allegiance in 1778 [Ref: C-23].

BROWN, Henry. Associator in December, 1775 [Ref: E-164]. Juror to the Oath of Allegiance in 1778 [Ref: C-23].

BROWN, Jacob. Petitioned the General Assembly under the Act of July 3, 1780, stating he had been a non-juror to the Oath of Allegiance and Fidelity in 1778 due to "ignorance" and now desired relief under the Act and to take the Oath [Ref: L-101].

BROWN, John. Associator in December, 1775 [Ref: E-164]. Juror to the Oath of Allegiance in 1778 [Ref: C-23, S-263]. Private who enlisted on June 15, 1778, for 3 years [Ref: A-326].

BROWN, John. Associator in December, 1775 [Ref: E-164]. Private who enlisted on July 19, 1776 [Ref: A-51]. Sergeant in the 6th Maryland Regiment. Disabled at the Battle of Camden, and his invalid pension commenced on November 29, 1783, but it ceased on March 29, 1786, with the cause of pension ceasing noted as "removed or dead." [Ref: A-630, A-631, F-475].

BROWN, John. Militia substitute from May to December 10, 1781, and "marched to Annapolis." [Ref: A-653].

BROWN, John (of Edward). Petitioned the General Assembly under the Act of July 3, 1780, stating he had been a non-juror to the Oath of Allegiance and Fidelity in 1778 due to "ignorance" and now desired relief under the Act and to take the Oath [Ref: L-101].

BROWN, John Jr. Associator in December, 1775 [Ref: E-164]. Juror to the Oath of Allegiance in 1778 [Ref: C-23].

BROWN, Joshua. Non-Enroller who was fined by the Committee of Observation in May, 1776, but he apparently enrolled because the fine was remitted in June, 1776 [Ref: E-248]. Private, 1st Maryland Regiment, enlisted on April 23, 1778, and served in the Southern Army of the United States under Lt. William Lamar in the late Capt. Beatty's company until discharged on April 23, 1781 [Ref: A-391]. Private in the 7th Maryland Regiment in 1780 [Ref: A-189].

BROWN, Margaret. See "Thomas Stone," q.v.

BROWN, Robert. Sergeant in Capt. William Shields' company of militia in 1775 [Ref: E-56]. Provided wheat for the military in July, 1782 [Ref: R-533].

BROWN, Thomas. Juror to the Oath of Allegiance in March, 1778 [Ref: S-263, but not listed in Ref: C-22]. Private who enlisted on May 1, 1778, and served in the 2nd Maryland Regiment [Ref: A-294, A-321].

BROWN, Thomas. Private in the 7th Maryland Regiment who enlisted in Frederick Town between January and April, 1780, and reported "gone to Camp" [Ref: A-334].

BROWN, William. Private who was enlisted on July 20, 1776 by Capt. Jacob Good [Ref: A-46].

BROWNE, Hugh. Associator in December, 1775 [Ref: E-164]. (This name appeared twice on the list of Associators). One subscribed to the Oath of Allegiance in 1778 [Ref: C-23].

BROWNE, Joshua. Associator in December, 1775 [Ref: E-164]. Juror to the Oath of Allegiance in 1778 [Ref: C-23].

BROWNE, William. Associator in December, 1775 [Ref: E-164]. Juror to the Oath of Allegiance in 1778 [Ref: C-23].

BROWNING, Basil. Associator in December, 1775 [Ref: E-164]. Juror to the Oath of Allegiance in 1778 [Ref: C-23].

BROWNING, Benjamin. Associator in December, 1775 [Ref: E-164]. Juror to the Oath of Allegiance in 1778 [Ref: C-23].

BROWNING, Jeremiah. Non-Enroller who was fined by the Committee of Observation in April, 1776 [Ref: E-248].

BROWNING, Zephaniah. Private in militia in July, 1776 [Ref: A-42].

BRUBOI, Rudolph. 1st lieutenant in Capt. Michael McGuire's company of militia in the 3rd Battalion, November, 1775 [Ref: E-56, B-57].

BRUCE, Andrew (Pipe Creek Hundred). Appointed by the Committee of Correspondence to solicit subscriptions in 1775 to purchase arms and ammunition [Ref: I-86]. Served on the Committee of Observation in 1775 [Ref: I-85].

BRUCE, Normand [Norman]. Captain of a company of militia, November 11, 1775 [Ref: E-54, B-57]. Associator in December, 1775 [Ref: E-163]. Colonel of the 3rd Battalion on December 28, 1776 [Ref: E-58, H-17, X-555]. Juror to the Oath of Allegiance in 1778 [Ref: C-23]. County Lieutenant on April 24, 1779 [Ref: B-57]. Colonel in the Frederick Town Battalion of Militia in 1779 [Ref: V-295]. A Justice of the Peace and a Judge of the Orphans' Court in 1777. Served in the House of Delegates in 1780 [Ref: F-476, F-479]. Col. Normand Bruce died on April 25, 1811 [Ref: F-471]. "On Friday, February 22, 1805, Susanna Bruce, wife of

Normand Bruce, Esq., of Frederick County, died (age not stated). They had been married upwards of 44 years." [Ref: N-57]. Born in Scotland and immigrated as a freeman in 1748, Normand Bruce died in 1811 [Ref: P-177].

BRUCE, Townley. Associator in December, 1775 [Ref: E-164]. Juror to the Oath of Allegiance in 1778 [Ref: C-23].

BRUCE, William. Associator in December, 1775 [Ref: E-164]. Juror to the Oath of Allegiance in 1778 [Ref: C-23].

BRUCHER, John. Corporal in the German Regiment, 1779 [Ref: A-264].

BRUEBACK, Rudolph. Juror to the Oath of Allegiance in March, 1778 [Ref: S-263, but not listed in Ref: C-22].

BRUFF, William. Corporal, 1st Maryland Regiment, 1781, and served in the Southern Army of the United States under Lt. William Lamar in the late Capt. Beatty's company [Ref: A-389].

BRUGH, Philip. Private who enlisted on July 19, 1776 [Ref: A-51].

BRUIN, Peter. Associator in December, 1775 [Ref: E-164]. Juror to the Oath of Allegiance in 1778 [Ref: C-23].

BRUNNER, Anna Barbara. See "Baltzer Getzendanner," q.v.

BRUNNER, Anna Maria and Anna Catherine. See "John Ramsburg," q.v.

BRUNNER, Elias. Served on the Committee of Observation in 1775 [Ref: I-85]. Ensign in Capt. John Haass' company of militia in the 1st Battalion, November 29, 1775 [Ref: E-53, B-57]. Associator in December, 1775 [Ref: E-164]. Juror to the Oath of Allegiance in 1778 [Ref: C-23]. One "Elias Brunner Jr. (1756-1826) married Maria Elizabeth Zimmerman (b. 1761) at Frederick Reformed Church." [Ref: O-123]. Another "Elias Brunner (born 1723) was a son of Joseph Brunner (1676-1752?) who arrived in the Monocacy area by 1736." [Ref: O-105]. One Elias Brunner died testate in 1783, leaving a wife Albertina and sons Peter and Stephen [Ref: M-6:83].

BRUNNER, Henry. Associator in December, 1775 [Ref: E-164]. Juror to the Oath of Allegiance, 1778 [Ref: C-23, and S-263, which spelled the name "Henry Brooner."]. One "Henry Brunner (died 1776) married Anna Catherine Zimmerman (born 1752) at Frederick Lutheran Church." [Ref: O-123]. Another Henry Brunner (born 1715 - died by January, 1776) married Magdalena ---- and was a son of Joseph (1676-1752?), of the Monocacy area. Henry's will was probated January 12, 1776, naming wife Magdaline, sons Henry, Valentine, and Jacob, and daughters Barbara, Mary, Susannah, and Margaretha [Ref: O-105, M-4:183, M-4:184]. Also, see "Henry Brother," q.v.

BRUNNER, Jacob. Private who enlisted on July 20, 1776 [Ref: A-50]. "Jacob Bunner" was a captain in the German Regiment by 1779 [Ref: A-271]. "Jacob Bruner" died March 5, 1822, aged 63 [Ref: F-472]. One "Jacob Bruner applied for pension (W332) on September 8, 1832, in Greene County, Tennessee, aged 79, stating that he enlisted at Frederick Town, Maryland, and married Margaret Cline in Frederick County, Maryland. Soldier died August 10, 1847, and widow died May 15, 1849. In 1852 the surviving children were: Mary Ann, widow of George Mercer; Jacob Bruner; Henry Bruner; Elizabeth, widow of Thomas Starns; Margaret, wife of William Baylie, of Indiana; Eliza Bruner, of Illinois; and, Daniel, Othniel, and Samuel Bruner, of Greene County, Tennessee. Soldier's son Joseph, aged 54, applied March 6, 1854, Greene County, Tennessee, for final payment. Births of soldier's children that were translated from German were: Ann Maria, born March 1, 1785; Maria "Mary" Elizabeth, born January 25, 1787; John or Jacob, born March 9, 1789; John, born November 21, 1793; a daughter, born December 3, year not shown; Henry, born November 22, year not shown; Elias, born April 26, 1797; Joseph, born April 26, 1799; and, Samuel, born in 1801. Soldier's son Othniel was aged 44 in 1854." A second "Jacob Bruner was a soldier in the Maryland and Pennsylvania Lines who applied for a pension (S357792) on November 8, 1821, in Boone County, Kentucky, aged 62, with a wife aged 60 (the mother of 14 children) and a daughter aged 17 at home. He died February 14, 1845, leaving a widow. In 1851 six children of the soldier were: Moses, aged 54; Solomon and Simeon, aged 51; Lydia Rowan, aged 49; Samuel, no age stated; and, David, no age stated. In 1823 a Christian Bruner signed an affidavit in Jessamine County, Kentucky, relationship not stated." [Ref: T-441]. "Jacob Bruner (February 12, 1763 - August 10, 1847) was a son of Johann Peter Bruner (August 30, 1724 - October 2, 1821) and Maria Ann Storm (Sturm), and a grandson of Johann Jacob Bruner and Maria Barbara Storm (Sturm) of Schifferstadt, Germany, and Frederick County, Maryland [Ref: U-2910, citing *The Genealogy of the Bruner Family*, by A. Fisher, and *Knowing the Bruners*, by Donald Osborn].

BRUNNER, Jacob and Margaret. See "Joseph Doll," q.v.

BRUNNER, John. Associator in December, 1775 [Ref: E-164]. Juror to the Oath of Allegiance in 1778 [Ref: C-23]. "John Brunner" died on February 26, 1819, "John Bruner, miller," died December 14, 1821, and "John Brunner" died on May 28, 1829, aged 81 [Ref: F-471, F-472, F-473]. The John who died in 1819 was born in 1745, a son of Jacob and

Maria Brunner, and he married Christina Storm [Ref: O-105]. John Brunner (1730-1776) married Ann Mary ---- in 1751 and a son Stephen (b. 1754) married Madeline ---- in 1776 [Ref: U-1031, which source states this John Brunner was the Associator in 1775].

BRUNNER [BRUNER], Peter. Associator in December, 1775 [Ref: E-164], and a Juror to the Oath of Allegiance in 1778 [Ref: C-23, and S-263, which spelled the name as "Brooner."]. "Peter Bruner" provided wheat for the military in May, 1782 [Ref: R-515]. "Peter Brunner" died testate in 1784, and left his entire estate to his wife Maria Catherine [Ref: M-6:123]. A "Peter Brumer [sic] died on October 2, 1821, aged 97, the oldest inhabitant of the county." [Ref: F-472].

BRUNNER, Stephen (born 1754). Son of John Brunner (1730-1776) and Ann Mary ----. He married to Madeline ---- in 1776 [Ref: U-1031]. A non-Enroller who was fined by the Committee of Observation in April, 1776 [Ref: E-248], "Stephen Brooner" subscribed to the Oath of Allegiance in March, 1778 [Ref: S-263].

BRUNNER, Valentine. Associator in December, 1775 [Ref: E-163]. Private who enlisted on July 1, 1776 in Capt. Peter Mantz's company; marched from Frederick Town to Leonardtown, and from there to Philadelphia, arriving on August 23, 1776 [Ref: A-47]. Juror to the Oath of Allegiance in 1778 [Ref: C-23]. Pensioned in 1831, aged 76 [Ref: J-33; however, Ref: T-441 states he pensioned in 1832, aged 74]. "Valentine Brother" was Sheriff of Frederick County in 1779 [Ref: F-480]. "Valentine Brunner, a Revolutionary soldier, died on June 29, 1841, aged 84." [Ref: F-473]. Valentine Brunner was a soldier in the Maryland Line who applied for pension on December 27, 1832, in Frederick County, Maryland, aged 74, a resident of Frederick Town. He married in 1804 to Elizabeth (no last name given) and died in June, 1841. His widow applied for a pension (W633) on June 9, 1853, in Frederick County, Maryland, aged 78." [Ref: T-441]. See "Valentine Brother," q.v.

BRUSELTON, Isaac. Associator in December, 1775 [Ref: E-164]. Juror to the Oath of Allegiance in 1778 [Ref: C-23].

BRYAN, Daniel. Private in the Middle District Militia in 1776 [Ref: A-72]. Juror to the Oath of Allegiance in 1778 [Ref: C-23]. "Daniel Bryon" was a substitute on June 13, 1781; marched with Capt. Dyer [Ref: D-1814].

BRYAN, David. Associator in December, 1775 [Ref: E-163].

BRYAN, Edward. "Draught," May to December 10, 1781, and "marched to Annapolis." [Ref: A-653].

BRYAN, Gilbert. Private in the militia in July, 1776 [Ref: A-42].

BRYAN, John. Private in the 7th Maryland Regiment from June 10, 1777, through at least November 1, 1780 [Ref: A-188].

BRYANT, James. Private who enlisted on August 5, 1776 in the Flying Camp under Capt. Philip Meroney [Ref: A-45, N-30:112].

BUCHLUP [BURKLUP], Charles. Private in the 1st Maryland Regiment who was disabled at the Battle of Eutaw Springs. His invalid's pension commenced on November 29, 1783, and ceased on November 1, 1789 [Ref: A-630, A-631]. Another source also states that "George Burklup" was a soldier in the First Maryland Regiment who was wounded at the Battle of Eutaw [Springs]. [Ref: F-475].

BUCK, George. Private in the 1st Maryland Regiment, 1781, who served in the Southern Army of the United States under Lt. William Lamar in the late Capt. Beatty's company [Ref: A-390]. "George Buch" was a private in the German Regiment, roll dated October 23, 1776 [Ref: A-264], and fought in the Battle of White Plains on September 5, 1778, under Lt. Col. Ludwick Weltner [Ref: A-266].

BUCKEY, Matthias. See "Matthias Bokey," q.v.

BUCKHANNON, James. Private in the Middle District Militia in 1776 [Ref: A-72].

BUDDELL, Andrew. Associator in December, 1775 [Ref: E-164]. Juror to the Oath of Allegiance in 1778 [Ref: C-23].

BULGER, Cornelius. Private who enlisted in 1780 [Ref: A-345].

BULLEN, James. Associator in December, 1775 [Ref: E-164]. Juror to the Oath of Allegiance in 1778 [Ref: C-23].

BULLENER, Peter. Associator in December, 1775 [Ref: E-163]. Juror to the Oath of Allegiance in 1778 [Ref: C-23].

BULLENER, Stephen. Associator in December, 1775 [Ref: E-163]. Juror to the Oath of Allegiance in 1778 [Ref: C-23].

BULLER, James. Private who enlisted on August 5, 1776 in the Flying Camp under Capt. Philip Meroney [Ref: A-45, N-30:113].

BUMGARDNER, Michael. Drafted June 13, 1781; provided a substitute [Ref: D-1814].

BUNNER, Jacob. See "Jacob Brunner," q.v.

BURAST, Peter. Associator in December, 1775 [Ref: E-163]. Juror to the Oath of Allegiance in 1778 [Ref: C-23].

BURCH, Thomas. Militia substitute from May to December 10, 1781, and "marched to Annapolis." [Ref: A-653].

BURCKHART, John Sr. Associator in December, 1775 [Ref: E-164]. Juror to the Oath of Allegiance in 1778 [Ref: C-23].

BURCKHART, Nathaniel. Non-Enroller who was fined by the Committee of Observation in April, 1776 [Ref: E-248].

BURCKHART, Peter. Ensign in Capt. William Duvall's company of militia in the 4th Battalion in November, 1775 [Ref: E-54, B-58].

BURCKHARTT, Christian. Associator in December, 1775 [Ref: E-163]. Juror to the Oath of Allegiance in 1778 [Ref: C-23].

BURCKHARTT, George. Associator in December, 1775 [Ref: E-163]. Juror to the Oath of Allegiance in 1778 [Ref: C-23]. "George Burkhart," an old merchant, died in Frederick County on April 10, 1805 [Ref: F-470]. "George Burck-Hartt died Tuesday evening [April 10, 1805] at 6 p.m., within two months of being 80 years old, of this town [Frederick]. Left 11 children, 74 great-grandchildren and 21 great-great-grandchildren." [Ref: N-57].

BURGE, William. Captain in the 29th Battalion of militia on June 26, 1776 [Ref: B-58].

BURGESS, Benjamin. Private in the militia, July, 1776 [Ref: A-42].

BURGESS, Edward (lower part of New Foundland). Appointed by the Committee of Correspondence to solicit subscriptions in 1775 to purchase arms and ammunition [Ref: I-85]. Served on the Committee of Observation in 1775 [Ref: I-85]. Associator in December, 1775 [Ref: E-163]. Gave money in the amount of 4 lbs. for arms and ammunition for the militia in 1775 [Ref: E-63]. Captain in the Lower District Militia [now Montgomery County] in 1776 [Ref: A-42]. Juror to the Oath of Allegiance, 1778 [Ref: C-23]. One Edward Burgess "applied for pension (S37813) on March 5, 1822, in Fayette County, Pennsylvania, aged 70, stating he served in the Maryland Line and had a wife Margaret, aged 56." [Ref: T-469].

BURGESS, James. Juror to the Oath of Allegiance in March, 1778 [Ref: S-263, but not listed in Ref: C-22].

BURGESS, Josiah. Private, 1st Maryland Regiment, enlisted on April 19, 1778, and served in the Southern Army of the United States under Lt. William Lamar in the late Capt. Beatty's company until transferred to the light infantry on March 12, 1781 [Ref: A-390].

BURGESS, Mathias. Ensign in the Frederick Town Battalion of militia on January 23, 1782 [Ref: B-58].

BURGESS, Richard. Private in the militia in July, 1776 [Ref: A-42].

BURGESS, William. Militia substitute from May to December 10, 1781, and "marched to Annapolis." [Ref: A-653].

BURINGER, Adam. Associator in December, 1775 [Ref: E-163]. Juror to the Oath of Allegiance in 1778 [Ref: C-23].

BURK, James. Private who enlisted on May 16, 1778 [Ref: A-322]. Private in the 2nd Maryland Regiment whow as disabled at the Battle of Cowpens. His invalid pension commenced on February 10, 1784, and ceased on March 10, 1788, with the cause of the pension ceasing as "dead." [Ref: A-630, A-631, F-475].

BURK, Thomas. Associator in December, 1775 [Ref: E-164]. Private who enlisted on May 18, 1778 [Ref: A-324]. Juror to the Oath of Allegiance in 1778 [Ref: C-23].

BURK, Walter. Private, enlisted in Frederick on July 27, 1780, and subsequently reported as "deserted" (no date given). [Ref: A-344].

BURKETT, Christopher. Served on the Committee of Observation in 1775 [Ref: I-85]. Recommended to be commissioned a 1st lieutenant on October 13, 1777 [Ref: H-26].

BURKETT, George Jr. Recommended to be commissioned a captain on October 13, 1777 [Ref: H-26].

BURKETT, Joseph. Non-Enroller who was fined by the Committee of Observation in April, 1776 [Ref: E-248].

BURKETT, Nathaniel. Drafted on June 2, 1783 [Ref: B-169]. One Nathaniel Burkett died testate in 1791, leaving a wife Margaret and a daughter Margaret [Ref: M-8:86].

BURKHART, George. See "George Burckhartt," q.v.

BURKHOLDER, Veronica Magdalena. See "Yost Blickenstiffe," q.v.

BURKLUP, George. See "Charles Bucklup (Burklup)," q.v.

BURNESTON, William. Associator in December, 1775 [Ref: E-163]. Juror to the Oath of Allegiance in 1778 [Ref: C-23].

BURNEY, Thomas. Private in the German Regiment, muster roll dated October 23, 1776 [Ref: A-264].

BURNGARDENER, John. Associator in December, 1775 [Ref: E-164]. Juror to the Oath of Allegiance in 1778 [Ref: C-23].

BURNHART, Anthony. Non-Enroller who was fined by the Committee of Observation in May, 1776 [Ref: E-248].

BURNHART, ---- [blank] (son of Anthony). Non-Enroller who was fined by the Committee of Observation in May, 1776 [Ref: E-248].

BURNS, James. Private in the 7th Maryland Regiment who enlisted in Frederick Town between January and April, 1780, and reported as "gone to Camp" [Ref: A-334].

BURNS, John. Private who enlisted on May 20, 1778, and served in the 2nd Maryland Regiment [Ref: A-294, A-323].

BURNS, Thomas. Private in the 7th Maryland Regiment who enlisted in Frederick Town between January and April, 1780 [Ref: A-334].

BURRAWL, George. Private in the Middle District Militia in 1776 [Ref: A-72].

BURRIER, Philip. "Philip Barrier" was an Associator in December, 1775 [Ref: E-164], and also Juror to the Oath of Allegiance in 1778 [Ref: C-22]. "Philip Burrier" was born before 1740 and died in Frederick County prior to 1807. He married Maria Barbara ---- circa 1765, and Maria Barbara "Burger" was a communicant at Frederick Reformed Church on Easter, 1767. In 1785 "Philip Burger" had resurveyed tract "Hitchbaugh." Barbara Burrier died testate in 1821. Their children were John (1766-1840, Carroll County, Ohio), Barbara, Anna Margaretha, Mary, Catherine, George (c1774-1831, Jefferson County, Ohio), Magdalene, Elizabeth, and Esther [Ref: M-6:5, 6].

BURTON, Henry. Private who enlisted on July 29, 1776 [Ref: A-43]. Juror to the Oath of Allegiance in March, 1778 [Ref: S-263, but not listed in Ref: C-22].

BURTON, Isaac. Corporal in Capt. Samuel Plummer's company of militia in 1775 [Ref: E-54].

BURTON, Jacob. Private who enlisted on August 5, 1776 in the Flying Camp under Capt. Philip Meroney [Ref: A-45, N-30:112].

BURTON, James. Private who enlisted on August 5, 1776 in the Flying Camp under Capt. Philip Meroney [Ref: A-45, N-30:112].

BURTON, John. Sergeant in Capt. Michael Troutman's company of militia in 1775 [Ref: E-51]. Associator in December, 1775 [Ref: E-164]. Juror to the Oath of Allegiance in 1778 [Ref: C-23].

BURWELL, Ephraim. Associator in December, 1775 [Ref: E-164]. Juror to the Oath of Allegiance in 1778 [Ref: C-23].

BUSEY, Ann. See "Benjamin Popham," q.v.

BUSEY, Charles. Sergeant in Capt. Samuel Plummer's company of militia in 1775 [Ref: E-54].

BUSEY, Henry. Corporal in Capt. William Duvall's company of militia in 1775 [Ref: E-54].

BUSEY, Samuel. Private who enlisted on July 22, 1776 or August 5, 1776 [Ref: A-45, A-49, N-30:112].

BUSH, Herman. "Herman Bush" was an Associator in December, 1775 [Ref: E-164]. "Harmon Bush" was a non-enroller who was fined by the Committee of Observation in April, 1776 [Ref: E-248]. "Herman Bush" was a juror to the Oath of Allegiance in 1778 [Ref: C-23]. "Harman Bush" provided wheat for the military in May, 1782 [Ref: R-515].

BUSH, John. Non-Enroller who was fined by the Committee of Observation in April, 1776 [Ref: E-248].

BUSH, Lewis. Ensign in Capt. Philip Thomas' company of militia in 1775 [Ref: E-50]. "Louis Bush" was quartermaster in the First Battalion in 1776 [Ref: I-95].

BUTLER, Edward. Private in the Skipton District Militia under Capt. Thomas Waring on April 16, 1776 [Ref: B-167, D-1814]. He provided wheat for the military in May, 1782 [Ref: R-515].

BUTLER, Henry (Lower Antietam Hundred). Appointed by the Committee of Correspondence to solicit subscriptions in 1775 to purchase arms and ammunition [Ref: I-86].

BUTLER, Peter. Militia substitute from May to December 10, 1781, and "marched to Annapolis." [Ref: A-653].

BUTLER, Richard (upper part of Monocacy Hundred). Appointed by the Committee of Correspondence to solicit subscriptions in 1775 to purchase arms and ammunition [Ref: I-86]. Associator in December, 1775 [Ref: E-163]. Gave money in the amount of 5 lbs. 11 sh. 9 p. for arms and ammunition for the militia in 1775 [Ref: E-62]. Clerk of the Circuit Court from 1775 to 1779 [Ref: F-480. However, Ref: Y-468 states he was appointed clerk on January 17, 1778, upon the resignation of Richard Potts]. Quartermaster in the 37th Battalion of militia on December 28, 1776, under Col. Johnson [Ref: B-58, X-555]. Juror to the Oath of Allegiance in 1778 [Ref: C-23]. Appointed Deputy Quartermaster General on September 14, 1779 [Ref: Z-525].

BUTLER, Tobias. Associator in December, 1775 [Ref: E-163]. Juror to the Oath of Allegiance in 1778 [Ref: C-23].

BUXTON, Abijah. Private, 7th Maryland Regiment, 1780, enlisted in Frederick Town between January and April, 1780, and reported as "gone to Camp" [Ref: A-334].

BUZARD [BUZZARD], Andrew. Petitioned the General Assembly under the Act of May 12, 1780, stating he had been a non-juror to the Oath of Allegiance and Fidelity in 1778 due to "ignorance" and now desired relief under the Act and to take the Oath [Ref: L-101].

BUZARD, Daniel. Non-Enroller who was fined by the Committee of Observation in April, 1776 [Ref: E-248]. "Settler Daniel Bussard or Bossert married Sophia Renner. The best known was their son Peter (1761-1802) who married Margaret or Becky Householder (1762-1839) and lived at Bussard Flats, west of Catoctin Furnace." [Ref: O-98].

BUZARD [BUZZARD], Jacob. Provided wheat for the military in May, 1782 [Ref: R-516].

BUZARD, Samuel. Associator in December, 1775 [Ref: E-164]. Juror to the Oath of Allegiance in 1778 [Ref: C-23].

BUZARD, Samuel Jr. Associator in December, 1775 [Ref: E-164]. Juror to the Oath of Allegiance in 1778 [Ref: C-23].

BYE, John. Provided wheat for the military in 1782 [Ref: R-516].

BYER, William. Private who enlisted on August 5, 1776 in the Flying Camp under Capt. Philip Meroney [Ref: A-45, N-30:112].

BYERLY, Michael. 2nd lieutenant in the militia, April 15, 1778 [Ref: H-16].

BYFIELD, Robert. Juror to the Oath of Allegiance in March, 1778 [Ref: S-263, but not listed in Ref: C-22].

BYRN, Charles. Private who enlisted on July 18, 1776 [Ref: A-49].

BYSER, Daniel. Associator in December, 1775 [Ref: E-164]. Juror to the Oath of Allegiance in 1778 [Ref: C-23].

CADWELL, John. Substitute on June 13, 1781, but the roster noted that he was "non-resident." [Ref: D-1814].

CAHILL, Timothy. Private who enlisted on April 27, 1778 [Ref: A-321]. Served as a private in the German Regiment at White Plains on September 5, 1778, under Lt. Col. Ludwick Weltner [Ref: A-266].

CAIN, William. Petitioned the General Assembly under the Act of May 12, 1780, stating he had been a non-juror to the Oath of Allegiance and Fidelity in 1778 due to "ignorance" and now desired relief under the Act and to take the Oath [Ref: L-101].

CALBERT, William. Associator in December, 1775 [Ref: E-165]. Juror to the Oath of Allegiance in 1778 [Ref: C-23].

CALLAHAN, Samuel. Enlisted on March 13, 1781, for 3 years, and was subsequently reported as "deserted" (no date given). [Ref: D-1814].

CALLIHAN, Edward. Associator in December, 1775 [Ref: E-165]. Juror to the Oath of Allegiance in 1778 [Ref: C-23].

CALVERT, William. Private who enlisted on August 5, 1776 in the Flying Camp under Capt. Philip Meroney [Ref: A-45, N-30:112].

CAMBLER, Michael. Private in the German Regiment, muster roll dated October 23, 1776 [Ref: A-264]. Also, see "Michael Gambler," q.v.

CAMMELL, James. Associator in December, 1775 [Ref: E-165]. Juror to the Oath of Allegiance in 1778 [Ref: C-23]. Private in the Middle District Militia in 1776 [Ref: A-72].

CAMMELL, John. Militia substitute on June 8, 1778 [Ref: A-325].

CAMMELL, Matthew. Associator in December, 1775 [Ref: E-165]. Juror to the Oath of Allegiance in 1778 [Ref: C-23].

CAMMELL, Nicholas. Private who enlisted on April 21, 1778 [Ref: A-320].

CAMMELL, Thomas. Private in Capt. Charles Baltzel's Company, served 3 years, and discharged July 17, 1779 at Camp Wyoming [Ref: A-271].

CAMPBELL, Aeneas (Sugarland Hundred). Appointed by the Committee of Correspondence to solicit subscriptions in 1775 to purchase arms and ammunition [Ref: I-86]. Served on the Committee of Observation in 1775 [Ref: I-85]. Captain in the Upper District Militia [now Washington County] in 1776 [Ref: A-48].

CAMPBELL, Aeneas Jr. Cadet who enlisted on July 18, 1776 [Ref: A-49]. "Eneas or Enos Campbell" applied for a pension (R1627) stating he was born October 3, 1757, served in the Maryland Line during the Revolution, and married Elizabeth Ann Belt on February 25, 1791. He died on October 15, 1828, his widow (born February 20, 1767) died on January 3, 1853, and they had these children: Thomas (born April 10, 1793); Elijah (January 17, 1795); Umphrey (born February 18, 1797); Esther (born January 3, 1799, married a Nichbell); Asa (born March 28, 1791); Rutha (born May 27, 1803); Belt (born September 9, 1805); Elizabeth C. (born September 23, 1807, married a Tiner); and, David (born February 26, 1810). Asa Swann, aged 91 in 1855, stated he knew the soldier and his second wife Liza Ann Belt. On August 6, 1855, soldier's son David C. Campbell, of Wilkes County, Georgia, applied for pension due his father or mother [Ref: T-522].

CAMPBELL, James. Private who was enlisted on July 20, 1776, by Capt. Jacob Good [Ref: A-46].

CAMPBELL, John. Associator in December, 1775 [Ref: E-165]. Petitioned the General Assembly under the Act of May 12, 1780, stating he had been a non-juror to the Oath of Allegiance and Fidelity in 1778 due to "ignorance" and now desired relief under the Act and to take the Oath [Ref: L-101].

CAMPBELL, John. Sergeant in Capt. David Moore's company of militia in 1775 [Ref: E-56]. Associator in December, 1775 [Ref: E-165]. Subscribed to the Oath of Allegiance in 1778 [Ref: C-23, S-263].

CAMPEN, William. Associator in December, 1775 [Ref: E-165]. Juror, Oath of Allegiance in 1778 [Ref: C-23]. "William Campian" was a private who enlisted on July 19, 1776 [Ref: A-51].

CANDRY, Thomas. Private in the Skipton District Militia under Capt. Thomas Waring on April 16, 1776 [Ref: B-167, D-1814].

CANE, Edward. Private who enlisted on August 8, 1776 [Ref: A-49].

CANFIELD, Thomas. Militia substitute from May to December 10, 1781, and "marched to Annapolis." [Ref: A-653].

CANNON, Patrick. See "Patrick Conan," q.v.

CANNON, Starlin. Associator in December, 1775 [Ref: E-165]. Juror to the Oath of Allegiance in 1778 [Ref: C-23].

CAPPLE, Jacob. Corporal in Capt. John Carmack's company of militia in 1775 [Ref: E-56].

CAPPLE, William. Associator in December, 1775 [Ref: E-165]. Juror to the Oath of Allegiance in 1778 [Ref: C-23].

CARBERY, Henry (General). Died May 26, 1822, aged 66 [Ref: F-472].

CAREY, John Due. Captain in the Frederick Town Battalion of Militia in September, 1780 [Ref: V-295].

CAREY, Michael. Drummer, 1st Maryland Regiment, who enlisted on February 10, 1780, and served in the Southern Army of the United States under Lt. William Lamar in the late Capt. Beatty's company [Ref: A-389]. "Michael Ceary" was a private in the 7th Maryland Regiment who enlisted in Frederick Town in 1780, and was reported as "gone to Camp" by April, 1780 [Ref: A-197, A-334].

CAREY, Owen. "Owen Cary" was an Associator in December, 1775 [Ref: E-165]. Corporal, 1st Maryland Regiment, enlisted February 1, 1780, and served in the Southern Army of the United States under Lt. Wm. Lamar in the late Capt. Beatty's company, and subsequently became a sergeant. Was reported dead in March, 1781, while serving in the light infantry [Ref: A-389]. "Owen Cary" subscribed to the Oath of Allegiance in 1778 [Ref: C-23]. "Owen Ceary" was a private in the 7th Maryland Regiment who enlisted in Frederick Town in 1780, and was reported as "gone to Camp" [Ref: A-334].

CAREY [CARY], John. "John Cary" was an Associator in December, 1775 [Ref: E-165]. "John Carey" took the Oath of Allegiance in 1778 [Ref: C-23]. "John Due Carey" was captain in Frederick Town Battalion of militia from September 18, 1780, to January 23, 1782 [Ref: B-59]. "Capt. John D. Cary died the Saturday before October 19, 1804, in this town [Frederick], no age stated, a soldier at the time that tried men's souls." [Ref: N-56].

CAREY [CARY], Patrick. Private who enlisted on May 20, 1778, and served in the 2nd Maryland Regiment [Ref: A-294, A-323].

CAREY, William. Private who enlisted in the 7th Maryland Regiment on May 21, 1778, and was missing on August 16, 1780 (after the Battle of Camden, South Carolina). [Ref: A-197].

CARLILE, David. Associator in December, 1775 [Ref: E-165]. Juror to the Oath of Allegiance in 1778 [Ref: C-23].

CARLIN, William. Private who enlisted on July 29, 1776 [Ref: A-43].

CARLLEY, Barbara and Reuben R. See "Peter Zollinger," q.v.

CARMACK, Aquila. Associator in December, 1775 [Ref: E-165]. Juror to the Oath of Allegiance in 1778 [Ref: C-23]. "Aquilla Carmack" was a 2nd sergeant in the Middle District Militia in 1776 [Ref: A-72].

CARMACK, Cornelius. Soldier in the Virginia Line who "applied for pension (S2420) on October 30, 1832, in Overton County, Tennessee, aged 73 on January 3, 1832, stating he was born January 8, 1759, in Frederick County, Maryland and lived in Montgomery (now Washington) County, Virginia at enlistment. Died July 28, 1848." [Ref: T-542].

CARMACK, Elizabeth. See "William Beatty," q.v.

CARMACK, Even. Associator in December, 1775 [Ref: E-165]. Juror to the Oath of Allegiance in 1778 [Ref: C-23]. "Evan Carmack (1740-1830), son of William Carmack and Jane MacDonald, married Mary Wolf (1784-1805)." [Ref: O-258].

CARMACK, John. Captain of a company of militia in the 2nd Battalion on November 29, 1775, and a captain in the Catoctin Battalion on August 16, 1781 [Ref: E-56, B-60]. Associator in December, 1775, and was appointed "to hand about the Association paper" in Manor Hundred [Ref: E-165, E-305]. (This name appeared twice on the list of Associators). Took the Oath of Allegiance, 1778 [Ref: C-23]. "John Commack" was a captain in the Lower District, January 19, 1776 [Ref: B-64]. "John Cormacks" was captain in the 37th Battalion on June 22, 1776 [Ref: B-64]. Another "John Carmack applied for pension (R21699) on October 22, 1832, in Washington County, Virginia, aged 74 or 75, stating he was born in Frederick County, Maryland, and his father moved to Washington County, Virginia in 1773. John enlisted there in the Virginia Line during the Revolutionary War." [Ref: T-542]. One "John C. Carmack (May 12, 1742 - June 13, 1803), son of William (died 1776) and Jane Carmack, married Sarah Wolfe (1748-1822) in Frederick County, and was a captain during the Revolutionary War. A son, Paul Carmack (1786-1877), married Catherine Stimmel (1794-1867) in 1812 and lived at Walkersville, Maryland." [Ref: U-2531].

CARMACK, Levi [Levy]. Sergeant in Capt. Joseph Wood, Jr.'s company of militia in 1775 [Ref: E-53]. Associator in December, 1775 [Ref: E-165]. Juror to the Oath of Allegiance in 1778 [Ref: C-23]. "Levi Carmack" died testate in 1785, leaving wife Susanna and children Ephraim, Cathrine [sic] and Susanna, and his (Levi's) brother William [Ref: M-6:189].

CARMACK, William. 1st lieutenant in Capt. Smith's company in the 37th Battalion of militia on May 15, 1776, and captain on April 24, 1779 [Ref: B-59, B-60]. Associator in December, 1775 [Ref: E-165]. "William

Cormack" was a captain in the Catoctin Battalion on August 16, 1781 [Ref: B-64].

CARMACK, William Jr. Ensign in Capt. Joseph Wood's company in the 2nd Battalion of militia on November 29, 1775, and 1st lieutenant in Capt. Joseph Wood, Jr.'s company of militia in 1776 [Ref: E-53, W-427]. Associator in December, 1775 [Ref: E-165]. Juror to the Oath of Allegiance in 1778 [Ref: C-23]. Captain in the militia on April 27, 1779 [Ref: H-16, Z-368]. Ed. Note: There is a possibility that William (above) and William, Jr. were the same person (?).

CARMICLE, John. Juror to the Oath of Allegiance in March, 1778 [Ref: S-263, but not listed in Ref: C-23].

CARN, Jacob. Drafted on June 13, 1781, and provided a substitute [Ref: D-1814].

CARN, John. Ensign in the 34th Battalion (no date). [Ref: B-60].

CARN, Michael. Drafted on June 2, 1783; "discharged; hath a family, is poor, and had just served his tour in the mill" [sic]; probably an abbreviation of either militia or military?]. [Ref: B-168].

CARNAFF, Adam. Associator in December, 1775 [Ref: E-165]. Juror to the Oath of Allegiance in 1778 [Ref: C-23].

CARNANT, Jacob. Private who enlisted on July 1, 1776 in Capt. Peter Mantz's company; marched from Frederick Town to Leonardtown, and from there to Philadelphia, arriving August 23, 1776 [Ref: A-47]. Served in 1st Maryland Regiment, 1780, in the Southern Army of the United States under Lt. William Lamar in the late Capt. Beatty's company until transferred to the light infantry on March 12, 1781 [Ref: A-390].

CARNER, Lennard. Private in militia on March 9, 1776 [Ref: B-166].

CARNEY, Thomas. Private who enlisted on April 3, 1778 [Ref: A-315]. Corporal in Capt. William Beatty's company, 7th Maryland Regiment, 1779 [Ref: A-310].

CARNS, Arthur. Private who enlisted on July 22, 1776 [Ref: A-49].

CARNS, Francis. Private in the German Regiment who served at the Battle of White Plains on September 5, 1778, under Lt. Col. Ludwick Weltner [Ref: A-266].

CARR, Stephen. Private, 1st Maryland Regiment, 1781, and served in the Southern Army of the United States under Lt. William Lamar in the late Capt. Beatty's company [Ref: A-390].

CARRICK, Joseph. Private who enlisted on July 25, 1776 [Ref: A-51].

CARRICK, Samuel. Served on the Committee of Observation in 1775 [Ref: I-85].

CARRILL [CARROLL], George. Private who was enlisted on July 20, 1776, by Capt. Jacob Good [Ref: A-46]. "George Carrill" subscribed to the Oath of Allegiance in 1778 [Ref: C-23]. "George Carrill" was an Associator in December, 1775 [Ref: E-164].

CARRILL [CARROLL], John. Private who enlisted on May 18, 1778 [Ref: A-323]. "John Carrill" took the Oath of Allegiance in 1778 [Ref: C-23, S-263]. "John Carrill" was an Associator in December, 1775 [Ref: E-164].

CARRILL [CARROLL], William. Private who enlisted on August 8, 1776 [Ref: A-49]. "William Carrill" subscribed to the Oath of Allegiance in 1778 [Ref: C-23]. "William Carrill" was an Associator in December, 1775 [Ref: E-164]. "William Carrol or Carel applied for a pension (S2107) on August 8, 1832, in Gallia County, Ohio, and was a resident of Raccoon Township, Adams County, Ohio, in 1822, stating he was born in November, 1757, and lived in Frederick County, Maryland, at the time of his enlistment. In 1822 George Carel lived in Morgan County, Ohio (no relationship to soldier was stated)." [Ref: T-554].

CARROLL, Joseph. Enlisted on March 11, 1781, for 3 years, and was subsequently reported as "deserted" (no date given). [Ref: D-1814].

CARROLL, Patrick. Private who enlisted August 5, 1776 [Ref: A-44].

CARSON, John. Enlisted on January 24, 1781, for the duration of the war, and was later reported as "deserted" (no date). [Ref: D-1814].

CARTER, George. Private stationed at Fort Frederick on June 27, 1778, in Capt. John Kershner's company, and guarding prisoners of war [Ref: A-328].

CARTER, James. Private in the militia in July, 1776 [Ref: A-42].

CARTER, Michael. Private who enlisted August 5, 1776 [Ref: A-44].

CARTER, Samuel. Associator in December, 1775 [Ref: E-165]. Private in the militia in July, 1776 [Ref: A-42]. Juror to the Oath of Allegiance in 1778 [Ref: C-23].

CARTNEY, William. Private who enlisted April 25, 1778 [Ref: A-321].

CARTY, Daniel. Private who enlisted on July 19, 1776 [Ref: A-51].

CARTY, James. "James Carty" was a private who enlisted on August 5, 1776 in the Flying Camp under Capt. Philip Meroney [Ref: N-30:112, A-45]. "James Carte" took the Oath of Allegiance in 1778 [Ref: C-23]. "James Carte" was an Associator in December, 1775 [Ref: E-165].

CARTY, Lawrence. Defective from the Maryland Line in May, 1781 [Ref: A-415].

CARY, John. Served on Committee of Observation in 1775 [Ref: I-85].

CARY, Owen and John. See "John and Owen Carey," q.v.

CASERLINGS, Ludowick. Corporal in Capt. Robert Beatty's company of militia in 1775 [Ref: E-55].
CASEY, John. Militia substitute from May to December 10, 1781, and "marched to Annapolis." [Ref: A-653].
CASEY, William. Private who enlisted on July 19, 1776 [Ref: A-51]. Private, 1st Maryland Regiment, in 1781, and served in the Southern Army of the United States under Lt. William Lamar in the late Capt. Beatty's company. Record indicates he was in the hospital in July, 1781 [Ref: A-392].
CASH, John. Private who enlisted on August 5, 1776 in the Flying Camp under Capt. Philip Meroney [Ref: A-45, N-30:112].
CASH, William. Private who enlisted on August 5, 1776 in the Flying Camp under Capt. Philip Meroney [Ref: A-45, N-30:112].
CASNER, Christian. Private who enlisted May 20, 1778 [Ref: A-323]. "Christian Castner" was a private in the German Regiment at White Plains on September 5, 1778, under Lt. Col. Weltner [Ref: A-266].
CASSELL [CASTLE], Abraham. "Abraham Castle" was a corporal in Capt. William Beatty's company of militia in 1775 [Ref: E-55]. "Abraham Cassell, or Abram Cassel, was a soldier in the Maryland Line who applied for a pension on February 11, 1833, in Jessamine County, Kentucky, stating he was born September 25, 1756, and enlisted in Frederick County, Maryland. He married Catharine Lingenfelter, or Caterena Lingenfetter, on April 24, 1782, in Frederick County, and he died May 26, 1844. His widow applied for a pension (W2916) on December 21, 1844, in Jessamine County, Kentucky, stating their children were: Mary, born January 17, 1783; Johen [sic], born January 10, 1785, and died March 30, 1815; Elizabeth, born January 1, 1787, and died June 6, 1789; 'a little one,' born and died in March, 1790; Caterena, born October 21, 1791; Barbarah [sic], born August 15, 1794; Susannah, born November 22, 1798; and, Thomas Jefferson Cassel, born August 30, 1803. In 1833 a John Lingefetter was a resident of Fayette County, Kentucky, but no relationship to the widow was stated." [Ref: T-572].
CASSEL [CASSIL], Martin. Served on the Committee of Observation in 1775 [Ref: I-85]. Non-Enroller who was fined by the Committee of Observation in April, 1776 [Ref: E-248].
CASSELL, Jacob. Associator in December, 1775 [Ref: E-165]. "Jacob Cassall" was a non-enroller who was fined by the Committee of Observation in May, 1776 [Ref: E-248]. "Jacob Cassell" was a juror to the Oath of Allegiance in 1778 [Ref: C-23].

CASSELL [CASTLE], Peter. Juror to the Oath of Allegiance in 1778 [Ref: C-23, S-263]. "Peter Cassel" was one of those who were appointed "to hand about the Association paper" in the Upper Monocacy Hundred in 1775 [Ref: E-305]. "Peter Casel" was an Associator in December, 1775 [Ref: E-165]. "Peter Castle" was paid for recruiting services for the 7th Maryland Regiment on January 11, 1780 [Ref: V-54].

CASSOVER, Jacob. Associator in December, 1775 [Ref: E-165]. Juror to the Oath of Allegiance in 1778 [Ref: C-23].

CASTLE, Ann. See "Jacob Staley," q.v.

CASTLE, George. Associator in December, 1775 [Ref: E-164]. Juror to the Oath of Allegiance in 1778 [Ref: C-23]. "George Castle, of Upper Kittockten Hundred, farmer," died testate in 1782, leaving a wife Margaret and children Mary, James, Thomas, John, and George [Ref: M-6:27].

CASTLE, Jacob. Juror to the Oath of Allegiance in March, 1778 [Ref: S-263, but not listed in Ref: C-23].

CASTLE, John. Associator in December, 1775 [Ref: E-164]. Juror to the Oath of Allegiance in 1778 [Ref: C-23]. One John Castle died testate in 1778, leaving a wife Martha, a son John, and daughters Deliverance and Rebecca (all children under age). [Ref: M-5:87].

CASTLE, Thomas. Sergeant in Capt. Michael Troutman's company of militia in 1775 [Ref: E-51].

CASWELL, Richard. See "Isaac Shelby," q.v.

CAVENOR, John. Private who enlisted on August 5, 1776 [Ref: A-44].

CEARY, Michael and Owen. See "Michael and Owen Ceary," q.v.

CENEDEY, Philip. Private who was enlisted on July 20, 1776, by Capt. Jacob Good [Ref: A-46].

CEPHLNIGER, Martin. Sergeant in Capt. Herman Yost's company of militia in 1775 [Ref: E-52].

CHAMBERLAIN, James. Juror to the Oath of Allegiance in March, 1778 [Ref: S-267, but not listed in Ref: C-30].

CHAMBERLAIN, Jeremiah. Juror to the Oath of Allegiance in March, 1778 [Ref: S-267, but not listed in Ref: C-30].

CHAMBERLAIN, John. Associator in December, 1775 [Ref: E-165]. Juror to the Oath of Allegiance in 1778 [Ref: C-23]. "John Chamberlin," private, enlisted on July 20, 1776 by Capt. Jacob Good [Ref: A-46]. He died testate in 1782, leaving wife a Mary and sons Abner and Hops (minors). [Ref: M-5:171].

CHAMBERLAIN, John Jr. Associator in December, 1775 [Ref: E-165]. Juror to the Oath of Allegiance in 1778 [Ref: C-23].

CHAMBERLAIN, William. Private in the 7th Maryland Regiment, 1780. Enlisted in Frederick Town between January and April, 1780, and subsequently reported as "deserted" (no date given). [Ref: A-334].

CHAMBERLIN, Jonas [Jones]. Private who enlisted on May 20, 1778, and served in the 2nd Maryland Regiment [Ref: A-294, A-323].

CHAMBERS, Thomas. Non-Enroller who was fined by the Committee of Observation in May, 1776 [Ref: E-248].

CHAMBERS, William. Private who enlisted on April 27, 1778 [Ref: A-324]. Defective from the Maryland Line on February 14, 1781 [Ref: A-414].

CHAMBERS, William (of Thomas). Non-Enroller who was fined by the Committee of Observation in May, 1776 [Ref: E-248].

CHAMPNIS, James. Private who enlisted on May 6, 1778 [Ref: A-322]. "James Champness" was at White Plains on September 5, 1778, under Lt. Col. Ludwick Weltner [Ref: A-266].

CHANDLER, James. Private, 7th Maryland Regiment, 1780, enlisted in Frederick Town between January and April, 1780, and reported as "gone to Camp" [Ref: A-334].

CHANDLER, William. Fifer in Capt. Samuel Plummer's company of militia in 1775 [Ref: E-54]. Private who enlisted on August 5, 1776 in the Flying Camp under Capt. Philip Meroney [Ref: A-45, N-30:112].

CHAPLINE, James. Quartermaster in the 36th Battalion of militia on January 6, 1776. 1st lieutenant in the Upper District on July 4, 1776, under Capt. Joseph Chapline [Ref: B-61, O-104, W-546]. Served in the Select Militia of Washington County, 1778-1781 [Ref: B-61].

CHAPLINE, Joseph (Sharpsburg). Appointed by the Committee of Correspondence to solicit subscriptions in 1775 to purchase arms and ammunition [Ref: I-86]. Gave money in the amount of 5 lbs. for arms and ammunition for the militia in Frederick County in 1775 [Ref: E-62]. Served on the Committee of Observation in 1775 [Ref: I-85]. Captain in Frederick County's Upper District on July 4, 1776, and captain of Select Militia in Washington County from June 22, 1778 to March 30, 1781 [Ref: B-241, B-61, O-104, W-546, Z-145].

CHAPLINE, Moses. 1st lieutenant in the Upper District militia of Frederick County [now Washington County] in 1776 [Ref: A-48]. Also, one Moses Chapline was a private in Capt. Joseph Chapline's militia company in Washington County in 1777 [Ref: B-242].

CHAPMAN, Abraham. Private who enlisted July 25, 1776 [Ref: A-50].

CHAPMAN, Nathan. Corporal in Capt. Samuel Plummer's company of militia in 1775 [Ref: E-54].

CHAPPELL, Archibald. Private who enlisted July 22, 1776 [Ref: A-49].
CHAPPELL, Thomas. Private who enlisted July 22, 1776 [Ref: A-49].
CHARLES, Adam. Private in the German Regiment, 1776, in Capt. Henry Fister's company under the command of Col. Hussecker [Ref: A-261].
CHARLTON, John Usher. 2nd lieutenant in Capt. P. Thomas' militia company in 1775 [Ref: E-50, B-61]. Associator in December, 1775 [Ref: E-165]. Juror to the Oath of Allegiance in 1778 [Ref: C-23]. "John Usher Charlton" was captain in 34th Battalion of militia on May 15, 1776 [Ref: B-61, W-426]. "John Charlton" petitioned to form the horse troops in 1781 [Ref: B-167]. "Usher Charlton" was a private in the horse troops in June, 1781 [Ref: B-167].
CHATTELL, Thomas. Private who enlisted July 29, 1776 [Ref: A-44].
CHEATHAM, Aquilla. Sergeant, 1st Maryland Regiment, 1781, and served in the Southern Army of the United States under Lt. William Lamar in the late Capt. Beatty's company, but was "recruiting in Maryland from January to July, 1781." [Ref: A-389].
CHENOWETH, Arthur. Private in the Skipton District Militia under Capt. Thomas Waring on April 16, 1776 [Ref: B-167, D-1814].
CHENOWETH, Thomas. Private in the Skipton District Militia under Capt. Thomas Waring on April 16, 1776 [Ref: B-167, D-1814].
CHERRY, Benjamin. Non-Enroller who was fined by the Committee of Observation in April, 1776 [Ref: E-248].
CHILLON, Mark. Private who enlisted on July 18, 1776 [Ref: A-49].
CHILTON, John. Associator in December, 1775 [Ref: E-165]. Juror to the Oath of Allegiance in 1778 [Ref: C-23].
CHINAT, Charles. Associator in December, 1775 [Ref: E-165]. Juror to the Oath of Allegiance in 1778 [Ref: C-23].
CHRIESMAN, Frederick. Associator in December, 1775 [Ref: E-165], and a Juror to the Oath of Allegiance in 1778 [Ref: C-23]. Also, see "Frederick Christman," q.v.
CHRIESMAN, Frederick Jr. Petitioned the General Assembly under the Act of July 3, 1780, stating he had been a non-juror to the Oath of Allegiance and Fidelity in 1778 due to "ignorance" and now desired relief under the Act and to take the Oath [Ref: L-101].
CHRIESMAN, John. Associator in December, 1775 [Ref: E-165]. Juror to the Oath of Allegiance in 1778 [Ref: C-23].
CHRISMAN, George Jr. Associator in December, 1775 [Ref: E-165]. Juror to the Oath of Allegiance in 1778 [Ref: C-23].
CHRIST, Anna Barbara. See "Matthias Young," q.v.

CHRIST [CRIST], Jacob. Captain in the 37th Battalion of militia on April 15, 1778 [Ref: H-16, B-66, Z-35]. One "Jacob Crist" died in 1793, leaving a wife Catherine, and heirs Henry, Jacob, Elizabeth, Mary, Philip, and Catherine [Ref: M-4:13].

CHRIST [CRIST], Philip. 4th sergeant in Capt. Christopher Stull's company of militia in 1775 [Ref: E-50]. "Philip Crist" was ensign in the 37th Battalion of militia in April, 1779 [Ref: H-16, B-66]. "Philip Christ" was compensated in May, 1782, for wintering a bull for the military [Ref: R-515].

CHRISTIAN, John. Sergeant in the 7th Maryland Regiment from May 22, 1777, until October, 1777, when reported "off rolls" [Ref: A-195].

CHRISTMAN, Frederick. Soldier in the Maryland Line who applied for pension (R1942) on September 22, 1843, aged 88, in Indiana County, Pennsylvania, a resident of Blacklick Township, Pennsylvania. He was born in 1755 in Frederick County, Maryland, and lived there at the time of enlistment. After the war he moved to Cumberland [sic] County, Maryland, and then to Huntingdon County, Pennsylvania. In 1833 he moved to Indiana County, Pennsylvania, and died on July 8, 1844. His grandson, Jonathan Hartsock, wrote a letter of inquiry on February 14, 1884 [record mistakenly states 1784] at Blairsville, Pennsylvania. When Frederick Christman died he left no widow, but his surviving children were Susanna Hartsock, Elijah Christman, John Christman, and Samuel Christman." [Ref: T-630].

CHRISTMAN, Margaret and Nicholas. See "James Yule," q.v.

CHRISTMAN, Paul. Ensign in the German Regiment in July, 1776, under Capt. William Heiser, and on the muster roll dated October 23, 1776 [Ref: A-263, X-48].

CHRISTON, Charles. Associator in December, 1775 [Ref: E-165]. Juror to the Oath of Allegiance in 1778 [Ref: C-23].

CHRISTOPHER, Thomas. Private, 1st Maryland Regiment, 1781, and served in the Southern Army of the United States under Lt. William Lamar in the late Capt. Beatty's company. Record indicates he "deserted" in March, 1781 [Ref: A-391].

CHURCHILL, John. Private in the 7th Maryland Regiment from January 10, 1777, until May, 1777, when reported "off rolls" [Ref: A-195].

CHURCHWELL, John. Private who enlisted on August 5, 1776, in the Flying Camp under Capt. Philip Meroney [Ref: A-45, N-30:111].

CIFERD, John. Private in the Middle District Militia in 1776 [Ref: A-72].

CLABAUGH, Charles. Juror to the Oath of Allegiance in March, 1778 [Ref: S-263, but not listed in Ref: C-23].

CLABAUGH, Frederick. Corporal in Capt. Normand Bruce's company of militia in 1775 [Ref: E-55]. Associator in December, 1775 [Ref: E-165]. Juror to the Oath of Allegiance in 1778 [Ref: C-23]. "Frederick Cleabaugh" was sergeant in Capt. John Carmack's company of militia in 1775 [Ref: E-56]. A "Frederick Claybaugh" died testate in 1781, leaving wife Sarah and children Samuel, Frederick, Catherine, Ann, Jacob, James, and Juddy (daughter). [Ref: M-6:167].

CLABAUGH, John. Associator in December, 1775 [Ref: E-165]. Juror to the Oath of Allegiance in 1778 [Ref: C-23]. "John Cleabaugh" was a sergeant in Capt. J. Carmack's militia company in 1775 [Ref: E-56].

CLABAUGH, John Jr. Juror to the Oath of Allegiance in March, 1778 [Ref: S-263, but not listed in Ref: C-23].

CLABAUGH [CLAUBAUGH, Martin. Soldier in the Pennsylvania Line who married Margaret (no last name given) about 1772 in Hagerstown, Maryland, and enlisted there at the time of the Revolution. He applied for a pension on April 14, 1818, in Huntingdon County, Pennsylvania. In 1820 he was aged 77 with a wife Margaret aged 69. He died July 15, 1822. His widow applied for a pension (W3222) on March 25, 1840, in Huntingdon County, aged about 88, stating they had moved from Maryland in 1801 or 1802. The soldier's daughter Catharine Clabaugh, aged 54, applied July 23, 1850, in Huntingdon County, Pennsylvania, for herself and the other children of the deceased widow, to wit: Martin Claubaugh, Margaret Summers, Jacob Claubaugh, Elizabeth Nightime, Catharine Claubaugh, and Abraham Claubaugh. Widow died on March 3, 1848." [Ref: T-665].

CLAGETT, Alexander (upper part of Potomac Hundred). Appointed by the Committee of Correspondence to solicit subscriptions in 1775 to purchase arms and ammunition [Ref: I-86].

CLAGETT, Postumus. Private in militia, March 9, 1776 [Ref: B-166].

CLANCER, Charles. Associator in December, 1775 [Ref: E-165]. Juror to the Oath of Allegiance in 1778 [Ref: C-23].

CLANCEY, Edward. Drummer or fifer, 1st Maryland Regiment, 1781, and served in the Southern Army of the United States under Lt. William Lamar in the late Capt. Beatty's company [Ref: A-389].

CLAPSADDLE, George. Juror to the Oath of Allegiance in March, 1778 [Ref: S-263, but not listed in Ref: C-23].

CLAPSADDLE [CLAPSADEL], John. Associator in December, 1775 [Ref: E-165]. Juror to the Oath of Allegiance in 1778, Frederick County [Ref: C-23, S-263].

CLAPSADDLE, Michael. Juror to the Oath of Allegiance in March, 1778 [Ref: S-263, but not listed in Ref: C-23].
CLARK, Elisha. See "John Clarke," q.v.
CLARK, Henry. Private in the militia in July, 1776 [Ref: A-42].
CLARK, Richard. Private who enlisted April 24, 1778 [Ref: A-320].
CLARK, Samuel. Enlisted in the 7th Maryland Regiment on July 20, 1780 [Ref: V-224]. Private in the 1st Maryland Regiment, 1781, and served in the Southern Army of the United States under Lt. William Lamar in the late Capt. Beatty's company [Ref: A-390].
CLARKE, Barzellia. Private in the Skipton District Militia under Capt. Thomas Waring on April 16, 1776 [Ref: B-167, D-1814].
CLARKE, John. Soldier in the Maryland Line who "applied for pension (S3158) on October 5, 1832, in Warren County, Ohio, a resident of Deerfield Township, stating he was born near Mt. Holly, New Jersey, and was raised at Old Town in Frederick County, Maryland, where he lived at the time of his enlistment. Also mentioned was an Elisha Clark, but no relationship was stated." [Ref: T-663].
CLARKE, Jonathan. Private in the Skipton District Militia under Capt. Thomas Waring on April 16, 1776 [Ref: B-167, D-1814].
CLARKE, Joseph. Petitioned the General Assembly under the Act of July 3, 1780, stating that he had been a non-juror to the Oath of Allegiance and Fidelity in 1778 due to "ignorance" and now desired relief under the Act and to take the Oath [Ref: L-101].
CLARKE, William. Private who was in the 7th Maryland Regiment by November 2, 1778, and transferred to the 2nd Maryland Regiment on January 11, 1779 [Ref: A-197].
CLARY, Adieni [?]. Petitioned the General Assembly under the Act of May 12, 1780, stating that he had been a non-juror to the Oath of Allegiance and Fidelity in 1778 due to "ignorance" and now desired relief under the Act and to take the Oath [Ref: L-101].
CLARY, Benjamin Jr. Petitioned the General Assembly under the Act of May 12, 1780, stating he had been a non-juror to the Oath of Allegiance and Fidelity in 1778 due to "ignorance" and now desired relief under the Act and to take the Oath [Ref: L-101].
CLARY, Benjamin. Drafted on June 2, 1783, but he was "discharged... is poor and has a family." [Ref: B-169].
CLARY, Dennis. Private who enlisted on August 5, 1776 [Ref: A-44].
CLARY, John. Associator in December, 1775 [Ref: E-165]. Juror to the Oath of Allegiance in 1778 [Ref: C-23].
CLASS, John. Private who enlisted on July 18, 1776 [Ref: A-50].

CLASS, Martin. Private who enlisted in the 7th Maryland Regiment on June 9, 1778, and served to at least March 1, 1779 [Ref: A-196].
CLAYBAUGH, Frederick and John. See "Frederick and John Clabaugh."
CLEM, George. Petitioned the General Assembly under the Act of May 12, 1780, stating he had been a non-juror to the Oath of Allegiance and Fidelity in 1778 due to "neglect" and now desired relief under the Act and to take the Oath [Ref: L-101].
CLEMENTS, Henry. Private who enlisted on August 5, 1776, in the Flying Camp under Capt. Philip Meroney [Ref: A-45, N-30:112]. One "Henry Clemments" took the Oath of Allegiance in 1778 [Ref: C-23]. One "Henry Clements" was a substitute from May to December 10, 1781, and also "marched to Annapolis." [Ref: A-653]. "Henry Clemments" was an Associator in December, 1775 [Ref: E-165]. "Henry Clemens" was paid for services rendered to the military in 1779 (nature not stated). [Ref: V-44].
CLEMENTS [CLEMONTS], James. Private, 7th Maryland Regiment, 1780, enlisted in Frederick Town between January and April; subsequently reported as "deserted" (no date given). [Ref: A-334]. Private, 1st Maryland Regiment, 1781, who served in the Southern Army of the United States under Lt. William Lamar in the late Capt. Beatty's company. Record states he "deserted" on June 22, 1781 [Ref: A-391].
CLICE, Henry. Private in the Middle District Militia in 1776 [Ref: A-72].
CLICKETT, Captain. See "David Love," q.v.
CLIFTON, Thomas. Private in the German Regiment; roll dated October 23, 1776 [Ref: A-264]. Discharged on July 26, 1779 [Ref: A-265].
CLINE, Daniel. "Daniel Cline" was a private who enlisted on July 19, 1776 [Ref: A-51]. "Daniel Clyne" took the Oath of Allegiance in March, 1778 [Ref: S-263, but not listed in Ref: C-23]. Also, see "Daniel Kline," q.v.
CLINE, Jacob. Juror to the Oath of Allegiance in March, 1778 [Ref: S-263, but not listed in Ref: C-23]. Also, see "Jacob Klein," q.v.
CLINE, Margaret. See "Jacob Brunner," q.v.
CLINE, Peter. 1st lieutenant in the Linganore Battalion of militia, 1778-1779 [Ref: H-16, B-63].
CLINK, Henry. Non-Enroller who was fined by the Committee of Observation in May, 1776 [Ref: E-248].
CLINK, John. Non-Enroller who was fined by the Committee of Observation in May, 1776 [Ref: E-248].
CLINTON, Charles (Cumberland Hundred). Appointed by the Committee of Correspondence to solicit subscriptions in 1775 to purchase arms and ammunition [Ref: I-86]. Served on the Committee of Observation in

1775 [Ref: I-85]. Private in the Skipton District Militia under Capt. Thomas Waring on April 16, 1776 [Ref: B-167, D-1814]. Captain in the Skipton District Militia on July 27, 1776, and a captain in Washington County in 1778, "on the frontier." [Ref: X-127, B-63].

CLINTON, George. Private in the German Regiment in 1776 in Capt. Fister's company under the command of Col. Hussecker [Ref: A-261].

CLISCE, Christeen. Private who was enlisted on July 20, 1776, by Capt. Jacob Good [Ref: A-46]. Also, see "Christopher Klise," q.v.

CLOSE, Charles. Defective from the Maryland Line on March 15, 1781 [Ref: A-414].

CLOSS, John. Private who enlisted on July 19, 1776 [Ref: A-51].

CLOSSON, Garrett. Private who enlisted July 20, 1776 [Ref: A-50].

CLOTZ, John. Associator in December, 1775 [Ref: E-165]. Juror to the Oath of Allegiance in 1778 [Ref: C-23].

CLOUSE, William. Private in the Skipton District Militia under Capt. Thomas Waring on April 16, 1776 [Ref: B-167, D-1814].

CLYNE, Daniel. See "Daniel Cline," q.v.

CNOUFF, Peter. See "Peter Knouff," q.v.

COAM, Michael. Associator in December, 1775 [Ref: E-165]. Juror to the Oath of Allegiance in 1778 [Ref: C-23].

COBBLE, George. 1st lieutenant in Linganore Battalion of militia on January 17, 1777, under Capt. Henry Baker [Ref: B-63, Y-54].

COBOLENCE [COBLENCE], Herman. "Herman Cobolence" was an Associator in December, 1775 [Ref: E-165], and Juror to the Oath of Allegiance in 1778 [Ref: C-23]. "Harmon Covelince" provided wheat for the military, May, 1782 [Ref: R-517].

COBOLENCE [COBLENCE], Peter. Provided wheat for the military in May, 1782 [Ref: R-517].

COCHINDERFER, Michael. On July 29, 1776, the Treasurer of the Western Shore was directed "to pay to Michael Cochinderfer, of Frederick County, 300 pounds to enable him to carry on a stocking manufactory." [Ref: X-134].

COCHRAN, James. Juror to the Oath of Allegiance in 1778 [Ref: C-23].

COCHRAN, James Henry (July 4, 1763 - July 12, 1840). Associator in December, 1775 [Ref: E-165]. "James Cochran" was a private in the Maryland Line from August 1, 1780 until discharged on November 29, 1783 [Ref: A-529, U-2616]. "James Cochrane," aged 77, was on the 1840 pension list, residing in the 3rd District of Frederick County [Ref: J-37]. "On February 13, 1837, the Treasurer of the Western Shore was directed to pay to 'James Cochran,' the half pay of a private during his life, as a further remuneration for his services during the Revolutionary War. On January 18, 1847 the Treasurer of the Western Shore was directed to pay to 'Ann Mary Cockrane,' of Frederick County, widow of 'James Cockrane,' who was a private in the Revolutionary War, or to her order, quarterly, during her life, commencing on January 1, 1847, a sum equal to the half pay of a private, as further remuneration for the services of her deceased husband." [Ref: G-329]. The widow of "James Cochran" applied for his pension (W25438) on July 17, 1846, in Frederick County, aged 76 years, 5 months, and 23 days, stating her name before marriage on May 12, 1793, was Ann Mary Ahalt. Her husband, the soldier, was born July 4, 1763 and died July 12, 1840. Their children were: Elizabeth Cochran, born September 30, 1793; John Cochran, born November 12, 1795, and died February 3, 1802; Henry Cochran, born September 7, 1797; Jacob Cochran, born February 9, 1800; Daniel Cochran, born May 26, 1803; Anna Mary Cochran, born June 22, ----; and, James Cochran, Jr., born March 17, 1806 and died at age of 3 months." [Ref: T-688, U-2616].

COCHRAN, John. Associator in December, 1775 [Ref: E-165]. Juror to the Oath of Allegiance in 1778 [Ref: C-23]. "John Cockran" was a private in the Skipton District Militia under Capt. Thomas Waring on April 16, 1776 [Ref: B-167, D-1814]. Private in the 7th Maryland Regiment who enlisted in Frederick Town between January and April, 1780 [Ref: A-334, V-175]. Private in the 1st Maryland Regiment in 1781, and served in the Southern Army of the United States under Lt. William Lamar in the late Capt. Beatty's company. This record indicates he was killed on March 15, 1781 [Ref: A-391].

COCHRAN, Robert. Associator in December, 1775 [Ref: E-165]. Juror to the Oath of Allegiance in 1778 [Ref: C-23].

COCK, Henry. Served on the Committee of Observation in 1775 [Ref: I-85].

COFFEEROTH, William. Private who enlisted on July 18, 1776 [Ref: A-50]. Juror to the Oath of Allegiance in 1778 [Ref: C-23]. "William Cofferoth" was an Associator in December, 1775 [Ref: E-165]. "William Cofferot" was a sergeant in Capt. Herman Yost's company of militia in 1775 [Ref: E-52].

COH, Jacob. Associator in December, 1775 [Ref: E-165]. Juror to the Oath of Allegiance in 1778 [Ref: C-23].

COLBERT, Simon. "Simon Colibert" was a private in the 7th Maryland Regiment, enlisted in Frederick Town between January and April, 1780, and reported as "gone to Camp" [Ref: A-334]. "Simon Colbert" was a private in the 1st Maryland Regiment in 1781, and served in the Southern Army of the United States under Lt. William Lamar in the late Capt. Beatty's company until reported "deserted" in February, 1781 [Ref: A-390].

COLE, Benjamin. Private who enlisted on May 20, 1778 [Ref: A-323]. Served as a private in the German Regiment at the Battle of White Plains on September 5, 1778, under Lt. Col. Weltner [Ref: A-266].

COLE, James. Non-Enroller who was fined by the Committee of Observation in April, 1776 [Ref: E-248].

COLE, James. Petitioned the General Assembly under the Act of May 12, 1780, stating he had been a non-juror to the Oath of Allegiance and Fidelity in 1778 due to "ignorance" and now desired relief under the Act and to take the Oath [Ref: L-101].

COLEMAN, John B. See "Matthias Young," q.v.

COLLER, Michael. Associator in December, 1775 [Ref: E-164]. (This name appeared twice on the list of Associators. One was spelled "Coller" and the other was spelled "Collar."). "Michael Coller" subscribed to the Oath of Allegiance in 1778 [Ref: C-23]. A "John Collar" was captain of militia in Washington County in 1777 [Ref: B-246].

COLLESS, Pompey. Militia substitute from May to December 10, 1781, and "marched to Annapolis." [Ref: A-653].

COLLEY, George. Private who enlisted on July 19, 1776 [Ref: A-51].

COLLIER, Isaac. Private in the Skipton District Militia under Capt. Thomas Waring on April 16, 1776 [Ref: B-167, D-1814].

COLLIER, Michael. Private in the Skipton District Militia under Capt. Thomas Waring on April 16, 1776 [Ref: B-167, D-1814].

COLLINS, Edmund. Defective from the Maryland Line on November 6, 1780 [Ref: A-414].

COLLINS, Jacob. Associator in December, 1775 [Ref: E-165]. Juror to the Oath of Allegiance in 1778 [Ref: C-23]. Captain in the Catoctin Battalion on August 16, 1781 [Ref: B-64].

COLLINS, James. Private who was enlisted on July 20, 1776 by Capt. Jacob Good [Ref: A-46]. Juror to the Oath of Allegiance in 1778 [Ref: C-23]. This or another James Collins enlisted on May 2, 1781, for three years, and marched with Capt. Lynn [Ref: D-1814].

COLLINS, John. Associator in December, 1775 [Ref: E-164]. Private who enlisted on July 19, 1776 or July 29, 1776 [Ref: A-44, A-51].

COLLINS, Thomas. Private who enlisted on July 19, 1776 [Ref: A-51].

COLLYBERGER, John. See "John Kallenberger," q.v.

COLMORE, Ann. See "Patrick Connor," q.v.

COLOUR, Philip. Private in German Regiment, 1776, in Capt. Henry Fister's company under the command of Col. Hussecker [Ref: A-261].
COMBS, Henry. Associator in December, 1775 [Ref: E-165]. Juror to the Oath of Allegiance in 1778 [Ref: C-23].
COMP[?], John. Juror to the Oath of Allegiance in March, 1778 [Ref: S-263, but not listed in Ref: C-23].
COMPTON, John. Private who enlisted July 18, 1776 [Ref: A-49]. 2nd lieutenant, May 12, 1779, and 1st lieutenant, September 18, 1780, in Frederick Town Battalion of Militia [Ref: H-15, B-64, V-295].
CONAN, Patrick. Associator in December, 1775 [Ref: E-165]. "Patrick Connan," private, enlisted on August 5, 1776 in the Flying Camp under Capt. Philip Meroney [Ref: N-30:112, A-45, which latter source spelled his name "Patrick Cannon."]. "Patrick Conan" subscribed to the Oath of Allegiance in 1778 [Ref: C-23]. "Patrick Cunnan" was drafted on June 2, 1783 [Ref: B-169].
CONELL, Morgan Charles. Non-Enroller who was fined by the Committee of Observation in May, 1776 [Ref: E-248].
CONN, John. Corporal in Capt. John Kershner's company; guarded prisoners at Fort Frederick, 1777-1778; discharged June 21, 1778 [Ref: A-328].
CONN, Peter. Corporal at Fort Frederick on June 27, 1778, in Capt. John Kershner's company, and guarded prisoners of war [Ref: A-328].
CONN, Timothy. Private in Capt. Charles Baltzel's Company, served 3 years, and discharged July 19, 1779 at Camp Wyoming [Ref: A-271].
CONN, William Young. Private in militia in July, 1776 [Ref: A-42].
CONNELLY, Edward. Private who enlisted April 14, 1778 [Ref: A-315].
CONNELLY, John. Substitute on June 13, 1781, and marched with Capt. Dyer [Ref: D-1814].
CONNER, David. Private who enlisted in the 2nd Maryland Regiment in 1778 and was "disabled by sickness." His invalid pension commenced on November 29, 1783, and ceased on March 29, 1784, with the cause of the pension ceasing noted as "dead." [Ref: A-294, A-630, A-631].
CONNER [CONNOR], Patrick. Drummer in Capt. Normand Bruce's company of militia in 1775 [Ref: E-55]. "Bounty land warrant numbers 12873 and 14102-100-24, February, 1795, were issued to Francis Sherrard, assignee of Ann Colmore, administratrix, stating the soldier was a private in the Maryland Line." [Ref: T-738].
CONNER, Thomas. Ensign in the Lower District Militia in the 16th Battalion on May 20, 1776, in Capt. Owens' company [Ref: W-432].

CONNOLLY, Patrick. Soldier in the Maryland Line who "applied for a pension (S35861) on March 27, 1818, in Kent County, Delaware, aged 61, stating he had enlisted at Fredericktown, Maryland. In 1820 he was a resident of Dover, Delaware, with no family, and was the postmaster there." [Ref: T-738].

CONNOWAY, James. Private who enlisted on May 15, 1778 [Ref: A-322].

CONRAD [CONROD], Henry. Private in the Skipton District Militia under Capt. Thomas Waring on April 16, 1776 [Ref: B-167, D-1814].

CONRAD, John. Private who enlisted on July 1, 1776 in Capt. Peter Mantz's company; marched from Frederick Town to Leonardtown, and from there to Philadelphia, arriving August 23, 1776 [Ref: A-47].

CONRAD, Nicholas. Associator in December, 1775 [Ref: E-165]. Juror to the Oath of Allegiance in 1778 [Ref: C-23]. "Nicholas Conrad, turner," died testate in 1786, leaving a wife Elizabeth and seven children (not named in the will). [Ref: M-7:31].

CONRAD [CONROD], William. Ensign at Fort Frederick in 1778 in Capt. John Kershner's company, guarding prisoners of war [Ref: A-328].

CONROY, Patrick. Associator in December, 1775 [Ref: E-165]. Juror to the Oath of Allegiance in 1778 [Ref: C-23].

CONSELLA, Hermon. Private who enlisted July 20, 1776 [Ref: A-50].

CONWAY, Robert. Associator in December, 1775 [Ref: E-165]. Juror to the Oath of Allegiance in 1778 [Ref: C-23].

COOE, Job. Associator in December, 1775 [Ref: E-165]. Juror to the Oath of Allegiance in 1778 [Ref: C-23].

COOE, John Jr. Associator in December, 1775 [Ref: E-165]. Juror to the Oath of Allegiance in 1778 [Ref: C-23].

COOK, Henry. Associator in December, 1775 [Ref: E-165]. Juror to the Oath of Allegiance in 1778 [Ref: C-23].

COOK, John. Non-Enroller who was fined by Committee of Observation in May, 1776 [Ref: E-248]. Enlisted on August 5, 1776 [Ref: A-44]. Drafted on June 13, 1781, and was discharged, "being upwards of 50 years old." [Ref: D-1814].

COOK, Thomas. Associator in December, 1775 [Ref: E-165]. Juror to the Oath of Allegiance in 1778 [Ref: C-23]. Private in the Middle District Militia in 1776 [Ref: A-72].

COOKE, George (Captain). Loaned $1,000 for the use of the State of Maryland in June, 1780 [Ref: V-520].

COOKE, John. Associator in December, 1775 [Ref: E-165]. Juror to the Oath of Allegiance in 1778 [Ref: C-23].

COOKE, Richard. Private who enlisted on July 29, 1776 [Ref: A-44].

COOKSON, Samuel (Burnt House Woods Hundred). Non-Enroller who was fined by the Committee of Observation in August, 1776 [Ref: E-248].
COOMPTH, Peter. Associator in December, 1775 [Ref: E-165]. Juror to the Oath of Allegiance in 1778 [Ref: C-23].
COON, Adam. Private in Capt. John Kershner's company; guarded prisoners at Fort Frederick, 1777-1778; discharged June 5, 1778 [Ref: A-328].
COONE, Philip. Juror to the Oath of Allegiance in March, 1778 [Ref: S-263, but not listed in Ref: C-23].
COONSE, Henry. "Henry Coonse" was a private who enlisted on July 18, 1776 [Ref: A-50]. "Henry Coontz" took the Oath of Allegiance in March, 1778 [Ref: S-263].
COONSE, Martin. "Martin Coonse" was an Associator in December, 1775 [Ref: E-165], and a Juror to the Oath of Allegiance in 1778 [Ref: C-23]. "Martin Coontz" took the Oath of Allegiance in March, 1778 [Ref: S-263].
COONSE [CONSE], Patrick. Juror to the Oath of Allegiance in March, 1778 [Ref: S-263, but not listed in Ref: C-23].
COOPER, Archibald. Provided wheat for the military in May, 1782 [Ref: R-516].
COOPER, Christopher. Associator in December, 1775 [Ref: E-165]. Juror to the Oath of Allegiance in 1778 [Ref: C-23]. Private in the Middle District Militia in 1776 [Ref: A-72].
COOPER, James. Associator in December, 1775 [Ref: E-165]. Juror to the Oath of Allegiance in 1778 [Ref: C-23].
COOPER, Thomas. See "John Barlow," q.v.
COPE, Philip. Associator in December, 1775 [Ref: E-165]. Juror to the Oath of Allegiance in 1778 [Ref: C-23].
COPPEL, Jacob. Associator in December, 1775 [Ref: E-165]. Juror to the Oath of Allegiance in 1778 [Ref: C-23].
COPPERSMITH, John. Associator in December, 1775 [Ref: E-165]. Juror to the Oath of Allegiance in 1778 [Ref: C-23].
COPPERSMITH, Peter. Associator in December, 1775 [Ref: E-164]. Juror to the Oath of Allegiance in 1778 [Ref: C-23].
COPPLE, Peter. Private in the German Regiment, 1776, in Capt. Henry Fister's company under the command of Col. Hussecker [Ref: A-261].
CORKERY, William. Private in the 6th Maryland Regiment from March 31, 1778 until July 10, 1780 when reported "deserted" [Ref: A-193].

CORNALL, Benjamin. in Capt. Samuel Shaw's company of militia in 1775 [Ref: E-51].

CORRELL, Andrew. Non-Enroller who was fined by the Committee of Observation in April, 1776 [Ref: E-248].

CORT, Jacob. Paid for services rendered to the military in April, 1780 (nature of the services not stated). [Ref: V-151].

CORTER, Thomas. Private, 7th Maryland Regiment, 1780, enlisted in Frederick Town between January and April, 1780, and subsequently reported "deserted and in Baltimore goal" (jail). [Ref: A-334].

CORTZ [COTZ], Jacob. 1st lieutenant in the German Regiment under Capt. William Heiser in July, 1776 [Ref: X-48].

CORTZ, Michael. Private who enlisted on July 25, 1776 [Ref: A-51].

CORTZ [CURTS], Christopher. Private who enlisted on July 18, 1776 [Ref: A-50].

COSGROVE, Mathias. Private who enlisted May 12, 1778 [Ref: A-322].

COST, Francis. Associator in December, 1775 [Ref: E-164]. Juror to the Oath of Allegiance in 1778 [Ref: C-23]. "Francis Cost, farmer" died testate in 1782, leaving wife (not named) and children George Cost, Jacob Cost, and Cathren Kitschurner [Ref: M-5:170, U-910].

COST, Jacob. Associator in December, 1775 [Ref: E-164]. Juror to the Oath of Allegiance in 1778 [Ref: C-23].

COST, John. Juror to the Oath of Allegiance in March, 1778 [Ref: S-263, but not listed in Ref: C-23].

COST, Philip. Associator in December, 1775 [Ref: E-165]. Juror to the Oath of Allegiance in 1778 [Ref: C-23].

COUGHLAN, Michael. Private who enlisted May 14, 1778 [Ref: A-322].

COUNSTON, Henry. Petitioned the General Assembly under the Act of May 12, 1780, stating that he had been a non-juror to the Oath of Allegiance and Fidelity in 1778 due to "ignorance" and now desired relief under the Act and to take the Oath [Ref: L-101].

COURTNEY, William. Private who enlisted in the 2nd Maryland Regiment in 1778 [Ref: A-294].

COVE, John. Private who enlisted on July 25, 1776 [Ref: A-51].

COVENTRY, Jacob. Non-Enroller who was fined by the Committee of Observation in April, 1776 [Ref: E-248]. Drafted on June 2, 1783, but "hath not appeared." [Ref: B-168].

COVER, Archart [Areheart]. Associator in December, 1775 [Ref: E-165]. Juror to the Oath of Allegiance in 1778 [Ref: C-23, S-263].

COVER, Jost [Yost]. Associator in December, 1775 [Ref: E-165]. Juror to the Oath of Allegiance in 1778 [Ref: C-23, S-263].

COVILE, Jonathan. Petitioned the General Assembly under the Act of May 12, 1780, stating that he had been a non-juror to the Oath of Allegiance and Fidelity in 1778 due to "ignorance" and now desired relief under the Act and to take the Oath [Ref: L-101].

COWEN, Samuel. Associator in December, 1775 [Ref: E-165]. Juror to the Oath of Allegiance in 1778 [Ref: C-23].

COWIN, William. Private in the Skipton District Militia under Capt. Thomas Waring on April 16, 1776 [Ref: B-167, D-1814].

COWLAND, George. Private in the 7th Maryland Regiment who enlisted in Frederick Town between January and April, 1780 [Ref: A-334].

COX, Clarkeson. Private in the 7th Maryland Regiment who enlisted on June 7, 1778, and was discharged on March 30, 1779 [Ref: A-197].

COX, Ezekiel (Fort Frederick Hundred). Appointed by the Committee of Correspondence to solicit subscriptions in 1775 to purchase arms and ammunition [Ref: I-86]. Gave money in the amount of 12 lbs. 3 sh. 4 p. for arms and ammunition for the militia in 1775 [Ref: E-62]. 2nd lieutenant in the Skipton District militia on July 27, 1776, in Capt. Andrew Hynes' company [Ref: B-65, X-127, X-337].

COX, Henry (upper part of Monocacy Hundred). Appointed by the Committee of Correspondence to solicit subscriptions in 1775 to purchase arms and ammunition [Ref: I-86].

COX, Isaac. Soldier in the Maryland Line who "applied for pension (S32186) on September 22, 1832, in Rush County, Indiana, aged 77, a resident of Noble Township, stating he enlisted in Washington County (that part which was formerly Frederick County), Maryland. It was stated that since 1818 he had neither a wife or children. In 1826 Jacob Cox made affidavit in Hamilton County, Ohio, and in 1828 Daniel Cox was postmaster at Pleasant Ridge, Rush County, Indiana, and in 1833 Rev. Elmer H. Cox lived in Rush County, Indiana, but no relationship to soldier was stated for these 3 men." [Ref: T-788].

COX, John. 1st lieutenant in Capt. Jacob Snowdenberger's company of militia in the 2nd Battalion, November 29, 1775 [Ref: E-56, B-65].

COX, Joshua. Enlisted on April 20, 1781, for 3 years, but was later reported as "deserted" (no date given). [Ref: D-1814].

COX, Matthew. Private who enlisted on March 3, 1778 [Ref: A-315].

COX [COCKS], William. Private, 7th Maryland Regiment, who enlisted in Frederick Town between January and April, 1780 [Ref: A-334].

COYEL, Michael. Associator in December, 1775 [Ref: E-165]. Juror to the Oath of Allegiance in 1778 [Ref: C-23].

COZZENS, William. Associator in December, 1775 [Ref: E-165]. Juror to the Oath of Allegiance in 1778 [Ref: C-23].

CRABB, Richard (Seneca). Appointed by the Committee of Correspondence to solicit subscriptions in 1775 to purchase arms and ammunition [Ref: I-86]. Served on the Committee of Observation in 1775 [Ref: I-85]. Associator in December, 1775 [Ref: E-165]. Commissioned a 2nd major in the 16th Battalion on January 3, 1776 [Ref: H-9]. Reviewed and passed recruits in 1776 [Ref: A-43]. Juror to the Oath of Allegiance in 1778 [Ref: C-23].

CRABBS, Elizabeth. See "Peter Zollinger," q.v.

CRABEAL, John. Non-Enroller who was fined by the Committee of Observation in April, 1776 [Ref: E-248].

CRABS, Christian. Sergeant in Capt. William Blair's company of militia in 1775 [Ref: E-55]. Ensign in the 35th Battalion on November or December 28, 1776 [Ref: B-65, X-555].

CRABS, John. Corporal in Capt. William Blair's company of militia in 1775 [Ref: E-55]. "John Crabbs" was drafted on June 13, 1781, but provided a substitute [Ref: D-1814].

CRAFFORD, Robert Beall. Private who enlisted on July, 1776 [Ref: A-49].

CRAFT, Frederick. Private stationed at Fort Frederick in June, 1778 [Ref: A-328].

CRAFT, John. Private in the German Regiment; roll dated October 23, 1776 [Ref: A-264]. Discharged on July 26, 1779 [Ref: A-265].

CRAIL, Peter. Associator in December, 1775 [Ref: E-165]. Juror to the Oath of Allegiance in 1778 [Ref: C-23]. Also, see "Christian Crall," q.v.

CRAIL, William. Private, 1st Maryland Regiment, 1780, and served in the Southern Army of the United States under Lt. William Lamar in the late Capt. Beatty's company in 1781, until he was assigned to Major Roxburgh to serve as a waiter in July, 1781 [Ref: A-390].

CRALE, James. Private who enlisted on July 19, 1776 [Ref: A-51].

CRALE, William. Private who enlisted on July 19, 1776 [Ref: A-51].

CRALL, Christian. Associator in December, 1775 [Ref: E-165]. Juror to the Oath of Allegiance in March, 1778 [Ref: C-23]. "Christian Crall, yeoman," died testate in 1784, leaving a wife Barbara and children Ann, Mary, Catherina, Peter, Elizabeth, and Hannah [Ref: M-6:88].

CRALL, Isaac Jr. Associator in December, 1775 [Ref: E-165]. Juror to the Oath of Allegiance in 1778 [Ref: C-23].

CRAMBAUGH, Jacob. Non-Enroller who was fined by the Committee of Observation in April, 1776 [Ref: E-248].

CRAMER, Daniel. See "Daniel Creamer," q.v.

CRAMER, John. Juror to the Oath of Allegiance in 1778 [Ref: C-23].
CRAMER, Michael. Private who enlisted July 1, 1776 in Capt. Peter Mantz's company; marched from Frederick Town to Leonardtown, and from there to Philadelphia, arriving August 23, 1776 [Ref: A-47]. Michael Cramer died testate in 1790, leaving a wife Mary "to raise my small children (names not given in the will)." [Ref: M-8:33].
CRAMER, Peter, Margaret, and Philip. See "Peter Creamer," q.v.
CRAMER, William. Associator in December, 1775 [Ref: E-165]. Juror to the Oath of Allegiance in 1778 [Ref: C-23].
CRAMPHIN, Thomas. Served on the Committee of Observation in 1775 [Ref: I-85]. This name appeared twice on the list of men who were appointed by the Committee of Correspondence to solicit funds by subscription in 1775 so as to purchase arms and ammunition. One was in Rock Creek Hundred and one in Lower Antietam [Ref: I-86]. Also, "Thomas Cramplin" gave money in the amount of 3 lbs. 3 sh. 4 p. for arms and ammunition for the militia in 1775 [Ref: E-62].
CRAMPTON, James. 2nd lieutenant in the Upper District Militia on July 4, 1776 [Ref: B-66].
CRAMPTON, Thomas. Gave money in the amount of 3 lbs. 15 sh. and then 6 lbs. 10 sh. 1 p. for arms and ammunition for the Frederick County militia in 1775 [Ref: E-62]. "On March 16, 1835, Treasurer of the Western Shore was directed to pay to Thomas Crampton, a soldier of the Revolution, the half pay of a private, in quarterly payments during life." [Ref: G-331]. However, Thomas Crampton was a 2nd lieutenant in Capt. Joseph Chapline's company of militia in Frederick [now Washington] County from July 4, 1776, through at least June 4, 1781 [Ref: B-66, W-546].
CRAPER, Jacob. Associator in December, 1775 [Ref: E-165]. Juror to the Oath of Allegiance in 1778 [Ref: C-23].
CRAPSTER, Abraham. Sergeant in Capt. Abraham Hayter's company of militia in 1775 [Ref: E-52].
CRATON, John. Petitioned the General Assembly under the Act of May 12, 1780, stating he had been a non-juror to the Oath of Allegiance and Fidelity in 1778 due to "ignorance" and now desired relief under the Act and to take the Oath [Ref: L-101].
CRAVER, Jacob. Corporal stationed at Fort Frederick in 1778 [Ref: A-328].
CRAWFORD, James. Associator in December, 1775 [Ref: E-165]. Juror to the Oath of Allegiance in 1778 [Ref: C-23]. Private, Maryland Line, age 82, resided in Frederick County, and pensioned January 6, 1819, at

$96 per annum from May 5, 1818 [Ref: G-331, citing the U. S. Pension Rolls of 1835]. "Applied for pension (S34720) in Frederick County, Maryland, on May 5 1818, aged 60, stating he had enlisted in the Maryland Line in Baltimore. In 1820 he had wife Catherine, aged about 50, and daughter Elizabeth, aged 25. James died on February 12, 1839, in Carroll County (formerly part of Frederick County), leaving no widow and his only surviving child (in 1839) was Miss Elizabeth Crawford." [Ref: T-808, J-25].

CRAWFORD, John. Corporal in Capt. Jacob Good's company of militia in 1775 [Ref: E-51].

CRAWFORD, Jonas. Associator in December, 1775 [Ref: E-165]. Juror to the Oath of Allegiance in 1778 [Ref: C-23].

CRAWL, Henry. Served on the Committee of Observation in 1775 [Ref: I-85].

CRAWLL, Nicholas. Associator in December, 1775 [Ref: E-165]. Juror to the Oath of Allegiance in 1778 [Ref: C-23].

CRAWLY, Joseph. Private who enlisted on July 29, 1776 [Ref: A-43].

CRAWMORE, Philip. Non-Enroller who was fined by the Committee of Observation in April, 1776 [Ref: E-248].

CRAY, John. Paid for services rendered to the military in December, 1779 (nature of the services not stated). [Ref: V-44].

CREAGER, Adam. Ensign in Capt. Valentine Creager's militia company in the Catoctin Battalion on November 29, 1775 [Ref: E-53, B-66, O-239]. He died in the morning on the Wednesday before September 6, 1805, aged 68 [Ref: N-58].

CREAGER, Benjamin. "Benjamin Cregar" was an Associator in December, 1775 [Ref: E-165]. "Benjamin Creigor" took the Oath of Allegiance in 1778 [Ref: C-23].

CREAGER, Conrad. Associator in December, 1775 [Ref: E-165]. Juror to the Oath of Allegiance in 1778 [Ref: C-23].

CREAGER, Daniel. Captain in the Revolutionary War [Ref: O-239].

CREAGER, George. Associator in December, 1775 [Ref: E-165]. Juror to the Oath of Allegiance in 1778 [Ref: C-23].

CREAGER, Henry. Associator in December, 1775 [Ref: E-165]. Juror to the Oath of Allegiance in 1778 [Ref: C-23].

CREAGER, John. Associator in December, 1775 [Ref: E-165]. (This name appeared twice on the list of Associators). One subscribed to the Oath of Allegiance in 1778 [Ref: C-23]. "John Creager, son of Handel," was appointed "to hand about the Association paper" in Upper Monocacy Hundred in 1775 [Ref: E-305].

CREAGER, Lawrence. Associator in December, 1775 [Ref: E-165]. Juror to the Oath of Allegiance in 1778 [Ref: C-23]. "Laurence Krieger, Sr., of Frederick County, near Catoctin Mountain, yeoman," died testate in 1785, leaving wife Mary Elizabeth and children John (eldest son), Laurence, Margaret, Mary Barbara, and Elizabeth (and several grandchildren). [Ref: M-6:128].

CREAGER, Lawrence Jr. Associator in December, 1775 [Ref: E-165]. Juror to the Oath of Allegiance in 1778 [Ref: C-23]. "Lawrence Creager, Jr." was an ensign in the militia in 1778 [Ref: H-16]. "Lawrence Creagar" was an ensign in the militia on April 15, 1778 [Ref: B-66, O-239, Z-35].

CREAGER, Michael. Associator in December, 1775 [Ref: E-165]. Juror to the Oath of Allegiance in 1778 [Ref: C-23]. Ensign in the 37th Battalion on April 15, 1778 [Ref: B-66, O-239, Z-35].

CREAGER, Nathaniel. Captain in the militia, 1778-1779 [Ref: H-16].

CREAGER [CREGAR], Pheba (Phoebe). See "Peter Hedges," q.v.

CREAGER, Valentine. "Valentine Creager" was a captain of a company of militia in the 2nd Battalion on November 29, 1775 [Ref: E-53, B-66, O-239]. Associator in December, 1775 [Ref: E-165]. "Valentine Creagar" was a captain in the Middle District on October 3, 1776 [Ref: A-72, B-66, X-317]. "Valentine Cregar" was a captain in the Catoctin Battalion on June 29, 1782 [Ref: B-66]. "Valentine Creager" signed as a Juror to the Oath of Allegiance in 1778 [Ref: C-23]. Resident of Manor Hundred, he was appointed by the Committee of Correspondence to solicit subscriptions in 1775 to purchase arms and ammunition [Ref: I-86]. Also, see "Frederick Beard," q.v.

CREAL, Richard. Associator in December, 1775 [Ref: E-164]. Juror to the Oath of Allegiance in 1778 [Ref: C-23].

CREAMER [CREMER], Daniel. Soldier in the Maryland and Virginia Lines who "applied for a pension (R2477) on September 5, 1833, in Greene County, Tennessee, stating he was born in March, 1757, in York County, Pennsylvania, and when very young his father moved to Frederick County, Maryland, where he enlisted in the Revolution. Daniel died in Tennessee in April 3, 1840. He had married Sarah Wilson on December 9, 1790, at the home of Joseph Roberts in Greene County, Tennessee, and they were married by a Joseph Wilson, a Justice of the Peace (no relationship stated). Widow died June 29, 1840, and raised their 6 children, of which 5 survived the widow, but only a daughter Polly was named. In 1852 she signed by mark as Polly Creamer and was a resident of Greenville, Tennessee, and she mentioned her brothers, but did not name them. A daughter living in Georgia had been mentioned, but whether this was Polly or not was not stated. In 1833 the soldier's brother (not named) was living in Ohio." [Ref: T-811, T-812].

CREAMER [CRAMER], Peter (1740-1812). Associator in December, 1775 [Ref: E-165]. Juror to the Oath of Allegiance in 1778 [Ref: C-23]. He married Margaret ---- in 1765 and a daughter Mary Barrick Cramer (1789-1853) married Philip Henry Cramer (1781-1853) in 1817 [Ref: U-1016].

CREAT, Thomas. Associator in December, 1775 [Ref: E-165]. Juror to the Oath of Allegiance in 1778 [Ref: C-23].

CREEKPAUM, Conrad. "Conrad Crickbone" was ensign in Capt. Stull's company of militia in the 1st Battalion on November 29, 1775 [Ref: E-50, B-66]. "Conrard Creekpaum" was a 1st lieutenant in the 37th Battalion of militia on April 27, 1779 [Ref: H-16, B-66, Z-368]. Probably related to "Philip Creekbaum" who enlisted in Hagerstown, Maryland, and pensioned in Fayette County, Pennsylvania (S40860). He served in the Maryland Line and died March 2, 1826 [Ref: T-812].

CREELY, Michael. Associator in December, 1775 [Ref: E-165]. Juror to the Oath of Allegiance in 1778 [Ref: C-23].

CREIGER, Peggy. See "Matthias Young," q.v.

CREIGH [CRIEGH], Phillip. Private in Capt. John Kershner's company; guarded prisoners at Fort Frederick, 1777-1778; discharged June 14, 1778 [Ref: A-328].

CREIGHTON, Thomas. Associator in December, 1775 [Ref: E-165]. Juror to the Oath of Allegiance in 1778 [Ref: C-23].

CREPELL [CRAPPELL], Jacob. Private who enlisted on July 1, 1776, in Capt. Peter Mantz's company, and marched from Frederick Town to Leonardtown, and from there to Philadelphia, arriving on August 23, 1776 [Ref: A-47].

CREPELL, Peter. Associator in December, 1775 [Ref: E-165]. Juror to the Oath of Allegiance in 1778 [Ref: C-23]. One Peter Crepell died testate in 1791, leaving his children Jacob, Margaret, Elizabeth, Rachel, and mentioning a son-in-law Richard Hardin [Ref: M-8:88].

CRESAP, Daniel. Commissioned a captain in the Frederick County militia in the Skipton District on July 27, 1776, and captain in the Washington County militia, "on the frontier" on May 13, 1778, and commissioned again June 22, 1778 [Ref: B-66, X-127, Z-145].

CRESAP, Thomas (Skipton). Appointed by Committee of Correspondence to solicit subscriptions in 1775 to purchase arms and ammunition [Ref: I-85]. Served on the Committee of Observation in 1775 [Ref: I-85]. Associator in December, 1775 [Ref: E-165]. Juror to the Oath of

Allegiance in 1778 [Ref: C-23. The Cresaps were prominent in western Maryland in the early 1700's. For more data on this family consult J. Thomas Scharf's *History of Western Maryland*, Volume I.]

CRETSINGER, Solomon. Associator in December, 1775 [Ref: E-165]. Juror to the Oath of Allegiance in 1778 [Ref: C-23].

CRICKBONE, Conrad. See "Conrad Creekpaum," q.v.

CRIDER, John and Rebecca. See "Levi Davis," q.v.

CRISE, Peter. Associator in December, 1775 [Ref: E-165]. Juror to the Oath of Allegiance in 1778 [Ref: C-23].

CRIST, Jacob. Non-Enroller who was fined by the Committee of Observation in April, 1776 [Ref: E-248].

CRIST, Philip. Juror to the Oath of Allegiance in March, 1778 [Ref: S-263, but not listed in Ref: C-23].

CRISTBARRICK, John. Associator in December, 1775 [Ref: E-165]. Juror to the Oath of Allegiance in 1778 [Ref: C-23. Ed. Note: It is possible this name could be John Crist Barrick, rather than John Cristbarrick (?).]

CROCE, Henry. Associator in December, 1775 [Ref: E-165]. Juror to the Oath of Allegiance in 1778 [Ref: C-23].

CROM [CRUM], Adam. Soldier in the Maryland Line who "applied for a pension (W2069) on May 12, 1818, in Monroe County, Ohio, aged 69, stating in 1820 that he had a wife Mary, aged 50, and children as follows: David, aged 20; William, aged 17; and, Mary, aged 14. Soldier's son Henry applied June 4, 1852, in Monroe County, Ohio, for himself and surviving children, to wit: David, William, and Mary Crum, plus himself. He also stated the soldier had died on February 26, 1831, and his widow died on April 29, 1851, and that his parents had married before 1800. In 1851 the children were aged as follows: Henry, aged 53 on April 29, 1851; David, aged 51 on June 16, 1851; William, aged 48 on June 7, 1851; and, Mary, aged 47 on October 3, 1851." [Ref: T-831].

CROM, Gilbert. Associator in December, 1775 [Ref: E-164]. Juror to the Oath of Allegiance in 1778 [Ref: C-23]. Gilbert Crum, son of Gilbert (1700-1762), was born about 1735 in New Jersey and was in Monocacy Manor, Frederick County, Maryland, by 1756 [Ref: O-170].

CROM [CRUM], John. Soldier in the Maryland Line who "applied for a pension (S12624) on February 26, 1833, in Huntington County, Pennsylvania, a resident of Barre Township, stating he was born in New Jersey in 1761 and lived in Frederick County, Maryland, at the time of his enlistment. He lived there until 1801 when he moved to Huntington County, Pennsylvania." [Ref: T-831].

CROM [KRUM], William (1731-1790). Son of Gilbert Crum (1700-1762) and wife Martha Jansen, of New Jersey, and later Monocacy Manor, married Mary Ann Barrick [Ref: O-170]. Associator in December, 1775 [Ref: E-165], and a Juror to the Oath of Allegiance in 1778 [Ref: C-23]. "William Krum" died testate in 1790, leaving a wife Mary and children Mary, Sarah, Abraham, and William [Ref: M-8:36].

CROM [CRUM], William (1741-1810). Son of Abraham Crum (1708-1787) and wife Aeltje Pieterse, of New Jersey and later Frederick County, married first Catherine ---- and secondly Amelia Wise [Ref: O-170]. Associator in December, 1775 [Ref: E-164]. Juror to the Oath of Allegiance, 1778 [Ref: C-23].

CRONISE, Henry. Private, German Regiment, 1776, with Capt. Henry Fister's company under the command of Col. Nicholas Hussecker, and discharged on July 24, 1779 [Ref: A-198, A-261]. "Heinrich Croneis, or Kroneis (1758-1815), son of George and Anna, married Barbara Wort (1761-1804)." [Ref: O-145].

CRONISE [KRONISE], John (November 25, 1748 - September 29, 1803). Associator in December, 1775. He married Mary Fey (1753-1823) in 1773, and a son John Cronise (born 1774) married Rachel Saum (born 1785) in 1797, and a son George Cronise (1782-1850) married Elizabeth Beeler (1786-1858) in 1806. [Ref: U-1092, U-1819, E-169]. He also signed as a Juror to the Oath of Allegiance in 1778 [Ref: C-26]. Loaned $1,000 for the use of the State of Maryland in 1780 [Ref: V-520].

CROOK, Henry. Private, 1st Maryland Regiment, was disabled at the Battle of Guilford Court House, and invalid pension commenced on November 29, 1783, and ceased on March 29, 1784, with the cause of pension ceasing as "removed or supposed dead." [Ref: A-630, A-631].

CROOK, John. Private in the militia in July, 1776 [Ref: A-42].

CROPP, John. Private in the German Regiment, muster roll dated October 23, 1776 [Ref: A-264].

CROSS, George. Juror to the Oath of Allegiance in March, 1778 [Ref: S-263, but not listed in Ref: C-23].

CROUMER, Jacob. Private in German Regiment, 1776, in Capt. Henry Fister's company under the command of Col. Hussecker [Ref: A-261].

CROUSE, Jacob. 2nd lieutenant in the Linganore Battalion of militia on January 17, 1777, under Capt. Basil Dorsey [Ref: B-66, Y-55].

CROUSE, John. 2nd lieutenant in the Linganore Battalion of militia on June 22, 1778 [Ref: H-17, B-66, Z-145]. One John Crouse was a soldier in the Maryland Line who "applied for a pension (R2535) on June 13,

1833, in Ross County, Ohio, aged 73, stating he enlisted in the revolution in Frederickstown, Maryland." [Ref: T-828].

CROUSE, Valentine. Fifer in Capt. Abraham Hayter's company of militia in 1775 [Ref: E-52].

CROW, Adam. Private in the 1st Maryland Regiment who enlisted on April 28, 1778, and served in the Southern Army of the United States under Lt. William Lamar in the late Capt. Beatty's company until discharged on April 28, 1781 [Ref: A-391].

CROW, Edward. 1st lieutenant in the Lower District Militia in the 16th Battalion on May 20, 1776 [Ref: W-432].

CROW, William. Private in the militia in July, 1776 [Ref: A-42].

CROWELL [CROWLE], Henry (Burnt Woods Hundred). Appointed by the Committee of Correspondence to solicit subscriptions in 1775 to purchase arms and ammunition [Ref: I-86]. Associator in December, 1775 [Ref: E-165]. Juror to the Oath of Allegiance in 1778 [Ref: C-23]. He died testate in 1784, leaving wife Margaret and children Devalt, Henry, Michael, Barbara Young, John, and Sevile, plus a son-in-law Daniel Root, husband of daughter Elizabeth Crowell [Ref: M-6:125, U-938].

CROWL, Michael. Associator in December, 1775 [Ref: E-165]. Juror to the Oath of Allegiance in 1778 [Ref: C-23].

CROWL, Peter. Associator in December, 1775 [Ref: E-165]. Juror to the Oath of Allegiance in 1778 [Ref: C-23].

CROWLEY, Darby. Private who enlisted on February 25, 1778 [Ref: A-314].

CROWN, Conrad. Associator in December, 1775 [Ref: E-165]. Juror to the Oath of Allegiance in 1778 [Ref: C-23].

CROWS, Samuel. Associator in December, 1775 [Ref: E-165]. Juror to the Oath of Allegiance in 1778 [Ref: C-23].

CRUM, Adam, John, and William. See "Adam, John, and William Crom."

CRUMBECKER, Abraham (Unity Hundred). Non-Enroller who was fined by the Committee of Observation in June, 1776 [Ref: E-248].

CRUMMITT, Jacob. Ensign in the German Regiment in Capt. Fister's company in July, 1776 [Ref: X-48].

CRUSH, Adam. 1st lieutenant in the 33rd Battalion of militia on December 28, 1776 [Ref: B-66].

CRY, John. Non-Enroller who was fined by the Committee of Observation in May, 1776 [Ref: E-248].

CRYDER, John. Juror to the Oath of Allegiance in March, 1778 [Ref: S-263, but not listed in Ref: C-23].

CUDY, Philip. Provided wheat for the military in July, 1782 [Ref: R-533].

CULLEM, George. Commissioned 1st lieutenant in the Lower District Militia on March 26, 1776 [Ref: W-287].

CULLER, John. See "John Keller," q.v.

CULVER, Samuel. Private in the militia in July, 1776 [Ref: A-42].

CUMBAKER, John. Associator in December, 1775 [Ref: E-165]. Juror to the Oath of Allegiance in 1778 [Ref: C-23].

CUMBER, Christian. 4th sergeant in the Middle District Militia in 1776 in Capt. Valentine Creager's company [Ref: A-72].

CUMBERIDGE, Joseph. Drafted on June 2, 1783, but "will not appear." [Ref: B-168].

CUMMING, Anna. See "William Cumming," q.v.

CUMMING, James. Associator in December, 1775 [Ref: E-165]. Juror to the Oath of Allegiance in 1778 [Ref: C-23].

CUMMING, William. "William Comming" was a private, 1st Maryland Regiment, 1781, and served in the Southern Army of the United States under Lt. William Lamar in the late Capt. Beatty's company. Record indicates he was a prisoner of war on April 25, 1781 [Ref: A-391]. "William Cumming" died testate in 1793, leaving children Anna Cumming, Elizabeth Hobbs, Sarah Dorsey, Catharine Simpson, Jane Mackelfresh, and Robert and Thomas Cumming [Ref: M-8:180].

CUMMINGS, James. Associator in December, 1775 [Ref: E-165]. Juror to the Oath of Allegiance in 1778 [Ref: C-23]. It appears that another James Cummings petitioned the General Assembly under the Act of May 12, 1780, stating he had been a non-juror to the Oath of Allegiance and Fidelity in Maryland in 1778 due to "ignorance" and now desired relief under the Act and to take the Oath [Ref: L-101].

CUMMINGS, Robert. Major General and commander of the 2nd Division of Maryland Militia, died November 14, 1824, aged 72 [Ref: F-472].

CUMMINGS, William. Provided wheat for the military in June, 1782 [Ref: R-517].

CUMPTON, Ignatius. Private, 1st Maryland Regiment, 1780, and served in the Southern Army of the United States under Lt. William Lamar in the late Capt. Beatty's company in 1781; "sick in July." [Ref: A-389].

CUMSTON, Jacob (Lower Monocacy Hundred). Non-Enroller who was fined by the Committee of Observation in April, 1776 [Ref: E-248]. "Jacob Cumstone" petitioned the General Assembly under the Act of May 12, 1780, stating he had been a non-juror to the Oath of Allegiance and Fidelity in 1778 due to "ignorance" and now desired relief under the Act and to take the Oath [Ref: L-101].

CUMSTON, John. Non-Enroller who was fined by the Committee of Observation in April, 1776 [Ref: E-248]. "John Cumstone" petitioned the General Assembly under the Act of May 12, 1780, stating he had been a non-juror to the Oath of Allegiance and Fidelity in 1778 due to "ignorance" and now desired relief under the Act and to take the Oath [Ref: L-101].

CUNIUS, William. Private in the German Regiment, 1776 [Ref: A-266].

CUNNINGHAM, James. Private who enlisted July 24, 1776 [Ref: A-50].

CUNNINGHAM, Jona. Private who enlisted on May 8, 1778 [Ref: A-322].

CUNNINGHAM, Peter. Private, 7th Maryland Regiment. Disabled in South Carolina; invalid pension commenced on September 19, 1784, and ceased on March 29, 1789, with the cause of pension ceasing as "removed or supposed dead." [Ref: A-630, A-631, F-475].

CURPMAN [CURFMAN?], Philip. Juror to the Oath of Allegiance in March, 1778 [Ref: S-267, but not listed in Ref: C-30].

CURRANCE, William. Associator in December, 1775 [Ref: E-165]. Juror to the Oath of Allegiance in 1778 [Ref: C-23].

CURRENS, William Jr. Sergeant in Capt. William Blair's company of militia in 1775 [Ref: E-55].

CURRENT [CURRIN], James. Private, 1st Maryland Regiment, 1781, and served in the Southern Army of the United States under Lt. William Lamar in the late Capt. Beatty's company. Record indicates he was a prisoner of war on April 25, 1781 [Ref: A-391]. "James Currin or Current received a disability pension (S34724) from May 4, 1789, and bounty land warrant #2-100-5 in May, 1803, for his services in the Maryland Line. In 1820 he was a resident of Frederick County, Maryland, aged 68. His records were burned in the War Office fire of 1800 or either when the British burned Washington, D.C. in 1814. He reapplied on November 11, 1818, in Montgomery County, Maryland, aged 66, and in 1820 stated that he had no family." [Ref: T-845].

CURRINGTON, John. Private who enlisted July 29, 1776 [Ref: A-43].

CURTIS, Michael. Private, 1st Maryland Regiment, 1781, and served in the Southern Army of the United States under Lt. William Lamar in the late Capt. Beatty's company [Ref: A-389].

CUSTARD, Michael. Non-Enroller who was fined by the Committee of Observation in June, 1776 [Ref: E-248].

CUSTER, John. See "Peter Grossnickle," q.v.

CUSTOR [CUSTER], George. Non-Enroller who was fined by the Committee of Observation in April, 1776 [Ref: E-248].

CUTLER, Edmund. Associator in December, 1775 [Ref: E-165]. Juror to the Oath of Allegiance in 1778 [Ref: C-23].

CYESTER, Henry. Soldier in the Maryland Line who "applied for a pension (S8275) on December 29, 1835, aged 78, Washington County, Maryland, a resident of Williamsport, stating he enlisted in what was then Frederick County, Maryland, but later became Washington County. He was born at Reading in Berks County, Pennsylvania on August 28, 1757, and when age 9 his father moved to Frederick (now Washington) County, Maryland. After the war he moved to Pennsylvania for a few months and then moved to Virginia for a few months and then returned to Williamsport." [Ref: T-859].

CYPHER, Mathias. Enlisted on April 10, 1781, for 3 years; marched with Capt. Dyer [Ref: D-1814].

CYSARD, David. Private in the Skipton District Militia under Capt. Thomas Waring on April 16, 1776 [Ref: B-167, D-1814].

DAGER, Michael. Non-Enroller who was fined by the Committee of Observation in April, 1776 [Ref: E-248].

DAILEY, John. Private in the 7th Maryland Regiment from May 6, 1778 to May, 1780, when he was reported as "deserted." [Ref: A-202].

DALEY, Thomas. Private who enlisted on May 16, 1778, and served in the 2nd Maryland Regiment [Ref: A-294, A-322].

DALLAG [sic], Charles. Associator in December, 1775 [Ref: E-166]. Juror to the Oath of Allegiance in 1778 [Ref: C-24].

DALTON, John. Private who enlisted on April 22, 1778 [Ref: A-320].

DANNER, Jacob. Non-Enroller who was fined by the Committee of Observation in April, 1776, but he apparently enrolled because the fine was remitted in June, 1776 [Ref: E-248].

DANNER, Samuel. Non-Enroller who was fined by the Committee of Observation in April, 1776 [Ref: E-248].

DARBY, Joseph. Petitioned the General Assembly under the Act of May 12, 1780, stating he had been a non-juror to the Oath of Allegiance and Fidelity in 1778 due to "ignorance" and now desired relief under the Act and to take the Oath [Ref: L-101].

DARE, George. Associator in December, 1775 [Ref: E-165]. Juror to the Oath of Allegiance in 1778 [Ref: C-24].

DARLIN, Philip. Associator in December, 1775 [Ref: E-166]. Juror to the Oath of Allegiance in 1778 [Ref: C-24].

DARNALL, Henry. 2nd major in the 34th Battalion of militia on January 6, 1776 [Ref: B-67].

DARNALL, John (Lower Monocacy). Appointed by the Committee of Correspondence to solicit subscriptions in 1775 to purchase arms and ammunition [Ref: I-86]. Served on the Committee of Observation in 1775 [Ref: I-85]. Associator in December, 1775 [Ref: E-165]. Juror to the Oath of Allegiance in 1778 [Ref: C-24].

DARNALL, Thomas. Provided wheat for the military in May, 1782 [Ref: R-514].

DARNER, Anna Maria. See "John Shafer," q.v.

DAUGHERTY, Patrick. Private in the Middle District Militia in 1776, in Capt. Valentine Creager's company [Ref: A-72].

DAUGHERTY, Stephen and Jane. See "James Smith," q.v.

DAVID, George. Private in the Middle District Militia in 1776, in Capt. Valentine Creager's company [Ref: A-72].

DAVID, William. Associator in December, 1775 [Ref: E-166]. Juror to the Oath of Allegiance in 1778 [Ref: C-24].

DAVIDSON, James. Sergeant in the 7th Maryland Regiment in 1778 [Ref: A-202].

DAVIDSON, Thomas. Provided beef for the military in May, 1782 [Ref: R-516].

DAVIS, Abraham. Associator in December, 1775 [Ref: E-166]. Juror to the Oath of Allegiance in 1778 [Ref: C-24].

DAVIS, Francis. Petitioned the General Assembly under the Act of May 12, 1780, stating that he had been a non-juror to the Oath of Allegiance and Fidelity in 1778 due to "ignorance" and now desired relief under the Act and to take the Oath [Ref: L-101].

DAVIS, Jarrard. Provided wheat for the military in June, 1782 [Ref: R-520].

DAVIS, John. Sergeant in Capt. Henry Baker's company of militia in 1775 [Ref: E-54]. Associator in December, 1775 [Ref: E-166]. Juror to the Oath of Allegiance in 1778 [Ref: C-24].

DAVIS, Josey. Drafted on June 2, 1783 [Ref: B-168].

DAVIS, Joshua. Private in the Skipton District Militia under Capt. Thomas Waring on April 16, 1776 [Ref: B-167, D-1814].

DAVIS, Levi. Sergeant in Capt. Samuel Plummer's company of militia in 1775 [Ref: E-54]. "On June 1, 1847, Ebenezer Davis, of Pickaway County, Ohio, brother of Levi, stated that Levi had died March 6, 1846. He was born in Hampshire County, Virginia, and at age 5 or 6 his parents moved to Frederick County, Maryland, where he lived at enlistment. In 1813 Levi moved from Maryland to Kentucky and then to Indiana. Levi's son James stated in 1846 that Levi died March 8,

1847, leaving a widow Hannah (who was deceased in 1847) and these children: Irena (who married John Hendrix), Rachael (who married Solomon Ritchey), Sarah (who married Shelby Harney), Stephen, James, Rebecca (who married John Crider), Effee (who married Aaron Gelstrap), Jane (who married Samuel Starr, and he was deceased in 1847), and Nancy (who married John McNeeley, who were both deceased in 1847 and left children Isaac and Levi McNeeley). James Davis was the administrator of the estate of levi Davis on November 10, 1851, in Jackson County, Indiana." [Ref: T-904].

DAVIS, Lodowick. Private who enlisted on July 29, 1776 [Ref: A-44].

DAVIS, Nathan. Associator, 1775 [Ref: E-166]. Non-Enroller who was fined by the Committee of Observation in May, 1776 [Ref: E-248]. Juror, Oath of Allegiance in 1778 [Ref: C-24].

DAVIS, Philip. Corporal in Capt. Basil Dorsey's company of militia in 1775 [Ref: E-52].

DAVIS, Rezin. Associator in December, 1775 [Ref: E-165]. (This name appeared twice on the lists of Associators, one of whom made his "X" mark). Ensign in the militia company of Capt. Young on February 21, 1776 [Ref: B-68]. Took the Oath of Allegiance in 1778 [Ref: C-24].

DAVIS, Richard (Marsh Hundred). Appointed by the Committee of Correspondence to solicit subscriptions in 1775 to purchase arms and ammunition [Ref: I-86]. Associator in December, 1775 [Ref: E-166]. Gave money in the amount of 3 lbs. 13 sh. 9 p. for arms and ammunition for the militia in 1775 [Ref: E-62]. One Richard Davis was a 2nd lieutenant in the militia on June 6, 1776, and a 1st lieutenant on August 29, 1777. Another was a 1st major on January 6, 1776, and a lieutenant colonel on April 20, 1776 [Ref: B-68, W-356]. One was Juror to the Oath of Allegiance in 1778 [Ref: C-24]. One Richard Davis (1751-1791), son of John Davis (1706-1774) and Elizabeth Anderson, formerly of Chester County, Pennsylvania, before coming to western Maryland, married Catherine Hinkle and moved to a farm near New Market with 7 children. Their son George Davis (1775-1850) married Elizabeth Hyatt [Ref: O-82].

DAVIS, Richard Jr. (Skipton District). Appointed by the Committee of Correspondence to solicit subscriptions in 1775 to purchase arms and ammunition [Ref: I-85]. Served on the Committee of Observation in 1775 [Ref: I-85]. See "Richard Davis" above.

DAVIS, Robert. Associator in December, 1775 [Ref: E-166]. Juror to the Oath of Allegiance in 1778 [Ref: C-24].

DAVIS, Samuel. Private who enlisted on May 19, 1778 [Ref: A-323]. Sergeant, 1st Maryland Regiment, 1780, and served in the Southern Army of the United States under Lt. William Lamar in the late Capt. Beatty's company, and was "recruiting in Maryland from January to July, 1781." [Ref: A-389].

DAVIS, Thomas. Drummer in Capt. Robert Wood's company of militia in 1775 [Ref: E-53].

DAVIS, William. Private who enlisted on July 18 or 19, 1776 [Ref: A-49, A-51], and "applied for a pension (S34731) on August 5, 1819, in Bedford County, Pennsylvania, aged 62, stating he had enlisted at Fredericktown, Maryland, in the Maryland Line. In 1820 he had a wife Mary, aged 59, and on September 17, 1830, he had moved back to Maryland (location not indicated)." [Ref: T-912]. One William Davis was quartermaster in the 7th Maryland Regiment from 1777 to March 2, 1780, when he was discharged [Ref: A-201].

DAVISON, Lewis. Private in the Skipton District Militia under Capt. Thomas Waring on April 16, 1776 [Ref: B-167, D-1814].

DAVY, Alexander W. Associator in December, 1775 [Ref: E-165]. Juror to the Oath of Allegiance in 1778 [Ref: C-24].

DAWNER, Benjamin. Juror to the Oath of Allegiance in March, 1778 [Ref: S-264, but not listed in Ref: C-24].

DAWSON, John. Private in the 7th Maryland Regiment who enlisted on February 29, 1780 [Ref: A-312, A-334, V-175].

DAWSON, Nicholas. Private in the horse troops in 1781 [Ref: B-167].

DAY, John. Private who enlisted on April 2, 1778, and served in the 2nd Maryland Regiment [Ref: A-294, A-320].

DAYLEY, John. Private who enlisted some time in 1780 [Ref: A-345].

DAYLEY, Patrick. Private in the Middle District Militia in 1776 in Capt. Valentine Creager's company [Ref: A-72].

DAYNE, Jacob. Enlisted on April 10, 1781, for 3 years; marched with Capt. Lynn [Ref: D-1814].

DEAKINS, Francis (Sugar Loaf Hundred). Appointed by the Committee of Correspondence to solicit subscriptions in 1775 to purchase arms and ammunition [Ref: I-86]. Served on the Committee of Observation in 1775 [Ref: I-85]. Associator in December, 1775 [Ref: E-166]. Gave money in the amount of 6 lbs. 12 sh. 8 p. for arms and ammunition for the militia in 1775 [Ref: E-62]. Major in the Upper District Militia [now Washington County] in 1776 [Ref: A-48]. Juror to the Oath of Allegiance in 1778 [Ref: C-24].

DEAKINS, Leonard. Captain in the Lower District Militia [now Montgomery County] in 1776 [Ref: A-42]. "Leonard M. Deakins" reviewed troops in 1781 [Ref: B-168].

DEAKINS, William Jr. (Georgetown). Appointed by the Committee of Correspondence to solicit subscriptions in 1775 to purchase arms and ammunition [Ref: I-85]. Collected 52 lbs. 4 sh. 4 p. for arms and ammunition for the militia in 1775 [Ref: E-63]. "Will. Deakins, Jr." reviewed and passed recruits in 1776 [Ref: A-44]. Served on the Committee of Observation in 1775 [Ref: I-85].

DEALE, George. Private who enlisted on July 18, 1776 [Ref: A-50].

DEAN, Rodger. Private who enlisted on July 25, 1776 [Ref: A-51].

DEANES, James. Provided wheat for the military in May, 1782 [Ref: R-516].

DEAVER, Abraham. Petitioned the General Assembly under the Act of May 12, 1780, stating that he had been a non-juror to the Oath of Allegiance and Fidelity in 1778 due to "ignorance" and now desired relief under the Act and to take the Oath [Ref: L-101].

DEAVER, Miscal. "Applied for a pension (S34738) in Frederick County on January 22, 1819, aged 66. He served in the Maryland Line and in 1820 had a wife Sarah, aged about 70, and a son Henry Deaver, aged about 17. An Abraham Deaver (no relationship stated) made affidavit on October 8, 1819 in Muskingum County, Ohio, that he knew of the soldier's service." [Ref: T-931, J-25].

DEBOY, John. Private in the militia on March 9, 1776 [Ref: B-166].

DEBOY, Joseph. Juror to the Oath of Allegiance in March, 1778 [Ref: S-264, but not listed in Ref: C-24].

DECAMP, Henry. Associator in December, 1775 [Ref: E-166]. Juror to the Oath of Allegiance in 1778 [Ref: C-24]. Private, Middle District Militia in 1776, in Capt. Valentine Creager's company [Ref: A-72].

DEDIE, Abraham. Associator in December, 1775 [Ref: E-166]. Juror to the Oath of Allegiance in 1778 [Ref: C-24].

DEEFHEM, Frederick. Private stationed at Fort Frederick in June, 1778 [Ref: A-328].

DEERDOFF, Anthony. Non-Enroller who was fined by the Committee of Observation in April, 1776 [Ref: E-248]. "Anthony Deardurf" was drafted on June 2, 1783 [Ref: B-168].

DEILMAN, John. Militia substitute from May to December 10, 1781, and "marched to Annapolis." [Ref: A-652].

DELAPLANE, John. Associator in December, 1775 [Ref: E-165]. Juror to the Oath of Allegiance in 1778 [Ref: C-24].

DELAPLANE, Joshua. Associator in December, 1775 [Ref: E-165]. One "Joshua Delaplain" was ensign in Capt. John Carmack's company of militia on November 29, 1775 [Ref: E-56, B-69]. "Joshua Delophain" was appointed ensign in Capt. Cormack's company on June 19, 1776, and wrote the Council of Safety to advise them that he "was then unable to serve, but shall always be willing and able to serve as a soldier whenever it lied within his power." [Ref: B-69, W-503].

DELASHMUTT [DELASHMET], Lindsey. Son of Capt. Elias Delashmutt and Elizabeth Nelson. Associator in December, 1775. On March 11, 1778, Col. Thomas Price's report of Frederick County recruiting efforts included 3 soldiers enlisted by "Mr. Lindsey Delashmed," Recruiting Officer. On June 12, 1782, "Linsey Delashmett" was compensated for wheat and mutton purchased for military use [Ref: M-5:59, E-166, R-523]. "Lindsey Delashmet" was a Juror to the Oath of Allegiance in 1778 [Ref: C-24]. On February 22, 1779, marriage license was issued for "Lindsey Delashmutt" and Sarah Trammell. Their children were Jean/Jane, Trammell, John, and Sampson. Lindsey's will was probated November 10, 1791. His widow married Ralph Briscoe on March 8, 1792. Ralph subsequently moved to Kentucky and died in 1831 in Missouri [Ref: M-5:59, 60, 61, 62, and information provided by a descendant, Miss Frederika ver Hulst, of Omaha, Nebraska (1995), who stated that Ralph Briscoe's first wife was Ann Mackall and Ralph was the son of John Briscoe and Ann Wood, of Charles County]. "Lindsey Delashmutt" died testate in late 1791, leaving wife Sarah and minor children Trammell, John, Sampson and Jean [Ref: M-8:132]. Also, see "Ralph Briscoe," q.v.

DELASHMUTT, Nancy and Sarah. See "Richard Ankrim, Sr.," q.v.

DELAWTER, Henry. Sergeant in Capt. Michael Troutman's company of militia in 1775 [Ref: E-51].

DELAWTER [DELAUTER], Henry (May 16, 1758 - c1788). Private in the German Regiment in 1776 in Capt. Henry Fister's company under the command of Col. Nicholas Hussecker. A son, Jacob Delawter, married Catherine Main (Mahn) on February 21, 1790 [Ref: A-261, U-2687].

DELL, Nicholas. See "Nicholas Dill," q.v.

DELOZIER, Phoebe. See "Richard Elder," q.v.

DEMMINE, John. Associator in December, 1775 [Ref: E-166]. Juror to the Oath of Allegiance in 1778 [Ref: C-24].

DEMORNEY [?], Jno. Juror to the Oath of Allegiance in March, 1778 [Ref: S-264, but not listed in Ref: C-24].

DENELEY, Patrick. Private who was enlisted on July 20, 1776, by Capt. Jacob Good [Ref: A-46].

DENISON, John. Corporal in Capt. William Beatty's company, 7th Maryland Regiment, 1779 [Ref: A-310]

DENNY [DENNEY], Samuel. Private in the 1st Maryland Regiment who enlisted March 2, 1778 (or May 9, 1778). Corporal, January 1, 1780. Sergeant in the 7th Maryland Regiment on April 1, 1780. Discharged on March 2, 1781 [Ref: A-202, A-388].

DENNY, William. Associator in December, 1775 [Ref: E-166]. Juror to the Oath of Allegiance in 1778 [Ref: C-24].

DENT, George. Took the oath of office as Surveyor for Frederick County in June, 1782 [Ref: R-523].

DERBIN, Thomas. 1st lieutenant in the 35th Battalion of militia on December 28, 1776, in Capt. Little's company [Ref: B-69, X-555].

DERR, John. See "John Stoner (Steiner)," q.v.

DERR, John Martin. "John Martin Dor" was a second lieutenant in Capt. James Johnson's company of militia in 1775 [Ref: E-52]. "John Martin Derr" was a captain in the Catoctin Battalion of militia (no date given in record). [Ref: B-69]. "John Martindear, or Martinder" was a 1st lieutenant in the 37th Battalion of militia on May 15, 1776, and a captain on January 17, 1777 [Ref: B-101, W-427].

DERR, William. Associator who was appointed "to hand about the Association paper" in Israel Creek Hundred in October, 1775, in the room of John Remsburgh [Ref: E-308].

DERRY, Baltser (Bolser). Petitioned the General Assembly under the Act of May 12, 1780, stating he had been a non-juror to the Oath of Allegiance and Fidelity in 1778 due to "ignorance" and now desired relief under the Act and to take the Oath [Ref: L-101].

DERRY, Peter. Petitioned the General Assembly under the Act of May 12, 1780, stating he had been a non-juror to the Oath of Allegiance and Fidelity in 1778 due to "ignorance" and now desired relief under the Act and to take the Oath [Ref: L-101].

DERRY, Philip. Petitioned the General Assembly under the Act of May 12, 1780, stating he had been a non-juror to the Oath of Allegiance and Fidelity in 1778 due to "ignorance" and now desired relief under the Act and to take the Oath [Ref: L-101].

DERTZBACH, Peter. Associator in December, 1775 [Ref: E-166]. Juror to the Oath of Allegiance in 1778 [Ref: C-24].

DESMOREAUX [DESORMEAUX], Baptiste. Private, 7th Maryland Regiment, enlisted in Frederick Town on February 11, 1780, and subsequently reported as "deserted" (no date given). [Ref: A-312, A-334].

DEVENISH, George. Private in the 7th Maryland Regiment in 1779 and reported missing on August 16, 1780 (after the Battle of Camden, South Carolina). [Ref: A-202].

DEVILBISS, Adam (September 18, 1750 - September 12, 1794). Son of George Devilbiss and Anna Catherine Stull. Non-Enroller who was fined by the Committee of Observation in April, 1776. He married Catherine Barrick on May 27, 1778 [Ref: E-248, O-208, U-1989B].

DEVILBISS, Anna Elizabeth. See "Jacob Ramsburg," q.v.

DEVILBISS, Catharine. See "William Barrick," q.v.

DEVILBISS, Christian. Associator in December, 1775 [Ref: E-166]. Juror to the Oath of Allegiance in 1778 [Ref: C-24].

DEVILBISS, Elizabeth and George. See "Alexander Ogle," q.v.

DEVILBISS, Frederick (born 1760), of George. Non-Enroller fined by the Committee of Observation in April, 1776 [Ref: E-248, O-208]. One Frederick Devilbiss was an ensign in the Catoctin Battalion of militia on June 29, 1782, in Capt. Barrick's company [Ref: B-69].

DEVILBISS, George (1715-1785). Performed the patriotic service of lending money ($900) to the State of Maryland to issue Continental Loan Office certificates. George married Anna Catherine Stull and a son Adam (1750-1794) married Catherine Barrick in 1778 [Ref: V-520, and U-1989B, citing *Archives of Maryland*, Vol. 45, p. 52].

DEVILBISS, George (1747-1813), son of Casper. Non-Enroller fined by the Committee of Observation in April, 1776 [Ref: E-248, O-208]. He provided wheat for the military in May, 1782 [Ref: R-515].

DEVILBISS, John (1750-1827), son of Casper. Non-Enroller fined by the Committee of Observation in April, 1776 [Ref: E-248, O-208].

DEVILBISS, John (1743-1804), of Casper. Non-Enroller fined by the Committee of Observation in April, 1776 [Ref: E-248, O-208]. "John Devilbliss" died October 4, 1804, "an old resident." [Ref: N-56].

DEVILBISS, Rebecca and John. See "Alexander Ogle," q.v.

DEVILBISS, Susanna. See "Philip Ramsburg," q.v.

DEVIT, George. Private, 7th Maryland Regiment, 1779 [Ref: A-311]. Private, 1st Maryland Regiment, 1780, and served in the Southern Army of the United States under Lt. William Lamar in the late Capt. Beatty's company in 1781; "sick in July." [Ref: A-389].

DEWELL, Thomas. Associator in December, 1775 [Ref: E-165]. Juror to the Oath of Allegiance in 1778 [Ref: C-24].

DEWITT, Valentine. Militia substitute from May to December 10, 1781, and "marched to Annapolis." [Ref: A-653].

DICHOR, Thomas. Associator in December, 1775 [Ref: E-166]. Juror to the Oath of Allegiance in 1778 [Ref: C-24].
DICK, Peter. Private in the Middle District Militia in 1776, in Capt. Valentine Creager's company [Ref: A-72]. There was also a Peter Dick who was the 4th corporal in Capt. Christopher Stull's company of militia in 1775 [Ref: E-50].
DICKERSON, Solomon. Private in the militia, July, 1776 [Ref: A-42].
DICKS, John. Private who enlisted on July 19, 1776 [Ref: A-51].
DICKSON, George. Associator in December, 1775 [Ref: E-165]. Juror to the Oath of Allegiance in 1778 [Ref: C-24].
DICKSON, Thomas. Sergeant in Capt. Normand Bruce's company of militia in 1775 [Ref: E-54]. Also, see "Thomas Dixon," q.v.
DIFFENTALER, Michael. Associator in December, 1775 [Ref: E-166]. Juror to the Oath of Allegiance in 1778 [Ref: C-24, and S-264, which spelled the name "Michael Diffendaller."
DIGGS, Ignatius and Mary. See "Thomas Sim Lee," q.v.
DIGMAN, Peter. Private who enlisted on July 19, 1776 [Ref: A-51].
DILL, Nicholas. Associator in December, 1775 [Ref: E-166]. Juror to the Oath of Allegiance in 1778 [Ref: C-24]. Nicholas Dill died testate in 1785, naming his wife Esther and children Nicholas and Hannah [Ref: M-7:26].
DILL, Nicholas Jr. Associator in December, 1775 [Ref: E-166]. Juror to the Oath of Allegiance in 1778 [Ref: C-24].
DIVERS, William. Private who enlisted on July 19, 1776 [Ref: A-51].
DIXON, Thomas. Enlisted March 11, 1781 for 3 years; "sent back by General William Smallwood and since has been sick." [Ref: D-1814]. Also, see "Thomas Dickson," q.v.
DIXON, William. Private who enlisted on July 18, 1776 [Ref: A-49].
DIXSON, Nathaniel. Corporal in the militia on March 9, 1776 [Ref: B-166].
DOBSON, Samuel. "Draught," May to December 10, 1781, and "marched to Annapolis." [Ref: A-653].
DOBSON, William. Militia substitute from May to December 10, 1781, and "marched to Annapolis." [Ref: A-653].
DODD, James. Militia substitute on June 6, 1778 [Ref: A-325].
DODSON, John. Associator in December, 1775 [Ref: E-166]. Juror to the Oath of Allegiance in 1778 [Ref: C-24].
DODSON, Michael. Associator in December, 1775 [Ref: E-166]. Private who was enlisted on July 20, 1776, by Capt. Jacob Good [Ref: A-46]. Provided wheat for the military in July, 1782 [Ref: R-530].

DODSON, Thomas. Juror to the Oath of Allegiance in March, 1778 [Ref: S-264, but not listed in Ref: C-24].
DODSON, William. Militia substitute on June 13, 1778 [Ref: A-326].
DOFLAR [DOFLER], Peter. Associator in December, 1775 [Ref: E-166]. Furnished powder to the militia in 1775 [Ref: E-59]. Juror to the Oath of Allegiance in 1778 [Ref: C-24]. See "Peter Duffler," q.v.
DOGHERTY, Neil. Private who enlisted on July 29, 1776 [Ref: A-43].
DOINER, Samuel. Petitioned the General Assembly under the Act of May 12, 1780, stating that he had been a non-juror to the Oath of Allegiance and Fidelity in 1778 due to "ignorance" and now desired relief under the Act and to take the Oath [Ref: L-101].
DOLL, Conrod. "Conrad Dolle" was an Associator in December, 1775 [Ref: E-165]. "Conrod Doll" was 1st lieutenant in the Frederick Town Battalion of militia on May 12, 1779, and lieutenant in the Select Militia on August 3, 1781 [Ref: B-70, Z-387, and H-15, which latter source misspelled his name as "Ennod Doll"]. "Conrad Dolle" was Juror to the Oath of Allegiance in 1778 [Ref: C-24]. "Settler Conrad Dolle emigrated from Barbelroth between Landau and Karlsruhe. The census of 1800 in Fredericktown spelled the name Dull (close to the pronunciation of Doll in German). Conrad and Joseph were over 45 years old. Conrad apparently lived with a son and 2 daughters under 26 years. Joseph had 3 sons and 4 daughter under 16 years. Joseph Jr. and wife, 26-45, had 3 children under 10 years. The Reformed Church records at Frederick and gravestones disclose the following early Dolls: Conrad married 1761, Anne Maria Schisler; Conrad and Anna [sic] Maria (1745-1798) had daughter Maria in 1762; Joseph and Charlotta had Joseph in 1769; Joseph and Catherine (died 1822) had Ezra in 1800; John married 1800, Susan Kortz, witnesses were Joseph Doll, Sr. and Jr... Doll families also have lived in Adams County, Pennsylvania." [Ref: O-84].
DOLL [DOLLE], Joseph (1748-1819). "Joseph Dolle" was an Associator in December, 1775 [Ref: E-165]. "Joseph Doll" was sergeant in Capt. Haass' company of militia in 1775 [Ref: E-53]. Juror to the Oath of Allegiance in 1778 [Ref: C-24]. Joseph Doll married Charlotte ---- (died February 3, 1832) in 1767, and their children were: Joseph (born September 1, 1769, and married Catherine ----); Elizabeth (born October 1, 1771, and married Valentine Hoffman in 1791); Charlotte (born March 17, 1773, married Peter Hardt or Hart (1776-1821) in 1795, and died November 5, 1845); John (born November 4, 1775, and married Susanna Kortz in 1800); George (born April 17, 1778, and married Catherine Schmit in 1799); Catherine (born March 1, 1782, and married George Gebbard in

1803); Mary (born April 12, 1784, and married John Shook); Margaret (born March 4, 1786, and married Jacob Brunner in 1807); Susanna (born October 23, 1787, and married George Lore in 1807); Peter (born October 15, 1789); Jacob (born August 21, 1791, and married Mary Myers in 1812); Michael (born December 6, 1794). [Ref: U-1089, U-1542]. Also, see comments under "Conrod Doll," q.v.

DOLLER, Jacob. Associator in December, 1775 [Ref: E-166]. Juror to the Oath of Allegiance in 1778 [Ref: C-24].

DOLLINCE, Patrick. Associator in December, 1775 [Ref: E-165]. Juror to the Oath of Allegiance in 1778 [Ref: C-24].

DOLTON, Jacob. Private in the German Regiment. Served at White Plains on September 5, 1778, under Lt. Col. Weltner [Ref: A-267].

DOMER, George. Juror to the Oath of Allegiance in March, 1778 [Ref: S-264, but not listed in Ref: C-24].

DONACK, John. Private who enlisted on August 5, 1776 in the Flying Camp under Capt. Philip Meroney [Ref: A-45, N-30:112].

DONAH, John. See "John Dorah," q.v.

DONALLY, James. Non-Enroller who was fined by the Committee of Observation in April, 1776 [Ref: E-248].

DONAR, George. Provided wheat for the military in May, 1782 [Ref: R-512].

DONLON, Thedy. Militia substitute from May to December 10, 1781, and "marched to Annapolis." [Ref: A-653].

DONNELL, Hugh. Sergeant in Capt. Robert Beatty's company of militia in 1775 [Ref: E-55].

DONNELLY [DONNALLY], Patrick. Private in the 7th Maryland Regiment who enlisted on July 22, 1777, and was discharged on July 22, 1780 [Ref: A-200]. "In December, 1815, the Treasurer of the Western Shore was directed to pay to 'Patrick Donally' of Frederick County, half pay of a private, as a further remuneration to him for those services by which his country has been so essentially benefitted. On February 20, 1829, the Treasurer was directed to pay 'Elizabeth Donnelly,' widow of the late Patrick Donnelly, of Frederick County, whatever sum may have been due to said Patrick Donnelly from the State of Maryland at the time of his decease, on account of his revolutionary services. On March 6, 1832 the Treasurer was directed to pay to Elizabeth Donnelly, of Frederick County, widow of Patrick Donnelly, a soldier of the Revolutionary War, during her widowhood, half yearly, half pay of a private, for services rendered by her husband during said war." [Ref: G-336].

103

DOOMBAUGH, Jno. Juror to the Oath of Allegiance in March, 1778 [Ref: S-264, but not listed in Ref: C-24].

DOR, John Martin. See "John Martin Derr," q.v.

DORAH [DONAH?], John. "John Dorah" subscribed to the Oath of Allegiance in 1778 [Ref: C-24]. "John Donah" was an Associator in December, 1775 [Ref: E-165].

DORAH [DORON?], Dineas [Dinnis?]. Private who enlisted on June 26, 1780, for 3 years, in Capt. Michael Bayer's company. [Ref: A-268].

DORFF, Samuel. Paid for services rendered to the military in December, 1779 (nature of services not stated). [Ref: V-44].

DORRAN, William. Served on the Committee of Observation in 1775 [Ref: I-85].

DORSEY, Basil (Linganore Hundred). Appointed by the Committee of Correspondence to solicit subscriptions in 1775 to purchase arms and ammunition [Ref: I-86]. Served on the Committee of Observation in 1775 [Ref: I-85]. Captain of a company of militia on November 29, 1775 [Ref: E-52, B-70]. Associator who was appointed "to hand about the Association paper" in the Linganore Hundred in 1775 [Ref: E-305]. Captain in the Linganore Battalion of militia from December 28, 1776, through at least March 11, 1777 [Ref: B-70, X-555, Y-54]. Justice of the Peace in 1777 [Ref: F-476]. Apparently, there was another Basil Dorsey who petitioned the General Assembly under the Act of May 12, 1780, stating he had been a non-juror to the Oath of Allegiance and Fidelity in 1778 due to "ignorance" and now desired relief under the Act and to take the Oath [Ref: L-101].

DORSEY, Charles. Petitioned the General Assembly under the Act of May 12, 1780, stating that he had been a non-juror to the Oath of Allegiance and Fidelity in 1778 due to "ignorance" and now desired relief under the Act and to take the Oath [Ref: L-101]. Also, see "Charles Lowrey, alias Dorsey," q.v.

DORSEY, Edward. Petitioned the General Assembly under the Act of May 12, 1780, stating that he had been a non-juror to the Oath of Allegiance and Fidelity in 1778 due to "ignorance" and now desired relief under the Act and to take the Oath [Ref: L-101]. Provided wheat for the military in June, 1782 [Ref: R-522].

DORSEY, Henry. Corporal in Capt. David Moore's company of militia in 1775 [Ref: E-56].

DORSEY, Henry Griffin. Petitioned the General Assembly under the Act of May 12, 1780, stating he had been a non-juror to the Oath of Allegiance and Fidelity in 1778 due to "ignorance" and now desired relief under the Act and to take the Oath [Ref: L-101].

DORSEY, John. Recommended on August 21, 1776, to be a surgeon of the militia in Frederick County [Ref: X-231].

DORSEY, Josiah. Petitioned the General Assembly under the Act of May 12, 1780, stating that he had been a non-juror to the Oath of Allegiance and Fidelity in 1778 due to "ignorance" and now desired relief under the Act and to take the Oath [Ref: L-101].

DORSEY, Richard. 3rd lieutenant in a rifle company in July, 1776 [Ref: X-54].

DORSEY, Sarah. See "William Cumming," q.v.

DORSEY, Sophia and Basil. See "Upton Sheredine," q.v.

DORSEY, William. Petitioned the General Assembly under the Act of May 12, 1780, stating that he had been a non-juror to the Oath of Allegiance and Fidelity in 1778 due to "ignorance" and now desired relief under the Act and to take the Oath [Ref: L-101].

DOSTMAN, Martin. Associator in December, 1775 [Ref: E-166]. Juror to the Oath of Allegiance in 1778 [Ref: C-24, and S-264, which spelled the name "Dustman."].

DOTTS, George. Private in the Middle District Militia in 1776 in Capt. Valentine Creager's company [Ref: A-72].

DOUBEMAN, Peter. Corporal in Capt. Herman Yost's company of militia in 1775 [Ref: E-52].

DOVE, John. Sergeant in the 7th Maryland Line on May 1, 1778, and field and staff quartermaster on July 20, 1778 [Ref: A-202].

DOWLEN [DOWLING], James. Private, 1st Maryland Regiment, enlisted January 26, 1777, and served in the Southern Army of the United States under Lt. William Lamar in the late Capt. Beatty's company. Corporal, June 8, 1777. Sergeant, November 1, 1777. Private, August 6, 1777. Sergeant, January 1, 1780 [Ref: A-201]. Record indicates he was a prisoner of war on April 25, 1781 [Ref: A-391].

DOWNEY, Cornelius. Associator in December, 1775 [Ref: E-166]. Juror to the Oath of Allegiance in 1778 [Ref: C-24]. Private in the Middle District Militia in 1776 in Capt. Valentine Creager's company [Ref: A-72].

DOWNEY, Frederick. Private in German Regiment, 1776 [Ref: A-266].

DOWNING, Francis. Private who enlisted July 29, 1776 [Ref: A-43].

DOWNING, Timothy. Private in the Skipton District Militia under Capt. Thomas Waring on April 16, 1776 [Ref: B-167, D-1814].

DOWRY, Charles. Associator in December, 1775 [Ref: E-166]. Juror to the Oath of Allegiance in 1778 [Ref: C-24].

DRAKE, Robert. Private who enlisted on August 5, 1776 [Ref: A-44].

DRAKE, William. Drafted on June 13, 1781, and was later reported "deserted" (no date given). [Ref: D-1814].

DRAPER, William. Private who enlisted on July 13, 1776 [Ref: A-43].

DRAPIER [DRAPER], John. Private who enlisted on May 15, 1778, and served in the 2nd Maryland Regiment [Ref: A-294, A-322].

DROME, William. Private who was enlisted on July 20, 1776 by Capt. Jacob Good [Ref: A-46].

DRUMBO, Conrad. Associator in December, 1775 [Ref: E-166]. Juror to the Oath of Allegiance in 1778 [Ref: C-24, S-264].

DRUMBRO, John. Non-Enroller who was fined by the Committee of Observation in May, 1776 [Ref: E-248].

DUCMAN, John. Associator in December, 1775 [Ref: E-165]. Juror to the Oath of Allegiance in 1778 [Ref: C-24].

DUDDERER, Conrad (May 26, 1728 - May, 1831). 2nd lieutenant in the Linganore Battalion. He married Margaret Pennetecker (1742-1797), and a son Conrad (1773-1836) married Margaret Baker [Ref: U-2911]. "Conrad Dutterow" was an Associator who was appointed "to hand about the Association paper" in Burnt House Woods Hundred in 1775 [Ref: E-305]. Grandson of "George Philip Dodderer" from Sinsheim who had emigrated to Pennsylvania in 1724. "Georg Philip Duddra" settled in Montgomery County, Maryland, and "Conrad Dutterow" (his grandson) settled in Frederick County [Ref: O-124]. There was also a "Conrad Dudderar" (1712-1801) living at this time [Ref: U-1199].

DUDDERER [DUTTERO], Jacob (c1733-1806). Son of Conrad Dudderar, or Dudderer (1712-1801) and Magdalena ---- (1715-1797), Jacob enlisted on April 22, 1781, for 3 years, and marched with Capt. Lynn [Ref: D-1814]. He was a grandson of "Georg Philip Dodderer" from Sinsheim who had emigrated to Pennsylvania in 1724. "George Philip Duddra" settled in Montgomery County, Maryland, and "Jacob Duttero" (his grandson) settled in Frederick County [Ref: O-124, U-1199].

DUDDERER [DUTTERER], John. "John Dutterer" was a private who enlisted on July 1, 1776 in Capt. Peter Mantz's company; marched from Frederick Town to Leonardtown, and from there to Philadelphia, arriving on August 23, 1776 [Ref: A-47]. "John Duderow" pensioned in 1831 [Ref: J-33]. "On March 12, 1828, the Treasurer of the Western Shore was directed to pay to 'John Dotrow,' of Frederick County, during life, half yearly, sum of money equal to the half pay of a private, as further remuneration for his services during the Revolutionary War." [Ref: G-337]. Also, see "John Tuttro," q.v.

DUDEROW, John. See "John Dutterer," q.v.

DUFFLER, Peter. Non-Enroller fined by the Committee of Observation in April, 1776 [Ref: E-248]. "Peter Doefler" took the Oath of Allegiance in March, 1778 [Ref: S-267]. Also, see "Peter Dofler," q.v.

DUGMORE, John. Associator in December, 1775 [Ref: E-166]. Juror to the Oath of Allegiance in 1778 [Ref: C-24].

DUGUD, Robert. Associator in December, 1775 [Ref: E-166]. Juror to the Oath of Allegiance in 1778 [Ref: C-24].

DULANY, Benjamin Tasker. "Numerous writers have stated falsely that all Dulanys were Royalists, or Tories, whose lands were confiscated after the Revolutionary War. Daniel Dulany, the Elder, who founded Fredericktown, died in 1753. His son Daniel II, or the Younger, was neutral and his lands were not confiscated. His son Benjamin Tasker Dulany was a patriot and a close friend of George Washington... A tradition that may be true is that Benjamin Tasker Dulany and wife Elizabeth presented to George Washington the horse 'Blueskin' from their pasture at Prospect Hill. Washington rode 'Blueskin' on ceremonial occasions as depicted on entering New York City by Currier and Ives. Since 'Blueskin' was gun-shy and light in color, George used his other, dark horse, 'Nelson,' more often in battle. The tradition that 'Blueskin' was buried on Prospect Hill may be doubted, since when the old horse was returned to the Dulanys after 1785, they lived in Alexandria, Virginia." [Ref: O-186].

DULL, Peter. Associator in December, 1775 [Ref: E-166]. Juror to the Oath of Allegiance in 1778 [Ref: C-24].

DULLIS, Charles. Private who enlisted on August 5, 1776, in the Flying Camp under Capt. Philip Meroney [Ref: A-45, N-30:112].

DUMATT, Edward. Private who enlisted on July 18, 1776 [Ref: A-50].

DUNCAN, James. Private who enlisted on July 19, 1776 [Ref: A-51]. Private in the German Regiment, on muster roll dated October 23, 1776, and was discharged on July 16, 1779 [Ref: A-264].

DUNCAN, Jessee. Sergeant in the 7th Maryland Regiment in 1778 and discharged January 5, 1779 [Ref: A-202].

DUNCAN, John. Private who was enlisted on July 20, 1776, by Capt. Jacob Good [Ref: A-46].

DUNCAN [DUNKIN], Robert. Private in the 1st Maryland Regiment, enlisted August 7, 1777, and served in the Southern Army of the United

States under Lt. William Lamar in the late Capt. Beatty's company through at least November, 1780 [Ref: A-202, A-389].

DUNKLE, Jacob. Sergeant in Capt. Ludowick Kemp's company of militia in 1775 [Ref: E-52]. Associator in December, 1775 [Ref: E-166]. Juror to the Oath of Allegiance in 1778 [Ref: C-24].

DUNKLE, Mathias. Private in the German Regiment, muster roll dated October 23, 1776 [Ref: A-264].

DUNLOP, Collin. Furnished powder and lead for use of the militia in Frederick Town in 1775 [Ref: E-60, E-61].

DUNN, William. Militia substitute from May to December 10, 1781, and "marched to Annapolis." [Ref: A-652].

DUNWOLTE, Frederick. Associator in December, 1775 [Ref: E-166]. Juror to the Oath of Allegiance in 1778 [Ref: C-24].

DURBIN, Benjamin. Associator in December, 1775 [Ref: E-166]. Juror to the Oath of Allegiance in 1778 [Ref: C-24]. Apparently, another Benjamin Durbin petitioned the General Assembly under the Act of May 12, 1780, stating that he had been a non-juror to the Oath of Allegiance and Fidelity in 1778 due to "ignorance" and now desired relief under the Act and to take the Oath [Ref: L-101].

DURBIN, Christopher. Associator in December, 1775 [Ref: E-166]. Juror to the Oath of Allegiance in 1778 [Ref: C-24].

DURBIN, Philip. Petitioned the General Assembly under the Act of May 12, 1780, stating that he had been a non-juror to the Oath of Allegiance and Fidelity in 1778 due to "ignorance" and now desired relief under the Act and to take the Oath [Ref: L-101].

DURBIN, Samuel. Associator in December, 1775 [Ref: E-166]. Juror to the Oath of Allegiance in 1778 [Ref: C-24].

DURBIN, Thomas. Associator in December, 1775 [Ref: E-166]. Juror to the Oath of Allegiance in 1778 [Ref: C-24].

DURBIN, William (Burnt House Woods Hundred). Non-Enroller who was fined by the Committee of Observation in August, 1776 [Ref: E-248].

DURGAN, Anthony. Militia substitute on June 13, 1778 [Ref: A-326]. Served in the 7th Maryland Regiment as a private until December, 1779, when he was reported "absent without leave." [Ref: A-200].

DUSSEY, John. Non-Enroller who was fined by the Committee of Observation in April, 1776 [Ref: E-248].

DUSTMAN, Martin. See "Martin Dostman," q.v.

DUTROW, Martha. See "William Rice," q.v.

DUVALL, Marrion. Associator in December, 1775 [Ref: E-165]. Juror to the Oath of Allegiance in 1778 [Ref: C-24].

DUVALL, Samuel. Associator in December, 1775 [Ref: E-166]. Juror to the Oath of Allegiance in 1778 [Ref: C-24]. Private in the horse troops in June, 1781 [Ref: B-167]. Served in the House of Delegates in 1782 [Ref: F-479]. Loaned $1,000 for the use of the State of Maryland in June, 1780 [Ref: V-520]. "Samuel Duvall, surveyor, died on January 17, 1811." [Ref: F-471].

DUVALL, William (Linganore Hundred). Appointed by the Committee of Correspondence to solicit subscriptions in 1775 to purchase arms and ammunition [Ref: I-86]. Captain of a militia company in the 4th Battalion on November 29, 1775 [Ref: E-54, B-72]. Gave money in the amount of 1 lb. 15 sh. for arms and ammunition for the militia in 1775 [Ref: E-63].

DWIER, Thomas. Defective from Maryland Line in 1780 [Ref: A-415].

DWYRE, John. Private who was enlisted on July 20, 1776 by Capt. Jacob Good [Ref: A-46].

DYCUS, Philip. Associator in December, 1775 [Ref: E-166]. Juror to the Oath of Allegiance in 1778 [Ref: C-24].

DYE, Benjamin. Private who enlisted on July 25, 1776 [Ref: A-51].

DYER, Aaron. Non-Enroller who was fined by the Committee of Observation in May, 1776 [Ref: E-248].

DYER, Edward. Associator who was appointed "to hand about the Association paper" in Sugar Loaf Hundred in 1775 [Ref: E-305].

DYER, James. Private who enlisted on May 2, 1778 [Ref: A-321]. Served in the German Regiment at the Battle of White Plains on September 5, 1778, under Lt. Col. Ludwick Weltner [Ref: A-267].

DYER, Joseph. Non-Enroller who was fined by the Committee of Observation in May, 1776 [Ref: E-248].

DYER, Thomas. Captain in 1781 [Ref: D-1814]. Another Thomas Dyer apparently enlisted on April 11, 1781, for 3 years and marched with Capt. Lynn [Ref: D-1814].

DYTCH, George. Militia substitute from May to December 10, 1781, and "marched to Annapolis." [Ref: A-653].

EAKIN, Daniel. Associator in December, 1775 [Ref: E-166]. Juror to the Oath of Allegiance in 1778 [Ref: C-24].

EAKIN, Marmaduke. Associator in 1775 [Ref: E-166].

EAMICK, Peter. Defective from Maryland Line in 1781 [Ref: A-415].

EARBOCK, William. Associator in December, 1775 [Ref: E-166]. Juror to the Oath of Allegiance in 1778 [Ref: C-24].

EAREL, James. "Applied for a pension (S34790) in Frederick County, Maryland, on September 20, 1821, aged 75, stating he had enlisted in the Pennsylvania Line in Cumberland County, Pennsylvania. In 1821 he had a wife Susannah, aged 69. On January 18, 1929 [1829?] one A. M. Earel, of Hoopeston, Illinois, stated that the soldier was born in April, 1746, married Susanna Uleguyer, and died about 1830, but this was not confirmed." [Ref: T-1065, J-25].

EASTERDAY, Christian. See "Christian Yesterday," q.v.

EASTBURN, Benjamin (Upper Catoctin). Appointed by the Committee of Correspondence to solicit subscriptions in 1775 to purchase arms and ammunition [Ref: I-85]. "Benjamin Easburn" was an Associator in December, 1775 [Ref: E-166]. Juror to the Oath of Allegiance in 1778 [Ref: C-24]. "Benjamin Eastburn" gave money in the amount of 18 sh. 4 p. for arms and ammunition for the militia in 1775 [Ref: E-62]. "Benjamin Eastbun" was a 1st lieutenant in the 34th Battalion of militia on June 11, 1776, and "Benjamin Eastbrun" was a captain on August 22, 1781 [Ref: B-73, W-476].

EASTHAP, Thomas. Petitioned the General Assembly under the Act of May 12, 1780, stating that he had been a non-juror to the Oath of Allegiance and Fidelity in 1778 due to "ignorance" and now desired relief under the Act and to take the Oath [Ref: L-101].

EASTHAP, William. Petitioned the General Assembly under the Act of May 12, 1780, stating that he had been a non-juror to the Oath of Allegiance and Fidelity in 1778 due to "ignorance" and now desired relief under the Act and to take the Oath [Ref: L-101].

EATCHBERRIGER, Devall. Associator in December, 1775 [Ref: E-166]. Juror to the Oath of Allegiance in 1778 [Ref: C-24].

EBERLEY, Nicholas. Associator in December, 1775 [Ref: E-166]. Juror to the Oath of Allegiance in 1778 [Ref: C-24].

EBERT, Andrew. Transported flour for the military in May, 1782 [Ref: R-511].

ECK, Matthias. See "Matthias Ack," q.v.

EBERT, John Adam. Associator in December, 1775 [Ref: E-166]. Juror to the Oath of Allegiance in 1778 [Ref: C-24].

ECKMER, Jacob. Associator in December, 1775 [Ref: E-166]. Juror to the Oath of Allegiance in 1778 [Ref: C-24].

ECKMER, Jacob Jr. Associator in December, 1775 [Ref: E-166]. Juror to the Oath of Allegiance in 1778 [Ref: C-24].

EDDY, James. Private who enlisted on May 4, 1778, and served in the 2nd Maryland Regiment [Ref: A-294, A-321].

EDELIN, Bartholomew. Private, enlisted July 13, 1776 [Ref: A-43].

EDELIN [EDELEN], Christopher. Served in the French and Indian War, 1756. Chosen to serve on the Committee of Observation in 1775 [Ref: E-302, I-85]. Associator in December, 1775 [Ref: E-166], a member of the State Constitutional Convention in 1776, a Justice for Frederick County in 1777, and Sheriff on October 14, 1779 [Ref: E-302]. Juror to the Oath of Allegiance in 1778 [Ref: C-24]. Member of the House of Delegates in 1776, Election Judge in the Middle District on July 2, 1776, Justice of the Peace in 1777, Sheriff from 1779 to at least 1782 [Ref: F-476, F-479, F-480, Z-555]. He died circa 1786 in Frederick County, Maryland [Ref: P-298].

EDELIN, Elizabeth. See "Mountjoy Bailey," q.v.

EDELMAN, Michael. Private who enlisted July 20, 1776 [Ref: A-50]. "Michael Edleman applied for a pension (S38678) on October 28, 1829, in Greene County, Tennessee, aged 74, stating served in the Maryland Line. He also stated he had lost his wife, three children, and a grandchild within 6 months, and he still had a son and three daughters living, all on his land: Jacob (aged 31), Betsey (aged 30), Caty (aged 26), and Sally (aged 19)." [Ref: T-1083].

EDLEMAN [EDELMAN], Leonard. He was probably related to the Michael Edelman above. Leonard who was born near Hagerstown, Maryland, in 1761, and served in the Maryland Line. After the war he also moved to Greene County, Tennessee, and then on to Kentucky, Indiana, and back to Harrison County, Kentucky, where he applied for a pension (S30397) on September 22, 1832. His wife (no name given) died on April 3, 1839. Leonard returned to Kentucky in 1840 and lived with a son. An Aaron Edelman is mentioned in his pension [Ref: T-1083].

EDGE, Peter. Militia substitute from May to December 10, 1781, and "marched to Annapolis." [Ref: A-653].

EDISON, James. Associator in December, 1775 [Ref: E-166]. Juror to the Oath of Allegiance in 1778 [Ref: C-24].

EDISON, Thomas. Associator in December, 1775 [Ref: E-166]. Juror to the Oath of Allegiance in 1778 [Ref: C-24]. One Thomas Edison was a private in the Middle District Militia in 1776 in Capt. Valentine Creager's company [Ref: A-72]. Also, Thomas Edison was adjutant in the 37th Battalion of militia in 1776 [Ref: B-73, W-526, X-555].

EDMONDSON, Thomas. Ensign in the Lower District Militia [now Montgomery County] in 1776 [Ref: A-42]. "Thomas Edmonston" was 1st lieutenant in the Lower District Militia [now Montgomery County] under Capt. Edward Burgess on August 7, 1776 [Ref: A-42].

EDORS, Abraham. Associator in December, 1775 [Ref: E-166]. Juror to the Oath of Allegiance in 1778 [Ref: C-24].

EDWARDS, John. Juror to the Oath of Allegiance in March, 1778 [Ref: S-264, but not listed in Ref: C-24].

EDWARDS, Robert. Juror to the Oath of Allegiance in March, 1778 [Ref: S-264, but not listed in Ref: C-24].

EDWARDS, Samuel. Private who enlisted on May 19, 1778 [Ref: A-323]. Served as a private in the 7th Maryland Regiment 1779 [Ref: A-204].

EGGMAN, Jacob. Private in the German Regiment, 1776, in Capt. Henry Fister's company under the command of Col. Hussecker [Ref: A-261].

EIGINOR, Benedict. Private who enlisted July 18, 1776 [Ref: A-50].

EILER [ILER], Conrad. Drafted on May 4, 1781; provided a substitute [Ref: D-1814]. Probably related to Conrad Eyler from Manheim Twp., York County, Pennsylvania, who died in 1751 near Friend's Mountain (near Emmittsburg), Frederick County, Maryland [Ref: O-81].

EILER [EYLER], Frederick (1741-1821). Associator in December, 1775 [Ref: E-166], and signed as a Juror to the Oath of Allegiance in 1778 [Ref: C-24]. Frederick Eyler and wife Barbara are buried at Apples Church near Thurmont, Maryland [Ref: O-81].

EILER [OLER], Peter. "Peter Eiler" was a non-enroller who was fined by the Committee of Observation in April, 1776 [Ref: E-248]. "Peter Oler" was 2nd lieutenant in Capt. Robert Beatty's militia company in the 3rd Battalion on November 29, 1775 [Ref: E-55, B-108].

EILER, Valentine. Non-Enroller who was fined by the Committee of Observation in April, 1776 [Ref: E-248].

EIMBACH, Jacob. Associator in December, 1775 [Ref: E-166]. Juror to the Oath of Allegiance in 1778 [Ref: C-24].

EIRHEART, George. Non-Enroller who was fined by the Committee of Observation in April, 1776 [Ref: E-248].

ELDER, Aloysius (1757-1827). Son of William Elder and his second wife Jacoba Clementina Livers. Married Elizabeth Mills (1757-1802) and secondly Mary Josephine Green Hayden (1775-1842). [Ref: O-81]. Petitioned the General Assembly under the Act of May 12, 1780, stating that he had been a non-juror to the Oath of Allegiance and Fidelity in 1778 due to "ignorance" and now desired relief under the Act and to take the Oath [Ref: L-101].

ELDER, Arnold (1745-1812). Son of William Elder and his second wife Jacoba Clementina Livers. He married Clotilda Phoebe Green (1752-1833); no issue [Ref: O-80]. Associator in December, 1775 [Ref: E-166]. Juror to the Oath of Allegiance in 1778 [Ref: C-24].

ELDER, Charles (1730-1804). Son of William Elder and his first wife Ann Wheeler (1709-1739). He married Julia Ward (1737-1814). [Ref: O-80]. Associator in December, 1775 [Ref: E-166]. Juror to Oath of Allegiance, 1778 [Ref: C-24].

ELDER, Francis (1755-1816). Son of William Elder and his second wife Jacoba Clementina Livers. He married Catherine Spalding (1766-1809). [Ref: O-81]. Ensign in the 37th Battalion of militia on February 1, 1777 [Ref: B-73].

ELDER, Guy (1731-1805). Son of William Elder and his first wife Ann Wheeler. He married first Eleanor Wickham (died 1759) and secondly Eleanor Ogle Beall, the widow of Ninian Magruder Beall [Ref: O-80]. Associator in December, 1775 [Ref: E-166]. Juror to the Oath of Allegiance in 1778 [Ref: C-24, S-264].

ELDER, Hugh. Private who enlisted on July 22, 1776 [Ref: A-49].

ELDER, Ignatius (1749-c1800). Son of William Elder and his second wife Jacoba Clementina Livers. He married Elizabeth ---- and moved to Washington County, Kentucky, circa 1792 [Ref: O-81]. Associator in December, 1775 [Ref: E-166]. Ensign in the 37th Battalion of militia on May 15, 1776, to at least February 1, 1777 [Ref: W-427, B-73]. Juror to the Oath of Allegiance in 1778 [Ref: C-24].

ELDER, Richard (1734-1790). Son of William Elder and his first wife Ann Wheeler. Richard married Phoebe Delozier in 1764 [Ref: O-80]. Associator in December, 1775 [Ref: E-166]. Juror to the Oath of Allegiance in 1778 [Ref: C-24]. He died testate in 1790, leaving a wife Phoebe and children Benedick (oldest son), Elizabeth (oldest daughter), Lucy (youngest daughter), Benjamin, Richard, and Joseph [Ref: M-8:33].

ELDER, Thomas (1748-1832). Son of William Elder and his second wife Jacoba Clementina Livers. He married Elizabeth Spalding (1750-1848) in 1771, and removed to Bardstown, Kentucky [Ref: O-81]. Associator in December, 1775 [Ref: E-166]. Juror to the Oath of Allegiance in 1778 [Ref: C-24]. He was commissioned a 2nd lieutenant in the Catoctin Battalion of militia under Capt. Simpkins on October 13, 1777 [Ref: B-73, H-13].

ELDER, William (of Guy). "Native of Calvert County and a resident of Emmittsburg Hundred or District in Frederick County, near the Pennsylvania line, during the Revolutionary period. As early as 1770 he took an active part in the Tom's Creek and Monocacy Valleys in rousing the people of that section to resist the encroachments of the British government against the rights and privileges of the American colonies and to throw off their allegiance to George III. Mr. Elder belonged to a

Quaker family, and when he espoused the American cause it is said to have 'created no little flutter in the royal camp.' He helped to organize and equip the Gamecock Company of Frederick County, so called from their jaunty cap and waving plume or cockade, the distinguished frontiersmen of Tom' Creek. Of this company, William Blair was elected captain, Henry Williams was first lieutenant, and George Hockensmith was second lieutenant. Mr. Elder was also a member of this organization." [Ref: F-461]. Also, William Elder, of Guy, was a corporal in Capt. Benjamin Ogle, Jr.'s company of militia in 1775 [Ref: E-54]. He was the son of Guy Elder (1731-1805) and Eleanor Wickham (who died in 1759). [Ref: O-80].

ELDER, William Jr. Associator in December, 1775 [Ref: E-166]. Juror to the Oath of Allegiance in 1778 [Ref: C-24]. One "William Elder III" (1729-1804) was a son of William Elder and his first wife Ann Wheeler (1707-1739). He married Sabina Wickham (who died 1786). [Ref: O-80].

ELDER, William Sr. Associator in December, 1775 [Ref: E-166]. Juror to the Oath of Allegiance in 1778 [Ref: C-24]. One William Elder (1707-1775) married Ann Wheeler (1709-1739) and secondly Jacoba Clementina Livers (1717-1807). He settled near Payne's Hill between what later was Mount St. Mary's and Thurmont [Ref: O-80]. Also, see "Arnold Livers," q.v.

ELDRIDGE, Mary. See "Michael Waltman," q.v.

ELEY, David. Private who enlisted on July 1, 1776 in Capt. Peter Mantz's company; marched from Frederick Town to Leonardtown, and from there to Philadelphia, arriving August 23, 1776 [Ref: A-47].

ELEY, Isaac. Drafted on June 13, 1781, and provided a substitute [Ref: D-1814].

ELKINS, William. Private who enlisted in Frederick on August 8, 1780, and marched to Annapolis under Capt. Beatty [Ref: A-344].

ELLIOTT, Benjamin. "Benjamin Ellit" was a private, enlisted on July 25, 1776 [Ref: A-49]. "Benjamin Ellott" was a private, enlisted on May 20, 1778 [Ref: A-323]. "Benjamin Elliott" was a private in the German Regiment at White Plains on September 5, 1778, under Lt. Col. Ludwick Weltner [Ref: A-266].

ELLIS, James. Corporal in Capt. Samuel Shaw's company of militia in 1775 [Ref: E-51].

ELLIS, John. Private who enlisted on July 25, 1776 [Ref: A-49].

ELLIS, Samuel. Associator in December, 1775 [Ref: E-166].

ELLIS, Zacharias. Served on the Committee of Observation in 1775 [Ref: I-85].

ELLISON, Richard. Private in the 7th Maryland Regiment from May 2, 1778, until reported dead on May 26, 1779 [Ref: A-204].

ELLSPERGER, Wolfgang. Private in the German Regiment until July 16, 1779, when he was discharged [Ref: A-204].

ELWOOD, John. Private in the militia in July, 1776 [Ref: A-42].

EMMIT, Elis. Juror to the Oath of Allegiance in 1778 [Ref: C-24].

EMMIT [EMMET], Samuel. Served on the Committee of Observation in 1775 [Ref: I-85]. Associator in December, 1775 [Ref: E-166]. Juror to the Oath of Allegiance in 1778 [Ref: C-24].

EMRICH, Joseph. Private who enlisted on July 20, 1776 [Ref: A-50].

ENGEL, Bartle. Private in the German Regiment, 1776, in Capt. Henry Fister's company under the command of Col. Hussecker [Ref: A-261].

ENGEL, Peter. Associator in December, 1775 [Ref: E-166]. Juror to the Oath of Allegiance in 1778 [Ref: C-24]. One Peter Engel died testate in 1792, leaving a wife Elizabeth and children Justinus (oldest son living in York County, Pennsylvania), Charlotte, and Peter, and also sons-in-law Adam Warner, John Nichlos Warner, and Abraham Yingling [Ref: M-8:178]. "Peter Engellee, or Angel" was a private in the German Regiment until August 14, 1779 [Ref: A-204].

ENGELS, Peter. Associator in 1775 [Ref: E-166].

ENGELS, Samuel. Associator in December, 1775 [Ref: E-166]. Juror to the Oath of Allegiance in 1778 [Ref: C-24].

ENGLAND, John (Burn House Woods Hundred). Non-Enroller who was fined by the Committee of Observation in June, 1776 [Ref: E-248].

ENGLAR, Jacob. Juror to the Oath of Allegiance in March, 1778 [Ref: S-264, but not listed in Ref: C-24].

ENGLAR, Philip. See "Philip Angler," q.v.

ENGLEMAN, Ludwick. Associator in December, 1775 [Ref: E-166]. Juror to the Oath of Allegiance in 1778 [Ref: C-24].

ENGLISH, Robert. Private who enlisted on July 19, 1776 [Ref: A-51].

ENOS, Samuel. Associator in December, 1775 [Ref: E-166]. Juror to the Oath of Allegiance in 1778 [Ref: C-24].

ENSMINGER, John. Associator in December, 1775 [Ref: E-166]. Juror to the Oath of Allegiance in 1778 [Ref: C-24].

ENSMINGER, Philip. Associator in December, 1775 [Ref: E-166]. Juror to the Oath of Allegiance in 1778 [Ref: C-24].

EPPART, Andrew. "Andrew Eppart" was an ensign in the Linganore Battalion of militia on January 17, 1777, and "Andrew Eppard" was a 1st lieutenant on June 22, 1778 [Ref: B-74, Y-54, Z-145].

ERB, Christopher. Associator in December, 1775, who "assisted in handing about the Association paper" in 1776 [Ref: E-166, E-245]. Juror to the Oath of Allegiance in 1778 [Ref: C-24, S-267].

ERBACH, Anna Maria. See "Devalt Samsel," q.v.

ERBACH, Jacob. Associator in December, 1775 [Ref: E-166]. Juror to the Oath of Allegiance in 1778 [Ref: C-24]. "Jacob Erbaugh" died testate in 1790, leaving a wife Margaret and three children (only mentioning Henry, who was under 21, in his will). [Ref: M-7:189].

ERHAL, Matthias. Associator in December, 1775 [Ref: E-166]. Juror to the Oath of Allegiance in 1778 [Ref: C-24].

ERHART, George. Associator in December, 1775 [Ref: E-166]. Juror to the Oath of Allegiance in 1778 [Ref: C-24].

ERVIN [ERWIN, IRVINE], James. Soldier in the Maryland Line who "applied for a pension on June 2, 1818, on Frederick County, Maryland, aged 60, stating he had enlisted at Frederick Town. On November 18, 1820, he was then a resident of Montgomery County, Maryland, and stated he was still age 60? with a wife Sarah, aged 55, and a daughter Mary, aged 25, and sons Thomas, aged 16, and Alfred, aged 10. Soldier's son Samuel Irvine applied (W9430) on February 25, 1841, in Frederick County, stating his father had died June 28, 1827, and his mother had died August 18, 1838, and that they had married on December 20, 1787. Widow died leaving children: Mary (aged 52 on September 26, 1840); John (aged 50 on November 1, 1840); Jane (aged 58 on February 6, 1841, and wife of Frederick Brown, of Frederick County); James (aged 45 on April 2, 1840; Samuel (aged 43 on August 16, 1840); Thomas (aged 38 on August 16, 1840); and, Alfred (aged 30 on February 22, 1841). All were living in 1841. The widow's name before marriage was Sarah Harrison, and their son Samuel Irvin [sic] married Eleanor Hollis on January 22, 1839, and their daughter Mary C. Ervin [sic] was born August 19, 1840. Soldier's children's births were: Mary (born September 26, 1788); John (born November 1, 1790); Jane (born February 6, 1793); James (born April 2, 1795); Samuel (born August 16, 1797); William (born February 3, 1800); Thomas (born August 16, 1802); Rebekah (born January 20, 1804); and, Alfred (born February 22, 1811); and, Eleanor (born April 25, 1817). Also, James Ervin, Sr. died August 18, 1838, probably soldier's son." [Ref" T-1125].

ESHOME, Josh. Drummer in Capt. William Beatty's company in the 7th Maryland Regiment in 1779 [Ref: A-310].

ESTEP, Alexander. 2nd lieutenant in the Lower District Militia [now Montgomery County] under Capt. Edward Burgess on August 7, 1776

[Ref: A-42]. Lieutenant in the 7th Maryland Regiment from February 20, 1777, until October 13, 1777, when he resigned [Ref: A-203].

ESTEP, Joseph. Private in the militia in July, 1776 [Ref: A-42].

ESTEP [EASTEP], William. Associator in December, 1775 [Ref: E-166]. Juror to the Oath of Allegiance in 1778 [Ref: C-24].

ESTEP [EASTUP], Jacob. Associator in December, 1775 [Ref: E-166]. Juror to the Oath of Allegiance in 1778 [Ref: C-24].

ESTEP [ESSTEP], Thomas. Associator in December, 1775 [Ref: E-166]. Juror to the Oath of Allegiance in 1778 [Ref: C-24]. "Thomas Estep, Jr. served in the Revolutionary War." [Ref: Information contained in a query from direct descendant Virgil B. Long, of Seymour, Indiana, in the *Maryland Genealogical Society Bulletin*, Vol. 25:3, p. 342 (1984).]

ESTEP [ESTUP], James. Private who was enlisted on July 20, 1776 by Capt. Jacob Good [Ref: A-46].

ETHER, Christopher. Non-Enroller who was fined by the Committee of Observation in April, 1776 [Ref: E-248].

ETNIER, John. Private in the German Regiment until discharged on July 26, 1779 [Ref: A-265].

ETSLER, Macbelena. See "William Albaugh," q.v.

ETTLEMAN, George. Private who was enlisted on July 20, 1776, by Capt. Jacob Good [Ref: A-46].

EVANS, Benjamin. Private who enlisted April 23, 1778 [Ref: A-324].

EVANS, Edward. Associator in December, 1775 [Ref: E-166]. Juror to the Oath of Allegiance in 1778 [Ref: C-24].

EVANS, Elijah. Associator in December, 1775 [Ref: E-166]. Juror to the Oath of Allegiance in 1778 [Ref: C-24].

EVANS, Ezekiel. Non-Enroller who was fined by the Committee of Observation in April, 1776 [Ref: E-248]. Petitioned the General Assembly under the Act of May 12, 1780, stating that he had been a non-juror to the Oath of Allegiance and Fidelity in Maryland in 1778 due to "ignorance" and now desired relief under the Act and to take the Oath [Ref: L-101].

EVANS, John. Private who enlisted on August 5, 1776 [Ref: A-44].

EVANS, Seth. Associator in December, 1775 [Ref: E-166]. Juror to the Oath of Allegiance in 1778 [Ref: C-24].

EVANS, Thomas. Soldier in the Maryland Line, "applied for a pension (S34821) on October 2, 1818 in Baltimore County, Maryland, aged 64, stating he enlisted at Hagerstown, Maryland. In 1820 he had a wife Elenor, aged about 57, and in 1824 he made affidavit in Washington, D. C. (residence not stated). He died on September 2, 1833." [Ref: T-1135].

"On March 1, 1830, the Treasurer of the Western Shore was directed to pay to Thomas Evans, of Frederick County, during life quarterly, the half pay of a private, as further remuneration for his services during the Revolutionary War. On March 4, 1834, the Treasurer was directed to pay to Eleann Evans, widow of Thomas, of Frederick County, during life, quarterly, half pay of a private, for the services rendered by her husband in the war." [Ref: G-340].

EVANS, William. Private in the 6th Maryland Regiment from July 21, 1777, to October 12, 1778; deserted; rejoined twice [Ref: A-203].

EVANS, Zachariah. Private who enlisted August 5, 1776 [Ref: A-44].

EVERHART, Lawrence. "Born on May 6, 1755, in Frederick County and lived in Taneytown at the time of his enlistment in the Continental and Maryland Lines. He received a disability pension from January 1, 1803, and reapplied on April 7, 1834, in Frederick County "where he had always lived except for 3 or 4 years." Lawrence married in the fall of 1781 or early 1782 to Anne Mary Beckenbaugh, daughter of Casper Beckenbaugh, of Middletown Valley in Frederick County, Virginia [sic]. Anne was born in October, 1755. Lawrence died on August 2 or 3, 1840, and his widow applied for his pension (W9431) on August 24, 1840, at Middletown Valley, Maryland [sic], and she was still there in 1845. She died on July 4, 1848. Their children were: William Everhart, born January 1, 1783; Elizabeth Everhart, born April 10, 1784; Jacob Everhart, born April 25, 1786; Mary Everhart, born February 10, 1788; Nancy Everhart, born February 28, 1790; John Everhart, born August 24, 1791; Catherine Everhart, born January 31, 1793; Sarah Everhart, born October 21, 179[5?]; and, George Everhart, born September 6, 1798. In 1840 six of their children were still living, but no names were given. Lawrence's son-in-law Henry Smeltzer (name of wife not stated) was born on the last day of February, 1774, at Middletown Valley, Maryland, married in 1799, and was still living in 1848. Lawrence's brother, Philip Everhart, was born on April 5, 1770, and lived in Frederick County, Maryland, in 1840." [Ref: T-1138, J-8]. "His company was commanded by Capt. Jacob Goode. Everheart [sic] was then [1776] in his 22nd year and was a tall, stalwart youth, of great physical endurance and indomitable pluck. With his regiment he joined the brigade commanded by Gen. Rezin Beall, which was then stationed at New York. He was, with the other Maryland troops, at the Battle of White Plains, and also at Fort Washington. When the latter was surrendered, however, he managed to escape. In 1778, after the expiration of his term of service, he enlisted at Frederick, with a number of others, in Colonel Washington's regiment of cavalry. At the Battle of Cowpens he was wounded and captured by the enemy. Everheart, with seventeen men, was selected by Colonel Washington to reconnoitre Col. Tarleton's command. As the enemy's horses, impressed from the South Carolina plantations, were much fleeter than those of Everheart and his companions, the scouting party was overtaken. A bloody contest ensued, and Everheart was captured after his horse had been shot under him. He was taken before Tarleton" and a conversation ensued which, in part, upset Tarleton and caused him to state "I am Colonel Tarleton, sir!" and to which came the reply "And I am Sergeant Everheart, sir!" Finding that they could no longer keep him in their possession during the course of the battle, the British "shot him in the head, over one of his eyes. The wound was not serious, and Washington's cavalry being then intermingled with the British, Everheart pointed out to Col. James Simons the man who had shot him. The British soldier was at once shot down, and his horse was handed over to Everheart." Soon thereafter, "Sergeant Everheart sprang forward and saved Colonel Washington by disabling a [British] officer's sword arm... On returning from the pursuit, Washington embraced Everheart and sent him to the rear, where his wounds were dressed. He was disabled for active service for some time, but was present at the surrender at Yorktown, where he made the acquaintance of Lafayette. In 1782 he was honorably discharged. He returned to Middletown Valley and settled on a farm. He then married and was the father was several children. He afterwards became a Methodist minister. Colonel Washington paid him a visit in 1799, and on meeting the veterans 'rushed into each other's arms, kissed, and gave vent to their feelings in tears of joy.' Everheart died in 1839." [Ref: F-454, F-455]. Sergeant on the 1840 list of pensioners in the 3rd District of Frederick County, aged 85 [Ref: J-37]. A chapter of the Maryland Society, Sons of the American Revolution, was named in his honor in 1920 [Ref: Henry C. Peden, Jr.'s *Centennial History of the Maryland Society, Sons of the American Revolution, 1889-1989*]. "In his will probated in 1840 Lawrence Everhart (Eberhardt) named his friend Middletown Valley, Jacob Flook of John, as executor. He willed wife Mary 18 acres, a cow of choice, the choice of all my German books, and his pension of $1,000 yearly. His daughters Elizabeth Jackson and Catharine Nickum lived in Indiana. Daughter Sarah married Henry Smelzer." [Ref: O-14]. Lawrence Everhart was born in Hessheim near Worms, Germany, to Christian Eberhardt (born

1729). He emigrated to Middletown Valley, Frederick County, Maryland, in 1764 [Ref: O-99].

EVERHART, Martin. To the General Assembly of Maryland: "That your petitioner having neglected to take the Oath of Fidelity to this State as by law he was injoined to do, is thereby burthened with a treeble tax on his property, a continuation whereof will inevitably reduce your petitioner to beggary and the greatest distress that your petitioners neglect in this instance, arose wholly from an incapacity to judge, of the nature and principles of government, or the allegiance due thereto, and not from any interested views or inimical principles, held by your petitioner. That your petitioner is a German, by birth, and did not understand the nature of the said Oath, but being led by the example and influence of designing men is now grievously distressed with the said treeble tax. Your petitioner therefore most humbly prays your Honourable House to take his case into consideration and to grant him relief from said treeble tax in such manner as you in your wisdom and goodness shall think meet." Dated at Frederick County, May 22, 1780 [Ref: V-500].

EVERLY, Jacob. Provided wheat for the military in June, 1782 [Ref: R-519].

EVERLY, John. Associator in December, 1775 [Ref: E-166]. Juror to the Oath of Allegiance in 1778 [Ref: C-24].

EVERLY [EVERLEY], Leonard. "Leonard Everley" was a private in the German Regiment, 1776, in Capt. Henry Fister's company under the command of Col. Nicholas Hussecker [Ref: A-261]. "Leonard Everly" was drafted on June 2, 1783 [Ref: B-168].

EVERTS, Matthew. Associator in December, 1775 [Ref: E-166]. Juror to the Oath of Allegiance in 1778 [Ref: C-24].

EYSSELL, John. Private in the German Regiment in 1776 [Ref: A-266].

FAHNAR, John. Associator in December, 1775 [Ref: E-166]. Juror to the Oath of Allegiance in 1778 [Ref: C-24].

FALCONER, Gilbert. Provided wheat for the military in May, 1782 [Ref: R-512].

FALLER, Margaret. See "Yost Blickenstiffe," q.v.

FALLING, John. Corporal, 1st Maryland Regiment, 1780, and served in the Southern Army of the United States under Lt. William Lamar in the late Capt. Beatty's company until he joined the State Regiment on March 12, 1781 [Ref: A-389].

FANGLAR, George. Sergeant at Fort Frederick in 1778, with Capt. John Kershner's company, guarding prisoners of war [Ref: A-328].

FANNELL, John. Private who enlisted on May 20, 1778 [Ref: A-323]. Also, see "John Fennell," q.v.

FANNER, William. Private who enlisted on July 25, 1776 [Ref: A-51].

FANSLAR, Henry. Private who was enlisted on July 20, 1776 by Capt. Jacob Good [Ref: A-46].

FANTZ, Jacob. Private in the German Regiment, 1776, in Capt. Henry Fister's company under the command of Col. Hussecker [Ref: A-261].

FARBER, Jacob. Private in the German Regiment, 1776, in Capt. Henry Fister's company under the command of Col. Hussecker [Ref: A-261].

FARDO, Absalom. Private in Capt. Beatty's company, 7th Maryland Regiment, in 1779 [Ref: A-311]. "Absolum Fardo" was a private in the 1st Maryland Regiment in 1781, and served in the Southern Army of the United States under Lt. William Lamar in the late Capt. Beatty's company [Ref: A-390].

FARE, Charles. Corporal in Capt. Jacob Good's company of militia in 1775 [Ref: E-51].

FARIS, John. Juror to the Oath of Allegiance in March, 1778 [Ref: S-264, but not listed in Ref: C-24]. Also, see "John Forris," q.v.

FARIS, Robert (Burnt House Woods Hundred). Non-Enroller who was fined by the Committee of Observation in June, 1776 [Ref: E-248].

FARLME, Benjamin. Corporal in Capt. Michael McGuire's company of militia in 1775 [Ref: E-57].

FARMEVALD, Lawrence. See "Lawrence Firmwald," q.v.

FARQUHAR, Allen Jr. Non-Enroller who was fined by the Committee of Observation in April, 1776 [Ref: E-248].

FARQUHAR, Allen Sr. Non-Enroller who was fined by the Committee of Observation in April, 1776, but he apparently enrolled because the fine was remitted in June, 1776 [Ref: E-248].

FARQUHAR, Moses. Non-Enroller who was fined by the Committee of Observation in April, 1776 [Ref: E-248].

FARQUHAR, Samuel. Non-Enroller who was fined by the Committee of Observation in April, 1776 [Ref: E-248].

FARQUHAR, Thomas. Non-Enroller who was fined by the Committee of Observation in April, 1776 [Ref: E-248].

FARQUHAR, William (of Allen). Non-Enroller who was fined by the Committee of Observation in April, 1776 [Ref: E-248].

FARQUHAR, William (of William). Non-Enroller who was fined by the Committee of Observation in April, 1776 [Ref: E-248].

FARRAN, John. Sergeant in the 7th Maryland Regiment from April 20, 1777, until October, 1778, when reported "deserted." [Ref: A-207].

FARRELL, John. Private in the 7th Maryland Regiment from December 3, 1776, until January 5, 1780, when discharged [Ref: A-207].

FARRELL, Walter. Militia substitute from May to December 10, 1781, and "marched to Annapolis." [Ref: A-653].

FARTHING, Aaron. Militia substitute from May to December 10, 1781, and "marched to Annapolis." [Ref: A-653].

FARTHING, James. Drafted on June 2, 1783; "never appointed, and discharged on account of poverty and having family." [Ref: B-168].

FAUT, Peter. Associator in December, 1775 [Ref: E-166]. Juror to the Oath of Allegiance in 1778 [Ref: C-24].

FAVOR, Henry. Associator in December, 1775 [Ref: E-167]. Juror to the Oath of Allegiance in 1778 [Ref: C-24].

FAW, Abraham. Served on the Committee of Observation in 1775 [Ref: I-85]. Associator in December, 1775 [Ref: E-166]. Juror to the Oath of Allegiance in 1778 [Ref: C-24]. Responsible for condition and maintenance of the Frederick Town Barracks for the Maryland Regiment in 1777-1779, and appointed the Collector of Clothing in Frederick County on November 27, 1777, by the Council of Maryland [Ref: V-32, Y-418]. Served as State Senator from 1781 to 1785 [Ref: F-478], and he loaned $1,000 for the use of the State of Maryland in June, 1780 [Ref: V-520]. Also, an Abraham Faw was a private in the horse troops in June, 1781 [Ref: B-167].

FAWNER, Jacob. Provided wheat for the military in May, 1782 [Ref: R-515].

FAWNER, John. Non-Enroller who was fined by the Committee of Observation in April, 1776 [Ref: E-248].

FEELY, Charles. Private who enlisted on July 19, 1776 [Ref: A-51].

FEETER, Abraham. Private stationed at Fort Frederick in June, 1778 [Ref: A-328].

FEILSON, James. Private who enlisted on May 26, 1778, for 3 years [Ref: A-326].

FEISTER, John and Susanna. See "Henry Bear," q.v.

FELMOT, Dorest. Private in the 1st Maryland Regiment who enlisted May 5, 1778, and served in the Southern Army of the United States under Lt. William Lamar in the late Capt. Beatty's company until discharged on May 5, 1781 [Ref: A-391].

FELTON, Henry. Provided wheat for the military in May, 1782 [Ref: R-516].

FENLY, Thomas. Private who enlisted on August 5, 1776 in the Flying Camp under Capt. Philip Meroney [Ref: A-45, N-30:112].

FENNELL, John. Private in the German Regiment. Served at White Plains on September 5, 1778, under Lt. Col. Weltner [Ref: A-266].

FERGUSON, Daniel. Private who enlisted July 25, 1776 [Ref: A-50].

FERGUSON, James. Associator in December, 1775 [Ref: E-166]. Juror to the Oath of Allegiance in 1778 [Ref: C-24].

FERGUSON, John. Ensign in Capt. Charles Beatty's militia company in the 1st Battalion, November 29, 1775 [Ref: E-51, B-75]. Associator in December, 1775 [Ref: E-167]. Furnished powder and lead for use of the militia in Frederick Town in 1775 [Ref: E-60, E-61]. 1st lieutenant in the Middle District Militia on March 26, 1776 [Ref: B-75, W-199, W-287]. Juror to the Oath of Allegiance, 1778 [Ref: C-24].

FERGUSON, John. Private who enlisted on July 18, 1776 [Ref: A-50]. He also enrolled as an Associator in December, 1775 [Ref: E-166].

FERGUSON, Josias. Associator in December, 1775 [Ref: E-167]. Juror to the Oath of Allegiance in 1778 [Ref: C-24].

FERGUSON, William. Associator in December, 1775 [Ref: E-166]. Juror to the Oath of Allegiance in 1778 [Ref: C-24].

FERO, Henry. See "Henry Firor (Fero)," q.v.

FERRELL, James. Private who enlisted on March 24, 1778, and served in the 2nd Maryland Regiment [Ref: A-294].

FERRELL, Jeremiah. Private in the militia, July, 1776 [Ref: A-42].

FERRELL, John. Private who enlisted on July 25, 1776 [Ref: A-42, A-49].

FERRELL [FERROL], Joseph. Private, 7th Maryland Regiment, enlisted on June 8, 1780 [Ref: A-312].

FERRELL, Thomas. Private who enlisted on May 5, 1778, and served in the 2nd Maryland Regiment [Ref: A-294, A-322].

FERRENCE [FERRINS], Henry. Private who enlisted on May 20, 1778 [Ref: A-323]. "Henry Ferrins" was in the German Regiment at White Plains on September 5, 1778, under Lt. Col. Weltner [Ref: A-267].

FERRENCE [FARRANCE], Nicholas. Private in the 7th Maryland Regiment from April 22, 1778 until discharged on April 1, 1779 [Ref: A-206].

FERROLLET, Leonard. Non-Enroller who was fined by the Committee of Observation in April, 1776 [Ref: E-248].

FERVER, Leonard. Juror to the Oath of Allegiance in March, 1778 [Ref: S-264, but not listed in Ref: C-24].

FERVER, Philip. Juror to the Oath of Allegiance in March, 1778 [Ref: S-264, but not listed in Ref: C-24].

FETTIE, Abraham. Private in German Regiment, 1776, in Capt. Henry Fister's company under the command of Col. Hussecker [Ref: A-261].

FEUERSTEIN, Nicholas and Mathias. See "Nicholas Firestone," q.v.

FEVOTT, John Peter. Defective from the Maryland Line on May 4, 1780 [Ref: A-414].

FEY, Mary. See "John Cronise," q.v.

FICHE, John. Private stationed at Fort Frederick on June 27, 1778, in Capt. John Kershner's company, guarding prisoners of war [Ref: A-328].

FICKLE, Benjamin. Private who enlisted April 6, 1778 [Ref: A-315]. Sergeant, 7th Maryland Regiment, involved in recruiting in 1780 [Ref: V-176]. "Officer entitled to promotion in his own regiment previous to January 1, 1781." [Ref: A-365]. "On March 2, 1827, the Treasurer of the Western Shore of Maryland was directed to pay to Benjamin Fickle, of Muskingum County, Ohio, during life, half yearly, the half pay of a lieutenant, for his services during the Revolutionary War." [Ref: G-341].

FICKLE, Isaac. Substitute on June 13, 1781, and marched with Capt. Dyer [Ref: D-1814].

FIEGLEY, George. Private who enlisted on July 19, 1776 [Ref: A-51].

FIEGLEY, Peter. Private who enlisted on July 19, 1776 [Ref: A-51].

FIFER, George. Juror to the Oath of Allegiance in 1778 [Ref: C-24].

FILENBOCH, Christian. Associator in December, 1775 [Ref: E-167]. Juror to the Oath of Allegiance in 1778 [Ref: C-24].

FILLAR, Jacob. Associator in December, 1775 [Ref: E-167]. Juror to the Oath of Allegiance in 1778 [Ref: C-24].

FILLER, Andrew. Corporal in the German Regiment, muster roll dated October 23, 1776 [Ref: A-263].

FILLER, Frederick. Private in the German Regiment, on muster roll dated October 23, 1776 [Ref: A-264]. One "Fredrik. Filter" was a private in the German Regiment until discharged on July 26, 1779 [Ref: A-265].

FILSON [FILLSON], James. Private in the 7th Maryland Regiment on May 25, 1778, and subsequently "deserted from the hospital, time unknown." [Ref: A-207].

FILSON, Samuel. Associator in December, 1775 [Ref: E-166]. Juror to the Oath of Allegiance in 1778 [Ref: C-24]. Private who enlisted on April 18, 1778 [Ref: A-315]. Sergeant in the 7th Maryland Regiment on December 16, 1779, and in the 1st Maryland Regiment in 1781, and served in the Southern Army of the United States under Lt. William Lamar in the late Capt. Beatty's company. Assigned to "recruiting in Maryland from January to July, 1781." [Ref: A-207, A-389].

FINACY, John. Militia substitute on June 6, 1778 [Ref: A-325]. Private in the 7th Maryland Regiment from July 1, 1778, through December, 1778, when discharged [Ref: A-206].

FINACY [FINNESSEE], Robert. "Robert Finnessee" was a substitute on June 13, 1781, and marched with Capt. Lynn [Ref: D-1814].

FINACY [FINNISEE], William. "William Finacy" was a substitute on June 6, 1778 [Ref: A-325]. "William Finnisee" signed as a Juror to the Oath of Allegiance in March, 1778 [Ref: S-264, but not listed in Ref: C-24]. "William Finacy" was a private in the 7th Maryland Regiment from July 1, 1778, to December, 1779, when "absent without leave." [Ref: A-206].

FINCH, Joseph. Private who enlisted on July 24, 1776 [Ref: A-50].

FINDLAY, William. Soldier of the Revolution who died in Frederick County on April 5, 1821 [Ref: F-471].

FINE, Peter. Private who enlisted on July 1, 1776, in Capt. Peter Mantz's company; marched from Frederick Town to Leonardtown, and from there to Philadelphia, arriving on August 23, 1776 [Ref: A-47]. Applied for a pension (S2209) in Knox County, Ohio, a resident of Wayne Township, Ohio, on September 27, 1832, aged 82, stating he was born in Morristown, New Jersey in 1750 and removed at age 21 to Frederick County, Maryland [Ref: T-1191 mistakenly states Frederick County, MA (Massachusetts) rather than MD (Maryland), which is an apparent typographical error in that source]. Peter volunteered "about the last of July or first of August, 1776, and left it about last of November or first of December of same year having served 4 months." He marched from Maryland to Philadelphia and then to New York, and fought in the Battle of White Plains on October 28, 1776. Shortly afterward he was put into a hospital as a nurse, where he continued until he was taken sick and was removed with the rest of the sick back to Philadelphia where he remained until he was discharged. He again entered the service about August 1, 1777, as a volunteer and left it about the middle of November the same year, serving about two and a half months. He marched from Fredericktown to Leonards Town in Pennsylvania and joined General Wayne at Peola. From there he went to Perqueyous Creek and joined Gen. Washington and they fought in the Battle of Germantown on October 4, 1777. He returned to camp and was subsequently discharged, which paper he has lost. At the time of his application for a pension, he stated he "had a record of his age on a blank leaf of his father's big Bible which he believes is now in his trunk, but he has been blind and unable to see for more than 14 years. Christopher Myers, William Myers, John Bates, Henry Rhodes, and others of his neighborhood can testify to his character for truth and veracity and good behavior." On August 2, 1837, Peter made another application stating that his certificate had been lost some time between

September 4, 1835 and the first of March, 1836, at his residence in Wayne Township in Knox County, Ohio. "He has no recollection of seeing it after the drawing of his pension on September 4, 1835." [Ref: T-1191, K-26].

FINER, Daniel. Associator in December, 1775 [Ref: E-166]. Juror to the Oath of Allegiance in 1778 [Ref: C-24].

FINK, Nicholas. See "David Stottlemeyer," q.v.

FINLEY, Peter. Drummer in the German Regiment, 1776 [Ref: A-266].

FINNESSEE, Robert and William. See "Robert and William Finacy."

FIRESTONE, Matthias (April 5, 1744 - 1829). Matthias Feuerstein [Firestone] married about 1774 Mary Ann Beaver (Bieber). During the Revolution he served in the militia of York County, Pennsylvania. They settled on a farm in Frederick before 1787. In 1790 Mathias and Mary Ann were living in Frederick County with the following of their 14 children. Later the family except for Jacob moved to southwestern Pennsylvania and Ohio: Jacob Firestone (1775-1830) married Mary Mohl (1780-1832), both buried at Mt. Olivet Cemetery at Frederick; Sarah Firestone (born 1778) married Daniel Perky (died 1854) and lived in Holmes County, Ohio; John F. Firestone (born 1782, Frederick Lutheran Church) married Rachel Rowler (died 1848) and lived in Columbiana County, Ohio; George Firestone (born 1784) married Rebecca Karl (died 1851) and lived in Wayne County, Ohio; Solomon Firestone (born 1786) married Elizabeth Baird (died 1841) and lived in Stark County, Ohio; Mary Firestone (born 1788) married Richard Karl and lived in Columbiana County, Ohio; and, Daniel F. Firestone (born 1796). "Descendants of Jacob Firestone made notable contributions to Frederick, Maryland, but now the name has almost disappeared from the county." [Ref: O-46, U-2593].

FIRESTONE, Nicholas Jr. Nicholas Feuerstein [Firestone] arrived at Philadelphia [from northern Alsace] in 1753 and in 1761 married Eva Catharina Schwab. After living in Bedford County, Pennsylvania and serving in the Revolutionary War, they settled in 1786 on a farm near Trapp (later Jefferson) in southern Middletown Valley. In 1796 they sold their Maryland farm and purchased a farm three miles from Natural Bridge, Virginia. Of their eight children, none apparently remained in Frederick County, but migrated on to Virginia, Ohio, Tennessee, and Pennsylvania. [Ref: O-46. Also, see Ref: M-9:2-14].

FIRMWALD, Lawrence. Associator in December, 1775 [Ref: E-167]. Juror to the Oath of Allegiance in 1778 [Ref: C-24, and S-624, which spelled the name "Lawr. Farmevald."].

FIROR [FERO], Henry. "Henry Firor" served in the militia (no dates given), and pensioned in 1831 [Ref: J-33]. "Henry Fero" was paid for services rendered to the military in April, 1780 [Ref: V-151].

FIRTHHUNT, Henry. 2nd lieutenant in the 35th Battalion of militia on December 28, 1776, in Capt. Little's company [Ref: B-75, X-555].

FISH, Thomas. Private who enlisted on July 19, 1776 [Ref: A-51].

FISHBURN, Philip. Served on the Committee of Observation in 1775 [Ref: I-85].

FISHER, A. See "Jacob Brunner," q.v.

FISHER, Adam (1736 - August 27, 1787). Dr. Fisher was a graduate of "a German University" and had a large practice in Frederick County [Ref: E-303]. Chosen to serve on the Committee of Observation in 1775 [Ref: E-302, I-85], and enrolled as an Associator in December, 1775 [Ref: E-166]. Member of the State Constitutional Convention in 1776. Commissioned as Surgeon in Col Beatty's Battalion on January 10, 1777 [Ref: E-303]. "Adam Fischer" was noted on July 13, 1776, by Col. Charles Beatty, as "a man of credit and may be depended on." [Ref: A-47]. Juror to the Oath of Allegiance in March, 1778 [Ref: C-24]. "Adam Fischer" served in the House of Delegates from the Middle District on August 14, 1776 [Ref: F-476, F-479]. "Adam Fisher" died testate on August 27, 1787 and his will was probated on September 18, 1787, naming wife Margaret and children John, Adam, Elizabeth, Catharine, Christianna, Amelia, and Barbara "Fischer." [Ref: M-7:90, F-470].

FISHER, Balser. Private in the German Regiment, muster roll dated October 23, 1776 [Ref: A-264].

FISHER, Daniel. Private who enlisted on July 19, 1776 [Ref: A-51].

FISHER, George. Sergeant in Capt. Abraham Hayter's company of militia in 1775 [Ref: E-52].

FISHER, Henry. Private who enlisted on August 5, 1776 in the Flying Camp under Capt. Philip Meroney [Ref: A-45, N-30:112]. Private who enlisted on April 21, 1778 [Ref: A-320]. Served in the German Regiment at White Plains on September 5, 1778, under Lt. Col. Weltner [Ref: A-267].

FISHER, Jacob. Associator in December, 1775 [Ref: E-167]. Non-Enroller who was fined by the Committee of Observation in May, 1776 [Ref: E-248]. Juror to the Oath of Allegiance in 1778 [Ref: C-24].

FISHER, Philip. Private in the German Regiment, roll dated October 23, 1776, and was discharged on July 26, 1779 [Ref: A-264, A-265]. Enlisted again in Frederick County on July 25, 1780, and marched to Annapolis under Capt. Beatty [Ref: A-344]. Private in 1st Maryland Regiment, disabled at Battle of Guilford Court House, his invalid's pension commenced on November 29, 1783, and ceased on November 1, 1789 [Ref: A-630, A-631]. Philip Fisher, private, German Regiment, Revolutionary Army, pensioned on February 8, 1828 at $40 per annum from March 4, 1789, under Act of June 7, 1785. Private in Maryland Line, aged 86, from Frederick County, pensioned January 26, 1819, at $96 per annum from April 8, 1818 [Ref: G-341, citing the U. S. Pension Rolls of 1835]. However, Ref: T-1200 states Philip Fisher applied for a pension on April 8, 1818, aged 70 (not 86) and in 1820 he stated he was aged "75?". He married Margaret Albrecht on June 27, 1790, in Frederick County and in 1820 he had a wife named Catherine, aged about 63, plus a daughter Mary, aged 25, and son Henry, aged 11. Philip died on February 8, 1839, and his widow received a pension (W3972). She died on February 10, 1844. A son John Fisher applied on October 29, 1844, in Frederick County, aged 43, referring to his mother's name as both Margaret and Mariah. He applied for himself and his siblings: Philip Fisher, Henry Fisher, Mary Johnson (wife of Thomas Johnson), Susanna Powell (wife of William Powell), and Catharine Fisher. [Ref: T-1200, J-25, F-475].

FISTER, Henry. Associator in December, 1775 [Ref: E-167]. Captain in the German Regiment in July, 1776, under Colonel Nicholas Hussecker [Ref: A-261, X-48]. Juror to Oath of Allegiance in March, 1778 [Ref: C-24].

FISTER, John. Associator in December, 1775 [Ref: E-167]. Juror to the Oath of Allegiance in 1778 [Ref: C-24].

FITCHER, Geo. Lodo. [George Lodowick]. Militia substitute from May to December 10, 1781, and "marched to Annapolis." [Ref: A-653].

FITZGERALD, Benjamin. Sergeant, 1st Maryland Regiment, enlisted in October, 1779, and served in the Southern Army of the United States under Lt. William Lamar in the late Capt. Beatty's company. He was "recruiting in Maryland from January to July, 1781." [Ref: A-389]. "On March 7, 1834, the Treasurer of the Western Shore of Maryland was directed to pay to Benjamin Fitzgerald, of Kentucky, during life, quarterly, the half pay of a quartermaster sergeant, for the services rendered by him during the Revolution." [Ref: G-341]. "Benjamin Fitzjarrald" was a militia private in 1776 [Ref: A-42].

FITZGERALD, Henry. Private in the 7th Maryland Regiment from July 20, 1778, to April 9, 1779, when he was discharged [Ref: A-208].

FITZGERALD, James. Private who enlisted April 3, 1778, and served in the 2nd Maryland Regiment [Ref: A-294]. A "James Fitzjarrold" enrolled as an Associator in December, 1775 [Ref: E-166]. Juror to the Oath of Allegiance in 1778 [Ref: C-24].

FITZGERALD [FITZJARLD], Michael. Private, 7th Maryland Regiment, from May 28, 1777, until August 16, 1780, when reported missing (after the Battle of Camden, South Carolina). [Ref: A-207, A-311].

FITZGERALD [FITZJAROLD], Nicholas. Private, 1st Maryland Regiment, enlisted on May 2, 1778, and served in the Southern Army of the United States under Lt. William Lamar in the late Capt. Beatty's company and the light infantry until discharged on May 2, 1781 [Ref: A-391]. "On February 16, 1820, the Treasurer of the Western Shore was directed to pay to Nicholas Fitzgerald, of Washington County, half pay of a private for his Revolutionary War services." [Ref: G-341]. Served in the 7th Maryland Regiment [Ref: A-207].

FITZJAROLD, ---ar'y [sic]. Private, 1st Maryland Regiment, 1781, and served in the Southern Army of the United States under Lt. William Lamar in the late Capt. Beatty's company. Record indicates he was in the hospital in July, 1781 [Ref: A-392].

FITZPATRICK, Lawrence. Private who enlisted on April 29, 1778, and served in the 2nd Maryland Regiment [Ref: A-294].

FITZPATRICK, Philip. Militia substitute on June 6, 1778 [Ref: A-325]. Served as a private in the German Regiment at White Plains on September 5, 1778, under Lt. Col. Ludwick Weltner [Ref: A-266].

FLACK, James. Private stationed at Fort Frederick on June 27, 1778, in Capt. John Kershner's company, guarding prisoners of war [Ref: A-328].

FLACK, Lucas. Sergeant in Capt. John Stoner's company of militia in 1775 [Ref: E-56].

FLACK, Philip. Private who enlisted July 1, 1776 or July 19, 1776 [Ref: A-47, A-51].

FLAHERTY, Stephen. Private, 7th Maryland Regiment, 1780, enlisted in Frederick Town between January and April, 1780, and reported as "gone to Camp" [Ref: A-334]. "Stephen Flaharty" was a sergeant in the 1st Maryland Regiment in 1781, and served in the Southern Army of the United States under Lt. Wm. Lamar in the late Capt. Beatty's company; "in hospital from June 19 to July, 1781." [Ref: A-389].

FLANNIGAN, Richard. Private in the 7th Maryland Regiment from January to May, 1778 [Ref: A-207].

FLAUTT, Jacob. See "John Wolf (Woolf)," q.v.

FLECK [FLICK, FLEEK], George. "George Fleek" was an Associator in December, 1775 [Ref: E-166], and Juror to the Oath of Allegiance in 1778 [Ref: C-24]. "George Flick" was a private who enlisted on July 20,

1776 [Ref: A-50]. "George Fleck" died testate in 1786, leaving a wife Eva Elizabeth and children Jacob, George, Philip, and Peter [Ref: M-7:29].

FLECK [FLICK], John. "John Flick" was a private in the German Regiment on the muster roll dated October 23, 1776 [Ref: A-264]. "John Fliet" [Flick?] was a private in the German Regiment until discharged on July 26, 1779 [Ref: A-265].

FLECK [FLEEK], Philip. "Philip Fleek" was an Associator in 1775 [Ref: E-166]. "Philip Fleck" was a Juror to the Oath of Allegiance in 1778 [Ref: C-24].

FLECKINGER [FLICKINGER], Andrew. Non-Enroller who was fined by the Committee of Observation in April, 1776 [Ref: E-248].

FLECKINGER, Michael. "Draught," May to December 10, 1781, and "marched to Annapolis." [Ref: A-653].

FLEGLE, Charles. Juror to the Oath of Allegiance in March, 1778 [Ref: S-264, but not listed in Ref: C-24].

FLEMING [FLEMMING], James. Associator who was appointed "to hand about the Association paper" in Upper Kittockton [Catoctin] Hundred in 1775 [Ref: E-305]. 1st lieutenant in Capt. Michael Troutman's militia company in the 4th Battalion from November 29, 1775, to at least October 13, 1777, Catoctin Battalion [Ref: E-51, H-14, B-75]. Justice of the Peace in 1777 [Ref: F-476].

FLEMING [FLIMING], Patrick. Private in the German Regiment until discharged on August 9, 1779 [Ref: A-265].

FLEMMING, Nathaniel and Jennet. See "Nathaniel Patterson," q.v.

FLEMMING, Samuel. Associator in December, 1775 [Ref: E-166]. Juror to the Oath of Allegiance in 1778 [Ref: C-24]. Loaned $1,000 for the use of the State of Maryland in June, 1780 [Ref: V-520]. Provided wheat for the military in May, 1782 [Ref: R-516]. One Samuel Flemming died testate in 1788, naming wife Allice and children Arthur, Joseph, Thomas, Samuel (deceased), John, and Robert, and daughter Allice [Ref: M-7:92].

FLEMMING, Thomas ("T. Flemming, Rock Creek Hundred"). Appointed by the Committee of Correspondence to solicit subscriptions in 1775 to purchase arms and ammunition [Ref: I-86]. 1st lieutenant in the 34th Battalion of militia on May 15, 1776 [Ref: B-75, W-426].

FLETCHER, Jacob. "Jacob Fletser" was a sergeant in Capt. Samuel Shaw's company of militia in 1775 [Ref: E-51]. "Jacob Fletcher" was 2nd lieutenant in Capt. Watson's company in the 33rd Battalion on January 10, 1777 [Ref: B-75].

FLETCHER, John (Sugarland Hundred). Appointed by the Committee of Correspondence to solicit subscriptions in 1775 to purchase arms and ammunition [Ref: I-86].

FLETCHER, Martin. Private who was enlisted on July 20, 1776 by Capt. Jacob Good [Ref: A-46].

FLETCHER, Philip. Private who was enlisted on July 20, 1776 by Capt. Jacob Good [Ref: A-46].

FLETCHER, Richard. Private who enlisted on August 5, 1776 in the Flying Camp under Capt. Philip Meroney [Ref: A-45, N-30:112].

FLETCHER, Samuel. Private who enlisted May 20, 1778 [Ref: A-323].

FLICK, George and John. See "George and John Fleck," q.v.

FLICKINGER, Andrew. See "Andrew Fleckinger," q.v.

FLIGH, Nal. [sic]. Juror to the Oath of Allegiance in March, 1778 [Ref: S-264, but not listed in Ref: C-24].

FLINT, Joseph (Linton Hundred). Appointed by the Committee of Correspondence to solicit subscriptions in 1775 to purchase arms and ammunition [Ref: I-86]. Gave money in the amount of 2 lbs. 5 sh. for arms and ammunition for the militia in 1775 [Ref: E-62].

FLOARY, Robert. Ensign in the Skipton District Militia on July 27, 1776, in Capt. Andrew Hynes' company [Ref: B-75, X-127].

FLOHRE, John. Associator in December, 1775 [Ref: E-166]. Juror to Oath of Allegiance in 1778 [Ref: C-24]. "John Floore" was drafted June 2, 1783 [Ref: B-169].

FLOOK, Jacob (of John). See "Lawrence Everhart," q.v.

FLOROUGH, Jacob Jr. Non-Enroller who was fined by the Committee of Observation in April, 1776 [Ref: E-248].

FLOROUGH, Jacob Sr. Non-Enroller who was fined by the Committee of Observation in April, 1776 [Ref: E-248].

FLOWDEN, John. Associator in December, 1775 [Ref: E-167]. Juror to the Oath of Allegiance in 1778 [Ref: C-24].

FLOWER, Jacob. Militia substitute from May to December 10, 1781, and "marched to Annapolis." [Ref: A-653].

FOGEL [FOGLE], Andrew [Andreas Vogler]. (July 19, 1727 - July 27, 1786, Woodsboro, Maryland). Associator in December, 1775 [Ref: E-166]. Juror to the Oath of Allegiance in 1778 [Ref: C-24]. Loaned $400 for the use of the State of Maryland in June, 1780 [Ref: V-520]. "Andrew (Andreas) Vogel, or Fogle (1727-1786), from Hettenhausen near Fulda, Germany, about 1747 settled near Rocky Hill Church. He married Susannah Catherine Bager (or Baugher) and had these children baptized at Rocky Hill Church: Mattheis, 1768; Johan Baltzer, 1771;

Elizabeth, 1773." [Ref: O-152]. "Andrew Fogle" died testate in 1786, leaving a wife Susanna Catharine and children Mathias, Balser, Philip, Henry, Susanna, and Catharine [Ref: M-7:30]. Another source states Andrew Fogle (or Andreas Vogler) married Susanna Catharine Barth in November, 1753, and they are buried at Grace Evangelical Church, Frederick County. A son, Balser Fogle (Johann Balthasar Vogel) was born on May 6, 1771 and married Catharine Hertzog on August 18, 1789 [Ref: U-2715].

FOGEL [FOGLE], David. Associator in December, 1775 [Ref: E-167]. Juror to the Oath of Allegiance in 1778 [Ref: C-24].

FOGEL [FOGLE], Henry. Private in the Middle District Militia in 1776 in Capt. Valentine Creager's company [Ref: A-72].

FOGEL [FOGLE], John. Drummer in Capt. Joseph Wood, Jr.'s company of militia in 1775 [Ref: E-53]. Private in the German Regiment, muster roll dated October 23, 1776 [Ref: A-264].

FOGEL [FOGLE], Michael. Associator in December, 1775 [Ref: E-167]. Juror to the Oath of Allegiance in 1778 [Ref: C-24].

FOGELY, Chr. Private who enlisted on July 19, 1776 [Ref: A-51].

FOGLER, Simon. Private in the German Regiment, muster roll dated October 23, 1776 [Ref: A-264].

FOGLESONG, George. Juror to the Oath of Allegiance in March, 1778 [Ref: S-264, but not listed in Ref: C-24].

FOGWELL, George. Sergeant in the 7th Maryland Regiment on January 16, 1777, until reported "deserted" on January 23, 1778. Re-joined as a private on July 26, 1778 [Ref: A-207].

FOLLENWIDER, Henry. Associator in December, 1775 [Ref: E-167]. Juror to the Oath of Allegiance in 1778 [Ref: C-24].

FORACH [?], Daniel. Juror to the Oath of Allegiance in March, 1778 [Ref: S-264, but not listed in Ref: C-24].

FORBEY, William. Private who enlisted on May 19, 1778, and served in the 2nd Maryland Regiment [Ref: A-294, A-323].

FORD, Benjamin. Associator in December, 1775 [Ref: E-166]. Clerk of the Committee of Observation in 1776 [Ref: E-242]. Juror to the Oath of Allegiance in 1778 [Ref: C-24].

FOREMAN, Daniel. Associator in December, 1775 [Ref: E-167]. Juror to the Oath of Allegiance in 1778 [Ref: C-24].

FOREMAN, Jacob. Juror to the Oath of Allegiance in March, 1778 [Ref: S-264, but not listed in Ref: C-24].

FOREMAN [FORMAN], John. Juror to the Oath of Allegiance in March, 1778 [Ref: S-264, but not listed in Ref: C-24].

FORNEY, James. Private in the German Regiment until discharged on July 26, 1779 [Ref: A-208, A-265].

FORNEY, Mary Catherine. See "Nicholas Keefhover (Kefauver)," q.v.

FORQUER, William. "Draught," May to December 10, 1781, and "marched to Annapolis." [Ref: A-653].

FORRIS, John. 1st lieutenant in Capt. William Shields' company in the 35th Battalion of militia on December 28, 1776 [Ref: B-76, X-555]. Also, see "John Faris," q.v.

FORSHEY, Mary. See "John Baum," q.v.

FORSYTHE, Jacob. Private who enlisted on July 25, 1776 [Ref: A-51].

FORTNEY (FORTENEY), Margaret. See "Jacob Schley," q.v., and "John Thomas Schley," q.v.

FORTUNE, William. Militia substitute on June 3, 1778 [Ref: A-325].

FOSNEY, David. Private stationed at Fort Frederick on June 27, 1778, in Capt. John Kershner's company, and guarding prisoners of war [Ref: A-328].

FOSTER, George. Associator in December, 1775 [Ref: E-167]. Juror to the Oath of Allegiance in 1778 [Ref: C-24].

FOSTER, John. Private who enlisted on July 1, 1776 in Capt. Peter Mantz's company; marched from Frederick Town to Leonardtown, and from there to Philadelphia, arriving August 23, 1776 [Ref: A-47].

FOSTER, Moses. Private who enlisted on April 23, 1778 [Ref: A-320]. Private in the 1st Maryland Regiment in 1780 who served in the Southern Army of the United States under Lt. William Lamar in the late Capt. Beatty's company, 1781. He also served as a "B. Smith" [Blacksmith] in July, 1781 [Ref: A-391].

FOUNGER, ---- [blank]. Lieutenant in the militia on December 6, 1781 [Ref: B-76].

FOUT, Adam. See "Adam Psaut," q.v.

FOUT [FAUTH], Maria Margaretha. See "John Shellman," q.v.

FOUT, Peter. See "Peter Faut," q.v.

FOUT, William. Associator in December, 1775 [Ref: E-166]. Juror to the Oath of Allegiance in 1778 [Ref: C-24].

FOUTH, Henry. Associator in December, 1775 [Ref: E-166]. Juror to the Oath of Allegiance in 1778 [Ref: C-24].

FOUTS, Baltis. Corporal in Capt. William Duvall's company of militia in 1775 [Ref: E-54].

FOUTS, Michael (Pipe Creek Hundred). Non-Enroller who was fined by the Committee of Observation in May, 1776 [Ref: E-248].

FOWEE, Jacob. Private in the German Regiment, muster roll dated October 23, 1776 [Ref: A-264].
FOWLER, Clement. Associator in December, 1775 [Ref: E-166, which misspelled his name "Cement Fowler."]. Juror to Oath of Allegiance in 1778 [Ref: C-24].
FOWLER, John. Associator in December, 1775 [Ref: E-166]. (This name appeared twice on the list of Associators). One subscribed to the Oath of Allegiance in 1778 [Ref: C-24]. One was a 2nd lieutenant in the Frederick County militia in the Linganore Battalion, with Capt. Winchester's company, on January 17, 1777, and one (or the same person) was a 2nd lieutenant in the Washington County militia in Capt. Spires' company on June 22, 1778 [Ref: B-76, Y-54, Z-145].
FOWLER, Thomas. Private who enlisted on July 18, 1776 [Ref: A-50].
FOX, Balser. Associator in December, 1775 [Ref: E-166]. Juror to the Oath of Allegiance in 1778 [Ref: C-24]. Frederick Lutheran records show a Balthasar Fox (or Fuchs) and wife Juliana had a child baptized in 1775 (no name given). [Ref: O-99].
FOX, Christopher. Served in the militia during the Revolutionary War (no dates given). Frederick Lutheran records show a Christopher Fox (or Fuchs) and wife Magdalena had a child baptized in 1765 (no name given). [Ref: O-99].
FOX, Edward. Served in the militia during the Revolutionary War (no dates given). [Ref: O-99].
FOX, Elijah. Served in the militia during the Revolutionary War (no dates given). [Ref: O-99].
FOX, Frederick. Served in the militia during the Revolutionary War (no dates given). [Ref: O-99].
FOX, Henry. Associator in December, 1775 [Ref: E-166]. Private in the Middle District Militia in 1776 in Capt. Valentine Creager's company [Ref: A-72]. Juror to the Oath of Allegiance in 1778 [Ref: C-24]. Frederick Lutheran records show Henry Fox (or Fuchs) and wife Anna Eva had a child baptized in 1775 (no name given). [Ref: O-99].
FOX, Jeremiah. 1st lieutenant in Fredericktown Battalion of militia on January 23, 1782, in Capt. Shellman's company [Ref: B-76].
FOX, Jophel. Associator in December, 1775 [Ref: E-166]. Juror to the Oath of Allegiance in 1778 [Ref: C-24].
FOX, Michael. Associator in December, 1775 [Ref: E-166]. Private in the Middle District Militia in 1776 in Capt. Valentine Creager's company [Ref: A-72, O-99]. Juror to the Oath of Allegiance in 1778 [Ref: C-24].

Frederick Lutheran records show a Michael Fox (or Fuchs) and wife Anna Maria had a child baptized in 1778 (no name given). [Ref: O-99].

FOX, Peter. Associator in December, 1775 [Ref: E-166]. Juror to the Oath of Allegiance in 1778 [Ref: C-24]. Frederick Lutheran records show a Peter Fox (or Fuchs) and wife Margaretha had a child baptized in 1769 (no name given). [Ref: O-99].

FOY, John. Drafted on June 13, 1781, and marched with Capt. Dyer [Ref: D-1814].

FRALEY, Henry. See "Johan Heinrich Froelich," q.v.

FRANCE [FRANTZ], Abram. Private in the German Regiment until discharged on July 19, 1779 [Ref: A-208].

FRANCE, Christian. Private who enlisted July 24, 1776 [Ref: A-50].

FRANCE, Nicholas. Private who enlisted July 20, 1776 [Ref: A-50].

FRANKLIN, Charles. See "Jacob Gilbert," q.v.

FRANKLIN, John. Militia substitute from May to December 10, 1781, and "marched to Annapolis." [Ref: A-653].

FRANKLIN, William. Private who enlisted July 18, 1776 [Ref: A-49].

FRASHER, John. 2nd lieutenant in the 34th Battalion of militia on June 11, 1776, in Capt. Thomas Frazer's company [Ref: B-76, W-476]. Also, see "John Frazier," q.v.

FRAZER, Jonathan. Juror to the Oath of Allegiance in March, 1778 [Ref: S-264, but not listed in Ref: C-24].

FRAZER [FRAZIER], Thomas. "Thomas Frazer" was 1st lieutenant in Capt. William Luckett, Jr.'s company in the 4th (34th?) Battalion on November 11, 1775 [Ref: E-55, B-76]. "Thomas Frazier" was an Associator in December, 1775 [Ref: E-166]. Juror to the Oath of Allegiance in 1778 [Ref: C-24, and S-624, which spelled the name "Frazer."]. Captain in the 34th Battalion of militia on June 11, 1776 [Ref: W-476].

FRAZIER, Henry. Associator in December, 1775 [Ref: E-166]. Juror to the Oath of Allegiance in 1778 [Ref: C-24].

FRAZIER, John. Associator in December, 1775 [Ref: E-166]. Juror to the Oath of Allegiance in 1778 [Ref: C-24]. See "John Frasher," q.v.

FRAZIER, William. Associator in December, 1775 [Ref: E-166]. Juror to the Oath of Allegiance in 1778 [Ref: C-24].

FREAM, William. Sergeant in Capt. Abraham Hayter's militia company in 1775 [Ref: E-52]. Militia substitute from May to December 10, 1781, and "marched to Annapolis." [Ref: A-653].

FREAS, Michael. Associator in December, 1775 [Ref: E-166]. Juror to the Oath of Allegiance in 1778 [Ref: C-24].

FREDERICK, John. Militia substitute from May to December 10, 1781, and "marched to Annapolis." [Ref: A-653].

FREE, George. Private who was enlisted on July 20, 1776, by Capt. Jacob Good [Ref: A-46].

FREELAND, Benjamin. Private in the Skipton District Militia under Capt. Thomas Waring on April 16, 1776 [Ref: B-167, D-1814].

FREEMAN, Francis. Private who enlisted on August 5, 1776, in the Flying Camp under Capt. Philip Meroney [Ref: A-45, N-30:112].

FREEMAN, Jacob. Private who was enlisted on July 20, 1776, by Capt. Jacob Good [Ref: A-46].

FREEMAN, Thomas. Private in the militia in July, 1776 [Ref: A-42].

FREMBACH, Jacob. Associator in December, 1775 [Ref: E-166]. Juror to the Oath of Allegiance in 1778 [Ref: C-24].

FREN, Andrew. See "Andrew Friend," q.v.

FRENCH, George. Associator in December, 1775 [Ref: E-166]. Non-Enroller who was fined by the Committee of Observation in April, 1776 [Ref: E-248]. Juror to the Oath of Allegiance in 1778 [Ref: C-24]. Private in the Skipton District Militia under Capt. Thomas Waring on April 16, 1776 [Ref: B-167, D-1814]. Also, see "Joshua Testill," q.v.

FRENCH, Israel. Non-Enroller who was fined by the Committee of Observation in April, 1776 [Ref: E-248].

FRENCH, Thomas. Associator in December, 1775 [Ref: E-166]. Sheriff in 1775 [Ref: F-480]. Juror to the Oath of Allegiance in 1778 [Ref: C-24].

FRESHOR, Jacob. See "Jacob Froushoir," q.v.

FRESHOUR, Adam. See "Adam Froshour," q.v.

FREY [FRYE], Abrm. Juror to the Oath of Allegiance in March, 1778 [Ref: S-264, but not listed in Ref: C-24].

FREY [FRY], Barnard. Corporal in the German Regiment, muster roll dated October 23, 1776 [Ref: A-263]. "Bernard Fry" was a corporal in the German Regiment in 1779 [Ref: A-264].

FREY, Daniel. Non-Enroller who was fined by the Committee of Observation in April, 1776 [Ref: E-248].

FREY, Enoch. Associator in December, 1775 [Ref: E-166]. Juror to the Oath of Allegiance in 1778 [Ref: C-24].

FREY [FRY, FRYE], Isaac. Associator in December, 1775 [Ref: E-167]. Juror to the Oath of Allegiance in 1778 [Ref: S-264, C-24]. Isaac Fry [sic] died testate in early 1783, leaving a wife Margaret, and nephew Isaac Frey [sic], son of Abraham Frey [sic]. [Ref: M-6:32].

FREY [FRY], Jonathan. Associator in December, 1775 [Ref: E-166]. Non-Enroller who was fined by the Committee of Observation in April, 1776

[Ref: E-248]. Juror to the Oath of Allegiance in 1778 [Ref: C-24]. "Jonathan Fry" provided wheat for the military in June, 1782 [Ref: R-525].

FREY [FRYE], Nicholas. Associator in December, 1775 [Ref: E-166], and Juror to the Oath of Allegiance in 1778 [Ref: C-24]. "Nicholas Frye" was a private in German Regiment in 1776 in Capt. Henry Fister's company under the command of Col. Nicholas Hussecker [Ref: A-261].

FRICKER, John. Private who enlisted on May 13, 1778, and served in the 2nd Maryland Regiment [Ref: A-294, A-322].

FRIDDLE, Jno. Juror to the Oath of Allegiance in March, 1778 [Ref: S-264, but not listed in Ref: C-24].

FRIEND [FREN], Andrew. Private in the 7th Maryland Regiment from December 30, 1777, to February 8, 1778; "deserted." [Ref: A-207].

FRIEND, Charles. Private who was enlisted on July 20, 1776, by Capt. Jacob Good [Ref: A-46].

FRIEND, Jacob (Conococheague). Appointed by the Committee of Correspondence to solicit subscriptions in 1775 to purchase arms and ammunition [Ref: I-86].

FRIEND [FRIND], Nicholas. Associator in December, 1775 [Ref: E-167]. Juror to the Oath of Allegiance in 1778 [Ref: C-24].

FRIEND, Tobias. Private in the German Regiment, muster roll dated October 23, 1776 [Ref: A-264].

FRINGER, Nicholas. 2nd lieutenant in the Linganore Battalion of Militia on June 22, 1778 [Ref: Z-144].

FRITCHY, Caspar. Associator in December, 1775 [Ref: E-166]. Juror to the Oath of Allegiance in 1778 [Ref: C-24].

FROELICH, Christian. Soldier in the Revolutionary War who died in Frederick County on March 23, 1830, aged 75 [Ref: F-473].

FROELICH, Johan Heinrich (1756-1830). Born at Wichmannshausen in northeastern Hesse, Heinrich Froelich (or "Henry Fraley") was a soldier in the Revolutionary War "who was interned at the barracks in Frederick during the war... and deserted from the barracks in 1783." He lived in the Emmittsburg District in 1800. [Ref: O-172].

FROGGAT, Richard. Private who enlisted on March 17, 1777, and in Capt. William Beatty's company, 7th Maryland Regiment, 1779 [Ref: A-311].

FROM [FRUM], William. "William From" was a private in the Middle District Militia in 1776, with Capt. Valentine Creager's company [Ref: A-72]. "William Frum" was a substitute on June 13, 1781 [Ref: D-1814]. Also, see "William Fream," q.v.

137

FROSHOUR, Adam. Private in the German Regiment in 1776, with Capt. Henry Fister's company under the command of Col. Nicholas Hussecker [Ref: A-261]. Mrs. Catharine Baker, daughter of Adam Freshour, died on the Wednesday before January 11, 1805, in Frederick [Ref: N-57].

FROUSHOIR, Jacob. Associator in December, 1775 [Ref: E-166]. Juror to the Oath of Allegiance in 1778 [Ref: C-24]. "Jacob Freshor" was 2nd Corporal in Capt. Christopher Stull's company of militia in 1775 [Ref: E-50].

FRUMANTLE, Francis. Private who enlisted July 19, 1776 [Ref: A-51].

FRY, Bernard, Isaac, Nicholas. See "Bernard, Isaac, Nicholas Frey."

FRYBACK, George. Private in the militia in July, 1776 [Ref: A-42].

FRYBACK, John. Private in the militia in July, 1776 [Ref: A-42].

FULFORD, John (Major). Passed recruits in Frederick County in July, 1776 [Ref: A-49].

FULHAM, Charles. Private who enlisted April 23, 1778 [Ref: A-320]. Served as a private in the German Regiment at the Battle of White Plains on September 5, 1778, under Lt. Col. Weltner [Ref: A-267].

FULLAM, Michael. Militia substitute on June 2, 1778 [Ref: A-324].

FULLER, Robert. Associator in December, 1775 [Ref: E-166]. Juror to the Oath of Allegiance in 1778 [Ref: C-24].

FULSOM, Jeremiah. Corporal in the militia, March 9, 1776 [Ref: B-166]. Also, "Jeremiah Fulsome" was a private who enlisted August 8, 1776 [Ref: A-49].

FULTON, Robert. Associator in December, 1775 [Ref: E-166]. Juror to the Oath of Allegiance in 1778 [Ref: C-24].

FUNDENBERGH, Daniel. Non-Enroller who was fined by the Committee of Observation in April, 1776 [Ref: E-248].

FUNDENBERGH, Lazarus. Non-Enroller who was fined by the Committee of Observation in April, 1776 [Ref: E-248].

FUNK, Henry. Gave money in the amount of 6 lbs. 15 sh. 10 p. for arms and ammunition for the militia in 1775 [Ref: E-63].

FUNK, Jacob (Upper Antietam). Appointed by the Committee of Correspondence to solicit subscriptions in 1775 to purchase arms and ammunition [Ref: I-86]. Served in the House of Delegates in 1774 [Ref: F-479]. Served on the Committee of Observation in 1775 [Ref: I-85]. Gave money in the amount of 9 lbs. 7 sh. 6 p. for arms and ammunition for the militia in 1775 [Ref: E-62].

FUNK, Peter. Associator in December, 1775 [Ref: E-166]. Juror to the Oath of Allegiance in 1778 [Ref: C-24].

FUNNER, John M. Private in the 1st Maryland Regiment in 1781 who served in the Southern Army of the United States under Lt. William Lamar in the late Capt. Beatty's company. Record indicates he was a prisoner of war on April 25, 1781 [Ref: A-391].

FURNEY, Abraham. Non-Enroller who was fined by the Committee of Observation in April, 1776 [Ref: E-248].

FURNEY [FURNY], Daniel. Associator in December, 1775 [Ref: E-166]. Juror to the Oath of Allegiance in 1778 [Ref: C-24].

FURNEY, Jacob. Non-Enroller who was fined by the Committee of Observation in April, 1776 [Ref: E-248].

FURNEY [FURNY], Michael. Ensign in the 35th Battalion of militia on December 28, 1776, in Capt. Peppel's company [Ref: B-76, X-555].

FURNIER, James. Private in the German Regiment, muster roll dated October 23, 1776 [Ref: A-264].

FY, John Simon. Associator in December, 1775 [Ref: E-166]. Juror to the Oath of Allegiance in 1778 [Ref: C-24].

GABER, Peter. Non-Enroller who was fined by the Committee of Observation in April, 1776 [Ref: E-248].

GABERT, Daniel. 1st lieutenant in Capt. Rodenbieler's company of militia in the 4th Battalion, November 29, 1775 [Ref: E-51, B-77].

GABLE, George. Captain in the militia on June 22, 1778 [Ref: Z-145, H-17, which spelled his name "Gabble."]. See "George Gobble," q.v.

GABLE, John. Private stationed at Fort Frederick on June 27, 1778, in Capt. John Kershner's company, and guarding prisoners of war [Ref: A-328].

GAITHER, Benjamin. 1st lieutenant in Capt. Pigman's company in the 29th Battalion, Frederick [now Montgomery] County, in March, 1776. [Ref: D-1814, W-289; but, Ref: B-77 indicates September 12, 1777].

GAITHER, Greenbury. 1st lieutenant in the Lower District Militia of Frederick [now Montgomery] County, under Capt. Edward Burgess on August 7, 1776 [Ref: A-42, although Ref: X-187 states he had been commissioned on July 26, 1776, and served under Capt. Benjamin Spyker]. Quartermaster in Montgomery County on August 30, 1777, in the 16th Battalion of militia [Ref: B-77].

GAITHER, Henry Sr. (upper part of New Foundland). Appointed by the Committee of Correspondence to solicit subscriptions in 1775 to purchase arms and ammunition [Ref: I-86].

GAITHER, John. 1st lieutenant in the Lower District Militia [now Montgomery County] under Capt. Edward Burgess on August 7, 1776 [Ref: A-42]. Captain in Montgomery County in 1777 [Ref: B-77].

GAITHER, Nicholas. Private who enlisted July 29, 1776 [Ref: A-44].
GAITHER, William. Ensign in Capt. Nathaniel Pigman's company, 29th Battalion, in Frederick [now Montgomery] County, on May 14, 1776. [Ref: D-1814, W-424, and B-77, which latter states May 15, 1776].
GALE, Edward. Ensign in Capt. Thomas Richardson's company in the Lower District Militia on April 20, 1776 [Ref: B-77, W-356].
GALLOWAY, Mary. See "David Lynn," q.v.
GALMAN, Henry. Corporal in Capt. Herman Yost's company of militia in 1775 [Ref: E-52].
GAMBER, Jacob, John and Peter. See "Jacob, John and Peter Gombar."
GAMBLER, Michael. Private in the German Regiment in 1779 [Ref: A-264]. Also, see "Michael Cambler," q.v.
GANDY, Jacob. Militia substitute on June 4, 1778 [Ref: A-325].
GANDY, Samuel. Ensign in the Linganore Battalion of militia on June 22, 1778, in Capt. Meridith's company [Ref: B-77, Z-144].
GANTT, Fielder. "Fielder Gaunt" was an Associator in December, 1775 [Ref: E-167], and a juror to the Oath of Allegiance in 1778 [Ref: C-24]. "Fielder Gantt" served in the House of Delegates, 1779-1780 [Ref: F-479].
GARCY, Samuel. Private, 1st Maryland Regiment who enlisted on April 27, 1778, and served in the Southern Army of the United States under Lt. William Lamar in the late Capt. Beatty's company until he transferred to the light infantry on March 12, 1781 [Ref: A-390].
GARDNER, George. Private who enlisted on May 17, 1778 [Ref: A-322].
GARDNER, Jacob. Associator in December, 1775 [Ref: E-167]. Juror to the Oath of Allegiance in 1778 [Ref: C-24].
GAREY, Henry. Associator in December, 1775 [Ref: E-167]. Juror to the Oath of Allegiance in 1778 [Ref: C-24].
GARNER, Edward (D. S. T.). Private who enlisted on July 25, 1776 [Ref: A-51].
GARRETT [GARROTT], Allen. Provided wheat for the military in June, 1782 [Ref: R-520].
GARRETT [GARRET], Barton. Private in the militia on March 9, 1776 [Ref: B-166]. Juror to the Oath of Allegiance in March, 1778 [Ref: S-264, but not listed in Ref: C-24].
GARRETT [GARROTT], John. Associator in December, 1775 [Ref: E-167]. Juror to the Oath of Allegiance in 1778 [Ref: C-24, S-264].
GARRISH, Francis. Defective from Maryland Line, 1780 [Ref: A-414].
GARTEN, William. Private in the militia in July, 1776 [Ref: A-42].

GARTH, James. Private, 4th Maryland Regiment. Disabled at the Battle of Ninety-Six; invalid pension commenced on November 29, 1783, and ceased on November 1, 1789 [Ref: A-630, A-631, F-475, which latter source stated he was in the 2nd Maryland Regiment].

GARTRELL, Charles. Private in the militia, July, 1776 [Ref: A-42].

GARTRELL, Joseph. Private in the militia, July, 1776 [Ref: A-42].

GARTRELL, Stephen. Private in the militia, July, 1776 [Ref: A-42].

GARVER, John Jr. Non-Enroller who was fined by the Committee of Observation in April, 1776 [Ref: E-248].

GARVER, John Sr. Non-Enroller who was fined by the Committee of Observation in April, 1776, but he apparently enrolled because the fine was remitted in June, 1776 [Ref: E-248].

GARVER, Martin. Non-Enroller who was fined by the Committee of Observation in April, 1776 [Ref: E-248].

GARVER, Martin (of John). Non-Enroller who was fined by the Committee of Observation in April, 1776 [Ref: E-248].

GARVER, Samuel. Non-Enroller who was fined by the Committee of Observation in April, 1776 [Ref: E-248].

GARVER, Samuel (of John). Non-Enroller who was fined by the Committee of Observation in April, 1776 [Ref: E-248].

GASKIN, John. Private who enlisted on August 5, 1776 [Ref: A-44].

GASSAWAY, Benjamin. Associator in December, 1775 [Ref: E-167]. Juror to the Oath of Allegiance in 1778 [Ref: C-24]. Apparently, another Benjamin Gassaway petitioned the General Assembly under the Act of May 12, 1780, stating he had been a non-juror to the Oath of Allegiance and Fidelity in 1778 due to "ignorance" and now desired relief under the Act and to take the Oath [Ref: L-101].

GASSAWAY, Richard. Non-Enroller who was fined by the Committee of Observation in June, 1776 [Ref: E-248]. Petitioned the General Assembly under the Act of May 12, 1780, stating that he had been a non-juror to the Oath of Allegiance and Fidelity in 1778 due to "ignorance" and now desired relief under the Act and to take the Oath [Ref: L-101].

GASSAWAY, Robert. Associator in December, 1775 [Ref: E-167]. Juror to the Oath of Allegiance in 1778 [Ref: C-24]. One Robert Gassaway was a private in the militia, but on February 26, 1776, he spoke out, advising "the poor people to lay down their arms and pay the duties and taxes laid upon by the King and Parliament.. [rather than]... be brought into slavery..." However, when formally charged, Robert informed the Council of Safety that he had signed the Association and had duly enrolled

141

himself in a company of militia in Frederick County, and "acknowledged at the time he had greatly misconducted himself, and was sorry that it should be thought that he would do anything to disunite the people of this province." He was fined and discharged from custody, and returned to duty [Ref: W-309, W-310].

GATHER, Richard. See "Joseph Holland," q.v.

GAUFF, James. Private who enlisted on July 13, 1776 [Ref: A-43].

GAUFF, John Baptist. Private who enlisted on July 13, 1776 [Ref: A-43].

GAUL, Richard. Private who enlisted on May 16, 1778 [Ref: A-322]. Served as a private in the German Regiment at the Battle of White Plains on September 5, 1778, under Lt. Col. Weltner [Ref: A-266].

GAVER, Daniel. Juror to the Oath of Allegiance in March, 1778 [Ref: S-264, but not listed in Ref: C-25].

GAVIN, Francis. Private in the German Regiment until discharged on July 26, 1779 [Ref: A-265].

GEASEY, Henry. Private in the militia who served in the Maryland Line. He applied for a pension (S8554) on November 14, 1832, aged 78, stating he lived in Frederick County at the time of enlistment [Ref: T-1329, and J-33, which latter source states he was aged 77].

GEBBARD, George. See "Joseph Doll," q.v.

GEBERT, John. Sergeant in Capt. Philip Rodenbieler's company of militia in 1775 [Ref: E-51].

GEBHART, Jacob. Associator in December, 1775 [Ref: E-167]. Juror to the Oath of Allegiance in 1778 [Ref: C-24].

GEDDIS, John. Substitute on May 4, 1781, and marched with Capt. Dyer [Ref: D-1814].

GEDULTIGH, Conrad. Corporal in Capt. John Stoner's company of militia in 1775 [Ref: E-56].

GEE, Richard. Private in the 1st Maryland Regiment in 1780, and served in the Southern Army of the United States under Lt. William Lamar in the late Capt. Beatty's company in 1781. Also served as a hospital orderly in July, 1781 [Ref: A-391].

GEEHAN, John. Private in the militia in July, 1776 [Ref: A-42].

GEERHERT, Jacob. Private in Capt. John Kershner's company; guarded prisoners at Fort Frederick, 1777-1778; and, discharged on June 5, 1778 [Ref: A-328].

GEIGER, Jacob. Associator in December, 1775 [Ref: E-167]. Juror to the Oath of Allegiance in 1778 [Ref: C-24].

GEISBERT, Jane. See "Andrew Michael," q.v.

GEISTE [?], Allen. Juror to the Oath of Allegiance in March, 1778 [Ref: S-264, but not listed in Ref: C-25].

GELSTRAP, Aaron and Effee. See "Levi Davis," q.v.

GENTILE, George. Private who enlisted July 18, 1776 [Ref: A-49].

GENTILE, Stephen. Private who enlisted July 25, 1776 [Ref: A-49].

GENTNER, Adam. Associator in December, 1775 [Ref: E-167]. Juror to the Oath of Allegiance in 1778 [Ref: C-24]. Private in the German Regiment, 1776, in Capt. Henry Fister's company under the command of Col. Nicholas Hussecker [Ref: A-261].

GEORGE, Martin Smith. Petitioned the General Assembly under the Act of May 12, 1780, stating that he had been a non-juror to the Oath of Allegiance and Fidelity in 1778 due to "ignorance" and now desired relief under the Act and to take the Oath [Ref: L-101].

GEORGE, Michael. Private in militia on March 9, 1776 [Ref: B-166].

GERINGER, David. Sergeant in Capt. Philip Rodenbieler's company of militia in 1775 [Ref: E-51].

GERRAND, Adam. Associator in December, 1775 [Ref: E-167]. Juror to the Oath of Allegiance in 1778 [Ref: C-24].

GETIG [GETTING], George. See "George Gittin (Getting)," q.v.

GETZENDANNER, Baltzer, or Baltis (1735-1795). Son of Christian Getzendanner (Giezendanner) and Anna Barbara Brunner, of Klein Schifferstadt, Germany, and grandson of Johan Jacobus Getzendanner of Wattwil, Switzerland [Ref: O-244]. "Baltis Ketzendanner" was 2nd lieutenant in Capt. John Stoner's militia company in 1775 [Ref: E-56, B-95]. "Baltzer Gitzadanner" was 1st lieutenant in Frederick Town Battalion of militia on May 12, 1779 [Ref: H-16, B-79, Z-387].

GETZENDANNER, Margaret. See "Frederick Kemp," q.v.

GETZENDANNER [GETZENDAMIER], Solomon. Soldier who served in the Maryland Militia and pensioned on December 29, 1827 [Ref: J-8, but not found in Ref: T-1336].

GEYER, Henry. Associator in December, 1775 [Ref: E-167]. Juror to the Oath of Allegiance in 1778 [Ref: C-25].

GHEEN [GHEIN], James. Corporal in Capt. John Haass' company of militia in 1775 [Ref: E-53]. Associator in December, 1775 [Ref: E-167]. Juror to the Oath of Allegiance in 1778 [Ref: C-25].

GHISELIN, John. 2nd lieutenant in the Middle District Militia in 1776 [Ref: A-44]. Captain of militia on January 4, 1777. Captain in the 7th Maryland Regiment from June 20, 1777, until June 1, 1779, when he resigned [Ref: A-210, A-326, B-78].

GIBBENEY, David. Associator in December, 1775 [Ref: E-167]. Juror to the Oath of Allegiance in 1778 [Ref: C-25].

GIBBONS, John. Private who enlisted on April 20, 1778 [Ref: A-324].

GIBBS, Abraham. "Abraham Gips" was an Associator in December, 1775 [Ref: E-167], and a Juror to the Oath of Allegiance in 1778 [Ref: C-25]. One "Abraham Gibbs, of Frederick Town," died testate in 1784, naming children Nicholas, Abraham, Elizabeth, and Rebecca [Ref: M-6:121].

GIBHART, George. Private who enlisted on February 27, 1778 [Ref: A-314].

GIBSON, Gideon. Non-Enroller who was fined by the Committee of Observation in April, 1776 [Ref: E-248]. "Gideon Gibson, sawyer" died testate in 1786, leaving a wife (not named) and "all my children," but only naming his daughter Ann [Ref: M-7:28].

GIDDY, Peter. Private who was enlisted on July 20, 1776 by Capt. Jacob Good [Ref: A-46].

GIESER, Mathias. Private in the German Regiment, muster roll dated October 23, 1776 [Ref: A-264].

GIGER, George. Drafted on June 2, 1783 [Ref: B-169].

GILBERT, Frederick. Associator in December, 1775 [Ref: E-167]. Juror to the Oath of Allegiance in 1778 [Ref: C-25].

GILBERT, Jacob. Petitioned the General Assembly under the Act of May 12, 1780, stating that he had been a non-juror to the Oath of Allegiance and Fidelity in 1778 due to "ignorance" and now desired relief under the Act and to take the Oath [Ref: L-101]. Jacob Gilbert died testate in 1790, leaving wife Magdalene and children Magdalene (wife of Jacob Haines and mother of Polly), Elizabeth (wife of Andrew Ridinger), Catherine, Hannah (wife of George Beamer), Margaret (wife of Amos Goslin), Susannah (wife of Charles Franklin), Eve, John (and grandson John Gilbert). [Ref: M-8:35].

GILBERT, Thomas. Served on the Committee of Observation in 1775 [Ref: I-85]. Associator in December, 1775 [Ref: E-167]. Non-Enroller who was fined by the Committee of Observation in April, 1776 [Ref: E-248]. Juror to the Oath of Allegiance in 1778 [Ref: C-25]. "Thomas Gilbert (died 1793) acquired land northwest of Harmony in Middletown Valley in 1752. He and wife Elizabeth had children Rebecca, Elizabeth, Susanna and Jeremiah (c1751-1822), who by wives Magdalena Catherine Weaver and Zepporah Powell had 23 children born in Frederick County. Most of the children and grandchildren lived in Montgomery County, Ohio, or Indiana." [Ref: O-175].

GILL, Thomas. Private who enlisted on August 5, 1776 in the Flying Camp under Capt. Philip Meroney [Ref: A-45, N-30:112]. Also, Thomas Gill, private, enlisted on January 28, 1778 [Ref: A-314].

GILLUM, John. Private who enlisted on July 18, 1776 [Ref: A-49].

GILMAN, William. Ensign in the Linganore Battalion of militia on January 17, 1777, in Capt. Meredith's company [Ref: B-78, Y-54].

GILMORE [GILMOUR], William. Private who enlisted on August 5, 1776 in the Flying Camp under Capt. Philip Meroney [Ref: N-30:111]. Reported as "deserted" (no date given). [Ref: A-45].

GIPS, Abraham. See "Abraham Gibbs," q.v.

GISINGER, John. Private who enlisted on July 1, 1776 in Capt. Peter Mantz's company; marched from Frederick Town to Leonardtown, and from there to Philadelphia, arriving August 23, 1776 [Ref: A-47].

GIST, Mordecai, Nathaniel, and John. See "John Sponseller," q.v.

GITTIN [GETTING, GETIG], George. Drummer in the German Regiment, muster roll dated October 23, 1776 [Ref: A-263]. "George Getting" was a private in the German Regiment until discharged on July 26, 1779 [Ref: A-212, A-265]. Possibly related to George Adam Geeting, or Guding (1741-1812), who settled near Keedysville in Washington County, Maryland [Ref: M-8:146].

GITTIN, Jacob. Fifer in the German Regiment, muster roll dated October 23, 1776 [Ref: A-263].

GITTIN, Peter. Private in the German Regiment, muster roll dated October 23, 1776 [Ref: A-264].

GITTINGS, Jeremiah. Paid for supplying horses for the military on September 1, 1780 [Ref: V-273].

GITTINGS, Thomas. Private in the militia, July, 1776 [Ref: A-42].

GITZADANNER, Baltzer. See "Baltzer Getzendanner," q.v.

GIVENS, Daniel. Sergeant in militia on March 9, 1776 [Ref: B-166].

GIVENS, Ezekiel. Private in the 7th Maryland Regiment from June 11, 1778, until April 11, 1779, when he was discharged [Ref: A-211].

GLADHILL, William. Private in militia, March 9, 1776 [Ref: B-167].

GLATZ, John. Drafted on June 13, 1781, and provided a substitute [Ref: D-1814].

GLAZE, James. Private who enlisted on July 22, 1776 [Ref: A-49].

GLAZE, Nathaniel. Private who enlisted July 25, 1776 [Ref: A-50].

GLORY, William. Private who enlisted on July 29, 1776 [Ref: A-43].

GLOVER, Richart [sic]. Provided wheat for the military in July, 1782 [Ref: R-534].

GLUMPHY, Mary W. See "Andrew Pees," q.v.

GOBBLE, Christeen. Private who was enlisted on July 20, 1776, by Capt. Jacob Good [Ref: A-46].

GOBBLE, George. Private who was enlisted on July 20, 1776, by Capt. Jacob Good [Ref: A-46]. Captain in the Linganore Battalion of militia on June 22, 1778 [Ref: B-79]. See "George Gable," q.v.

GODMAN, William. Age 21 (height 5' 8") when enlisted on January 24, 1776 (born in Frederick County, Maryland) to serve as a corporal in the First Company of Matrosses under Captain Nathaniel Smith. His occupation at the time was listed as a "labourer." [Ref: A-563].

GOFF, John. 1st sergeant in Capt. Philip Thomas' company of militia in 1775 [Ref: E-50]. Associator in December, 1775 [Ref: E-167]. Juror to the Oath of Allegiance in 1778 [Ref: C-25]. Also, see "John Baptist Gauff," q.v.

GOFF, Richard. Defective from the Maryland Line in August, 1780 [Ref: A-414].

GOLB, Michael. Associator in December, 1775 [Ref: E-167]. Juror to the Oath of Allegiance in 1778 [Ref: C-25].

GOLDERMAN, Jacob. Associator in December, 1775 [Ref: E-167]. Juror to the Oath of Allegiance in 1778 [Ref: C-25].

GOMBAR [GOMBER], Jacob. Associator in December, 1775 [Ref: E-167]. Juror to the Oath of Allegiance in 1778 [Ref: C-25]. Petitioned to form the horse troops in 1781 [Ref: B-167]. Together with Laurence Bringle he loaned $4,000 for the use of the State of Maryland in June, 1780 [Ref: V-520].

GOMBAR, John. Private in the Flying Camp. Disabled at the Battle of York Island. Invalid pension commenced on June 9, 1788, and ceased on November 1, 1789 [Ref: A-630, A-631]. "John Gombare, Jr." was a private, enlisted on July 1, 1776, in Capt. Peter Mantz's company; marched from Frederick Town to Leonardtown, and from there to Philadelphia, arriving on August 23, 1776 [Ref: A-47]. "Jacob Gumbare" was a private in the horse troops in June, 1781 [Ref: B-167]. "John Gombur" and "John Gombur, Jr." subscribed to the Oath of Allegiance in 1778 [Ref: C-25]. "John Gombur" and "John Gombur, Jr." were Associators in December, 1775 [Ref: E-167]. "On February 18, 1825, the Treasurer of the Western Shore was directed to pay John Gomber, of Frederick County, during life, half pay of a private, further compensation for his Revolutionary War services." [Ref: G-347]. "John Gombare" received a disability pension (S25111) for his services in the Maryland Line from November 1789; no papers. [Ref: T-1375, J-8]. One "John Gambier" died February 11, 1801, aged 78 [Ref: F-470].

GOMBAR, Peter. Associator in December, 1775 [Ref: E-167]. Juror to the Oath of Allegiance in 1778 [Ref: C-25].

GONDY, Samuel. Ensign in the militia on June 22, 1778 [Ref: H-16]. See "Samuel Gandy," q.v.

GOOD, Adam. Paid for recruiting services for the 7th Maryland Regiment on January 11, 1780 [Ref: V-54].

GOOD, Henry. Non-Enroller who was fined by the Committee of Observation in May, 1776, but he apparently enrolled because the fine was remitted in June, 1776 [Ref: E-248].

GOOD, Jacob (Piney Creek Hundred). Appointed by the Committee of Correspondence to solicit subscriptions in 1775 to purchase arms and ammunition [Ref: I-86]. Served on the Committee of Observation in 1775 [Ref: I-85]. Captain of a militia company on November 29, 1775 [Ref: E-51, A-44, A-46, B-79]. Associator who was appointed "to hand about the Association paper" in Piney Creek Hundred in 1775 [Ref: E-305]. Gave money in the amount of 8 lbs. 17 sh. 6 p. for ammunition and arms for the local militia in 1775 [Ref: E-62]. "Jacobe Goode" was commissioned a colonel in the 25th Battalion and "Jacob Good" was commissioned a colonel in the 35th Battalion, both on January 3, 1776 (Note:Obviously, this is the same man, but an error in the battalion number). [Ref: H-3, H-17, B-79]. One "Jacob Good, of Taney Town" died testate in 1783, leaving wife Eleanor and daughter Mary, also mentioning his mother Elizabeth Good, and his nephew Jacob Good (son of Adam), plus his (the deceased's) brothers Adam and George, and sisters Magdalene, Mary, and Catherine [Ref: M-6:33]. Also, see "Lawrence Everhart," q.v.

GOODEN, Benjamin. Private in the Skipton District Militia under Capt. Thomas Waring on April 16, 1776 [Ref: B-167, D-1814].

GOODEN, Joseph. Private in the Skipton District Militia under Capt. Thomas Waring on April 16, 1776 [Ref: B-167, D-1814].

GOODEN, Moses. Private in the Skipton District Militia under Capt. Thomas Waring on April 16, 1776 [Ref: B-167, D-1814].

GOODWIN, Edward. Private who enlisted on July 29, 1776 [Ref: A-43].

GORDIER, Maria Elizabeth. See "Elias Williard," q.v.

GORDON, Daniel. Associator in December, 1775 [Ref: E-167]. Juror to the Oath of Allegiance in 1778 [Ref: C-25].

GORDON [GORDAN], Joseph. Private, 1st Maryland Regiment, enlisted on May 1, 1778, and served in the Southern Army of the United States under Lt. William Lamar in the late Capt. Beatty's company until discharged on May 1, 1781 [Ref: A-391].

GORDON [GORDEN], William. Private in the Skipton District Militia under Capt. Thomas Waring on April 16, 1776 [Ref: B-167, D-1814].

GORE, Sarah. See "Laurence Myer," q.v.

GORMAN, John. Private who enlisted on July 29, 1776 [Ref: A-43].

GOSLIN, Amos. See "Jacob Gilbert," q.v.

GOTARD, Valentine. Juror to the Oath of Allegiance in March, 1778 [Ref: S-264, but not listed in Ref: C-24].

GOTSHALL, Earnest. Drafted on June 2, 1783; "hath not appeared." [Ref: B-169].

GOTTSHULL, John. Associator in December, 1775 [Ref: E-167]. Juror to the Oath of Allegiance in 1778 [Ref: C-25].

GOULDY, Samuel. Associator in December, 1775 [Ref: E-167]. Juror to the Oath of Allegiance in 1778 [Ref: C-25].

GRABEL, Peter. Provided wheat for the military in May, 1782 [Ref: R-515].

GRABICH, John. Non-Enroller who was fined by the Committee of Observation in April, 1776 [Ref: E-248].

GRAFF, Peter. Private in the German Regiment, 1776, in Capt. Henry Fister's company under the command of Col. Hussecker [Ref: A-261].

GRAMER [GRAMMER], Jacob. "John Grammer" was an Associator in December, 1775 [Ref: E-167]. Juror to the Oath of Allegiance in 1778 [Ref: C-25, S-624]. "Jacob Gramer" was 1st lieutenant in the Linganore Battalion of militia on June 22, 1778 [Ref: H-17, B-79, Z-145].

GRANADAM, Francis. "Francis Granadam" was an Associator in December, 1775 [Ref: E-167]. Juror to the Oath of Allegiance in 1778 [Ref: C-25]. "Francis Grand Adain" petitioned the General Assembly under the Act of July 3, 1780, stating that he had been a non-juror to the Oath of Allegiance and Fidelity in 1778 due to "ignorance" and now desired relief under the Act and to take the Oath [Ref: L-101].

GRANDLER, Philip. Associator in December, 1775 [Ref: E-167]. Juror to the Oath of Allegiance in 1778 [Ref: C-25].

GRANT, John. Private who enlisted July 19, 1776 [Ref: A-51]. Also, a John Grant, private, enlisted on February 20, 1778 [Ref: A-314].

GRANTHAM, Henry. Private who enlisted on May 5, 1778 [Ref: A-322].

GRASS, Jacob. Private in the German Regiment, muster roll dated October 23, 1776 [Ref: A-264].

GRAWLEY, Nicholas. Non-Enroller who was fined by the Committee of Observation in April, 1776 [Ref: E-248].

GRAWLEY, Peter. Non-Enroller who was fined by the Committee of Observation in April, 1776 [Ref: E-248].

GRAY, Richard. Private who enlisted on February 3, 1778 [Ref: A-314]. On April 14, 1779, Ann Gray, wife of Richard Gray, a soldier in the Continental service, petitioned the Frederick County Court for assistance for herself and two children. She was granted 20 lbs. for one year's subsistence [Ref: Q-6835].

GRAYBILL, Nancy. See "Joseph Wood," q.v.

GREATHOUSE, Jacob. Private in the German Regiment, muster roll dated October 23, 1776 [Ref: A-264].

GREATHOUSE, Rachel (Bratton). See "John Wood," q.v.

GREECHBAUM, Phillip. Private in the German Regiment, muster roll dated October 23, 1776 [Ref: A-264].

GREEN, Clotilda Phoebe. See "Arnold Elder," q.v.

GREEN, David. Private who enlisted on July 13, 1776 [Ref: A-43].

GREEN, Henry. Juror to the Oath of Allegiance in March, 1778 [Ref: S-264, but not listed in Ref: C-25].

GREEN, James. Private who enlisted on July 19, 1776 [Ref: A-51].

GREEN, Nathan. Private who enlisted on July 29, 1776 [Ref: A-43].

GREEN, Robert. Sergeant in Capt. William Beatty's company, 7th Maryland Regiment. Enlisted on January 8, 1777 and discharged on January 4, 1780 [Ref: A-310].

GREEN, Thomas. Enlisted on April 10, 1781, for 3 years, and was subsequently reported as "deserted" (no date given). [Ref: D-1814].

GREENTREE, Benjamin. "On February 12, 1820, the Treasurer of the Western Shore was directed to pay to Benjamin Greentree, of Montgomery County, during life, quarterly, half pay of a private, for his services during the Revolutionary War. On March 3, 1840, the Treasurer was directed to pay to Mary Greentree, of Frederick County, widow of Benjamin Greentree, a soldier of the revolution, or her order, the sum of $10 for one quarter pension due her late husband at the time of his death. Treasurer also directed to pay to the said Mary Greentree, during life, from January 1, 1840, the half pay of a private, in consideration of the services of her late husband during the Revolutionary War. On January 26, 1848 the State Treasurer was directed to pay to Elizabeth Beall, or her order, any money due to Mary Greentree at time of her death." [Ref: G-348].

GREENWALD, Philip. Corporal in Capt. Henry Baker's company of militia in 1775 [Ref: E-54].

GREENWOOD, Philip. Associator in December, 1775 [Ref: E-167]. Private in the Middle District Militia in 1776 in Capt. Valentine Creager's company [Ref: A-72]. Juror to the Oath of Allegiance in 1778

[Ref: C-25]. "Philip Greenwood, blacksmith" died testate in 1780, leaving wife Catherine and children Barbary, Yost, Philip, Margaret, Susannah, and Adam [Ref: M-5:165].

GREER, John. Commissisoned to be Assistant Deputy Quartermaster General of the Army of the United States in the lower part of Frederick and the upper part of Baltimore Counties on November 1, 1778, and empowered to act on September 17, 1779 [Ref: Z-529].

GREFF, Peter. Associator in December, 1775 [Ref: E-167]. Juror to the Oath of Allegiance in 1778 [Ref: C-25].

GRICE, Henry. Non-Enroller who was fined by the Committee of Observation in May, 1776 [Ref: E-248].

GRIDLEY [GRIDLER], Martin. Militia substitute on June 9, 1778 [Ref: A-325]. Private in the 6th Maryland Regiment from July 1, 1778, to October 10, 1778, at which time he was reported dead [Ref: A-210].

GRIEG, Harvy. Private in the 7th Maryland Regiment from May 5, 1778 until October 3, 1778, when he was reported dead [Ref: A-211].

GRIFFITH, Charles Greenbury. (Linganore Hundred). Served on the Committee of Observation in 1775 [Ref: I-85]. Appointed by the Committee of Correspondence to solicit subscriptions in 1775 to purchase arms and ammunition [Ref: I-96]. On July 30, 1776, he was "appointed colonel of the Battalion of Militia to be raised in Frederick County for the Flying Camp in the room of Otho Holland Williams who resigned." [Ref: X-140]. Source Ref: A-45 indicates that "Charles E. Griffith" reviewed new recruits in 1776, but this apparently was "Charles G. Griffith," not "Charles E. Griffith."

GRIFFITH, Chisholm. Juror to the Oath of Allegiance in March, 1778 [Ref: S-264, but not listed in Ref: C-24].

GRIFFITH, Dennis. Private who enlisted July 13, 1776 [Ref: A-43]. Ensign in the Lower District Militia [now Montgomery County] under Capt. Edward Burgess on August 7, 1776 [Ref: A-42].

GRIFFITH, Elisha. Sergeant in Capt. Samuel Plummer's company of militia in 1775 [Ref: E-54].

GRIFFITH, Greenbury. Served on the Committee of Observation in 1775 [Ref: I-85].

GRIFFITH, Henry (upper part of New Foundland). Appointed by the Committee of Correspondence to solicit subscriptions in 1775 to purchase arms and ammunition [Ref: I-86]. Served on the Committee of Observation in 1775 [Ref: I-85]. Petitioned the General Assembly under the Act of May 12, 1780, stating he had been a non-juror to the Oath of Allegiance and Fidelity in 1778 due to "ignorance" and now desired relief under the Act and to take the Oath [Ref: L-101]. A Henry Griffith served in House of Delegates in 1774 [Ref: F-479].

GRIFFITH, Henry Jr. Served on the Committee of Observation in 1775 [Ref: I-85]. Gave money in the amount of 19 lbs. 13 sh. 4 p. for arms and ammunition for the militia in 1775 [Ref: E-63].

GRIFFITH, Philemon. Captain in the Virginia (?) Line who pensioned in Frederick County, Maryland, in 1831 [Ref: J-33]. Another source states that he served in the Maryland Line. He applied for pension (S8617) on July 26, 1832, in Frederick County, Maryland, stating he was born in August, 1756. Philemon died on April 29, 1838, and the final payment was made to 2 of 3 surviving children (no names were given) on January 22, 1840 [Ref: T-1442]. "Col. Philemon Griffith, an officer of the Revolutionary War, died at New Market, Maryland, on April 29, 1838, aged 82." [Ref: F-473].

GRIFFITH, Samuel. Served on the Committee of Observation in 1775 [Ref: I-85].

GRIFFITH, Zadock. Corporal in Capt. Samuel Plummer's company of militia in 1775 [Ref: E-54]. Private who enlisted on August 5, 1776 in the Flying Camp under Capt. Philip Meroney [Ref: A-45, N-30:112].

GRIM, Jacob. Corporal in the militia, March 9, 1776 [Ref: B-166].

GRIMBER, John. Served on the Committee of Observation in 1775 [Ref: I-85]. (This is probably "John Gombar," q.v.)

GRIMES, Archibald. Drafted on June 2, 1783; "never appointed, and discharged on account of poverty and having family." [Ref: B-168].

GRIMES, Martin. Associator in December, 1775 [Ref: E-167]. Juror to the Oath of Allegiance in 1778 [Ref: C-25].

GRIMM, Alexander. Private in militia on March 9, 1776 [Ref: B-167].

GRINGER, Nicholas. 2nd lieutenant in the militia, 1778 [Ref: H-17].

GRISEL, Henry. Associator in December, 1775 [Ref: E-167]. Juror to the Oath of Allegiance in 1778 [Ref: C-25].

GRIST, Peter. Associator in December, 1775 [Ref: E-167]. Juror to the Oath of Allegiance in 1778 [Ref: C-25].

GRITZER, William. Associator in December, 1775 [Ref: E-167]. Juror to the Oath of Allegiance in 1778 [Ref: C-25].

GROFF, Henry. See "Henry Grose," q.v.

GROFF, Peter. Associator who assisted the Committee of Observation in handing about the Association paper by having it "lodged" [at his place of business] in March, 1776 [Ref: E-244].

GROFF, Philip. Associator in December, 1775 [Ref: E-167]. Juror to the Oath of Allegiance in 1778 [Ref: C-25].

GROMMET [GROMATH], Jacob. "Jacob Grommet" was ensign in the German Regiment, 1776, in Capt. Henry Fister's company under the command of Col. Nicholas Hussecker [Ref: A-261]. "Jacob Gromath" was a lieutenant from January 4, 1778, until declared a supernumerary on January 1, 1781 [Ref: A-365]. Also, see "Jacob Crummitt," q.v.

GROOP, John. Private in the German Regiment until discharged on July 26, 1779 [Ref: A-265].

GROOS, Paul. Associator in December, 1775 [Ref: E-167]. Juror to the Oath of Allegiance in 1778 [Ref: C-25].

GROSE, Henry. Private who enlisted on July 1, 1776 in Capt. Peter Mantz's company; marched from Frederick Town to Leonardtown, and from there to Philadelphia, arriving August 23, 1776 [Ref: A-47]. "Henry Gross" was private in the horse troops, June, 1781 [Ref: B-167]. A "Henry Groff" died February 22, 1823, aged 64 [Ref: F-472].

GROSE, Peter. "Peter Grose" was an Associator in December, 1775 [Ref: E-167]. "Peter Groos" was a juror to the Oath of Allegiance in 1778 [Ref: C-25]. Also, see "Peter Grosh," q.v.

GROSE, William. Associator in December, 1775 [Ref: E-167]. Juror to the Oath of Allegiance in 1778 [Ref: C-25].

GROSH, Adam. 1st lieutenant in Capt. Peter Mantz's militia company on November 29, 1775 [Ref: E-50, B-81]. Associator in December, 1775 [Ref: A-167]. 1st lieutenant in the Middle District Militia on March 26, 1776, and captain by May, 1778 [Ref: A-44, A-326, and W-287, which latter source spelled his name "Adam Grash." Source X-140 stated "Adam Grost" was 1st lieutenant in the Flying Camp Militia on July 1, 1776]. Juror to the Oath of Allegiance in 1778 [Ref: C-25]. "Adam Grosh" was a captain in the 7th Maryland Regiment on December 26, 1776, a major on June 8, 1779, and, resigned on March 30, 1780 [Ref: A-211].

GROSH, Andrew. Non-Enroller who was fined by the Committee of Observation in April, 1776 [Ref: E-248].

GROSH, Conrad. Chosen to serve on the Committee of Observation in 1775 [Ref: R-302, I-85]. Associator in December, 1775 [Ref: E-167]. Justice of the Court of Appeals on May 23, 1778 [Ref: E-302, E-303, and Z-109, which latter source spelled his name "Comard Grosh."]. Juror to the Oath of Allegiance in March, 1778 [Ref: C-25]. He loaned $300 for the use of the State of Maryland in June, 1780 [Ref: V-520]. One "John Conrad Grosh" died testate in 1794 [Ref: M-9:40].

GROSH, Mary Dorathy. See "William Beatty, Jr.," q.v.

GROSH, Michael. Served on the Committee of Observation in 1775 [Ref: I-85]. 2nd lieutenant in Capt. John Haass' company of militia in 1775 [Ref: E-53]. Associator in December, 1775 [Ref: E-167]. Juror to the Oath of Allegiance in 1778 [Ref: C-25]. "Michael Grosch" was a 2nd lieutenant in the 1st Battalion of militia on November 29, 1775 [Ref: B-81. It appears that this Michael Grosh was probably the Lieutenant Grosch who was killed at the Battle of Brunswick]. Also, see "Charles Beatty," q.v.

GROSH, Michael. Private in Capt. George Keeports' company in the German Regiment from July 15, 1776 through at least August 1, 1780. He was the ancestor of Senator Charles McCurdy Mathias, Jr., of Maryland [Ref: U-1600, A-212].

GROSH, Peter. Served on the Committee of Observation in 1775 [Ref: I-85]. Associator in December, 1775 [Ref: E-167]. Juror to the Oath of Allegiance in 1778 [Ref: C-25]. "Peter Grosch" was a captain in the Frederick Town Battalion of militia on September 19, 1780 [Ref: B-81]. He loaned $2,000 for the use of the State of Maryland in June, 1780 [Ref: V-520]. Also, see "Peter Grose," q.v.

GROSH, Peter. Private in the horse troops, June, 1781 [Ref: B-167].

GROSSNICKLE, John. Non-Enroller who was fined by the Committee of Observation in April, 1776 [Ref: E-248]. "John Grossnickel is believed to have come to Middletown Valley from near Littlestown, Pennsylvania... The first Grossnickel record in the courthouse in Frederick is in 1767 when John registered the mark used to identify his cattle, sheep and hogs... Wills of John probated in 1782 and wife Susannah in 1803 show no direct descendants. Thus, the many Grossnickle descendants of our area are believed to come largely from Peter, Sr. and his son Peter II... Many moved to Washington County, to Indiana, and further." [Ref: O-223]. "John Grossnickle, of Upper Part of Kitocton Hundred, farmer," died testate in 1782, leaving wife Susannah, but no children were named [Ref: M-6:29].

GROSSNICKLE, Peter (1750-1822). Non-Enroller who was fined by the Committee of Observation in April, 1776 [Ref: E-248]. Hauled beef and flour for the military in July, 1782 [Ref: R-535]. (Bernard) Peter Grossnickel, son of Peter Grossnickel Jr., married Christina Studebaker (1754-1836) and had a daughter Susanna (1775-1839) who married John Custer (1774-1843). [Ref: O-90].

GROUSE, Michael Jr. Non-Enroller who was fined by the Committee of Observation in April, 1776 [Ref: E-248].

GROVE, David. Private who enlisted on July 18, 1776 [Ref: A-50].

GROVE, Peter. Loaned $500 for the use of the State of Maryland in June, 1780 [Ref: V-520].

GUEST, James. Private in the Skipton District Militia under Capt. Thomas Waring on April 16, 1776 [Ref: B-167, D-1814].

GUIN, John. Associator in December, 1775 [Ref: E-167]. Juror to the Oath of Allegiance in 1778 [Ref: C-25].

GULDY, Frederick. Associator in December, 1775 [Ref: E-167]. Juror to the Oath of Allegiance in 1778 [Ref: C-25].

GUMP, John. Sergeant in Capt. Jacob Ambrose's company of militia in 1775 [Ref: E-54]. Associator in December, 1775 [Ref: E-167]. Juror to the Oath of Allegiance in 1778 [Ref: C-25]. Paid for services rendered to the military in 1779 (nature of the services not stated). [Ref: V-44].

GUMPF, Rosina. See "Elias Williard," q.v.

GUN, Christopher. Associator in December, 1775 [Ref: E-167]. Non-Enroller who was fined by the Committee of Observation in April, 1776 [Ref: E-248]. Juror to the Oath of Allegiance, 1778 [Ref: C-25].

GWINN, Joseph. Associator in December, 1775 [Ref: E-167]. Juror to the Oath of Allegiance in 1778 [Ref: C-25].

GWYNNE, Evan. Associator in December, 1775 [Ref: E-167]. Juror to the Oath of Allegiance in 1778 [Ref: C-25].

GYSE, Nicholas. Associator in December, 1775 [Ref: E-167]. Juror to the Oath of Allegiance in 1778 [Ref: C-25].

HAASS, John. Served on the Committee of Observation in 1775 [Ref: I-85]. Captain of a company of militia in the 1st Battalion on November 29, 1775 [Ref: E-53, B-81]. Associator in December, 1775 [Ref: E-167]. 1st major in the 1st Battalion in 1776 [Ref: E-57]. Chosen to serve on the Committee of Observation on September 12, 1775 [Ref: E-302]. Juror to the Oath of Allegiance in 1778 [Ref: C-25]. Court Justice on November 21, 1778 [Ref: E-303]. Justice of the Peace in 1777 [Ref F-476]. "John Haas" died testate in 1779, leaving two sons, Michael and Frederick, and daughter Christiana; also, he mentioned his deceased wife Barbara, daughter of Michael Raymer [Ref: M-5:134].

HACK, David. Militia substitute from May to December 10, 1781, and "marched to Annapolis." [Ref: A-653].

HACKETT, Jonathan. Private in the German Regiment, 1779, and was reported as "deserted" on August 25, 1779 [Ref: A-264].

HADEN [HADON], William. "William Hader" [Haden?] was an Associator in December, 1775 [Ref: E-168], and Juror to the Oath of Allegiance in 1778 [Ref: C-25, S-264, which latter source spelled the name "William Hadon."].

HAFF, Abraham. 1st lieutenant in Capt. William Beatty's company of militia in the 1st Battalion, November 29, 1775 [Ref: E-55, B-81, B-82]. Associator in December, 1775 [Ref: E-167]. Juror to the Oath of Allegiance in 1778 [Ref: C-25]. "Major Abraham Haff" loaned $350 for the use of the State of Maryland in June, 1780 [Ref: V-520]. Provided wheat for the military in May, 1782 [Ref: R-516]. Captain and then a major in the Frederick Town Battalion of militia on May 12, 1779 [Ref: B-82, Z-387, and H-15, which latter source misspelled his name as "Hoff."]. "Major Abraham Haff was drafted on June 2, 1783, but discharged on account of sickness." [Ref: B-168].

HAFF, Garrett. Associator in December, 1775 [Ref: E-168]. Juror to the Oath of Allegiance in 1778 [Ref: C-25].

HAFF, John. Associator in December, 1775 [Ref: E-168]. Juror to the Oath of Allegiance in 1778 [Ref: C-25].

HAFF, Laurence. Associator in December, 1775 [Ref: E-167]. Juror to the Oath of Allegiance in 1778 [Ref: C-25].

HAFF, Richard. 1st lieutenant in Capt. Ludowick Kemp's company of militia on November 29, 1775 [Ref: E-52, B-82]. "Richard Haff, or Hoff" was captain in charge of the magazine at Frederick Town from October 29, 1779, through July 22, 1780 [Ref: V-5, V-113, V-226].

HAFF, Robert. Drummer in Capt. William Beatty's company of militia in 1775 [Ref: E-55].

HAFFLEY [HAFLEY], Stephen. Militia substitute from May to December 10, 1781, and "marched to Annapolis." [Ref: A-652]. "On February 18, 1830, the Treasurer of the Western Shore was directed to pay to 'Stephen Hafley," of Frederick County, during life, quarterly, half pay of a private, for his services during the Revolutionary War." [Ref: G-349]. "On February 9, 1839, the Treasurer was directed to pay to John B. Boyle, as per order of 'Mary Magdalene Hofley,' widow of Stephen Hofley, a Revolutionary War pensioner, $31.22 for 9 months and 11 days pension, due said Stephen Hofley at the time of death. Further ordered that the Treasurer pay to Mary Magdalene Hofley, widow of Stephen Hofley, a Revolutionary War soldier, or her order, half pay of a soldier of the Revolutionary War during her life, commencing January 1, 1839." [Ref: G-354].

HAFFLEY [HAIFLEY], Jacob. Private who deserted from the German Regiment and was jailed on April 19, 1778 [Ref: A-327]. However, "Jacob Haseligh" [Hafeligh?] was listed as "present" on August 1, 1780 [Ref: A-217].

HAFFLEY [HAVELAY, HAVCLAY], Peter. Private who enlisted on July 20, 1776 by Capt. Jacob Good [Ref: A-46]. "Peter Haflegh" was a private stationed at Fort Frederick in June, 1778, in Capt. John Kershner's company, guarding prisoners of war [Ref: A-328].

HAFLICH [HAFLIGH], Frederick. Associator in December, 1775 [Ref: E-167]. Juror to the Oath of Allegiance in 1778 [Ref: C-25]. Also, see "Frederick Hufligh," q.v.

HAGAN, Alexander Jr. Juror to the Oath of Allegiance in March, 1778 [Ref: S-264, but not listed in Ref: C-25].

HAGAN, Alexander Sr. Juror to the Oath of Allegiance in March, 1778 [Ref: S-264, but not listed in Ref: C-25].

HAGAN, Leonard. "Leonard Hagon," private, enlisted on July 13, 1776 [Ref: A-43]. "Leonard Hagan," private in the 1st Maryland Regiment, enlisted on January 1, 1780, and served in the Southern Army of the United States under Lt. William Lamar in the late Capt. Beatty's company, 1781 [Ref: A-390].

HAGAN, Michael. Private who enlisted on July 18, 1776 [Ref: A-49].

HAGAN, Walter. Private, 1st Maryland Regiment, enlisted February 1, 1780, and served in the Southern Army of the United States under Lt. W. Lamar in the late Capt. Beatty's company, 1781 [Ref: A-390].

HAGARTY, John. Non-Enroller who was fined by the Committee of Observation in April, 1776 [Ref: E-248].

HAGARTY, Paul. Private, 1st Maryland Regiment. Disabled at Battle of Brandywine; invalid pension commenced on December 27, 1784, and ceased on November 1, 1789 [Ref: A-630, A-631, F-476].

HAGER, John. Private who enlisted on July 19, 1776 [Ref: A-51].

HAGER, Jonathan (Salisbury Hundred). Appointed by the Committee of Correspondence to solicit subscriptions in 1775 to purchase arms and ammunition [Ref: I-85]. Served in the House of Delegates, 1773-1775 [Ref: F-479]. Served on the Committee of Observation in 1775 [Ref: I-85].

HAGER, Shadrick. Associator in December, 1775 [Ref: E-167]. Juror to the Oath of Allegiance in 1778 [Ref: C-25].

HAGERTY [HEGERTY], George. Private who enlisted on May 17, 1778, and served in the 2nd Maryland Regiment [Ref: A-294, A-322].

HAGERTY, John Jr. Associator in December, 1775 [Ref: E-167]. Juror to the Oath of Allegiance in 1778 [Ref: C-25].

HAGERTY, Thomas. Associator in December, 1775 [Ref: E-168]. Juror to the Oath of Allegiance in 1778 [Ref: C-25].

HAGS, John. Associator in December, 1775 [Ref: E-167]. Juror to the Oath of Allegiance in 1778 [Ref: C-25].

HAIDEN, Philip. Petitioned the General Assembly under the Act of May 12, 1780, stating that he had been a non-juror to the Oath of Allegiance and Fidelity in 1778 due to "ignorance" and now desired relief under the Act and to take the Oath [Ref: L-101].

HAIL, James. Enlisted on April 13, 1781 for 3 years; marched with Capt. Lynn [Ref: D-1814].

HAILEY, Michael. Private in the 6th Maryland Regiment from April 20, 1777, until April 12, 1779, when reported dead [Ref: A-214].

HAIN, Henry. Private in the German Regiment, 1776, in Capt. Henry Fister's company under the command of Col. Hussecker [Ref: A-261].

HAIN, Jacob Jr. Associator in December, 1775 [Ref: E-168]. Juror to the Oath of Allegiance in 1778 [Ref: C-25].

HAIN, Jacob Sr. Associator in December, 1775 [Ref: E-168]. Juror to the Oath of Allegiance in 1778 [Ref: C-25].

HAINES, Jacob. See "John Myers," q.v., and "Jacob Gilbert," q.v.

HAINES, Peter. Private who enlisted on July 19, 1776 [Ref: A-51].

HAINS, Joseph. Non-Enroller who was fined by the Committee of Observation in April, 1776 [Ref: E-248].

HAINS, Mordecai. Non-Enroller who was fined by the Committee of Observation in April, 1776 [Ref: E-248].

HAINS, Nathan. Non-Enroller who was fined by the Committee of Observation in May, 1776 [Ref: E-248].

HALE, James. Non-Enroller who was fined by the Committee of Observation in April, 1776 [Ref: E-248].

HALE, Michael. Private who enlisted on August 5, 1776 in the Flying Camp under Capt. Philip Meroney [Ref: A-45, N-30:112].

HALFPENNY, Thomas. Juror to the Oath of Allegiance in March, 1778 [Ref: S-264, but not listed in Ref: C-25]. Private who enlisted on April 22, 1778 [Ref: A-320], served as a private in the German Regiment at White Plains on September 5, 1778, under Lt. Col. Ludwick Weltner [Ref: A-266], and was in the service to at least August 1, 1780 [Ref: A-217]. In August, 1779, Ann Halfpenny, wife of Thomas Halfpenny, a soldier in the German Regiment under Col. Weltner, petitioned the Frederick County Court for assistance for herself and 3 children. She was granted 30 lbs. for one year's subsistence [Ref: Q-6835].

HALIN, John. Petitioned the General Assembly under the Act of July 3, 1780, stating he had been a non-juror to the Oath of Allegiance and

Fidelity in 1778 due to "ignorance" and now desired relief under the Act and to take the Oath [Ref: L-101].

HALL, Andrew Jr. Juror to the Oath of Allegiance in March, 1778 [Ref: S-264, but not listed in Ref: C-25].

HALL, Daniel. Private, 7th Maryland Regiment, who enlisted July 9, 1779, served in the 1st Maryland Regiment in 1780, and also in the Southern Army of the United States under Lt. William Lamar in the late Capt. Beatty's company in 1781. He also served as a hospital orderly in July, 1781 [Ref: A-217, A-391].

HALL, Edward. Private in the horse troops, June, 1781 [Ref: B-168]. One Edward Hall died testate in 1785; not married. [Ref: M-6:185].

HALL, Gabriel. Provided wheat for the military in June, 1782 [Ref: R-520].

HALL, John. Private who enlisted on May 15, 1778 [Ref: A-324], and reported a defective from the Maryland Line in 1780 [Ref: A-414]. He was drafted on June 2, 1783, but was "discharged, as rendered unfit for duty by sickness." [Ref: B-169].

HALL, Nicholas. Recommended and was appointed a captain upon the resignation of William Brashears, Jr. on June 10, 1778, and served through at least 1779 [Ref: H-5, H-17, B-82, Z-128]. Provided wheat for the military in June, 1782 [Ref: R-520].

HALL, William. Provided wheat for the military in June, 1782 [Ref: R-520].

HALLER, Godfrey. Associator in December, 1775 [Ref: E-168]. Juror to the Oath of Allegiance in 1778 [Ref: C-25]. "The early Hallers flourished around Jefferson in southern Middletown Valley. There are numerous Hallers in the records of Frederick Lutheran Church. Gottfried Haller married Elizabeth Abel in 1777." [Ref: O-69]. One "Godfried Hallow" was paid for services rendered to the military in December, 1779 (nature of the services not stated). [Ref: V-45].

HALLER, Mary Magdelen. See "Jacob Storm," q.v.

HALTER, Henry. Associator in December, 1775 [Ref: E-167]. Juror to the Oath of Allegiance in 1778 [Ref: C-25].

HAMAN, John. Associator in December, 1775 [Ref: E-168]. Juror to the Oath of Allegiance in 1778 [Ref: C-25].

HAMILTON, Anthony. Private in German Regiment, 1776, in Capt. Henry Fister's company under the command of Col. Hussecker [Ref: A-261].

HAMILTON, James. Brigadier General in the militia on October 30, 1781 [Ref: B-82].

HAMILTON, James Jr. Militia substitute from May to December 10, 1781, and "marched to Annapolis." [Ref: A-653].

HAMILTON, John. Juror to the Oath of Allegiance in March, 1778 [Ref: S-264, but not listed in Ref: C-25]. Private who enlisted on April 24, 1778 [Ref: A-320]. Also, this or another John Hamilton enlisted as a private on February 17, 1778 [Ref: A-314].

HAMILTON, Samuel. Private who was enlisted on July 20, 1776 by Capt. Jacob Good [Ref: A-46].

HAMILTON, William. Militia substitute from May to December 10, 1781, and "marched to Annapolis." [Ref: A-653].

HAMMER, Jacob. Private in the German Regiment, 1776, in Capt. Henry Fister's company under the command of Col. Hussecker [Ref: A-261].

HAMMER, Tobias. Private who was enlisted on July 20, 1776 by Capt. Jacob Good [Ref: A-46].

HAMMERSLY, John. Private who enlisted April 27, 1778 [Ref: A-321]. "John Ammersley" was a private in German Regiment at White Plains on September 5, 1778, under Lt. Col. Ludwick Weltner [Ref: A-266]. "John W. Hammersly, or Amersly" was listed "deserted" on the muster payroll of the German Regiment on August 1, 1780 [Ref: A-217].

HAMMITT [HAMETT], James. Juror to the Oath of Allegiance in March, 1778 [Ref: S-264, but not listed in Ref: C-25].

HAMMITT, Robert. Corporal in Capt. William Duvall's militia company in 1775 [Ref: E-54]. Also, drafted on June 2, 1783 [Ref: B-169].

HAMMOND, Charles. Militia substitute from May to December 10, 1781, and "marched to Annapolis." [Ref: A-653]. Provided wheat for the military in June, 1782 [Ref: R-526].

HAMMOND, John. Associator in December, 1775 [Ref: E-168]. Juror to the Oath of Allegiance in 1778 [Ref: C-25].

HAMMOND, Nathan. Served in House of Delegates in 1783 [Ref: F-479].

HAMMOND, Peter. Private in Maryland Line, aged 79, from Frederick County, pensioned on April 3, 1819, at $96 per annum from April 8, 1818. "On March 5, 1844, the Treasurer of the Western Shore was directed to pay to Elizabeth Hammond, of Frederick County, during her life, the half pay of a private, in consideration of services rendered by her husband during the Revolutionary War." [Ref: G-350, citing the U. S. Pension Rolls of 1835]. "Peter Hawman or Hammond" applied for a pension on April 8, 1818, aged 64, in Frederick County, MA (Massachusetts; an obvious typographical error since he lived in MD, i. e., Maryland) and he died on October 31, 1820. His widow Elizabeth applied for a pension (W9474) in Frederick County, MD (Maryland, not

Massachusetts) on December 2, 1842, aged 84. Peter Hammond married Elizabeth Heldelrand on August 17, 1781, and they had 12 children, of which only 3 survived in 1842, to wit: Frederick Hawman, Philip Hawman (both of Fredericktown, Maryland), and Margaret, wife of John Sta?? [sic]. In 1842, Catherine Peters, aged 80, stated she knew Elizabeth from childhood. [Ref: T-1572]. Source F-471 states that "Peter Hawman" died on November 5, 1820.

HAMMOND, William. See "Upton Sheredine," q.v.

HAMON, William. Private who enlisted on May 11, 1778 [Ref: A-322].

HAMSTON, William. Private, in 1st Maryland Regiment, enlisted on January 31, 1780, and served in the Southern Army of the United States under Lt. William Lamar in the late Capt. Beatty's company in 1781 [Ref: A-390].

HAN, David. Fifer in the Pennsylvania Line, aged 78, from Frederick County, who pensioned April 3, 1819, at $96 per annum from January 29, 1819. [Ref: G-350, citing the U. S. Pension Rolls of 1835]. However, Ref: T-1503 states he applied for a pension (S34918) in Frederick County on January 25, 1819, aged 63, and in 1820 he was aged "70?". He had enlisted at Shippensburg, Pennsylvania, and had no family in 1820. [Ref: T-1503, J-25].

HANCE, Jacob. Associator in December, 1775 [Ref: E-167]. Juror to the Oath of Allegiance in 1778 [Ref: C-25].

HANCE, John. Substitute on June 13, 1781, and marched with Capt. Boyer [Ref: D-1814].

HANCE, Martin. Corporal in Capt. Michael McGuire's company of militia in 1775 [Ref: E-57].

HANCKS, Matthias. Associator in December, 1775 [Ref: E-167]. Juror to the Oath of Allegiance in 1778 [Ref: C-25].

HANEE, Kinsey. Private in the militia in July, 1776 [Ref: A-42].

HANEY, James. Enlisted on April 10, 1781, for 3 years, and was later reported as "deserted" (no date given). [Ref: D-1814].

HANEY, John. Private who enlisted in April 6, 1778, and served in the 2nd Maryland Regiment [Ref: A-294].

HANEY, Patrick. Sergeant in Capt. William Shields' company of militia in 1775 [Ref: E-56].

HANGER, John. Associator in December, 1775 [Ref: E-168]. Juror to the Oath of Allegiance in 1778 [Ref: C-25].

HANNAN, Jacob. Associator in December, 1775 [Ref: E-168]. Juror to the Oath of Allegiance in 1778 [Ref: C-25].

HANNISS, Samuel. Soldier from Frederick County who was wounded during the Revolutionary War [Ref: F-475].

HANSON, Alexander Contee. Son of John Hanson, Jr. and Jane Contee. Served on the Committee of Observation in 1775 [Ref: I-85], and was appointed a Judge of the General Court [Chancellor of Maryland] on March 9, 1778 [Ref: F-478]. He died January 16, 1806 [Ref: F-470]. Also, see "James Johnson," q.v.

HANSON, John Jr. (April 3, 1721 - November 15, 1783). Son of Samuel and Elizabeth Hanson, he was born in Charles County, Maryland where he served in the Assembly from 1757 until he removed to Frederick County in 1773. Member of the Provincial Convention in 1774, and elected Treasurer of Frederick County on June 2, 1775 [Ref: E-303]. Associator in December, 1775, and chosen to serve on Committee of Observation on September 12, 1775. Elected Chairman on September 14, 1775 [Ref: E-167, E-302, I-85]. Member of the General Assembly, 1777-1779. Delegate to Congress from 1779-1781. Elected President of the United States in Congress Assembled on November 5, 1781 [Ref: E-303. Also, see Dr. Edward Papenfuse's *A Biographical Dictionary of the Maryland Legislature, 1635-1789*, Volume I, for more information on this very prominent Marylander]. He was juror to the Oath of Allegiance in 1778 [Ref: C-25]. "Upon the formation of the Committee of Observation for Frederick County, in September, 1775, Hanson was elected chairman, and retained that position until the Constitution of 1776 was carried into effect. He also filled positions on various important committees, among them the Provincial Committee for Licensing suits, the provincial Committee of Correspondence, and the Committee for the building of a military jail, or barracks, at Frederick, where a large number of prisoners were confined. During his chairmanship of the Committee of Observation the formidable Tory conspiracy of Lord Dunmore and White Eyes, an Indian chief, was discovered and frustrated. In 1775 he was commissioned Treasurer of the county, and was appointed by the Convention of Maryland to establish a gun-lock factory at Frederick. He was appointed member of a commission by the Convention of Maryland, October 9, 1776, to appoint officers and to encourage the re-enlistment of Maryland militia and regular troops whose terms of service in the Continental Army was about expiring. Mr. Hanson was elected to the Continental Congress, and presented his credentials February 22, 1781. He was elected President on the 5th of November following... He signed the Articles of Confederation on March 1, 1781... He married Miss Jane Contee and had a number of children, among them Alexander Contee Hanson, afterwards Chancellor; another son, Samuel Hanson, was surgeon of Washington's Life-Guards; and, still another, Peter Contee Hanson, was a lieutenant in the First Battalion, Maryland Infantry, and was mortally wounded at Fort Washington in 1776. John Hanson died November 22, 1783, at Oxen Hill, Prince George's County, while visiting his nephew, Thomas Hanson." [Ref: F-449, F-478, F-479]. Mrs. Jane Hanson, relict of Hon. John Hanson, died on February 21, 1822, aged 85 [Ref: F-471].

HANSON, Peter Contee. Son of John Hanson, Jr. and Jane Contee. 2nd lieutenant in the Upper District Militia [now Washington County] in 1776 [Ref: A-48]. "Peter C. Hanson" was an Associator in December, 1775 [Ref: E-167]. 1st lieutenant in a rifle company in July, 1776, under Capt. Barrett [Ref: X-54]. Juror to the Oath of Allegiance, 1778 [Ref: C-25].

HANSON, Rezin [Reson]. Militia substitute on June 6, 1778 [Ref: A-325]. Private, 6th Maryland Regiment, June 6, 1778, and corporal on September 1, 1778; reported "deserted" July 23, 1780 [Ref: A-215].

HANSON, Samuel. Son of John Hanson, Jr. and Jane Contee. Associator in December, 1775 [Ref: E-167]. Surgeon in the 34th Battalion of militia on September 4, 1777 [Ref: B-84]. Juror to the Oath of Allegiance in 1778 [Ref: C-25]. Appointed the Surveyor for Frederick County on November 6, 1779 [Ref: V-10]. He also petitioned to form the horse troops in 1781 [Ref: B-167].

HANY, Michael. Private in the militia, March 9, 1776 [Ref: B-167].

HARBIN, Joshua. Associator in December, 1775 [Ref: E-167]. Private who enlisted on July 25, 1776 [Ref: A-49]. Juror to the Oath of Allegiance in 1778 [Ref: C-25].

HARBOUGH [HARBAUGH], Christian. Ensign in 34th Battalion of militia on March 29, 1779, under Col. J. Johnson [Ref: H-15, B-84, Z-331]. "Christian Herbach" was a son of Ludwig (1729-1809). [Ref: O-128].

HARBOUGH [HERBAUGH], John. "John Herbaugh" was an Associator in December, 1775 [Ref: E-167]. "John Harbough" was a militia substitute, May to December 10, 1781, and "marched to Annapolis." [Ref: A-653]. "John Harbough" was drafted on June 2, 1783, but was "discharged, being very poor and having a wife and three children." [Ref: B-168]. "John Herbaugh" took the Oath of Allegiance in 1778 [Ref: C-25]. One "John Herbach" was a son of Ludwig (1729-1809) and Christiana (1727-1797) another "John Herbach (1735-1803)" was a son of Jost Herbach who died in York County, Pennsylvania, in 1792, and a third "John Herbach" was a son of George (1726-1787) and Catherine (1721-1791) who were born in Switzerland and emigrated in 1736 [Ref: O-128].

HARBOUGH [HARBAUGH], Margaret. See "Andrew Williard," q.v.

HARDEN, Edward. Private in the militia in July, 1776 [Ref: A-42].

HARDEN, Elias. Captain in the 29th Battalion of militia on May 14, 1776. [Ref: W-424, D-1814]. Also, see "Samuel Swearingen," q.v.

HARDESTY, George. "George Hardastee (Lower Monocacy Hundred)" was a non-enroller who was fined by the Committee of Observation in June, 1776 [Ref: E-248]. "George Hardesty" was drafted on June 2, 1783 [Ref: B-168].

HARDESTY, Peter. Private who enlisted on July 25, 1776 [Ref: A-50].

HARDEY, Isaac. Private who enlisted on July 19, 1776 [Ref: A-51].

HARDEY, Solomon. Associator in December, 1775 [Ref: E-168]. Juror to the Oath of Allegiance in 1778 [Ref: C-25].

HARDEY, William. Juror to the Oath of Allegiance in March, 1778 [Ref: S-264, but not listed in Ref: C-25].

HARDIN, Richard. See "Peter Crepell," q.v.

HARDING, Gray [Garah]. "Garah Harding" was a private who enlisted on August 5, 1776, in the Flying Camp under Capt. Philip Meroney [Ref: A-45, N-30:111]. "Gray Harding" was captain in the Frederick Town Battalion of militia on September 18, 1780 [Ref: B-84, V-295].

HARDING, John. Private in the militia in July, 1776 [Ref: A-42].

HARDING, Josiah. Private in the militia in July, 1776 [Ref: A-42].

HARDING, Philip. Provided wheat for the military in June, 1782 [Ref: R-522].

HARDMAN, Abraham. Non-Enroller who was fined by the Committee of Observation in April, 1776 [Ref: E-248].

HARDMAN. Anthony. Non-Enroller who was fined by the Committee of Observation in April, 1776 [Ref: E-248].

HARDMAN, Anthony Jr. Non-Enroller who was fined by the Committee of Observation in April, 1776 [Ref: E-248].

HARDMAN, Daniel. Non-Enroller who was fined by the Committee of Observation in April, 1776 [Ref: E-248]. Provided wheat for the military in July, 1782 [Ref: R-533].

HARDMAN, Frederick. Private in the Middle District Militia in 1776 in Capt. Valentine Creager's company [Ref: A-72].

HARDMAN, George. Non-Enroller who was fined by the Committee of Observation in April, 1776 [Ref: E-248].

HARDMAN, Henry. Associator in December, 1775 [Ref: E-167]. 2nd lieutenant in the 34th Battalion of militia on May 15, 1776 [Ref: B-84, W-426]. Captain in the Upper District Militia [now Washington County] in July, 1776 [Ref: A-48]. Juror to Oath of Allegiance in 1778 [Ref: C-25, S-264]. One Henry Hardman was a militia substitute from May to December 10, 1781, and "marched to Annapolis." [Ref: A-653]. "Major Henry Hardman, an old soldier, died in 1799." [Ref: F-470].

HARDMAN, Joseph. Associator in December, 1775 [Ref: E-168]. Juror to the Oath of Allegiance in 1778 [Ref: C-25].

HARDMAN, Michael. Private who enlisted April 20, 1778 [Ref: A-320]. Served as a private in the German Regiment at the Battle of White Plains on September 5, 1778, under Lt. Col. Weltner [Ref: A-267].

HARDY, Rodolph [Rudolph]. Associator in December, 1775 [Ref: E-168]. Juror to the Oath of Allegiance in 1778 [Ref: C-25].

HARES, James. Corporal in Capt. Michael McGuire's company of militia in 1775 [Ref: E-57]. Also, see "James Harris," q.v.

HARGETT [HARGIS], Abraham (1753-1824). "Served as a 1st lieutenant and then captain-lieutenant in the 10th Pennsylvania Regiment from January 1, 1777, to June 24, 1778. Resigned July 1, 1778, to fight the Indians. He married Mary Pentrim (1755-1831) in 1779, and a son John Hargett (1787-1859) married Barbara Shafer Thomas (1780-1856) in 1810. Abraham was born in Pennsylvania and died in Frederick County, Maryland, on March 3, 1824." [Ref: U-1454, U-2086].

HARGRADER, Henry. Associator in December, 1775 [Ref: E-168]. Juror to the Oath of Allegiance in 1778 [Ref: C-25].

HARGRADER, Jacob. Associator in December, 1775 [Ref: E-168]. Juror to the Oath of Allegiance in 1778 [Ref: C-25].

HARGRADER, Philip. Associator in December, 1775 [Ref: E-168]. Juror to the Oath of Allegiance in 1778 [Ref: C-25].

HARKINS, William. Non-Enroller who was fined by the Committee of Observation in May, 1776 [Ref: E-248].

HARLAN, John Jr. Non-Enroller who was fined by the Committee of Observation in April, 1776 [Ref: E-248].

HARLAN, John Sr. Associator in December, 1775 [Ref: E-167]. Juror to the Oath of Allegiance in 1778 [Ref: C-25]. One "John Harlon" died testate in 1787, naming children Elizabeth, John, Hannah, and Joel [Ref: M-7:90].

HARLIN, Joel. Petitioned the General Assembly under the Act of July 3, 1780, stating he had been a non-juror to the Oath of Allegiance and

Fidelity in 1778 due to "ignorance" and now desired relief under the Act and to take the Oath [Ref: L-101].

HARLING, Cornelius. Private who enlisted July 18, 1776 [Ref: A-49].

HARM, Jonathan. Associator in December, 1775 [Ref: E-168]. Juror to the Oath of Allegiance in 1778 [Ref: C-25].

HARMER, James. Private who enlisted in 1778 and served in the 2nd Maryland Regiment [Ref: A-294].

HARMON, Marcus. Associator in December, 1775 [Ref: E-168]. Juror to the Oath of Allegiance in 1778 [Ref: C-25].

HARMONY, George. Private in the German Regiment, muster roll dated October 23, 1776 [Ref: A-264].

HARMOR, Joseph. Private who enlisted on May 12, 1778 [Ref: A-324].

HARNY, John. Associator in December, 1775 [Ref: E-167]. Juror to the Oath of Allegiance in 1778 [Ref: C-25].

HARPER, Robert Goodloe. See "John Stricker," q.v.

HARPER, Stephen. Private who enlisted August 5, 1776 [Ref: A-44].

HARPS, Michael. Associator in December, 1775 [Ref: E-167]. Juror to the Oath of Allegiance in 1778 [Ref: C-25]. "Michael Harp emigrated to western Maryland via Philadelphia in 1740. John Harp, doubtless a relative of Michael, came to Middletown Valley from Reading, Pennsylvania in 1750 along with several brothers... Gravestone records show the early Harp families belonged to the Church of the Brethren at Grossnickle Meeting House in upper Middletown Valley.." [Ref: O-100].

HARRIS, Francis. Non-Enroller who was fined by the Committee of Observation in April, 1776, but he apparently enrolled because the fine was remitted in June, 1776 [Ref: E-248].

HARRIS, James. Private in the Skipton District Militia under Capt. Thomas Waring on April 16, 1776 [Ref: B-167, D-1814].

HARRIS, Samuel Jr. Private in the Skipton District Militia under Capt. Thomas Waring on April 16, 1776 [Ref: B-167, D-1814].

HARRIS, Stephen. Private in the Skipton District Militia under Capt. Thomas Waring on April 16, 1776 [Ref: B-167, D-1814].

HARRISON, Elizabeth. See "Roger Nelson," q.v.

HARRISON, John. Private who was enlisted on July 20, 1776 by Capt. Jacob Good [Ref: A-46].

HARRISON, John. Juror to the Oath of Allegiance in March, 1778 [Ref: S-264; not listed in Ref: C-25]. Orphans' Court Judge in 1783 [Ref: F-480].

HARRISON, Josiah (of William). Petitioned the General Assembly under the Act of May 12, 1780, stating he had been a non-juror to the Oath of

Allegiance and Fidelity in 1778 due to "ignorance" and now desired relief under the Act and to take the Oath [Ref: L-101].

HARRISON, Samuel. Substitute on June 13, 1781; marched with Capt. Boyer [Ref: D-1814].

HARRISON, Sarah. See "James Ervin (Irvine)," q.v.

HARRISON, Thomas. Non-Enroller who was fined by the Committee of Observation in April, 1776 [Ref: E-248]. Private in militia, March 9, 1776 [Ref: B-167]. Also, Thomas Harrison, private, enlisted on August 5, 1776, in the Flying Camp under Capt. Philip Meroney [Ref: A-45, N-30:112]. He was drafted on June 2, 1783, and was "ordered to pay 6.75 pounds, but hath not done it." [Ref: B-168].

HARRY, Martain. Private stationed at Fort Frederick on June 27, 1778, in Capt. John Kershner's company, and guarding prisoners of war [Ref: A-328].

HARSBERGER, Barnard. Associator in December, 1775 [Ref: E-168]. Juror to the Oath of Allegiance in 1778 [Ref: C-25].

HART, ---- (no first name given). Paid for recruiting services for the 7th Maryland Regiment on January 11, 1780 [Ref: V-54].

HART, Chr. Private who enlisted on July 19, 1776 [Ref: A-51]. Both "Christr. Hart" and "Christn. Hart" took the Oath of Allegiance in March, 1778 [Ref: S-264, but they are not listed in Ref: C-25].

HART, John. Private who enlisted on February 18, 1778, and served in the 2nd Maryland Regiment [Ref: A-294].

HART, Noah. Election Judge in the Upper District on July 2, 1776 [Ref: F-476].

HART (HARDT), Peter and Charlotte. See "Joseph Doll," q.v.

HART, Susannah. See "Isaac Shelby," q.v.

HART, Valentine. See "Valentine Heart," q.v.

HARTER, Adam. Petitioned the General Assembly under the Act of May 12, 1780, stating he had been a non-juror to the Oath of Allegiance and Fidelity in 1778 due to "ignorance" and now desired relief under the Act and to take the Oath [Ref: L-101].

HARTER, Christian. Petitioned the General Assembly under the Act of May 12, 1780, stating that he had been a non-juror to the Oath of Allegiance and Fidelity in 1778 due to "ignorance" and now desired relief under the Act and to take the Oath [Ref: L-101].

HARTER, George. Petitioned the General Assembly under the Act of May 12, 1780, stating that he had been a non-juror to the Oath of Allegiance and Fidelity in 1778 due to "ignorance" and now desired relief under the Act and to take the Oath [Ref: L-101].

HARTLY, Michael. Private stationed at Fort Frederick in June, 1778 [Ref: A-328].

HARTNESS, Robert. Private in the German Regiment, muster roll dated October 23, 1776 [Ref: A-264].

HARTSOCK [HARTSUCK], George. "George Hartsuck" was enrolled as an Associator in December, 1775 [Ref: E-168]. Juror to the Oath of Allegiance in 1778 [Ref: C-25].

HARTSOCK [HEARTSOOK], Henry. "Henry Heartsook" was enrolled as an Associator in December, 1775 [Ref: E-168]. Juror to the Oath of Allegiance in 1778 [Ref: C-25].

HARTSOCK [HARTSUCK], John. Associator in December, 1775 [Ref: E-168]. Juror to the Oath of Allegiance in 1778 [Ref: C-25].

HARTSOCK [HORTSOOK], Nicholas. "Nicholas Hortsook" enrolled as an Associator in December, 1775 [Ref: E-168]. Juror to the Oath of Allegiance in 1778 [Ref: C-26].

HARTSOCK [HARTSOKE], Peter. "Peter Hartsoke" was a "Draught," May to December 10, 1781, and "marched to Annapolis." [Ref: A-653].

HARTSOCK, Susanna and Jonathan. See "Frederick Christman," q.v.

HARTSOCK [HARTSUCK], William. "William Hartsuck" enrolled as an Associator in December, 1775 [Ref: E-168]. Juror to the Oath of Allegiance in 1778 [Ref: C-25].

HARTWELL, Thomas. Drafted on June 2, 1783, and "discharged, having a wife and eight children and is poor." [Ref: B-169].

HARTWICK, George. Associator in December, 1775 [Ref: E-168]. Juror to the Oath of Allegiance in 1778 [Ref: C-25]. These same sources also listed a "George Hartweak" (same person listed twice perhaps?).

HARTY, Frederick. Militia substitute on June 13, 1778 [Ref: A-326]. Private, 1st Maryland Regiment, 1780, and served in the Southern Army of the United States under Lt. William Lamar in the late Capt. Beatty's company until transferred to light infantry in 1781 [Ref: A-390].

HARTZELL, George. Private in Capt. Baltzel's Company, served three years, and discharged July 19, 1779, at Camp Wyoming [Ref: A-271].

HARVEY, Shelby and Sarah. See "Levi Davis," q.v.

HARWOOD, Samuel (Northwest Hundred). Appointed by the Committee of Correspondence to solicit subscriptions in 1775 to purchase arms and ammunition [Ref: I-86].

HASE, James. Private in the militia on March 9, 1776 [Ref: B-166].

HASELIGH, Jacob. See "Jacob Haffley (Haifley)," q.v.

HASSELBACK, Nicholas. Private who enlisted on July 20, 1776 [Ref: A-50].

HATCHCRAFT, James. See "James Hutchcraft," q.v.

HATFIELD, John. Private in the German Regiment until discharged on July 26, 1779 [Ref: A-265].

HATMAN, Michael. Private in Capt. Christian Myer's Company, served 3 years, and discharged July 17, 1779 at Camp Wyoming [Ref: A-271].

HAUCK, John. Provided wheat for the military in 1782 [Ref: R-533].

HAUER, Catherine. See "Peter Mantz," q.v.

HAULP, Nicholas. Associator in December, 1775 [Ref: E-167]. Juror to the Oath of Allegiance in 1778 [Ref: C-25].

HAULTZ, Nicholas. Associator in December, 1775 [Ref: E-168]. Juror to the Oath of Allegiance in 1778 [Ref: C-25].

HAUMAN, John. Petitioned the General Assembly under the Act of May 12, 1780, stating he had been a non-juror to the Oath of Allegiance and Fidelity in 1778 due to "ignorance" and now desired relief under the Act and to take the Oath [Ref: L-101].

HAUSMAN, Michael. Private in Capt. Bayer's company; served three years; discharged on July 25, 1779, at Camp Wyoming [Ref: A-271].

HAVELY, Anthony. Petitioned the General Assembly under the Act of July 3, 1780, stating that he had been a non-juror to the Oath of Allegiance and Fidelity in 1778 due to "ignorance" and now desired relief under the Act and to take the Oath [Ref: L-101]. Also, see "Anthony Heafley," q.v.

HAVER, Daniel. Associator in December, 1775 [Ref: E-167]. Juror to the Oath of Allegiance in 1778 [Ref: C-25].

HAVER, Jacob. Private in the German Regiment until discharged on October 12, 1779 [Ref: A-265].

HAVERT, Michael. Associator in December, 1775 [Ref: E-167]. Juror to the Oath of Allegiance in 1778 [Ref: C-25].

HAWK, Andrew. Associator in December, 1775 [Ref: E-168]. Juror to the Oath of Allegiance in 1778 [Ref: C-25].

HAWK, George Michael. Private who enlisted on July 1, 1776 in Capt. Peter Mantz's company; marched from Frederick Town to Leonardtown, and from there to Philadelphia, arriving on August 23, 1776 [Ref: A-47]. Also, see "George Michael Hook," q.v.

HAWK, Henry. Associator in December, 1775 [Ref: E-168]. Juror to the Oath of Allegiance in 1778 [Ref: C-25]. Private in the German Regiment, 1776, in Capt. Henry Fister's company under the command of Col. Nicholas Hussecker [Ref: A-261].

HAWK, John. Corporal in Capt. William Shields' company of militia in 1775 [Ref: E-56].

HAWKE, Jacob. Juror to the Oath of Allegiance in March, 1778 [Ref: S-264, but not listed in Ref: C-25].

HAWKERSMITH, George, et al. See "George Hockersmith," q.v.

HAWKINS, Thomas. Served on the Committee of Observation in 1775 [Ref: I-85]. Associator in December, 1775, appointed "to hand about the Association paper" in Lower Kittockton [Catoctin] Hundred [Ref: E-168, E-305]. (This name appeared twice on the list of Associators). Took the Oath of Allegiance in 1778 [Ref: C-25]. Loaned $1,000 for the use of the State of Maryland in June, 1780 [Ref: V-520].

HAWMAN, Peter. See "Peter Hammond," q.v.

HAWN, George. Juror to the Oath of Allegiance in March, 1778 [Ref: S-264, but not listed in Ref: C-25]. (This name was listed twice). Drafted on June 13, 1781; marched with Capt. Boyer [Ref: D-1814].

HAWN [HAWNE], Michael. Juror to the Oath of Allegiance in March, 1778 [Ref: S-264, but not listed in Ref: C-25].

HAWN, Sarah. See "John Smith," q.v.

HAY, Thomas. Private in the 1st Maryland Regiment who enlisted on April 25, 1778, and served in the Southern Army of the United States under Lt. William Lamar in the late Capt. Beatty's company until discharged on April 25, 1781 [Ref: A-391].

HAYDEN, Mary Josephine Green. See "Aloysius Elder," q.v.

HAYES, Jonathan. Juror to the Oath of Allegiance in March, 1778 [Ref: S-264, but not listed in Ref: C-25].

HAYMAN, Charles. Provided wheat for the military in July, 1782 [Ref: R-536].

HAYMON, Owen. Private in the militia in July, 1776 [Ref: A-42].

HAYNES, John. Militia substitute from May to December 10, 1781, and "marched to Annapolis." [Ref: A-653].

HAYS, John. Drafted on June 13, 1781, but "since proved under age." [Ref: D-1814].

HAYS, John. Private in the Skipton District Militia under Capt. Thomas Waring on April 16, 1776 [Ref: B-167, D-1814]. Ensign in Capt. C. Clinton's company on July 27, 1776 [Ref: B-86, X-127].

HAYS, Thomas. Ensign in a cadet company in the Lower District on March 26, 1776 [Ref: W-287].

HAYS, William. Private who enlisted on May 15, 1778 [Ref: A-324].

HAYS, William. Private who enlisted on July 13, 1776 [Ref: A-43].

HAYTER, Abraham. Captain of a company of militia in 3rd Battalion on November 29, 1775 [Ref: E-52, B-86]. Name also spelled "Abram Heyter." [Ref: E-312]. "Abraham Heiter" was an Associator who was appointed "to hand about the Association paper" in Piney Creek Hundred in 1775 [Ref: E-305].

HAZEL, Strutton. Private who enlisted on July 29, 1776 [Ref: A-43].

HAZLEWOOD, Thomas. Private who enlisted May 2, 1778 [Ref: A-321].

HAZELIP, Richard. Private who enlisted on April 1 or 24, 1778 [Ref: A-217, A-320, which latter source misspelled his name as "Haylip"]. Served with the German Regiment at the Battle of White Plains on September 5, 1778, under Lieut. Col. Ludwick Weltner [Ref: A-266]. "On February 16, 1820, Treasurer of the Western Shore was directed to pay to Richard Hazelip, of Washington County, the half pay of a private, for his services during the Revolutionary War." [Ref: G-353]. "Richard Azelip" applied for a pension (S34630) in Frederick County on April 6, 1818, aged 65, for his service in the Continental and Maryland Lines [Ref: T-102. However, Ref: J-25 mistakenly states he was age 54 at time of application].

HEAD, Bigger [Biggar]. Associator in December, 1775 [Ref: E-168], and a Juror to the Oath of Allegiance in 1778 [Ref: C-25]. Ensign on November 29, 1775 in Capt. Wood's company of militia, 2nd lieutenant on May 15, 1776, and 1st lieutenant on December 28, 1776 in the 37th Battalion of militia [Ref: B-86, E-53, W-427, X-555]. "Bigger Head" provided wheat for the military in June, 1782 [Ref: R-521].

HEAD, George. Private in the 7th Maryland Regiment from December 30, 1777, to February 8, 1778, when "deserted." [Ref: A-216].

HEAD, William. Associator in December, 1775 [Ref: E-168]. Juror to the Oath of Allegiance in 1778 [Ref: C-25].

HEAD, William Beckwith. "William Bth. Head" was an Associator in December, 1775 [Ref: E-168]. "William Beckwith Head" was a 2nd lieutenant in Capt. Wood's company of militia in the 2nd Battalion on November 29, 1775, 1st lieutenant on May 15, 1776, and captain on November 28, 1776, in the 37th Battalion of militia [Ref: E-53, B-86, W-427, X-555]. Juror to the Oath of Allegiance in 1778 [Ref: C-25].

HEAD, William Edward (1748, Frederick County, Maryland - c.1790, Washington County, Kentucky). He enrolled as an Associator in December, 1775 [Ref: E-168], and signed as a Juror to the Oath of Allegiance in 1778 [Ref: C-25]. He served as a private in the 3rd Maryland Regiment in Capt. Chew's Company. His daughter Elizabeth Head (1779-1859) married Daniel Rodman (1781-1859) in 1801 in Kentucky [Ref: U-2842].

HEAFLEY, Anthony. Juror to the Oath of Allegiance in 1778 [Ref: C-25]. Associator in December, 1775 [Ref: E-168]. Also, see "Anthony Havely," q.v.

HEAGHER, Laurence. Associator in December, 1775 [Ref: E-168]. Juror to the Oath of Allegiance in 1778 [Ref: C-25].

HEAGLE, Jacob. Ensign in the Skipton District Militia on July 27, 1776, in Capt. Daniel Cresap's company [Ref: B-86, X-127].

HEALE, James. Associator in December, 1775 [Ref: E-167]. Juror to the Oath of Allegiance in 1778 [Ref: C-25].

HEAP, Anthony. Associator in December, 1775 [Ref: E-168]. Juror to the Oath of Allegiance in 1778 [Ref: C-25].

HEART, Chr. See "Chr. Hart," q.v.

HEART, Noah. See "Noah Hart," q.v.

HEART, John. Private who enlisted on August 8, 1776 [Ref: A-49].

HEART, Valentine. Associator in December, 1775 [Ref: E-168]. Juror to the Oath of Allegiance in 1778 [Ref: C-25]. "Valentine Hart" died testate in 1785, leaving a wife Anne Maria and 11 children: John, Christopher, Valentine, Jacob, Christian, Michael, Adam, Catherine, Elizabeth, Anne Maria, and Anne; plus "one to come into the world." [Ref: M-6:128].

HEART, Valentine Jr. Associator in December, 1775 [Ref: E-168]. Juror to the Oath of Allegiance in 1778 [Ref: C-25].

HEARTY, James. Militia substitute on June 6, 1778 [Ref: A-325].

HEARTY, Nicholas. Private, 1st Maryland Regiment, enlisted on April 24, 1778 and served in the Southern Army of the United States under Lt. William Lamar in the late Capt. Beatty's company until discharged on June 2, 1781 [Ref: A-391].

HEATER, George. Private who enlisted August 5, 1776 [Ref: A-44].

HEATHMAN, George. Private who enlisted August 5, 1776 [Ref: A-44].

HEBERLIN, Andrew. Juror to the Oath of Allegiance in 1778 [Ref: C-25].

HEBINER, George. Non-Enroller who was fined by the Committee of Observation in May, 1776 [Ref: E-248].

HEBINER, Michael. Non-Enroller who was fined by the Committee of Observation in May, 1776 [Ref: E-248].

HECK, Balser. Associator in December, 1775 [Ref: E-167]. Juror to the Oath of Allegiance in 1778 [Ref: C-25]. Balser Heck died testate in 1790, leaving wife Eve Margaret and his minor children Charles, Margaret, and Maria [Ref: M-8:34, M-8:35].

HECK, Daniel. Associator in December, 1775 [Ref: E-168]. Juror to the Oath of Allegiance in 1778 [Ref: C-25].

HECKET, Jonathan. Private in the German Regiment, muster roll dated October 23, 1776 [Ref: A-264].

HECKETHORN, Jacob. Associator in December, 1775 [Ref: E-167]. Juror to the Oath of Allegiance in 1778 [Ref: C-25, and S-264, which spelled the name "Heckathorn."].

HECKETON, George. Corporal in Capt. James Johnson's company of militia in 1775 [Ref: E-52].

HECKETORN, Martin. Militia substitute from May to December 10, 1781, and "marched to Annapolis." [Ref: A-653]. "Martin Heckenton" was a private who enlisted on July 1, 1776 in Capt. Peter Mantz's company, and marched from Frederick Town to Leonardtown, and from there to Philadelphia, arriving on August 23, 1776 [Ref: A-47].

HEDGES [HEDGE], Absolom. Associator in December, 1775 [Ref: E-168]. Juror to the Oath of Allegiance in 1778 [Ref: C-25].

HEDGES, Charles. Associator in December, 1775 [Ref: E-167]. (This name appeared twice on the list of Associators). One subscribed to the Oath of Allegiance in 1778 [Ref: C-25]. Charles Hedges, Sr. married Isabella ---- and died in 1795. A son Shadrach Hedges (1757-1846) married Mary Magdalene Miller (died in 1867), and their son Rev. Shadrach Abram Hedges, of Middletown, Maryland (aged 87 in 1923, thus born in 1836) joined the Sons of the American Revolution, stating "my father Shadrach Hedges told me that, in crossing the Delaware River while he was in the service during the Revolution, the chimney smoked so much that the stove could not be used and the soldiers dances all night to keep warm." He also noted that his grandfather Charles Hedges was an Associator in Frederick County [Ref: U-957].

HEDGES, Jacob. Juror to the Oath of Allegiance in 1778 [Ref: C-25].

HEDGES, James. Associator in December, 1775 [Ref: E-167]. Juror to the Oath of Allegiance in 1778 [Ref: C-25].

HEDGES [HEDGE], Joseph. 2nd Sergeant in Capt. Christopher Stull's company of militia in 1775 [Ref: E-50]. Associator in December, 1775 [Ref: E-167]. Juror to the Oath of Allegiance in 1778 [Ref: C-25]. "Joseph Hedge" was ensign in Capt. Michael Troutman's militia company in the 4th Battalion on November 29, 1775 [Ref: E-51, B-86, O-148]. Associator in December, 1775 [Ref: E-168]. Juror to the Oath of Allegiance in 1778 [Ref: C-25]. (Note: It is unclear whether William Hedge and William Hedges were the same person or different men since they are listed twice in both Ref: E-167 and Ref: C-25).

HEDGES, Josiah. Sergeant in Capt. Valentine Creager's company of militia in 1775 [Ref: E-53]. Associator in December, 1775 [Ref: E-167].

Juror to the Oath of Allegiance in 1778 [Ref: C-25]. Served as 3rd sergeant in the Middle District Militia in 1776, with Capt. Valentine Creager's company [Ref: A-72].

HEDGES, Mary. See "Joseph Wood," q.v.

HEDGES, Moses. Associator in December, 1775 [Ref: E-167]. Juror to the Oath of Allegiance in 1778 [Ref: C-25].

HEDGES, Peter. Associator in December, 1775 [Ref: E-167]. Juror to the Oath of Allegiance in 1778 [Ref: C-25]. Provided wheat for the military in July, 1782 [Ref: R-532]. Peter Hedges died testate in early 1792, leaving a wife Elizabeth and children Peter, William, Josiah, Caleb, John, and Pheba Cregar [Ref: M-8:135, M-8:136].

HEDGES, Shadrach. Soldier in the Maryland Line. See comments under "Charles Hedges," q.v. [Ref: U-957].

HEDGES, William (1742 - April 19, 1777). Associator in December, 1775 [Ref: E-167]. Juror to the Oath of Allegiance in 1778 [Ref: C-25]. William died testate in 1777, leaving wife Elizabeth and sons William and Andrew (among others). [Ref: M-5:171, and U-2564, which latter source states he served as a lieutenant in the Revolutionary War]. "William Hedge" was a 1st lieutenant in Capt. Christopher Stull's company of militia in the 1st Battalion on November 29, 1775, and in the 33rd Battalion of militia on March 3, 1777 [Ref: E-50, B-86, O-148].

HEEMS, Henry. Enlisted on April 10, 1781, for 3 years, and marched with Capt. Lynn [Ref: D-1814].

HEETER, Frederick. Private who enlisted on July 1, 1776 in Capt. Peter Mantz's company; marched from Frederick Town to Leonardtown, and then to Philadelphia, arriving on August 23, 1776 [Ref: A-47].

HEFFNER, Eva Maria. See "Lodwick Bireley," q.v.

HEFFNER [HEEFNER], Jacob. Private in the German Regiment, muster roll dated October 23, 1776 [Ref: A-264]. Discharged on October 12, 1779 [Ref: A-265].

HEFFNER, John. Drummer in Capt. Christopher Stull's company of militia in 1775 [Ref: E-50]. Drummer in the German Regiment, 1776, in Capt. Henry Fister's company under the command of Col. Nicholas Hussecker [Ref: A-261].

HEFFNER, Maria Juliana. See "Joseph Staley," q.v.

HEGERTY, George. See "George Hagerty," q.v.

HEIPNER, Gutlip. Non-Enroller who was fined by the Committee of Observation in April, 1776 [Ref: E-248].

HEISER, William. See "William Heyser," q.v.

HEITER, Abraham. See "Abraham Hayter," q.v.

HELDEBRIDLE, Solomon. Juror to the Oath of Allegiance in 1778 [Ref: C-25].

HELDELBRAND, Elizabeth. See "Peter Hammond," q.v.

HELDERBAND, Henry. Corporal in Capt. Ludowick Kemp's company of militia in 1775 [Ref: E-52].

HELLEN, John. 2nd lieutenant in the Middle District Militia in 1776 [Ref: A-44].

HELLMAN, William. Private, 1st Maryland Regiment, 1781, and served in the Southern Army of the United States under Lt. William Lamar in the late Capt. Beatty's company [Ref: A-392].

HELMES, John. Militia substitute from May to December 10, 1781, and "marched to Annapolis." Discharged by Gen. William Smallwood (no date was given). [Ref: A-653].

HELTEBIDLE, Jacob. Associator in December, 1775 [Ref: E-168]. Juror to the Oath of Allegiance in 1778 [Ref: C-25].

HEMINGER, Conrad. Juror to the Oath of Allegiance in 1778 [Ref: C-25].

HENCKEL, Maria Catherine. See "Peter Apple," q.v.

HENDERSON, Daniel. Private who enlisted July 19, 1776 [Ref: A-51].

HENDERSON, John. Private who was enlisted on July 20, 1776 by Capt. Jacob Good [Ref: A-46].

HENDERSON, Judge. See "Isaac Shelby," q.v.

HENDRICKS, Albert. Private in the German Regiment. Served at White Plains on September 5, 1778, under Lt. Col. Weltner [Ref: A-266].

HENDRICKSON, Albert. Militia substitute, June 3, 1778 [Ref: A-325].

HENDRICKSON, Henrick. Sergeant in Capt. William Duvall's company of militia in 1775 [Ref: E-54].

HENDRICKSON, John. Associator in December, 1775 [Ref: E-168]. Private who enlisted on July 1, 1776 in Capt. Peter Mantz's company; marched from Frederick Town to Leonardtown, and from there to Philadelphia, arriving on August 23, 1776 [Ref: A-47]. Juror to the Oath of Allegiance in 1778 [Ref: C-25].

HENDRICKSON, William. Private who enlisted on July 1, 1776 in Capt. Peter Mantz's company; marched from Frederick Town to Leonardtown, and then to Philadelphia, arriving on August 23, 1776 [Ref: A-47].

HENDRIX, John and Irena. See "Levi Davis," q.v.

HENEP [HENOP], Frederick. Associator in December, 1775 [Ref: E-168]. Juror to the Oath of Allegiance in 1778 [Ref: C-25]. One "Frederick Ludwick Henop, of Prince George's County," died testate in Frederick County in 1784, leaving a son James and mentioning his sister Susan Baily [Ref: M-6:127]. "Frederick Henop" loaned $400 for the use of the

State of Maryland in June, 1780 [Ref: V-520]. Also, see "Lodowick Weltner," q.v.

HENET, John. 2nd lieutenant in the Skipton District Militia on July 27, 1776, in Capt. Daniel Cresap's company [Ref: B-86, X-127].

HENNING, John. Associator in December, 1775 [Ref: E-168]. Juror to the Oath of Allegiance in 1778 [Ref: C-25].

HENNINGER, Ulrick. Associator in December, 1775 [Ref: E-168]. "Ulrick Henningher" was a non-enroller who was fined by the Committee of Observation in April, 1776 [Ref: E-248]. "Ulrick Henninger" was a juror to the Oath of Allegiance in 1778 [Ref: C-25].

HENNINGHOUSE, Frederick. Private in the German Regiment, 1776, in Capt. Henry Fister's company under the command of Col. Nicholas Hussecker [Ref: A-261].

HENNIS, Samuel. Private in the militia who was disabled at White Horse. His invalid's pension commenced on September 20, 1777, and ceased on November 1, 1789 [Ref: A-630, A-631].

HENNISY [HENESSEY], James. Private who enlisted on May 11, 1778, and served in the 2nd Maryland Regiment [Ref: A-294, A-322]. One "James Hannesey, who was sent to camp as a vagrant from Frederick County, returned by General Smallwood and sent on board the Gallies and appearing to be unfit for duty, is hereby discharged from the service" on September 30, 1778 [Ref: Z-213].

HENRICK, Conrad. Associator in December, 1775 [Ref: E-167]. Juror to the Oath of Allegiance in 1778 [Ref: C-25].

HENRY, John. Private who enlisted on July 18, 1776 [Ref: A-49].

HENRY, Patrick. See "Isaac Shelby," q.v.

HENSY, John. Associator in December, 1775 [Ref: E-168]. Juror to the Oath of Allegiance in 1778 [Ref: C-25].

HEO, Simeon. Drafted on June 2, 1783 [Ref: B-168].

HER, John. Petitioned the General Assembly under the Act of May 12, 1780, stating he had been a non-juror to the Oath of Allegiance and Fidelity in 1778 due to "ignorance" and now desired relief under the Act and to take the Oath [Ref: L-101].

HERBAUGH, John. See "John Harbough" and "John Herboch," q.v.

HERBERT, Mary and Zephaniah. See "Peter Zollinger," q.v.

HERBOCH, Jacob (1730-1818). Son of Jost Herbach who died in 1792 in York County, Pennsylvania. Non-Enroller who was fined by the Committee of Observation in April, 1776 [Ref: E-248, O-128].

HERBOCK, George (1726-1787). Son of Jost Herbach who died in 1792 in York County, Pennsylvania. Non-Enroller who was fined by the Committee of Observation in April, 1776 [Ref: E-248, O-128].

HERBOCK, John (1735-1803). Son of Jost Herbach who died in 1792 in York County, Pennsylvania. Non-Enroller who was fined by the Committee of Observation in April, 1776 [Ref: E-248, O-128].

HERBOCK, Ludwick (1729-1809). Son of Jost Herbach who died in 1792 in York County, Pennsylvania. Non-Enroller who was fined by the Committee of Observation in April, 1776 [Ref: E-248, O-128].

HERD, Bennett. Private who enlisted on July 29, 1776 [Ref: A-44].

HERD, Jacob. Petitioned the General Assembly under the Act of May 12, 1780, stating he had been a non-juror to the Oath of Allegiance and Fidelity in 1778 due to "ignorance" and now desired relief under the Act and to take the Oath [Ref: L-101].

HERITAGE, Thomas. Private in the 7th Maryland Regiment from August 3, 1777, to September 11, 1777, when reported missing [Ref: A-216].

HERLIN, James. Juror to the Oath of Allegiance in March, 1778 [Ref: S-264, but not listed in Ref: C-25].

HERMINGER, Conrad. Associator in December, 1775 [Ref: E-167].

HERMINGER, John. Associator in December, 1775 [Ref: E-167]. Juror to the Oath of Allegiance in 1778 [Ref: C-25].

HERN, John. Associator in December, 1775 [Ref: E-168]. Juror to the Oath of Allegiance in 1778 [Ref: C-25].

HERR (HERRMANN), Juliana. See "Jacob Storm," q.v.

HERRING, Henry. Private in German Regiment, 1776, in Capt. Henry Fister's company under the command of Col. Hussecker [Ref: A-261].

HERRIOT, John. Served on the Committee of Observation in 1775 [Ref: I-85].

HERSHBERGER, Barnet. Provided beef for the military in May, 1782 [Ref: R-505].

HERSHBERGER, Dorothea. See "Frederick Kemp," q.v.

HERSHBERGER, Henry. Non-Enroller who was fined by the Committee of Observation in April, 1776 [Ref: E-248].

HERTER, Adam. Corporal in Capt. Jacob Snowdenberger's company of militia in 1775 [Ref: E-56].

HERTZOG, Catherine. See "Andrew Fogel (Vogler)," q.v.

HERUPELY, Michael. Associator in December, 1775 [Ref: E-167]. Juror to the Oath of Allegiance in 1778 [Ref: C-25].

HESSONG, Balser. Juror to the Oath of Allegiance in March, 1778 [Ref: S-264, but not listed in Ref: C-25].

HEVERON, Peter. Private in the Middle District Militia in 1776 in Capt. Valentine Creager's company [Ref: A-72].

HEVLIN, Debora Ann. See "Matthias Young," q.v.

HEVNER, John. Associator in December, 1775 [Ref: E-167]. Juror to the Oath of Allegiance in 1778 [Ref: C-25].

HEWITT, Elijah. Private in the Skipton District Militia under Capt. Thomas Waring on April 16, 1776 [Ref: B-167, D-1814].

HEYL, Leonard. Associator in December, 1775 [Ref: E-168]. Juror to the Oath of Allegiance in 1778 [Ref: C-25].

HEYSER [KEYSER?], Nicholas. Private in the German Regiment in 1776 [Ref: A-266].

HEYSER [HEISER], William. Captain in the German Regiment in July, 1776, and on muster roll dated October 23, 1776 [Ref: A-263, X-48].

HICKE, William. Private in the militia in July, 1776 [Ref: A-42].

HICKELTHORN, Michael. Associator in December, 1775 [Ref: E-168]. Juror to the Oath of Allegiance in 1778 [Ref: C-25].

HICKS, Laben. Drafted on June 2, 1783; "gone to Montgomery County." [Ref: B-168].

HIDE, John. Corporal in Capt. Joseph Wood, Jr.'s company of militia in 1775 [Ref: E-53]. Associator in December, 1775 [Ref: E-168]. Juror to the Oath of Allegiance in 1778 [Ref: C-25].

HIGDON, John Jr. Private who enlisted on July 22, 1776 [Ref: A-49].

HIGDON, Mary Ellen. See "Leonard Watkins," q.v.

HIGH, John. Paid by the Committee of Observation "for carriage of 13 casks of bullets" in 1775 [Ref: E-65].

HIGHLER, Nicholas. Associator in December, 1775 [Ref: E-168]. Juror to the Oath of Allegiance in 1778 [Ref: C-25].

HILAND, George. Private, 7th Maryland Regiment, 1780, enlisted in Frederick Town between January and April, 1780, and reported as "gone to Camp" [Ref: A-334].

HILDEBRAND, Henry. Private in German Regiment, 1776, in Capt. Henry Fister's company under the command of Col. Hussecker [Ref: A-261].

HILDEBRAND, Nicholas. Sergeant in Capt. John Haass' militia company in 1775 [Ref: E-53]. "Nicholas Hielderbrand" was an Associator in December, 1775 [Ref: E-168]. Also signed as a Juror to the Oath of Allegiance, 1778 [Ref: C-25].

HILDEBRIDLE, Jacob. Juror to the Oath of Allegiance in March, 1778 [Ref: S-264, but not listed in Ref: C-25].

HILDROP, John. Private who enlisted February 11, 1778 [Ref: A-314].

HILER, Abraham (Piney Creek Hundred). Appointed by the Committee of Correspondence to solicit subscriptions in 1775 to purchase arms and ammunition [Ref: I-86].

HILL [HILE], Conrad. Associator in December, 1775 [Ref: E-168], and signed as a Juror to the Oath of Allegiance in 1778 [Ref: C-25].

HILL, Abraham. 1st lieutenant in Capt. Abraham Hayter's company of militia in the 3rd Battalion, November 29, 1775 [Ref: E-52, B-87].

HILL, Cosomer. Private who enlisted February 27, 1778 [Ref: A-314]. "Casimir Hill" was a private in the German Regiment at White Plains on September 5, 1778, under Lt. Col. Ludwick Weltner [Ref: A-267]. On April 15, 1779, Colonel Weltner petitioned the Frederick County Court in behalf of "Casmer Hill," a soldier in his regiment, and his wife (no name given) and 2 children. Mrs. Hill was subsequently granted 20 lbs. for one year's subsistence [Ref: Q-6835]. "Casamore Hiel" enrolled as an Associator in December, 1775 [Ref: E-168], and signed as a Juror to the Oath of Allegiance in 1778 [Ref: C-25]. "Casimer Hull" was a private in the German Regiment to at least August 1, 1780 [Ref: A-217].

HILL, Edward. 1st lieutenant in the Light Infantry Company of the 31st Battalion of militia on May 15, 1776 [Ref: B-87].

HILL, George. Private who enlisted on August 5, 1776, in the Flying Camp under Capt. Philip Meroney [Ref: A-45, N-30:111].

HILL, John. Militia substitute on June 8, 1778 [Ref: A-325].

HILL, Joseph. 2nd lieutenant in the militia on November 9, 1776 [Ref: B-87, X-432].

HILL, Joseph Jr. Juror to the Oath of Allegiance in March, 1778 [Ref: S-264, but not listed in Ref: C-25].

HILL, Joseph Sr. Juror to the Oath of Allegiance in March, 1778 [Ref: S-264, but not listed in Ref: C-25].

HILL, Thomas. Juror to the Oath of Allegiance in March, 1778 [Ref: S-264, but not listed in Ref: C-25]. Ensign in the Frederick Town Battalion of Militia on September 18, 1780 [Ref: V-295].

HILL, William. 1st lieutenant in the 34th Battalion of militia on May 15, 1776 [Ref: W-426].

HILLARY, Ralph. 1st lieutenant in Capt. Samuel Plummer's company of militia in the 1st Battalion, November 29, 1775 [Ref: E-54, B-87]. "Ralph Hilleary" was a captain in the 33rd Battalion of militia on March 3, 1777, and captain in the Select Militia on August 16, 1781 [Ref: B-87].

HILLARY, Thomas. "Thomas Hillery" was a private who enlisted August 5, 1776 in the Flying Camp under Capt. Philip Meroney [Ref: A-45, and

N-30:112, which spelled his name "Hilleary"]. "Thomas Hilleary" was an ensign in the Select Militia on August 16, 1781 [Ref: B-87].

HILLEGAS, Albright. Associator in December, 1775 [Ref: E-168]. Juror to the Oath of Allegiance in 1778 [Ref: C-25].

HILLS, Charles. Private who enlisted April 28, 1778 [Ref: A-321].

HILLS, Richard. Associator in December, 1775 [Ref: E-168]. Juror to the Oath of Allegiance in 1778 [Ref: C-25].

HILTON, James Jr. Juror to the Oath of Allegiance in March, 1778 [Ref: S-264, but not listed in Ref: C-25].

HILTON, James Sr. Juror to the Oath of Allegiance in March, 1778 [Ref: S-264, but not listed in Ref: C-25].

HILTON, John. Juror to the Oath of Allegiance in March, 1778 [Ref: S-264, but not listed in Ref: C-25].

HILTON, Trueman. Juror to the Oath of Allegiance in March, 1778 [Ref: S-264, but not listed in Ref: C-25].

HILTON, William. Private who enlisted on August 5, 1776 in the Flying Camp under Capt. Philip Meroney [Ref: A-45, N-30:112].

HILTT, John (Colonel). See "Conrad Hogmire," q.v.

HIME, Laurence. Associator in December, 1775 [Ref: E-168]. Juror to the Oath of Allegiance in March, 1778 [Ref: C-25]. A David Hime died testate in 1786, naming his wife Margaret and a son Larance [sic], among others. [Ref: M-7:28].

HINCKEL [HINCKELL], John. Ensign in Capt. Henry Baker's company of militia from November 29, 1775, through at least December 28, 1776 [Ref: E-54, B-87, X-555].

HINDMARSH, John. Petitioned the General Assembly under the Act of May 12, 1780, stating that he had been a non-juror to the Oath of Allegiance and Fidelity in 1778 due to "ignorance" and now desired relief under the Act and to take the Oath [Ref: L-101].

HINDON, Philip. Private who enlisted on August 5, 1776 [Ref: A-44].

HINDS, Daniel. Private who enlisted on July 1, 1776 in Capt. Peter Mantz's company; marched from Frederick Town to Leonardtown, and from there to Philadelphia, arriving August 23, 1776 [Ref: A-47].

HINDS, Henry. Private who enlisted on July 1, 1776 in Capt. Peter Mantz's company; marched from Frederick Town to Leonardtown, and from there to Philadelphia, arriving August 23, 1776 [Ref: A-47]. "Henry Hines" was ensign in 1778 and 2nd lieutenant on August 16, 1779, in the Frederick Town Battalion of militia [Ref: H-15, B-87].

HINKEL, Baltis. Associator in December, 1775 [Ref: E-168]. Juror to the Oath of Allegiance, 1778 [Ref: C-25]. "Baltzel Hinkle" died on February 18, 1804 [Ref: F-470].
HINKLE, Catherine. See "Richard Davis," q.v.
HINKLE, Jacob Jr. Drafted on June 2, 1783 [Ref: B-168].
HINKLE, Philip. Militia substitute on June 2, 1778 [Ref: A-324]. "Philip Hinkel," private in the German Regiment at White Plains on September 5, 1778, under Lt. Col. Ludwick Weltner [Ref: A-267].
HINKLE, Maria Catherine. See "Maria Catherine Henckel," q.v.
HINTON, John. Sergeant in Capt. Samuel Plummer's company of militia in 1775 [Ref: E-54].
HINTON, Richard. Juror to the Oath of Allegiance in March, 1778 [Ref: S-264, but not listed in Ref: C-25].
HINTZ, Henry. Sergeant in Capt. William Beatty's company of militia in 1775 [Ref: E-55].
HINTZ, Ridolf. Corporal in Capt. William Beatty's company of militia in 1775 [Ref: E-55].
HIRSCH, Jacob. Associator in December, 1775 [Ref: E-168]. "Jacob Hirsh" was a private, enlisted on July 19, 1776 [Ref: A-51]. "Jacob Hirsch" took the Oath of Allegiance in 1778 [Ref: C-25].
HIRSHMAN, Christian. Non-Enroller who was fined by the Committee of Observation in April, 1776 [Ref: E-248].
HISER, Godfrey. Petitioned the General Assembly under the Act of May 12, 1780, stating that he had been a non-juror to the Oath of Allegiance and Fidelity in 1778 due to "ignorance" and now desired relief under the Act and to take the Oath [Ref: L-101].
HISLER, Nicholas. Sergeant in Capt. Charles Beatty's company of militia in 1775 [Ref: E-51], and 2nd lieutenant on May 12, 1779 [Ref: H-15, Z-387].
HOAN, David. Associator in December, 1775 [Ref: E-168]. Juror to the Oath of Allegiance in 1778 [Ref: C-25].
HOARN [HORAN], Patrick. Private who enlisted on May 22, 1777, and served in Capt. William Beatty's company in 7th Maryland Regiment in 1779 [Ref: A-311].
HOBBINS, Moses. Private who enlisted on July 18, 1776 [Ref: A-50].
HOBBS, Elizabeth. See "William Cumming," q.v.
HOBBS, Greenbury. Corporal in Capt. Basil Dorsey's company in 1775 [Ref: E-52]. "Greenbury Hobs" petitioned the General Assembly under the Act of May 12, 1780, stating that he had been a non-juror to the

Oath of Allegiance and Fidelity in 1778 due to "ignorance" and now desired relief under the Act and to take the Oath [Ref: L-101].

HOBBS, Joseph. 1st lieutenant in Capt. Basil Dorsey's company of militia on November 29, 1775, to at least December 28, 1776 [Ref: E-52, B-87, X-555]. Petitioned the General Assembly under the Act of May 12, 1780, stating he had been a non-juror to the Oath of Allegiance and Fidelity in 1778 due to "ignorance" and now desired relief under the Act and to take the Oath [Ref: L-101]. Provided wheat for the military in June, 1782 [Ref: R-526].

HOBBS, Joshua. Drafted on June 2, 1783 [Ref: B-169].

HOBBS, Nicholas (Linganore Hundred). Appointed by the Committee of Correspondence to solicit subscriptions in 1775 to purchase arms and ammunition [Ref: I-86]. 2nd lieutenant in Capt. Basil Dorsey's company of militia on November 29, 1775, to at least November 28, 1776 [Ref: E-52, X-555]. Associator who was appointed "to hand about the Association paper" in Linganore Hundred in 1775 [Ref: E-305]. Nicholas Hobbs petitioned the General Assembly under the Act of January 14, 1781, stating he had been a non-juror to the Oath of Allegiance and Fidelity in 1778 due to "ignorance" and now desired relief under the Act and to take the Oath [Ref: L-101].

HOBBS, Samuel. 1st lieutenant in the Skipton District Militia on July 27, 1776, in Capt. Daniel Cresap's company [Ref: B-88, X-127].

HOBBS, William (Burnt Woods Hundred). Appointed by the Committee of Correspondence to solicit subscriptions in 1775 to purchase arms and ammunition [Ref: I-86]. Served on the Committee of Observation in 1775 [Ref: I-85]. Associator who was appointed "to hand about the Association paper" in Linganore Hundred in 1775 [Ref: E-305]. Petitioned the General Assembly under the Act of May 12, 1780, stating that he had been a non-juror to the Oath of Allegiance and Fidelity in 1778 due to "ignorance" and now desired relief under the Act and to take the Oath [Ref: L-101]. One William Hobbs was a coroner in Frederick County in 1777 [Ref: F-476].

HOBLITZELL, Adrian (February 5, 1745 - June 20, 1820). Private who enlisted on July 1, 1775, in Frederick County, in the company of Capt. Michael Cresap's Maryland Riflemen. Subsequently lived in the part of Frederick County that became Washington County in 1777. He also subscribed to the Oath of Allegiance in Washington County in 1778. Adrian Hoblitzell, of Lorraine, Germany, married Martha Barton in 1774 and a son Jacob Hoblitzell died in 1834 [Ref: U-2827].

HOBS, Leonard. Petitioned the General Assembly under the Act of May 12, 1780, stating he had been a non-juror to the Oath of Allegiance and Fidelity in 1778 due to "ignorance" and now desired relief under the Act and to take the Oath [Ref: L-101].

HOBS, Samuel (of Samuel). Petitioned the General Assembly under the Act of May 12, 1780, stating he had been a non-juror to the Oath of Allegiance and Fidelity in 1778 due to "ignorance" and now desired relief under the Act and to take the Oath [Ref: L-101].

HOBS, William. Petitioned the General Assembly under the Act of May 12, 1780, stating he had been a non-juror to the Oath of Allegiance and Fidelity in 1778 due to "ignorance" and now desired relief under the Act and to take the Oath [Ref: L-101].

HOBSON, Richard. Militia substitute on June 9, 1778 [Ref: A-325].

HOCKERSMITH, C. Jr. Associator in December, 1775 [Ref: E-167]. Juror to the Oath of Allegiance in 1778 [Ref: C-25].

HOCKERSMITH, C. Sr. Associator in December, 1775 [Ref: E-167]. Juror to the Oath of Allegiance in 1778 [Ref: C-25].

HOCKERSMITH [HAWKERSMITH], George. 1st lieutenant in Capt. Blair's company of militia in the 3rd Battalion on November 29, 1775 [Ref: E-55, B-88]. Associator in December, 1775 [Ref: E-167]. "George Hawkersmith" was a captain in the 35th Battalion of militia on November 28, 1776 [Ref: B-86]. Served in Col. Bruce's battalion on December 28, 1776 [Ref: X-555]. "George Hockersmith" was a Juror to Oath of Allegiance in 1778 [Ref: C-25]. See "William Elder, of Guy," q.v.

HOCKERSMITH [HAWKERSMITH], Jacob. Ensign in Capt. William Blair's company of militia in the 3rd Battalion on November 29, 1775 [Ref: E-55, B-88]. Associator in December, 1775 [Ref: E-167]. "Jacob Hawkersmith" was 2nd lieutenant in the 35th Battalion of militia on November or December 28, 1776 [Ref: B-86, X-555]. "Jacob Hockersmith" was a Juror to the Oath of Allegiance, 1778 [Ref: C-25].

HOCKERSMITH [HAWKERSMITH], Michael. 2nd lieutenant in Capt. William Shields' company of militia in the 3rd Battalion from November 29, 1775, to at least December 26, 1776 [Ref: E-55, B-86, B-88, X-555].

HOCKMAN, John. Non-Enroller who was fined by the Committee of Observation in April, 1776 [Ref: E-248]. Juror to the Oath of Allegiance in March, 1778 [Ref: S-264, but not listed in Ref: C-25].

HOCKWATER, Michael. Associator in December, 1775 [Ref: E-168]. Juror to the Oath of Allegiance in 1778 [Ref: C-25].

HODGKISS, Edward. Associator in December, 1775 [Ref: E-168]. Juror to the Oath of Allegiance in 1778 [Ref: C-25].

HOEY, Peter. Private who enlisted on July 29, 1776 [Ref: A-43].

HOFF, Abraham (Manor Hundred). Appointed by the Committee of Correspondence to solicit subscriptions in 1775 to purchase arms and ammunition [Ref: I-86]. Served on the Committee of Observation in 1775 [Ref: I-85]. (Note: This is probably "Abraham Haff," q.v.)

HOFFHART, Daniel. Associator in December, 1775 [Ref: E-168]. Juror to the Oath of Allegiance in 1778 [Ref: C-25].

HOFFHART, John. Juror to the Oath of Allegiance in 1778 [Ref: C-25].

HOFFHART, Philip. Associator in December, 1775 [Ref: E-168]. Juror to the Oath of Allegiance in 1778 [Ref: C-25].

HOFFLER, David. Non-Enroller who was fined by the Committee of Observation in April, 1776 [Ref: E-248].

HOFFMAN, Christopher. Substitute on June 13, 1781, and subsequently reported as "deserted" (no date given). [Ref: D-1814].

HOFFMAN, Francis. Ensign in Capt. Ludowick Kemp's company of militia on November 29, 1775 [Ref: E-52, B-88].

HOFFMAN, Henry. Soldier in the Pennsylvania Line who "applied for pension (R5096) in Frederick County, Maryland, on October 29, 1834, aged 77, stating he had lived there at the time of his enlistment. Received bounty land warrant #2135-100. On October 23, 1846, a son Henry Hoffman applied and stated his father had married Elizabeth Wickard of Lancaster, Pennsylvania in August, 1783. His father died in November, 1838, his mother died on February 19, 1842, and left these heirs: George, Caspar, John, and Henry Hoffman, Catharine Travise, Rebecca Hill, and Charlotte Hoffman, heirs of Adam and Jacob Hoffman, the only heirs of Elizabeth Hoffman." [Ref: T-1666].

HOFFMAN, Jacob. Associator in December, 1775 [Ref: E-167, E-168]. (This name appeared twice on the list of Associators). One subscribed to the Oath of Allegiance in 1778 [Ref: C-25].

HOFFMAN, John. Associator in December, 1775 [Ref: E-167]. (This name appeared twice on the list of Associators). One subscribed to the Oath of Allegiance in 1778 [Ref: C-25].

HOFFMAN, Peter (Fredericktown Hundred). Appointed by the Committee of Correspondence to solicit subscriptions in 1775 to purchase arms and ammunition [Ref: I-86]. Served on the Committee of Observation in 1775 [Ref: I-85]. Associator in December, 1775 [Ref: E-167]. Furnished lead and flints for use of the militia in Frederick Town in 1775 [Ref: E-61]. Collected 12 lbs. 19 sh. 3 p. for arms and ammunition for the militia in 1775 [Ref: E-63]. Juror to the Oath of Allegiance in 1778 [Ref: C-25, S-267].

HOFFMAN, Valentine and Elizabeth. See "Joseph Doll," q.v.
HOFFSTATTER [HOSTETER], Abraham. Served on the Committee of Observation in 1775 [Ref: I-85].
HOFFSTATTER, Adam. Associator in December, 1775 [Ref: E-167]. Juror to the Oath of Allegiance in 1778 [Ref: C-25].
HOFFSTATTER [HOUSTETLER], Frederick. Juror to the Oath of Allegiance in March, 1778 [Ref: S-264, but not listed in Ref: C-25].
HOFFSTATTER, Henry. Associator in December, 1775 [Ref: E-167]. Juror to the Oath of Allegiance in 1778 [Ref: C-25]. "Henry Hoofstadler" was sergeant in Capt. Charles Beatty's company of militia in 1775 [Ref: E-51]. "Henry Hupstadler" was an ensign in the Frederick Town Battalion of militia on May 12, 1779, under Capt. Thomas Beatty [Ref: B-90, H-15, Z-387]. "Henry Hoffstadler" was an ensign in the Select Militia on August 3, 1781 [Ref: B-88].
HOG, Thomas (Lower Antietam Hundred). Appointed by the Committee of Correspondence to solicit subscriptions in 1775 to purchase arms and ammunition [Ref: I-86]. Served on the Committee of Observation in 1775 [Ref: I-85].
HOGGY, ----. Lieutenant in militia on December 6, 1781 [Ref: B-88].
HOGMIRE, Conrad (Upper Antietam Hundred). Appointed by the Committee of Correspondence to solicit subscriptions in 1775 to purchase arms and ammunition [Ref: I-86]. Served on the Committee of Observation in 1775 [Ref: I-85]. Associator in December, 1775 [Ref: E-167]. Juror to the Oath of Allegiance in 1778 [Ref: C-25]. Commissioned a captain in the 32nd Battalion under Col. John Hiltt on January 3, 1776 [Ref: H-19, B-88]. Captain in militia of Washington County on October 10, 1776, to 1777 [Ref: B-244, B-88].
HOGSHIELD, Justinius. Private in the German Regiment in 1776 in Capt. Henry Fister's company under the command of Col. Nicholas Hussecker [Ref: A-261].
HOHL, Mary. See "Mathias Firestone," q.v.
HOHN [HONIN], Catherine, et al. See "John Smith," q.v.
HOLDERMAN, Jacob. Associator in December, 1775 [Ref: E-168]. Juror to the Oath of Allegiance in 1778 [Ref: C-25].
HOLDEN, John. Private who enlisted in 1778 and served in the 2nd Maryland Regiment [Ref: A-294].
HOLDUP, Thomas. Private who enlisted April 27, 1778 [Ref: A-321].
HOLLAND, Benjamin. Private who enlisted August 5, 1776 [Ref: A-44].
HOLLAND, Gabriel. Private who enlisted April 30, 1778 [Ref: A-321].
HOLLAND, John. Private who enlisted February 19, 1778 [Ref: A-314].

HOLLAND, Joseph. Private, Maryland Line, from Frederick County, who pensioned on October 8, 1818, at $96 per annum from April 1, 1818 [Ref: G-355, citing the U. S. Pension Rolls of 1835]. He was aged 62 when he applied for a pension on April 1, 1818 (S34924), stating he had wife Lurana, aged 58, daughter Elizabeth, aged about 29, and daughter Comfort, aged 15, and also a "granddaughter" [sic] Richard Gather, aged 3 years and 9 months [Ref: T-1680, J-25].

HOLLAND, William. Private who enlisted July 29, 1776 [Ref: A-43].

HOLLAR, Godfrey. Corporal in Capt. Peter Mantz's company of militia in 1775 [Ref: E-50].

HOLLIDAY, George. Private who enlisted August 5, 1776 in the Flying Camp under Capt. Philip Meroney [Ref: A-45, N-30:111]. Also, George Holliday, a private, enlisted on January 29, 1778 [Ref: A-314].

HOLLINGS, William. Private who enlisted on August 5, 1776 in the Flying Camp under Capt. Philip Meroney [Ref: A-45, N-30:112].

HOLLIT, John. Private in the Skipton District Militia under Capt. Thomas Waring on April 16, 1776 [Ref: B-167, D-1814].

HOLLON, Reson. Private in the militia in July, 1776 [Ref: A-42].

HOLLOWAY, John. Corporal in the 7th Maryland Regiment on May 18, 1778, private on January 1, 1779, and reported "deserted" April 8, 1779 [Ref: A-217].

HOLLYDAY, Clement. 1st lieutenant in the Upper District Militia [now Washington County] in 1776 [Ref: A-48].

HOLMES, Thomas. Petitioned the General Assembly under the Act of May 12, 1780, stating that he had been a non-juror to the Oath of Allegiance and Fidelity in 1778 due to "ignorance" and now desired relief under the Act and to take the Oath [Ref: L-101].

HOLMS, Thomas. Associator in December, 1775 [Ref: E-168]. Juror to the Oath of Allegiance in 1778 [Ref: C-25].

HOLS, Jacob. See "Jacob Holtz," q.v.

HOLSAPPLE, Frederick. See "Frederick Holtzable," q.v.

HOLTON, George. Substitute on June 13, 1781, for 3 years; marched with Capt. Boyer [Ref: D-1814].

HOLTZ, Eleanora. See "John Zimmerman," q.v.

HOLTZ, Jacob. Private who enlisted on August 5, 1776 in the Flying Camp under Capt. Philip Meroney [Ref: A-45, N-30:112]. "Jacob Hols" subscribed to the Oath of Allegiance in 1778, as did one "J. Holz." [Ref: C-25]. Both "Jacob Hols" and J. Holtz" were Associators in 1775 [Ref: E-167].

HOLTZABLE [HULTZAPPLE, HOLSAPPLE], Frederick. "Frederick Holtzable" was a non-enroller who was fined by the Committee of Observation in April, 1776. It was later determined that he was over age and the fine was remitted, June, 1776 [Ref: E-248]. "Frederick Hultzapple" provided wheat for the military in 1782 [Ref: R-522]. "Frederick Holsapple" died testate and his will was probated on January 4, 1786, naming wife Mary and children Frederick, Abraham, Daniel, Catherine, Mary, Salome, Susannah, and Regina [Ref: M-7:27].

HOLTZMAN, Henry. Associator in December, 1775 [Ref: E-167]. Juror to the Oath of Allegiance in 1778 [Ref: C-25]. Enlisted as a sergeant on May 11, 1778, and served in the 7th Maryland Regiment; private on September 20, 1779, and discharged by Gen. William Smallwood on March 26, 1780 [Ref: A-216, A-322]. Served as a substitute in 1781, and "marched to Annapolis." [Ref: A-653]. A Frederick Holtzman died testate in 1793, leaving a wife Margaret and a son Henry Holtzman (among others). [Ref: M-9:33].

HOLTZMAN, Jacob. Private in the Middle District Militia in 1776 in Capt. Valentine Creager's company [Ref: A-72].

HOLVERSTOT, Margaret. See "Philip Angler (Englar)," q.v.

HOM, Michael. Associator in December, 1775 [Ref: E-168]. Juror to the Oath of Allegiance in 1778 [Ref: C-25].

HOMMER, Jacob. Militia substitute on June 3, 1778 [Ref: A-325].

HOOD, John. Private who enlisted on July 24, 1776 [Ref: A-50].

HOOFMAN, Henry. Associator in December, 1775 [Ref: E-168]. Juror to the Oath of Allegiance in 1778 [Ref: C-25].

HOOK, Daniel. Drafted on June 2, 1783 [Ref: B-168].

HOOK, George Michael. Private in the horse troops in 1781 [Ref: B-168]. Also, see "George Michael Hawk," q.v.

HOOK, James. Associator in December, 1775 [Ref: E-168]. Juror to the Oath of Allegiance in 1778 [Ref: C-25].

HOOK, James Jr. Private in horse troops in June, 1781 [Ref: B-167].

HOOK, James Samuel. Associator in December, 1775 [Ref: E-168]. Juror to the Oath of Allegiance in 1778 [Ref: C-26].

HOOK, John Snowden. Associator in December, 1775 [Ref: E-168]. Juror to the Oath of Allegiance in 1778 [Ref: C-26]. "John Snowden Hooke," private, enlisted August 8, 1776 [Ref: A-49].

HOOK, Joseph. Soldier in the Maryland Line. Applied for pension on April 15, 1818, aged 76. [Ref: J-25, but not found in Ref: T-1697. There is a Joseph Hook who pensioned from Baltimore in Ref: T-1697, but Ref: J-25 states Joseph Hook was a Frederick County pensioner].

HOOK, Sarah. See "Abraham Lakin," q.v.

HOOK, Stephen. Associator in December, 1775 [Ref: E-168]. Juror to Oath of Allegiance in 1778 [Ref: C-26]. Applied for pension (S8733) for his services in Maryland Line, on July 8, 1833, in Allegheny County, Virginia, stating he was born in Frederick County, Maryland in 1756. [Ref: T-1697].

HOON, John. Associator in December, 1775 [Ref: E-168]. Juror to the Oath of Allegiance in 1778 [Ref: C-26].

HOOPER, James. Sergeant in Capt. William Beatty's militia company in 1775 [Ref: E-55]. Ensign in the Frederick Town Battalion of militia on August 16, 1779, in Capt. Salmon's company [Ref: B-88].

HOOVER [HUVER], Adam. Associator in December, 1775 [Ref: E-167]. Juror to the Oath of Allegiance in 1778 [Ref: C-26]. Also, see "Adam Hower," q.v.

HOOVER, Christian. Non-Enroller who was fined by the Committee of Observation in April, 1776 [Ref: E-248].

HOOVER, George. Corporal in Capt. John Haass' company of militia in 1775 [Ref: E-53]. Corporal in the German Regiment, 1776, in Capt. Henry Fister's company under the command of Col. Nicholas Hussecker [Ref: A-261].

HOOVER, Grandmother. See "William Blair (Captain)," q.v.

HOOVER, Jacob. Private in the German Regiment, muster roll dated October 23, 1776 [Ref: A-264].

HOOVER, John. Corporal in Capt. John Haass' company of militia in 1775 [Ref: E-53]. Associator in December, 1775 [Ref: E-168]. Juror to the Oath of Allegiance in 1778 [Ref: C-26].

HOOVER, Nicholas. Associator in December, 1775 [Ref: E-168]. Juror to the Oath of Allegiance in 1778 [Ref: C-26]. One Nicholas Hoover died testate in 1784, leaving a wife Mary (daughter of Jacob Keller) and children Cathrine [sic], Philip, Margaret, and Jacob [Ref: M-6:124, 125]. Also, see "Nicholas Hower," q.v.

HOOVER, Peter. Private in the German Regiment, 1776, in Capt. Henry Fister's company under the command of Col. Hussecker [Ref: A-261].

HOPKINS, Levy. Non-Enroller who was fined by the Committee of Observation in April, 1776 [Ref: E-248].

HOPKINS, William. Private in the militia, July, 1776 [Ref: A-42].

HORINE, Adam. Corporal in Capt. Michael Troutman's company of militia in 1775 [Ref: E-51]. "Adam Horine, son of Tobias, was born January 11, 1753, in Montgomery County, Pennsylvania, and baptized 'George Adam Harrein' in 1753. He was confirmed by the Evangelical Lutheran Church in Frederick on June 5, 1772, and married Elizabeth Wollenschlaeger on April 19, 1774. Died in 1831." [Ref: M-1:103].

HORINE, Charles. Associator in December, 1775 [Ref: E-168]. Juror to the Oath of Allegiance in 1778 [Ref: C-26].

HORINE, Jacob. Private who was enlisted on July 20, 1776 by Capt. Jacob Good [Ref: A-46].

HORINE, Michael. Associator in December, 1775 [Ref: E-168]. Juror to the Oath of Allegiance in 1778 [Ref: C-26].

HORMAN, Abraham. Fifer in Capt. John Carmack's company of militia in 1775 [Ref: E-56].

HORN, Peter. Associator in December, 1775 [Ref: E-168]. Juror to the Oath of Allegiance in 1778 [Ref: C-26].

HORN, Valentine. Fifer in the Skipton District Militia under Capt. Thomas Waring on April 16, 1776 [Ref: B-167, D-1814].

HORNER, Daniel. Loaned $500 for the use of the State of Maryland in June, 1780 [Ref: V-520].

HORNER, Thomas. Associator in December, 1775 [Ref: E-168]. Juror to the Oath of Allegiance in 1778 [Ref: C-26].

HORNICKER, Isaac. Juror to the Oath of Allegiance in March, 1778 [Ref: S-264, but not listed in Ref: C-25].

HORNICKER, John. Juror to the Oath of Allegiance in March, 1778 [Ref: S-264, but not listed in Ref: C-25].

HORSEFIELD [HORSFIELD], James. Private who enlisted in 1778 and served in the 2nd Maryland Regiment [Ref: A-294].

HORSEFIELD, Joseph. Private who enlisted May 20, 1778 [Ref: A-323].

HORSEFIELD, Luke. Private who enlisted on May 20, 1778, and served in the 2nd Maryland Regiment [Ref: A-323].

HOSE, Jacob. Sergeant in the German Regiment, muster roll dated October 23, 1776 [Ref: A-263], and discharged on July 26, 1779 [Ref: A-264].

HOSKIN, John. Associator in December, 1775 [Ref: E-168]. Juror to the Oath of Allegiance in 1778 [Ref: C-26].

HOSKINS, Charles. Private who enlisted July 18, 1776 [Ref: A-49].

HOSKINS, George. Private who enlisted on July 18, 1776 [Ref: A-49].

HOSKINSON, Archibald. Private in militia on July, 1776 [Ref: A-42].

HOSLER, Jacob. Private who enlisted on July 18, 1776 [Ref: A-50].

HOSPELHORN, George. Corporal in Capt. Jacob Snowdenberger's company of militia in 1775 [Ref: E-56].

HOSSILTON, Edward. Private in the Middle District Militia in 1776 in Capt. Valentine Creager's company [Ref: A-72].

HOTTENSTEIN, Samuel. Private who enlisted on April 30, 1778 [Ref: A-321].

HOTTFIELD, John. Private in the German Regiment, muster roll dated October 23, 1776 [Ref: A-264].

HOUBERT, Nicholas. Associator in December, 1775 [Ref: E-168]. Juror to the Oath of Allegiance in 1778 [Ref: C-26].

HOUBRE, Jacob. Associator in December, 1775 [Ref: E-168]. Juror to the Oath of Allegiance in 1778 [Ref: C-26].

HOUCK, Jacob. Paid for services he rendered to the military in December, 1779 (nature of the services not stated). [Ref: V-45].

HOUCK, John. Juror to the Oath of Allegiance in March, 1778 [Ref: S-267, but not listed in Ref: C-30].

HOUKS, Mathias. Private who enlisted on July 19, 1776 [Ref: A-51].

HOULDEN, John. Private who enlisted on April 22, 1778 [Ref: A-320].

HOUPERT, Nicholas. Associator in December, 1775 [Ref: E-168]. Juror to the Oath of Allegiance in 1778 [Ref: C-26].

HOUPTMAN, George. Associator in December, 1775 [Ref: E-168]. Juror to the Oath of Allegiance in 1778 [Ref: C-26].

HOURE, George. Associator in December, 1775 [Ref: E-168]. Juror to the Oath of Allegiance in 1778 [Ref: C-26].

HOUSE, Elizabeth. See "James Yule," q.v.

HOUSE, John. 2nd lieutenant in Frederick County militia, Skipton District, on July 27, 1776, and 2nd lieutenant in the Washington County militia on June 22, 1778 [Ref: B-89, X-127, Z-145].

HOUSE [HOUS, HOUSZ], William. "William Hous" was an Associator in December, 1775 [Ref: E-168]."William House" was enlisted on August 5, 1776, as private [Ref: A-44]. "William Hous" took the Oath of Allegiance in 1778 [Ref: C-26]. Loaned $300 for the use of the State of Maryland in 1780 [Ref: V-520]. "William Housz" died March 1, 1822, aged 90 [Ref: F-472].

HOUSEHOLDER, Margaret or Becky. See "Daniel Buzard," q.v.

HOUSEMAN, Conrad. Private in the German Regiment, 1776, in Capt. Henry Fister's company under the command of Col. Nicholas Hussecker [Ref: A-261].

HOUSER, Jacob. Associator in December, 1775 [Ref: E-167]. Juror to the Oath of Allegiance in 1778 [Ref: C-26].

HOUSLEY, William. Private who enlisted July 18, 1776 [Ref: A-49].

HOUSMAN, Jacob. Drummer in Capt. James Johnson's company of militia in 1775 [Ref: E-52].

HOUSTETLER, Francis. See "Francis Hoffstatter," q.v.

HOUSTON, James. Private who enlisted January 28, 1778 [Ref: A-314].
HOUSTON, Thomas. Militia substitute from May to December 10, 1781, and "marched to Annapolis." [Ref: A-653].
HOUTZ, Frederick. Associator in December, 1775 [Ref: E-168]. Juror to the Oath of Allegiance in 1778 [Ref: C-26].
HOW, George. Private who enlisted on July 19, 1776 [Ref: A-51].
HOWARD, Clement. Private who enlisted on July 25, 1776 [Ref: A-51].
HOWARD, Ephraim (1745-1788). Appointed in Burnt Woods Hundred by the Committee of Correspondence to solicit subscriptions in 1775 to purchase arms and ammunition [Ref: I-86]. Served on the Committee of Observation in 1775 [Ref: I-85]. 1st lieutenant in Capt. David Moore's company of militia in Frederick County on November 29, 1775 [Ref: E-56, B-88]. Associator in December, 1775 [Ref: E-168]. 2nd major in Frederick County from November 28, 1776, through at least January 2, 1777. Surgeon in the Severn Battalion in Anne Arundel County on September 3, 1777 [Ref: B-89, B-90, X-555, P-465]. Justice of the Peace in 1777 [Ref: F-476]. Juror to the Oath of Allegiance in 1778, Frederick County [Ref: C-26].
HOWARD, John. Associator in December, 1775 [Ref: E-168]. Juror to the Oath of Allegiance in 1778 [Ref: C-26]. Private who enlisted on February 25, 1778 [Ref: A-314].
HOWARD, William. Associator in December, 1775 [Ref: E-168]. Juror to the Oath of Allegiance in 1778 [Ref: C-26]. One William Howard died testate in 1786, leaving wife Martha and children Cornelius, Ann, Elizabeth, Benjamin, Margaret, and Richard [Ref: M-7:29]. One William Howard was a private in the 7th Maryland Regiment from May 8, 1778, to May 21, 1778, when reported "deserted." [Ref: A-216].
HOWE, William Robert. Militia substitute, June, 1778 [Ref: A-326].
HOWELL, Stephen. Drafted on June 2, 1783 [Ref: B-168].
HOWER, Adam. Corporal in Capt. Valentine Creager's company of militia in 1775 [Ref: E-53]. Also, see "Adam Huver," q.v.
HOWER, George. Private who enlisted on July 1, 1776 in Capt. Peter Mantz's company; marched from Frederick Town to Leonardtown, and from there to Philadelphia, arriving August 23, 1776 [Ref: A-47].
HOWER, Nicholas. Served on the Committee of Observation in 1775 [Ref: I-85]. Furnished lead for use of the militia in Frederick Town in 1775 [Ref: E-61]. Loaned $1,000 for the use of the State of Maryland in June, 1780 [Ref: V-520].
HOWIE [HOURIE], David. Drafted on June 13, 1781, and provided a substitute [Ref: D-1814].

HOYLE, Conrod. Private in the German Regiment, muster roll October 23, 1776 [Ref: A-264]. Discharged on July 20, 1779 [Ref: A-265].

HOYLE, Frederick. Juror to the Oath of Allegiance in March, 1778 [Ref: S-264, but not listed in Ref: C-25].

HUBARD, Peter. Non-Enroller who was fined by the Committee of Observation in May, 1776, but he apparently enrolled because the fine was remitted in June, 1776 [Ref: E-248].

HUBOR, Melchor. Drafted on June 2, 1783 [Ref: B-169].

HUDSON, George. Private stationed at Fort Frederick in June, 1778 [Ref: A-328].

HUDSON, James. Private who enlisted on August 5, 1776 in the Flying Camp under Capt. Philip Meroney [Ref: A-45, N-30:112].

HUES, James. Associator in December, 1775 [Ref: E-168]. Juror to the Oath of Allegiance in 1778 [Ref: C-26].

HUFF, Jacob. Juror to the Oath of Allegiance in March, 1778 [Ref: S-264, but not listed in Ref: C-25].

HUFF, Philip. Juror to the Oath of Allegiance in March, 1778 [Ref: S-264, but not listed in Ref: C-25].

HUFFMAN, David. Juror to the Oath of Allegiance in March, 1778 [Ref: S-264, but not listed in Ref: C-25].

HUFFMAN, Henry. Private who enlisted on July 1, 1776 in Capt. Peter Mantz's company; marched from Frederick Town to Leonardtown, and from there to Philadelphia, arriving August 23, 1776 [Ref: A-47].

HUFFMAN, John. Loaned $500 for the use of the State of Maryland in June, 1780 [Ref: V-520].

HUFFORD, Christian. Associator in December, 1775 [Ref: E-167]. Juror to the Oath of Allegiance in 1778 [Ref: C-26]. "Christian Huffert, farmer," died testate in 1788, leaving his wife Ann and children Christian, Christiana, Philip, Margaret, Daniel, John, Casper, Catharine, Elizabeth, Adam, Hannah, Jacob, Susanna, Magdalene, Rebecca, and Barbara [Ref: M-7:135, M-7:136].

HUFFORD, John. Associator in December, 1775 [Ref: E-167]. Juror to the Oath of Allegiance in 1778 [Ref: C-26].

HUFFSTADLER, Henry. See "Henry Hoffstatter," q.v.

HUFLIGH, Frederick. Associator in December, 1775 [Ref: E-168]. Juror to the Oath of Allegiance in 1778 [Ref: C-26]. Also, see "Frederick Haflich," q.v.

HUGH, Andrew (lower part of Potomac Hundred). Appointed by the Committee of Correspondence to solicit subscriptions in 1775 to purchase arms and ammunition [Ref: I-86].

HUGHES, Daniel and Samuel. Manufactured cannons for the Maryland military at their ironworks in Antietam [Ref: W-288, W-289].
HUGHES, Elizabeth. See "Richard Potts," q.v.
HUGHES, Jacob. Associator in December, 1775 [Ref: E-167]. Juror to the Oath of Allegiance in 1778 [Ref: C-26].
HUGHES, James. "James Hughs" provided wheat for the military in May, 1782 [Ref: R-513].
HUGHES, Jesse. Non-Enroller who was fined by the Committee of Observation in June, 1776 [Ref: E-248].
HUGHES, John. Associator in December, 1775 [Ref: E-167]. Juror to the Oath of Allegiance in 1778 [Ref: C-26].
HUGHES, Samuel. Served on the Committee of Observation in 1775 [Ref: I-85]. Election Judge in the Upper District on August 14, 1776 [Ref: F-476, F-479]. See "Daniel and Samuel Hughes," q.v.
HUGHMORE, John. Private in the German Regiment. Served at White Plains on September 5, 1778, under Lt. Col. Weltner [Ref: A-267].
HULET, Samuel. Associator in December, 1775 [Ref: E-168]. Juror to the Oath of Allegiance in 1778 [Ref: C-26].
HULING, Michael. Private in the German Regiment, 1776 [Ref: A-266].
HULL, Andrew. Associator in December, 1775 [Ref: E-168]. Juror to the Oath of Allegiance in 1778 [Ref: C-26. S-267]. Andrew Hull died testate in 1791, leaving wife Catherine and children Andrew, John, and Jacob (youngest son). [Ref: M-8:87].
HULL, John. Juror to the Oath of Allegiance in March, 1778 [Ref: S-264, but not listed in Ref: C-25].
HULSE, Samuel. Associator in December, 1775 [Ref: E-168]. Private in Middle District Militia in 1776 in Capt. Valentine Creager's company [Ref: A-72]. Juror to the Oath of Allegiance in 1778 [Ref: C-26].
HULSMAN, Henry. Private who enlisted on July 1, 1776 in Capt. Peter Mantz's company; marched from Frederick Town to Leonardtown, and from there to Philadelphia, arriving August 23, 1776 [Ref: A-47].
HUMBERT, Frederick. Associator in December, 1775 [Ref: E-168]. Juror to the Oath of Allegiance in 1778 [Ref: C-26].
HUMBERT, Michael. Associator in December, 1775 [Ref: E-168]. Juror to the Oath of Allegiance in 1778 [Ref: C-26].
HUMPHREYS, Thomas. Served on the Committee of Observation in 1775 [Ref: I-85]. 2nd lieutenant in the Skipton District Militia under Capt. Thomas Waring on April 16, 1776 [Ref: B-167, D-1814, W-427]. One Thomas Humphreys was a private in the 7th Maryland Regiment from

July 20, 1778, until February 22, 1779, when he was discharged [Ref: A-217].

HUNT, Gilbert. Militia substitute from May to December 10, 1781, and "marched to Annapolis." [Ref: A-653].

HUNT, Jacob. Militia substitute on June 13, 1778 [Ref: A-326]. Private in the 1st Maryland Regiment, and in the 7th Maryland Regiment, who served in the Southern Army of the United States under Lt. William Lamar in the late Capt. Beatty's company, 1780-1781 [Ref: A-217, A-390].

HUNT, Robert (Pipe Creek Hundred). Non-Enroller who was fined by the Committee of Observation in June, 1776 [Ref: E-248].

HUNTER, Henry. Associator in December, 1775 [Ref: E-167]. Juror to the Oath of Allegiance in 1778 [Ref: C-26].

HUNTER, William. Militia substitute from May to December 10, 1781, and "marched to Annapolis." [Ref: A-653].

HUNTSINGER, Elizabeth. See "Peter Shull," q.v.

HUNTSUCKER, Mary M. See "Peter Shull," q.v.

HURDLE, Laurance. Private in the militia, July, 1776 [Ref: A-42]. "Lawrence Hurdle" was a private, 1st Maryland Regiment, and also in the 7th Maryland Regiment, who served in the Southern Army of the United States under Lt. William Lamar in the late Capt. Beatty's company in 1780-1781 [Ref: A-216, A-390].

HURLEY, John. Private who enlisted on July 18, 1776 [Ref: A-50].

HURLY, William. Private, 1st Maryland Regiment, 1781, and served in the Southern Army of the United States under Lt. William Lamar in the late Capt. Beatty's company [Ref: A-390].

HURVY, James. Private in the militia in July, 1776 [Ref: A-42].

HUSSECKER, Nicholas. Colonel, German Regiment, 1776 [Ref: A-261].

HUSTON, Thomas. Juror to the Oath of Allegiance in March, 1778 [Ref: S-264, but not listed in Ref: C-25].

HUTCHCRAFT, James. Private who enlisted on August 5, 1776, in the Flying Camp, under Capt. Philip Meroney [Ref: A-45, and N-30:112, which latter source spelled his named "James Hatchcraft."]. Served in the 7th Maryland Regiment from January 6, 1777, until April, 1780, when he was reported "deserted." [Ref: A-216]. It should be noted that Ref: A-310 mistakenly listed him as "Jos. Hutchcraft."

HUTCHCRAFT, Thomas. Private who enlisted on May 19, 1778 [Ref: A-323]. "Thomas Hutchcrofft" was a private in the German Regiment at White Plains on September 5, 1778, under Lt. Col. Weltner [Ref: A-

267]. "Thomas Hutchcraft" was a drummer in the German Regiment from May 16, 1778, through at least August 1, 1780 [Ref: A-217].

HUTCHINS, Caleb. Private in the 7th Maryland Regiment from May 11, 1778, until April 18, 1779, when reported "deserted." [Ref: A-217].

HUTCHINSON, Archibald. Associator in December, 1775 [Ref: E-168]. Juror to the Oath of Allegiance in 1778 [Ref: C-26].

HUTCHINSON, John. Private who enlisted on August 5, 1776, in the Flying Camp under Capt. Philip Meroney [Ref: A-45, N-30:112, which latter source spelled his name "John Hutchison."].

HUTCHINSON, Nicholas. Private in the 7th Maryland Regiment who enlisted January 16, 1777, and was discharged on January 12, 1780 [Ref: A-215]. He reenlisted in Frederick Town and was a Sergeant in the 7th Maryland Regiment before July 20, 1780 [Ref: A-334, V-224].

HUTER, Jacob. Associator in December, 1775 [Ref: E-167]. Juror to the Oath of Allegiance in 1778 [Ref: C-26].

HUTTON, Samuel. Non-Enroller who was fined by the Committee of Observation in April, 1776 [Ref: E-248].

HUTTON, William. Private in the 7th Maryland Regiment from April 23, 1778, to September 12, 1778, when he was reported "deserted." [Ref: A-216, which source listed this name twice on the muster].

HYATT, Abednego. Non-Enroller who was fined by the Committee of Observation in April, 1776 [Ref: E-248].

HYATT [HIATT], Asa. Applied for a pension (R4943) in Parke County, Indiana, on May 12, 1835, aged 81, stating he was born about nine miles from Fredericktown in Frederick County, MA (Massachusetts, an obvious typographical error since he lived in Maryland which is MD) and lived there with his father who was aged about 50 when he (Asa) enlisted in the Maryland Line. Asa moved to Parke County, Indiana about 1826 or 1827. [Ref: T-1620, and Ref: J-8 mistakenly listed his name as "Jose Hyatt." Such a name not found in Ref: T-1620].

HYATT, Elizabeth. See "Richard Davis," q.v.

HYDER, William. Associator in December, 1775 [Ref: E-167]. Juror to the Oath of Allegiance in 1778 [Ref: C-26].

HYNES, Andrew. Captain in the Skipton District Militia on July 27, 1776 [Ref: X-127, X-337].

HYNES, Henry. Ensign in the Frederick Town Battalion of militia on May 26, 1778, under Capt. Abraham Haff [Ref: B-91].

HYNES, Thomas. Associator in December, 1775, in Frederick County [Ref: E-167]. Juror to the Oath of Allegiance in March, 1778 [Ref: C-26].

1st lieutenant in the Washington County militia on May 16, 1778, under Capt. Pindell [Ref: B-91].

HYRINGER, George. Militia substitute from May to December 10, 1781, and "marched to Annapolis." [Ref: A-653].

HYTER, Christopher. Associator in December, 1775 [Ref: E-168]. Juror to the Oath of Allegiance in 1778 [Ref: C-26].

HYTESHU [sic], Jacob. Associator in December, 1775 [Ref: E-168]. Juror to the Oath of Allegiance in 1778 [Ref: C-26].

IDEN, John. Private who enlisted on July 25, 1776 [Ref: A-51].

IEDEN [IODON], Francis. Corporal in Capt. Samuel Shaw's company of militia in 1775 [Ref: E-51].

IGENBREAD, John Yost. Juror to the Oath of Allegiance in March, 1778 [Ref: S-264, but not listed in Ref: C-25].

IHER, Joseph. Non-Enroller who was fined by the Committee of Observation in May, 1776, but he apparently enrolled because the fine was remitted in June, 1776 [Ref: E-248].

IKENBURY, John. Juror to the Oath of Allegiance in March, 1778 [Ref: S-264, but not listed in Ref: C-25].

ILER, Conrad. See "Conrad Eiler," q.v.

IMFELD, John. Private in the German Regiment, 1776, in Capt. Henry Fister's company under the command of Col. Hussecker [Ref: A-261].

INFEAT, John. Associator in December, 1775 [Ref: E-168]. Juror to the Oath of Allegiance in 1778 [Ref: C-26].

INGRAM, John (Upper Antietam Hundred). Appointed by the Committee of Correspondence to solicit subscriptions in 1775 to purchase arms and ammunition [Ref: I-86].

INGRAM [INGEAM], Thomas. Associator in December, 1775 [Ref: E-168]. Juror to the Oath of Allegiance in 1778 [Ref: C-26].

IRELAND, Alexander. Corporal in Capt. William Luckett, Jr.'s company of militia in 1775 [Ref: E-55]. Associator in December, 1775 [Ref: E-168]. Juror to the Oath of Allegiance in 1778 [Ref: C-26, S-264].

IRONS, Edward. Private in the Skipton District Militia under Capt. Thomas Waring on April 16, 1776 [Ref: B-167, D-1814].

IRONS, Jonathan. Private in the Skipton District Militia under Capt. Thomas Waring on April 16, 1776 [Ref: B-167, D-1814].

IRWIN, Samuel. Associator in December, 1775 [Ref: E-168]. Juror to the Oath of Allegiance in 1778 [Ref: C-26].

ISENBERGER, Gabriel. Non-Enroller who was fined by the Committee of Observation in April, 1776 [Ref: E-248].

ISENBERGER, Jacob. Non-Enroller who was fined by the Committee of Observation in April, 1776 [Ref: E-248].

ISENBERGER, John. Non-Enroller who was fined by the Committee of Observation in April, 1776 [Ref: E-248].

ISENBERGER, Michael. Non-Enroller who was fined by the Committee of Observation in April, 1776 [Ref: E-248].

ISGRIG, Michael. "Michael Isgreeg" was a sergeant in Capt. Michael McGuire's company of militia in 1775 [Ref: E-56]. "Michael Isgrig" was an Associator in December, 1775 [Ref: E-168]. Juror to the Oath of Allegiance in 1778 [Ref: C-26].

ISHOME, Joshua. Drummer or fifer, 1st Maryland Regiment, 1781, and served in the Southern Army of the United States under Lt. William Lamar in the late Capt. Beatty's company [Ref: A-389].

ISIMINGER, Adam. "Adam Iseminger" was a sergeant in Capt. Yost's company in 1775 [Ref: E-52]. "Adam Isiminger" was an Associator in December, 1775 [Ref: E-168], and a Juror to the Oath of Allegiance in 1778 [Ref: C-26]. "Adam Iseminger" hauled flour for the military in 1782 [Ref: R-515].

ISIMINGER, Philip. Juror to the Oath of Allegiance in 1778 [Ref: C-26]. "Philip Isingminger" was a private in the German Regiment, 1776, in Capt. Henry Fister's company under the command of Col. Nicholas Hussecker [Ref: A-261].

ITNIER, John. Private in the German Regiment, muster roll dated October 23, 1776 [Ref: A-264].

JACKSON, Elizabeth. See "Lawrence Everhart," q.v.

JACKSON, John. Private in the 7th Maryland Regiment from June 12, 1779, to December 8, 1779, when discharged [Ref: A-220, A-345].

JACOB, Gabriel. Private in the Skipton District Militia under Capt. Thomas Waring on April 16, 1776 [Ref: B-167, D-1814].

JACOB, John Conrad. Provided wheat for the military in June, 1782 [Ref: R-524].

JACOB, John Jeremiah. Ensign in the Skipton District Militia on April 16, 1776 [Ref: B-91, B-167, D-1814, W-427, X-337].

JACOB, Philip. Associator in December, 1775 [Ref: E-168]. Private who was enlisted on July 20, 1776 by Capt. Jacob Good [Ref: A-46]. Also, signed as a Juror to the Oath of Allegiance in 1778 [Ref: C-26].

JACOBS, Adam. Loaned $200 for the use of the State of Maryland in June, 1780 [Ref: V-520].

JACOBS, Benjamin. Drafted on June 13, 1781; provided a substitute [Ref: D-1814].

JACOBS, Jesse. Sergeant in Capt. Jacob Good's company of militia in 1775 [Ref: E-51].

JACOBS, William. Private who enlisted on August 5, 1776, in the Flying Camp under Capt. Philip Meroney [Ref: A-45, N-30:111]. Petitioned to form the horse troops in 1781 [Ref: B-167]. Private in the horse troops in June, 1781 [Ref: B-168].

JACQUES, Lancelot. Judge of the Court of Appeals for Frederick County, appointed on May 23, 1778 [Ref: Z-109].

JAMES, Daniel. Associator in December, 1775 [Ref: E-169]. Juror to the Oath of Allegiance in 1778 [Ref: C-26]. Daniel died testate in 1793, leaving a wife Lucy (died 1827) and children Daniel, Joseph, John, James, Margaret (married Henry Poole), Elizabeth, Achsah, and Rebecca, and "my mother Margret Justis." Daniel was also appointed Collector of Fines and Receiver of Arms in Unity Hundred on April 29, 1776 [Ref: M-9:34, U-1195].

JAMES, Thomas. Private in the 7th Maryland Regiment from May 13, 1778, to August 16, 1780, when he was reported taken a prisoner (after the Battle of Camden, South Carolina). [Ref: A-220].

JAMES, William. Associator in December, 1775 [Ref: E-168]. Juror to the Oath of Allegiance in 1778 [Ref: C-26].

JAMESON, Henry. Associator in December, 1775 [Ref: E-168]. Juror to the Oath of Allegiance in 1778 [Ref: C-26]. Provided wheat for the military in June, 1782 [Ref: R-520].

JAMISON, Benedict (Colonel). Died on March 23, 1804 [Ref: F-470].

JAMISON, Leonard and Mary. See "Leonard Smith," q.v.

JANTZ, John. Associator in December, 1775 [Ref: E-168]. Juror to the Oath of Allegiance in 1778 [Ref: C-26].

JANUS, Daniel. Sergeant in Capt. David Moore's company of militia in 1775 [Ref: E-56].

JAQUET [JACQUET], John Daniel. "Daniel Jaquet" was a sergeant in the German Regiment, on muster roll October 23, 1776 [Ref: A-263]. "Jno. Danl. Jacquet" was a sergeant in the German Regiment until discharged on July 26, 1779 [Ref: A-220, A-264]. "In December, 1815, Treasurer of the Western Shore was directed to pay 'John D. Jaquet,' a sergeant in the Revolutionary War, quarterly, the half pay of a sergeant for life, as a further remuneration for those services by which his country has been so essentially benefitted." [Ref: G-359].

JARVIS, Cato. Private in the 7th Maryland Regiment from May 18, 1778, until April 9, 1778, when he was discharged [Ref: A-220].

JARVIS, John. Private who enlisted February 21, 1778 [Ref: A-314].

JEANS, John. Private who enlisted on July 25, 1776 [Ref: A-50].
JEFFERSON, Thomas. See "Isaac Shelby," q.v.
JEMISON, Samuel. Juror to the Oath of Allegiance in March, 1778 [Ref: S-267, but not listed in Ref: C-30].
JENNINGS, George. Private who enlisted in 1780 [Ref: A-345].
JERBO, William. Private who enlisted on August 5, 1776 [Ref: A-44].
JERMAN, Benjamin. Associator in December, 1775 [Ref: E-168]. Juror to the Oath of Allegiance in 1778 [Ref: C-26].
JESSERONG, Peter. Son of Daniel and Anna Margaret Jesserong, born March 2, 1747, Lancaster, Pennsylvania, and grandson of Bartholomew Jesserang who died testate in Frederick, Maryland, in 1764. He was an Associator in December, 1775 and Juror to the Oath of Allegiance in 1778 in Frederick County [Ref: C-26]. "Peter Yesseroon(e)" was a private in Capt. Parkeson's company of militia in the 5th battalion in Washington County, 1781-1782 [Ref: M-7:152, M-7:153, which contains a detailed genealogy].
JINKINGS, Edward. Private who enlisted July 13, 1776 [Ref: A-43].
JOEL, John. Private who enlisted on February 28, 1778, and served in the 2nd Maryland Regiment [Ref: A-294].
JOHN, Ebenezer. Non-Enroller who was fined by the Committee of Observation in June, 1776 [Ref: E-248].
JOHN, Thomas. Private who enlisted April 20, 1781 for 3 years, and marched with Capt. Lynn [Ref: D-1814]. Private, Maryland Line, age 84, from Frederick County, pensioned on August 8, 1821, at $96 per annum from July 16, 1821 [Ref: G-359, and citing the U. S. Pension Rolls of 1835. Ref: T-1839 states he applied for a pension (S34943) on July 16, 1821, aged 66, a former soldier of the Maryland Line].
JOHNS, James. Private in the 7th Maryland Regiment from June 30, 1778, until March 30, 1779, when he was discharged [Ref: A-220].
JOHNS, John. Private in the 7th Maryland Regiment from May 21, 1778, through at least November 1, 1780 [Ref: A-220].
JOHNS, Margaret A. See "Elisha Williams," q.v.
JOHNS, Thomas (Georgetown). Appointed by the Committee of Correspondence to solicit subscriptions in 1775 to purchase arms and ammunition [Ref: I-85]. Served on the Committee of Observation in 1775 [Ref: I-85]. Reviewed and passed recruits in 1776 [Ref: A-49].
JOHNSON, Baker, Benjamin, James, Roger, and Thomas. Collectively they loaned $12,000 for the use of the State of Maryland in June, 1780 [Ref: V-520].

JOHNSON, Baker (September 30, 1747 or 1749 - June 16, 1811). Lawyer and brother of Governor Thomas Johnson, sons of Thomas and Dorcas Johnson [Ref: F-454]. Resident of Fredericktown Hundred. Appointed by the Committee of Correspondence to solicit subscriptions in 1775 to purchase arms and ammunition [Ref: I-86]. Chosen to serve on Committee of Observation in 1775 [Ref: E-302, I-85]. 1st lieutenant in Capt. Charles Beatty's company of militia in the 1st Battalion on November 29, 1775 [Ref: E-51, B-92]. Collected 36 lbs. 16 sh. 7 1/2 p. for arms and ammunition for the militia in 1775 [Ref: E-63]. Associator in December, 1775 [Ref: E-168]. Served in the House of Delegates from the Middle District on December 7, 1775 [Ref: F-479]. Reviewed and passed recruits in 1776 [Ref: A-46]. Colonel of the 34th Battalion, 1776-1780 [Ref: E-302, H-15, B-92, O-189, P-491]. Juror to the Oath of Allegiance in 1778 [Ref: C-26]. County Lieutenant, 1780-1781 [Ref: B-92]. Col. Baker Johnson was "drafted June 2, 1783, says he furnished a recruit, but after repeated applications to him on the subject has never appeal" [appeared?]. [Ref: B-168]. "He commanded a battalion of infantry in his brother's, Gen. Johnson's, brigade in the summer and fall of 1776, and was at the Battle of Paoli, near Philadelphia, famous for the slaughter of Wayne's men. He married Kitty Worthington, eldest daughter of Col. Nicholas Worthington, of 'Summer Hill,' near Annapolis, by whom he had six sons and five daughters [not named here]. After the Revolution he was a leading member of the bar of Frederick and the General Court." [Ref: F-454]. Col. Baker Johnson died on June 16, 1811. His widow, Catherine, died on June 9, 1814 [Ref: F-471]. A son, also titled Col. Baker Johnson, formerly of Frederick County, died near Tallahassee, Florida, on July 13, 1838, aged 50, leaving a wife and 5 children (not named). [Ref: F-473].

JOHNSON, Benjamin. Served on the Committee of Observation in 1775 [Ref: I-85]. Associator in December, 1775 [Ref: E-168]. Quartermaster in the 1st Battalion in 1776 [Ref: E-57]. Juror to the Oath of Allegiance in 1778 [Ref: C-26]. 1st major in the 33rd Battalion of militia on January 6, 1776 [Ref: B-92]. Lieutenant Colonel in the militia in 1778-1779 [Ref: H-15], and colonel in the militia on December 6, 1781 [Ref: B-92, O-189]. Loaned $2,000 for the use of the State of Maryland in June, 1780 [Ref: V-520].

JOHNSON, Bradley T. See "Roger Johnson," q.v.

JOHNSON, Henry. Associator in December, 1775 [Ref: E-169]. Juror to the Oath of Allegiance in 1778 [Ref: C-26].

JOHNSON, James (September 30, 1736 - December 3, 1809). Son of Thomas and Dorcas Johnson, and brother of Gov. Thomas Johnson. "He emigrated to Frederick County, now Washington County, where he built the Green Spring Furnace for the firm of Jacques & Johnson, a mile from old Fort Frederick, where his son James was born on May 28, 1774, and also Licking Creek Forge at the mouth of said creek. In November 1774, he established himself permanently in Frederick County, where, in partnership with his brothers Thomas, Baker and Roger Johnson, be built Catoctin Furnace and Bush Creek Furnace, Johnson Furnace near the mouth of the Monocacy, and Potomac Furnace in Loudon County, Virginia, opposite the Point of Rocks. During the Revolutionary War, besides casting a number of cannon, he furnished the Continental Army with one hundred tons of bomb-shells, which assisted in bringing about the surrender of Cornwallis at Yorktown. He was for many years Justice of the Peace in Frederick County, a member of the court, and in 1779, in with Alexander C. Hanson and Upton Sheredine, composed a special court for the trial of the Tories who were executed on the Courthouse Creek in Frederick Town. He commanded a battalion of infantry in the Flying Camp under his brother, Brig. Gen. Thomas Johnson, in the Jerseys in the winter of 1776 and 1777, the most gloomy period of the Revolution. He married Miss Peggie Skinner, of Calvert County, by whom he had 3 children (not named here). [Ref: F-453, F-454, F-476]. Captain of a militia company on November 29, 1775 [Ref: E-52, B-92]. Associator in December, 1775 [Ref: E-168]. Served on the Committee of Observation in 1775 [Ref: I-85]. Colonel of the 2nd Battalion in 1776 [Ref: E-58], colonel of the 37th Battalion in 1776 [Ref: B-92, X-555], and colonel of the Catoctin Battalion in 1778-1779 [Ref: H-16, O-189]. Juror to the Oath of Allegiance in 1778 [Ref: C-26]

JOHNSON, James. Enlisted as a private on May 20, 1778 [Ref: A-323].

JOHNSON, John (August 9, 1745 - April, 1811). Son of Thomas and Dorcas Johnson. Associator in December, 1775 [Ref: E-169]. Recommended on August 21, 1776, to be a surgeon in the militia of Frederick County [Ref: X-231]. Juror to the Oath of Allegiance in 1778 [Ref: C-26]. Ensign on May 12, 1779 [Ref: H-15, Z-387], and 2nd lieutenant in the Frederick Town Battalion of Militia on September 18, 1780 [Ref: B-92, V-295]. Petitioned to form the horse troops in 1781 [Ref: B-167]. "He was a physician by profession, and a surgeon in the Maryland Line during the Revolution." [Ref: F-454]. Provided wheat for the military in May, 1782 [Ref: R-517].

JOHNSON, Joseph. 2nd lieutenant in Capt. Michael Troutman's company of militia in 1775 [Ref: E-51]. Associator in December, 1775 [Ref: E-169]. Juror to the Oath of Allegiance in 1778 [Ref: C-26].

JOHNSON, Martin (Linton Hundred). Appointed by the Committee of Correspondence to solicit subscriptions in 1775 to purchase arms and ammunition [Ref: I-86].

JOHNSON, Mary and Thomas. See "Philip Fisher," q.v.

JOHNSON, Nicholas. Private in Capt. Baltzel's Company, served three years, and discharged July 24, 1779, at Camp Wyoming [Ref: A-271].

JOHNSON, Peter. Associator in December, 1775 [Ref: E-168]. Juror to the Oath of Allegiance in 1778 [Ref: C-26].

JOHNSON, Reverdy. See "John Stricker," q.v.

JOHNSON, Robert. Associator in December, 1775 [Ref: E-169]. Juror to the Oath of Allegiance in 1778 [Ref: C-26]. Militia substitute from May to December 10, 1781, and "marched to Annapolis." [Ref: A-653].

JOHNSON, Roger (March 18, 1749 - March 3, 1831). Son of Thomas and Dorcas Johnson. "He was an iron-master, and built Bloomsburg Forge on Bennett's Creek, Frederick County. He was also major of his brother James' battalion in the Revolutionary War. He married Betsy Thomas, daughter of Richard Thomas, of Montgomery County, by whom he had seven sons and four daughters [no names given here]. General Bradley T. Johnson is a grandson of Baker Johnson." [Ref: F-454]. Resident of the upper part of Monocacy Hundred. Appointed by the Committee of Correspondence to solicit subscriptions in 1775 to purchase arms and ammunition [Ref: I-86]. Served on the Committee of Observation in 1775 [Ref: I-85]. Associator in December, 1775 [Ref: E-168]. Gave money in the amount of 11 lbs. 4 sh. 9 p. for arms and ammunition for the militia in 1775 [Ref: E-62]. 2nd major in the 2nd Battalion, 1776 [Ref: E-58], and 2nd major in the 37th Battalion, 1776 [Ref: B-93, O-148]. Juror to the Oath of Allegiance in 1778 [Ref: C-26].

JOHNSON, Simon. Private who enlisted April 30, 1778 [Ref: A-321].

JOHNSON, Thomas (November 4, 1732 - October 26, 1819). Son of Thomas Johnson and Dorcas Sedgwick, of Calvert County, he moved to Frederick County circa 1776 and settled at "Rose Hill." Resident of Upper Catoctin. Appointed by the Committee of Correspondence to solicit subscriptions in 1775 to purchase arms and ammunition [Ref: I-85]. Served in many capacities, as follows: Clerk of Indictments, 1760; Committee of Correspondence, 1774; Council of Safety, 1775; Governor of Maryland, 1777-1779, re-elected in 1788 but declined; Maryland State Elector, 1786; Constitution Ratification Convention, 1788; Judge, Court of Appeals for Tax Assessments, 1786; Chief Judge, General Court, 1790-1791; Justice of the Orphans' Court, 1799; and, served in the Maryland legislature from 1762 through 1788 [Ref: P-496]. Associator in December, 1775 [Ref: E-168]. Subscribed to the Oath of Allegiance in 1778 [Ref: C-26]. Elected senior brigadier general of the Flying Camp in the Maryland Militia in January, 1776, but was relieved from his duties so he could continue serving in the Convention in July, 1776. Commander of the Maryland troops sent to aid General Washington in his retreat through New Jersey, December, 1776 - February, 1777. Delegate to the Continental Congress, 1774-1776; elected in 1779, but did not attend; resigned March 28, 1780; elected 1780, but did not attend; resigned January 16, 1781; elected 1783, but again declined to serve (in 1784 also). Member of the Board of Commissioners for the District of Columbia, 1791-1794. Associate Justice of the U. S. Supreme Court, 1791-1793 (resigned). Selected, but declined to serve, in the following: U. S. District Judge for Maryland, 1789; Secretary of State, 1795; and, Chief Judge of the Circuit Court of the District of Columbia, 1801. Granted an allowance of 3,750 lbs. by the General Assembly in 1780, he spent most of it equipping Revolutionary War soldiers. He is buried in All Saints' Parish Cemetery in Frederick, Maryland [Ref: P-495, P-496, P-497, F-478, U-1018]. See "Adam Boone," q.v.

JOHNSON, Thomas. Corporal in the Skipton District Militia under Capt. Thomas Waring on April 16, 1776 [Ref: B-167, D-1814].

JOHNSON, Thomas Sr. Associator in December, 1775 [Ref: E-168]. Juror to the Oath of Allegiance in 1778 [Ref: C-26]. See "Thomas Johnson," q.v.

JOHNSON, William. Private who enlisted May 16, 1778 [Ref: A-322].

JOHNSTON, James. Private in the German Regiment. Served at White Plains on September 5, 1778, under Lt. Col. Weltner [Ref: A-267].

JOHNSTON, William. Private in the German Regiment. Served at White Plains on September 5, 1778, under Lt. Col. Weltner [Ref: A-266].

JOHNSTONE, Henry. Juror to the Oath of Allegiance in March, 1778 [Ref: S-264, but not listed in Ref: C-25].

JONES, Charles. Private who enlisted on May 20, 1778 [Ref: A-323]. He served as a private in the German Regiment at White Plains on September 5, 1778, under Lt. Col. Ludwick Weltner [Ref: A-266].

JONES, Charles (lower part of Potomac Hundred). Appointed by the Committee of Correspondence to solicit subscriptions in 1775 to purchase arms and ammunition [Ref: I-86].

JONES, David. Private who was enlisted on July 20, 1776, by Capt. Jacob Good [Ref: A-46].

JONES, David (Conococheague). Appointed by the Committee of Correspondence to solicit subscriptions in 1775 to purchase arms and ammunition [Ref: I-86].

JONES, Henry. Private who enlisted on July 22, 1776 [Ref: A-49]. Private who enlisted on April 17, 1778 [Ref: A-315]. Private in 7th Maryland Regiment, 1780. Enlisted in Frederick Town between January and April, 1780, and subsequently reported as "deserted" (no date given). [Ref: A-334]. (References could be to more than one Henry).

JONES, John. Private who enlisted on August 5, 1776 in the Flying Camp under Capt. Philip Meroney [Ref: A-45, N-30:112].

JONES, John. Private who enlisted on May 16, 1778 [Ref: A-322]. Private, 1st Maryland Regiment, 1781, and served in the Southern Army of the United States under Lt. Lamar in the late Capt. Beatty's company. Record indicates he had "deserted" on March 15, 1781 [Ref: A-391].

JONES, John. Sergeant in Capt. Jacob Good's company of militia in 1775 [Ref: E-51].

JONES, John. Substitute on June 13, 1781; marched with Capt. Dyer [Ref: D-1814].

JONES, John Court. 2nd Lieutenant in the Upper District Militia [now Washington County] in 1776 [Ref: A-48].

JONES, Jonathan. Private who enlisted July 1, 1776 in Capt. Peter Mantz's company; marched from Frederick Town to Leonardtown, and from there to Philadelphia, arriving August 23, 1776 [Ref: A-47].

JONES, Joseph. Associator in December, 1775 [Ref: E-168]. Juror to the Oath of Allegiance in 1778 [Ref: C-26].

JONES, Leonard. Associator in December, 1775 [Ref: E-168]. Juror to the Oath of Allegiance in 1778 [Ref: C-26].

JONES, Livie. Private who enlisted on July 19, 1776 [Ref: A-51].

JONES, Samuel. Militia substitute on June 6, 1778 [Ref: A-325].

JONES, Thomas. Private who enlisted on July 19, 1776 [Ref: A-51].

JONES, William. Militia substitute on June 5, 1778 [Ref: A-325].

JORDON, James. Private who enlisted on July 19, 1776 [Ref: A-51].

JURER, David. Drafted on June 2, 1783; "gone to Va." [Ref: B-169].

JUSTIS, Margret. See "Daniel James," q.v.

KAALBAUGH, Francis. Non-Enroller who was fined by the Committee of Observation in April, 1776 [Ref: E-248].

KALLENBERGER [COLLENBERGER], Christopher. Private who enlisted on July 1, 1776 in Capt. Peter Mantz's company; marched from Frederick Town to Leonardtown, and then to Philadelphia, arriving on August 23, 1776 [Ref: A-47]. "Christopher Kollenberger" was an Associator in December, 1775 [Ref: E-169]. "Christopher Kallenberger" took the Oath of Allegiance in 1778 [Ref: C-26]. "Christopher Collenberger" was a sergeant in Capt. Peter Mantz's militia company in 1775 [Ref: E-50].

KALLENBERGER, Frederick. Private who enlisted on July 1, 1776 in Capt. Peter Mantz's company, and marched from Frederick Town to Leonardtown, and from there to Philadelphia, arriving August 23, 1776 [Ref: A-47]. "Frederick Kallenburger" subscribed to the Oath of Allegiance in 1778 [Ref: C-26]. "Fred. Kallenburger" was an Associator in December, 1775 [Ref: E-169].

KALLENBURGER [COLLYBERGER], John. Captain in the Linganore Battalion of militia on June 22, 1778 [Ref: H-16, B-64, Z-144].

KALLOR, Michael. Associator in December, 1775 [Ref: E-169]. Juror to the Oath of Allegiance in 1778 [Ref: C-26].

KAMPER, Conrad. Associator in December, 1775 [Ref: E-169]. Juror to the Oath of Allegiance in 1778 [Ref: C-26].

KANE, John. Ensign in the 33rd Battalion of militia on January 17, 1777, under Capt. Van Swearingen [Ref: B-94, Y-54].

KARL, Rebecca and Richard. See "Mathias Firestone," q.v.

KARNES, Robert. Enlisted on April 3, 1781 for 3 years; marched with Capt. Lynn [Ref: D-1814].

KARR, Nicholas. Private who enlisted January 6, 1778 [Ref: A-314].

KASEBIER, William. Corporal in Capt. Philip Rodenbieler's company of militia in 1775 [Ref: E-51].

KASTOR, Andrew. Associator in December, 1775 [Ref: E-169]. Juror to the Oath of Allegiance in 1778 [Ref: C-26].

KAUFMAN, Jacob. Private who enlisted on May 10, 1778 [Ref: A-322]. "Jacob Kauffman" served in the German Regiment at White Plains on September 5, 1778, under Lt. Col. Ludwick Weltner [Ref: A-266].

KEEFF, Thomas. Private, 1st Maryland Regiment, 1781, and served in the Southern Army of the United States under Lt. William Lamar in the late Capt. Beatty's company. Record indicates he had "deserted" on March 15, 1781 [Ref: A-391].

KEEFHOVER [KIEFHABER, KEFAUVER], Nicholas (1751-1817). Son of Conrad Kiefhaber who was naturalized in 1764 in [now] Adams County, Pennsylvania. "Nicholas Kefauver" married Mary Catherine

Forney (1752-1798). [Ref: O-72]. "Nicholas Keefhover" was an Associator in December, 1775 [Ref: E-169], and a Juror to the Oath of Allegiance in 1778 [Ref: C-26].

KEEFOUVER [KEEFAUVER], Philip. Provided wheat for the military in May, 1782 [Ref: R-515].

KEEMER, John. Private who enlisted on July 29, 1776 [Ref: A-44].

KEEN, Richard. Private who enlisted April 27, 1778 [Ref: A-321].

KEEPERS, Isaac. Petitioned the General Assembly under the Act of May 12, 1780, stating that he had been a non-juror to the Oath of Allegiance and Fidelity in 1778 due to "ignorance" and now desired relief under the Act and to take the Oath [Ref: L-101].

KEEPHEART, George and Peter. See "George and Peter Kephart," q.v.

KEES, Charles. Private in Capt. Charles Baltzel's Company, served 3 years, and was discharged July 21, 1779, at Camp Wyoming, "as a good soldier from the time of his inlistment [sic]." [Ref: A-271].

KEESEY, Henry. "Henry Keesey" was drafted on June 13, 1781, and provided a substitute [Ref: D-1814]. "Henry Keisey" took the Oath of Allegiance in March, 1778 [Ref: S-265].

KEFAUVER, Nicholas and Philip. See "Nicholas and Philip Keefhover."

KEGAR, George. Associator in December, 1775 [Ref: E-169]. Juror to the Oath of Allegiance in 1778 [Ref: C-26].

KEILER, Christopher. Associator in December, 1775 [Ref: E-169]. Juror to the Oath of Allegiance in 1778 [Ref: C-26].

KEILER, Daniel. Associator in December, 1775 [Ref: E-169]. Juror to the Oath of Allegiance in 1778 [Ref: C-26].

KEIN, James. Associator in December, 1775 [Ref: E-169]. Juror to the Oath of Allegiance in 1778 [Ref: C-26].

KEISER, Christian and Mathias. See "Christian and Mathias Keyser."

KEISER, Sally. See "Matthias Young," q.v.

KEISEY, Henry. See "Henry Keesey," q.v.

KELAM, James. Private who enlisted on August 5, 1776, in the Flying Camp under Capt. Philip Meroney [Ref: A-45, N-30:112].

KELCHOLUMER, Baltzer. Served on the Committee of Observation in 1775 [Ref: I-85].

KELLER, Adam. Sergeant in Capt. Robert Wood's company of militia in 1775 [Ref: E-53]. Associator in December, 1775 [Ref: E-169]. This or another Adam Keller was a private who was enlisted on July 20, 1776, by Capt. Jacob Good [Ref: A-46]. One Adam Keller signed as a Juror to the Oath of Allegiance in 1778 [Ref: C-26].

KELLER [KELLAR], Andrew. Provided wheat for the military in July, 1782 [Ref: R-536].

KELLER [KELLAR], Jacob. Drafted on June 13, 1781, and provided a substitute [Ref: D-1814]. "Jacob Keller" provided wheat for the military in May, 1782, as did "Jacob Kellar" in June, 1782 [Ref: R-515, R-520]. One "Jacob Keller, an old inhabitant, no age given," died before August 31, 1804, in Frederick [Ref: N-56]. Also, see "Nicholas Hoover," q.v.

KELLER [KELLAR], John. Associator in December, 1775 [Ref: E-169]. (Name appeared three times on the list of Associators). Subscribed to the Oath of Allegiance in 1778 [Ref: C-26]. "John Kellar," private, enlisted on July 1, 1776, in Capt. Peter Mantz's company, and marched from Frederick Town to Leonardtown, and from there to Philadelphia, arriving on August 23, 1776 [Ref: A-47]. A "John Koller (c1742-1796), son of Jakob Koller (d. 1765), married Anna Maria Miller (no date given). [Ref: O-153].

KELLER, John Jr. Drafted June 2, 1783, "discharged from... having a subst. on duty and delca?... last furnished subst." [Ref: B-168].

KELLER, Wentch. Associator in December, 1775 [Ref: E-169]. Juror to the Oath of Allegiance in 1778 [Ref: C-26].

KELLEY, George. Associator in December, 1775 [Ref: E-169]. Juror to the Oath of Allegiance in 1778 [Ref: C-26]. Private in the Skipton District Militia under Capt. Thomas Waring on April 16, 1776 [Ref: B-167, D-1814]. Private who enlisted March 14, 1777, and served in Capt. William Beatty's company in the 7th Maryland Regiment in 1779 [Ref: A-311].

KELLEY, Hugh. Private, 7th Maryland Regiment, 1780, enlisted in Frederick Town between January and April, 1780, and reported as "gone to Camp" [Ref: A-334].

KELLEY, James. Private, 7th Maryland Regiment, 1780, enlisted in Frederick Town between January and April, 1780, and reported as "gone to Camp" [Ref: A-334]. Corporal, 1st Maryland Regiment, 1781, and served in the Southern Army of the United States under Lt. William Lamar in the late Capt. Beatty's company until transferred to the light infantry on March 12, 1781 [Ref: A-389].

KELLEY, Thomas. Private, 7th Maryland Regiment, 1780, enlisted in Frederick Town on February 15, 1780, and reported as "gone to Camp" [Ref: A-312, A-334].

KELLY, Barnaby. Private who enlisted in Frederick, August 14, 1780, and was "not marched [to Annapolis] for want of pay." [Ref: A-344].

KELLY, George. Private who enlisted on August 5, 1776, in the Flying Camp under Capt. Philip Meroney [Ref: A-45, N-30:112].

KELLY, George. Sergeant in Capt. William Blair's company of militia in 1775 [Ref: E-55].

KELLY, Hugh. Private in the 2nd Maryland Line who, in 1778, was referred to as an "old soldier." [Ref: A-294].

KELLY, Thomas. Private in the 7th Maryland Regiment from December 30, 1776, until August 16, 1780, when reported missing (after the Battle of Camden, South Carolina). [Ref: A-222].

KELSEY, Joseph. Private, 7th Maryland Regiment, 1780, enlisted in Frederick Town between January and April, 1780, and reported as "gone to Camp" [Ref: A-334].

KEMMER, Daniel. Private stationed at Fort Frederick on June 27, 1778, in Capt. John Kershner's company, and guarding prisoners of war [Ref: A-328].

KEMP, Christian. Provided wheat for the military in May, 1782 [Ref: R-516].

KEMP, Conrad. Associator in December, 1775 [Ref: E-169]. Juror to the Oath of Allegiance in 1778 [Ref: C-26, S-265].

KEMP, Frederick. Served on the Committee of Observation in 1775 [Ref: I-85]. Associator in December, 1775 [Ref: E-169]. Juror to the Oath of Allegiance in 1778 [Ref: C-26, S-267]. There were at least two men by the name of Frederick Kemp at this time. One, a son of Conrad and Maria Kemp (or Kaempf), was born in 1725, married Regina ----, had a son Peter Kemp (1749-1811, who was a founder of the Church of the Brethren), and died in 1804. Another Frederick Kemp (1747-1814), the son of Gilbert Kemp (1717-1794) and Margaret Getzendanner, married Dorothea Hershberger, or Hersperger (1753-1831); both are buried at Rocky Springs west of Frederick [Ref: O-72, O-73, O-198, O-199].

KEMP, Frederick Jr. Non-Enroller who was fined by the Committee of Observation in April, 1776 [Ref: E-248].

KEMP, Gabriel. Non-Enroller who was fined by the Committee of Observation in April, 1776 [Ref: E-248]. He was probably a son of Gilbert Kemp who died testate in early 1794 [Ref: M-9:36, M-9:37].

KEMP, Gilbert. Juror to the Oath of Allegiance in March, 1778 [Ref: S-267, but not listed in Ref: C-30].

KEMP, Henry. Non-Enroller who was fined by the Committee of Observation in April, 1776 [Ref: E-248]. He was probable a son of Gilbert Kemp who died testate in early 1794 [Ref: M-9:36, M-9:37].

KEMP, Jacob. Juror to the Oath of Allegiance in March, 1778 [Ref: S-265, but not listed in Ref: C-26].

KEMP, Lewis (Lower Monocacy Hundred). Appointed by the Committee of Correspondence to solicit subscriptions in 1775 to purchase arms and ammunition [Ref: I-86]. Served on the Committee of Observation in 1775 [Ref: I-85]. Associator who was appointed "to hand about the Association paper" in Lower Monocacy Hundred in 1775 [Ref: E-305]. Juror to the Oath of Allegiance in March, 1778 [Ref: S-267, but not listed in Ref: C-30]. "Louis Kemp" died on April 30, 1805 [Ref: F-470]. However, another source spelled the name "Lewis Kemp" and stated that he "died on the Tuesday before May 3, 1805, very old," in Frederick." [Ref: N-57].

KEMP, Ludowick. Captain of a militia company on November 29, 1775 [Ref: E-52, B-94]. 2nd major in 4th Battalion in 1776 [Ref: E-58].

KEMP, Ludowick. Corporal in Capt. John Stoner's company of militia in 1775 [Ref: E-56].

KEMP, Mary. See "Samuel Brandenburgh," q.v.

KEMP, Peter Jr. Non-Enroller who was fined by the Committee of Observation in April, 1776 [Ref: E-248]. Juror to the Oath of Allegiance in March, 1778 [Ref: S-267, but not listed in Ref: C-30].

KEMP, Peter Sr. Associator in December, 1775 [Ref: E-169]. Non-Enroller who was fined by the Committee of Observation in April, 1776 [Ref: E-248]. Juror to the Oath of Allegiance in 1778 [Ref: C-26].

KEMP, Wilhelm. Private in Capt. Myers' Company, German Regiment, served 3 years, and was discharged July 23, 1779, at Camp Wyoming [Ref: A-270].

KENDALL, Aron. Juror to the Oath of Allegiance in March, 1778 [Ref: S-265, but not listed in Ref: C-26].

KENDALL, Jacob. Loaned $500 for the use of the State of Maryland in June, 1780 [Ref: V-520].

KENDIT, Jacob. Associator in December, 1775 [Ref: E-169]. Juror to the Oath of Allegiance in 1778 [Ref: C-26].

KENDRICK, John. Substitute on May 28, 1778 [Ref: A-325]. Served in the German Regiment at White Plains on September 5, 1778, under Lt. Col. Ludwick Weltner [Ref: A-266].

KENNEDAY, Benjamin. Associator in December, 1775 [Ref: E-169]. Juror to the Oath of Allegiance in 1778 [Ref: C-26].

KENNEDAY, John. Private who enlisted on August 5, 1776, in the Flying Camp under Capt. Philip Meroney [Ref: A-45, N-30:112].

KENNEDY, John. Sergeant in Capt. Joseph Wood, Jr.'s company of militia in 1775 [Ref: E-53]. 2nd lieutenant in the 37th Battalion of militia on May 15, 1776, under Capt. Smith [Ref: B-95, W-427].
KENNEDY, Moses. Corporal in Capt. William Shields' company of militia in 1775 [Ref: E-56].
KENNEDY, Thomas. Sergeant in Capt. Jacob Snowdenberger's company of militia in 1775 [Ref: E-56].
KENNEDY, William. Militia substitute on June 9, 1778 [Ref: A-325]. Private in the 6th Maryland Regiment from June 11, 1778, until October 15, 1778, when he was reported dead [Ref: A-221].
KENNEDY, William. Enlisted in German Regiment in 1780 [Ref: V-126].
KENNEY, William. Private in the 7th Maryland Regiment who enlisted in Frederick Town between January and April, 1780, and reported as "gone to Camp" [Ref: A-334].
KENT, Jacob. "Jacob Ken" was an Associator in December, 1775 [Ref: E-169]. Juror to the Oath of Allegiance in 1778 [Ref: C-26]. "Jacob Kent" was a 2nd lieutenant in the 33rd Battalion on March 2, 1777 [Ref: B-95].
KEPHART, Adam. Private who enlisted January 12, 1778 [Ref: A-314]. "Adam Kephart or Keepheart" served in the Maryland Line and also received bounty land warrant #2404-100. See Revolutionary War Claim W4206 in which an "Adam Gibhart" stated he was the only soldier of that name in the 2nd Maryland Regiment. The heirs of "Adam Kephart" applied for his pension on July 27, 1846, in Frederick County, to wit: "Barbara Smith, Mary and Peter Kephart, Mary Magdalene Wisman, John and Elizabeth Kephart." [Ref: T-1930]. Also, "Adam Gibhart or Kibhart" applied for a pension (W4206) in Sumter District, South Carolina on February 13, 1819, aged about 60. In 1822 he stated he had lived in Sumter District for 39 years and prior to that he had lived in Maryland. [For more information, see Ref: T-1339, 1340].
KEPHART, George. "George Keephart" was a private in the German Regiment from February 3, 1778, to at least November, 1780 [Ref: A-223]. He was also drafted June 13, 1781, and provided a substitute [Ref: D-1814]. "George Keiphart or Kephart" applied for a pension (S36673) on August 21, 1819, aged 65, in Jackson County, Indiana, stating he served in the Continental and Maryland Lines. In 1820 he mentioned his wife Margaret, aged 64. [Ref: T-1906].
KEPHART, Martin. Soldier in the Maryland Line. Applied for pension (S41727) on June 10, 1818, aged 60, in Stark County, Ohio, stating he enlisted in Frederickstown, Maryland. In 1821 he had a wife aged nearly 60 and two daughters, the youngest aged 15 (no names given). He died

on July 5, 1832. [Ref: T-1930]. Martin served from the fall of 1775 until 1780, as a private in the 1st Maryland Regiment under Capt. George Stricker. He fought at the Battles of Long Island, White Plains, Trenton, Princeton, Brandywine, Germantown, Monmouth, and was discharged at Morristown, New Jersey. His occupation was a cooper and his property scheduled showed $314.39 total [Ref: K-47].

KEPHART [KEEPHEART], Peter. Captain in the Frederick Town Battalion of militia from 1778 through September 18, 1780 [Ref: H-15, B-94].

KEPLINGER, Christopher. Militia substitute on June 1, 1778 [Ref: A-324]. "Christopher Kepplinger" was a private in the German Regiment at the Battle of White Plains on September 5, 1778, under Lt. Col. Ludwick Weltner [Ref: A-267]. "Chresn. Keplinger" was a private in the German Regiment until discharged March 22, 1779 [Ref: A-222].

KERIGUEN, Lawrence. Corporal in Capt. Jacob Ambrose's company of militia in 1775 [Ref: E-54].

KERN, Jacob. Associator in December, 1775 [Ref: E-169]. Private who enlisted on July 1, 1776 in Capt. Peter Mantz's company; marched from Frederick Town to Leonardtown, and from there to Philadelphia, arriving August 23, 1776 [Ref: A-47]. Juror to Oath of Allegiance in 1778 [Ref: C-26].

KERN, John. Associator in December, 1775 [Ref: E-169]. Juror to the Oath of Allegiance in 1778 [Ref: C-26]. Ensign in the 33rd Battalion of militia, March 3, 1777 [Ref: B-95].

KERNAM, Michael. Private in Capt. John Kershner's company; guarded prisoners at Fort Frederick, 1777-1778; discharged on May 17, 1778 [Ref: A-328].

KERNEY, William. Private who enlisted on July 25, 1776 [Ref: A-51].

KERNS, Francis. Militia substitute on June 1, 1778 [Ref: A-324].

KERNS, Jacob. Private in the German Regiment in 1776 [Ref: A-266].

KERNS, Robert. Sergeant, 2nd Maryland Regiment, Disabled at the Battle of York [Yorktown]; invalid pension commenced on November 29, 1783, and ceased November 1, 1789 [Ref: A-630, A-631, F-475].

KERNY, Edward. Private who enlisted on July 20, 1776 [Ref: A-50].

KERR, Hugh. Ensign in Capt. Jacob Good's company of militia in 1775 and in the Select militia in December, 1781 [Ref: E-51, B-95]. One "Hugh Kerr, of Pipe Creek," died testate in 1784, leaving his wife Eleanor and naming "Hugh Ker," son of his brother "Robert Ker" and "Hugh Kerr," son of his sister "Elizabeth Ker." [Ref: M-6:86].

KERR, James. Corporal in Capt. Abraham Hayter's company of militia in 1775 [Ref: E-52].

KERR, Michael. Associator in December, 1775 [Ref: E-169]. Juror to the Oath of Allegiance in 1778 [Ref: C-26].

KERR, Robert. Corporal in Capt. Abraham Hayter's company of militia in 1775 [Ref: E-52].

KERSEY, Leven. Private who enlisted on August 5, 1776 [Ref: A-44].

KERSHNER, John. Captain at Fort Frederick, 1777-1778 [Ref: A-328]. One John Kershner was a 1st lieutenant in Capt. Martin Kershner's company of militia in Washington County in 1777 [Ref: B-247]. One John Kershner was captain of guards in Frederick County on March 20, 1779 [Ref: B-95].

KERSHNER, Michael. Private in the German Regiment from July 16, 1779, until discharged in 1780 [Ref: A-223]. Applied for a pension (S34947) on April 20, 1818, aged 67, in Allegany County, Maryland, receiving the half pay of a private, having enlisted in Baltimore. "On March 2, 1827, his pay went to Mary Ann Kershner, of Allegany County, for her late husband's service. On March 6, 1832, Treasurer of the Western Shore was directed to pay Jacob Lantz, for the use of Mrs. Mary C. Shryer, of Allegany, next and near friend of Mrs. Mary A. Kershner, deceased, late a pensioner of the state, $14.55, the balance due up to her decease." [Ref: G-362, T-1931, T-1967].

KESER, Stophel. 2nd lieutenant in the 29th Battalion of militia on August 29, 1777 [Ref: B-95].

KESLER, ---- (of John). Non-Enroller who was fined by the Committee of Observation in May, 1776 [Ref: E-248].

KESLER [KENSLER], James. Non-Enroller who was fined by the Committee of Observation in May, 1776 [Ref: E-248].

KESLER [KESSLER], George. Associator in December, 1775 [Ref: E-169]. Juror to the Oath of Allegiance in 1778 [Ref: C-26].

KESLER [KESSLER], George Barnhardt. "George Barnht. Kessler" was an Associator in December, 1775 [Ref: E-169]. "George Barnet Kesler" was a non-enroller who was fined by the Committee of Observation in April, 1776 [Ref: E-248]. "George Barnhardt Kessler" was a juror to the Oath of Allegiance in 1778 [Ref: C-26].

KESLER [KESSLER], John. "John Kessler" was an Associator in December, 1775 [Ref: E-169]. (Name appeared three times on a list of Associators). "John Kesler" was a non-enroller who was fined by the Committee of Observation in May, 1776 [Ref: E-248]. Subscribed to the Oath of Allegiance in 1778 [Ref: C-26].

KESLER, Peter. Non-Enroller who was fined by the Committee of Observation in May, 1776, but he apparently enrolled because the fine was remitted in June, 1776 [Ref: E-248].

KETTEL [KETTLE], Daniel. Private in the German Regiment from November 1, 1779, to at least August 1, 1780 [Ref: A-223].

KETTELL, Samuel. Associator in December, 1775 [Ref: E-169]. Juror to the Oath of Allegiance in 1778 [Ref: C-26].

KEY, Edmund. See "Thomas Stone," q.v.

KEY, John (Piney Creek Hundred). Appointed by the Committee of Correspondence to solicit subscriptions in 1775 to purchase arms and ammunition [Ref: I-86]. Served on Committee of Observation in 1775 [Ref: I-85].

KEY, John Ross. Captain in the 35th Battalion of militia on December 28, 1776. Lieutenant in the horse troops on February 2, 1781, and captain on June 25, 1781 [Ref: B-95, B-167, X-555]. "Gen. John Ross Key, close friend of Capt. Henry Williams, resided about 12 miles apart in Frederick. Both entered the Revolutionary War about the same time and both died about the same time. Key died at his residence near Middleburg on May 21, 1821 [although same source stated he died on October 17, 1821]. The people of Emmittsburg and Taneytown District, then Frederick County, passed resolutions at the time of their decease eulogizing their memories and extolling their public and private virtues." He was also an Associate Judge in the 5th Judicial District in 1791 [Ref: F-457, F-472, F-479].

KEY, Patrick. Private, 7th Maryland Regiment, 1779 [Ref: A-312].

KEYS, William. Private in the Skipton District Militia under Capt. Thomas Waring on April 16, 1776 [Ref: B-167, D-1814].

KEYSER [KEISER], Christian. Associator in December, 1775 [Ref: E-169]. Juror to the Oath of Allegiance in 1778 [Ref: C-26].

KEYSER, Jacob. Sergeant in the German Regiment from February 13, 1779, to at least August 1, 1780 [Ref: A-223].

KEYSER [KIEZER], Martin. Private who enlisted on July 18, 1776 [Ref: A-49].

KEYSER [KEISER], Mathias. Private in the German Regiment until discharged on July 24 or 26, 1779 [Ref: A-222, A-265].

KHUN, Peter. Associator in December, 1775 [Ref: E-169]. Juror to the Oath of Allegiance in 1778 [Ref: C-26].

KIBLER, John. Private in the German Regiment, muster roll dated October 23, 1776 [Ref: A-264]. "John Kebler" was a private in the German Regiment until discharged on July 26, 1779 [Ref: A-265].

KIDD, Benjamin. Associator in December, 1775 [Ref: E-169]. Juror to the Oath of Allegiance in 1778 [Ref: C-26].

KIDING, Ludowick. Private who enlisted July 18, 1776 [Ref: A-50].

KILER, George. Corporal in Capt. Henry Baker's company of militia in 1775 [Ref: E-54].

KILLENBERGER, Adam. Petitioned the General Assembly under the Act of May 12, 1780, stating he had been a non-juror to the Oath of Allegiance and Fidelity in 1778 due to "ignorance" and now desired relief under the Act and to take the Oath [Ref: L-101].

KIMBALL, Cathrina. See "William Beatty, Jr.," q.v.

KIMBERLY, John. Corporal in the Skipton District Militia under Capt. Thomas Waring on April 16, 1776 [Ref: B-167, D-1814].

KIMBOLE, William. Associator in December, 1775 [Ref: E-169]. Juror to the Oath of Allegiance in 1778 [Ref: C-26].

KINDLE, William. Private in the 1st Maryland Regiment, and in the 7th Maryland Regiment, who enlisted on April 25, 1778 and served in the Southern Army of the United States under Lt. Lamar in the late Capt. Beatty's company until discharged on April 25, 1781 [Ref: A-22, A-391]. "In December, 1817, the Treasurer of the Western Shore was directed to pay to Wm. Kindle, of Washington County, a private in the Revolutionary War, quarterly, half pay of a private, as a further remuneration to him for those services by which his country has been so essentially benefited." [Ref: G-362].

KING, George. Private who enlisted on February 28, 1778, and served in the 2nd Maryland Regiment [Ref: A-294].

KING, John. Private, 1st Maryland Regiment, enlisted on April 25, 1778, and served in the Southern Army of the United States under Lt. William Lamar in the late Capt. Beatty's company until transferred to the light infantry on March 12, 1781 [Ref: A-391].

KING, Joshua. See "Matthias Young," q.v.

KING, Mathias. Private in the German Regiment, 1776, in Capt. Henry Fister's company under the command of Col. Hussecker [Ref: A-261].

KING, Matthew. Private who was enlisted on July 20, 1776 by Capt. Jacob Good [Ref: A-46].

KING, Sarah and Eleanor. See "Isaac Rawlings," q.v.

KINGSTON, George. Private who enlisted August 8, 1776 [Ref: A-49].

KININGER, Jacob. Provided wheat for the military in July, 1782 [Ref: R-535].

KINSER, George. "George Kinser" was a militia substitute on June 4, 1778 [Ref: A-325]. "George Kinsor" took the Oath of Allegiance in 1778

[Ref: C-26]. "George Kinsor" was an Associator in December, 1775 [Ref: E-169].

KINSEY, George. Private who enlisted in Frederick on August 6, 1780, but later reported as "deserted" (no date). [Ref: A-344].

KINSY [KINSEY], John. Non-Enroller who was fined by the Committee of Observation in May, 1776 [Ref: E-248].

KINTZ [KIRTZ?], George. "George Kintz" was an Associator in December, 1775 [Ref: E-169], and a Juror to the Oath of Allegiance in 1778 [Ref: C-26, and S-265, which latter source spelled the name "George Kirtz."].

KIPPS, Abraham. Loaned $300 for the use of the State of Maryland in June, 1780 [Ref: V-520].

KIRCH, Anna Katherine. See "Elias Williard," q.v.

KIRGERY, Christian. Private stationed at Fort Frederick in June, 1778 [Ref: A-328].

KIRK, John. Private who enlisted on July 19, 1776 [Ref: A-51].

KIRK, Peter. Associator in December, 1775 [Ref: E-169]. Juror to the Oath of Allegiance in 1778 [Ref: C-26].

KIRK, Thomas. Ensign in Capt. Samuel Plummer's company of militia in the 1st Battalion on November 29, 1775 [Ref: E-54, B-95]. 1st lieutenant in the 33rd Battalion on March 3, 1777 [Ref: B-95]. Also, see "John Breeze," q.v.

KIRK, Thomas Jr. Private who enlisted August 5, 1776 in the Flying Camp under Capt. Philip Meroney [Ref: A-45, N-30:112]. Also, see "John Breeze," q.v.

KIRTZ, George. See "George Kintz," q.v.

KISBY, Richard. Private who enlisted on August 5, 1776 [Ref: A-44].

KISSINGER, John. Associator in December, 1775 [Ref: E-169]. Juror to the Oath of Allegiance in 1778 [Ref: C-26].

KIST, Godliff. 3rd Corporal in Capt. Christopher Stull's company of militia in 1775 [Ref: E-50].

KITELY, Francis. Private who enlisted on July 25, 1776 [Ref: A-50]. Private in 7th Maryland Regiment, 1779 [Ref: A-311]. Private in 1st Maryland Regiment, and served in the Southern Army of the United States under Lt. William Lamar in the late Capt. Beatty's company, 1781. Record indicates he was killed April 25, 1781 [Ref: A-391].

KITSCHURNER, Cathren. See "Francis Cost," q.v.

KITTAMAN, Peter. Non-Enroller who was fined by the Committee of Observation in April, 1776 [Ref: E-248].

KITTENGER, John. Private in Capt. Joseph Wood's company of militia in 1776 [Ref: E-244].

KITTSMILLER, Leonard. Non-Enroller who was fined by the Committee of Observation in May, 1776 [Ref: E-248].

KITZMILLER, George. See "Henry Baumgardner," q.v.

KLAISS, Frederick. Associator in December, 1775 [Ref: E-169]. Juror to the Oath of Allegiance in 1778 [Ref: C-26].

KLEIN, Daniel. See "Daniel Cline," q.v.

KLEIN, Frederick. Associator in December, 1775 [Ref: E-169]. Juror to the Oath of Allegiance in 1778 [Ref: C-26].

KLEIN, Gottlieb. Private in German Regiment, 1776, in Capt. Henry Fister's company under the command of Col. Hussecker [Ref: A-261].

KLEIN, Jacob. Third Sergeant in Capt. Philip Thomas' company of militia in 1775 [Ref: E-50]. Associator in December, 1775 [Ref: E-169]. "Jacob Klein" was a private in the German Regiment, muster roll dated October 23, 1776 [Ref: A-264]. "Jacob Kline" was a private in the German Regiment; discharged on July 26, 1779 [Ref: A-265]. "Jacob Klein" took the Oath of Allegiance in 1778 [Ref: C-26]. One "Jacob Klein, of Frederick Town," died testate in 1785, leaving wife Mary and "children who are mostly small" (not named). [Ref: M-6:188].

KLEIN, John. Associator in December, 1775 [Ref: E-169]. Private in the German Regiment, 1776, in Capt. Henry Fister's company under the command of Col. Nicholas Hussecker [Ref: A-261]. (Name appeared twice on the roster). Took the Oath of Allegiance in 1778 [Ref: C-26].

KLEINHOFF, John. 1st lieutenant in Capt. Jacob Good's company of militia on November 29, 1775 [Ref: E-51, B-96].

KLINE, Daniel. Associator in December, 1775 [Ref: E-169]. Juror to the Oath of Allegiance in 1778 [Ref: C-26]. Also, see "Daniel Cline," q.v.

KLINE, David. Petitioned the General Assembly under the Act of July 3, 1780, stating he had been a non-juror to the Oath of Allegiance and Fidelity in 1778 due to "ignorance" and now desired relief under the Act and to take the Oath [Ref: L-101].

KLINE, Jacob. Private in the German Regiment until discharged on August 26, 1780 [Ref: A-223].

KLINE, John. Private in the German Regiment until discharged on October 12, 1779 [Ref: A-222]. "On March 12, 1834, the Treasurer of the Western Shore was directed to pay to Mary M. Kline, widow of John Kline, of Frederick County, during life, quarterly, half pay of a private, for the service rendered by her husband during the Revolutionary War." [Ref: G-363].

KLINE, Nicholas. Associator in December, 1775 [Ref: E-169]. Juror to the Oath of Allegiance in 1778 [Ref: C-26].

KLISE, Christopher. Associator in December, 1775 [Ref: E-169]. Juror to the Oath of Allegiance in 1778 [Ref: C-26]. Also, see "Christeen Clisce," q.v.

KNAVE, Adam. Associator in December, 1775 [Ref: E-169]. Juror to the Oath of Allegiance in 1778 [Ref: C-26].

KNAVE, Bastian. "Bastian Knave" was a non-enroller who was fined by the Committee of Observation in April, 1776 [Ref: E-248]. "Bostian Nave" provided wheat for the military in May, 1782 [Ref: R-509].

KNAVE, Henry. Private who enlisted on July 18, 1776 [Ref: A-50].

KNAVE [NEAVE], John. "John Neave" was a militia substitute from May to December 10, 1781, and "marched to Annapolis." [Ref: A-653].

KNIGHT, Jacob. Private who enlisted on May 19, 1778, and served in the 2nd Maryland Regiment [Ref: A-294, A-323].

KNIGHT, Nicholas. Associator in December, 1775 [Ref: E-169]. Juror to the Oath of Allegiance in 1778 [Ref: C-26].

KNIGHT, Peter and William. See "Peter and William Night," q.v.

KNIGLY, Frederick. Associator in December, 1775 [Ref: E-169]. Juror to the Oath of Allegiance in 1778 [Ref: C-26].

KNOUFF, Peter. "Peter Cnouff" was an Associator in December, 1775 [Ref: E-165], and a Juror to the Oath of Allegiance in 1778 [Ref: C-23].

KNOWLAR, Thomas. Private who enlisted on July 29, 1776 [Ref: A-43].

KNOX, Thomas. Juror to the Oath of Allegiance in March, 1778 [Ref: S-265, but not listed in Ref: C-26].

KOFFMAN [KAUFMAN], Jacob. Private in the German Regiment until discharged on August 30, 1780 [Ref: A-223].

KOFFMAN, John. Associator in December, 1775 [Ref: E-169]. Juror to the Oath of Allegiance in 1778 [Ref: C-26].

KOLLER, Jakob. See "John Keller," q.v.

KOONCE, George. Associator in December, 1775 [Ref: E-169]. Juror to the Oath of Allegiance in 1778 [Ref: C-26]. "George Kunes" was a corporal in Capt. Jacob Ambrose's company of militia in 1775 [Ref: E-54].

KOONCE, Nicholas. Corporal in Capt. Robert Wood's company of militia in 1775 [Ref: E-53].

KOONS, Peter. Private in the German Regiment from June 1, 1778, to at least August 1, 1780 [Ref: A-223].

KOONTZ, Jacob. Sergeant in Capt. Basil Dorsey's company of militia in 1775 [Ref: E-52]. Provided wheat for the military in May, 1782 [Ref: R-516].

KOONTZ, Philip. Militia substitute from May to December 10, 1781, and "marched to Annapolis." [Ref: A-653].

KORTZ, Susan. See "Conrod Doll," q.v.

KORTZ, Susanna. See "Joseph Doll," q.v.

KOST, George. Associator in December, 1775 [Ref: E-169]. Juror to the Oath of Allegiance in 1778 [Ref: C-26].

KOTTZ, Jacob. 1st lieutenant in the German Regiment, muster roll dated October 23, 1776 [Ref: A-263]. Also, see "Jacob Cost," q.v.

KREBALL, David. Associator in December, 1775 [Ref: E-169]. Juror to the Oath of Allegiance in 1778 [Ref: C-26].

KREEBS, Henry. Associator in December, 1775 [Ref: E-169]. Juror to the Oath of Allegiance in 1778 [Ref: C-26].

KRIEGER, Laurence. See "Lawrence Creager," q.v.

KRISER, Henry. See "Matthias Young," q.v.

KROBLOCK, George. Petitioned the General Assembly under the Act of July 3, 1780, stating that he had been a non-juror to the Oath of Allegiance and Fidelity in 1778 due to "ignorance" and now desired relief under the Act and to take the Oath [Ref: L-101].

KRONICE, John. See "John Cronise," q.v.

KRUG, Andrew. Loaned $400 for the use of the State of Maryland in June, 1780 [Ref: V-520].

KRUGG, John Andrew. Associator in December, 1775 [Ref: E-169]. Juror to the Oath of Allegiance in 1778 [Ref: C-26].

KULBMAN, Philip. Associator in December, 1775 [Ref: E-169]. Juror to the Oath of Allegiance in 1778 [Ref: C-26].

KUNTZ, Jacob. Private in the German Regiment, 1776, in Capt. Henry Fister's company under the command of Col. Hussecker [Ref: A-261].

KUNTZ, Peter. Private in the German Regiment, 1776, in Capt. Henry Fister's company under the command of Col. Hussecker [Ref: A-261].

KURTZ, Jacob. Private in the German Regiment, 1776, in Capt. Henry Fister's company under the command of Col. Hussecker [Ref: A-261].

LABO, Adam. Associator in December, 1775 [Ref: E-169]. Juror to the Oath of Allegiance in 1778 [Ref: C-26].

LACKLAND, James. 2nd lieutenant in Capt. Elias Harden's Company, 29th Battalion of militia, on May 14, 1776. [Ref: W-424, D-1814]. Also, see "Samuel Swearingen," q.v.

LACY, Adam. 1st Corporal in Capt. Christopher Stull's company of militia in 1775 [Ref: E-50].

LAFAYETTE, Gen. See "Lawrence Everhart" and "John Stricker," q.v.

LAFEVER, Christian. See "Christian Lefever," q.v.

LAGO, Charles. Private who enlisted on April 1, 1780, for 3 years, in Capt. Michael Bayer's company, and served in the German Regiment [Ref: A-225, A-268].

LAKIN, Abraham. Associator in December, 1775 [Ref: E-169]. (This name appeared twice on the list of Associators). One subscribed to the Oath of Allegiance in 1778 [Ref: C-26]. "Abraham Lakin, Jr. (1713-1796)" had a wife named Sarah (1715-1797) and "Abraham Lakin, Jr. (1756-1799)" had a wife named Martha or Susan. Both men were "Jr." [Ref: O-109, O-132]. However, the following clarifies things: "Abraham Lakin 2nd (October 16, 1722 - 1796) married Sarah Hook (1724-1797) and lived in Jefferson, Frederick County, Maryland. Their son, Abraham Lakin 3rd (December 29, 1756 - July 2, 1799) married Mary Ungles (1766-1826) in 1788 and lived in Jefferson, Maryland." [Ref: U-2601].

LAKIN, Basil. Associator in December, 1775 [Ref: E-169]. Juror to the Oath of Allegiance in 1778 [Ref: C-26].

LAKIN, Daniel. Associator in December, 1775 [Ref: E-169]. Juror to the Oath of Allegiance in 1778 [Ref: C-26].

LAKIN, John. Associator in December, 1775 [Ref: E-169]. Juror to the Oath of Allegiance in 1778 [Ref: C-26].

LAKIN, Joseph. Associator in December, 1775 [Ref: E-169]. Juror to the Oath of Allegiance in 1778 [Ref: C-26].

LAKIN, Samuel. Associator in December, 1775 [Ref: E-169]. Juror to the Oath of Allegiance in 1778 [Ref: C-26].

LAMAR, Robert. Associator in December, 1775 [Ref: E-169]. Juror to the Oath of Allegiance in 1778 [Ref: C-26].

LAMAR, Thomas. Associator in December, 1775 [Ref: E-169]. Juror to the Oath of Allegiance in 1778 [Ref: C-26].

LAMAR, William. Private who enlisted on July 25, 1776 [Ref: A-50]. Ensign in the 7th Maryland Regiment on February 14, 1777, promoted to Lieutenant on December 28, 1777, and was acting quartermaster in July, 1778 [Ref: A-224]. Served in the late Capt. Charles Beatty's company in the 1st Maryland Regiment and in the Southern Army of the United States in 1780-1781 [Ref: A-390]. In February, 1800, he received bounty land warrant no. 1293-300-11, and he applied for a pension (S46388) on August 6, 1828, in Allegany County, Maryland. [Ref: T-1997, and Ref: J-35 states he applied on August 6, 1823].

LAMB, Edward. Associator in December, 1775 [Ref: E-169]. Juror to the Oath of Allegiance in 1778 [Ref: C-26]. "Edward Lamb, yeoman," died testate in 1785, leaving sons Frederick, William, and Pearce [Ref: M-6:185].

LAMB, Pearre [Pearce]. Son of Edward Lamb [Ref: M-6:185]. Associator in December, 1775 [Ref: E-169]. Juror to the Oath of Allegiance in 1778 [Ref: C-26].

LAMB, William (of Edward). Associator in December, 1775, and a Juror to the Oath of Allegiance in 1778 [Ref: E-169, C-26, M-6:185].

LAMBERT, Balser. Juror to the Oath of Allegiance in March, 1778 [Ref: S-265, but not listed in Ref: C-26].

LAMBERT, Christopher. Private in the 3rd Maryland Regiment who was disabled by fire in the Carolinas (no date given). His invalid's pension commenced on November 29, 1783, and ceased on November 1, 1789 (no reason was given). [Ref: A-630, A-631, F-475].

LAMBRECHT, Elizabeth. See "John Sponseller," q.v.

LAMBRIGHT, Henry. Associator in December, 1775 [Ref: E-169]. Juror to the Oath of Allegiance in 1778 [Ref: C-26]. "Henry Lambrecht, Sr., an old inhabitant, died on the Wednesday before April 5, 1805, in Frederick, Maryland." [Ref: N-57].

LANAUFF, Adam, Corporal in Capt. Benjamin Ogle, Jr.'s company of militia in 1775 [Ref: E-54].

LANCASTER, Abraham. Paid for recruiting services for the 7th Maryland Regiment on January 11, 1780 [Ref: V-54].

LANCASTER, Henry. Private who enlisted in Frederick on August 7, 1780, but was "not marched [to Annapolis] for want of pay." [Ref: A-344].

LANCY, John. Corporal in Capt. Normand Bruce's company of militia in 1775 [Ref: E-55].

LANDERS [LANDESS, LANDISS, LANDUS], Henry. Non-Enroller who was fined by the Committee of Observation in April, 1776 [Ref: E-248].

LANDERS [LANDESS, LANDISS, LANDUS], Roger. "Roger Landers" was a private who enlisted April 29, 1778, and served in the 2nd Maryland Regiment [Ref: A-294, A-321]. In August, 1779, Col. Thomas Price, in behalf of "Elizabeth Landiss, wife of Roger Landiss," a soldier in the 2nd Maryland Regiment, petitioned the Frederick County Court for assistance. Mrs. Landiss was granted subsistence for herself and their three children (no names were given). [Ref: Q-6835].

LANE [LAINE], Bartley. "Bartley Laine" was a private in 1778 who was referred to as an "old soldier" in the 2nd Maryland Regiment [Ref: A-294]. In August, 1779, Col. Thomas Price, in behalf of Catherine Lane, wife of Bartley Lane, a soldier in the 2nd Maryland Regiment, petitioned the Frederick County Court for assistance. She was granted 30 lbs. for one year's subsistence for herself and four children [Ref: Q-6835].

LANE, Henry. Private in Capt. Charles Baltzel's Company, served 3 years, and discharged July 19, 1779, at Camp Wyoming [Ref: A-271].

LANEHEART, Henry. Associator in December, 1775 [Ref: E-169]. Juror to the Oath of Allegiance in 1778 [Ref: C-26].

LANG, Anna Veronica. See "John Thomas," q.v.

LANGLEY, John. Private in the Middle District Militia in 1776 in Capt. Valentine Creager's company [Ref: A-72].

LANGTON, John. Private who enlisted on August 5, 1776 [Ref: A-44].

LANHAM, William. Private who enlisted on July 13, 1776 [Ref: A-43].

LANTZ, Jacob. See "Michael Kershner," q.v.

LANTZ [LONTZ, LOUTZ], Leonard. "Leonard Lantz" was an Associator in December, 1775 [Ref: E-169], and signed as a Juror to the Oath of Allegiance in 1778 [Ref: C-26]. "Leonard Lartz" was a sergeant in Capt. Peter Mantz's company of militia in 1775 [Ref: E-50]. "Leonard Lontz" was 2nd lieutenant in the militia, 1778-1779 [Ref: H-15, and Z-35, which latter source had spelled his name "Loutz."]. "Leonard Lantz" was 2nd lieutenant in the Frederick Town Battalion of militia on November 2, 1782, in Capt. White's company [Ref: B-96].

LANTZ, Martin. Private in the German Regiment until discharged on July 15, 1779 [Ref: A-225].

LARKINGS, John. Provided wheat for the military in May, 1782 [Ref: R-517].

LAROSE, John. Enlisted in the German Regiment in 1780 [Ref: V-126].

LARYMORE, Thomas. Enlisted in German Regiment in 1780 [Ref: V-126].

LASHORN [LEASHORN], Paul. Sergeant in Capt. Ludowick Kemp's company of militia in 1775 [Ref: E-52]. Juror to the Oath of Allegiance in March, 1778 [Ref: S-265, but not listed in Ref: C-26].

LASHYEAR, John. Private in the militia in July, 1776 [Ref: A-42].

LAVELY [LAVERTY], Jacob. "John Lavely" was a soldier in the Maryland Line in Anne Arundel County, Maryland, and applied for a pension (S34952) in Frederick County, Maryland, on June 9, 1818, aged 62. In 1820 he had a wife Sally, aged 54, and two children: William, aged 14, and Rachel, aged 11. He died on October 1, 1827, leaving 3 children (no names given). [Ref: T-2025]. However, Ref: J-25 states that "Jacob Laverty" was the pensioner on June 9, 1818, and he died on January 11, 1830.

LAWLER, Gudlip. Juror to the Oath of Allegiance in March, 1778 [Ref: S-265, but not listed in Ref: C-26].

LAWLESS, Philip. Soldier in the United States Infantry who applied for pension on June 9, 1815, and died March 1, 1830. [Ref: J-8, but a Revolutionary War pension abstract was not found in Ref: T-2026].

LAWMAN, Elizabeth. See "John Godlieb Boyer," q.v.

LAWRENCE, Jacob. Associator in December, 1775 [Ref: E-169]. Juror to the Oath of Allegiance in 1778 [Ref: C-26].

LAWRENCE, John (Burnt Woods Hundred). Appointed by the Committee of Correspondence to solicit subscriptions in 1775 to purchase arms and ammunition [Ref: I-86]. Served on the Committee of Observation in 1775 [Ref: I-85]. Clerk in Capt. David Moore's militia company in 1775 [Ref: E-56]. Justice of the Peace in 1777 [Ref: F-476]. One John Lawrence died testate in early 1782 (codicil) naming his wife Martha and children John Stephen, Upton, Ann, Susannah, Rachel, and Elizabeth (and Peggy, born after will was written). [Ref: M-6:27].

LAWS, William. Drafted on June 2, 1783 [Ref: B-168].

LAWSON, Luke. Soldier from Frederick County who was wounded at the battle of Guilford [Courthouse] while serving with the 1st Maryland Regiment [Ref: F-475].

LAYMAN, George. See "George Lemmon," q.v.

LAZARUS, Henry. Juror to the Oath of Allegiance in 1778 [Ref: C-26]. Died testate in 1779, naming his brother Sampson Lazarus and his niece Brandley Lazarus (to whom he bequeathed his entire estate). [Ref: M-5:133].

LAZARUS, Sampson. Associator in December, 1775 [Ref: E-169]. "Samson Lazarus" furnished lead for use of the militia in Fredericktown in 1775 [Ref: E-61]. Juror to the Oath of Allegiance in 1778 [Ref: C-26].

LAZENBY, Alexander. Private in the militia, July, 1776 [Ref: A-42].

LAZENBY, Henry. Private in the militia in July, 1776 [Ref: A-42].

LEACH, Benjamin. Non-Enroller who was fined by the Committee of Observation in May, 1776, but he apparently enrolled because the fine was remitted in June, 1776 [Ref: E-248].

LEACH, William. Non-Enroller who was fined by the Committee of Observation in May, 1776, but he apparently enrolled because the fine was remitted in June, 1776 [Ref: E-248].

LEAKIN, John. Provided wheat for the military in 1782 [Ref: R-515].

LEAKIN, William. Private, 1st Maryland Regiment, 1781, and served in the Southern Army of the United States under Lt. William Lamar in the late Capt. Beatty's company [Ref: A-390].

LEAMON, John. See "John Lemmon," q.v.

221

LEAR, Daniel. Non-Enroller who was fined by the Committee of Observation in April, 1776 [Ref: E-248].

LEARN, Margaret. See "George Zimmerman," q.v.

LEARY [LARREY], William. Private in the 7th Maryland Regiment who enlisted March 12, 1780 [Ref: A-312, A-334].

LEASE, William. Provided wheat for the military in July, 1782 [Ref: R-533].

LEATH, Samuel. Provided wheat for the military in June, 1782 [Ref: R-520].

LEATHER, John. Corporal in Capt. Ludowick Kemp's company of militia in 1775 [Ref: E-52]. Private in the German Regiment, 1776, in Capt. Henry Fister's company under the command of Col. Nicholas Hussecker [Ref: A-261]. Juror to the Oath of Allegiance in March, 1778 [Ref: S-265, but not listed in Ref: C-26]. "In December, 1816, the Treasurer of the Western Shore was directed to pay to John Leather, of Frederick County, an old revolutionary soldier, quarterly, a sum of money equal to half pay of a sergeant, or to his order during his life, as a further compensation for those services he rendered his country during the Revolutionary War." [Ref: G-365]. "John Leather, aged 76, a Revolutionary soldier, who was wounded at Brandywine, died on September 10, 1831. For a number of years he was an elder in the Lutheran Church." [Ref: F-473].

LEATHERMAN, Godfrey. 2nd lieutenant in Capt. Philip Rodenbieler's company of militia in the 4th Battalion in 1775 [Ref: E-51, B-97].

LEATHERMAN, Nicholas. Non-Enroller who was fined by the Committee of Observation in April, 1776 [Ref: E-248].

LEATHERMAN, Peter (1757-1845). Drafted on June 2, 1783 [Ref: B-168]. Married Mary Ann Swigart (1764-1835) and is buried at the Swigart-Ambrose family cemetery near Ellerton [Ref: O-126].

LEE, Andrew. Associator in December, 1775 [Ref: E-169]. Juror to the Oath of Allegiance in 1778 [Ref: C-26].

LEE, Dudley. Militia substitute on June 6, 1778 [Ref: A-325]. Private who enlisted in 1780 [Ref: A-345]. "In November, 1811, the Treasurer of the Western Shore was directed to pay to Dudley Lee, half payment of a soldier, as remuneration for services rendered his country in the Revolutionary War, and as a relief from the indigence and misery which attend his old age. On March 21, 1838, the Treasurer was directed to pay to Margaret Lee, widow of Dudley Lee, half pay of a private during her life, as further remuneration for his services during the Revolutionary War." [Ref: G-365].

LEE, James. Private who enlisted on some time in 1780 [Ref: A-345].

LEE, Joseph. Private, 7th Maryland Regiment, enlisted in Frederick Town on February 21, 1780, and reported as "gone to Camp" [Ref: A-312, A-334].

LEE, Mark. Private in the Skipton District Militia under Capt. Thomas Waring on April 16, 1776 [Ref: B-167, D-1814].

LEE, Thomas Sim (1745-1819). Born in Prince George's County (at his father's home) or in Charles County (at his grandfather's estate), Thomas Sim Lee became Governor of Maryland in 1779. However, he did not live in Frederick County until 1784 (after the Revolution) and then moved to Georgetown, D. C. in 1795, after serving a second term as governor, 1792-1794. He returned to Frederick County in 1811, where he lived until his death on November 9, 1819. He was also a Congressman, 1783-1784 [Ref: F-451, F-471, F-478, and P-529, which should be consulted for more genealogical information on this prominent Marylander]. Mrs. Mary Lee, wife of Thomas Sim Lee, Esq., former Governor of Maryland, and daughter of Ignatius Diggs, Esq., of Maryland, died on Monday, January 21, 1805 [Ref: N-57].

LEE, Timothy. Private in the 7th Maryland Regiment from January 18, 1778, until February 12, 1778, when he "deserted." [Ref: A-225].

LEEDY, Abraham. Private stationed at Fort Frederick on June 27, 1778, in Capt. John Kershner's company, and guarding prisoners of war [Ref: A-328].

LEFEVER, Christian. Sergeant in Capt. James Johnson's company of militia in 1775 [Ref: E-52]. "Christian Lafever" was 2nd lieutenant in the 37th Battalion of militia on February 1, 1777 [Ref: B-96, which source later misspelled his name as "Lasaver"]. "Christian Lefavor" provided hay for the military in May, 1782 [Ref: R-515].

LEGG, Arthur. Private in the militia in July, 1776 [Ref: A-42].

LEGG, Thomas. Associator in December, 1775 [Ref: E-169]. Juror to the Oath of Allegiance in 1778 [Ref: C-26].

LEINBAUGH, Daniel. Fifer in Capt. Benjamin Ogle, Jr.'s company of militia in 1775 [Ref: E-54]. A "Frederick Linebough" died testate in 1784 and his will named a son Daniel Linebough (among others). [Ref: M-6:124]. Also, see "Frederick Limebock," q.v

LEISER [LIESER], Adam. Private in the German Regiment, muster roll dated October 23, 1776 [Ref: A-264]. Son of "Youst Leezer, yeoman," who wrote his will in 1775 and died in 1784 [Ref: M-6:124].

LEISER [LEISOR], Peter. Non-Enroller who was fined by the Committee of Observation in April, 1776 [Ref: E-248]. Son of "Youst Leezer, yeoman" who wrote his will in 1775 and died in 1784 [Ref: M-6:124].

LEISER [LEESER], Yost. Provided wheat for the military in July, 1782 [Ref: R-534. Name looks like "Yost Luser" in this record]. "Youst Leezer, yeoman," died testate in 1784 [Ref: M-6:124].

LEISER, Zachariah. Non-Enroller who was fined by the Committee of Observation in April, 1776 [Ref: E-248]. Zachariah was a son of "Youst Leezer, yeoman," who died testate in 1784 [Ref: M-6:124].

LEITCH, William. Private who enlisted on July 29, 1776 [Ref: A-44].

LEITHUSIER, George. Private in the German Regiment until discharged on July 22, 1779 [Ref: A-225].

LEMASTER, Abraham. Associator in December, 1775 [Ref: E-169]. Juror to the Oath of Allegiance in 1778 [Ref: C-26].

LEMMON, Adam. Non-Enroller who was fined by the Committee of Observation in April, 1776 [Ref: E-248]. Petitioned the General Assembly under the Act of May 12, 1780, stating that he had been a non-juror to the Oath of Allegiance and Fidelity in 1778 due to "ignorance" and now desired relief under the Act and to take the Oath [Ref: L-101].

LEMMON [LAYMAN?], George. Non-Enroller fined by the Committee of Observation in May, 1776 [Ref: E-248]. "George Layman (Lemmons) was born in Frederick County, Maryland, and married Barbara Baumgardner (1763-1852) in 1785. They moved to Botetourt County, Virginia, and George served as a private in the Virginia Line. They are buried in the Laymantown Cemetery. George died in June, 1854." [Ref: U-2904].

LEMMON, Jacob. Non-Enroller who was fined by the Committee of Observation in April, 1776 [Ref: E-248]. Petitioned the General Assembly under the Act of May 12, 1780, stating that he had been a non-juror to the Oath of Allegiance and Fidelity in 1778 due to "ignorance" and now desired relief under the Act and to take the Oath [Ref: L-101].

LEMMON [LEAMON, LEMON], John. Sergeant in Capt. Robert Beatty's company of militia in 1775 [Ref: E-55]. Juror to the Oath of Allegiance in March, 1778 [Ref: S-265, but not listed in Ref: C-26]. One "John Leamon" died testate in early 1792, leaving wife Mary and son Peter (other children mentioned, but none were named in will). [Ref: M-8:134].

LEMMON, Lodowick. Provided wheat for the military in May, 1782 [Ref: R-517].

LENEGEN, John. Militia substitute from May to December 10, 1781, and "marched to Annapolis." [Ref: A-653].

LEONARD, Peter. Sergeant in Capt. Benjamin Ogle, Jr.'s company of militia in 1775 [Ref: E-53].

LESELAND, William. Private in 7th Maryland Regiment who enlisted in Frederick Town between January and April, 1780, and reported as "gone to Camp" [Ref: A-334].

LESH, George. Militia substitute from May to December 10, 1781, and "marched to Annapolis." [Ref: A-653].

LESSAR, Christian. Ensign in the 37th Battalion of militia on May 15, 1776, in Capt. Richard Balsell's company [Ref: B-97, W-427].

LESTER, Joshua. Private, 1st Maryland Regiment, 1780, and served in the Southern Army of the United States under Lt. William Lamar in the late Capt. Beatty's company in 1781; also served as a hospital orderly in July, 1781 [Ref: A-391].

LETT, Daniel. Militia substitute on June 6, 1778 [Ref: A-325].

LETT, James. Private who enlisted February 28, 1778 [Ref: A-314].

LETT, Rosalius. Private who enlisted on February 28, 1778 [Ref: A-314].

LEVISTON, James. Associator in December, 1775 [Ref: E-169]. Juror to the Oath of Allegiance in 1778 [Ref: C-26].

LEVY, David. Associator in December, 1775 [Ref: E-169]. Juror to the Oath of Allegiance in 1778 [Ref: C-26]. On April 15, 1779, Mary Levy petitioned the Frederick County Court, stating her husband David was a soldier in Col. Ludwick Weltner's regiment. She was granted 45 lbs. for one year's subsistence for herself and six children [Ref: Q-6835]. David Levy was paid for services rendered to (or while in) the military in December, 1779 [Ref: V-44].

LEWIS, Daniel. Private in the militia in July, 1776 [Ref: A-42].

LEWIS, George. Private in the militia, March 9, 1776 [Ref: B-167]. Substitute on May 1, 1781; marched with Capt. Boyer [Ref: D-1814].

LEWIS, Jacob. Associator in December, 1775 [Ref: E-169]. Non-Enroller who was fined by the Committee of Observation in April, 1776. He apparently enrolled because the fine was remitted in June, 1776 [Ref: E-248]. Juror to the Oath of Allegiance in 1778 [Ref: C-26].

LEWIS, Mary. On April 14, 1779, Mary Lewis petitioned the Frederick County Court for relief, stating her husband (name not given) was a soldier in the Revolutionary service. She was granted 30 lbs. for one year's subsistence for herself and 3 children [Ref: Q-6835].

LEWIS, Richard. Private who enlisted on July 18, 1776 [Ref: A-49].

LEWIS, Samuel. Associator in December, 1775 [Ref: E-169]. Juror to the Oath of Allegiance in 1778 [Ref: C-26].
LEWIS, William. Private who enlisted on July 22, 1776 [Ref: A-49]. Corporal in the German Regiment; muster roll dated October 23, 1776 [Ref: A-263]. Sergeant in the German Regiment who was discharged on July 16, 1779 [Ref: A-264].
LICKLITER, Peter. Private in the Middle District Militia in 1776 in Capt. Valentine Creager's company [Ref: A-72].
LIDES, Eliza. See "Peter Mantz," q.v.
LIGAMIRE, Jacob. Militia substitute from May to December 10, 1781, and "marched to Annapolis." [Ref: A-653].
LIGHTER, Peter. Fifer at Fort Frederick in 1778 with Capt. John Kershner's company; also guarded prisoners of war [Ref: A-328].
LIGHTFOOT, Thomas. Private who enlisted July 13, 1776 [Ref: A-43].
LILLGENGER, Henry. Associator in December, 1775 [Ref: E-169]. Juror to the Oath of Allegiance in 1778 [Ref: C-26].
LILLY, Richard. Associator in December, 1775 [Ref: E-169]. Juror to the Oath of Allegiance in 1778 [Ref: C-26]. He died testate in 1792, leaving a wife Mary and children Samuel, Ignatius, Joseph, and Mary [Ref: M-8:177].
LILLY, Samuel. Associator in December, 1775 [Ref: E-169]. Juror to the Oath of Allegiance in 1778 [Ref: C-26].
LIMEBOCK, Frederick. Associator in December, 1775 [Ref: E-169]. Juror to the Oath of Allegiance in 1778 [Ref: C-26]. See "Daniel Leinbaugh," q.v.
LIMES, Nicholas. Private in Capt. Charles Baltzel's Company, served 3 years, and discharged July 21, 1779 at Camp Wyoming [Ref: A-271].
LIMRICK, Patrick. Associator in December, 1775 [Ref: E-169]. Juror to the Oath of Allegiance in 1778 [Ref: C-26].
LINCH, John. Corporal in Cat. William Luckett, Jr.'s company of militia in 1775 [Ref: E-55].
LINCH, William. Private who was enlisted on July 20, 1776 by Capt. Jacob Good [Ref: A-46].
LINDER, Jacob. Private who enlisted on July 25, 1776 [Ref: A-51].
LINDER, Nathaniel. Private who enlisted July 20, 1776 [Ref: A-50].
LINDSAY [LINDSEY], Anthony. "Anthony Lindsey" was an Associator in December, 1775 [Ref: E-169]. Juror to the Oath of Allegiance in 1778 [Ref: C-26]. "Anthony Lindsay" was a 2nd lieutenant in Linganore Battalion of militia on January 17, 1777 under Capt. Baker [Ref: B-97, Y-54].

LINDSAY, John. Sergeant in Capt. Henry Baker's company of militia in 1775 [Ref: E-54]. Associator in December, 1775 [Ref: E-169]. Juror to the Oath of Allegiance in 1778 [Ref: C-26].

LINDSEY, John. Private who enlisted on July 19, 1776 [Ref: A-51].

LINDSEY, Oliver. Corporal in Capt. Robert Wood's company of militia in 1775 [Ref: E-53]. Associator in December, 1775 [Ref: E-169], and a Juror to the Oath of Allegiance in 1778 [Ref: C-26]. "Oliver Linsey" was a private in the Middle District Militia in 1776 in Capt. Valentine Creager's company [Ref: A-72]. He later served in the Maryland Line. In November, 1779, Nancy Lindsey, wife of "Olliver Lindsey," a soldier in the Continental service, petitioned the Frederick County Court for assistance. She was granted 120 lbs. for herself and 4 children [Ref: Q-6835].

LINEBOUGH, Frederick. See "Daniel Leinbaugh," q.v.

LINGAN, James. 2nd lieutenant in a rifle company in July, 1776, under Capt. Barrett [Ref: X-54].

LINGEFELTY, Felty. Associator in December, 1775 [Ref: E-169]. Juror to the Oath of Allegiance in 1778 [Ref: C-26].

LINGENFETTER, Ceterena and John. See "Abraham Cassell," q.v.

LINK, Adam. Loaned $800 for the use of the State of Maryland in June, 1780 [Ref: V-520].

LINK, John. 4th corporal in the Middle District Militia in 1775 in Capt. Valentine Creager's company [Ref: A-72]. Became an ensign in Capt. William Beatty's company of militia in the 1st Battalion on November 29, 1775 (or 1776?). [Ref: E-55, B-97]. 2nd lieutenant in the Frederick Town Battalion of militia on May 26, 1778, and 1st lieutenant on August 16, 1779. [Ref: H-15, B-97].

LINK, Nicholas. Associator in December, 1775 [Ref: E-169]. Juror to the Oath of Allegiance in 1778 [Ref: C-26, S-265].

LINKEN, John. Associator in December, 1775 [Ref: E-169]. Non-Enroller who was fined by the Committee of Observation in April, 1776 [Ref: E-248]. Juror to the Oath of Allegiance in 1778 [Ref: C-26].

LINN, David. See "David Lynn," q.v.

LINTHICUM, Nathan. Ensign in the Lower District Militia on March 26, 1776 [Ref: W-287].

LINTHICUM, Z. (Sugar Loaf Hundred). Appointed by the Committee of Correspondence to solicit subscriptions in 1775 to purchase arms and ammunition [Ref: I-86].

LINTON, Samuel. Sergeant in Capt. William Duvall's company of militia in 1775 [Ref: E-54].

LINTRIDGE, Samuel. Private who enlisted on July 18, 1776. Also, a Samuel Lintridge was a private who enlisted on April 21, 1778 [Ref: A-49, A-324].
LIPPS, Philip. See "Michael Smith," q.v.
LISLEND, William. Private in the 7th Maryland Regiment who enlisted February 29, 1780 [Ref: A-312].
LITTLE, Peter. Associator in December, 1775 [Ref: E-169]. Juror to the Oath of Allegiance in 1778 [Ref: C-26]. He may have been the Capt. Little in the 35th Battalion of militia on November 28, 1776 [Ref: B-98].
LITZINGER, William. Sergeant in German Regiment, 1776 [Ref: A-266].
LIVERS, Arnold. Associator in December, 1775 [Ref: E-169]. Juror to the Oath of Allegiance in 1778 [Ref: C-26]. "William Elder and his friend Arnold Livers moved to the frontier in 1734 to what later became Frederick County from Mt. Calvert in eastern Prince George's County, east of the area that became Washington, D. C." [Ref: O-80]. Arnold Livers died testate in 1779, leaving a wife Mary and children (not named in the will). [Ref: M-5:135].
LIVERS, Jacoba Clementina. See "William Elder, Sr.," q.v., "Francis Elder," q.v., "Arnold Elder," q.v., and "Aloysius Elder," q.v.
LIVERS, Robert. Associator in December, 1775 [Ref: E-169]. Juror to the Oath of Allegiance in 1778 [Ref: C-26].
LOAG, John. Fifer in Capt. Robert Wood's company of militia in 1775 [Ref: E-53].
LOAR, Peter. Private who enlisted on July 20, 1776 [Ref: A-50].
LOAR, Philip. Private who enlisted on July 20, 1776 [Ref: A-50].
LOCHER, Frederick. Private in the German Regiment, muster roll dated October 23, 1776 [Ref: A-264]. "Fredk. Locker," private in the German Regiment, was discharged August 9, 1779 [Ref: A-265].
LOCK, John. Private who enlisted on July 1, 1776 in Capt. Peter Mantz's company; marched from Frederick Town to Leonardtown, and from there to Philadelphia, arriving August 23, 1776 [Ref: A-47].
LOCKER, Shedereck. Private who enlisted July 18, 1776 [Ref: A-49].
LOCKMAN, Jacob. Associator in December, 1775 [Ref: E-169]. Juror to the Oath of Allegiance in 1778 [Ref: C-26].
LOCLEN, John W. Private, 1st Maryland Regiment, 1780, and served in the Southern Army of the United States under Lt. William Lamar in the late Capt. Beatty's company until his (Loclen's) death in March of 1781 (Name could be McLoclen rather than Loclen?). [Ref: A-390].
LODGEADE, Marthew. Private in the militia, July, 1776 [Ref: A-42].

LOE, Andrew. Private who enlisted on July 1, 1776 in Capt. Peter Mantz's company; marched from Frederick Town to Leonardtown, and from there to Philadelphia, arriving August 23, 1776 [Ref: A-47].

LOEHR, Daniel. Associator in December, 1775 [Ref: E-169]. Juror to the Oath of Allegiance in 1778 [Ref: C-26].

LOGAN, Joseph. Associator in December, 1775 [Ref: E-169]. Juror to the Oath of Allegiance in 1778 [Ref: C-26].

LOGE, John. Associator in December, 1775 [Ref: E-169]. Juror to the Oath of Allegiance in 1778 [Ref: C-27].

LOGSDON, Edward. Associator in December, 1775 [Ref: E-169]. Juror to the Oath of Allegiance in 1778 [Ref: C-27, S-265].

LOGSDON, John. Associator in December, 1775 [Ref: E-169]. Juror to the Oath of Allegiance in 1778 [Ref: C-27].

LOGSDON, John Jr. Associator in December, 1775 [Ref: E-169]. Juror to the Oath of Allegiance in 1778 [Ref: C-27, S-265].

LOGSDON, Lawrence. Associator in December, 1775 [Ref: E-169]. Juror to the Oath of Allegiance in 1778 [Ref: C-27].

LOGSDON, Ralph. Associator in December, 1775 [Ref: E-169]. Juror to the Oath of Allegiance in 1778 [Ref: C-27].

LOGSDON, William Sr. Associator in December, 1775 [Ref: E-169]. Juror to the Oath of Allegiance in 1778 [Ref: C-27].

LOKERIAS, Frederick. Militia substitute, June 4, 1778 [Ref: A-325].

LONG, Christopher. Associator in December, 1775 [Ref: E-169]. "Chris. Long" was also an Associator in December, 1775 [Ref: E-169]. One subscribed to the Oath of Allegiance in 1778 [Ref: C-27].

LONG, Daniel Jr. Non-Enroller who was fined by the Committee of Observation in May, 1776, but he apparently enrolled because the fine was remitted in June, 1776 [Ref: E-248].

LONG, Jacob. Private who enlisted on July 20, 1776 [Ref: A-50]. Juror to the Oath of Allegiance in March, 1778 [Ref: S-265, but not listed in Ref: C-26].

LONG, John. Corporal in Capt. William Shields' company of militia in 1775 [Ref: E-56]. Associator in December, 1775 [Ref: E-169]. Juror to the Oath of Allegiance in 1778 [Ref: C-27].

LONG, Nicholas Tom. Sergeant in Capt. Charles Beatty's company of militia in 1775 [Ref: E-51]. Also, see "Nicholas Thomlong," q.v.

LONG, Thomas. Ensign in the Frederick Town Battalion of militia on September 18, 1780, under Capt. Stoner [Ref: B-98], and paid for services rendered to the military in December, 1779 [Ref: V-45].

LONGFELLOW, Andrew. Private in the 7th Maryland Regiment from July 20, 1778, until discharged on February 12, 1779 [Ref: A-225].
LONGLEY, William. Private who enlisted July 13, 1776 [Ref: A-43].
LONGSWORTH, Solomon. Juror to the Oath of Allegiance in March, 1778 [Ref: S-265, but not listed in Ref: C-26].
LONTZ [LOUTZ], Leonard. See "Leonard Lantz," q.v.
LOOKENBEALL, Jacob. Non-Enroller who was fined by the Committee of Observation in April, 1776 [Ref: E-248].
LOOKENBEALL, Peter. Non-Enroller who was fined by the Committee of Observation in April, 1776 [Ref: E-248].
LOPER, Cutlip. Associator in December, 1775 [Ref: E-169]. Juror to the Oath of Allegiance in 1778 [Ref: C-27].
LORANTZ [LARANTZ], Frederick. Private in the German Regiment until discharged on July 15, 1779 [Ref: A-225].
LORANTZ, Vendel. Private in the German Regiment until discharged on July 20, 1779 [Ref: A-225].
LORE, George and Susanna. See "Joseph Doll," q.v.
LORE, Joseph. Served in the Maryland militia and pensioned in 1831, aged 76 [Ref: J-33]. However, source T-2107 states "Joseph Lohr" was born near Lebanon, Pennsylvania, on November 26, 1758, and he lived there at enlistment. He applied for pension (S8849) on July 15, 1828, in Frederick County, Maryland, a resident of Emmitsburg.
LOSINAR, Jacob. Associator in December, 1775 [Ref: E-169]. Juror to the Oath of Allegiance in 1778 [Ref: C-27].
LOUDEN, William. Private who enlisted on August 5, 1776, in the Flying Camp under Capt. Philip Meroney [Ref: A-45, N-30:112].
LOUGDON, Joseph. Militia substitute on June 13, 1778 [Ref: A-326].
LOUX, George. Militia substitute on June 1, 1778 [Ref: A-324].
LOUTZ, Leonard. See "Leonard Lantz (Lontz, Loutz)," q.v.
LOVE, David. Sergeant in the 1st Maryland Regiment, and the 7th Maryland Regiment, who enlisted September 8, 1779, and served in the Southern Army of the United States under Lt. William Lamar in 1780 in the late Capt. Beatty's company until transferred to the light infantry on March 12, 1781 [Ref: A-225, A-389]. He applied for pension (S18948) in Oldham County, Kentucky, on June 28, 1828, stating he had enlisted in the Continental Line of the Army of the Revolution and continued in service until its termination at which period he was a sergeant in Capt. Clickett's Company, 7th Maryland Regiment, in Fredericktown, Maryland, and that he was discharged in Baltimore at the close of the war, and his discharge has been long since lost." He died on December

6, 1830, leaving a widow Nancy and children: Joseph, John, and David Love. Nancy died on July 5, 1836. A copy of the soldier's will was in his pension file, in which he named his three sons and wife Agness. David Love, Jr., son of the soldier, made affidavit on April 21, 1856, that his father had lived in Shelby County, Kentucky, and then moved to Oldham County, Kentucky, where he lived for 6 years [Ref: T-2124, K-59].

LOVE, Thomas. Private who enlisted on July 29, 1776 [Ref: A-43].

LOVEDAY, John. Private, 1st Maryland Regiment, 1781, and served in the Southern Army of the United States under Lt. William Lamar in the late Capt. Beatty's company [Ref: A-389].

LOVELASS, Barton. Private who enlisted July 18, 1776 [Ref: A-49].

LOVELESS, Charles. Private who enlisted July 18, 1776 [Ref: A-49].

LOVET, William. Private who enlisted on July 13, 1776 [Ref: A-43].

LOVETH, Henry. Associator in December, 1775 [Ref: E-169]. Juror to the Oath of Allegiance in 1778 [Ref: C-27].

LOW, Andrew. Ensign in the Frederick Town Battalion of militia on January 23, 1782, under Capt. Shellman [Ref: B-98].

LOW, Jacob. Corporal in the German Regiment, 1776, in Capt. Henry Fister's company under the command of Col. Hussecker [Ref: A-261].

LOWER, John. Associator in December, 1775 [Ref: E-169]. Juror to the Oath of Allegiance in 1778 [Ref: C-27].

LOWREY, Charles (alias Dorsey). Enlisted on March 16, 1781 for the duration of the war, and later reported "deserted." [Ref: D-1814].

LOWRY, John. Private who enlisted on August 5, 1776 [Ref: A-44].

LOWRY, William. Private who enlisted on July 29, 1776 [Ref: A-44].

LOWTHER, James. Private who enlisted August 5, 1776, in the Flying Camp under Capt. Philip Meroney [Ref: A-45, N-30:112]. Served in the 6th Maryland Regiment from August 23, 1777, until November 24, 1778, when he was reported "deserted." [Ref: A-224].

LOYD, Thomas. Juror to the Oath of Allegiance in March, 1778 [Ref: S-265, but not listed in Ref: C-26].

LOYL, Frederick. Juror to the Oath of Allegiance in March, 1778 [Ref: S-265, but not listed in Ref: C-26].

LUCAS, Charles. Private who enlisted on July 25, 1776 [Ref: A-49].

LUCAS, William. Private who enlisted on July 18, 1776 [Ref: A-49].

LUCKETT, John (Sugarland Hundred). Appointed by the Committee of Correspondence to solicit subscriptions in 1775 to purchase arms and ammunition [Ref: I-86]. Gave money in the amount of 7 lbs. 2 sh. for arms and ammunition for the militia in 1775 [Ref: E-63].

LUCKETT, William Jr. (Catoctin Hundred). Appointed by the Committee of Correspondence to solicit subscriptions in 1775 to purchase arms and ammunition [Ref: I-86]. Served on the Committee of Observation in 1775 [Ref: I-85]. Captain of a company of militia in the 4th Battalion on November 29, 1775 [Ref: E-55, B-98]. Associator in December, 1775 [Ref: E-169]. Juror to the Oath of Allegiance in 1778 [Ref: C-27]. Commissioned a Justice of Frederick County on November 21, 1778 [Ref: E-303]. "William Luckett, Jr." was an Election Judge in the Middle District on July 2, 1776, and in 1777 [Ref: F-476. Ed. Note: It is possible that some of this information might apply to William Luckett, Sr. For more information, see Ref: P-553].

LUCKETT, William Sr. Captain in the French and Indian War, 1756. Chosen to serve on the Committee of Observation in 1775 [Ref: E-302, E-303, I-85]. Lieutenant Colonel in the 4th Battalion in 1776 [Ref: E-58, B-98]. "Col. William Luckett" reviewed and passed recruits in 1776 [Ref: A-49]. "William Luckett, Sr." was an Election Judge in the Lower District on July 2, 1776, and November 25, 1776 [Ref: F-476. Ed. Note: It is possible that some of this information may apply to William Luckett, Jr. See Ref: P-553].

LUDWICK, Leonard (c1750-1804). Private in the German Regiment in 1776 in Capt. Henry Fister's company under the command of Colonel Nicholas Hussecker [Ref: A-261]. "Leonard Lodwick" was a private in the militia on March 9, 1776 [Ref: B-166]. He served under Capt. Michael Bayer from July 15, 1776, to July 21, 1779. He married Catharine Rothrock (Katherine Rotbruck) and they later moved to Hampshire County, Virginia. A daughter, Ann Ludwick (born 1789), married John Whiteman (born 1783). [Ref: U-2532]. "Leonard Ludwick" was discharged July 24, 1779 from the German Regiment [Ref: A-225].

LUNLEY, Leonard. Ensign in the 34th Battalion of militia on June 6 or 11, 1776, in Capt. James Mackall's company [Ref: B-99, W-476].

LUTER, Michael Jr. Petitioned the General Assembly under the Act of May 12, 1780, stating that he had been a non-juror to the Oath of Allegiance and Fidelity in 1778 due to "ignorance" and now desired relief under the Act and to take the Oath [Ref: L-101].

LUTER, Michael Sr. Petitioned the General Assembly under the Act of May 12, 1780, stating that he had been a non-juror to the Oath of Allegiance and Fidelity in 1778 due to "ignorance" and now desired relief under the Act and to take the Oath [Ref: L-101].

LUTHER, Christopher. Drafted on June 13, 1781, and then discharged, "being unfit for duty." [Ref: D-1814].

LYERS, Patrick. Associator in December, 1775 [Ref: E-169].

LYETH, Samuel. Associator in December, 1775 [Ref: E-169]. Juror to the Oath of Allegiance in 1778 [Ref: C-27].

LYM, William. Associator in December, 1775 [Ref: E-169]. Juror to the Oath of Allegiance in 1778 [Ref: C-27].

LYMBAGH, Joseph. Associator in December, 1775 [Ref: E-169]. Juror to the Oath of Allegiance in 1778 [Ref: C-27].

LYNCH, John. Associator in December, 1775 [Ref: E-169]. Juror to the Oath of Allegiance in 1778 [Ref: C-27].

LYNCH, Patrick. Private who enlisted on May 22, 1777, and served in Capt. William Beatty's company in the 7th Maryland Regiment in 1779 [Ref: A-311].

LYNN, David. Associator in December, 1775 [Ref: E-169]. Ensign in the Upper District Militia [now Washington County] in July, 1776 [Ref: A-48]. "David Linn" was a first lieutenant in Capt. William Beatty's company, 7th Maryland Regiment on June 10, 1779 [Ref: A-310], and captain on May 22, 1779 [Ref: A-225] through 1781 [Ref: D-1814]. Juror to the Oath of Allegiance in 1778 [Ref: C-27]. "On February 28, 1836, the Treasurer of the Western Shore was directed to pay to Mary Lynn, the widow of David Lynn, a captain in the Revolutionary Army, half pay of a captain during her widowhood." [Ref: G-368]. "David Lynn applied for a pension in Allegany County, Maryland, on June 4, 1828, stating he married Mary Galloway on April 28, 1796, at West River in Anne Arundel County, Maryland. He also received bounty land warrant #1295-300-1 in February, 1790. David died on April 6, 1835, at Cumberland, Maryland, and his widow applied for a pension (W9151) in Allegany County on April 28, 1848, aged 74." [Ref: J-35, T-2153]. Francina Chestor Schley, wife of Frederick A. Schley, and daughter of Capt. David Lynn, of Allegany County, died on September 4, 1828 [Ref: F-473].

LYNN, Henry. Non-Enroller who was fined by the Committee of Observation in April, 1776 [Ref: E-248].

MACATEE, Leonard. Private who was enlisted on July 20, 1776, by Capt. Jacob Good [Ref: A-46].

MACH, John. Associator in December, 1775 [Ref: E-170]. Juror to the Oath of Allegiance in 1778 [Ref: C-27].

MACKALL, Ann. See "Lindsey Delashmutt" and "Ralph Briscoe," q.v.

MACKALL, James. Associator who was appointed "to hand about the Association paper" in Lower Monocacy Hundred in 1775 [Ref: E-305].

Captain of a militia company in the 34th Battalion on June 6 or 11, 1776 [Ref: E-239, E-243, B-99, W-476].

MACKALL, Thomas. "Thomas Mackell" was a private who enlisted on May 13, 1778 [Ref: A-322, which source spelled his name "Macrell," and Ref: R-167, which spelled his name "Mackrell."]. "Thomas Mackall" was a private in the German Regiment at the Battle of White Plains on September 5, 1778, under Lt. Col. Ludwick Weltner [Ref: A-267].

MACKELFRESH, Jane. See "William Cumming," q.v.

MACKELFRESH, John. Provided wheat for the military in June, 1782 [Ref: R-520].

MACKELFRESH [MACILFISH], John Jr. Petitioned the General Assembly under the Act of May 12, 1780, stating he had been a non-juror to the Oath of Allegiance and Fidelity in 1778 due to "ignorance" and now desired relief under the Act and to take the Oath [Ref: L-101].

MACKELFRESH [MACILFISH], John Sr. Petitioned the General Assembly under the Act of May 12, 1780, stating he had been a non-juror to the Oath of Allegiance and Fidelity in 1778 due to "ignorance" and now desired relief under the Act and to take the Oath [Ref: L-101].

MACKELFRESH [MACILFISH], Philip. Petitioned the General Assembly under the Act of May 12, 1780, stating he had been a non-juror to the Oath of Allegiance and Fidelity in 1778 due to "ignorance" and now desired relief under the Act and to take the Oath [Ref: L-101].

MACKIE, Henry. Private who enlisted on August 5, 1776 [Ref: A-44]. "Henry Mackey" was a private who enlisted February 16, 1778 [Ref: A-314].

MACKIE, William. 1st lieutenant in the militia on November 9, 1776, under Capt. Mackall [Ref: B-99, X-432].

MACKRELL, Thomas. See "Thomas Mackall," q.v.

MACLAMARY, Timothy. Private who enlisted July 29, 1776 [Ref: A-43].

MACNABB, Archibald. Associator in December, 1775 [Ref: E-170]. Juror to the Oath of Allegiance in 1778 [Ref: C-27].

MADCALF, Bennett. Private who enlisted July 25, 1776 [Ref: A-51].

MADDING, John. Private who enlisted on August 5, 1776 [Ref: A-44].

MADDOCKE, James. Associator in December, 1775 [Ref: E-170]. Juror to the Oath of Allegiance in 1778 [Ref: C-27].

MADDIN, Nathaniel. Sergeant in the 7th Maryland Regiment on October 28, 1778, and a private on February 20, 1779, he was reported as "deserted" on April 30, 1779 [Ref: A-233].

MADDON, Frederick. Juror to the Oath of Allegiance in March, 1778 [Ref: S-265, but not listed in Ref: C-27].

MADDOX, Ignatius. Private who enlisted August 8, 1776 [Ref: A-49].
MADERN, Adam. Private who enlisted on May 17, 1778 [Ref: A-322].
MADIERA, Jacob. Corporal in Capt. John Haass' company of militia in 1775 [Ref: E-53].
MAGEE, John. Private who enlisted on February 3, 1778 [Ref: A-314].
MAGERS, Elias. Associator in December, 1775 [Ref: E-170]. Juror to the Oath of Allegiance in 1778 [Ref: C-27].
MAGERS, Peter Jr. Associator in December, 1775 [Ref: E-170]. Juror to the Oath of Allegiance in 1778 [Ref: C-27].
MAGERS, Peter Sr. Associator in December, 1775 [Ref: E-170]. Juror to the Oath of Allegiance in 1778 [Ref: C-27].
MAGLOHEN, Charles. Private in militia, March 9, 1776 [Ref: B-166].
MAGRUDER, Alexander. Associator, and was appointed "to hand about the Association paper" in the Lower Monocacy Hundred in 1775 [Ref: E-305].
MAGRUDER, Hezekiah. Appointed an Inspector of the George Town Warehouses on September 21, 1776 [Ref: X-293]. 1st lieutenant in the 29th Battalion of militia from August 29, 1777, to at least May, 1782 [Ref: B-100].
MAGRUDER, Josiah. Ensign in the 29th Battalion of militia on August 29, 1777 [Ref: B-100].
MAGRUDER, Nathan. Served on the Committee of Observation in 1775 [Ref: I-85].
MAGRUDER, Samuel. Served on the Committee of Observation in 1775 [Ref: I-85]. Associator in December, 1775 [Ref: E-170]. Juror to the Oath of Allegiance in 1778 [Ref: C-27].
MAGRUDER, Samuel Jr. Juror to the Oath of Allegiance in March, 1778 [Ref: S-265, but not listed in Ref: C-27].
MAGRUDER, Samuel Wade (lower part of Potomac Hundred). Appointed by the Committee of Correspondence to solicit subscriptions in 1775 to purchase arms and ammunition [Ref: I-86]. Gave money in the amount of 17 lbs. 8 sh. 9 p. for arms and ammunition for the militia in Frederick County in 1775 [Ref: E-63]. Captain and then 2nd major in the Montgomery County militia from 1776 to 1777 [Ref: B-100].
MAGRUDER, William. Contractor for horses in Frederick County on September 1, 1780 [Ref: V-272]. Provided wheat for the military in June, 1782 [Ref: R-521].
MAGRUDER, Zadock (Rock Creek Hundred). Appointed by the Committee of Correspondence to solicit subscriptions in 1775 to purchase arms and ammunition [Ref: I-86]. Served on the Committee of Observation

in 1775 [Ref: I-85]. Associator in December, 1775 [Ref: E-170]. Gave money in the amount of 4 lbs. 5 sh. for arms and ammunition for the militia in 1775 [Ref: E-63]. Juror to the Oath of Allegiance in 1778 [Ref: C-27]. Election Judge in the Lower District of Frederick County on July 2, 1776 [Ref: F-476]. Colonel in Frederick County by March, 1776 [Ref: W-288]. Colonel in the 16th Battalion of militia in Montgomery County from 1777 through at least 1778 [Ref: B-100].

MAGUIRE, Nicholas. Militia substitute from May to December 10, 1781, and "marched to Annapolis." [Ref: A-652].

MAHONEY, Charles. Private who enlisted July 13, 1776 [Ref: A-43].

MAHONEY, Thomas. Private who enlisted April 2, 1778 [Ref: A-315]. "Thomas Mahony" was a private in German Regiment and served in the Battle of White Plains on September 5, 1778, under Lt. Col. Ludwick Weltner [Ref: A-267].

MAIN [MAHN], Catherine. See "Henry Delawter (Delauter)," q.v.

MAIN [MEHN], George (died 1822). Son of George Mehn (1722-1773) and wife Elizabeth who settled at High Knob (Gambrill Park), Frederick County [Ref: O-143]. He petitioned the General Assembly under the Act of May 12, 1780, stating he had been a non-juror to the Oath of Allegiance and Fidelity in 1778 due to "ignorance" and now desired relief under the Act and to take the Oath [Ref: L-101].

MAIN [MEHN], John (1756-1832). Son of George Mehn (1722-1773) and wife Elizabeth who settled at High Knob (Gambrill Park), Frederick County [Ref: O-143]. Associator in December, 1775 [Ref: E-170]. Juror to the Oath of Allegiance in 1778 [Ref: C-27].

MAINYARD, Henry. See "Henry Maynard," q.v.

MAIS, William. Private, 7th Maryland Regiment, 1780, who enlisted in Frederick Town between January and April, 1780 [Ref: A-334].

MAJOR, Thomas. Drafted on June 2, 1783 [Ref: B-168].

MAJORS, Elias. Petitioned the General Assembly under the Act of May 12, 1780, stating he had been a non-juror to the Oath of Allegiance and Fidelity in 1778 due to "ignorance" and now desired relief under the Act and to take the Oath [Ref: L-101]. Elias was a son of Peter Majors, Sr., who died testate in 1790 [Ref: M-7:189].

MAJORS, Peter Jr. Petitioned the General Assembly under the Act of July 3, 1780, stating that he had been a non-juror to the Oath of Allegiance and Fidelity in 1778 due to "ignorance" and now desired relief under the Act and to take the Oath [Ref: L-101]. Peter was a son of Peter Majors, Sr., who died testate, 1790 [Ref: M-7:189].

MAKELFRISH, John. Sergeant in Capt. Basil Dorsey's company of militia in 1775 [Ref: E-52]. Also, see "John Macilfish," q.v.

MALADY, John. Private who enlisted May 2, 1778 [Ref: A-321], and served with the German Regiment at the Battle of White Plains on September 5, 1778, under Lt. Col. Ludwick Weltner [Ref: A-267].

MALHONEY, Daniel. Private in militia on March 9, 1776 [Ref: B-167].

MALINIA, William. Private in the German Regiment. Served at White Plains on September 5, 1778, under Lt. Col. Weltner [Ref: A-266].

MALLEN, Andrew. Private, 1st Maryland Regiment, 1780, and served in the Southern Army of the United States under Lt. William Lamar in the late Capt. Beatty's company in 1781; served on hospital duty from March 15 to July, 1781 [Ref: A-391].

MALLONE, Daniel. Associator in December, 1775 [Ref: E-170]. Juror to the Oath of Allegiance in 1778 [Ref: C-27].

MALLOON, Thomas. Private who enlisted August 5, 1776 [Ref: A-44].

MALONEY, William (Burnt House Woods Hundred). Non-Enroller who was fined by the Committee of Observation in June, 1776 [Ref: E-248].

MALOY, Barkard. Associator in December, 1775 [Ref: E-170]. Juror to the Oath of Allegiance in 1778 [Ref: C-27].

MANAGE [MANAGA], James. Private in the 1st Maryland Regiment, and in the 7th Maryland Regiment, from May 1, 1778, and served in the Southern Army of the United States under Lt. William Lamar in the late Capt. Beatty's company. Reported "deserted" in January, 1781, but he returned to service on May 14, 1781 [Ref: A-233, A-390].

MANAHAN, Thomas. Corporal in Capt. Henry Baker's company of militia in 1775 [Ref: E-54]. Associator in December, 1775 [Ref: E-170]. Juror to the Oath of Allegiance in 1778 [Ref: C-27]. "Thomas Manohan" was an ensign in the militia, 1778-1779 [Ref: H-17]. "Thomas Monohan" was an ensign in the Linganore Battalion of militia on June 22, 1778, under Capt. Gobble [Ref: B-105, Z-145].

MANN, William. Private in the 1st Maryland Regiment in 1781, and served in the Southern Army of the United States under Lt. William Lamar in the late Capt. Beatty's company [Ref: A-390].

MANSELL, Richard. Enlisted on January 24, 1781, for the duration of the war and was subsequently reported as "deserted." [Ref: D-1814].

MANTZ, Casper. Associator in December, 1775 [Ref: E-170]. Furnished powder for use of the militia in Frederick Town in 1775 [Ref: E-60]. Juror to the Oath of Allegiance in 1778 [Ref: C-27]. "Caspar Mantz" died testate in 1791, leaving wife Christiana and children Francis, Peter, David, Isaac, John, Elizabeth, Catharine, Ester, and Mary [Ref: M-8:85].

MANTZ, David. Associator in 1775 [Ref: E-170].
MANTZ, Francis. Associator in December, 1775 [Ref: E-170]. Juror to the Oath of Allegiance in 1778 [Ref: C-27]. Provided wheat for the military in May, 1782 [Ref: R-516]. He died on May 22, 1823, aged 75 [Ref: F-472].
MANTZ, Peter (November 18, 1761 - January 16, 1833). Captain of a company of militia in the 1st Battalion on November 29, 1775 [Ref: E-50, B-100]. Associator in December, 1775 [Ref: E-170]. Quartermaster in the 33rd Battalion on March 2, 1776, and then captain on March 26, 1776 [Ref: B-100]. Captain in the Middle District Militia on July 1, 1776 [Ref: A-44, A-47, X-140]. One Peter Mantz was a captain in the 33rd Battalion in Frederick County on December 28, 1776, and one Peter Mantz was a major in the 16th Battalion in Montgomery County on December 10, 1776 (same person?). [Ref: B-100]. Juror to the Oath of Allegiance in 1778 [Ref: C-27, S-265]. "On February 20, 1846, Treasurer of the Western Shore was directed to pay Catharine Mantz, widow of Peter Mantz, a major of the revolution, during her life, quarterly, the half pay of a major, in consideration of the service of her husband." [Ref: G-372]. Peter Mantz also served in the House of Delegates in 1782 [Ref: F-479]. Major Peter Mantz died January 16, 1833, aged 81, in Frederick County [Ref: F-473]. Peter Mantz married Catherine Hauer on April 23, 1778, and a son Gideon Mantz was born on March 7, 1788, married Eliza Lides (1797-1867) in 1815, and died on November 30, 1846 [Ref: U-935].
MANYARD, Nathan. See "Nathan Maynard," q.v.
MARCKQUART, Nicholas. Associator in December, 1775 [Ref: E-170]. Juror to the Oath of Allegiance in 1778 [Ref: C-27].
MARHAY, Dennis. Private in the militia in July, 1776 [Ref: A-42].
MARHUR, Adam. Associator in December, 1775 [Ref: E-170]. Juror to the Oath of Allegiance in 1778 [Ref: C-27].
MARKELL, George. Juror to the Oath of Allegiance in March, 1778 [Ref: S-265, but not listed in Ref: C-27].
MARKELL, John. Lieutenant in the 6th Maryland Regiment from April 17, 1777, until August 15, 1777, when he resigned [Ref: A-229].
MARQUERT, John. Associator in December, 1775 [Ref: E-170]. Juror to the Oath of Allegiance in 1778 [Ref: C-27].
MARR, Paul. Militia substitute on June 8, 1778 [Ref: A-325].
MARSHALL, Benjamin. Private in the Pennsylvania Line, aged 74, from Frederick County, Maryland, pensioned on March 6, 1819, at $96 per annum from November 13, 1818. Issued a warrant for 50 acres of land

in Allegany County on March 9, 1826, "as a donation from the state to revolutionary soldiers who served in the Maryland Line, and to which they consider him entitled." [Ref: G-372]. Also, see Benjamin Marshall's pension W4279, which data may apply here. [Ref: T-2196].

MARSHALL, Catharine and Brooke. See "Elisha Williams," q.v.

MARSHALL, James. Associator in December, 1775 [Ref: E-170]. Juror to the Oath of Allegiance in 1778 [Ref: C-27].

MARSHALL, John. Private who enlisted on August 5, 1776 in the Flying Camp under Capt. Philip Meroney [Ref: A-45, N-30:112]. One John Marshall died on April 15, 1803, aged 74 [Ref: F-470].

MART, John. Associator in December, 1775 [Ref: E-170]. Juror to the Oath of Allegiance in 1778 [Ref: C-27].

MART, Peter. Associator in December, 1775 [Ref: E-170]. Juror to the Oath of Allegiance in 1778 [Ref: C-27].

MARTEL, John. Sergeant in Capt. Robert Beatty's company of militia in 1775 [Ref: E-55].

MARTIN, David. Non-Enroller who was fined by the Committee of Observation in April, 1776 [Ref: E-248].

MARTIN, George. Sergeant in Capt. Michael McGuire's company of militia in 1775 [Ref: E-57]. Associator in December, 1775 [Ref: E-170]. Juror to the Oath of Allegiance in 1778 [Ref: C-27].

MARTIN, Henry. "On February 5, 1818, the Treasurer of the Western Shore was directed to pay to Henry Martin, of Frederick County, during life, half yearly, half pay of a private, as further compensation for his services during the war." [Ref: G-373].

MARTIN, Jacob. Non-Enroller who was fined by the Committee of Observation in April, 1776 [Ref: E-248]. Private who was enlisted on July 20, 1776, by Capt. Jacob Good [Ref: A-46]. "On March 9, 1846, the Treasurer of Maryland was directed to pay to Margaret Martin, of Westmoreland County, Pennsylvania, the widow of Jacob Martin, a revolutionary soldier with the Maryland Troops, during life, quarterly, the half pay of a private, in consideration of services rendered by her husband during the war." [Ref: G-373].

MARTIN, James. Private who enlisted on July 19, 1776 [Ref: A-51].

MARTIN, John. Associator in December, 1775 [Ref: E-170]. Juror to the Oath of Allegiance in 1778 [Ref: C-27]. Private who enlisted on July 1 or July 18, 1776, and was referred to as an "old soldier" in the 2nd Maryland Regiment in 1778 [Ref: A-47, A-49, A-294].

MARTIN, Joseph. Enlisted in the German Regiment, 1780 [Ref: V-126].

MARTINDEAR [MARTINDER], John. See "John Martin Derr," q.v.

MARTZ, Balser [Baltzer]. Sergeant in Capt. Peter Mantz's company of militia in 1775 [Ref: E-50]. Associator in December, 1775 [Ref: E-170]. Juror to the Oath of Allegiance in 1778 [Ref: C-27]. "Balzer Martz" was ensign in the Frederick Town Battalion of militia on May 26, 1778, under Capt. White [Ref: H-15, B-101].

MARTZ, Deobalt. Associator in December, 1775 [Ref: E-170]. Juror to the Oath of Allegiance in 1778 [Ref: C-27]. "Theobald Martz, of Frederick Town," died testate in 1786, leaving children George, Balser, Peter, Henry, Elizabeth, and Catherine [Ref: M-6:186].

MARTZ, George. Associator in December, 1775 [Ref: E-170]. Juror to the Oath of Allegiance in 1778 [Ref: C-27].

MARZAR, Philip. Associator in December, 1775 [Ref: E-170]. Juror to the Oath of Allegiance in 1778 [Ref: C-27].

MASON, Captain. See "William Crail," q.v.

MASSBAUGH [MASEBOUGH], Jacob. "Jacob Massbaugh" was a non-enroller who was fined by the Committee of Observation in April, 1776 [Ref: E-248]. "Jacob Masebough" provided wheat for the military in June, 1782 [Ref: R-525].

MASSELHAMER, Peter. Associator in December, 1775 [Ref: E-170]. Juror to the Oath of Allegiance in 1778 [Ref: C-27].

MASTIN, Francis. Associator in December, 1775 [Ref: E-170]. Juror to the Oath of Allegiance in 1778 [Ref: C-27].

MATHERY, Jacob. Associator in December, 1775 [Ref: E-170]. Juror to the Oath of Allegiance in 1778 [Ref: C-27].

MATHIAS, Charles McCurdy, Jr. See "Michael Grosh," q.v.

MATHIAS, Jacob. Served on the Committee of Observation in 1775 [Ref: I-85].

MATTART, Jacob. "Jacob Mattard" was 2nd Sergeant in Capt. Philip Thomas' company of militia on November 29, 1775 [Ref: E-50]. "Jacob Mattart" was an Associator in December, 1775 [Ref: E-170]. Juror to the Oath of Allegiance in 1778 [Ref: C-27]. "Jacob Medtart" died on April 19, 1821, aged 67 [Ref: F-471].

MATTHEWS, Conrad. Sergeant in Capt. Benjamin Ogle, Jr.'s company of militia in 1775 [Ref: E-53]. Associator in December, 1775 [Ref: E-170]. Juror to the Oath of Allegiance in 1778 [Ref: C-27, S-265].

MATTHEWS, Daniel. Private who enlisted July 19, 1776 [Ref: A-51]. Provided wheat for the military in July, 1782 [Ref: R-536].

MATTHEWS, Francis. Non-Enroller who was fined by the Committee of Observation in April, 1776 [Ref: E-248].

MATTHEWS, George. Corporal in Capt. William Blair's company of militia in 1775 [Ref: E-55].

MATTHEWS, Henry. "Henry Matthews" was a 1st lieutenant in Capt. Benjamin Ogle, Jr.'s company of militia in the 2nd Battalion on November 29, 1775. "Henry Mathews" was a 1st lieutenant in the 37th Battalion of militia in Capt. James Ogle's company on May 15, 1776 [Ref: E-53, B-101, W-427].

MATTHEWS [MATHEWS], Jacob. Juror to the Oath of Allegiance in March, 1778 [Ref: S-265, but not listed in Ref: C-27].

MATTHEWS, John. Juror to the Oath of Allegiance in 1778 [Ref: C-27, S-265].

MATTHEWS [MATHEWS], Philip. Juror to the Oath of Allegiance in March, 1778 [Ref: S-265, but not listed in Ref: C-27].

MATTHEWS, Robert. Private who enlisted May 15, 1778 [Ref: A-322].

MATTHEWS, Thomas. Private who enlisted on February 25, 1778 [Ref: A-314].

MATTINGLY, Joseph. Private, 1st Maryland Regiment, 1781, and served in the Southern Army of the United States under Lt. William Lamar in the late Capt. Beatty's company [Ref: A-389].

MATTRIT, Adam. Fifer in the German Regiment. Served at White Plains on September 5, 1778, under Lt. Col. Ludwick Weltner [Ref: A-266].

MATTUNSS [sic], Henry. Associator in December, 1775 [Ref: E-170], and signed as a Juror to the Oath of Allegiance in 1778 [Ref: C-27].

MAUGENS, Conrad. Non-Enroller who was fined by the Committee of Observation in April, 1776 [Ref: E-248].

MAUGENS, Peter. Non-Enroller who was fined by the Committee of Observation in April, 1776 [Ref: E-248].

MAWK, Thomas. Associator in December, 1775 [Ref: E-170]. Juror to the Oath of Allegiance in 1778 [Ref: C-27].

MAXFIELD, Jon. Private in the 1st Maryland Regiment, and served in the Southern Army of the United States under Lt. William Lamar in the late Capt. Beatty's company in 1781 [Ref: A-389].

MAY, George. Private in Capt. John Kershner's company; guarded prisoners at Fort Frederick, 1777-1778; and, subsequently reported as "deserted" on June 2, 1778 [Ref: A-328].

MAY, Jacob. Associator in December, 1775 [Ref: E-170]. Juror to the Oath of Allegiance in 1778 [Ref: C-27].

MAY, Roland. Associator in December, 1775 [Ref: E-170]. Juror to the Oath of Allegiance in 1778 [Ref: C-27].

MAYBURY, Benjamin. Sergeant in the 7th Maryland Regiment on December 10, 1776, and private on July 1, 1777, who served until July, 1778, when he was reported "off rolls." [Ref: A-231].

MAYERS, Christian, or Christopher [sic]. Captain from March 12, 1778, until declared a supernumerary on January 1, 1781 [Ref: A-365]. Also, see "Christian or Christopher Myers," q.v.

MAYNARD, Henry Jr. Associator in December, 1775 [Ref: E-170]. Juror to the Oath of Allegiance in 1778 [Ref: C-27]. "Henry Mainyard" was a private in the horse troops in 1781 [Ref: B-167]. "Henry Mayner" enlisted on April 28, 1781 for 3 years, and was later reported as "deserted" (no date was given). [Ref: D-1814].

MAYNARD, John. Associator in December, 1775 [Ref: E-171]. Private who enlisted on August 5, 1776 in the Flying Camp under Capt. Philip Meroney [Ref: A-45, N-30:112]. Juror to the Oath of Allegiance in 1778 [Ref: C-27].

MAYNARD, Nathan. Ensign in Capt. Basil Dorsey's company of militia from 1775 to at least December 28, 1776 [Ref: E-52, X-555, B-100, B-101, which latter source spelled his name both as "Manard" and "Maynard"]. "Nathan Maniard" was a 1st lieutenant in the Linganore Battalion of militia on January 17, 1777 [Ref: B-100, Y-55]. "Nathan Maynard" (Esq.) was commissioned a captain on October 13, 1777 [Ref: H-26, G-373].

MAYNARD, Thomas. Corporal in Capt. Basil Dorsey's company of militia in 1775 [Ref: E-52].

MAYNER, Henry. See "Henry Maynard," q.v.

MAYNES [MAYNER?], John. Juror to the Oath of Allegiance in March, 1778 [Ref: S-265, but not listed in Ref: C-27].

McALISTER, Alexander. Provided wheat for the military in May, 1782 [Ref: R-517].

McALISTER [McCALLESTER], Archibald. Private in the militia on March 9, 1776 [Ref: B-166].

McALISTER [McCALLESTER], John (Piney Creek Hundred). Appointed by the Committee of Correspondence to solicit subscriptions in 1775 to purchase arms and ammunition [Ref: I-86]. Served on the Committee of Observation in 1775 [Ref: I-85]. Gave money in the amount of 6 lbs. 15 sh. for arms and ammunition for the militia in 1775 [Ref: E-62]. "John McCallester" was a private in the militia on March 9, 1776 [Ref: B-166].

McALLEN, Joseph. Associator in December, 1775 [Ref: E-170]. Private who enlisted on August 5, 1776, in the Flying Camp under Capt. Philip

Meroney [Ref: A-45, N-30:112]. Juror to Oath of Allegiance in 1778 [Ref: C-27].

McCABE, James. Private who enlisted on April 9, 1778 [Ref: A-315].

McCAIN, John. See "Matthias Young," q.v.

McCAIN, Marmaduke. Substitute on June 13, 1781; marched with Capt. Dyer [Ref: D-1814].

McCANN, Michael. "In December, 1817, the Treasurer of the Western Shore was directed to pay to Michael McCann, of Frederick County, an old revolutionary soldier, the half pay of a private during the remainder of his life, as remuneration for his meritorious service. "Michael McCam," private, Maryland Line, aged 88, from Frederick County, pensioned September 25, 1818, at $96 per annum from April 11, 1818. He died on May 4, 1827." [Ref: G-369, J-25]. "Michael McCann" applied for a pension (S34993) in Frederick County on April 11, 1818. He was aged 82 in 1821 and died in 1827. [Ref: T-2242].

McCARG, Walter. Associator in December, 1775 [Ref: E-170]. Juror to the Oath of Allegiance in 1778 [Ref: C-27].

McCARTY [McKARTY], Timothy. Private who enlisted on May 9, 1778, and served in the 2nd Maryland Regiment [Ref: A-294, A-322].

McCARTY [McCARTEY], William. Juror to the Oath of Allegiance in March, 1778 [Ref: S-265, but not listed in Ref: C-27].

McCHAN, John. Soldier in the Maryland Line, he applied for pension (S34995) in Frederick County on April 3, 1818, aged about 70. In 1820 he gave his age as 70 and stated he had an 11 year old son (no name given). [Ref: T-2245]. However, Ref: J-25 states he was aged 73 in 1818 and died in 1821.

McCLAIN, Dennis. Associator in December, 1775 [Ref: E-170]. Juror to the Oath of Allegiance in 1778 [Ref: C-27].

McCLAIN [McLANE], John. Juror to the Oath of Allegiance in March, 1778 [Ref: S-265, but not listed in Ref: C-27].

McCLAIN [McCLAINE] Joseph. Private who was enlisted on July 20, 1776 by Capt. Jacob Good [Ref: A-46]. Juror to the Oath of Allegiance in March, 1778 [Ref: S-265, but not listed in Ref: C-27]. "Joseph McClane" was in Col. Griffith's Regiment and was taken prisoner at Fort Washington on November 16, 1776, and returned on March 20, 1777 [Ref: Y-515].

McCLAIN, Josua [sic]. Juror to the Oath of Allegiance in March, 1778 [Ref: S-265, but not listed in Ref: C-27].

McCLAIN [McCLAND], Robert. Private who enlisted on May 2, 1778 [Ref: A-321].

McCLAIN [McCLANE], Simon. Private who enlisted on July 25, 1776 [Ref: A-51].

McCLAIN [McCLANE], William. "William McClane" was a private who was enlisted July 20, 1776, by Capt. Jacob Good [Ref: A-46]. "William McClain" died testate in 1794, leaving children Joshua, Maria, Susanna, and Mary [Ref: M-9:38]. Also, see "William McLane," q.v.

McCLANY, Alexander. Private in the Skipton District Militia under Capt. Thomas Waring on April 16, 1776 [Ref: B-167, D-1814].

McCLARY, John. Private who enlisted on August 5, 1776 in the Flying Camp under Capt. Philip Meroney [Ref: A-45, N-30:112].

McCLARY, William. Served on the Committee of Observation in 1775 [Ref: I-85].

McCLEAN [McKEAN?], Joseph. Juror to the Oath of Allegiance in March, 1778 [Ref: S-265, but not listed in Ref: C-27].

McCLEAN, William (Lower Monocacy Hundred). Non-Enroller who was fined by the Committee of Observation in June, 1776 [Ref: E-248]. Also, see "William McClane," q.v.

McCOLL, Thomas. Private in the militia, March 9, 1776 [Ref: B-166].

McCONEY, Philip. Petitioned to form the horse troops in 1781 [Ref: B-167].

McCONNELL, Robert. Associator in December, 1775 [Ref: E-170]. Juror to the Oath of Allegiance in 1778 [Ref: C-27].

McCORGAN, David. Sergeant in the German Regiment, muster roll dated October 23, 1776 [Ref: A-263].

McCORMACK, James. See "James McCormack Beall," q.v.

McCORMICK, Daniel. Associator in December, 1775 [Ref: E-170]. Non-Enroller who was fined by the Committee of Observation in April, 1776, but he was subsequently "discharged because ineffective" and the fine was remitted in June, 1776; yet, he "voluntarily agreed to give." [Ref: E-248]. Juror to the Oath of Allegiance in 1778 [Ref: C-27]. One Daniel McCormick also petitioned the General Assembly under the Act of May 12, 1780, stating that he had been a non-juror to the Oath of Allegiance and Fidelity in 1778 due to "ignorance" and now desired relief under the Act and to take the Oath [Ref: L-101].

McCOY, Hugh. Private in the militia on March 9, 1776 [Ref: B-166]. This or another Hugh McCoy was a private who enlisted on May 19, 1778 [Ref: A-323].

McCOY, James. Private who enlisted on August 5, 1776, in the Flying Camp under Capt. Philip Meroney [Ref: A-45, N-30:112].

McCOY [McKOY], William. Private who enlisted on April 30, 1778, and served in the 2nd Maryland Regiment [Ref: A-294, A-321].

McCOY, Zerelda. See "John Godlieb Boyer," q.v.

McCRACKEN, Joseph. Private who was enlisted on July 20, 1776, by Capt. Jacob Good [Ref: A-46].

McCRACKEN [McCRACKIN, MEKRAKIN, MERKREKIN], Isaac. 1st lieutenant in the Skipton District Militia in 1776 [Ref: B-103, X-127, X-337].

McCRAY, James. Private in the Maryland Line from August 7, 1781, to December 10, 1781 [Ref: A-410].

McCREA, James. Substitute on June 13, 1781, and marched with Capt. Boyer [Ref: D-1814].

McCRERY, John. Private who enlisted on August 5, 1776 in the Flying Camp under Capt. Philip Meroney [Ref: A-45, N-30:111].

McCULLIM, Thomas. Private stationed at Fort Frederick in June, 1778 [Ref: A-328].

McCULLOCH, David. Private in the 7th Maryland Regiment who enlisted in Frederick Town between January and April, 1780, and reported as "gone to Camp" [Ref: A-334].

McCULLOCH, James. Private who enlisted July 13, 1776 [Ref: A-43].

McCUNE, Samuel. Corporal in Capt. Abraham Hayter's company of militia in 1775 [Ref: E-52].

McCUNE, Thomas. 2nd lieutenant in Capt. A. Hayter's militia company in the 3rd Battalion on November 29, 1775 [Ref: E-52, B-102].

McDANIEL, John. Defective from the Maryland Line on August 18, 1780 [Ref: A-414].

McDANIEL, Joseph. Associator in December, 1775 [Ref: E-170]. Juror to the Oath of Allegiance in 1778 [Ref: C-27].

McDAVID, John. Private who enlisted on July 29, 1776 [Ref: A-43].

McDEED, James. Private who enlisted on July 13, 1776 [Ref: A-43].

McDONALD, Alexander. Drummer in Capt. Michael McGuire's company of militia in 1775 [Ref: E-57]. Associator in December, 1775 [Ref: E-170]. (This name appeared on the list of Associators twice). One subscribed to the Oath of Allegiance in 1778 [Ref: C-27]. One was a private who enlisted in March 12, 1778, and served in the 2nd Maryland Regiment [Ref: A-294].

McDONALD, George. Private in the Middle District Militia who enlisted on August 5, 1776 [Ref: A-45, A-72, N-30:112].

McDONALD, John. Associator in December, 1775 [Ref: E-171]. Associator in December, 1775 [Ref: E-170]. Juror to the Oath of Allegiance in 1778 [Ref: C-27]. Private who enlisted on February 18, 1778 [Ref: A-314].

McDONALD, Michael. Private who enlisted on March 6, 1778 [Ref: A-315]. "Michael McDonnold" was a private in Capt. Beatty's company, 7th Maryland Regiment. Reported "deserted" on August 12, 1779, but he was present and on duty in December, 1779 [Ref: A-311].

McDONALD, Robert. Private who enlisted on August 5, 1776 in the Flying Camp under Capt. Philip Meroney [Ref: A-45, N-30:112].

McDONALD, Thomas. Defective from the Maryland Line in October, 1780 [Ref: A-414].

McDONALL, Jonathan. Private who was enlisted on July 20, 1776 by Capt. Jacob Good [Ref: A-46].

McDONNAGH, John. "John McDonnagh" was a militia substitute on June 9, 1778 [Ref: A-325]. "John McDonnehough" was a private in the 7th Maryland Regiment from July 1, 1778, until November 24, 1778, when he was reported "deserted." [Ref: A-230].

McDONNEL, James. Private, 1st Maryland Regiment, 1780, and served in the Southern Army of the United States under Lt. William Lamar in the late Capt. Beatty's company in 1781, He also served as a waggoner from January to July, 1781 [Ref: A-390].

McDONNELL, James. Corporal in Capt. William Beatty's company of militia in 1775 [Ref: E-55].

McDONNOLD, James. Private, 7th Maryland Regiment, 1780, enlisted in Frederick Town between January and April, 1780 [Ref: A-334].

McELROY, James. Soldier in the Pennsylvania Line who applied for a pension (S34976) in Frederick County, Maryland, on May 21, 1818, aged 56, stating he enlisted in York County, Pennsylvania. In 1820 he gave his age as 60 and stated he had no family [Ref: T-2270].

McFADING, Edward. Sergeant in Capt. Robert Wood's company of militia in 1775 [Ref: E-53]. Associator in December, 1775 [Ref: E-170]. Juror to the Oath of Allegiance in 1778 [Ref: C-27].

McFADON, Alexander. 1st lieutenant in the Lower District Militia of Frederick County on April 20, 1776, and then a captain in the 29th Battalion in Montgomery County [Upper District] from September 12, 1777, to at least August 11, 1779 [Ref: W-356, B-102]. "Alexander McFadon, of Georgetown in Frederick County, was paid 300 pounds common money [by the Treasurer of Maryland] to enable him to carry on a linen manufactory" on June 10, 1776 [Ref: W-473].

McFARLING, Samuel. Gave money in the amount of 2 lbs. 16 sh. for arms and ammunition for the militia in 1775 [Ref: E-62].

McFERRAN, Samuel (Piney Creek Hundred). Appointed by the Committee of Correspondence to solicit subscriptions in 1775 to purchase arms and ammunition [Ref: I-86].

McGAREY, Alexander. Private who enlisted on March 24, 1778 [Ref: A-315].

McGAREY, Henry. Associator in December, 1775 [Ref: E-170]. Juror to the Oath of Allegiance in 1778 [Ref: C-27]. Militia substitute from May to December 10, 1781, and "marched to Annapolis." [Ref: A-653].

McGLOVAR, Charles. Associator in December, 1775 [Ref: E-170]. Juror to the Oath of Allegiance in 1778 [Ref: C-27].

McGRAW, James. Private who enlisted on February 18, 1778 [Ref: A-314].

McGRAW, John. Private who enlisted on May 5, 1778, and served in the 2nd Maryland Regiment [Ref: A-294. A-321].

McGRAW, Stephen. Private who enlisted April 24, 1778 [Ref: A-321]. "Stephen McGrough" was with the German Regiment at the Battle of White Plains on September 5, 1778, under Col. Weltner [Ref: A-266].

McGUIRE, Andrew. Associator in December, 1775 [Ref: E-171]. Juror to the Oath of Allegiance in 1778 [Ref: C-27]. One Andrew McGuire died testate in 1784, leaving children Jane, Cornelius, James, Lydia, and Sarah [Ref: M-6:121].

McGUIRE, James. Associator in December, 1775 [Ref: E-170]. Juror to the Oath of Allegiance in 1778 [Ref: C-27].

McGUIRE, Michael. Captain of a militia company in the 3rd Battalion on November 29, 1775 [Ref: E-56, B-103]. Associator who assisted in "handing about the Association paper" in 1776 [Ref: E-245].

McGUIRE, Nicholas. Associator in December, 1775 [Ref: E-170]. Juror to the Oath of Allegiance in 1778 [Ref: C-27].

McGUIRE, Thomas. Associator in December, 1775 [Ref: E-170]. Juror to the Oath of Allegiance in 1778 [Ref: C-27]. "Thomas McGuyer" was a private who enlisted on July 19, 1776 [Ref: A-51]. Thomas McGuire petitioned the General Assembly under the Act of July 3, 1780, stating that he had been a non-juror to the Oath of Allegiance and Fidelity in 1778 due to "ignorance" and now desired relief under the Act and to take the Oath [Ref: L-101].

McILVAIN, John. Corporal in Capt. Normand Bruce's company of militia in 1775 [Ref: E-55].

McINTIRE, Daniel. Associator in December, 1775 [Ref: E-170]. Private who was enlisted on July 20, 1776, by Capt. Jacob Good [Ref: A-46]. Juror to the Oath of Allegiance in 1778 [Ref: C-27].

McINTIRE, Patrick. Private who was enlisted on July 20, 1776, by Capt. Jacob Good [Ref: A-46].

McKACHON, Charles. Associator in December, 1775 [Ref: E-170]. Juror to the Oath of Allegiance in 1778 [Ref: C-27].

McKAY, William. Private who enlisted on August 5, 1776 in the Flying Camp under Capt. Philip Meroney [Ref: A-45, N-30:112].

McKEEN, James. Associator in December, 1775 [Ref: E-170]. Juror to the Oath of Allegiance in 1778 [Ref: C-27].

McKELLUP, Joseph. Quartermaster in the 35th Battalion on January 3, 1776, under Col. Jacob Good [Ref: H-25]. "Joseph McKillip" was a quartermaster in the 35th Battalion of militia in 1776 [Ref: B-103]. "Joseph McKilliss" was a quartermaster in the 3rd Battalion in 1775-1776 [Ref: E-58, which apparently misspelled his name, as Ref: I-95 and B-103 both indicate it was "Joseph McKillip."].

McKELSOM, William. Juror to the Oath of Allegiance in March, 1778 [Ref: S-265, but not listed in Ref: C-27].

McKENNY, John. Associator in December, 1775 [Ref: E-170]. Juror to the Oath of Allegiance in 1778 [Ref: C-27]. Private who enlisted on July 25, 1776 [Ref: A-51].

McKINNEY, John. Private who enlisted on April 18, 1778, and served in the 2nd Maryland Regiment [Ref: A-320].

McKINSEY, Daniel. Associator in December, 1775 [Ref: E-171]. Juror to the Oath of Allegiance in 1778 [Ref: C-27].

McKINSEY, Henry. "Henry McKinsey" was drafted on June 2, 1783 [Ref: B-169]. "Henry McKinsy" took the Oath of Allegiance in 1778 [Ref: C-27]. "Henry McKinsy" was an Associator in December, 1775 [Ref: E-171].

McKINSEY [McKENSEY], Jesse. Enlisted in the German Regiment in 1780 [Ref: V-126].

McKINSEY, Joshua. Private who enlisted April 28, 1778 [Ref: A-321]. Private in the German Regiment at the Battle of White Plains on September 5, 1778, under Lt. Col. Weltner [Ref: A-267]. Drummer in the German Regiment in 1779 [Ref: A-264].

McKINSEY, Moses. Private who enlisted April 28, 1778 [Ref: A-321]. Private in the German Regiment at the Battle of White Plains on September 5, 1778, under Lt. Col. Weltner [Ref: A-267]. Drummer in the German Regiment in 1779 [Ref: A-264]. "In December, 1815, the Treasurer of the Western Shore was directed to pay Moses McKinsey, of Allegany County, a sum of money annually during life, quarterly, equal to half pay of a drummer in the Revolutionary War. On March 9, 1827, the Treasurer was directed pay to Sarah McKinsey, of Allegany County, during life, half yearly, half pay of a private, for her husband Moses McKinsey's service during the Revolutionary War." [Ref: G-370].

McKINZIE, James. Private who enlisted on August 5, 1776, in the Flying Camp under Capt. Philip Meroney [Ref: A-45, N-30:112].

McKOY, Hugh. Private in the German Regiment. Served at White Plains on September 5, 1778, under Lt. Col. Ludwick Weltner [Ref: A-266]. Also, see "Hugh McCoy," q.v.

McKOY, Thomas (D. S. T.). Private who enlisted on July 18, 1776 [Ref: A-50].

McLANE, Enoch. Sergeant in the 7th Maryland Regiment from May 6, 1778, through at least November 1, 1780 [Ref: A-233].

McLANE, John. Juror to the Oath of Allegiance in March, 1778 [Ref: S-265, but not listed in Ref: C-27].

McLANE, William. Associator in December, 1775 [Ref: E-170]. Juror to the Oath of Allegiance in 1778 [Ref: C-27]. Also, see "William McClain (McClane)," q.v.

McLAUGHLIN, John. Lieutenant at Fort Frederick in 1778 with Capt. John Kershner's company, guarding prisoners of war [Ref: A-328].

McLEAN, Arthur. Sergeant in the 1st Maryland Regiment who enlisted on February 1, 1780, and served in the Southern Army of the United States under Lt. William Lamar in the late Capt. Beatty's company in 1781 [Ref: A-388].

McLEAN, Daniel. See "Daniel McLoan," q.v.

McLEAN, Enoch. Sergeant, 1st Maryland Regiment, and served in the Southern Army of the United States under Lt. William Lamar in the late Capt. Beatty's company in 1781 [Ref: A-388].

McLEAN, James. Private who enlisted on sometime in 1780 [Ref: A-345].

McLEAN, Joseph. Sergeant in Capt. Ludowick Kemp's company of militia in 1775 [Ref: E-52].

McLEOD, Robert. Private who was enlisted on July 20, 1776 by Capt. Jacob Good [Ref: A-46].

McLOAN, Daniel. Drummer in Capt. William Blair's company of militia in 1775 [Ref: E-55].

McLOCHEN, John. See "John W. Loclen," q.v.

McMAHON, John V. L. See "George Stricker," q.v.

McMAHON, Morris. Private who enlisted in Frederick on July 25, 1780 and was subsequently reported "deserted" (no date). [Ref: A-344].

McMANIS, Henry. Private who enlisted on May 12, 1778 [Ref: A-324].
McMIN, Joseph. Associator in December, 1775 [Ref: E-170]. Juror to the Oath of Allegiance in 1778 [Ref: C-27].
McMIN, Robert. Associator in December, 1775 [Ref: E-170]. Juror to the Oath of Allegiance, 1778 [Ref: C-27]. Drafted June 2, 1783; "called; says he was engaged as a cooper for the public but it was on wages; ordered to pay 7.10 pounds, of which he has paid 2 pounds." [Ref: B-169].
McMULLAN, John. Associator in December, 1775 [Ref: E-170]. Juror to the Oath of Allegiance in 1778 [Ref: C-27].
McMULLEN, Patrick. Juror to the Oath of Allegiance in March, 1778 [Ref: S-265, but not listed in Ref: C-27].
McMULLIN, James. See "John Messar," q.v.
McNABB, Charles. Associator in December, 1775 [Ref: E-170]. Militia substitute on June 3, 1778 [Ref: A-325]. Juror to the Oath of Allegiance in 1778 [Ref: C-27]. Sergeant, 1st Maryland Regiment, 1781, served in the Southern Army of the United States under Lt. William Lamar in the late Capt. Beatty's company, and "recruited in Maryland from January to July, 1781." [Ref: A-389].
McNALLEY, John. Private in the 1st Maryland Regiment who enlisted on April 27, 1778, and served in the Southern Army of the United States under Lt. Lamar in the late Capt. Beatty's company. Reported to be a prisoner of war on April 25, 1781 [Ref: A-321, A-391].
McNEAL, William. Militia substitute on June 6, 1778 [Ref: A-325].
McNEELEY, John and Nancy. See "Levi Davis," q.v.
McNEILL, John. Private who enlisted on March 17, 1781, for 3 years, and marched with Capt. Lynn [Ref: D-1814]. Juror to the Oath of Allegiance in March, 1778 [Ref: S-265, but not listed in Ref: C-27].
McNICHOLS, John. See "John Mc. Nichols," q.v.
McPAH, Patrick. Associator in December, 1775 [Ref: E-170]. Juror to the Oath of Allegiance in 1778 [Ref: C-27].
McPHERSON, John, Sr. Born in Pennsylvania in 1760, and removed to Frederick County in 1781. "Not long before the conclusion of the Revolutionary War he received a lieutenant's commission in the service of his native State, but as a cessation of hostilities soon after ensued, no demand was made upon him for active field duty. He went to Frederick as an agent for the supply of prisoners then quartered there. In 1783 he married there, which confirmed his residence in Frederick, where he lived until his death in December, 1829. He served with honor in the Legislature, and as an Associate Judge of the Court." [Ref: F-459]. Sarah McPherson, wife of a Col. John McPherson, died on July 8, 1821, aged

55 [Ref: F-471]. Harriet Brein, wife of John Brein, and daughter of Col. John McPherson, died at Catoctin Furnace on April 22, 1827, aged 43 [ref: F-472]. Col. John McPherson died on December 2, 1829 [Ref: F-473].

McPHERSON, Samuel Jr. Sergeant in Capt. Normand Bruce's company of militia in 1775 [Ref: E-54].

McTIER, Daniel. Private who was enlisted on July 20, 1776 by Capt. Jacob Good [Ref: A-46].

McVEY [McVAY], David. Private in the 1st Maryland Regiment, and in the 7th Maryland Regiment, from April 26, 1779, and served in the Southern Army of the United States under Lt. William Lamar in the late Capt. Beatty's company in 1780 [Ref: A-233, A-392].

MEANE, John. See "James Smith," q.v.

MEANS, Daniel. Private who was enlisted on July 20, 1776, by Capt. Jacob Good [Ref: A-46].

MEATHARD, Charles. Provided wheat for the military in July, 1782 [Ref: R-533].

MEDORF, Samuel. Associator in December, 1775 [Ref: E-170]. Juror to the Oath of Allegiance in 1778 [Ref: C-27].

MEDTART, Jacob. See "Jacob Mattart," q.v.

MEEK, Francis. Private in the 7th Maryland Regiment on December 10, 1776, and sergeant on May 6, 1777. Discharged on December 26, 1779 [Ref: A-231].

MEEK, John. Private, 7th Maryland Regiment. Disabled at Battle of Guilford Court House. his invalid pension commenced on November 29, 1783, and ceased on November 1, 1789 [Ref: A-630, A-631, F-475].

MEEKS, John. Private, 1st Maryland Regiment, 1781, and served in the Southern Army of the United States under Lt. William Lamar in the late Capt. Beatty's company. Record indicates he was killed on March 15, 1781 [Ref: A-391].

MEEM, Peter. Associator in December, 1775 [Ref: E-170]. Juror to the Oath of Allegiance in 1778 [Ref: C-27].

MEFFORD [MIFFORD], John. 2nd lieutenant in Capt. John Carmack's company of militia in 1775 [Ref: E-56]. Associator in December, 1775 [Ref: E-170]. Served as a militia substitute from May to December 10, 1781, and "marched to Annapolis." [Ref: A-653]. Juror to Oath of Allegiance in 1778 [Ref: C-27, S-265].

MEFFORD, William. Militia substitute on June 12, 1778 [Ref: A-325].

MEHN, George. See "George Main," q.v.

MEHONEY, Daniel. Militia substitute from May to December 10, 1781, and "marched to Annapolis." [Ref: A-653].

MEKRAKIN, Isaac. See "Isaac McCracken," q.v.

MELCHOR, Vendel. "Vendel Melchor" provided wheat for the military in July, 1782 [Ref: R-533]. "Ventch Melger" was an Associator in December, 1775 [Ref: E-170]. Also, see "Ventch Menger," q.v.

MELLOR, Thomas. Private in the Skipton District Militia under Capt. Thomas Waring on April 16, 1776 [Ref: B-167, D-1814].

MELTON, James. Juror to the Oath of Allegiance in March, 1778 [Ref: S-265, but not listed in Ref: C-27].

MENGEL, John. Associator in December, 1775 [Ref: E-171]. Juror to the Oath of Allegiance in 1778 [Ref: C-27].

MENGER [MENGES], Christian. Associator in December, 1775 [Ref: E-170]. Juror to the Oath of Allegiance in 1778 [Ref: C-27].

MENGER, Ventch. "Ventch Menger" was juror to the Oath of Allegiance in 1778 [Ref: C-27].

MENGER, William. Associator in December, 1775 [Ref: E-170]. Juror to the Oath of Allegiance in 1778 [Ref: C-27].

MENIX, Charles. Associator in December, 1775 [Ref: E-171]. 3rd Corporal in the Middle District Militia in 1776, with Capt. Valentine Creager's company [Ref: A-72]. Juror to the Oath of Allegiance in 1778 [Ref: C-27].

MENSH [MENCH], Adam. 2nd lieutenant in Capt. Herman Yost's company of militia, 1st Battalion, on November 29, 1775 [Ref: E-52, B-103]. Associator in December, 1775 [Ref: E-169]. Juror to the Oath of Allegiance in 1778 [Ref: C-27]. "Adam Mantch" was a 1st lieutenant in the 33rd Battalion of militia on March 3, 1777 [Ref: B-100]. "Adam Mench" provided wheat for the military in July, 1782 [Ref: R-526].

MENSH [MENCH], John. Provided wheat for the military in May, 1782 [Ref: R-514].

MENSON, Richard. Private stationed at Fort Frederick on June 27, 1778, in Capt. John Kershner's company, guarding prisoners of war [Ref: A-328].

MERCER, George and Mary. See "Jacob Brunner," q.v.

MERCHANT, Charles. Associator in December, 1775 [Ref: E-170]. Non-Enroller fined by the Committee of Observation in April, 1776 [Ref: E-248]. Juror who took the Oath of Allegiance in 1778 [Ref: C-27].

MERCKLE, George. Associator in December, 1775 [Ref: E-169]. Juror to the Oath of Allegiance in 1778 [Ref: C-27].

MEREDITH, Simon. Associator in December, 1775 [Ref: E-170]. Juror to the Oath of Allegiance in 1778 [Ref: C-27]. "Simon Meredith" was a captain in the Linganore Battalion from 1776-1777 [Ref: B-103, X-555, Y-54]. "Simon Meredeth" was captain of militia in 1778-1779 [Ref: H-16].

MERKREKIN, Isaac. See "Isaac McCracken (Merkrekin)," q.v.

MERONEY, Henry. Private who enlisted on August 5, 1776 in the Flying Camp under Capt. Philip Meroney [Ref: A-45, N-30:112]. "Henry Merony" was 2nd lieutenant on May 15, 1776, in 34th Battalion [Ref: B-103].

MERONEY, Philip. Captain in the Middle District Militia on May 15, 1776, and assigned to the 34th Battalion of Militia [Ref: A-44, E-245, B-103, W-427, and N-30:111, which latter source spelled his name "Maroney"]. "Philip Meroney" was an Associator who assisted the Committee of Observation in "handing about the Association paper" in March, 1776 [Ref: E-244]. "Philip Marony" was a cornet in the horse troops on February 2, 1781 [Ref: B-167, B-103, which source spelled his name "Merony"]. Capt. Philip Meroney was paid for recruiting services for the 7th Maryland Regiment in January, 1780 [Ref: R-260, V-54].

MESSAR, John. Private in the 7th Maryland Regiment on March 15, 1778, "in the place of James McMullin." [Ref: A-233].

MESSERSMITH, William. Private who enlisted on July 18, 1776 [Ref: A-50].

METTERT, Henry. Associator in December, 1775 [Ref: E-170].

METTS, Chr. Private who enlisted on July 19, 1776 [Ref: A-51].

METTZ, John. Private in the German Regiment, muster roll dated October 23, 1776 [Ref: A-264].

MICHAEL, Andrew (1720, Germany - March 3, 1800). Juror to the Oath of Allegiance in 1778. Andrew married Barbara Sinn (November 16, 1743 - 1814) before 1768. A son, Andrew Michael, Jr. (July 25, 1773 - October 25, 1851) married Jane Geisbert (1781-1840) on October 31, 1800 [Ref: U-2651].

MICHAEL, Henry. Private in the German Regiment, muster roll October 23, 1776, and discharged July 26, 1779 [Ref: A-234, A-264, A-265].

MICHAEL, Jacob. Sergeant in Capt. John Haass' company of militia in 1775 [Ref: E-53]. Associator in December, 1775 [Ref: E-170]. Juror to the Oath of Allegiance in 1778 [Ref: C-27]. "Jacob Michael, mason" died testate in 1783, leaving wife Catherine and children William, Jacob, Catherine, Mary, and Sophia [Ref: M-6:32, M-6:33].

MICHAEL, John. Associator in December, 1775 [Ref: E-170]. Private in the German Regiment by October 23, 1776, became a corporal, and was discharged on July 16, 1779 [Ref: A-234, A-264].
MICHAEL, Peter. Associator in December, 1775 [Ref: E-170]. Juror to the Oath of Allegiance in 1778 [Ref: C-27].
MICK, James. Private in the 7th Maryland Regiment who enlisted in Frederick Town between January and April, 1780 [Ref: A-334].
MICK, John. Private, 7th Maryland Regiment, from February 1, 1780, through at least November 1, 1780 [Ref: A-234].
MICKLER, Jacob. Associator in December, 1775 [Ref: E-170]. Juror to the Oath of Allegiance in 1778 [Ref: C-27].
MICKSELL, Martin. See "Martin Mikesell," q.v.
MIDDAGH [MEDDAGH, MILDAGH, MITTAG, MIDACH], Frederick. In November, 1801, the "several county courts of the Western and Eastern Shore respectively, do, and they are hereby authorized and required, upon the application of Frederick Meddagh, of Frederick County, an old and superannuated soldier of the late American Army, to grant him from year to year, during his life, a license to hawk and peddle, without his the said Frederick Meddagh paying anything there for." [Ref: G-374]. "Frederick Mildagh" was an Associator in December, 1775 [Ref: E-170]. Juror to the Oath of Allegiance in 1778 [Ref: C-27]. "Frederick Mittag" was a private in the German Regiment, 1776, in Capt. Henry Fister's company under the command of Col. Hussecker [Ref: A-261].
MIDDAGH [MIDACH, MITTAG], John. "John Middagh" was an Associator in December, 1775 [Ref: E-170]. "John Midach" was appointed "to hand about the Association paper" in Israel Creek Hundred in 1775 [Ref: E-305]. "John Middagh" subscribed to the Oath of Allegiance in 1778 [Ref: C-27]. One "John Middagh" died testate in 1778, leaving wife Mary, son John Gaites Middagh (under age), and mentioning a nephew John Rickey, son of his sister Mary Rickey [Ref: M-5:87].
MIDOUR, Andrew. Non-Enroller who was fined by the Committee of Observation in May, 1776, but he apparently enrolled because the fine was remitted in June, 1776 [Ref: E-248].
MIDOUR, Jacob. Non-Enroller who was fined by the Committee of Observation in May, 1776, but he apparently enrolled because the fine was remitted in June, 1776 [Ref: E-248].
MIDOUR, John. Non-Enroller who was fined by the Committee of Observation in May, 1776, but he apparently enrolled because the fine was remitted in June, 1776 [Ref: E-248].

MIELHOLAN, Peter. Associator in December, 1775 [Ref: E-170]. Juror to the Oath of Allegiance in 1778 [Ref: C-27].

MIER, Henry and John. See "Henry and John Myer (Myers)," q.v.

MIGEA, Spira. Soldier from Frederick County who was wounded while serving in the Maryland Line (no date given). [Ref: F-475].

MIKESELL, Andrew. Juror to the Oath of Allegiance in March, 1778 [Ref: S-265, but not listed in Ref: C-27].

MIKESELL, George. Sergeant in Capt. Jacob Snowdenberger's company of militia in 1775 [Ref: E-56].

MIKESELL, Jacob (November 2, 1756 - February 26, 1832). Sergeant in Capt. Jacob Snowdenberger's company of militia in 1775 [Ref: E-56]. He was born in Frederick County, Maryland, married Mary Valentine (1759-1846) in 1779, and later moved to Clark County, Indiana. A son Peter (1782-1860) died in Preble County, Ohio [Ref: U-1998].

MIKESELL, John. Drafted on June 2, 1783, and "was discharged; he has a wife, three small children, and is poor." [Ref: B-169].

MIKESELL, Martin. Ensign in the Linganore Battalion of militia on June 22, 1778 [Ref: B-104, Z-144]. "Martin Micksell" was an ensign in the militia, 1778-1779 [Ref: H-16].

MIKESELL [MIXSEL], Michael. Associator in December, 1775 [Ref: E-170]. Juror to the Oath of Allegiance in 1778 [Ref: C-27].

MILL, Jacob. Associator in December, 1775 [Ref: E-170]. Juror to the Oath of Allegiance in 1778 [Ref: C-27].

MILLAR, John. Associator in December, 1775 [Ref: E-170]. Juror to the Oath of Allegiance in 1778 [Ref: C-27].

MILLER, Abraham. Associator in December, 1775 [Ref: E-170]. Non-Enroller who was fined by the Committee of Observation in April, 1776 [Ref: E-248]. Private who enlisted on July 19, 1776 [Ref: A-51], and became 1st lieutenant on February 1, 1777, in the 37th Battalion of militia [Ref: B-104, O-99]. Juror to the Oath of Allegiance, 1778 [Ref: C-27].

MILLER, Abraham Jr. Substitute on June 3, 1778 [Ref: A-324]. Served as a private in the German Regiment at White Plains on September 5, 1778, under Lt. Col. Ludwick Weltner [Ref: A-267].

MILLER, Adam. Associator in December, 1775 [Ref: E-171]. Juror to the Oath of Allegiance in 1778 [Ref: C-27, S-265].

MILLER, Andrew. Associator in December, 1775 [Ref: E-170]. (This name appeared twice on the list of Associators). One subscribed to the Oath of Allegiance in 1778 [Ref: C-27]. Private in Capt. John Kershner's company; guarded prisoners at Fort Frederick in 1777-1778; and, discharged on June 8, 1778 [Ref: A-328].

MILLER, Anna Maria. See "John Keller," q.v.

MILLER, Anthony. Private in the German Regiment in 1776 with Capt. Henry Fister's company under the command of Col. Hussecker [Ref: A-261]. Juror to the Oath of Allegiance in March, 1778 [Ref: S-265, but not listed in Ref: C-27].

MILLER, Conrad. Associator in December, 1775 [Ref: E-170]. Juror to the Oath of Allegiance in 1778 [Ref: C-27, S-265]. Drafted on June 2, 1783 [Ref: B-168].

MILLER, Daniel (Pipe Creek Hundred). Non-Enroller who was fined by the Committee of Observation in May, 1776 [Ref: E-248].

MILLER, Daniel. Associator in December, 1775 [Ref: E-170]. Juror to the Oath of Allegiance in 1778 [Ref: C-27, S-265].

MILLER, David (Pipe Creek Hundred). Non-Enroller who was fined by the Committee of Observation in May, 1776 [Ref: E-248]. One David Miller died while serving in the Maryland Line (no date given). [Ref: F-475].

MILLER, Frederick. Associator in December, 1775 [Ref: E-170]. Juror to the Oath of Allegiance in 1778 [Ref: C-27].

MILLER, George. Private in the German Regiment, muster roll dated October 23, 1776 [Ref: A-264]. Militia substitute from May to December 10, 1781, and "marched to Annapolis." [Ref: A-653]. Drafted on June 2, 1783, but "never appeared." [Ref: B-168].

MILLER, Gollab. Associator in December, 1775 [Ref: E-170]. Juror to the Oath of Allegiance in 1778 [Ref: C-27].

MILLER, Henry. Non-Enroller who was fined by the Committee of Observation in April, 1776, but he apparently enrolled because the fine was remitted in June, 1776 [Ref: E-248]. One Henry Miller was enlisted July 20, 1776, by Capt. Jacob Good [Ref: A-46]. One Henry Miller was a sergeant in the 6th Maryland Regiment from July 30, 1777, to at least January, 1780 [Ref: A-228]. One Henry Miller died testate in 1793, leaving his wife Catherine and sons Joseph, David, John, and Jacob (under 18), plus daughters (names were not given in the will). [Ref: M-8:181].

MILLER, Isaac. Sergeant in Capt. Robert Wood's militia company in 1775 [Ref: E-53]. Ensign on May 15, 1776, and 2nd lieutenant on December 28, 1776, in the 37th Battalion of militia under Col. James Johnson [Ref: B-104, O-99, X-555].

MILLER, Jacob. Served on the Committee of Observation in 1775 [Ref: I-85]. 1st lieutenant in Capt. Thomas' militia company in the 4th Battalion, November 29, 1775 [Ref: E-50, B-104, O-99]. Associator in December, 1775 [Ref: E-170]. 2nd major in the 1st Battalion [Ref: E-57]. 1st major in the 34th Battalion on January 6, 1776 [Ref: B-104]. Juror to the Oath of Allegiance in 1778 [Ref: C-27]. Loaned $500 for the use of the State of Maryland in June, 1780 [Ref: V-520]. Major Jacob Miller died on November 25, 1810 [Ref: F-471].

MILLER, Jacob. Associator in December, 1775 [Ref: E-170]. Sergeant in German Regiment, muster roll on October 23, 1776 [Ref: A-263].

MILLER, Jacob. Associator in December, 1775 [Ref: E-170]. Private in the German Regiment in 1776, Capt. Henry Fister's company, under the command of Col. Nicholas Hussecker [Ref: A-261].

MILLER, Jacob. Non-Enroller who was fined by the Committee of Observation in April, 1776 [Ref: E-248].

MILLER, Jacob (of Adam). Non-Enroller who was fined by the Committee of Observation in April, 1776 [Ref: E-248].

MILLER, John. Fifer in Capt. Michael Troutman's company of militia in 1775 [Ref: E-51].

MILLER, John. Private who enlisted on August 5, 1776 in the Flying Camp under Capt. Philip Meroney [Ref: A-45, N-30:112]. Private in the German Regiment, in 1776, in Capt. Henry Fister's company under the command of Col. Nicholas Hussecker [Ref: A-261]. "Draught" from May to December 10, 1781, and "marched to Annapolis." [Ref: A-653]. There were two John Miller's who served as militia substitutes from May to December 10, 1781, and "marched to Annapolis." [Ref: A-653].

MILLER, Ludowick. Sergeant in Capt. Michael McGuire's company of militia in 1775 [Ref: E-57]. Juror to the Oath of Allegiance in March, 1778 [Ref: S-265, but not listed in Ref: C-27].

MILLER, Martin. Petitioned the General Assembly under the Act of July 3, 1780, stating that he had been a non-juror to the Oath of Allegiance and Fidelity in 1778 due to "ignorance" and now desired relief under the Act and to take the Oath [Ref: L-101]. A Martin Miller died testate in 1794, leaving wife Martha and children Peter (oldest son), Elizabeth, John, Mary, George, Jacob, and Christina [Ref: M-9:39].

MILLER, Michael. Associator in December, 1775 [Ref: E-170]. (This name appeared twice on the list of Associators). One subscribed to the Oath of Allegiance in 1778 [Ref: C-27].

MILLER, Moses. Associator in December, 1775 [Ref: E-170]. Juror to the Oath of Allegiance in 1778 [Ref: C-27].

MILLER, Peter. Non-Enroller who was fined by the Committee of Observation in April, 1776 [Ref: E-248].

MILLER, Philip. Sergeant in Capt. Michael Troutman's company of militia in 1775 [Ref: E-51]. Associator in December, 1775 [Ref: E-170]. 2nd lieutenant in the 33rd Battalion of militia on January 17, 1777 [Ref: B-104, O-99, Y-54]. Juror to the Oath of Allegiance in 1778 [Ref: C-27]. It appears that another Philip Miller was a Non-Enroller who was fined by the Committee of Observation in April, 1776 [Ref: E-248]. One Philip Miller died testate in 1793, leaving minor children Christiana, Sophia, and Catherine [Ref: M-9:34].

MILLER, Robert. Non-Enroller who was fined by the Committee of Observation in April, 1776 [Ref: E-248]. Drafted on June 2, 1783, and "appeared before Major Smallwood. Quaker suffered (?) to return him from Annapolis... paid 9.15 pounds." [Ref: B-168].

MILLER, Samuel. Associator in December, 1775 [Ref: E-170]. Juror to the Oath of Allegiance in 1778 [Ref: C-27].

MILLER, Solomon. Non-Enroller who was fined by the Committee of Observation in April, 1776 [Ref: E-248].

MILLER, Stephen. Associator in December, 1775 [Ref: E-170]. Non-Enroller who was fined by the Committee of Observation in 1776 [Ref: E-248]. Juror to the Oath of Allegiance in 1778 [Ref: C-27].

MILLER, Susan. See "Christian Orndorff," q.v.

MILLER, William. Sergeant in Capt. John Stoner's militia company in 1775 [Ref: E-56]. Juror to the Oath of Allegiance in March, 1778 [Ref: S-265, but not listed in Ref: C-27]. 2nd lieutenant in Frederick Town militia on May 12, 1779 [Ref: H-16, B-104, O-99, Z-387].

MILLS, Chs. Juror to the Oath of Allegiance, March, 1778 [Ref: S-265, but not in Ref: C-27].

MILLS, Elizabeth. See "Aloysius Elder," q.v.

MILLS, Jacob. Private who enlisted on July 22, 1776 [Ref: A-49].

MILLS, John. Associator in December, 1775 [Ref: E-170]. Juror to the Oath of Allegiance in 1778 [Ref: C-27]. Private who enlisted February 8, 1780, served in 1st and 7th Maryland Regiments, and served in the Southern Army of the United States under Lt. William Lamar in the late Capt. Beatty's company in 1781, and served as a waggoner from January to July, 1781 [Ref: A-234, A-345, A-390].

MILLS, William. Associator in December, 1775 [Ref: E-170]. Private who enlisted on July 1, 1776 in Capt. Peter Mantz's company; marched from Frederick Town to Leonardtown, and from there to Philadelphia, arriving August 23, 1776 [Ref: A-47]. Juror to Oath of Allegiance in 1778 [Ref: C-27].

MILSON, Jacob. Associator in December, 1775 [Ref: E-170]. Juror to the Oath of Allegiance in 1778 [Ref: C-27].

MING, William. "William Ming" was a private in the horse troops in June, 1781 [Ref: B-167]. "William Meng" petitioned to form the horse troops in 1781 [Ref: B-167].

MISBETT, Richard. Private who enlisted May 11, 1778 [Ref: A-324].

MISSELL, Casper. Corporal in Capt. Peter Mantz's company of militia in 1775 [Ref: E-50]. Associator in December, 1775 [Ref: E-170]. Juror to the Oath of Allegiance in 1778 [Ref: C-27].

MISSELL, Frederick. "Frederick Missel" was an Associator in 1775 [Ref: E-170]. "Frederick Missell" took the Oath of Allegiance in 1778 [Ref: C-27].

MITCHELL, David. Associator in December, 1775 [Ref: E-170]. Furnished powder for use of the militia in Frederick Town in 1775 [Ref: E-60]. Juror to the Oath of Allegiance in 1778 [Ref: C-27].

MITCHELL, Miles. Private in the militia in July, 1776 [Ref: A-42].

MITZAR, Michael. Associator in December, 1775 [Ref: E-170]. Juror to the Oath of Allegiance in 1778 [Ref: C-27].

MIXSEL, John and Michael. See "John and Michael Mikesell," q.v.

MOATS, George. "George Motes" was drafted on June 13, 1781, and discharged, "being upwards of 50 years old." [Ref: D-1814]. "George Moats" died testate in 1793, leaving wife Doraty [sic] and only son George [Ref: M-8:182].

MOBER, Ludwick. Private who was enlisted on July 20, 1776 by Capt. Jacob Good [Ref: A-46].

MOCKBEE, Allan. Private who enlisted on July 29, 1776 [Ref: A-43].

MOCKBEE, Brock. 2nd lieutenant in the Lower District Militia on March 26, 1776 [Ref: W-287].

MOCKBEE, Jeremiah. Associator in December, 1775 [Ref: E-170]. Juror to the Oath of Allegiance in 1778 [Ref: C-27].

MOCKBEE, Mary, Rebecca, Peter, et al. See "Peter Becraft," q.v.

MOCKBEE, Zephaniah. Private who enlisted July 22, 1776 [Ref: A-49].

MODE, William. Private, 1st Maryland Regiment, 1781, and served in the Southern Army of the United States under Lt. William Lamar in the late Capt. Beatty's company. Record indicates he had "deserted" in February, 1781 [Ref: A-391].

MOLLOY, John. Associator in December, 1775 [Ref: E-170]. Juror to the Oath of Allegiance in 1778 [Ref: C-27].

MOLNIX, William. Private who enlisted April 28, 1778 [Ref: A-321].
MONEY, John. Private who was enlisted on July 20, 1776, by Capt. Jacob Good [Ref: A-46]. 2nd lieutenant in the 34th Battalion of militia on March 29, 1779 [Ref: H-15, B-105, Z-331].
MONEY, Patrick. Private who was enlisted on July 20, 1776, by Capt. Jacob Good [Ref: A-46].
MONGRELL, John. Associator in December, 1775 [Ref: E-170]. Juror to the Oath of Allegiance in 1778 [Ref: C-27].
MONNIKEY, Joseph. Juror to the Oath of Allegiance in March, 1778 [Ref: S-265, but not listed in Ref: C-27].
MONOHAN, Thomas. See "Thomas Manahan," q.v.
MONTGOMERY, John. "Served in the Maryland Sea Service and Virginia Continental Line. John applied for a pension (S8901) in Frederick County, Maryland, on February 6, 1834, stating that he was born in Calvert County, Maryland and lived in Westmoreland County, Virginia at the time of his enlistment. He had lived in Frederick County 40 years prior to applying for his pension and in Maryland since 1782. He died March 2, 1846, leaving children: John and James Montgomery and Isabella Brian who died prior to June 28, 1853. In 1853 both John and James were living in Frederick County, Maryland." [Ref: T-2391]. John Montgomery, Sr. appeared on the 1840 list of pensioners in the 9th District of Frederick County, aged 80 [Ref: J-37].
MONTINI, Charles. Associator in December, 1775 [Ref: E-170]. Juror to the Oath of Allegiance in 1778 [Ref: C-27].
MOORE [MORE], Abraham. 2nd lieutenant in Capt. H. Baker's militia company from November 29, 1775, to at least December 28, 1776, under Capt. S. Meredith [Ref: E-54, B-105, X-555, Y-54]. Associator in December, 1775 [Ref: E-171]. Juror to the Oath of Allegiance in 1778 [Ref: C-27].
MOORE [MOOR], Alexander. 2nd lieutenant in the Linganore Battalion of militia on June 22, 1778 [Ref: B-105, Z-144, and H-16, which latter source apparently misspelled his name as "Alexander Moone"].
MOORE [MORE], Andrew. Private, 1st Maryland Regiment, 1780, and served in the Southern Army of the United States under Lt. William Lamar in the late Capt. Beatty's company. Record indicates he was killed on March 15, 1781 [Ref: A-391].
MOORE, Daniel. Private in the Middle District Militia in 1776 in Capt. Valentine Creager's company [Ref: A-72].
MOORE, David (Burnt Woods Hundred). Appointed by the Committee of Correspondence to solicit subscriptions in 1775 to purchase arms and

ammunition [Ref: I-86]. Captain of a company of militia on November 29, 1775 [Ref: E-56]. Associator in December, 1775 [Ref: E-171]. 1st major on December 28, 1776 [Ref: B-105, X-555]. Juror to the Oath of Allegiance in 1778 [Ref: C-27].

MOORE, Enoch. Associator in December, 1775 [Ref: E-171]. Juror to the Oath of Allegiance in 1778 [Ref: C-27].

MOORE, Henry. See "John Newman," q.v.

MOORE, Hugh. Private who enlisted on May 12, 1778 [Ref: A-322].

MOORE, Jahugh [Jehu]. Non-Enroller who was fined by the Committee of Observation in May, 1776 [Ref: E-248].

MOORE [MORE], John. Private, 1st Maryland Regiment, 1780, and served in the Southern Army of the United States under Lt. William Lamar in the late Capt. Beatty's company until transferred to the light infantry on March 12, 1781 [Ref: A-390].

MOORE, John. Associator in December, 1775 [Ref: E-171]. Militia substitute from May to December 10, 1781; "marched to Annapolis." [Ref: A-653]. Juror to the Oath of Allegiance in 1778 [Ref: C-27, S-265].

MOORE [MOOR], John. Private who enlisted July 19, 1776 [Ref: A-51].

MOORE, John Jr. Associator in December, 1775 [Ref: E-171]. Juror to the Oath of Allegiance in 1778 [Ref: C-27].

MOORE [MOOR], Joseph. Private who enlisted on July 25, 1776 [Ref: A-51].

MOORE, Robert. Associator in December, 1775 [Ref: E-170]. Juror to the Oath of Allegiance in 1778 [Ref: C-27].

MOORE, William. "Draught," from May through December 10, 1781, and "marched to Annapolis." [Ref: A-653].

MORGAN, David. Lieutenant in the Maryland Line from April 8, 1778, until declared a supernumerary on January 1, 1781 [Ref: A-365].

MORGAN, Johnsey. Private who enlisted on April 22, 1778, and served in the 2nd Maryland Regiment [Ref: A-294, A-320].

MORGAN, Richard. Private who enlisted on July 19, 1776 [Ref: A-51].

MORIAT, William. Associator in December, 1775 [Ref: E-170]. Juror to the Oath of Allegiance in 1778 [Ref: C-27].

MORLOCK, Michael. Associator in December, 1775 [Ref: E-170]. Juror to the Oath of Allegiance in 1778 [Ref: C-27].

MORNINGSTAR, Adam. Associator in December, 1775 [Ref: E-170]. Juror to the Oath of Allegiance, 1778 [Ref: C-27]. 2nd lieutenant in the 37th Battalion of militia on December 28, 1776 [Ref: B-105, X-555]. An "Adam Morningstar, of Manor Hundred," died testate in 1794, leaving a wife Christina and children Adam (oldest son under 21), Frederick, George, Elizabeth, Juliana and Mary [Ref: M-6:126].

MORNINGSTAR, Philip. Served in the horse troops, 1781 [Ref: B-168]. Captain by April, 1781 [Ref: K-73]. See "Christopher Myers," q.v.

MOROLF, Rudolph. Private who enlisted July 1, 1776 in Capt. Peter Mantz's company; marched from Frederick Town to Leonardtown, and from there to Philadelphia, arriving August 23, 1776 [Ref: A-47].

MORRIS, Cornelius. Private, 1st Maryland Regiment, 1780, and served in the Southern Army of the United States under Lt. William Lamar in the late Capt. Beatty's company in 1781. He also served as a waggoner in July, 1781 [Ref: A-390].

MORRIS, Evan. Private in the Middle District Militia in 1776 in Capt. Valentine Creager's company [Ref: A-72]. Also, Evan Morris was a private who enlisted on March 12, 1778 [Ref: A-315].

MORRIS, James. Militia substitute from May to December 10, 1781, and "marched to Annapolis." [Ref: A-653]. Enlisted on May 11, 1782 [Ref: R-508].

MORRIS, Jonathan. 4th Sergeant in Capt. Philip Thomas' company of militia on November 29, 1775 [Ref: E-50]. 2nd lieutenant in the Upper District Militia [now Washington County] in 1776 [Ref: A-48].

MORRIS, Nathaniel. Associator in December, 1775 [Ref: E-170]. Juror to the Oath of Allegiance in 1778 [Ref: C-27].

MORRIS, Samuel. Militia substitute on June 3, 1778 [Ref: A-325].

MORRISON, George. Private who enlisted July 19, 1776 [Ref: A-51].

MORRISS, John. Militia substitute from May to December 10, 1781, and "marched to Annapolis." [Ref: A-653].

MORSEL, William. Non-Enroller who was fined by the Committee of Observation in April, 1776 [Ref: E-248].

MORT [MORTT], John. "John Mortt" was a private in Middle District Militia in 1776 in Capt. Valentine Creager's company [Ref: A-72]. "John Mort" was an ensign in the Catoctin Battalion of militia on November 30, 1782 [Ref: B-105].

MORT, Matthias. Associator in December, 1775 [Ref: E-170]. Juror to the Oath of Allegiance in 1778 [Ref: C-27].

MOSASTER, Christian. Petitioned the General Assembly under the Act of May 12, 1780, stating he had been a non-juror to the Oath of Allegiance and Fidelity in 1778 due to "ignorance" and now desired relief under the Act and to take the Oath [Ref: L-101].

MOSASTER, Michael. Petitioned the General Assembly under the Act of May 12, 1780, stating that he had been a non-juror to the Oath of

Allegiance and Fidelity in 1778 due to "ignorance" and now desired relief under the Act and to take the Oath [Ref: L-101].

MOSER [MOSES], Conrad. Provided wheat for the military in June, 1782 [Ref: R-523].

MOSER, Francis. Militia substitute from May to December 10, 1781, and "marched to Annapolis." [Ref: A-653].

MOSER, Jacob. Associator in December, 1775 [Ref: E-170]. Juror to the Oath of Allegiance in 1778 [Ref: C-27]. "Jacob Moser" enlisted on May 12, 1778 [Ref: A-322]. "Jacob Mosen" was a private in the German Regiment in 1779 [Ref: A-264]. "Jacob Moser" served in the German Regiment at White Plains on September 5, 1778, under Lt. Col. Weltner [Ref: A-267].

MOSER, Leonard. Associator in December, 1775 [Ref: E-170]. Juror to the Oath of Allegiance in 1778 [Ref: C-27].

MOSER [MOUSER], Ludwick. Private in the Middle District Militia in 1776 in Capt. Valentine Creager's company [Ref: A-72].

MOSER, Michael. Private in the German Regiment in 1776 in Capt. Henry Fister's company under the command of Col. Nicholas Hussecker [Ref: A-261]. Militia substitute from May to December 10, 1781, and "marched to Annapolis." [Ref: A-653].

MOSER, Valentine. Non-Enroller who was fined by the Committee of Observation in April, 1776 [Ref: E-248].

MOSS, Nicholas. Private who enlisted in 1778 and served in the 2nd Maryland Regiment [Ref: A-294].

MOUNT, Thomas. Juror to the Oath of Allegiance in March, 1778 [Ref: S-265, but not listed in Ref: C-27].

MOURER [MOUER], John. Private who enlisted on July 1, 1776 in Capt. Peter Mantz's company; marched from Frederick Town to Leonardtown, and then to Philadelphia, arriving on August 23, 1776 [Ref: A-47].

MOWEN, John. Private who enlisted on July 19, 1776 [Ref: A-51].

MOXLEY, Daniel. Private who enlisted on July 18, 1776 [Ref: A-49].

MOXLEY, John. Private who enlisted on July 18, 1776 [Ref: A-49].

MOYER, Bostin. Associator in December, 1775 [Ref: E-170]. Juror to the Oath of Allegiance in 1778 [Ref: C-27].

MOYER, Daniel (Pipe Creek Hundred). Non-Enroller who was fined by the Committee of Observation in June, 1776 [Ref: E-248].

MOYER, Henry. Associator in December, 1775 [Ref: E-170]. Juror to the Oath of Allegiance in 1778 [Ref: C-27].

MUCKER, George. Ensign in Capt. Philip Rodenbieler's company of militia, 4th Battalion, on November 29, 1775 [Ref: E-51, B-106].

MUGG, Notley. Associator in December, 1775 [Ref: E-170]. Juror to the Oath of Allegiance in 1778 [Ref: C-27].
MULLHOLLAND, Arthur. Private who enlisted on May 19, 1778, and served in the 2nd Maryland Regiment [Ref: A-323].
MULLEN, Nicholas. Juror to the Oath of Allegiance in March, 1778 [Ref: S-265, but not listed in Ref: C-27].
MULLER, Michael. See "John Smith," q.v.
MULLICAN, Lewis. Private who enlisted July 29, 1776 [Ref: A-44].
MULLIHAN, Archibald. Private who enlisted on July 18, 1776 [Ref: A-50].
MUMMAW, Christian. Militia substitute on June 2, 1778 [Ref: A-324]. Private in the German Regiment who was reported dead on July 27, 1778 [Ref: A-267, and A-268, which spelled his name "Mummard."].
MUMMERT, William. Private who enlisted on April 25, 1778 [Ref: A-321]. "William Mummard" was a private in the German Regiment at White Plains on September 5, 1778, under Lt. Col. Ludwick Weltner [Ref: A-266, and A-234, which spelled his name as "Mummart."].
MUNN, James. Private who enlisted on July 19, 1776 [Ref: A-51].
MUNROW, Barney. Private, 1st Maryland Regiment, 1780, and served in the Southern Army of the United States under Lt. William Lamar in the late Capt. Beatty's company in 1781; also served on hospital duty from June 16 to July, 1781 [Ref: A-391].
MURDOCK, Benjamin. Captain in the Maryland militia who pensioned in 1831, aged 75 [Ref: J-33]. Another source indicated that he was a lieutenant during the war and received the half pay of a lieutenant during his life, effective December, 1817 [Ref: G-377]. His pension (S9046) on July 19, 1832, states he was born in 1759 in Frederick County and lived there since the Revolutionary War except for a few years in Montgomery County. His surviving children in 1852 were Richard B. Murdoch, ELiza Murdoch and Aritta Simmons [Ref: T-2456].
MURDOCK [MURDOCH], Eleanor. See "Richard Potts," q.v.
MURDOCK [MURDOCH], George. Sheriff of Frederick County in 1765 [Ref: E-303]. Associator in December, 1775. Chosen to serve on the Committee of Observation on September 12, 1775 [Ref: E-170, E-302]. Collector of 76 lbs. 5 sh. 3 p. for arms and ammunition for the militia in 1775 [Ref: E-63]. Juror to the Oath of Allegiance in 1778 [Ref: C-27]. Also served in the Continental Commissary and as Frederick County Register of Wills, 1776-1805 [Ref: E-303, F-476, F-480, Z-519]. "George Murdock, Register of Wills for this county, died on the Sunday morning prior to May 10, 1805, aged 66, with burial in the Episcopal Church-

yard." [Ref: N-58]. Harriet Tyler, wife of Dr. William Bradley Tyler, and daughter of George Murdock, died on August 31, 1831, in Frederick County [Ref: F-472].

MURDOCK, John. Served on the Committee of Observation in 1775 [Ref: I-85]. Reviewed and passed recruits in Frederick County in 1776 [Ref: A-43]. Colonel in the militia of Montgomery County, 29th Battalion, on January 1, 1776, and September 12, 1777 [Ref: B-106].

MURPHEY, Daniel. Private who enlisted on July 18, 1776 [Ref: A-50]. "Daniel Merfey" was a private who was enlisted on July 20, 1776, by Capt. Jacob Good [Ref: A-46].

MURPHY, James. Private who enlisted on April 27, 1778 [Ref: A-321]. Served in the German Regiment at White Plains on September 5, 1778, under Lt. Col. Ludwick Weltner [Ref: A-266].

MURPHY, John. Associator in December, 1775 [Ref: E-170]. Juror to the Oath of Allegiance in 1778 [Ref: C-27]. Private, 7th Maryland Regiment, 1780, who enlisted in Frederick Town between January and April, 1780 [Ref: A-334, V-175]. "Defective" from the Maryland Line on August 16, 1780. However, since this "defection" followed the Battle of Camden, South Carolina, he may have been missing or taken prisoner rather than actually "defecting." [Ref: A-415, V-175].

MURPHY, Joseph. Private, 7th Maryland Regiment, 1780, enlisted in Frederick Town between January and April, 1780, and reported as "gone to Camp in McCullum's place." [Ref: A-334].

MURPHY, Patrick. Private who enlisted on August 5, 1776, in the Flying Camp under Capt. Meroney [Ref: A-44, A-45, N-30:111]. Defective from the Maryland Line in October, 1780 [Ref: A-414].

MURPHY, William. Private who enlisted on July 29, 1776 [Ref: A-43].

MUSGROVE, Benjamin. Private in the horse troops, 1781 [Ref: B-168].

MUSGROVE, Henry. Private in the militia, March, 1776 [Ref: B-166].

MUSGROVE, Nathan. Private in the militia on July, 1776 [Ref: A-42].

MUSHLER, Adam. Private who enlisted on April 30, 1778 [Ref: A-321]. "Adam Mussler" was with the German Regiment at the Battle of White Plains on September 5, 1778, under Lt. Col. Weltner [Ref: A-266].

MUSRULPH, Rudolph. Corporal in Capt. James Johnson's company of militia on November 29, 1775 [Ref: E-52].

MYER, David. Juror to the Oath of Allegiance in March, 1778 [Ref: S-265, but not listed in Ref: C-27].

MYER, David Stattle. See "David Stottlemyer," q.v.

MYER, Henry. Private who enlisted on July 1, 1776 in Capt. Peter Mantz's company; marched from Frederick Town to Leonardtown, and from there to Philadelphia, arriving on August 23, 1776 [Ref: A-47]. "Henry Mier" subscribed to the Oath of Allegiance in 1778 [Ref: C-27]. "Henry Mier" was an Associator in December, 1775 [Ref: E-170]. "Henry Miers" was a captain in the Linganore Battalion of militia on June 22, 1778 [Ref: B-104, Z-145]. Also, see "Henry Myers," q.v.

MYER, Jacob. Associator in December, 1775 [Ref: E-170]. Non-Enroller who was fined by the Committee of Observation in April, 1776 [Ref: E-248]. Juror to the Oath of Allegiance in 1778 [Ref: C-27]. One Jacob Myer died testate in 1784, leaving a wife Magdalene and daughter Elizabeth [Ref: M-6:86, M-6:87].

MYER [MIER], John. "John Mier" was an Associator in December, 1775 [Ref: E-171]. "John Myer" was a non-enroller who was fined by the Committee of Observation in April, 1776 [Ref: E-248]. Private who enlisted on August 5, 1776, in the Flying Camp under Capt. Philip Meroney [Ref: A-45, N-30:112]. "John Mier" subscribed to the Oath of Allegiance in 1778 [Ref: C-27]. See "John Myers," q.v.

MYER, Joseph. Non-Enroller who was fined by the Committee of Observation in April, 1776 [Ref: E-248].

MYER, Philip. "Draught," May to December 10, 1781, and "marched to Annapolis." [Ref: A-653].

MYER, Sebastian. Juror to the Oath of Allegiance in March, 1778 [Ref: S-265, but not listed in Ref: C-27].

MYERS, Casper. Petitioned the General Assembly under the Act of May 12, 1780, stating he had been a non-juror to the Oath of Allegiance and Fidelity in 1778 due to "ignorance" and now desired relief under the Act and to take the Oath [Ref: L-101].

MYERS, Christopher [Christian?]. Private in 1st Maryland Regiment, and served in the Southern Army of the United States under Lt. Wm. Lamar in the late Capt. Beatty's company, 1781. "Christopher Myers was born in 1759 in Frederick County, Maryland, and lived there at the time of his enlistment on April 1, 1781, as a private in Capt. Philip Morningstar's Company, guarding prisoners at Fort Frederick. After the war he lived in Frederick County and moved about 5 miles from Winchester, Virginia, and then to Muskingum and Knox Counties, Ohio. On September 27, 1832, he applied for a pension (S2890) in Wayne Township, Knox County, Ohio. It is not stated whether he was ever married." [Ref: T-2465, K-73].

MYERS, Christopher. "Chrisr. Myers" was an Associator in December, 1775 [Ref: E-170]. "Christopher Myers" was commissioned a second lieutenant in the Linganore Battalion, Capt. Winchester's Company,

October 13, 1777 [Ref: H-28, B-106]. "Christopher Myers" took Oath of Allegiance in 1778 [Ref: C-27]. Also, see "Christian (or Christopher) Mayers," q.v., and "Peter Fine," q.v.

MYERS, Frances. Private in the German Regiment, muster roll dated October 23, 1776 [Ref: A-264].

MYERS, Frederick. Associator in December, 1775 [Ref: E-170]. Juror to the Oath of Allegiance in 1778 [Ref: C-27].

MYERS, Henry. Associator in December, 1775 [Ref: E-170]. Juror to the Oath of Allegiance in 1778 [Ref: C-27, S-265]. 2nd lieutenant on December 28, 1776, in the Linganore Battalion of militia under Col. Johnson [Ref: B-106, X-555, Y-54]. Captain in militia on June 22, 1778 [Ref: H-17, Z-145]. See "Henry Mier" and "Henry Miers," q.v.

MYERS, Jacob. Associator in December, 1775 [Ref: E-171]. Juror to the Oath of Allegiance in 1778 [Ref: C-27].

MYERS, John. Associator in December, 1775 [Ref: E-171]. Juror to the Oath of Allegiance in March, 1778 [Ref: C-27]. One John Myers died testate in 1783, leaving wife Elizabeth and son Henry, son John (deceased, leaving children Jacob and Elizabeth Myers), and son-in-law Jacob Haines [Ref: M-6:32].

MYERS, Joseph. "Joseph Myres" provided wheat for the military in May, 1782 [Ref: R-513].

MYERS, Laurence. Private who enlisted July 1, 1776 in Capt. Mantz's company, and marched from Frederick Town to Leonardtown, and from there to Philadelphia, arriving on August 23, 1776 [Ref: A-47]. "Lieut. Lawrence Meyers was married to Miss Sarah Gore, January 3, 1782. She was of the patriotic family that sent five brothers and two brothers-in-law into battle. Lieut. Meyers was of a German family from Frederick Town, Maryland. Besides having held several offices in the militia, he was for several years a magistrate, and in 1800 commissioner of the county. The plan of the courthouse, a cross, was introduced by him, taken from that at Frederick Town, which doubtless owes its origin to the Roman Catholic settlers of Maryland, under their liberal and tolerant founder, though that it was an emblem of Catholicism or had any Christian significance was probably not known to Mr. Meyers or those in Luzerne who approved thereof. The delight of his life was to talk of Frederick, and anything that existed or came from there was an object of his special regard." [Ref: F-461, quoting Miner's *History of Wyoming County, Pennsylvania.*]

MYERS, Mary. See "Joseph Doll," q.v.

MYERS, Post [Yost]. Non-Enroller who was fined by the Committee of Observation in May, 1776 [Ref: E-248]. "Yost Myers" died testate in 1787, naming a wife Anna Maria and children John, Jacob, Benjamin, David, Michael, Elizabeth, Anna Maria, and Rebecca, and he also mentioned his land in Kentucky County, Virginia [Ref: M-7:90].

MYERS, William. See "Peter Fine," q.v.

MYOR, Joseph. Petitioned the General Assembly under the Act of July 3, 1780, stating he had been a non-juror to the Oath of Allegiance and Fidelity in 1778 due to "ignorance" and now desired relief under the Act and to take the Oath [Ref: L-101].

MYSS, Nicholas. Private who enlisted April 13, 1778 [Ref: A-320].

NAGLE, Richard. Associator in December, 1775 [Ref: E-171]. Militia substitute, May to December 10, 1781, and "marched to Annapolis." [Ref: A-653]. Juror to the Oath of Allegiance in 1778 [Ref: C-27]. "On February 14, 1828, the Treasurer of Maryland was directed to pay to Richard Nagle, of Cambria County, Pennsylvania, during life, half yearly, half pay of a private, for his Revolutionary War services." [Ref: G-377]. "Richard Nagle, or Neagle, applied for a pension (S40195) on June 3, 1818, in Cambria County, Pennsylvania, aged 71, stating he had enlisted in Frederick County, Maryland, and served in the Maryland Line. One George M. Reed made inquiry for soldier's three surviving children (not named) on July 21, 1855, and stated soldier had died in March, 1837." [Ref: T-2468]. See "John Baum," q.v.

NAIL, David. Private who enlisted on July 1, 1776 in Capt. Peter Mantz's company; marched from Frederick Town to Leonardtown, and from there to Philadelphia, arriving August 23, 1776 [Ref: A-47].

NAILOR, Thomas. Private in the Middle District Militia in 1776 in Capt. Valentine Creager's company [Ref: A-72].

NAVE, Bastian, Henry and Adam. See "Bastian, Henry and Adam Knave."

NAYLOR, George. Associator in December, 1775 [Ref: E-171]. Juror to the Oath of Allegiance in 1778 [Ref: C-27].

NEADE, George. See "George Need," q.v.

NEAFF, Jacob (Burnt House Woods Hundred). Non-Enroller who was fined by the Committee of Observation in June, 1776, but he apparently enrolled because the fine was remitted in July, 1776 [Ref: E-248].

NEAL, Christopher. Associator in December, 1775 [Ref: E-171]. Private who enlisted on July 19, 1776 [Ref: A-51]. Juror to the Oath of Allegiance in 1778 [Ref: C-27].

NEAL, Jacob. Non-Enroller who was fined by the Committee of Observation in April, 1776 [Ref: E-248].

NEAL, Rudolf. Non-Enroller who was fined by the Committee of Observation in April, 1776, but he was subsequently "struck off because over age" and the fine was remitted in June, 1776; yet, he "agreed to contribute." [Ref: E-248].

NEALE, Elizabeth. See "Leonard Smith," q.v.

NEALL, Bennett. Private who enlisted on August 5, 1776, in the Flying Camp under Capt. Philip Meroney [Ref: A-45, N-30:112].

NEAVE, John. See "John Knave," q.v.

NEED, Christopher. Ensign in the Catoctin Battalion of militia on August 16, 1781; 2nd lieutenant on November 30, 1782 [Ref: B-106].

NEED [NEET, NEIT], George. 2nd lieutenant in Capt. Benjamin Ogle's company of militia on November 29, 1775 [Ref: E-53]."George Neet, or Neit" was a 2nd lieutenant in the Middle District Militia on October 3, 1776, in Capt. Valentine Creager's company [Ref: A-72, B-106, W-427, X-317]. "George Neade" took the Oath of Allegiance in 1778 [Ref: S-265]. "George Nead" died testate in 1782, leaving a wife Magdalena and children John (oldest son), George, Jacob, Henry, Anna Maria, Cathrine, Elizabeth, and youngest daughter (no name was given in his will). [Ref: M-5:170, M-5:171].

NEFF, Adam. Non-Enroller fined by the Committee of Observation in April, 1776, but he apparently enrolled because the fine was remitted in June, 1776 [Ref: E-248].

NEFF, Daniel. Non-Enroller fined by the Committee of Observation in April, 1776 [Ref: E-248].

NEFF [NEAFF], John. "John Neff" was a non-enroller who was fined by the Committee of Observation in April, 1776 [Ref: E-248]. "John Neaff" provided wheat for the military in July, 1782 [Ref: R-534].

NEICE, Matthias. Sergeant in Capt. Samuel Shaw's company of militia on November 29, 1775 [Ref: E-51].

NEILL, Thomas. Associator in December, 1775 [Ref: E-171]. Juror to the Oath of Allegiance in 1778 [Ref: C-27].

NELLEY, Jeremiah. Private in militia on March 9, 1776 [Ref: B-167].

NELSON, Arthur. Served on the Committee of Observation in 1775 [Ref: I-85].

NELSON, John. Associator in December, 1775 [Ref: E-171]. Juror to the Oath of Allegiance in 1778 [Ref: C-27].

NELSON, Peter. Drafted on June 2, 1783 [Ref: B-168].

NELSON, Roger. Lieutenant of cavalry of Frederick County, pensioned at $200 per annum on May 31, 1815, under the Act of March 3, 1803, dating from September 4, 1802. He died June 7, 1815. "On March 4,

1834, the Treasurer of the Western Shore was directed to pay to Eliza Nelson, widow of Roger, of Frederick County, a revolutionary officer, half pay during life, to which her husband would have been entitled. On March 27, 1839, the Treasurer was directed to pay to Eliza Nelson, widow of Roger, of Frederick County, or to her order, "half pay of a lieutenant in the Revolutionary Army, from July 1, 1815, up to the time she was placed on the pension roll, it being the amount to which she is entitled under the resolution of 1779." [Ref: G-378]. Roger Nelson received bounty land warrant #2843 for 1,000 acres and #2844 for 1666 2/3 acres, both in area northwest of the Ohio River in 1799. His widow Elizabeth, aged 87 [67?], applied for a pension (W1310) on January 15, 1849, in Frederick County, Maryland. Roger Nelson married Elizabeth Harrison on February 2, 1797, in Frederick County. Her sisters, Mrs. Sarah C. Waring and Mrs. Grace C. Tyler, of Prince George's County, gave affidavits in 1848." [Ref: T-2480, J-9]. "Roger Nelson, born in Frederick County, was a general in the Revolutionary Army, receiving several wounds at the Battle of Camden. He was a representative in Congress from Maryland from 1804 to 1810, and was for several years a member of the Virginia Legislature, and from 1810 to 1815 he was Judge of the Upper District of that State. He was the father of John Nelson, and died at Frederick, Maryland, on June 7, 1815." [Ref: F-470].

NERVEY, John. Private in the militia on March 9, 1776 [Ref: B-167]. Also, see "John Newey," q.v.

NESWANGHER [NEWSANGER, NISWANKER], John. "John Niswanker" was an Associator in December, 1775 [Ref: E-171]. "John Newsanger, or Neswangher" was a private, enlisted July 1, 1776 in Capt. Mantz's company; marched from Frederick Town to Leonardtown, and from there to Philadelphia, arriving on August 23, 1776 [Ref: A-47]. "John Newsanger" took the Oath of Allegiance in 1778 [Ref: C-28].

NETSLEY, John. Private who enlisted on July 1, 1776 in Capt. Peter Mantz's company; marched from Frederick Town to Leonardtown, and from there to Philadelphia, arriving August 23, 1776 [Ref: A-47].

NETT, George. See "George Neit," q.v.

NEVET, John. Private who enlisted on April 13, 1780, for 3 years, in Capt. Michael Bayer's company [Ref: A-268].

NEVIN, William. Private who enlisted on May 19, 1778 [Ref: A-323]. "William Neving" was with the German Regiment at White Plains on September 5, 1778, under Lt. Col. Ludwick Weltner [Ref: A-266].

NEWCOMER, John. Juror to the Oath of Allegiance in March, 1778 [Ref: S-265, but not listed in Ref: C-27].

NEWEY, John. Juror to the Oath of Allegiance in March, 1778 [Ref: S-265, but not listed in Ref: C-27]. Also, see "John Nervey," q.v.

NEWLAND, John. Private, 7th Maryland Regiment, 1780, enlisted in Frederick Town between January and April, 1780, and reported as "gone to Camp" [Ref: A-334].

NEWMAN, John. Private who enlisted on July 19, 1776 [Ref: A-51]. he applied for a disability pension from January 1, 1803, at which time he lived in Hampshire County, Virginia, and reapplied there on May 25, 1818, stating he had enlisted in Fredericktown, Maryland. In 1820 he was aged 67 with a wife Elizabeth aged 39 (her first husband was Henry Moore), and his son Michael P. Newman, aged 3 months, and a stepson (not named) aged 19; also stepchildren Nancy and Abraham Moore, with the oldest aged about 9 years. In 1823 he had in his family a wife and 4 children, aged 11, 9, and 3 years, and 5 months, but did not give their names. In 1809 Philip Nollart of Allegany County, Maryland, formerly of Frederick County, stated he had lived in the same house with the soldier in 1781, but no relationship was given. Soldier died July 26, 1826." [Ref: T-2488].

NEWMAN, John. Militia substitute on June 8, 1778 [Ref: A-325], and private in the 7th Maryland Regiment from June 1, 1778, until April 1, 1779, when he was discharged [Ref: A-235]. Enlisted on May 14, 1781, for 3 years, and marched with Capt. Dyer [Ref: D-1814].

NEWTON, Arnold. Associator in December, 1775 [Ref: E-171]. Juror to the Oath of Allegiance in 1778 [Ref: C-28]. One Arnold Newton petitioned the General Assembly under the Act of May 12, 1780, stating that he had been a non-juror to the Oath of Allegiance and Fidelity in 1778 due to "ignorance" and now desired relief under the Act and to take the Oath [Ref: L-101].

NIBLET, William. Private in the 1st and 7th Maryland Regiments, having enlisted May 15, 1778, and served in the Southern Army of the United States under Lt. Wm. Lamar in the late Capt. Beatty's company in 1780. Served as a waggoner in July, 1781 [Ref: A-391].

NICEWANGER, Christian. Petitioned the General Assembly under the Act of May 12, 1780, stating he had been a non-juror to the Oath of Allegiance and Fidelity in 1778 due to "ignorance" and now desired relief under the Act and to take the Oath [Ref: L-101].

NICHBELL, Esther. See "Aeneas Campbell, Jr., q.v.

NICHODEMUS, Henry. "Henry Nichodamus" was an Associator in 1775 [Ref: E-171], and a Juror to the Oath of Allegiance in 1778 [Ref: C-28]. One "Henry Nichodemus" (1728-1801) emigrated to this country in 1751 and is buried on his homestead near Westminster (now Carroll County), Maryland. He had a son, John L. Nichodemus (1758-1825). [Ref: O-256].

NICHOLAS, John. Provided wheat for the military in July, 1782 [Ref: R-533].

NICHOLASSON, Richard. Private in militia in July, 1776 [Ref: A-42].

NICHOLLS, Archibald. Sergeant in militia, March, 1776 [Ref: B-166].

NICHOLLS, Flayl. Private in militia on March 9, 1776 [Ref: B-166].

NICHOLLS, John. "John Nicholls" was a lieutenant in the militia on March 9, 1776 [Ref: B-166]. "John Nichols" was a 2nd lieutenant in the Upper District Militia on July 4, 1776 [Ref: B-107, W-546]. He was probably the "Capt. Nicholls" who served in Frederick County on December 6, 1781 [Ref: B-107]. Juror to the Oath of Allegiance in March, 1778 [Ref: S-265, but not listed in Ref: C-27].

NICHOLLS, Thomas. Juror to the Oath of Allegiance in March, 1778 [Ref: S-265, but not listed in Ref: C-27].

NICHOLLS, William. Sergeant in militia, March 9, 1776 [Ref: B-166].

NICHOLS, Edward. Defective from the Maryland Line in July, 1780 [Ref: A-414].

NICHOLS, John. Private in the militia in July, 1776 [Ref: A-42].

NICHOLS, John Haymond. Private who enlisted on July 29, 1776 [Ref: A-44].

NICHOLS, John Mc. Private in the 7th Maryland Regiment from June 28, 1778, until discharged on March 15, 1779 [Ref: A-235].

NICHOLS, Jossept [Jehosphet?]. Private in the Skipton District under Capt. Thomas Waring on April 16, 1776 [Ref: B-167, D-1814].

NICHOLS, Ninion. Private who enlisted on August 5, 1776, in the Flying Camp under Capt. Philip Meroney [Ref: A-45, N-30:112].

NICHOLS, Thomas. Private in the militia in July, 1776 [Ref: A-42].

NICHOLS, Walter. Private who enlisted August 5, 1776 [Ref: A-44].

NICKS, William. Private who enlisted on May 5, 1778 [Ref: A-322].

NICKUM, Catharine. See "Lawrence Everhart," q.v.

NIFE, Michael. Provided wheat for the military in June, 1782 [Ref: R-520].

NIGHHOOF, Frederick. Juror to the Oath of Allegiance in March, 1778 [Ref: S-265, but not listed in Ref: C-27].

NIGHSWANGER, Abraham. Non-Enroller who was fined by the Committee of Observation in April, 1776, but he apparently enrolled because the fine was remitted in June, 1776 [Ref: E-248].

NIGHT, Peter. Juror to the Oath of Allegiance in March, 1778 [Ref: S-265, but not listed in Ref: C-27].

NIGHT, William. Juror to the Oath of Allegiance in March, 1778 [Ref: S-265, but not listed in Ref: C-27].

NIGHTIME, Elizabeth. See "Martin Clabaugh," q.v.

NISBETT, Richard. Private who enlisted in 1778 and served in the 2nd Maryland Regiment [Ref: A-294].

NISWANKER, John. See "John Neswanger," q.v.

NITZLY, John. Associator in December, 1775 [Ref: E-171]. Juror to the Oath of Allegiance in 1778 [Ref: C-28].

NOBERT, Philip. Associator in December, 1775 [Ref: E-171]. Juror to the Oath of Allegiance in 1778 [Ref: C-28]. See "Philip Nollart (Nollert)," q.v.

NOCKEY, Christian. Private stationed at Fort Frederick in June, 1778 [Ref: A-328].

NOISE, Richard. Private who enlisted on July 19, 1776 [Ref: A-51].

NOLAND, Samuel. Petitioned to form the horse troops in 1781 [Ref: B-167].

NOLAND, Thomas. Gave money in the amount of 15 sh. for arms and ammunition for the militia in 1775 [Ref: E-62]. "Thomas Nolan" was a private in the horse troops in June, 1781 [Ref: B-167]. "Thomas Noland" died on April 13, 1811 [Ref: F-471].

NOLLART [NOLLERT], Philip. 2nd lieutenant in the 33rd Battalion of militia on March 3, 1777, and a captain in the 34th Battalion of militia on April 19, 1781 [Ref: B-107]. See "Philip Nobert," q.v., and also see "John Newman," q.v.

NORMAN, Bazel. Private, 1st Maryland Regiment, 1780, and served in the Southern Army of the United States under Lt. William Lamar in the late Capt. Beatty's company until transferred to the light infantry on March 12, 1781. He also served as a waiter to Capt. Anderson [Ref: A-390].

NORRIS, Benjamin. Private who was enlisted on July 20, 1776, by Capt. Jacob Good [Ref: A-46]. Petitioned the General Assembly under the Act of May 12, 1780, stating he had been a non-juror to the Oath of Allegiance and Fidelity in 1778 due to "ignorance" and now desired relief under the Act and to take the Oath [Ref: L-101].

NORRIS, George. 2nd lieutenant in a cadet company in the Lower District on March 26, 1776 [Ref: W-287].

NORRIS, John. 1st lieutenant in Capt. Henry Baker's militia company from November 29, 1775, to at least December 28, 1776 [Ref: E-54, B-107, X-555]. Associator in December, 1775 [Ref: E-171]. Juror to the Oath of Allegiance in 1778 [Ref: C-28]. Provided wheat for the military in July, 1782 [Ref: R-533].

NORRIS, Nathaniel (Pipe Creek Hundred). Appointed by the Committee of Correspondence to solicit subscriptions in 1775 to purchase arms and ammunition [Ref: I-86].

NORRIS, Patrick. Corporal in militia on March 9, 1776 [Ref: B-166].

NORRIS, Samuel. Associator in December, 1775 [Ref: E-171]. Juror to the Oath of Allegiance in 1778 [Ref: C-28].

NORRIS, Thomas. Juror to the Oath of Allegiance in March, 1778 [Ref: S-265, but not listed in Ref: C-27].

NORRIS, William. Associator in December, 1775 [Ref: E-171]. Private who enlisted May 4, 1778 [Ref: A-321]. Juror to Oath of Allegiance in 1778 [Ref: C-28].

NORTHCRAFT, Edward. Private who enlisted July 29, 1776 [Ref: A-43].

NORTHCRAFT, Richard. Served on the Committee of Observation in 1775 [Ref: I-85].

NORTON, John. Private in the 7th Maryland Regiment from November 16, 1777, until taken prisoner on April 26, 1779 [Ref: A-235].

NORWOOD, Richard. Non-Enroller who was fined by the Committee of Observation in April, 1776 [Ref: E-248].

NORWOOD, Samuel. Served on the Committee of Observation in 1775 [Ref: I-85].

NOSSINGER, John. Non-Enroller who was fined by the Committee of Observation in May, 1776 [Ref: E-248].

NOSSINGER [NOFFSINGER], John (of Peter). Non-Enroller who was fined by the Committee of Observation in April, 1776 [Ref: E-248].

NOSSINGER [NORTHSINGER], Mathias. Non-Enroller who was fined by the Committee of Observation in May, 1776 [Ref: E-248]. "Mathias Northsinger" was drafted on June 2, 1783 [Ref: B-168].

NOSSINGER, Peter. Non-Enroller who was fined by the Committee of Observation in May, 1776 [Ref: E-248].

NOSSINGER [NORTHSINGER], Samuel. Non-Enroller who was fined by the Committee of Observation in May, 1776 [Ref: E-248]. "Samuel Northsinger" was drafted on June 2, 1783, "paid 8.5 pounds in lieu of his service." [Ref: B-168].

NOWELL, John. Drummer in Capt. Robert Beatty's company of militia on November 29, 1775 [Ref: E-55].

NOWLAND, Thomas (Lower Monocacy Hundred). Appointed by the Committee of Correspondence to solicit subscriptions in 1775 to purchase arms and ammunition [Ref: I-86]. 1st lieutenant in the Lower District Militia [now Montgomery County] under Capt. Edward Burgess on August 7, 1776 [Ref: A-42].

NOWLES, Edward. Private who enlisted on July 24, 1776 [Ref: A-50].

NOWLES, James (D. S. T.). Private who enlisted on July 24, 1776 [Ref: A-50].

NULL, Michael. Ensign in Capt. Samuel Shaw's company of militia on November 29, 1775 [Ref: E-51]. Ensign in Capt. Watson's company of militia in the 33rd Battalion on January 10, 1777 [Ref: B-108]. Wendle Null died testate in 1793, leaving wife Mary and children Michael, John (youngest son under 21), and Mary [Ref: M-8:179].

NULL, Valentine. Corporal in Capt. Abraham Hayter's company of militia on November 29, 1775 [Ref: E-52]. Witnessed the will of Wendle Null in 1793 [Ref: M-8:179].

NULLER, ---- [no first name given]. Lieutenant in the militia on December 6, 1781 [Ref: B-108].

NUNAMAKER, Michael. Petitioned the General Assembly under the Act of July 3, 1780, stating he had been a non-juror to the Oath of Allegiance and Fidelity in 1778 due to "ignorance" and now desired relief under the Act and to take the Oath [Ref: L-101].

NYSMONGER [NYSWONGER], Christopher Jr. Associator in December, 1775 [Ref: E-171]. Juror to the Oath of Allegiance, 1778 [Ref: C-28].

NYSMONGER [NYSWONGER], Christopher Sr. Associator in December, 1775 [Ref: E-171]. Juror to the Oath of Allegiance, 1778 [Ref: C-28].

OAKLEY, Elijah. Private who enlisted on April 28, 1781 for 3 years; marched with Capt. Lynn [Ref: D-1814].

OBALAM, George. Private who was enlisted on July 20, 1776 by Capt. Jacob Good [Ref: A-46].

OBER, John. See "John Auber," q.v.

O'BRYAN, James. Private who enlisted on May 29, 1778 [Ref: A-324].

O'BRYAN, John. Private who was enlisted on July 20, 1776 by Capt. Jacob Good [Ref: A-46]. Private in the 1st Maryland Regiment in 1780, and served in the Southern Army of the United States under Lt. William Lamar in the late Capt. Beatty's company until he was reported dead on April 25, 1781 [Ref: A-390].

OCC [?], Adam. Juror to the Oath of Allegiance in March, 1778 [Ref: S-265, but not listed in Ref: C-27].

OCKERMAN, Jacob. Non-Enroller who was fined by the Committee of Observation in April, 1776 [Ref: E-248].

O'DANIEL, Richard. Private who enlisted July 13, 1776 [Ref: A-43].

ODLE [ODEL], Thomas. Associator, 1775 [Ref: E-171]. 1st lieutenant in the Upper District Militia on July 4, 1776 [Ref: B-108, B-166, W-546]. Juror to the Oath of Allegiance in 1778 [Ref: C-28].

OFALVEY, Patrick. Private who enlisted on February 23, 1778 [Ref: A-314].

OFFUTT, Nathaniel (upper part of Potomac Hundred). Appointed by the Committee of Correspondence to solicit subscriptions in 1775 to purchase arms and ammunition [Ref: I-86]. Served on the Committee of Observation in 1775 [Ref: I-85].

OGDON, John. Militia substitute from May to December 10, 1781, and "marched to Annapolis." [Ref: A-653].

OGG, Alexander. Paid for enlisting one recruit on October 29, 1779 [Ref: V-5].

OGLE, Alexander (1730-1783). "Brother of Major Joseph Ogle (1707-1756) who served with Cresap in the War with Pennsylvania." [Ref: O-273]. Associator in December, 1775 [Ref: E-171]. Juror to the Oath of Allegiance in 1778 [Ref: C-28]. Alexander Ogle died testate in 1783, leaving wife Martha and children Alexander Jr., Elizabeth (wife of George Devilbiss), Rebecca (wife of John Devilbiss), Martha (wife of John Wood), Jane, and Mary [Ref: M-6:85].

OGLE, Benjamin Jr. "Benjamin Ogle, Jr." was captain of a company of militia in the 2nd Battalion, November 29, 1775 [Ref: E-53, B-108]. Associator in 1775, appointed "to hand about the Association paper" in Tom's Creek Hundred [Ref: E-171, E-305]. Appointed by the Committee of Correspondence to solicit subscriptions in 1775 to purchase arms and ammunition [Ref: I-86]. "Benjamin Ogle" was 1st major in the 2nd Battalion, 1776 [Ref: E-58]. Juror to the Oath of Allegiance in 1778 [Ref: C-28]. "Benjamin Ogle, of Benjamin" was drafted June 2, 1783 [Ref: B-168]. "Benjamin Ogle" was a county coroner in 1777 [Ref: F-476]. He was probably a son of Benjamin Ogle (1715-1777), who was a brother of Major Joseph Ogle (1707-1756). [Ref: O-273]. "Benjamin Ogle" provided wheat and flour for the military in 1782 [Ref: R-522].

OGLE, James. "Draught," from May to December 10, 1781, and "marched to Annapolis." [Ref: A-653].

OGLE, James. Ensign in Capt. Benjamin Ogle, Jr.'s militia company in the 2nd Battalion on November 29, 1775 [Ref: E-53]. Associator in December, 1775 [Ref: E-171]. Captain in the 37th Battalion on May 15, 1776 [Ref: B-108, W-427]. Juror to the Oath of Allegiance in 1778 [Ref: C-28].

OGLE, Joseph. Associator in December, 1775 [Ref: E-171]. Juror to the Oath of Allegiance in 1778 [Ref: C-28].

OGLE, Thomas. Associator in December, 1775 [Ref: E-171]. (This name appeared twice on the list of Associators). Took the Oath of Allegiance in 1778 [Ref: C-28, S-265]. Loaned $600 for the use of the State of Maryland in June, 1780 [Ref: V-520]. One Thomas Ogle died testate in 1790, leaving wife Sebilla and minor children (names not given in his will). [Ref: M-8:36].

O'HARA, Henry. Associator in December, 1775 [Ref: E-171]. Juror to the Oath of Allegiance in 1778 [Ref: C-28].

OHAVEN, Christopher. Juror to the Oath of Allegiance in March, 1778 [Ref: S-265, but not listed in Ref: C-27].

OHAVEN, Conrad. Juror to the Oath of Allegiance in March, 1778 [Ref: S-265, but not listed in Ref: C-27].

OIK, Leonard. Associator in December, 1775 [Ref: E-171]. Juror to the Oath of Allegiance in 1778 [Ref: C-28].

OLDSTONE, Edward. Private in the 7th Maryland Regiment from April 13, 1778, to July 1, 1780, when reported "deserted." [Ref: A-236].

OLER, Peter. See "Peter Eiler," q.v.

OLIVER, William. Private who enlisted on July 25, 1776 [Ref: A-50].

OLNIGER, Peter. Associator in December, 1775 [Ref: E-171]. Juror to the Oath of Allegiance in 1778 [Ref: C-28].

O'NEAL, Bernard. Served on the Committee of Observation in 1775 [Ref: I-85].

O'NEAL, John. 2nd lieutenant in the Linganore Battalion of militia on June 22, 1778 [Ref: H-17, B-108, Z-145].

O'NEALE [ONEALE], John, Margaret, and Phebe. See "William Pack."

O'NEALE, Laurence. Associator in December, 1775 [Ref: E-171]. Juror to the Oath of Allegiance in 1778 [Ref: C-28].

O'NEILL, Bernard. Reviewed troops in June, 1781 [Ref: B-168].

O'NEILL, John. Militia substitute from May to December 10, 1781, and "marched to Annapolis." [Ref: A-653].

O'NEILL, Lawrence. Sheriff, 1773-1775 [Ref: F-480]. "Laurence O'Neil" provided wheat for the military in 1782 [Ref: R-513].

ONSTAD, John. Associator in December, 1775 [Ref: E-171]. Juror to the Oath of Allegiance in 1778 [Ref: C-28].

O'QUIN, Richard. Private in the German Regiment. Served at White Plains on September 5, 1778, under Lt. Col. Weltner [Ref: A-267]. Discharged on September 1, 1782, "Invalids dispd." [Ref: A-236].

O'RADY, Henry. Associator in December, 1775 [Ref: E-171]. Juror to the Oath of Allegiance in 1778 [Ref: C-28].

ORBESSON, Thomas. Non-Enroller who was fined by the Committee of Observation in May, 1776, but he apparently enrolled and the fine was remitted in June, 1776 [Ref: E-248]. "Thomas Orbison" died testate in

1779, leaving a wife Mary, sons William, Thomas, and James, daughters Susanna, Bethiah, and Jean, and mentioning his former wife Elizabeth (daughter of James Miller, late of Newcastle County). Will recorded at Carlisle, Pennsylvania [Ref: M-5:134].

ORME, Archibald. Served on the Committee of Observation in 1775 [Ref: I-85]. Associator in December, 1775 [Ref: E-171]. Gave money in the amount of 14 lbs. 6 p. for arms and ammunition for the militia in 1775 [Ref: E-63]. Juror to the Oath of Allegiance in 1778 [Ref: C-28].

ORME, Nathan. Private in the militia in July, 1776 [Ref: A-42].

ORME, Samuel Taylor. Private in militia in July, 1776 [Ref: A-42].

ORMES, Charles. Private, 1st Maryland Regiment, 1780, and served in the Southern Army of the United States under Lt. William Lamar in the late Capt. Beatty's company until transferred to the light infantry on March 12, 1781 [Ref: A-390].

ORNDORFF, Christian (November 15, 1726 - December 10, 1797). Served on the Committee of Observation in 1775 [Ref: I-85]. 2nd lieutenant in the Upper District Militia of Frederick [now Washington] County in 1776 [Ref: A-48]. On the same day, April 20, 1776, "Christian Orendorff" was listed as a captain and 2nd major in the Frederick County militia, 36th Battalion [Ref: B-108, W-356]. Election Judge in the Upper District on July 2, 1776 [Ref: F-476]. "On February 19, 1819, the Treasurer of the Western Shore was directed to pay him the half pay of a captain, during life." [Ref: G-379]. Jacob Orndorff, or Orendorff (1770-1830), son of Christian, married Susan Miller in 1794 [Ref: U-1164, which source also states Christian was a major in the militia, and he served on the Committee of Safety in the Sharpsburg community]. "Christian Orendorf" was appointed by the Committee of Correspondence to solicit subscriptions in 1775 so as to purchase arms and ammunition [Ref: I-86].

ORNDORFF, Christopher. Gave money in the amount of 3 lbs. for arms and ammunition for the militia in 1775 [Ref: E-63]. 2nd lieutenant in 36th Battalion of militia on April 20, 1776 in Frederick County, and major in 2nd Battalion of Washington County on June 22, 1778 [Ref: W-356, B-108]. "Christopher Orndorf, Jr." was 1st lieutenant in Washington County on June 22, 1778 [Ref: B-108, Z-145].

ORNDORFF [ORINGDURF], Conrad. Juror to the Oath of Allegiance in March, 1778 [Ref: S-265; not listed in Ref: C-27]. See "Michael Tawney," q.v.

ORNDORFF [ORNDOFF], Peter. Provided wheat for the military in May, 1782 [Ref: R-510].

ORPUTT [ORPUT], Richard. Drummer in Capt. David Moore's company of militia on November 29, 1775 [Ref: E-56]. Also, drafted on June 2, 1783 [Ref: B-169].

ORRIX, Michael. Associator in December, 1775 [Ref: E-171]. Juror to the Oath of Allegiance in 1778 [Ref: C-28].

ORT, Jacob. Non-Enroller who was fined by the Committee of Observation in April, 1776 [Ref: E-248].

ORTNER, Daniel. Corporal in Capt. Herman Yost's company of militia on November 29, 1775 [Ref: E-52]. "Daniel Otner" was an Associator in December, 1775 [Ref: E-171]. Juror to the Oath of Allegiance, 1778 [Ref: C-28].

OSBAND, John. Private in the 7th Maryland Regiment from April 14, 1777, to May 26, 1778; deserted; joined July 22, 1778 [Ref: A-236].

OSBORN, Donald. See "Jacob Brunner," q.v.

OSBURN, Benjamin. Private who enlisted July 18, 1776 [Ref: A-49].

OSLEY, William. See "William Housley," q.v.

OSTER, John. Drummer at Fort Frederick in 1778, with Capt. John Kershner's company; also guarded prisoners of war [Ref: A-328].

OSTER, Peter. Private stationed at Fort Frederick on June 27, 1778, in Capt. John Kershner's company, guarding prisoners of war [Ref: A-328].

OSTWABT, Henry. Private, 7th Maryland Regiment, who enlisted in Frederick Town between January and April, 1780, and reported as "gone to Camp" [Ref: A-334].

OTNER, Daniel. See "Daniel Ortner," q.v.

OTT, Barnett. Drafted on June 2, 1783 [Ref: B-168].

OTT, George. Provided wheat for the military in 1782 [Ref: R-513].

OTT, Jacob. Drafted on June 2, 1783; "not appeared." [Ref: B-169].

OTTO, William. Sergeant in Capt. Normand Bruce's company of militia on November 29, 1775 [Ref: E-54].

OUTHOUSE, Peter. Private in 7th Maryland Regiment who enlisted in Frederick Town between January and April, 1780 [Ref: A-334, V-175]. Private in 1st Maryland Regiment, 1781, and served in the Southern Army of the United States under Lt. William Lamar in the late Capt. Beatty's company [Ref: A-389].

OVELMAN, George. Maryland militiaman; pensioned in 1834, aged 74. He appeared on the 1840 list of pensioners in the 8th District of Frederick County, aged 81 [Ref: J-33, J-37]. George Ovelman served in the Maryland Line and "applied for a pension (S8914) on December 23, 1833, in Frederick County, aged 73 on October 29, 1833, stating he enlisted at Taneytown, Maryland." [Ref: T-2557].

279

OVERFELD [OVERFELT], Matthias. "Matthias Overfelt" was an Associator in December, 1775 [Ref: E-171]. "Matthias Overfeld" took the Oath of Allegiance in 1778 [Ref: C-28]. "Mathias Overfelt" enlisted on July 1, 1776, in Capt. Mantz's company, marched from Frederick Town to Leonardtown, and from there to Philadelphia, arriving August 23, 1776 [Ref: A-47].

OWEN, Robert. Captain in the Lower District Militia in the 16th Battalion on May 20, 1776 [Ref: W-432]. Associator in December, 1775 [Ref: E-171].

OWEN, Robert Jr. Associator in December, 1775 [Ref: E-171]. Juror to the Oath of Allegiance in 1778 [Ref: C-28].

OWEN, Thomas. Private who enlisted on July 25, 1776 [Ref: A-50].

OWENS, James. Non-Enroller who was fined by the Committee of Observation in April, 1776 [Ref: E-248].

OWENS, Thomas. Associator in December, 1775 [Ref: E-171]. Private in militia, March 9, 1776 [Ref: B-167]. Juror to Oath of Allegiance in 1778 [Ref: C-28].

OWLE, alias Ale [sic], Daniel. Juror to the Oath of Allegiance in March, 1778 [Ref: S-265, but not listed in Ref: C-27].

OWLER, Andrew. Juror to the Oath of Allegiance in March, 1778 [Ref: S-265, but not listed in Ref: C-27].

OWLER, George Adam. Non-Enroller who was fined by the Committee of Observation in April, 1776, but he apparently enrolled because the fine was remitted in June, 1776 [Ref: E-248].

OWLER, Laurence. Non-Enroller who was fined by the Committee of Observation in April, 1776, but he apparently enrolled because the fine was remitted in June, 1776 [Ref: E-248].

OWLER, Philip. Juror to the Oath of Allegiance in March, 1778 [Ref: S-265, but not listed in Ref: C-27]. Drafted on June 13, 1781, and provided a substitute [Ref: D-1814].

OYSTER, Henry. Private who enlisted on April 27, 1778, and served in the 2nd Maryland Regiment [Ref: A-294, A-321].

PACK, James. Private who enlisted on April 29, 1778 [Ref: A-321].

PACK, William. Private who enlisted on August 5, 1776 [Ref: A-44]. Soldier in the Maryland Line who "applied for a pension (R7852) on September 17, 1832, in Hamilton County, Ohio, stating he was a son of Thomas and Elizabeth Pack and was born on October 16, 1758, in Frederick County, Maryland. He lived there at the time of his enlistment and lived there until 1804 when he moved to Hamilton County, Ohio. He had married Phebe Oneale on April 11, 1782, in Montgomery

County, Maryland. She was born on June 16, 1760, the daughter of John and Margaret Oneale. William Pack died September 23, 1838, and his widow applied for a pension on August 5, 1839, in Hamilton County, Ohio. She was still there in 1842. Their children were: Mary Pack, born on August 13, 1783; John Oneale Pack, born on November 10, 1785; Enos Pack, born on January 12, 1788; and, Ann Pack, born on May 30, 1790." [Ref: T-2565].

PAIN, Edward. Private who enlisted on July 18, 1776 [Ref: A-50].

PAIN [PAYNE], Flayl. "Flall Payn" was an Associator in December, 1775 [Ref: E-171]. "Flayl Pain" was a private in the militia on March 9, 1776 [Ref: B-166]. "Flall Payn" took Oath of Allegiance in 1778 [Ref: C-28, and S-266, which latter source spelled his name "Frail Payne"]. He was the son of "Flayle Payne" who died testate in Frederick County in 1765 [Ref: M-4:52]. "Flayle Payne, Jr. moved to Bedford County, Virginia, in 1779, and died testate in 1784, naming wife Sarah and children Nancy, Thomas, Martha, and William. His brother John lived nearby." [Ref: M-4:101].

PAIN, George. Juror to the Oath of Allegiance in March, 1778 [Ref: S-266, but not listed in Ref: C-30]. Militia substitute on June 13, 1778 [Ref: A-326].

PAINTER, George. Juror to the Oath of Allegiance in March, 1778 [Ref: S-266, but not listed in Ref: C-30].

PAINTER, Henry. Private in the German Regiment until discharged on October 12, 1779 [Ref: A-191, A-240].

PAINTER, Jacob, John and Peter. See "Jacob, John and Peter Panter."

PALMER, Michael. Soldier in the Maryland Line who "applied for a pension (R7899) on February 19, 1835 in Frederick County, Maryland, stating he was born December 25, 1755, and at age 12 or 13 he moved with his father (name not given) to Washington County, Maryland. He lived there at enlistment and after the Revolution his father moved to Frederick County, Maryland." [Ref: T-2580].

PANNEBAUR, William. Associator in December, 1775 [Ref: E-171]. Juror to the Oath of Allegiance in 1778 [Ref: C-28]. One "William Pannebaker" died testate in 1776, leaving a wife Mary Jacobina, son William, daughter Magdalena (by his first wife), and 3 daughters by his second wife: Margareth, Barbara, and Elizabeth [Ref: M-5:81].

PANTER, Jacob. Juror to the Oath of Allegiance in March, 1778 [Ref: S-266, but not listed in Ref: C-30].

PANTER, John. Juror to the Oath of Allegiance in March, 1778 [Ref: S-266, but not listed in Ref: C-30].

PANTER, Peter. Juror to the Oath of Allegiance in March, 1778 [Ref: S-266, but not listed in Ref: C-30].

PARK, James. Corporal in Capt. William Blair's company of militia on November 29, 1775 [Ref: E-55].

PARKER, Charles. Private who enlisted on March 28, 1778, and served in the 2nd Maryland Regiment [Ref: A-294].

PARKER, John. Private who enlisted on April 18, 1778, and served in the 2nd Maryland Regiment [Ref: A-294, A-320].

PARKINSON, Edward. Associator in December, 1775 [Ref: E-171]. Juror to the Oath of Allegiance in 1778 [Ref: C-28].

PARKINSON, John. Sergeant in Capt. Joseph Wood, Jr.'s company of militia on November 29, 1775 [Ref: E-53]. Associator in December, 1775 [Ref: E-171]. "John Parkinson, or Parkison" was an ensign in the 37th Battalion of militia on May 15, 1776 [Ref: B-110, W-427], and served under Capt. Valentine Creager on October 3, 1776 [Ref: X-317]. Commissioned a 1st lieutenant on April 27, 1779 [Ref: H-16, Z-368]. Also, see "John Pirkinson," q.v.

PARKINSON, Thomas. Militia substitute from May to December 10, 1781, and "marched to Annapolis." [Ref: A-653]. Also, see "Thomas Pirkinson," q.v.

PARKS, James. Associator in December, 1775 [Ref: E-171]. Juror to the Oath of Allegiance in 1778 [Ref: C-28].

PARSON, Robert. Private in the Middle District Militia in 1776 in Capt. Valentine Creager's company [Ref: A-72].

PARSONS, John. Private in the 7th Maryland Regiment who enlisted in Frederick Town between January and April, 1780 [Ref: A-334].

PARSONS, William. Private in the 6th Maryland Regiment who enlisted on April 20, 1777, and was reported missing after the Battle of Camden, South Carolina, on August 16, 1780 [Ref: A-238]. He was apparently among those killed during the battle as another source states he was "a soldier from Frederick County who had died while serving in the Maryland Line." [Ref: F-475].

PASTERFIELD, Thomas. Private in the 7th Maryland Regiment and was in the hospital in Annapolis (no date was given). [Ref: A-239].

PATRICK, William. Private who enlisted July 18, 1776 [Ref: A-50].

PATTERN, William. Defective from Maryland Line, 1780 [Ref: A-414].

PATTERSON, John. Private who enlisted on some time in 1780 [Ref: A-345].

PATTERSON, Nathaniel. Associator in December, 1775 [Ref: E-171]. (He made his "X" mark). Non-Enroller who was fined by Committee of

Observation in April, 1776, but he was subsequently "struck off, he having satisfied the Committee that he is not an effective man" on April 29, 1776 [Ref: E-248]. Juror to the Oath of Allegiance in 1778 [Ref: C-28]. Nathaniel Patterson died testate in 1791, leaving son William Wood Patterson, daughter Margaret Porter, daughter Jennett Flemming, and grandsons Nathaniel Porter and Nathaniel Patterson Flemming [Ref: M-8:85].

PATTERSON, Robert. Juror to the Oath of Allegiance in March, 1778 [Ref: S-267, but not listed in Ref: C-30].

PATTERSON, William. Ensign in Capt. Robert Beatty's company of militia, 3rd Battalion, on November 29, 1775 [Ref: E-55, B-110].

PAUT, John. Associator in December, 1775 [Ref: E-171]. Juror to the Oath of Allegiance in 1778 [Ref: C-28].

PAYN, Flall. See "Flayl Pain," q.v.

PEACE, John. Corporal in the 7th Maryland Regiment on April 28, 1778; sergeant on May 16, 1779; and, sergeant major on March 2, 1780. In service until at least November 1, 1780 [Ref: A-239].

PEACOCK, Neal. Private, 1st Maryland Regiment, 1780, and served in the Southern Army of the United States under Lt. William Lamar in the late Capt. Beatty's company until transferred to the light infantry on March 12, 1781 [Ref: A-390]. He "received bounty land warrant no. 11601-100-7 in February, 1790. Applied for a pension (S40247) on May 1, 1818, in Harrison County, Ohio, stating he had enlisted at Fredericktown, Maryland. On July 31, 1820, he gave his age as 67 years, 11 months, and 1 day, and he then received his mail at Cadiz, Ohio. In 1820 he had with him a wife, a daughter aged 16 years, and a son aged 13 years (no names given). Neal died on August 17, 1827." [Ref: T-2629].

PEACOCK, Thomas. Private in the 1st and 7th Maryland Regiments from March 16, 1779 and served in the Southern Army of the United States under Lt. Lamar in the late Capt. Beatty's company in 1780. Served to at least November 1, 1780 [Ref: A-239, A-389].

PEAK, Lewis. Private who enlisted on July 22, 1776 [Ref: A-49].

PEARCE [PIERCE], Joshua. Private who enlisted on August 5, 1776 in the Flying Camp under Capt. Philip Meroney [Ref: A-45, N-30:112].

PEARL, Charles. Associator in December, 1775 [Ref: E-171]. Juror to the Oath of Allegiance in 1778 [Ref: C-28].

PEARSE, Benjamin. Private in the Skipton District Militia under Capt. Thomas Waring on April 16, 1776 [Ref: B-167, which spelled the name "Pearce," but D-1814 (the original) spelled it "Pearse."].

PEARSE, James. Private in the Skipton District Militia under Capt. Thomas Waring on April 16, 1776 [Ref: B-167, which spelled the name "Pearce," but Ref: D-1814 (the original) spelled it "Pearse."].

PEBBLE, William. Sergeant in Capt. Jacob Good's company of militia on November 29, 1775 [Ref: E-51]. Captain in the militia, 1778-1779 [Ref: H-17]. Also, see "William Pepple," q.v.

PECK, Andrew. Provided wheat for the military in June, 1782 [Ref: R-520].

PECKENBAGH, Casper. Associator in December, 1775 [Ref: E-171]. Juror to the Oath of Allegiance in 1778 [Ref: C-28].

PECKENBAGH, Peter. Associator in December, 1775 [Ref: E-171]. Juror to the Oath of Allegiance in 1778 [Ref: C-28].

PECKENPAUGH [PECKINBAUGH, BACKENBAUGH], Leonard. Soldier in the Maryland Line who applied for a pension on September 9, 1833, in Union County, Indiana, aged 72, stating he enlisted in Frederick County, Maryland, where he was born in 1760. Nineteen years after his discharge he moved to Fayette County, Pennsylvania, and lived there for 24 years. In 1822 he moved to Union County, Indiana. Michael Peckinpaugh, son of Leonard, stated his father and mother (Catharine) moved to Lebanon, Ohio in 1839 and his father died at his house on November 12, 1842. Christopher Shroyer, brother of Catharine Peckinpaugh, lived in Franklin County, Indiana, in 1848. Catharine stated she married Leonard in 1786 when she was age 16. She applied for a pension (W4122) on August 30, 1848 in Warren County, Ohio, aged 78, and died about May 6, 1856 [Ref: T-107].

PECKIN, James P. Associator in December, 1775 [Ref: E-171]. Juror to the Oath of Allegiance in 1778 [Ref: C-28].

PEDEN, Henry C. See "Lawrence Everhart" and "Ralph Briscoe," q.v.

PEEKLE, Nicholas. Drafted on June 13, 1781; provided a substitute [Ref: D-1814].

PEES, Andrew. Soldier in the Pennsylvania Line who was born near Baltimore, Maryland on November 2, 1763, and at the age of 4 moved with his parents to Fort Frederick, Maryland. At age 11 he moved to Washington County, Pennsylvania, and lived there at the time of his enlistment. Applied for pension (S22433) on December 26, 1832, and mentioned his sister Mary W. Glumphy and George Pees [Ref: T-2644].

PEGMAN, Edward. See "Edward Pigman (Pegman)," q.v.

PEIRR, John. Corporal in Capt. Jacob Snowdenberger's company of militia on November 29, 1775 [Ref: E-56].

PELLY, James. Private who enlisted on July 29, 1776 [Ref: A-44].

PELTZ, John Jr. Associator in December, 1775 [Ref: E-171]. Juror to the Oath of Allegiance in 1778 [Ref: C-28].

PELTZ, John Sr. Associator in December, 1775 [Ref: E-171]. Juror to the Oath of Allegiance in 1778 [Ref: C-28].

PENCE, Frederick. Associator in December, 1775 [Ref: E-171]. Juror to the Oath of Allegiance in 1778 [Ref: C-28].

PENCE, Martin. Associator in December, 1775 [Ref: E-171]. Juror to the Oath of Allegiance in 1778 [Ref: C-28].

PENN, Charles. 2nd lieutenant in the Lower District Militia in the 16th Battalion on May 20, 1776 [Ref: W-432].

PENN, Michael. Private, 1st Maryland Regiment, 1781, and served in the Southern Army of the United States under Lt. William Lamar in the late Capt. Beatty's company. Record indicates he had "deserted" in April, 1781 [Ref: A-391].

PENN, Shadrech. Private in the militia in July, 1776 [Ref: A-42].

PENNETECKER, Margaret. See "Conrad Dudderer," q.v.

PENNY, Joseph. Private who enlisted on July 29, 1776 [Ref: A-43].

PENNYWELL, Radcliffe. Private in the 7th Maryland Regiment from July 20, 1778, until discharged on April 9, 1779 [Ref: A-239].

PENROAD, Peter. Private who was enlisted on July 20, 1776 by Capt. Jacob Good [Ref: A-46].

PENTRIM, Mary. See "Abraham Hargett (Hargis)," q.v

PEPPER, Elijah. Private, 1st Maryland Regiment, 1781, and served in the Southern Army of the United States under Lt. William Lamar in the late Capt. Beatty's company [Ref: A-390].

PEPPLE, Philip. Private who was enlisted on July 20, 1776 by Capt. Jacob Good [Ref: A-46]. Around May 7, 1785, "Philip Pepple murdered his wife Christine with an ax and also similarly killed his eldest son Peter; his second child, a daughter, Elizabeth; third child, a son, Philip; and his fourth child, a son, Abram... between 5 and 7 p.m. on May 7, 1785, at his mother's house, Philip Pebble [sic] mortally wounded himself with a pen knife and later died in jail." [Ref: M-1:41, M-1:42].

PEPPLES, William. Captain of a militia company in Col. J. Johnson's battalion on December 28, 1776 [Ref: X-555]. He was probably the "Capt. Peppel" who served in the 35th Battalion [Ref: B-110]. Also, see "William Pebble," q.v.

PERKY, Daniel. See "Mathias Firestone," q.v.

PERRY, Charles (Seneca). Appointed by the Committee of Correspondence to solicit subscriptions in 1775 to purchase arms and ammunition

[Ref: I-86]. Associator in December, 1775 [Ref: E-171]. Juror to the Oath of Allegiance in 1778 [Ref: C-28].

PERRY, Joseph. Served on the Committee of Observation in 1775 [Ref: I-85]. Appointed by the Committee of Correspondence to solicit subscriptions to purchase arms and ammunition in Upper Antietam in 1775. This or perhaps another Joseph Perry was appointed for the same purpose in the lower part of New Foundland [Ref: I-85, I-86].

PETER, John. 2nd lieutenant in the Lower District Militia of Frederick County, 36th Battalion, on April 20, 1776 [Ref: W-356], and 1st lieutenant in the 29th Battalion in Montgomery County on September 12, 1777 [Ref: B-111].

PETER, Robert. Furnished powder and lead for use of the militia in Frederick Town on November 29, 1775 [Ref: E-60, E-61].

PETERSON, William. Sergeant in Capt. Henry Baker's company of militia on November 29, 1775 [Ref: E-54].

PETTY, William. Associator in December, 1775 [Ref: E-171]. Juror to the Oath of Allegiance in 1778 [Ref: C-28].

PEVERLER, Catharine and Lewis. See "Jacob Yoast (Yeast)," q.v.

PFISTER, John. Associator in December, 1775 [Ref: E-171]. Juror to the Oath of Allegiance in 1778 [Ref: C-28].

PHARES, John. 1st lieutenant in Capt. William Shields' company of militia, 3rd Battalion, on November 29, 1775 [Ref: E-55, B-111].

PHILIPS, John. Private who enlisted on February 24, 1778 [Ref: A-314]. One John Philips petitioned the General Assembly under the Act of May 12, 1780, stating he had been a non-juror to the Oath of Allegiance and Fidelity in 1778 due to "ignorance" and now desired relief under the Act and to take the Oath [Ref: L-101].

PHILIPS [PHILLIPS], William. Private who enlisted on May 1, 1778, and served in the 2nd Maryland Regiment [Ref: A-294, A-321].

PHILLIPS, George. Private in the 1st and 7th Maryland Regiments who enlisted on March 18, 1777, and served in the Southern Army of the United States under Lt. Lamar in the late Capt. Beatty's company. Record indicates he was dead in March, 1781 [Ref: A-239, A-391].

PHILPOT, Barton (Bartin). "Barton Philpott" was an Associator in December, 1775 [Ref: E-171]. "Bartin Philpot" was a lieutenant in the militia on March 9, 1776, and "Barton Philpot" was an ensign in the Upper District Militia on July 4, 1776 [Ref: B-111, B-166, W-546]. "Barton Philpott" subscribed to the Oath of Allegiance in 1778 [Ref: C-28, S-266].

PHILPOT, Charles. "Charles Philpott" was an Associator in December, 1775 [Ref: E-171]. "Charles Philpot" was a private in the militia on March 9, 1776 [Ref: B-167]. Sergeant in Capt. William Beatty's company, 7th Maryland Regiment; enlisted December 4, 1776; and, discharged December 5, 1779 [Ref: A-310]. "Charles Philpott" took the Oath of Allegiance in 1778 [Ref: C-28]. "Charles Philpott (taylor)" was a private who enlisted on August 5, 1776 in the Flying Camp under Capt. Philip Meroney [Ref: N-30:112, and A-45, although the name mistakenly appeared as "Charles Philpott Taylor" in this latter reference]. "Applied for a pension (S5924) on October 6, 1832, in Henry County, Virginia, stating he was born on November 20, 1753, and lived in Frederick County, Maryland, at enlistment." [Ref: T-2691].

PHILPOT, Charles Thomas. Private who enlisted on August 8, 1776 [Ref: A-49].

PHILPOT, Warran [Warren]. Private who enlisted on August 5, 1776 in the Flying Camp under Capt. Philip Meroney [Ref: A-45, N-30:112]. He "applied for pension (S31907) on December 12, 1833, in Washington County, Arkansas, stating he was born August 28, 1756, in Charles County, Maryland, and moved to Frederick County. In 1778 he moved to Bedford County, Virginia, and in 1779 he moved to Guilford County, North Carolina. In 1780 he returned to Bedford County and in 1784 moved to Franklin County, Georgia. In 1801 he moved to Pendleton County, South Carolina, and in 1807 he moved to Warren County, Tennessee. In 1830 he moved to Washington County in the Arkansas Territory." He also stated he was a soldier in the North Carolina Line, but did not mention Maryland service [Ref: T-2691].

PICKELHIMER, John. Non-Enroller who was fined by the Committee of Observation in May, 1776 [Ref: E-248].

PIDGEON, William. Non-Enroller who was fined by the Committee of Observation in April, 1776 [Ref: E-248].

PIER, Philip. Non-Enroller who was fined by the Committee of Observation in April, 1776 [Ref: E-248]. Juror to the Oath of Allegiance in March, 1778 [Ref: S-267, but not listed in Ref: C-30].

PIERCE, Joshua. See "Joshua Pearce," q.v.

PIERCE, Stephen. Drafted on June 2, 1783; "gone to the ancient..." [Ref: B-168].

PIERPOINT, Eli. Drafted on June 2, 1783; "dead." [Ref: B-168].

PIERPOINT, Francis. Non-Enroller who was fined by the Committee of Observation in April, 1776 [Ref: E-248].

PIERPOINT, Joseph. Non-Enroller who was fined by the Committee of Observation in April, 1776 [Ref: E-248].

PIERPOINT, Obediah. Non-Enroller who was fined by the Committee of Observation in April, 1776 [Ref: E-248].

PIETERSE, Aeltje. See "William Crom," q.v.

PIFER, Martin. Private in the German Regiment, muster roll dated October 23, 1776 [Ref: A-264]. "Martain Phipher" was a sergeant at Fort Frederick in 1778 [Ref: A-328].

PIFER, Philip. Associator in December, 1775 [Ref: E-171]. Juror to the Oath of Allegiance in 1778 [Ref: C-28]. Loaned $300 for the use of the State of Maryland in June, 1780 [Ref: V-520].

PIGMAN [PEGMAN], Edward. Private who was enlisted on July 20, 1776 by Capt. Jacob Good [Ref: A-46].

PIGMAN, Nathaniel. Captain in the 29th battalion on May 14, 1776, initially located in Frederick County. This battalion later became part of Montgomery County in 1777 [Ref: D-1814, B-111, W-289].

PILES, William. Lieutenant in the State Infantry Company on April 22, 1780, and lieutenant in the Guard Infantry Company on July 1, 1780 [Ref: B-111].

PINDELL, Captain. See "Thomas Hynes," q.v.

PINKLEY, Adam. Associator in December, 1775 [Ref: E-171].

PINKLEY [PINCTLY], John. Private in the 7th Maryland Regiment from February 2, 1777 to February, 1778, when "off rolls." [Ref: A-239].

PINKLEY, John Grist. Associator in December, 1775 [Ref: E-171].

PINKLEY [PINCKLEY], Michael. Private in the 7th Maryland Regiment from May 2, 1777, to August 16, 1780, when he was reported missing (after the Battle of Camden, South Carolina). [Ref: A-239].

PINKLEY, Nicholas. Private who enlisted July 20, 1776 [Ref: A-50].

PINKLEY, Peter. Associator in December, 1775 [Ref: E-171]. Juror to the Oath of Allegiance in 1778 [Ref: C-28].

PINN, Michael. Private in the 7th Maryland Regiment who enlisted in Frederick Town between January and April, 1780, and was reported as "gone to Camp" [Ref: A-334].

PINNALL [PANNELL], Joseph. Private who enlisted on July 1, 1776 in Capt. Peter Mantz's company, and marched from Frederick Town to Leonardtown, and from there to Philadelphia, arriving on August 23, 1776 [Ref: A-47].

PIPER, Jacob. Associator in December, 1775 [Ref: E-171]. Juror to the Oath of Allegiance in 1778 [Ref: C-28].

PIRKINSON, John. Ensign in the Middle District Militia in 1776 in Capt. Valentine Creager's company [Ref: A-72]. Also, see "John Parkinson," q.v.

PIRKINSON, Thomas. Private in the Middle District Militia in 1776 in Capt. Valentine Creager's company [Ref: A-72].

PITCHER, Thomas. Private who enlisted on July 18, 1776 [Ref: A-50].

PITTENGER [PETTINGER], Benjamin. Associator, 1775 [Ref: E-171]. Juror to the Oath of Allegiance in 1778 [Ref: C-28].

PLAIN, David. Associator in December, 1775 [Ref: E-171]. Non-Enroller who was fined by the Committee of Observation in April, 1776 [Ref: E-248]. Juror to the Oath of Allegiance in 1778 [Ref: C-28]. Also, a David Plain petitioned the General Assembly under the Act of May 12, 1780, stating he had been a non-juror to the Oath of Allegiance and Fidelity in 1778 due to "ignorance" and now desired relief under the Act and to take the Oath [Ref: L-101]. He appears to have been a brother of William Plain, of Liberty Town, who had died testate in 1788, and mentioned "my brother David's children." [Ref: M-7:136].

PLAISTER, John. Petitioned the General Assembly under the Act of May 12, 1780, stating that he had been a non-juror to the Oath of Allegiance and Fidelity in 1778 due to "ignorance" and now desired relief under the Act and to take the Oath [Ref: L-101].

PLANE, William. Drafted on June 2, 1783 [Ref: B-169].

PLUMB, Catharine and Jacob. See "George Arnold," q.v.

PLUMMER, Abraham. Non-Enroller who was fined by the Committee of Observation in April, 1776 [Ref: E-248].

PLUMMER, George. Associator in December, 1775 [Ref: E-171]. Juror to the Oath of Allegiance in 1778 [Ref: C-28]. Private who enlisted on July 1, 1776, in Capt. Peter Mantz's company, and marched from Frederick Town to Leonardtown, and from there to Philadelphia, arriving on August 23, 1776 [Ref: A-47].

PLUMMER, Jeremiah. Sergeant in Capt. William Duvall's company of militia on November 29, 1775 [Ref: E-54].

PLUMMER, John. Provided wheat for the military in June, 1782 [Ref: R-518].

PLUMMER, Joseph Jr. Non-Enroller who was fined by the Committee of Observation in April, 1776 [Ref: E-248].

PLUMMER, Joseph Sr. Non-Enroller who was fined by the Committee of Observation in April, 1776 [Ref: E-248].

PLUMMER, Joseph West. Petitioned the General Assembly under the Act of May 12, 1780, stating he had been a non-juror to the Oath of

Allegiance and Fidelity in 1778 due to "ignorance" and now desired relief under the Act and to take the Oath [Ref: L-101].

PLUMMER, L. (Sugar Loaf Hundred). Appointed by the Committee of Correspondence to solicit subscriptions in 1775 to purchase arms and ammunition [Ref: I-86].

PLUMMER, Robert. Non-Enroller who was fined by the Committee of Observation in April, 1776 [Ref: E-248].

PLUMMER, Samuel. Captain of a militia company in the 1st Battalion on November 29, 1775 [Ref: E-54, B-111]. Associator who assisted the Committee of Observation in "handing about the Association paper" in March, 1776 [Ref: E-244]. One Samuel Plummer was a non-enroller fined by the Committee of Observation in April, 1776 [Ref: E-248]. One Samuel Plummer died testate in 1777, leaving his wife Sarah and children Joseph, George, Thomas, and James, Mary, Martha, Jane, Ann, and Rachel [Ref: M-5:81]. Another Samuel Plummer died testate in 1791, leaving wife Mary and children Jonathan, Israel, Evan, Elizabeth, Sarah, Rachel, Ann, and Rebekah [Ref: M-8:137].

PLUMMER, Thomas. Petitioned the General Assembly under the Act of July 3, 1780, stating that he had been a non-juror to the Oath of Allegiance and Fidelity in 1778 due to "ignorance" and now desired relief under the Act and to take the Oath [Ref: L-101]. One Thomas Plummer died testate in 1784, leaving a wife Ellen and children Isaac, Jessee, William, and Ruth, and also mentioning his brother-in-law William Ballinger [Ref: M-6:126].

PLUMMER, Yate [Gate, Yates]. "Gate Plummer" was a non-enroller who was fined by the Committee of Observation in April, 1776 [Ref: E-248]. "Yate Plummer" was drafted on June 2, 1783 [Ref: B-169].

POE, George. Captain in the 34th Battalion of militia on June 11, 1776 [Ref: B-111, W-476].

POLAND, William. Private who enlisted on July 18, 1776 [Ref: A-49].

POLE, Lodowick. Militia substitute from May to December 10, 1781, and "marched to Annapolis." [Ref: A-653].

POLEHOUSE, Thomas. "Thomas Polhaus" was an Associator in December, 1775 [Ref: E-171]. "Thomas Polehouse" was a private in the German Regiment, 1776, in Capt. Henry Fister's company under command of Col. Hussecker [Ref: A-261]. "Thomas Polhaus" took the Oath of Allegiance in 1778 [Ref: C-28]. "Thomas Polhouse" was a substitute on June 2, 1778 [Ref: A-324]. "Thomas Polehouse" was a corporal in the German Regiment, having enlisted November 1, 1778, and served in the Battle of White Plains on September 5, 1778, under Lt. Col. Ludwick

Weltner [Ref: A-267, A-239]. On April 15, 1779, Colonel Weltner petitioned the Frederick County Court in behalf of "Thomas Pollhouse," a soldier in his regiment. Mrs. Pollhouse (name not stated) was granted 40 lbs. subsistence for herself and their 4 children [Ref: Q-6835].

POLHOWER, Andrew. Juror to the Oath of Allegiance in March, 1778 [Ref: S-266, but not listed in Ref: C-30].

POLLY, Charles. Associator in December, 1775 [Ref: E-171]. (This name appeared twice on the list of Associators). One subscribed to the Oath of Allegiance in 1778 [Ref: C-28].

POLSON, Andrew and James. See "Andrew and James Bolson," q.v.

POLSON, Cornelius. Associator in December, 1775 [Ref: E-171]. Juror to the Oath of Allegiance in 1778 [Ref: C-28].

POOLE, Henry. See "Daniel James," q.v.

POOLE, Thomas Samuel. Non-Enroller who was fined by the Committee of Observation in May, 1776 [Ref: E-248].

POPE, John. Private in the Maryland Line who "applied for pension (S35032) in Frederick County on April 10, 1818, aged 65 [or 68?], stating he enlisted in Montgomery County. In 1820 he stated he had no family. He died on March 3, 1821." [Ref: G-382, J-25, T-2729].

POPE, William. Private who enlisted on May 20, 1778 [Ref: A-323]. Served in the German Regiment at White Plains on September 5, 1778, under Lt. Col. Weltner [Ref: A-266]. A William Pope died testate in 1793, naming children Samuel, Margaret, Mary, Sarah, Rebecca, plus nephew Thomas King Clarke and cousin Anthony Swisher [Ref: M-9:33].

POPHAM, Benjamin. Recruited by Capt. David Lynn in Frederick Town in 1782 for 3 years [Ref: A-417]. "On March 27, 1827, the Treasurer of Maryland was directed to pay Benjamin Popham, of Anne Arundel County, during life, half yearly, the half pay of a private, for his services during the Revolutionary War." [Ref: G-382]. "On March 29, 1839, the Treasurer was directed to pay Ann Busey, sole legatee of Benjamin Topham [sic], deceased, who was a pensioner of this state, or her order, the arrear of pension due to said 'Topham' at time of death, under Resolution 63 passed in 1826." [Ref: G-400].

PORTER, Nathan. Petitioned the General Assembly under the Act of May 12, 1780, stating that he had been a non-juror to the Oath of Allegiance and Fidelity in 1778 due to "ignorance" and now desired relief under the Act and to take the Oath [Ref: L-101].

PORTER, Robert. Private who enlisted on May 15, 1778 [Ref: A-322]. Served with the German Regiment at the Battle of White Plains on September 5, 1778, under Lt. Col. Ludwick Weltner [Ref: A-266].

PORTER, Thomas. Non-Enroller who was fined by the Committee of Observation in June, 1776 [Ref: E-248].
PORTNEY, Anthony. Non-Enroller who was fined by the Committee of Observation in April, 1776 [Ref: E-248].
POST, Nal. [sic]. Juror to the Oath of Allegiance in March, 1778 [Ref: S-266, but not listed in Ref: C-30].
POSTLEWAIT, William. Private in the Skipton District Militia under Capt. Thomas Waring on April 16, 1776 [Ref: B-167, D-1814].
POTE, Michael. Private who enlisted on July 19, 1776 [Ref: A-51].
POTTS, Richard (June 19, 1753 - November 25, 1808). Clerk for the Committee of Observation in 1776 [Ref: E-242]. Ensign in the 34th Battalion of militia on May 15, 1776 [Ref: B-112, W-426]. Clerk of the Circuit Court from 1776-1778; House of Delegates in 1780; U.S. Congressman, 1781-1782; Chief Justice in the 5th Judicial District, 1791-1801; and, a Judge of the Court of Appeals, 1801 [Ref: F-478, F-480]. Elizabeth Hughes, the first wife of Judge Richard Potts, was born in 1761 and died on October 28, 1793. His second wife was Eleanor Murdoch (1744-1812). Miss Rebecca Potts, daughter of Richard Potts, died on February 21, 1804. George Murdoch Potts (1805-1893), a son of Richard Potts, married Cornelia Ringgold (1805-1868) in 1826 [Ref: F-470, F-471, O-217, P-658, U-2317].
POTTY, Thomas. Associator in December, 1775 [Ref: E-171]. Juror to the Oath of Allegiance in 1778 [Ref: C-28].
POULISS, Michael. Associator in December, 1775 [Ref: E-171]. Juror to the Oath of Allegiance in 1778 [Ref: C-28].
POWELL, John. Private who enlisted on July 25, 1776 [Ref: A-51].
POWELL, Susanna and William. See "Philip Fisher," q.v.
POWELL, Zepporah. See "Thomas Gilbert," q.v.
POWER, Essly. Private in the Skipton District Militia under Capt. Thomas Waring on April 16, 1776 [Ref: B-167, which spelled his name "Elsly," but Ref: D-1814 (original list) spelled it "Essly."].
POWER, James. Private in the Skipton District Militia under Capt. Thomas Waring on April 16, 1776 [Ref: B-167, D-1814].
POWLET, George. Associator in December, 1775 [Ref: E-171]. Juror to the Oath of Allegiance in 1778 [Ref: C-28].
PRANGLEY, William. Private who enlisted May 20, 1778 [Ref: A-323]. Private, 1st Maryland Regiment, 1781, and served in the Southern Army of the United States under Lt. William Lamar in the late Capt. Beatty's company. The record indicates he was a prisoner of war on April 25, 1781 [Ref: A-391].

PRATHER, Charles. Private in the Skipton District Militia under Capt. Thomas Waring on April 16, 1776 [Ref: B-167, D-1814].

PRATHER, James. Served on the Committee of Observation in 1775 [Ref: I-85]. 1st lieutenant in the Skipton District Militia in Frederick County under Capt. Waring on April 16, 1776 [Ref: B-167, D-1814, B-112, W-427]. Captain of a militia company in Washington County in 1777 and 1778. [Ref: B-112, B-242].

PRATHER, James. Private in Capt. James Prather's company of militia in 1777 [Ref: B-242].

PRATHER, Samuel. Associator in December, 1775 [Ref: E-171]. Juror to the Oath of Allegiance in 1778 [Ref: C-28]. "Samuel Prater" was a private on March 9, 1776 [Ref: B-166]. "Samuel Prator" provided wheat for the military in July, 1782 [Ref: R-539]. "Samuel Prather, planter," died testate in 1785, leaving wife Elizabeth and children John, Jean, Enos, Erasmus, Rhoda, and Silas [Ref: M-6:185].

PRATHER, Samuel. Served on the Committee of Observation in 1775 [Ref: I-85].

PRESTON, Andrew. Private who enlisted on May 19, 1778, and served in the 2nd Maryland Regiment [Ref: A-294, A-323].

PRESTON, John. Associator in December, 1775 [Ref: E-171]. Juror to the Oath of Allegiance in 1778 [Ref: C-28].

PRESTON, Stephen. Private who enlisted July 19, 1776 [Ref: A-51].

PRESTON, William. Private in the Middle District Militia in 1776 in Capt. Valentine Creager's company [Ref: A-72].

PRICE, John. Private in Capt. Philip Meroney's company in the Flying Camp in August, 1776, and subsequently reported "deserted" (no date was given). [Ref: N-30:112]. Also, see "John Rite," q.v.

PRICE, Samuel. Petitioned to form horse troops, 1781 [Ref: B-167].

PRICE, Thomas (Fredericktown Hundred). Appointed by the Committee of Correspondence to solicit subscriptions in 1775 to purchase arms and ammunition [Ref: I-86]. Served on the Committee of Observation in 1775 [Ref: I-85]. Associator in December, 1775 [Ref: E-171]. Juror to the Oath of Allegiance in 1778 [Ref: C-28]. "Colonel Thomas Price, son of Capt. John Price, was born in Philadelphia in 1732 and died in Frederick County in 1795." [Ref: O-157]. "Thomas Price, Jr." was a colonel in the 2nd Maryland Regiment in 1779 [Ref: Q-6835]. Col. Thomas Price was Commissary for Purchases from July 8, 1780, through 1782 [Ref: V-215, R-526]. Also, see "Bartley Lane," q.v., and "Roger Landess," q.v.

PRICE, William. Private who was enlisted on July 20, 1776 by Capt. Jacob Good [Ref: A-46].

293

PRICHARD, John. Private in the Skipton District Militia under Capt. Thomas Waring on April 16, 1776 [Ref: B-167, D-1814].

PRINGLE, Christian. Associator in December, 1775 [Ref: E-171]. Juror to the Oath of Allegiance in 1778 [Ref: C-28].

PROCTOR, Thomas. Private in the German Regiment who enlisted on May 4 1778, served at the Battle of White Plains on September 5, 1778, and was in service at least to January 1, 1781 [Ref: A-239, A-266].

PROCTOR, William. Soldier in the Maryland Line who "applied for a pension (S1711) on November 17, 1832, in Sumner County, Tennessee, stating he was born November 22, 1749, in Maryland and lived there at enlistment. After the Revolution he moved to Rockingham County, North Carolina, and moved to Tennessee in 1806." [Ref: T-2778].

PRODBECK, Margaret. See "William Albaugh," q.v.

PROTZMAN, Daniel. Corporal in Capt. Benjamin Ogle, Jr.'s company of militia on November 29, 1775 [Ref: E-54].

PROTZMAN, Lawrence. Sergeant in Capt. Benjamin Ogle, Jr.'s company of militia on November 29, 1775 [Ref: E-53]. Named as a son in the will of Lodewick Protzman, probated on May 16, 1778 [Ref: M-5:85].

PROTZMAN [PROTSMAN], John. Associator in December, 1775 [Ref: E-171]. Juror to the Oath of Allegiance in 1778 [Ref: C-28]. Named as a son in the will of Lodewick Protzman, probated May 16, 1778 [Ref: M-5:85].

PRYER, Peter. Sergeant in Capt. Jacob Snowdenberger's company of militia on November 29, 1775 [Ref: E-56].

PSAUT, Adam. Associator in December, 1775 [Ref: E-171]. Also, see "Adam P. Saut," q.v.

PUGH, Thomas. Private in the 7th Maryland Regiment, having enlisted on July 2, 1779 [Ref: A-239].

PURCELL, John. Private in the Skipton District Militia under Capt. Thomas Waring on April 16, 1776 [Ref: B-167, D-1814].

PURCELL, Thomas. Private in the Skipton District Militia under Capt. Thomas Waring on April 16, 1776 [Ref: B-167, D-1814].

PURDY, Edward. Private in the 6th Maryland Regiment from February 5, 1780, to at least November 1, 1780 [Ref: A-238].

PURDY, Henry. Private in the 6th Maryland Regiment from February 5, 1780, to at least November 1, 1780 [Ref: A-238].

PURDY, John. Private in the 6th Maryland Regiment from February 20, 1780, to at least November 1, 1780 [Ref: A-238].

PURDY [PURDAY], William. 1st lieutenant in Capt. William Duvall's company of militia in the 4th Battalion on November 29, 1775 [Ref: E-54, B-113].

PURGETT, Henry. Soldier in the Virginia Line who "applied for a pension (S18170) on June 24, 1833 in Hampshire County, Virginia, where he had lived since the end of the Revolutionary War. He was born near Fredericktown, Maryland, in 1753." [Ref: T-2787].

PURNAL, Samuel. Private in the militia in July, 1776 [Ref: A-42].

PURTELFARTHING, James. Petitioned the General Assembly under the Act of May 12, 1780, stating he had been a non-juror to the Oath of Allegiance and Fidelity in 1778 due to "ignorance" and now desired relief under the Act and to take the Oath [Ref: L-101].

PUTES, Ludlow. "Ludw. Putes" was an Associator in December, 1775 [Ref: E-171]. "Ludlow Putes" subscribed to the Oath of Allegiance in 1778 [Ref: C-28].

PUTTEE, James. Private in the Skipton District Militia under Capt. Thomas Waring on April 16, 1776 [Ref: B-167, D-1814].

QUEAH, Menasses. Militia substitute from May to December 10, 1781, and "marched to Annapolis." [Ref: A-653].

QUEEN, Walter. Adjutant in the 29th Battalion in Frederick County on August 29, 1777 [Ref: B-113].

QUEEN, William. Juror to the Oath of Allegiance in March, 1778 [Ref: S-266, but not listed in Ref: C-30].

QUEENER, John. Soldier in the Maryland Line who "applied for a pension (S1584) on September 4, 1832, in McMinn County, Tennessee, aged 71, stating he lived in Frederick County, Maryland, at time of enlistment. His application was witnessed by a Jacob Queener and a Daniel Queener, but no relationships were given." [Ref: T-2794].

QUEER, Henry. Private in the German Regiment, muster roll dated October 23, 1776 [Ref: A-264]. "Henry Quier" was a private in the German Regiment; discharged on July 29, 1779 [Ref: A-240, A-265].

QUIN [QUINN, QUYNN], Francis. Private who enlisted on August 5, 1776 in the Flying Camp under Capt. Philip Meroney [Ref: A-45, N-30:112].

QUIN, Richard. Private who enlisted on May 1, 1778 [Ref: A-321].

QUIN [QUYNN], Timothy. Private in the 7th Maryland Regiment from March 30, 1777, until August 16, 1780, when he was reported missing (after the Battle of Camden, South Carolina). [Ref: A-240].

QUINLIN, Cornelius. Private, German Regiment. Served at White Plains on September 5, 1778, under Lt. Col. Weltner [Ref: A-266].

QUINLEY, Levin. Private in the 7th Maryland Regiment from May 4, 1778, until reported "deserted" in December, 1779 [Ref: A-240].

QUINTON, William. Private in the 1st and 7th Maryland Regiments, 1780, and served in the Southern Army of the United States under Lt. Lamar in the late Capt. Beatty's company [Ref: A-240, A-390].

RADER, Michael. Associator in December, 1775 [Ref: E-171]. Juror to the Oath of Allegiance in 1778 [Ref: C-28].

RADFORD, William. Associator in December, 1775 [Ref: E-171]. Juror to the Oath of Allegiance in 1778 [Ref: C-28].

RAGER, Peter. Non-Enroller who was fined by the Committee of Observation in April, 1776, but he was subsequently determined to be "over age" and the fine was remitted in June, 1776 [Ref: E-248].

RAGON, Daniel. Associator in December, 1775 [Ref: E-172]. Juror to the Oath of Allegiance in 1778 [Ref: C-28].

RAGON, Joshua. Associator in December, 1775 [Ref: E-172]. Juror to the Oath of Allegiance in 1778 [Ref: C-28].

RAIDY, James. Private who enlisted on July 18, 1776 [Ref: A-49].

RAIT, John. Provided wheat for the military in 1782 [Ref: R-533].

RALEY, Walter. Private who enlisted on July 22, 1776 [Ref: A-49].

RAMSBERG [REMSBURG], Ann Margaret. See "John Thomas," q.v.

RAMSBERG [RAMSBURGH], George. Corporal in Capt. Ludowick Kemp's militia company on November 29, 1775 [Ref: E-52]. "George Ransberg" was Associator in December, 1775 [Ref: E-171]. Juror to the Oath of Allegiance in 1778 [Ref: C-28]. "George Ransburgh" died testate in 1794, leaving wife Christina and children (not named in his will). [Ref: M-9:40].

RAMSBERG [REMSBURG, REMSBURGH] John (c1741-1807). Son of Stephen Reimensperger (1711-1789) and Anna Catherine Bruñner. Served on the Committee of Observation in 1775 [Ref: I-85]. Associator who was appointed "to hand about the Association paper" in Israel Creek Hundred on November 29, 1775 [Ref: E-305]. Was appointed by the Committee of Correspondence to solicit subscriptions to purchase arms and ammunition in Manor Hundred in 1775 [Ref: I-86]. Anna Maria, widow of John Ramsburg, Sr., died on February 3, 1825, aged 84 [Ref: F-472]. John Ramsburg (Reimensperger) married Anna Maria Brunner (c1741-1825). Their children were Jacob, John, Stephen, Catherine, and Elizabeth [Ref: O-57]. See "William Derr," q.v.

RAMSBERG [RANSBERG], Philip (c1752-1807). Son of Stephen Ramsburg or Reimensperger or Rannesperger (1711-1789) and Anna Catherine Brunner, of Germany [Ref: U-2320]. Philip enrolled as an

Associator in December, 1775 [Ref: E-171], and signed as a Juror to the Oath of Allegiance in 1778 [Ref: C-28]. A (Philip) Henry Ramsberg (Reimensperger) married Susanna Devilbiss and moved to Strasburg, Virginia. Their children were Stephen, John, Henry, Christian, Casper, Susanna. Philip (Henry) married second to Catherine Stickley, of Virginia, and returned to Middletown. Their children were Elizabeth, Israel, Joseph, Anna, and Samuel [Ref: O-58]. He was probably the "Henry Remsburg?" who was a private in the 9th Company of Infantry in 1776 [Ref: A-20].

RAMSBURG, Catharine Elizabeth. See "John Stoner," q.v.

RAMSBURG, Elizabeth. See "John Shafer," q.v.

RAMSBURGH, Christian (born c1743). Son of Stephen Reimensperger and Anna Catherine Brunner, he was an ensign in Capt. John Stoner's company of militia in the 1st Battalion on November 29, 1775 [Ref: E-56, B-114]. "Christian Ransberg" was an Associator in December, 1775 [Ref: E-171]. Juror to the Oath of Allegiance in 1778 [Ref: C-28]. He married Susanna ---- and had a son Stephen and a daughter Catherine [Ref: O-57]. "Christian Ramsburg" died testate in 1793, leaving a wife Susannah and children Catharine and Stephen. [Ref: M-9:33, M-9:34].

RAMSBURGH, Jacob (born c1747). Son of Stephen Reimensperger and Anna Catherine Brunner. 3rd Sergeant in Capt. Christopher Stull's company of militia, November 29, 1775 [Ref: E-50]. "Jacob Ramsburg" was a 2nd lieutenant in the militia on 37th Battalion on April 27, 1779 [Ref: B-114, Z-368, and H-16, which latter source misspelled his name "Ramsbury"]. He married Anna Elizabeth Devilbiss and their children were Elizabeth, John George, Susanna, John, Jacob, Casper, Christian, Frederick, Henry, Catherine, and Uriah D. [Ref: O-58].

RAMSBURGH [RANSBURGH], Stephen. Provided wheat for the military in July, 1782 [Ref: R-530].

RAMSEY, William. Associator in December, 1775 [Ref: E-171]. Juror to the Oath of Allegiance in 1778 [Ref: C-28, S-266].

RANDLE, John. Private who enlisted on July 20, 1776 [Ref: A-50].

RANEY, Maria. See "Humphrey Beckett," q.v.

RAPE, Martin. Associator in December, 1775 [Ref: E-172]. Juror to the Oath of Allegiance in 1778 [Ref: C-28].

RAVEN [RAWEN], Patrick. Private who enlisted on May 5, 1778, and served in the 2nd Maryland Regiment [Ref: A-294, A-322].

RAVER, Christopher. Private in the German Regiment until discharged on July 26, 1779 [Ref: A-243, A-265].

RAWLINGS, Isaac. Soldier in the Maryland Line "who died a single unmarried man. His sister Sarah King received bounty land warrant no. 1130-200-6 in August, 1825, as one of his heirs. An Eleanor King also made affidavit (no relationship was given). Both resided in Frederick County, Maryland, in 1825." [Ref: T-2818].

RAWLINGS, Moses (Skipton). Appointed by Committee of Correspondence to solicit subscriptions in 1775 to purchase arms and ammunition [Ref: I-85]. "Commissioned on the 1st of July, 1776, lieutenant colonel of the rifle regiment of which Col. Stevenson was commander and Otho Holland Williams, major. In the absence of the colonel he commanded the regiment at Fort Washington, but during the assault by the Hessians was badly wounded, and when the fort capitulated he fell into the hands of the enemy with the rest of the command. At this time Washington said of him, 'I entertain a very high opinion of Col. Rawlings and his officers, and have interested myself much in their behalf.' His four companies of riflemen were joined to the German Battalion, and the command was afterwards known as the 8th Maryland Regiment. In 1779 he was ordered by Washington to Fort Pitt (on the present site of the city of Pittsburgh), and on the refusal of Washington to permit the German troops to accompany him he resigned, in April, 1779. Capt. Beale took charge of his command at Fort Frederick, and in May, 1779, marched with it to Fort Pitt. On September 27, 1779, Col. Rawlings was placed in charge of the prisoners at Frederick Town, where he remained until the close of the war. In 1794, there being danger of a war with Great Britain, the militia of Maryland was reorganized, and Col. Rawlings was appointed brigadier general for Washington and Allegany Counties. He died in Hampshire County, Virginia, in May, 1809." [Ref: F-452, Z-520]. Also, Moses was appointed Assistant Deputy Commissary of Purchases for Washington County on September 10, 1779 [Ref: Z-518].

RAWLINGS, Solomon. Militia substitute from May to December 10, 1781, and "marched to Annapolis." [Ref: A-653]. "Solomon Rawlins [sic] applied for a pension (S35039) on March 1, 1818, in Washington County, Maryland, for his service in the Maryland Line. In 1820 he was aged 77 with wife (no name was given) aged 67, and daughter Elizabeth, aged 30." [Ref: T-2818].

RAY, John. Private in the militia in July, 1776 [Ref: A-42].

RAY, Joseph. Private who was enlisted on July 20, 1776, by Capt. Jacob Good [Ref: A-46].

RAYBERT, Chs. or Chrisr. [sic]. Private in the German Regiment until discharged on July 20, 1779 [Ref: A-243].

RAYMER, Michael. Lieutenant in the French and Indian War in 1756. Chosen to serve on the Committee of Observation in 1775 [Ref: I-85, E-302, E-303]. Loaned $1,630 for the use of the State of Maryland in June, 1780 [Ref: V-520]. Also, see "John Haas (Haass)," q.v.

RAZOR, Jacob. Made an agreement on September 15, 1777, with the Governor and Council of Maryland "to make and in a workman like manner compleat and finish one hundred musquets fixed with bayonets and steel rammers, swivels, priming wires, and brushes at 3 pounds 15 shillings each, and within two months from this day will deliver at least twelve and so from month to month thereafter at least twelve of the said musquets the deliveries to be at Frederick Town to Charles Beatty or such other appointed person..." [Ref: Y-376].

READ, Christopher. Associator in December, 1775 [Ref: E-172]. Juror to the Oath of Allegiance in 1778 [Ref: C-28].

READER, Michael. Juror to the Oath of Allegiance in March, 1778 [Ref: S-267, but not listed in Ref: C-30].

READER, William. Associator in December, 1775 [Ref: E-171]. Juror to the Oath of Allegiance in 1778 [Ref: C-28].

REAL, Alexander. Associator in December, 1775 [Ref: E-172]. (This name appeared twice on the list of Associators). One subscribed to the Oath of Allegiance in 1778 [Ref: C-28].

REALLEY, Dennis. Private who enlisted July 1, 1776 in Capt. Peter Mantz's company; marched from Frederick Town to Leonardtown, and from there to Philadelphia, arriving August 23, 1776 [Ref: A-47].

REAM, Balser. Associator in December, 1775 [Ref: E-171]. Juror to the Oath of Allegiance in 1778 [Ref: C-28].

REASER, Jacob. Corporal in Capt. Charles Beatty's militia company on November 29, 1775 [Ref: E-51]. Associator in December, 1775 [Ref: E-172]. Wrote to the General Assembly on June 9, 1779, and offered to manufacture guns [Ref: R-124].

REASOR, John. Non-Enroller who was fined by the Committee of Observation in April, 1776 [Ref: E-248].

REB, Valentine. Associator in December, 1775 [Ref: E-172].

REBLER, Michael. Associator in December, 1775 [Ref: E-171].

REBSTOCK, Anna Margaret. See "Jacob Staley," q.v.

REDDLEY, Drue. Private who enlisted on April 25, 1778 [Ref: A-321].

REDENOUR, Jacob. See "Jacob Ridenour," q.v.

REECE, Jacob. Associator in December, 1775 [Ref: E-171]. Juror to the Oath of Allegiance in 1778 [Ref: C-28].

REED, Ann. See "Joseph Wood," q.v.

REED, George. See "Richard Nagle," q.v.

REED, Henry. Associator in December, 1775 [Ref: E-171].

REED, James. Paid by the Committee of Observation "for carriage of 13 casks of bullets" on November 29, 1775 [Ref: E-65].

REED, Philip. Lieutenant in the militia on February 23, 1776 [Ref: B-114].

REEDER, Jesse. Associator in December, 1775 [Ref: E-172]. Juror to the Oath of Allegiance in 1778 [Ref: C-28].

REEL, Joseph. Associator in December, 1775 [Ref: E-171]. Juror to the Oath of Allegiance in 1778 [Ref: C-28].

REELEY, Owen. Associator in December, 1775 [Ref: E-172]. Juror to the Oath of Allegiance in 1778 [Ref: C-28].

REESE, Andrew. Juror to the Oath of Allegiance in March, 1778 [Ref: S-266, but not listed in Ref: C-30].

REESE, Frederick. "Frederick Reese" took the Oath of Allegiance in March, 1778 [Ref: S-266]. One "Frederick Reess" was a 2nd lieutenant in the militia from 1778 to 1779 [Ref: H-17]. "Frederick Rease" was 2nd lieutenant in Linganore Battalion on June 22, 1778 [Ref: B-114, Z-145].

REESE, Henry. Private, 1st Maryland Regiment, 1780, who served in the Southern Army of the United States under Lt. William Lamar in the late Capt. Beatty's company in 1781, until assigned to Major Roxburgh to serve as a waiter in July, 1781 [Ref: A-390].

REETER, Elias. Private stationed at Fort Frederick on June 27, 1778, in Capt. John Kershner's company, and guarding prisoners of war [Ref: A-328].

REEVER [RIEBER], (Johann) Ulrich (April 16, 1738 - February 24, 1817). Born in Ebingen, Wurttenberg, Germany, son of Jorg Phillip Rieber and Margarethe Beck, Ulrich served in the Lancaster County, Pennsylvania militia, died in Frederick County, Maryland, and is buried in Trinity Lutheran Church Cemetery at Taneytown in Carroll County, Maryland. Son, Phillip Reaver or Reever (1766-1844), born in Lancaster County, is buried in Carroll County [Ref: T-2520].

REEVER, Stuffle. Private in the German Regiment, muster roll dated October 23, 1776 [Ref: A-264].

REEVES, Jonathan. Juror to the Oath of Allegiance in March, 1778 [Ref: S-266, but not listed in Ref: C-30].

REGALMAN, George. "George Regalman" was a private in the German Regiment until discharged on October 12, 1779 [Ref: A-243]. "George Riggleman" was a private in the German Regiment, muster roll dated October 23, 1776 [Ref: A-264]. "George Regliman" was a private in the German Regiment; discharged on October 12, 1779 [Ref: A-265].

REICH, Henry. Private in the Middle District Militia in 1776 in Capt. Valentine Creager's company [Ref: A-72].

REID, Joseph. Sergeant in the Skipton District Militia under Capt. Thomas Waring on April 16, 1776 [Ref: B-167, D-1814].

REILL, Frederick. Associator in December, 1775 [Ref: E-172]. Juror to the Oath of Allegiance in 1778 [Ref: C-28].

REINTZELL, Anthony. Associator in December, 1775 [Ref: E-172]. Juror to the Oath of Allegiance in 1778 [Ref: C-28, S-266].

REISER, Frederick. Provided wheat for the military in June, 1782 [Ref: R-518].

REMSBURG, John. See "John Ramsburg," q.v.

RENCH, Andrew (gentleman). Commissioned a lieutenant colonel in the 32nd Battalion on January 3 or 6, 1776 [Ref: H-32, G-384, B-115].

RENCH, John (Elizabeth Hundred). Appointed by the Committee of Correspondence to solicit subscriptions in 1775 to purchase arms and ammunition [Ref: I-86]. Ensign in the Upper District Militia [now Washington County] in July, 1776 [Ref: A-48].

RENDEL, Jacob. Associator in December, 1775 [Ref: E-172]. Juror to the Oath of Allegiance in 1778 [Ref: C-28].

RENHARD, Andrew. Militia substitute on June 9, 1778 [Ref: A-326].

RENNER, Philip. Served in the Maryland Militia during the Revolutionary War (no dates given). [Ref: O-56].

RENNER, Sophia. See "Daniel Buzard," q.v.

RENNER, William (1742-1793). Associator in December, 1775 [Ref: E-172]. Juror to the Oath of Allegiance in 1778 [Ref: C-28]. Buried at Rocky Hill Church Cemetery near Woodsboro, Maryland [Ref: O-56]. William Renner died testate in 1793, leaving wife Mary and children (only named Daniel in his will), plus his (William's) brother John. [Ref: M-9:34].

RENTCH, Andrew. Associator in December, 1775 [Ref: E-171]. Juror to the Oath of Allegiance in 1778 [Ref: C-28].

RETTLEMOSER, Michael. Provided wheat for the military in May, 1782 [Ref: R-516].

REYNER, Abraham. Non-Enroller who was fined by the Committee of Observation in April, 1776 [Ref: E-248].

REYNOLDS, Catherine. See "Joseph Wood," q.v.

REYNOLDS, Charles Maccubin. Private in militia in 1776 [Ref: A-42].

REYNOLDS, Francis. Private, 1st Maryland Regiment, 1781, who served in the Southern Army of the United States under Lt. William Lamar in the late Capt. Beatty's company. Record indicates he was in the hospital in July, 1781 [Ref: A-392].

REYNOLDS, George. Private who enlisted July 24, 1776 [Ref: A-50].

REYNOLDS, John. Captain in the Upper District Militia of Frederick [now Washington] County, 36th Battalion, on April 20, 1776 [Ref: A-48, B-115, W-356]. Captain in the 7th Maryland Line on December 10, 1776 [Ref: A-242].

REYNOLDS, John. Private who enlisted on July 29, 1776 [Ref: A-43].

REYNOLDS, Thomas. Petitioned the General Assembly under the Act of May 12, 1780, stating that he had been a non-juror to the Oath of Allegiance and Fidelity in 1778 due to "ignorance" and now desired relief under the Act and to take the Oath [Ref: L-101].

REYNOLDS, William. Associator in December, 1775 [Ref: E-171]. Juror to the Oath of Allegiance in 1778 [Ref: C-28].

RHODES, Elisha. Private who enlisted on August 5, 1776, in the Flying Camp under Capt. Philip Meroney [Ref: A-45, N-30:112].

RHODES, Henry. See "Peter Fine," q.v.

RHODES, Jacob. "Jacob Rhodes" was a private who enlisted on August 5, 1776, in the Flying Camp, with Capt. Philip Meroney's company [Ref: N-30:112, A-45]. "Jacob Rhoads" was a private in Capt. Joseph Wood's company early in 1776 [Ref: E-244]. "Jacob Roades" took the Oath of Allegiance an Fidelity to the State of Maryland in March, 1778 [Ref: S-266].

RIAN, Burnett. See "Burnett Ryan," q.v.

RIBGER, Matthias. Juror to the Oath of Allegiance in 1778 [Ref: C-28].

RICE, Benjamin. Associator in December, 1775 [Ref: E-172]. Juror to the Oath of Allegiance in 1778 [Ref: C-28]. "Draught," May to December 10, 1781, and "marched to Annapolis." [Ref: A-653]. Drafted on June 2, 1783, "appeared ready to march after siege of York." [Ref: B-168].

RICE, Frederick. Associator in December, 1775 [Ref: E-172]. Juror to the Oath of Allegiance in 1778 [Ref: C-28].

RICE, George. Drummer in Capt. Jacob Good's company of militia on November 29, 1775 [Ref: E-51]. Private who was enlisted on July 20, 1776 by Capt. Jacob Good [Ref: A-46].

RICE, John. Associator in December, 1775 [Ref: E-171]. (This name appeared twice on the list of Associators). One subscribed to the Oath of Allegiance in 1778 [Ref: C-28].

RICE, Thomas. 2nd lieutenant in Capt. Michael McGuire's company of militia, 3rd Battalion, on November 29, 1775 [Ref: E-56, B-115].

RICE, William (c1734-1788). Sergeant in Capt. William Beatty's militia company on November 29, 1775 [Ref: E-55], and commissioned 1st lieutenant in the German Regiment on September 25, 1778, and captain on January 4, 1778 [Ref: A-182]. William died testate in 1788, leaving a wife Ann and children James, William, Peregrine (1767-1841, married Martha Dutrow in 1794), Elizabeth, and Rebecca [Ref: M-7:136, U-1865].

RICHARDS, Abraham. Private in militia, March 9, 1776 [Ref: B-167].

RICHARDS, Caleb. Associator in December, 1775 [Ref: E-171]. Juror to the Oath of Allegiance in 1778 [Ref: C-28].

RICHARDS, David. Served on the Committee of Observation in 1775 [Ref: I-85].

RICHARDS, Jacob. Petitioned the General Assembly under the Act of July 3, 1780, stating that he had been a non-juror to the Oath of Allegiance and Fidelity in 1778 due to "ignorance" and now desired relief under the Act and to take the Oath [Ref: L-101].

RICHARDS, John. Non-Enroller who was fined by the Committee of Observation in April, 1776 [Ref: E-248]. Private who enlisted on May 20, 1778, and served in the German Regiment at White Plains on September 5, 1778, under Lt. Col. Weltner [Ref: A-323, A-266].

RICHARDS, Joshua. Associator in December, 1775 [Ref: E-172]. Juror to the Oath of Allegiance in 1778 [Ref: C-28].

RICHARDS, Richard. Associator in December, 1775 [Ref: E-171]. Juror to the Oath of Allegiance in 1778 [Ref: C-28]. Loaned $200 for the use of the State of Maryland in June, 1780 [Ref: V-520]. Petitioned to form the horse troops in 1781 [Ref: B-167].

RICHARDS, Thomas. Private who enlisted on February 23, 1778 [Ref: A-314].

RICHARDSON, John. Ensign in the Middle District Militia on July 1, 1776 [Ref: A-44, X-140].

RICHARDSON, Richard (Lower Monocacy Hundred). Non-Enroller who was fined by the Committee of Observation in June, 1776 [Ref: E-248].

RICHARDSON, Samuel. Private who enlisted July 19, 1776 [Ref: A-51].

RICHARDSON, Thomas. Furnished powder for use of the militia in Frederick Town on November 29, 1775 [Ref: E-60]. Captain in the

Lower District Militia, 36th Battalion, in 1776 [Ref: W-356]. Provided wheat for the military in May, 1782 [Ref: R-509]. One Thomas Richardson died testate in 1783, leaving a wife Ursula and children Anne, Mary, Elizabeth, William, and Thomas [Ref: M-6:33].

RICHARDSON, William. Militia substitute, May to December 10, 1781 [Ref: A-653]. Private who enlisted on July 1, 1776, in Capt. Peter Mantz's company; marched from Frederick Town to Leonardtown, and from there to Philadelphia, arriving August 23, 1776 [Ref: A-47].

RICHE, Isaac. Associator in December, 1775 [Ref: E-172]. Juror to the Oath of Allegiance in 1778 [Ref: C-28].

RICHEY, William. Private who enlisted on April 22, 1778, and served in the 2nd Maryland Regiment [Ref: A-294, A-320]. See "William Ritchie," q.v.

RICKENBAUGH, Martin. Private who enlisted on July 19, 1776 [Ref: A-51].

RICKER, Conrad. Sergeant in Capt. William Luckett, Jr.'s company of militia on November 29, 1775 [Ref: E-55]. Ensign in Capt. Frazer's company in the 34th Battalion on June 11, 1776 [Ref: W-476].

RICKER, Peter. Juror to the Oath of Allegiance in March, 1778 [Ref: S-266, but not listed in Ref: C-30].

RICKETS, Robert. Private who enlisted August 5, 1776 [Ref: A-44].

RICKEY, John and Mary. See "John Middagh," q.v.

RICKNAGLE, Joseph. Private in the German Regiment until discharged on July 26, 1779 [Ref: A-243].

RICKS, John and Catharine. See "John Smith," q.v.

RIDDLE, Benjamin. Provided wheat for the military in June, 1782 [Ref: R-520].

RIDENHOUSE, John. Sergeant in Capt. James Johnson's company of militia on November 29, 1775 [Ref: E-52].

RIDENOUR, Barnard. Militia substitute on June 3, 1778 [Ref: A-324]. "Bernhard Rodenhour" was a private in the German Regiment at White Plains on September 5, 1778. under Lt. Col. Weltner [Ref: A-267].

RIDENOUR, Jacob. Private stationed at Fort Frederick on June 27, 1778, in Capt. John Kershner's company, guarding prisoners of war [Ref: A-328]. "Jacob Ridingour" enlisted on July 20, 1776 by Capt. Jacob Good [Ref: A-46]. "Jacob Redenour" was a private pensioned in Frederick County on November 19, 1819, at $60 per annum under the Act of March 3, 1809, dating from April 10, 1806. [Ref: G-384]. "Jacob Ridenour applied for pension (S4075) in Washington County, Maryland, on October 30, 1819." [Ref: T-2885, J-9].

RIDENOUR [RIDENHOUR], John. Private in the German Regiment in 1776, in Capt. Henry Fister's company under the command of Col. Hussecker [Ref: A-261]. "John Redenour" was a private who enlisted on July 1, 1776, in Capt. Peter Mantz's company; marched from Frederick Town to Leonardtown, and from there to Philadelphia, arriving on August 23, 1776 [Ref: A-47].

RIDENOUR, Magdalena. See "John Smith," q.v.

RIDER, William. Private who enlisted on May 20, 1778 [Ref: A-323]. Served in the German Regiment at White Plains on September 5, 1778, under Lt. Col. Ludwick Weltner [Ref: A-266].

RIDGE, Cornelius. Associator in December, 1775 [Ref: E-172]. Juror to the Oath of Allegiance in 1778 [Ref: C-28].

RIDGE, William (cooper). Militia substitute on June 6, 1778 [Ref: A-325]. Militia substitute from May to December 10, 1781, and "marched to Annapolis." [Ref: A-653].

RIDGE, William. Sergeant in Capt. Robert Wood's company of militia on November 29, 1775 [Ref: E-53]. Associator in December, 1775 [Ref: E-172]. Ensign in 37th Battalion of militia on December 28, 1776, under Col. James Johnson [Ref: B-116, X-555]. Juror to the Oath of Allegiance in 1778 [Ref: C-28].

RIDGELY [RIDGLEY], Frederick. Surgeon in the 34th Battalion on January 10, 1777 [Ref: B-116].

RIDGELY [RIDGLEY], Jacob. Sergeant in Capt. William Luckett, Jr.'s company of militia on November 29, 1775 [Ref: E-55]. Associator in December, 1775 [Ref: E-172]. Juror to the Oath of Allegiance in 1778 [Ref: C-28].

RIDGELY [RIDGLEY], Westall (Catoctin Hundred). Appointed by the Committee of Correspondence to solicit subscriptions in 1775 to purchase arms and ammunition [Ref: I-86]. Served on the Committee of Observation in 1775 [Ref: I-85]. 1st lieutenant in Capt. Herman Yost's company of militia in the 1st Battalion on November 29, 1775 [Ref: E-52, B-116]. Associator in December, 1775 [Ref: E-172]. Juror to the Oath of Allegiance in 1778 [Ref: C-28].

RIDGELY [RIDGLEY]. Richard. Sergeant in Capt. Herman Yost's company of militia on November 29, 1775 [Ref: E-52].

RIDING, John. Defective from Maryland Line in 1780 [Ref: A-414].

RIDINGER, Andrew. See "Jacob Gilbert," q.v.

RIEKEBROAD, Godlip. Associator in December, 1775 [Ref: E-172]. Juror to the Oath of Allegiance in 1778 [Ref: C-28].

305

RIELY, Barny. Private who enlisted on July 19, 1776 [Ref: A-51]. "Bernard Riely" was a private in the German Regiment who was reported "deserted" on November 6, 1780 [Ref: A-243].

RIELY, Conrad. Private in the German Regiment until discharged on July 24, 1779 [Ref: A-243].

RIELY [RIELEY], John. Private in the 7th Maryland Regiment from April 25, 1778, until February 20, 1780, when reported "deserted." [Ref: A-243]. He apparently enlisted again in Frederick Town some time between January and April, 1780 [Ref: A-334].

RIELY [RILEY], Patrick. Corporal in the 7th Maryland Regiment on May 3, 1778, and a private on October 6, 1778 [Ref: A-241, A-321]. Private in the 1st Maryland Regiment, and served in the Southern Army of the United States under Lt. William Lamar in the late Capt. Beatty's company in 1780 [Ref: A-390]. He was reported "deserted" on August 15, 1780 (the day before the Battle of Camden), but he apparently served as a wagoner in July, 1781 [Ref: A-241, A-390].

RIENAKER, Paul. Associator in December, 1775 [Ref: E-171]. Juror to the Oath of Allegiance in 1778 [Ref: C-28].

RIEVENOCK, Philip. Associator in December, 1775 [Ref: E-172]. Juror to the Oath of Allegiance in 1778 [Ref: C-28]. "Philip Reevenach" was a corporal in the German Regiment, on muster roll dated October 23, 1776 [Ref: A-263].

RIGGLEMAN, George. See "George Regalman," q.v.

RIGGS, Amon [Amos]. "Amos Riggs" served on Committee of Observation in 1775 [Ref: I-85]. "Amon Riggs" was commissioned captain in the Lower District Militia on March 26, 1776 [Ref: W-287].

RIGGS, John. Private in the 7th Maryland Regiment who enlisted in Frederick Town on May 6, 1780 [Ref: A-334, V-175]. Drummer in the 1st Maryland Regiment in the Southern Army of the United States under Lt. William Lamar in the late Capt. Beatty's company until transferred to the light infantry on March 12, 1781 [Ref: A-389].

RIGGS, Samuel. 2nd lieutenant in Capt. N. Pigman's company, 29th Battalion of militia, on May 14, 1776. [Ref: D-1814, W-289, W-424].

RIGHTMYER [RIGHTMIRE], Michael. Private who enlisted on February 1, 1780, for 3 years, in Capt. Michael Bayer's company in the German Regiment [Ref: A-268, V-126].

RIGNALL, Jacob. Private in the Middle District Militia in 1776 in Capt. Valentine Creager's company [Ref: A-72].

RILEY, Patrick. See "Patrick Riely," q.v.

RILEY, Thomas. Associator in December, 1775 [Ref: E-172]. Juror to the Oath of Allegiance in 1778 [Ref: C-28].

RILY, Michael. Private who enlisted on August 5, 1776 [Ref: A-44].

RILY, Zachariah. Private who enlisted on July 29, 1776 [Ref: A-43].

RINE, Casper. Drafted June 2, 1783; "never appeared." [Ref: B-169].

RINE, Patrick. Private who enlisted on July 25, 1776 [Ref: A-49].

RINEHART, Andrew. Private in the 6th Maryland Regiment from July 1, 1778, until April 1, 1779, when he was discharged [Ref: A-242].

RINEHART, Simon. Private in the German Regiment, 1776 [Ref: A-266].

RINER, George. Juror to the Oath of Allegiance in March, 1778 [Ref: S-266, but not listed in Ref: C-30].

RINGER, Andrew. Private who enlisted on July 1, 1776 in Capt. Peter Mantz's company; marched from Frederick Town to Leonardtown, and from there to Philadelphia, arriving August 23, 1776 [Ref: A-47]. Private in Capt. William Beatty's company, 7th Maryland Regiment, 1779 [Ref: A-310].

RINGER, Jacob. Private in the Middle District Militia, 1776, in Capt. Valentine Creager's company [Ref: A-72].

RINGER, John. Associator in December, 1775 [Ref: E-172]. Private in German Regiment in 1776, in Capt. Henry Fister's company under the command of Col. Nicholas Hussecker [Ref: A-261]. Juror to the Oath of Allegiance in 1778 [Ref: C-28].

RINGER, Matthias (Middle Monocacy). Appointed by the Committee of Correspondence to solicit subscriptions in 1775 to purchase arms and ammunition [Ref: I-86]. Associator in December, 1775, who was appointed "to hand about the Association paper in Middle Monocacy Hundred." [Ref: E-171, E-305].

RINGGOLD, Cornelia. See "Richard Potts," q.v.

RINKER, John. Private in the militia on March 9, 1776 [Ref: B-167].

RIPPLE, Edward. Non-Enroller who was fined by the Committee of Observation in April, 1776 [Ref: E-248].

RISMEL, George. Private who enlisted on July 19, 1776 [Ref: A-51].

RISNAR, Tobias. Associator in December, 1775 [Ref: E-172]. Juror to the Oath of Allegiance in 1778 [Ref: C-28].

RISSER, Conrad. Associator in December, 1775 [Ref: E-172]. Juror to the Oath of Allegiance in 1778 [Ref: C-28].

RISTON, Samuel (Burnt House Woods Hundred). Non-Enroller who was fined by the Committee of Observation in June, 1776 [Ref: E-248].

RITCHEY, Solomon and Rachael. See "Levi Davis," q.v.

RITCHIE, John (Colonel). Died on November 16, 1826, age 70. Anna Ritchie, wife of John, died December 15, 1826, age 55 [Ref: F-472].
RITCHIE [RICHEY], William. "William Richey" was an Associator in December, 1775 [Ref: E-172]. Juror to the Oath of Allegiance in 1778 [Ref: C-28]. "William Ritchie" was a quartermaster in the 33rd Battalion of militia on March 26, 1776 [Ref: B-116]. Clerk for the Council of Safety in 1776 [Ref: W-199]. Clerk of the Circuit Court, 1779-1815 [Ref: F-480]. Also, see "William Richey," q.v.
RITE, John. Private who enlisted on August 5, 1776, in the Flying Camp under Capt. Philip Meroney, and reported as "deserted" (no date given). [Ref: A-45]. However, Ref: N-30:112 listed this name as "John Price" and indicated he had "deserted" (no date given).
RITMEYER, Conrad. Soldier in the Maryland Line who "applied for a pension (R8817) on February 27, 1841, in Frederick County, aged 77, stating he lived there at the time of enlistment in Frederick Town. He was born March, 1764, at Reading, Berks County, Pennsylvania." [Ref: T-2897].
RITMIRE, Michael. Private in the German Regiment from February 1, 1780, to at least January 1, 1781 [Ref: A-243].
RITTER, Tobias. Drafted on May 1, 1781; "marched." [Ref: D-1814].
RITTLEMEYER, George. Private in the German Regiment until he was discharged on August 11, 1779 [Ref: A-2432].
ROACH, John. Private who enlisted on April 21, 1778 [Ref: A-324]. Served in the German Regiment at White Plains on September 5, 1778, under Lt. Col. Ludwick Weltner [Ref: A-266].
ROAD, Henry. Associator in December, 1775 [Ref: E-172]. Juror to the Oath of Allegiance in 1778 [Ref: C-28].
ROADES, Jacob. See "Jacob Rhodes," q.v.
ROBERTS, Archibald. Militia substitute from May to December 10, 1781, and "marched to Annapolis." [Ref: A-653]. "Archibald Roberts, or Robards, applied for a pension on May 21, 1832, in Hardy County, Virginia, aged 68 or 69, stating he was born in Frederick County, Maryland, and married Mary Ann Bosley there in August, 1787, and enlisted in the Maryland Line. They moved to Hardy County around 1802, where he died April 18, 1836. His widow applied for pension (W5737) on December 4, 1839, in Hardy County, Virginia, aged 74, and applied for bounty land warrant no. 11395-160-55 on April 13, 1855, at which time her age was 90." [Ref: T-2900].
ROBERTS, Henry. Drafted on June 2, 1783 and "appeared before Gen. William Smallwood and suffered (?) to return home." [Ref: B-169].

ROBERTS, John. Juror to the Oath of Allegiance in March, 1778 [Ref: S-266, but not listed in Ref: C-30].

ROBERTS, Nathan. Private who enlisted August 5, 1776 [Ref: A-44].

ROBERTS, Richard. Non-Enroller who was fined by the Committee of Observation in April, 1776 [Ref: E-248].

ROBERTS, Robert. Associator in December, 1775 [Ref: E-171]. Juror to the Oath of Allegiance in 1778 [Ref: C-28].

ROBERTS, Thomas. Private who enlisted March 10, 1778 [Ref: A-315].

ROBERTS, William. Associator in December, 1775 [Ref: E-171]. Juror to the Oath of Allegiance in 1778 [Ref: C-28].

ROBERTS, William Jr. Associator in December, 1775 [Ref: E-172]. Juror to the Oath of Allegiance in 1778 [Ref: C-28].

ROBERTSON, Edward. Private in the German Regiment in 1776 in Capt. Henry Fister's company under the command of Col. Nicholas Hussecker [Ref: A-261].

ROBERTSON, James. Associator in December, 1775 [Ref: E-171]. Juror to the Oath of Allegiance in 1778 [Ref: C-28].

ROBERTSON, John. Private who was enlisted on July 20, 1776 by Capt. Jacob Good [Ref: A-46]. Private in the German Regiment, roll dated October 23, 1776 [Ref: A-264].

ROBESON, William. Associator in December, 1775 [Ref: E-171]. Juror to the Oath of Allegiance in 1778 [Ref: C-28].

ROBINSON, Andrew. Drafted on June 2, 1783 [Ref: B-168].

ROBINSON, Charles. Sergeant in Capt. William Shields' company of militia on November 29, 1775 [Ref: E-55]. Ensign in Capt. John Shields' company of militia on December 26, 1776 [Ref: X-555].

ROBINSON, Edward. Militia substitute from May to December 10, 1781, and "marched to Annapolis." [Ref: A-653].

ROBINSON, James. Soldier who served in the Maryland, New Jersey, and Pennsylvania Lines and "applied for a pension (S7432) on March 19, 1833, in Harrison County, Virginia, aged 85, stating he lived in Frederick County, Maryland, at enlistment and in 1785 moved to Virginia." [Ref: T-2919].

ROBINSON, John. Private stationed at Fort Frederick on June 27, 1778, in Capt. John Kershner's company, and guarding prisoners of war [Ref: A-328].

ROBINSON, Richard. Associator in December, 1775 [Ref: E-171]. Juror to the Oath of Allegiance in 1778 [Ref: C-28].

ROBINSON, Sarah Ann. See "Benjamin Yates (Yeats)," q.v.

ROBISON, Abram. Provided wheat for the military in May, 1782 [Ref: R-515].

ROBISON, Thomas. Private who enlisted on July 19, 1776 [Ref: A-51].

ROCHE, John. Drummer in Capt. Benjamin Ogle, Jr.'s company of militia on November 29, 1775 [Ref: E-54].

RODDY, Henry. Petitioned the General Assembly under the Act of May 12, 1780, stating he had been a non-juror to the Oath of Allegiance and Fidelity in 1778 due to "ignorance" and now desired relief under the Act and to take the Oath [Ref: L-101].

RODENBUSH, Daniel. Associator in December, 1775 [Ref: E-172]. Juror to the Oath of Allegiance in 1778 [Ref: C-28, and S-266, which latter source spelled his name "Daniel Roudabush."].

RODENPIELLER, Philip. "Philip Rodenbeiler" was captain of a company of militia, 4th Battalion, on November 29, 1775 [Ref: E-51, B-117]. "Philip Rodenpillar" was a captain in the 3rd Battalion on November 29, 1775 [Ref: E-312]. "Capt. Philip Rodenpieller, drafted June 2, 1783, says he is over age and refuses to pay... he was a commission [officer]... and is sick." [Ref: B-168]. "Philip Rodenpiller" died testate in 1793, leaving a wife Rachel and mentioning friend Jacob Wise and brother-in-law Conrad Shafer [Ref: M-8:182].

RODMAN, Daniel. See "William Edward Head," q.v.

ROE, Obediah. Private in the 7th Maryland Regiment from May 9, 1778 to July, 1778, when reported "off rolls." [Ref: A-243].

ROE, William. Defective from Maryland Line in 1780 [Ref: A-414].

ROGERS, John. Associator in December, 1775 [Ref: E-171]. Juror to the Oath of Allegiance in 1778 [Ref: C-28].

ROGERS [RODGERS], John. "Pardon [was] granted to John Rodgers of Frederick County convicted at the last March Court for said county on condition that he forthwith enlist himself into one of the regiments of the quota of this State in the Continental Army and do not desert therefrom, that he pay all charges incurred in carrying on the prosecution, pay four fold to the persons injured, and that he do not in future reside in the neighborhood where the offence was committed." [Ref: V-141]. "John Rogers" enlisted on April 10, 1780, for 3 years in Capt. Michael Bayer's company [Ref: A-268].

ROHR, Michael. Associator in December, 1775 [Ref: E-172]. Juror to the Oath of Allegiance in 1778 [Ref: C-28].

ROHRAR [RHOAR, ROHR], Jacob. "Jacob Rohrar" was an Associator in December, 1775 [Ref: E-172]. "Jacob Rhoar" was a corporal in Capt. Charles Beatty's company of militia on November 29, 1775 [Ref: E-51].

"Jacob Rorer" was a private in Capt. John Kershner's company, guarded prisoners at Fort Frederick, 1777-1778, until discharged on May 20, 1778 [Ref: A-328]. "Jacob Rohrar" subscribed to the Oath of Allegiance, 1778 [Ref: C-28].

ROHRAR, Rudolph. Associator in December, 1775 [Ref: E-172].

ROLAND, Abraham. Non-Enroller who was fined by the Committee of Observation in May, 1776 [Ref: E-248].

ROLE, John Jr. Associator in December, 1775 [Ref: E-171]. Juror to the Oath of Allegiance in 1778 [Ref: C-28].

ROLE, John Sr. Associator in December, 1775 [Ref: E-171]. Juror to the Oath of Allegiance in 1778 [Ref: C-28].

RONENBERGER, Charles. Private in the German Regiment from June 6, 1780, to at least January 1, 1781 [Ref: A-243].

ROOT, Daniel. See "Henry Crowell," q.v.

ROPP, Jacob. Associator in December, 1775 [Ref: E-172]. Juror to the Oath of Allegiance in 1778 [Ref: C-28].

ROPP, Philip. Drafted June 2, 1783; "paid 6 pounds." [Ref: B-168].

ROPP, Simon. Corporal in Capt. John Stoner's company of militia on November 29, 1775 [Ref: E-56]. Associator in 1775 [Ref: E-172]. Juror to the Oath of Allegiance in 1778 [Ref: C-28].

RORER, Jacob. See "Jacob Rohrar," q.v.

ROSE, Edward. Private in the militia who was disabled in New Jersey and his invalid pension commenced on April 24, 1786, and ceased on October 24, 1788, with the cause of pension ceasing as "removed or supposed dead." [Ref: A-630, A-631, F-476].

ROSENSTEIL, George. "George Rosensteel" was 3rd corporal in Capt. Philip Thomas' company of militia on November 29, 1775 [Ref: E-50]. "George Rosensteil" was an Associator in December, 1775 [Ref: E-172]. Juror to the Oath of Allegiance in 1778 [Ref: C-28].

ROSS, Alexander. Private, 1st Maryland Regiment, 1781, who served in the Southern Army of the United States under Lt. William Lamar in the late Capt. Beatty's company [Ref: A-389].

ROSS, General. See "John Stricker," q.v.

ROSS, John. Private in the 7th Maryland Regiment who enlisted in Frederick Town between January and April, 1780, and was reported as "gone to Camp" [Ref: A-334].

ROSS, Joseph. Private who enlisted on August 5, 1776 [Ref: A-44].

ROSSTELL, Joseph. Private in the 7th Maryland Regiment from January 12, 1778, until February 8, 1778, when he "deserted." [Ref: A-243].

ROTE, Christian. Non-Enroller who was fined by the Committee of Observation in April, 1776 [Ref: E-248].

ROTHE, John. Private in the German Regiment, muster roll dated October 23, 1776 [Ref: A-264].

ROTHROCK, Catherine. See "Leonard Ludwick," q.v.

ROUDABUSH, Daniel. See "Daniel Rodenbush," q.v.

ROUGH, Peter. Private stationed at Fort Frederick on June 27, 1778, with Capt. John Kershner's company, and guarded prisoners of war [Ref: A-328].

ROUSER, John. Associator in December, 1775 [Ref: E-171]. Juror to the Oath of Allegiance in 1778 [Ref: C-28]. One Henry Rouser died testate in 1794, leaving wife Eve and several children, including a son John Rouser [Ref: M-9:40].

ROUTSANG, Conrad. Fifer in Capt. Michael McGuire's company of militia on November 29, 1775 [Ref: E-57].

ROUZER, Daniel. See "Peter Shover," q.v.

ROW, Andrew. Associator in December, 1775 [Ref: E-171]. Juror to the Oath of Allegiance in 1778 [Ref: C-28].

ROW, Arthur. Corporal in Capt. Blair's militia company on November 29, 1775 [Ref: E-55]. Associator in December, 1775 [Ref: E-171]. Juror to the Oath of Allegiance in 1778 [Ref: C-28].

ROW, George. Associator in December, 1775 [Ref: E-171]. Juror to the Oath of Allegiance in 1778 [Ref: C-28].

ROW, John. Drummer in Capt. Peter Mantz's company of militia on November 29, 1775 [Ref: E-50]. Associator in December, 1775 [Ref: E-172]. (This name appeared twice on the list of Associators). One subscribed to the Oath of Allegiance in 1778 [Ref: C-28].

ROW, Michael. Associator in December, 1775 [Ref: E-171]. Juror to the Oath of Allegiance in 1778 [Ref: C-28].

ROWE, George. Associator in December, 1775 [Ref: E-172]. Juror to the Oath of Allegiance in 1778 [Ref: C-28].

ROWAN, Lydia. See "Jacob Brunner," q.v.

ROWIN, Patrick. Private in the Middle District Militia in 1776 in Capt. Valentine Creager's company [Ref: A-72].

ROWLANDS, Thomas. Militia substitute on June 6, 1778 [Ref: A-325]. He served as a private in the German Regiment at White Plains on September 5, 1778, under Lt. Col. Ludwick Weltner [Ref: A-267].

ROWLER, Rachel. See "Mathias Firestone," q.v.

ROWLINS, Solomon. 2nd corporal in the Middle District Militia in 1776 in Capt. Valentine Creager's company [Ref: A-72].

ROWSON, Christian. Petitioned the General Assembly under the Act of July 3, 1780, stating that he had been a non-juror to the Oath of Allegiance and Fidelity in 1778 due to "ignorance" and now desired relief under the Act and to take the Oath [Ref: L-101].

ROXBURGH, Major. See "Henry Reese," q.v.

RUBEL, Peter. Provided wheat for the military in July, 1782 [Ref: R-529].

RUDISCAL, Michael. Associator in December, 1775 [Ref: E-172]. Juror to the Oath of Allegiance in 1778 [Ref: C-28].

RUDRIECK, Mathew. Private who enlisted July 1, 1776 in Capt. Peter Mantz's company; marched from Frederick Town to Leonardtown, and from there to Philadelphia, arriving August 23, 1776 [Ref: A-47].

RUDY, Daniel. Non-Enroller who was fined by the Committee of Observation in April, 1776 [Ref: E-248].

RUDY, Tarter. Associator in December, 1775 [Ref: E-172]. Juror to the Oath of Allegiance in 1778 [Ref: C-28].

RUHOR, Peter. Provided wheat for the military in May, 1782 [Ref: R-518].

RULOFF, Gilbert. Provided wheat for the military in July, 1782 [Ref: R-535].

RUNEY, John. Drafted on June 13, 1781, and "sick." [Ref: D-1814].

RUNION, Isaac. Corporal in Capt. Jacob Good's company of militia on November 29, 1775 [Ref: E-51].

RUNKLE, Jacob. Associator in December, 1775 [Ref: E-172]. Juror to the Oath of Allegiance in 1778 [Ref: C-28, S-266].

RUPPERT, Jacob. Private in the German Regiment from 1776 until he was discharged on July 15, 1779 [Ref: A-243, A-266].

RUSH, Lewis. Appointed in early 1776 to be quartermaster to the 33rd battalion in Frederick County, but declined because he had accepted a commission in the Pennsylvania troops [Ref: W-198].

RUSS, Adam. Corporal in Capt. Carmack's militia company on November 29, 1775 [Ref: E-56]. Associator in December, 1775 [Ref: E-171]. Private in the Middle District Militia in 1776 in Capt. Creager's company [Ref: A-72]. Juror to the Oath of Allegiance in 1778 [Ref: C-28].

RUSS, John. Associator in December, 1775 [Ref: E-171]. Juror to the Oath of Allegiance in 1778 [Ref: C-28].

RUSSEL, Caleb. Private in the Skipton District Militia under Capt. Thomas Waring on April 16, 1776 [Ref: B-167, D-1814].

RUTHERFORD, Alliner. Private who enlisted in 1780 [Ref: A-345].

RUTLIDGE, Stephen. Private who enlisted July 19, 1776 [Ref: A-51].

313

RYAN, Burnett. "Burnett Rian" provided wheat for the military in May, 1782 [Ref: R-514].

RYAN, Edward and Polly. See "Matthias Young," q.v.

RYAN, John. Private in the militia in July, 1776 [Ref: A-42].

RYAN, William. Associator in December, 1775 [Ref: E-172]. Juror to the Oath of Allegiance in 1778 [Ref: C-28].

RYLET, Edward. Private who enlisted in Frederick on August 1, 1780, but "not marched [to Annapolis] for want of pay." [Ref: A-344].

RYLEY, Patrick. Private who enlisted on July 19, 1776 [Ref: A-51].

SABATER, William. Private in militia on March 9, 1776 [Ref: B-167].

SAFFLE, Charles. Private who enlisted on July 29, 1776 [Ref: A-44].

SAFLEY [SAFTLY], Henry. "Henry Saftly" was a private who enlisted on July 24, 1776 [Ref: A-50]. "Henry Safley applied for a pension (S4809) on April 20, 1833, in Champaign County, Ohio, stating he served in the Maryland and Virginia Lines. He was born in November, 1759, in York County, Pennsylvania, and lived in Frederick County, Maryland at the time of his first enlistment. He later moved to Augusta County, Virginia, and also enlisted there. He lived there after the Revolution, and moved to Rockingham County, Virginia and then to Botetourt County, Virginia. In 1820 he moved to Champaign County, Ohio." [Ref: T-2996].

SAGE, Thomas. Juror to the Oath of Allegiance in March, 1778 [Ref: S-266, but not listed in Ref: C-30].

SAILOR, Alexander. Private in the German Regiment, muster roll dated October 23, 1776 [Ref: A-264].

SALEGH, Nicholas. Private in the 7th Maryland Regiment from May 18, 1778 until August 16, 1780, when reported missing (after the Battle of Camden, South Carolina). [Ref: A-249].

SALMON, Edward. Private who enlisted on August 5, 1776, in the Flying Camp under Capt. Philip Meroney [Ref: A-45, N-30:112]. 1st lieutenant in the Frederick Town Battalion of militia on April or May 15, 1778, and a captain on August 16, 1779 [Ref: H-15, B-118, Z-35]. He died on June 30, 1808 [Ref: F-471].

SAMSEL, Devalt (March 17, 1741 - September 19, 1804). Private in Bucks County, Pennsylvania, in 1775, he married Anna Maria Erbach and a daughter Elizabeth Samsel was born on July 28, 1783, in Montgomery County, Pennsylvania. Devalt (Dewald) Samsel died in Middletown, Frederick County, Maryland, in 1804." [Ref: U-2928].

SANDS, Alexander. Soldier in the Maryland Line who "applied for a pension (R9191) on September 28, 1835, Monroe County, Ohio, stating he was born on January 16, 1760, in Baltimore County, Maryland, and lived there at enlistment. He lived in Frederick County and Anne Arundel County, Maryland, before moving to Monroe County, Ohio." [Ref: T-3014, but not listed in *Archives of Maryland, Volume 18*].

SANDS, Thomas. Private who enlisted on July 24, 1776 [Ref: A-50].

SANKY, John. Private in the 7th Maryland Regiment from May 16, 1778 until reported dead on May 13, 1779 [Ref: A-250].

SANSON, Luke. Private, 1st Maryland Regiment, who was disabled at the Battle of Guilford Courthouse. His invalid pension commenced on November 16, 1783, and ceased on October 16, 1785, with the cause of pension ceasing as "dead." [Ref: A-630, A-631].

SAPPS, Jacob. Private in the Skipton District Militia under Capt. Thomas Waring on April 16, 1776 [Ref: B-167, D-1814].

SAUM, Rachel. See "John Cronise," q.v.

SAUNDERS, John. Private who enlisted in Frederick on August 21, 1780, and "marched to Annapolis" under Capt. Beatty [Ref: A-344].

SAUT, Adam P. Associator in December, 1775 [Ref: E-172]. Juror to the Oath of Allegiance in 1778 [Ref: C-28]. See "Adam Psaut," q.v.

SAYLER, Christian. Non-Enroller who was fined by the Committee of Observation in April, 1776 [Ref: E-248].

SAYLER, Daniel. Non-Enroller who was fined by the Committee of Observation in April, 1776 [Ref: E-248].

SCAGGS, Christopher. "Draught," May to December 10, 1781, and "marched to Annapolis." [Ref: A-653].

SCAGGS, Richard. Sergeant in Capt. William Duvall's company of militia on November 29, 1775 [Ref: E-54].

SCAGGS, William. "Draught," May to December 10, 1781, and "marched to Annapolis." [Ref: A-653]. Drafted on June 2, 1783; "marched with cattle to Fredericksburg." [Ref: B-168].

SCHAAFF, Caspar. Served on the Committee of Observation in 1775 [Ref: I-85].

SCHAPPART, Nicholas. Associator in December, 1775 [Ref: E-173]. (This name appeared twice on the list of Associators). Subscribed to the Oath of Allegiance in 1778 [Ref: C-28].

SCHAPPART, Philip. Associator in December, 1775 [Ref: E-173]. Juror to the Oath of Allegiance in 1778 [Ref: C-28].

SCHARF, J. Thomas. See "Thomas Cresap," q.v.

SCHARTZ, Samuel. Non-Enroller who was fined by the Committee of Observation in April, 1776, but was subsequently determined to be "ineffective" and the fine was remitted in June, 1776 [Ref: E-248].

SCHEFFE, Adam. Associator in December, 1775 [Ref: E-173]. Juror to the Oath of Allegiance in 1778 [Ref: C-28].
SCHEVEL, John. Private who enlisted on April 10, 1778 [Ref: A-315].
SCHILDKNECHT, Calvin E. See "John Smith (Johan Schmidt)," q.v.
SCHISLER, Anne (Anna) Maria. See "Conrod Doll," q.v.
SCHLEY, Francina and Frederick. See "David Lynn," q.v.
SCHLEY, Jacob. 1st lieutenant in Capt. John Haass' company of militia on November 29, 1775 [Ref: E-53, B-118]. Associator in December, 1775 [Ref: E-173]. Juror to the Oath of Allegiance in 1778 [Ref: C-28]. Contracted to "supply 10 large rifles carrying a ball of four ounces weight for a sum not exceeding 15 lbs. each." [Ref: W-353]. Loaned $1,000 for the use of the State of Maryland in June, 1780 [Ref: V-520]. "(George) Jacob Schley (1735-1811) married 1761 at Lancaster, Pennsylvania, to Margaret Fortney (c1743-1821). He was a gunsmith and served in the Revolution. Had a son John George (1767-1835)." [Ref: O-39]. Also, see "John Thomas Schley," q.v.
SCHLEY, John. Juror to the Oath of Allegiance in 1778 [Ref: C-28].
SCHLEY, John Jacob. Associator in December, 1775 [Ref: E-173]. Juror to the Oath of Allegiance in 1778 [Ref: C-28]. Together with John Shellman he loaned $1,000 for the use of the State of Maryland in June, 1780 [Ref: V-520]. "John Jacob Schley, born in Frederick County, died on October 16, 1829, aged 77, in Louisville, Jefferson County, Georgia [sic], and was the father of Frederick A. Schley." (An obvious mistake since Louisville is in Jefferson County, Kentucky, not Georgia). [Ref: F-473].
SCHLEY, John Thomas (1712-1790). He came to Maryland in 1744 from Moerzheim, south Pfalz, Germany, settling at Frederick [Ref: O-38]. He married Margaret Von Wintz in 1735 in Germany, and a son George Jacob Schley (1735-1811) married Margaret Forteney in 1765. John Thomas Schley served on the Committee of Correspondence in 1774 and on the Committee of Observation in 1775 [Ref: U-1032]. He built the first house in Frederick in 1746, and died on November 24, 1790, aged 78 [Ref: F-470]. Also, see "Jacob Schley," q.v.
SCHLEY, Paul. Private who enlisted on July 19, 1776 [Ref: A-51].
SCHLEY, Thomas. Associator in December, 1775, and appointed "to hand about the Association paper" in Frederick Town [Ref: E-173, E-305]. Juror to the Oath of Allegiance in 1778 [Ref: C-28]. Loaned $600 for the use of the State of Maryland in June, 1780 [Ref: V-520].
SCHLEY, Thomas Jr. Associator in December, 1775 [Ref: E-173]. Non-Enroller fined by the Committee of Observation in April, 1776 [Ref: E-

248]. Juror to the Oath of Allegiance in 1778 [Ref: C-28]. Loaned $200 for the use of the State of Maryland in June, 1780 [Ref: V-520]. Yet, when drafted June 2, 1783, he was excused as he "has a large family and is poor but... pay a small sum of money." [Ref: B-168].

SCHLIFER, John. Non-Enroller who was fined by the Committee of Observation in April, 1776 [Ref: E-248].

SCHLIM, Elizabeth. See "Andrew Williard," q.v.

SCHMID [SCHMIDT], Johannes, et al. See "John Smith," q.v.

SCHMIT, Catherine. See "Joseph Doll," q.v.

SCHMITIN, Julia Ann. See "Christian Shank," q.v.

SCHNEBELY, Henry. Served in the House of Delegates from the Upper District on August 14, 1776 [Ref: F-476, F-479].

SCHNEIDER, Christopher. 4th Corporal in Capt. Philip Thomas' company of militia on November 29, 1775 [Ref: E-50]. Associator in December, 1775 [Ref: E-173]. Juror to the Oath of Allegiance in 1778 [Ref: C-28].

SCHNEIDER, Conrad. Associator in December, 1775 [Ref: E-173]. Juror to the Oath of Allegiance in 1778 [Ref: C-28].

SCHNEIDER, George. Associator in December, 1775 [Ref: E-173]. Juror to the Oath of Allegiance in 1778 [Ref: C-28].

SCHNEIDER, Jacob. Associator in December, 1775 [Ref: E-173]. Juror to the Oath of Allegiance in 1778 [Ref: C-28].

SCHNEIDER, John (of Jacob). Non-Enroller who was fined by the Committee of Observation in April, 1776 [Ref: E-248].

SCHNERTZELL, George. "George Schnertzell" was an Associator in December, 1775 [Ref: E-173]. Juror to the Oath of Allegiance in 1778 [Ref: C-28, S-266]. Petitioned to form horse troops in 1781 [Ref: B-167]. "George Schnertzell, Sr." died on November 22, 1810 [Ref: F-471].

SCHRINER [SHRINER, SHINER], John. Soldier in the Maryland, New Jersey and Pennsylvania Lines who "applied for a pension (R9632) on May 29, 1834, in Wayne County, Ohio, stating he was born February 21, 1753, in Bucks County, Pennsylvania. He lived there at the time of his enlistment, but his parents lived in Frederick County, Maryland, where he enlisted for his 3rd and 4th tours. He moved to Wayne County, Ohio, in 1821 [no date of death shown]. His widow Barbary applied for a pension (no number given) on October 3, 1853, in Morrow County, Ohio, aged 86." [Ref: T-3124].

SCHRINER, Valentine. Associator in December, 1775 [Ref: E-173]. Juror to the Oath of Allegiance in 1778 [Ref: C-28]. "Valentine Sheiner" provided wheat for the military in May, 1782 [Ref: R-515]. "Valentine

Shriner" married in 1751 to Anna Elizabeth Wolf, of Lancaster, and moved to Frederick about 1756. Their children were Eva Margaret (born 1757), Susanna (born 1759), Charlotte Amalia (born 1761), and John George (born 1771). [Ref: O-219]. "Valentine Shriner" died on May 8, 1812 [Ref: F-471].

SCHRIVER, David (Pipe Creek Hundred). Appointed by the Committee of Correspondence to solicit subscriptions in 1775 to purchase arms and ammunition [Ref: I-86]. Served on the Committee of Observation in 1775 [Ref: I-85].

SCHULTZ, Daniel. Associator in December, 1775 [Ref: E-173]. Juror to the Oath of Allegiance in 1778 [Ref: C-28].

SCHULTZ, Valentine. Sergeant in Capt. Baltzel's Company, served 3 years, and discharged August 13, 1779, at Camp Tioga [Ref: A-271].

SCHUYLER, Philip. Major General who died in Frederick, Maryland some time before December 7, 1804, aged 70 [Ref: N-57].

SCHWAB, Eva Catharine. See "Nicholas Firestone Jr.," q.v.

SCOTT, George (1736-1809). Served on the Committee of Observation in 1775 [Ref: I-85]. Associator in December, 1775 [Ref: E-173]. Juror to the Oath of Allegiance in 1778 [Ref: C-28, S-266]. Justice of the Peace in 1777. Judge of the Orphans' Court in 1783 [Ref: F-476, F-480]. Appointed the Solicitor for Frederick County to raise funds for the use of the State of Maryland on June 6, 1780 [Ref: V-510]. He married Mary Ann Young by 1769, and their known children were George and Eleanor; perhaps 3 others [Ref: P-715].

SCOTT, Hugh. Non-Enroller who was fined by the Committee of Observation in April, 1776 [Ref: E-248]. Provided wheat for the military in May, 1782 [Ref: R-517].

SCOTT, John. Private in the Skipton District Militia under Capt. Thomas Waring on April 16, 1776 [Ref: B-167, D-1814]. Sergeant in the 1st Maryland Regiment, enlisted on July 9, 1780, and served in the Southern Army of the United States under Lt. William Lamar in the late Capt. Beatty's company. Reported to have joined the State Regiment on March 12, 1781 [Ref: A-389].

SCOTT, Patrick. Private who enlisted on August 5, 1776, in the Flying Camp under Capt. Philip Meroney [Ref: A-45, N-30:112].

SCOTT, Samuel. Juror to the Oath of Allegiance in March, 1778 [Ref: S-266, but not listed in Ref: C-30].

SCYBERT, George. Private who enlisted August 5, 1776 [Ref: A-44].

SCYBERT, Nicholas. Ensign in the Lower District Militia [now Montgomery County] under Capt. Edward Burgess on August 7, 1776 [Ref: A-42, although Ref: X-187 states he was commissioned on August 5, 1776, and served under Capt. Benjamin Spyker].

SEABURN, Peter. Private who enlisted on July 24, 1776 [Ref: A-50].

SEBURN, John. Private in the 7th Maryland Regiment from April 26, 1777, until May, 1780, when he was discharged [Ref: A-248].

SECHRIT, George. Associator in December, 1775 [Ref: E-173]. Juror to the Oath of Allegiance in 1778 [Ref: C-28].

SECREST, Chs. Paid for the services he rendered to the military in December, 1779 (nature of the services not stated). [Ref: V-44].

SECRIST, Margaret. See "Michael Waltman," q.v.

SEDGWICK, Dorcas. See "Thomas Johnson," q.v.

SEEBRUCKS, Richard. "Draught," May to December 10, 1781, and "marched to Annapolis." [Ref: A-653].

SEEMAN, Balser. Juror to the Oath of Allegiance in March, 1778 [Ref: S-266, but not listed in Ref: C-30].

SEHOM, John. Private who enlisted on August 5, 1776, in the Flying Camp under Capt. Philip Meroney [Ref: A-45, N-30:112].

SEIDEL, Ann Catharina. See "George and John Zimmerman," q.v.

SEIPER, Christian. Juror to the Oath of Allegiance in March, 1778 [Ref: S-266, but not listed in Ref: C-30].

SELF, John. Private who enlisted on July 25, 1776 [Ref: A-50].

SELL, Henry. Associator in December, 1775 [Ref: E-172]. Juror to the Oath of Allegiance in 1778 [Ref: C-28].

SELLERS, Jacob (Salisbury Hundred). Appointed by the Committee of Correspondence to solicit subscriptions in 1775 to purchase arms and ammunition [Ref: I-85].

SELLERS, Robert. Corporal in Capt. Joseph Wood, Jr.'s company of militia on November 29, 1775 [Ref: E-53]. Associator in December, 1775 [Ref: E-172]. Juror to the Oath of Allegiance in 1778 [Ref: C-28]. Private in the Middle District Militia in 1776 in Capt. Valentine Creager's company [Ref: A-72].

SELLMAN, Jonathan. Associator in December, 1775 [Ref: E-173]. Juror to the Oath of Allegiance in 1778 [Ref: C-28].

SELMAN, John. Petitioned the General Assembly under the Act of May 12, 1780, stating he had been a non-juror to the Oath of Allegiance and Fidelity in 1778 due to "ignorance" and now desired relief under the Act and to take the Oath [Ref: L-101]. This or another John Selman also petitioned the General Assembly under the Act of January 14, 1781, stating he had been a non-juror to the Oath of Allegiance and Fidelity in 1778 due to "ignorance" and now desired relief under the Act and to take the Oath [Ref: L-101].

SENSER, George. Associator in December, 1775 [Ref: E-173]. Juror to the Oath of Allegiance in 1778 [Ref: C-28].

SERESHFIELD, Joshua. Sergeant in the Skipton District Militia under Capt. Thomas Waring on April 16, 1776 [Ref: B-167, D-1814].

SERGEANT, Elijah. Associator in December, 1775 [Ref: E-172]. Juror to the Oath of Allegiance in 1778 [Ref: C-28].

SERGEANT, Elisha. Juror to the Oath of Allegiance in March, 1778 [Ref: S-266, but not listed in Ref: C-28].

SERGEANT [SERJEANT], George. Private in the Middle District Militia in 1776 in Capt. Valentine Creager's company [Ref: A-72].

SERGEANT, James Jr. Associator in December, 1775 [Ref: E-172]. Juror to the Oath of Allegiance in 1778 [Ref: C-29].

SERGEANT, James Sr. Associator in December, 1775 [Ref: E-172]. Juror to the Oath of Allegiance in 1778 [Ref: C-29, S-266].

SERGEANT, John. Associator in December, 1775 [Ref: E-172]. Juror to the Oath of Allegiance in 1778 [Ref: C-29].

SERGEANT, Richard. Sergeant in Capt. William Luckett, Jr.'s militia company on November 29, 1775 [Ref: E-55]. Associator in December, 1775 [Ref: E-172]. Juror to the Oath of Allegiance, 1778 [Ref: C-29].

SERGEANT, Richard Jr. Associator in December, 1775 [Ref: E-172]. Juror to the Oath of Allegiance in 1778 [Ref: C-29]. "Richard Sarjeant, Jr.," private, enlisted on August 8, 1776 [Ref: A-49].

SERGEANT, Snowden. Associator in December, 1775 [Ref: E-172]. Juror to the Oath of Allegiance in 1778 [Ref: C-29].

SERGEANT [SARJENT], Thomas. Private who enlisted in 1778 and served in the 2nd Maryland Regiment [Ref: A-294].

SERGEANT, William. Associator in December, 1775 [Ref: E-173]. Juror to the Oath of Allegiance in 1778 [Ref: C-29]. Drafted on June 2, 1783 [Ref: B-168].

SERMAN, Benjamin. Associator in December, 1775 [Ref: E-172]. Juror to the Oath of Allegiance in 1778 [Ref: C-29].

SETTLEMEYER, Chr. Private in the German Regiment until discharged on July 20, 1779 [Ref: A-250].

SEWELL, John. Militia substitute on June 8, 1778 [Ref: A-325].

SEXTON, George. Non-Enroller who was fined by the Committee of Observation in April, 1776 [Ref: E-248].

SHAAFF, Casper. Associator in December, 1775 [Ref: E-173]. Juror to the Oath of Allegiance in 1778 [Ref: C-29].

SHAAFF, George. Juror to the Oath of Allegiance in 1778 [Ref: C-29]. "George Shoaff" was an Associator in December, 1775 [Ref: E-172].

SHACKLER, Frederick. Private stationed at Fort Frederick in June, 1778, in Capt. John Kershner's company, guarding prisoners of war [Ref: A-328].

SHAD, Samuel. Associator in December, 1775 [Ref: E-172]. Juror to the Oath of Allegiance in 1778 [Ref: C-29].

SHADE, Jacob. Private who enlisted on July 1, 1776 in Capt. Peter Mantz's company; marched from Frederick Town to Leonardtown, and from there to Philadelphia, arriving August 23, 1776 [Ref: A-47]. He "applied for a pension (S6082) on February 4, 1833, stating he was born June 24, 1757, in Germany, and lived in Frederick County, Maryland, at enlistment and where he applied for his pension. He said he served in the Maryland and Virginia Lines." [Ref: T-3077].

SHAFER [SHAFFER], Adam. Private in the German Regiment until discharged on July 20, 1779 [Ref: A-251].

SHAFER [SHAFFER], Conrad. Associator in December, 1775 [Ref: E-173]. Juror to the Oath of Allegiance, 1778 [Ref: C-29, S-266]. Also, see "Philip Rodenpieller," q.v.

SHAFER [SHAFFER], Henry. Associator in December, 1775 [Ref: E-173]. Juror to the Oath of Allegiance in 1778 [Ref: C-29].

SHAFER [SHAFFER], John. Associator in December, 1775 [Ref: E-173]. Juror to the Oath of Allegiance in 1778 [Ref: C-29]. He may have been the John Shafer, Jr. (1753-1825) who married Anna Maria Darner (1754-1837) and had a son George Shafer (1787-1857) who married Elizabeth Ramsburg [Ref: O-171]. "John Shaffer" was a private in the German Regiment until discharged on July 19, 1779 [Ref: A-250].

SHAFFY, Adam. See "Adam Sheffey," q.v.

SHAHAN, Daniel. Private who enlisted on February 11, 1778 [Ref: A-314].

SHAME, Joseph. Private who enlisted on July 1, 1776 in Capt. Peter Mantz's company; marched from Frederick Town to Leonardtown, and from there to Philadelphia, arriving August 23, 1776 [Ref: A-47].

SHANK [SCHENCK], Christian. Soldier in the Maryland and New Jersey Lines who "applied for a pension on August 27, 1832, in Morgan County, Virginia, stating he was born January 1, 1751, in Germany and lived near Middletown, New Jersey at enlistment and later moved to Middletown, Frederick County, Maryland, and also enlisted there. He married Juliana or Julia Ann Schmitin (born June 4, 1762) on May 30, 1781, and died on March 21, 1836. His widow applied for pension

(W29344) on September 11, 1837, in Morgan County, Virginia, stating their children were: George (born July 12, 1782); Christian (born April 10, 1784); John (born April 6, 1787); Anna Maria (born February 25, 1788); Catharina (born November 25, 1789); Jacob (born May 29, 1792 and died September 23, 1793); Elizabeth (born April 3, 1794); Susanna (born March 9, 1797); Anna (born August 26, 1800); and, Sara (born August 19, 1803)." [Ref: T-3080].

SHANK, John. Private who enlisted on August 5, 1776, in the Flying Camp under Capt. Philip Meroney [Ref: A-45, N-30:112]. "John George Schenck (born 1739), son of Andreas Schenck [Andrew Shank], settled near Woodsboro." [Ref: O-188].

SHANK, Michael. Associator in December, 1775 [Ref: E-172]. Juror to the Oath of Allegiance in 1778 [Ref: C-29]. "John Michael Schenck (born 1749), son of Andreas Schenck [Andrew Shank], settled near Woodsboro." [Ref: O-188].

SHANK, Philip. Non-Enroller who was fined by the Committee of Observation in April, 1776 [Ref: E-248].

SHARER, Valentine. Sergeant in Capt. Robert Beatty's company of militia on November 29, 1775 [Ref: E-55].

SHARPE, Governor. See "Michael Bayer (Boyer)," q.v.

SHATE, Adam. Private who enlisted in Frederick on July 18, 1780, and later marched to Annapolis under Capt. Beatty [Ref: A-344].

SHATE, Philip. Corporal in Capt. Charles Beatty's company of militia on November 29, 1775 [Ref: E-51].

SHATZ, John. Private in the German Regiment, 1776, in Capt. Henry Fister's company under the command of Col. Hussecker [Ref: A-261].

SHAVER, Adam. 2nd lieutenant in Capt. Ludowick Kemp's company of militia on November 29, 1775 [Ref: E-52. However, Ref: B-120 indicates he was a 1st lieutenant on November 29, 1775]. Juror to the Oath of Allegiance in March, 1778 [Ref: S-266, but not listed in Ref: C-30].

SHAVER, Christian. Sergeant in Capt. John Stoner's company of militia on November 29, 1775 [Ref: E-56].

SHAVER, Henry. Non-Enroller fined by the Committee of Observation in April, 1776 [Ref: E-248]. "Henry Shaver, farmer," died testate in 1790, naming a son Henry Shaver (among others). [Ref: M-7:189].

SHAVER, Jacob. Non-Enroller who was fined by the Committee of Observation in April, 1776 [Ref: E-248].

SHAVER, John. Corporal in Capt. Jacob Ambrose's company of militia on November 29, 1775 [Ref: E-54]. Associator in December, 1775 [Ref: E-173]. Juror to the Oath of Allegiance, 1778 [Ref: C-29].

SHAVER, Peter. Private in the 7th Maryland Regiment from June 1, 1778, until discharged on April 1, 1779 [Ref: A-249].

SHAW, Neal. Associator in December, 1775 [Ref: E-172]. Juror to the Oath of Allegiance in 1778 [Ref: C-29].

SHAW, Samuel. Captain of a militia company on November 29, 1775 [Ref: E-51, B-120]. 2nd major in the 3rd Battalion in 1776 [Ref: E-58. Note: Ref: H-36 and B-120 state he was commissioned 1st major in the 35th Battalion on January 3 or 6, 1776, under Col. Good].

SHAW, Victor. Sergeant in Capt. Samuel Shaw's company of militia on November 29, 1775 [Ref: E-51].

SHAWMAN [SHAWNAN], David. "David Shawnan" was an Associator in December, 1775 [Ref: E-172]. "David Shawman" took the Oath of Allegiance, 1778 [Ref: C-29].

SHAWRIET, Lawrence. Associator in December, 1775 [Ref: E-173]. Juror to the Oath of Allegiance in 1778 [Ref: C-29].

SHAWS, Samuel. Drafted on June 2, 1783; "discharged, being very poor... and two young children." [Ref: B-168].

SHEAFER, Christian. Private in the German Regiment, 1776, in Capt. Henry Fister's company under the command of Col. Nicholas Hussecker [Ref: A-261].

SHEAFER, Jacob. Private in the German Regiment in 1776, with Capt. Henry Fister's company under the command of Col. Nicholas Hussecker [Ref: A-261].

SHEALES, William. See "William Shields," q.v.

SHEAN, James. Private, 2nd Maryland Regiment., who was disabled at the Battle of Monmouth. His invalid pension commenced on November 29, 1783, and ceased on April 29, 1787, with the cause of the pension ceasing as "dead." [Ref: A-630, A-631].

SHEAN, Patrick. Private who enlisted on May 19, 1778 [Ref: A-323].

SHEARER, Andrew. Corporal in Capt. Samuel Shaw's company of militia on November 29, 1775 [Ref: E-51].

SHECKLES, Richard. "Rchd. Sheckles" petitioned to form the horse troops in 1781 [Ref: B-167]. "Richard Sheckells" was a private in the horse troops in June, 1781 [Ref: B-167].

SHEE, Murphy. Militia substitute from May to December 10, 1781, and "marched to Annapolis." [Ref: A-653].

SHEEKELS, John. Private in the militia in July, 1776 [Ref: A-42].

SHEEKELS, Thomas. Private in the militia in July, 1776 [Ref: A-42].

SHEERLOCK, Salathiel. Private in the 7th Maryland Regiment from December 24, 1777, until February 8, 1778, when reported "deserted" [Ref: A-249].

SHEESE, Peter. Private in the German Regiment, muster roll dated October 23, 1776 [Ref: A-264].

SHEETS, Jacob. "On January 26, 1828, the Treasurer of the Western Shore was directed to pay to Hannah Sheets, of Frederick County, during life, in half yearly payments, the half pay of a private, as further remuneration for her husband Jacob Sheets' services during the Revolutionary War." [Ref: G-391].

SHEFFEY, Adam. "Adam Shaffy" was a non-enroller who was fined by the Committee of Observation in 1776 [Ref: E-248]. "Adam Sheffey" died testate in 1793, leaving a wife Magdalene and children Elizabeth, Catharine, Magdalene, Daniel, John, and Henry [Ref: M-8:181].

SHEFFEY, Casper. "Casper Sherfe" was a non-enroller who was fined by the Committee of Observation in May, 1776 [Ref: E-248].

SHEHAN, Daniel. Private who enlisted on August 5, 1776, in the Flying Camp under Capt. Philip Meroney [Ref: A-45, N-30:111].

SHEHAN, James. "James Shehon" was a private who enlisted April 29, 1778, and served in the 2nd Maryland Regiment [Ref: A-294, A-324]. "James Shehan" was wounded at the battle of Monmouth while serving with the 2nd Maryland Regiment [Ref: F-475].

SHEIBLER [SHEIBELER], Frederick. Soldier in the Virginia Line who "applied for a pension (S23910) on August 20, 1832, in Westmoreland County, Pennsylvania, aged 69, stating he was born in 1763 near Philadelphia, Pennsylvania and enlisted at Fredericktown, Maryland. After the war he lived near Hagerstown, Maryland, for 2 years and then moved to Westmoreland County, Pennsylvania." [Ref: T-3097].

SHEILOR, Daniel. See "Daniel Shelor (Sheilor)," q.v.

SHEINER, Valentine. See "Valentine Schriner," q.v.

SHELBY, Evan. "General Evan Shelby was a man distinguished for indomitable courage, iron constitution, and clear intellect. A Welshman by birth, Gen. Evan Shelby came to this country a mere lad, who settled near Hagerstown, then in Frederick, but now in Washington County, Maryland. In 1758 he distinguished himself as a captain of rangers under Gen. Forbes, leading the advance upon Fort Duquesne. In 1772 he removed to the West, and in 1774 commanded a company, under Lewis and Dunmore, in an expedition against the Indians on the Scioto River. In 1779 he led a strong force against the Chicamauga Indians on the Tennessee River, and for his services and gallantry was appointed a brigadier general by the State of Virginia, the first officer of that grade appointed in the West. Such was the father of Isaac Shelby." [Ref: F-450].

SHELBY, Isaac. "Born near Hagerstown, now Washington County, but then in Frederick County, Maryland, December 11, 1750, and blessed with a firm and herculean frame, inured to the use of arms, capable of sustaining great fatigue, he was peculiarly fitted for the scenes in which he was destined to become so prominent an actor. In the great battle of Kanawha, October 10, 1774, on the Ohio River, he had his first experience of fighting as a lieutenant in a company commanded by his father [Shelby Evans]. He was employed as a surveyor under Judge Henderson's company in Kentucky, amid the dangers, privations, and difficulties that beset the 'dark and bloody ground,' under which his health gave way, and he returned home. In 1777, Governor Patrick Henry, of Virginia, appointed him commissary of supplies for a large body of troops guarding the frontier. In 1778 he represented Washington County in the Virginia House of Delegates, and was appointed by Governor Thomas Jefferson a major in the escort of guards to the commissioners for extending the boundary line between Virginia and North Carolina; by this line as established his residence was found to be in North Carolina, and he was appointed by Governor Richard Caswell, of North Carolina, a colonel of Sullivan County. The fall of Charleston in 1780 recalled him from his surveying and locating of lands in Kentucky, and he enlisted for the war. Having performed his service, he returned to Boonsboro, Kentucky, and married Susanna Hart. He was a member of the Convention in Kentucky, and was a member of the Convention in April, 1792, that formed the constitution of the State, and was elected the first Governor of Kentucky. He was again elected governor in 1812-1816, and, though 63 years of age, he headed in person four thousand troops and marched under Gen. Harrison in 1813 to Canada, and for his gallantry at the Battle of the Thames, the U.S. Congress honored him with a gold medal. In February, 1820, he was attached by a paralytic affection [sic], and expired in Lincoln County, Kentucky, on July 18, 1826, from a stroke of apoplexy, in the 79th year of his age. In honor of him nine counties in the States of Alabama, Texas, Tennessee, kentucky, Ohio, Indiana, Illinois, Iowa, Missouri, as well as several towns and one college now perpetuate his name. His son, Gen. James Shelby, was born in 1784 and died September, 1848. He was a major in the campaign of 1813 [Ref: F-450, F-451].

SHELL, Charles. Associator in December, 1775 [Ref: E-173]. Juror to the Oath of Allegiance in 1778 [Ref: C-29]. Loaned $500 for the use of the State of Maryland in June, 1780 [Ref: V-520].

SHELLMAN, Elizabeth. See "Henry Bear," q.v.

SHELLMAN [SHELMAN], Jacob. Loaned $200 for the use of the State of Maryland in June, 1780 [Ref: V-520].

SHELLMAN, John Jr. Associator in December, 1775 [Ref: E-173]. Juror to the Oath of Allegiance in 1778 [Ref: C-29]. "John Shelman, Jr." was a private in the horse troops in 1781 [Ref: B-168]. "John Shellman applied for a pension (S31960) on February 25, 1833, in Savannah, Chatham County, Georgia and stated he was aged 77 and was born in Fredericktown, Maryland. He lived there at enlistment in the Maryland Line and in 1784 moved to Georgia. He died on May 12, 1838, and his widow (not named) died in February, 1845, in Savannah, Georgia. A daughter, Catharine Ann (Shellman) Wilcox or Willcox, was aged 40 in 1852, a resident of New Haven County, Connecticut, and the wife of Jacob Willcox. The father of the soldier (not named) died in 1816 [sic]. The soldier's oldest brother (not named) was living in Fredericktown, Maryland in 1833. Also mentioned in 1852 were Norris and Cyprian Willcox of New Haven, Connecticut, but no relationship was given." [Ref" T-3100].

SHELLMAN, John Sr. Associator in December, 1775 [Ref: E-173]. Juror to the Oath of Allegiance in 1778 [Ref: C-29]. A "John Shelman" enlisted on July 1, 1776, in Capt. Peter Mantz's company; marched from Frederick Town to Leonardtown, and from there to Philadelphia, arriving August 23, 1776 [Ref: A-47]. "John Shellman" was a 1st lieutenant on September 18, 1780, and was a captain on January 23, 1782, in the Frederick Town Battalion of Militia [Ref: B-120, V-295]. Together with John Jacob Schley he loaned $1,000 for the use of the State of Maryland in June, 1780 [Ref: V-520]. "The emigrant Col. Johannes Mathias Schellman (1724-1814) married Maria Margaretha Fauth (or Fout) [and] John Schellman who arrived here in 1743 helped to lay out Fredericktown and was a leading carpenter for the first buildings of the town." [Ref: O-211].

SHELOR [SHEILOR], Daniel. "Daniel Shelor" was a 1st lieutenant in Capt. John Carmack's company of militia on November 29, 1775 [Ref: E-56, but Ref: B-120 listed his name as "David Shelor"]. Associator in December, 1775 [Ref: E-172]. Juror to the Oath of Allegiance in 1778 [Ref: C-29]. "Daniel Sheilor" was a captain in the Catoctin Battalion of militia on August 16, 1781, through at least November 30, 1782 [Ref: B-120].

SHENK, John. Private who enlisted on July 1, 1776 in Capt. Peter Mantz's company; marched from Frederick Town to Leonardtown, and from there to Philadelphia, arriving August 23, 1776 [Ref: A-47]. Also, see "John Shank," q.v.

SHEPHARD, John. Private in the Skipton District Militia under Capt. Thomas Waring on April 16, 1776 [Ref: B-167, D-1814].

SHEPHARD, Samuel. Private in the Skipton District Militia under Capt. Thomas Waring on April 16, 1776 [Ref: B-167, D-1814].

SHEPPART, Thomas. Private who enlisted August 5, 1776 [Ref: A-44].

SHEREDINE [SHERIDAN], Upton (1740 - January 14, 1800). Son of Major Thomas and Ellenor Sheredine, Upton was born in Baltimore County and subsequently moved near Liberty in Frederick County. Second lieutenant in Capt. David Moore's company of militia on November 29, 1775 [Ref: E-56, B-120]. Chosen to serve on the Committee of Observation in 1775 [Ref: I-85]. Member of State Constitutional Convention in 1776. State Senator, 1776. Colonel of the Linganore Battalion on December 28, 1776 [Ref: B-120, X-555]. Judge of the Orphans' Court, 1777-1800, and a Delegate to the Second Congress, 1791-1793 [Ref: E-302]. "Upton Sheredine took a most active part in the struggle for independence, was a member of the first State Constitutional Convention, was elected to the First Congress, was a Justice of the County and Orphans' Court, and held many other prominent positions. He married Sophia, daughter of Basil Dorsey, Jr., and left no children. His property, after providing for his widow, was willed to his nephews, Daniel Sheredine and William Hammond." [Ref: F-456]. He was also an Election Judge in the Upper District on July 2, 1776, was State Senator, 1776-1780, was Justice of the Peace in 1777, served in the House of Delegates in 1777, and was Judge of the Orphans' Court from 1777 to 1782 [Ref: F-476 to F-480]. "Mrs. Eleanor Sheredine, wife of Upton Sheredine, of Midhill, died on December 30, 1797. Upton Sheredine died, at Midhill, of yellow fever. He was the first U.S. Tax Commissioner for the State of Maryland." [Ref: F-470, P-731]. Also, see "James Johnson," q.v.

SHEREMAN, Jacob. Associator in December, 1775 [Ref: E-172]. Juror to the Oath of Allegiance in 1778 [Ref: C-29].

SHEREMAN [SHREMAN], Peter. Associator in December, 1775 [Ref: E-172]. Juror to the Oath of Allegiance in 1778 [Ref: C-29].

SHERFE, Casper. See "Casper Sheffey," q.v.

SHERRARD, Francis. See "Patrick Conner," q.v.

SHIELDS, James Sr. Sergeant in Capt. William Shields' company of militia on November 29, 1775 [Ref: E-56].

SHIELDS, John. Ensign in Capt. William Shields' company of militia in the 3rd Battalion on November 29, 1775 [Ref: E-55]. Captain in the 35th Battalion on December 28, 1776 [Ref: B-120, X-555].

SHIELDS, William. Captain of a company of militia on November 29, 1775 [Ref: E-55, B-120]. Associator, 1775, appointed "to hand about the Association paper" in Toms Creek Hundred [Ref: E-172, E-305]. Commissioned a 2nd major in the 35th Battalion on January 3 or 6, 1776 [Ref: H-36, B-120]. 1st major in the 3rd (or 35th) Battalion on October 7, 1776 [Ref: E-58, B-120]. Juror to the Oath of Allegiance in 1778 [Ref: C-29]. "William Sheales" was appointed by the Committee of Correspondence to solicit subscriptions to purchase arms and ammunition in Tom's Creek Hundred in 1775 [Ref: I-86].

SHIFFER, John. Militia substitute from May to December 10, 1781, and "marched to Annapolis." [Ref: A-653].

SHILLING, Conrad. Juror to the Oath of Allegiance in March, 1778 [Ref: S-266, but not listed in Ref: C-30].

SHIMER, Abraham. Associator in December, 1775 [Ref: E-173]. Juror to the Oath of Allegiance in 1778 [Ref: C-29].

SHINGLETAKER, Andrew. 2nd lieutenant in the 35th Battalion of militia on November or December 28, 1776 [Ref: B-120, X-555].

SHINKMYER, John. Associator in December, 1775 [Ref: E-173]. "John Shinkmeyer" subscribed to the Oath of Allegiance in 1778 [Ref: C-29].

SHIPPER, William. Associator in December, 1775 [Ref: E-173]. Juror to the Oath of Allegiance in 1778 [Ref: C-29].

SHIPPLE, George Michael. Non-Enroller who was fined by the Committee of Observation in May, 1776 [Ref: E-248].

SHIRTS, George. Juror to the Oath of Allegiance in March, 1778 [Ref: S-266, but not listed in Ref: C-30].

SHISLER, Jacob. Associator in December, 1775 [Ref: E-173]. Juror to the Oath of Allegiance in 1778 [Ref: C-29].

SHISTAKER, John. 2nd lieutenant in the 37th Battalion of militia on May 15, 1776, under Capt. Richard Balsell [Ref: B-121, W-427].

SHITENHELM, Frederick. Fifer in Capt. William Beatty's company of militia on November 29, 1775 [Ref: E-55].

SHITTERHELMS, Michael. Associator in December, 1775 [Ref: E-173]. Juror to the Oath of Allegiance in 1778 [Ref: C-29].

SHIVELY, John. Private who enlisted on March 1, 1778, and served in the German Regiment at the Battle of White Plains on September 5, 1778, under Lt. Col. Ludwick Weltner [Ref: A-250, A-266, A-321].

SHOCK, Chris. Private in Capt. John Kershner's company who guarded prisoners at Fort Frederick, 1777-1778, and was discharged June 19, 1778 [Ref: A-328].

SHODE, Philip. Associator in December, 1775 [Ref: E-173]. Juror to the Oath of Allegiance in 1778 [Ref: C-29].

SHOEMAKER, Frederick. Corporal in the German Regiment who enlisted on May 8, 1778, and was in the Battle of White Plains on September 5, 1778, under Lt. Col. Ludwick Weltner [Ref: A-250, A-267, R-166].

SHOEMAKER [SHUMAKER], Harmon. Soldier in the Maryland and North Carolina Lines who "applied for a pension (S32512) on May 12, 1834, in Fayette County, Alabama, aged about 73, stating he had enlisted at Fredericktown, Maryland, and he later moved to Randolph County, North Carolina with his relations, and also enlisted there in 1779. He stated he was of Dutch descent, born in the Dutch settlement on the Delaware River in New Jersey, and was living at Fredericktown, Maryland, at enlistment." [Ref: T-3126, 3127].

SHOEMAKER, Herbert. Private who enlisted on August 5, 1776, in the Flying Camp under Capt. Philip Meroney [Ref: A-45, N-30:112].

SHOEMAKER, Jacob. Associator in December, 1775 [Ref: E-173]. Juror to the Oath of Allegiance in 1778 [Ref: C-29].

SHOEMAKER, John. Associator in December, 1775 [Ref: E-172]. Juror to the Oath of Allegiance in 1778 [Ref: C-29]. Private in the German Regiment on muster roll dated October 23, 1776 [Ref: A-264]. 2nd lieutenant in Catoctin Battalion of militia on August 16, 1781, and 1st lieutenant on November 20, 1782 [Ref: B-121].

SHOEMAKER, Michael. Private in the German Regiment in 1776 in Capt. Henry Fister's company under the command of Col. Nicholas Hussecker until he was discharged on July 24, 1779 [Ref: A-250, A-261].

SHOEMAKER, Peter. Private who enlisted May 17, 1778, and served in the 7th Maryland Regiment until August 16, 1780, when he was killed (at the Battle of Camden, South Carolina). [Ref: A-249, A-322]. One Peter Shoemaker died testate and his will was probated in October, 1781, naming wife Dorothea and 8 children: Hester, Catharine, Mary, Margaret, Julian, Elizabeth, Peter, and Jacob [Ref: M-5:169, 170].

SHOEMAKER, Philip. Associator in December, 1775 [Ref: E-173]. Juror to the Oath of Allegiance in 1778 [Ref: C-29].

329

SHOLLY, Luke. Sergeant at Fort Frederick in 1778 with Capt. John Kershner's company, guarding prisoners of war [Ref: A-328].

SHOLLY, Peter. Commissioned a captain in the 36th Battalion on January 3, 1776, under Col. Samuel Beale [Ref: H-36, B-121].

SHOOK, John. Sergeant in Capt. James Johnson's company of militia on November 29, 1775 [Ref: E-52]. Also, see "Joseph Doll," q.v.

SHOPE, Catherine. See "John Sponseller," q.v.

SHOPP, Henry. Juror to the Oath of Allegiance in 1778 [Ref: C-29].

SHOPPER, Philip. Sergeant in the German Regiment, 1776, in Capt. Henry Fister's company under the command of Col. Nicholas Hussecker [Ref: A-261].

SHOREMAN, Jacob. Associator in December, 1775 [Ref: E-172]. Juror to the Oath of Allegiance in 1778 [Ref: C-29].

SHORT, James. Associator in December, 1775 [Ref: E-173]. Juror to the Oath of Allegiance in 1778 [Ref: C-29].

SHORT, Richard. Private who enlisted on July 29, 1776 [Ref: A-44].

SHOTS [SCHATZ], John. Soldier in the Maryland Line who "applied for a pension on April 14, 1818, in Frederick County, Maryland, stating he married Elizabeth Leschorn on September 18, 1791, in Frederick Town, Maryland. In 1820 he was aged 64 with a wife and 6 children (no names given). He died November 16, 1824, and his widow applied for pension (W25128) on March 28, 1846 in Madison County, Illinois. A son Henry Shotts, of Madison County, was aged 50 in 1846 and stated his father died in Frederick County, Virginia." [Ref: T-3123 and J-25, which latter source states he was in Pennsylvania Line].

SHOTTER, Valentine. Private in the German Regiment, 1776, in Capt. Henry Fister's company under the command of Col. Nicholas Hussecker [Ref: A-261].

SHOUP [SHOUPE], Martin. Non-Enroller who was fined by the Committee of Observation in April, 1776 [Ref: E-248]. "Martin Shoup" died testate in 1783, leaving wife Sofia and children George, Catharine, Sofia, Christian, Peter, and Samuel [Ref: M-6:84, M-6:85].

SHOUP, Samuel. Associator in December, 1775 [Ref: E-173]. Juror to the Oath of Allegiance in 1778 [Ref: C-29].

SHOUTS, John. Non-Enroller who was fined by the Committee of Observation in April, 1776 [Ref: E-248]. See "John Shots," q.v.

SHOVELL, John. Private who enlisted on April 6, 1778, and served in the 2nd Maryland Regiment [Ref: A-294]. Private in the 6th Maryland Regiment who was disabled at the Battle of Camden; invalid pension commenced on March 29, 1786, and ceased on November 1, 1789 (no reason was given). [Ref: A-294, A-630, A-631, F-476].

SHOVER, Henry. Associator in December, 1775 [Ref: E-173]. Juror to the Oath of Allegiance in 1778 [Ref: C-29].

SHOVER, Peter. 1st lieutenant in Capt. Jacob Ambrose's company of militia in 2nd Battalion on November 29, 1775 [Ref: E-54, B-121]. Associator in December, 1775 [Ref: E-172]. Provided wheat for the military in May, 1782 [Ref: R-516]. Juror to the Oath of Allegiance in 1778 [Ref: C-29, S-266. Also, see "Peter Shrover," q.v.]. This or perhaps another Peter Shover (1745-1813), of Frederick County, was a corporal in the 4th Philadelphia County Battalion of Militia and entered the service on December 28, 1776. His wife, Sophia ----, died in 1822, and their daughter Sophia (1772-1810) married Daniel Rouzer (1767-1850) in 1791 in Hagerstown, Maryland [Ref: T-2122].

SHOW, Jacob. Associator in December, 1775 [Ref: E-173]. Juror to the Oath of Allegiance in 1778 [Ref: C-29].

SHRADER, Conrad. Drafted on June 2, 1783 [Ref: B-168].

SHRANTZ, George. Private in the German Regiment, 1776, in Capt. Henry Fister's company under the command of Col. Nicholas Hussecker [Ref: A-261].

SHRAYER, Matthias. Corporal in Capt. Samuel Shaw's company of militia on November 29, 1775 [Ref: E-51]. Served in the German Regiment until discharged on October 1, 1779 [Ref: A-250].

SHRIBER, John. Private stationed at Fort Frederick on June 27, 1778, in Capt. John Kershner's company, and guarding prisoners of war [Ref: A-328].

SHRINER, Valentine. See "Valentine Schriner," q.v.

SHRIVER, David. "David Schriver" was an Associator in December, 1775, and "David Shriver" was appointed to "assist in handing about the Association paper" in Pipe Creek Hundred on November 29, 1775 [Ref: E-173, E-245, E-305]. Juror to the Oath of Allegiance in 1778 [Ref: C-28]. Election Judge in the Middle District on July 2, 1776, and served in the House of Delegates from 1776 to 1782 [Ref: F-476, F-479].

SHRIVER, George. Private in Capt. Charles Baltzel's Company, served 3 years, and discharged August 11, 1779 at Camp Tioga [Ref: A-271].

SHROOP, Philip. Sergeant in the German Regiment, 1776, in Capt. Henry Fister's company under the command of Col. Nicholas Hussecker [Ref: A-261].

SHROVER, Peter. Private in Capt. Christian Myers' Company, served 3 years and discharged July 29, 1779 at Camp Wyoming [Ref: A-270]. Also, see "Peter Shover," q.v.

SHROYER, Christopher and Catharine. See "Leonard Peckenpaugh," q.v.

SHRUPP, Henry. Associator in December, 1775 [Ref: E-173]. Juror to the Oath of Allegiance in 1778 [Ref: C-29]. Lieutenant in the German Regiment who pensioned in 1820 [Ref: G-391].

SHRYER, Frederick. Drafted on June 2, 1783; "never appeared." [Ref: B-169].

SHRYER, Leonard. Associator in December, 1775 [Ref: E-173]. Juror to the Oath of Allegiance in 1778 [Ref: C-29].

SHRYER, Mary C. See "Michael Kershner," q.v.

SHRYOCK, Henry. 1st major in 32nd Battalion of militia, January 6, 1776 [Ref: B-121]. Reviewed and passed recruits, 1776 [Ref: A-51].

SHRYOCK, John. "On March 16, 1835, the Treasurer of the Western Shore was directed to pay John Shryock, soldier of the revolution, half pay of a private, quarterly, during his life." [Ref: G-391]. There was also a Lt. John Shryock (and a Lt. Leonard Shryock) in Washington County during the Revolutionary War [Ref: O-52]. "John Shrayock" was a private in the German Regiment until discharged on July 20, 1779 [Ref: A-250].

SHUGART, Martin. Lieutenant from 1778 until declared supernumerary on January 1, 1781 [Ref: A-365].

SHULER, Andrew. Private who enlisted on May 6, 1778 [Ref: A-322].

SHULER, George. Juror to the Oath of Allegiance in March, 1778 [Ref: S-267, but not listed in Ref: C-30].

SHULL, Frederick. Private in the horse troops in June, 1781 [Ref: B-167].

SHULL, Peter. "Born January 11, 1761 in Frederick County, Maryland, he lived in York County, Pennsylvania at the time of his enlistment in the Revolutionary War. Three or four years after the war he moved to Maryland and lived some 11 miles from Fort Cumberland for 2 1/2 years and then moved to Fayette County, Pennsylvania for 7 years. He then moved to Kentucky for 35 years and then to Illinois. He applied for a pension on September 5, 1832, in White County, and died in November, 1834, in Henderson County, Kentucky. He married Anna Dorotha "Dorothy" ---- [name not stated] on March 5, 1782, in Pennsylvania. She applied for a pension (W9289) and died on January 2, 1849, in Ohio County, Kentucky, leaving children Peter Shull (who was aged 63 in 1852) and Samuel Shull. Other heirs included Mrs. Elizabeth Huntsinger, Mrs. Catharine Bottoms, and Mrs. Mary M. Huntsucker." [Ref: T-3126].

SHULTZ, Frederick. Sergeant in Capt. Jacob Ambrose's company of militia on November 29, 1775 [Ref: E-54]. Associator in December, 1775 [Ref: E-173]. Juror to the Oath of Allegiance, 1778 [Ref: C-29].

SHUMAN, Jacob (Pipe Creek Hundred). Non-Enroller who was fined by the Committee of Observation in May, 1776 [Ref: E-248].

SHUPER, Christopher. Associator in December, 1775 [Ref: E-172]. Juror to the Oath of Allegiance in 1778 [Ref: C-29].

SHUPP, Henry. Associator in December, 1775 [Ref: E-173].

SHUSH, Andrew. Provided wheat for the military in June, 1782 [Ref: R-521].

SHUTTER, Christian, Juror to the Oath of Allegiance in March, 1778 [Ref: S-267, but not listed in Ref: C-30].

SHWARTZ, Valentine. Associator in December, 1775 [Ref: E-173]. Juror to the Oath of Allegiance in 1778 [Ref: C-29].

SHYTACRE, John. Ensign in Capt. James Johnson's militia company on November 29, 1775 [Ref: E-52]. "John Shytaker" was 1st lieutenant in the 37th Battalion of militia on January 17, 1777 [Ref: B-121].

SIBELL, Conrod. Ensign in the 35th Battalion of militia on November or December 28, 1776, under Capt. Little [Ref: B-121, X-555].

SICKFREED, Andrew. Associator in December, 1775 [Ref: E-173]. Juror to the Oath of Allegiance in 1778 [Ref: C-29].

SIDES, Christian. Private in the German Regiment, muster roll dated October 23, 1776 [Ref: A-264].

SIDLE, Godlip (Israel's Creek Hundred). Non-Enroller who was fined by the Committee of Observation in April, 1776 [Ref: E-248].

SIEGFRIED [SEIKFRET], George. Private who enlisted on July 1, 1776, in Capt. Peter Mantz's company, and marched from Frederick Town to Leonardtown, and from there to Philadelphia, arriving on August 23, 1776 [Ref: A-47]. "George Seikfret" took the Oath of Allegiance in March, 1778 [Ref: S-266].

SIFER, John. Militia substitute on June 5, 1778 [Ref: A-325].

SIGENFOOSE [SIGERFOOSE], George. "George Sigerfoose" took the Oath of Allegiance in March, 1778 [Ref: S-266]. "George Sigenfoose" was drafted on June 13, 1781, and provided a substitute [Ref: D-1814].

SIGHAS, Joseph. Associator in December, 1775 [Ref: E-172]. Juror to the Oath of Allegiance in 1778 [Ref: C-29].

SIGLER, Henry. Corporal in Capt. Michael Troutman's company of militia on November 29, 1775 [Ref: E-51]. Also, see "Henry Zislar," and "Henry Ziegler," q.v.

SIGLOR, Jacob. Associator in December, 1775 [Ref: E-172]. Juror to the Oath of Allegiance in 1778 [Ref: C-29]. "Jacob Sigler" was a drummer in Capt. Michael Troutman's company of militia on November 29, 1775 [Ref: E-51].

SILL, John. Private who was enlisted on July 20, 1776 by Capt. Jacob Good [Ref: A-46].

SILVER, George. Private who enlisted on March 31, 1778, for 3 years, in Capt. Michael Bayer's company, and served in the 7th Maryland Regiment to at least August 1, 1780 [Ref: A-250, A-268]. "George Silver, Sr." died testate in 1785, leaving a wife Lyssy Market Silver, son George, and daughter Elizabeth [Ref: M-6:189].

SILVER, James. Private in the Middle District Militia in 1776 in Capt. Valentine Creager's company [Ref: A-72].

SILVER, John. Associator in December, 1775 [Ref: E-172]. Juror to the Oath of Allegiance in 1778 [Ref: C-29].

SILVER, Samuel. Private who enlisted on August 5, 1776, in the Flying Camp under Capt. Philip Meroney [Ref: A-45, N-30:112].

SIM, Joseph. Colonel who died on November 27, 1793 [Ref: F-470].

SIMM, William. Private in the horse troops in 1781 [Ref: B-167].

SIMMON [SIMON], Adam. Private in the Middle District Militia in 1776 in Capt. Valentine Creager's company [Ref: A-72].

SIMMONS, Aritta. See "Benjamin Murdock," q.v.

SIMMONS, Baltsar. Petitioned the General Assembly under the Act of July 3, 1780, stating that he had been a non-juror to the Oath of Allegiance and Fidelity in 1778 due to "neglect" and now desired relief under the Act and to take the Oath [Ref: L-101].

SIMMONS, James. Sergeant in Capt. William Beatty's company of militia on November 29, 1775 [Ref: E-55].

SIMMONS, John. Defective from the Maryland Line in August, 1780 [Ref: A-414].

SIMMONS, Samuel. Associator in December, 1775 [Ref: E-172]. Juror to the Oath of Allegiance in 1778 [Ref: C-29].

SIMMS, Alexcious. Private in the militia, July, 1776 [Ref: A-42].

SIMONS, James (Colonel). See "Lawrence Everhart," q.v.

SIMPKINS, Charles. Private, 1st Maryland Regiment, 1780, and served in the Southern Army of the United States under Lt. W. Lamar in the late Capt. Beatty's company in 1781; "sick in July." [Ref: A-389].

SIMPKINS, Dickerson (or Dickson). Private in the Skipton District Militia of Frederick County under Capt. Thomas Waring on April 16, 1776 [Ref: B-167, D-1814]. "Dickson Simkins" was 1st lieutenant in the Skipton District Militia on July 27, 1776, under Capt. Charles Clinton [Ref: X-127], and 1st lieutenant in the Washington County militia on June 22, 1778, under Capt. Clinton [Ref: B-121, Z-145].

SIMPKINS, John. Captain in the militia, 1778-1779 [Ref: H-15].

SIMPKINS, Syrus. Sergeant in the Skipton District Militia under Capt. Thomas Waring on April 16, 1776 [Ref: B-167, D-1814].

SIMPSON, Catharine. See "William Cumming," q.v.

SIMPSON, John. Associator in December, 1775 [Ref: E-172]. Juror to the Oath of Allegiance in 1778 [Ref: C-29].

SIMPSON, Luke. Private, 1st Maryland Regiment, 1781, and served in the Southern Army of the United States under Lt. William Lamar in the late Capt. Beatty's company [Ref: A-390].

SIMPSON, Musgrove. Non-Enroller who was fined by the Committee of Observation in April, 1776, but he apparently enrolled because the fine was remitted in June, 1776 [Ref: E-248].

SIMPSON, Richard. Associator in December, 1775 [Ref: E-173]. Juror to the Oath of Allegiance in 1778 [Ref: C-29, S-266].

SIMPSON, Richard Jr. Associator in December, 1775 [Ref: E-173]. Juror to the Oath of Allegiance in 1778 [Ref: C-29].

SIMPSON, Solomon (Sugarland Hundred). Appointed by the Committee of Correspondence to solicit subscriptions in 1775 to purchase arms and ammunition [Ref: I-86].

SINN, Barbara. See "Andrew Michael," q.v.

SINN [SIN], Philip. Associator in December, 1775 [Ref: E-172]. Juror to the Oath of Allegiance in 1778 [Ref: C-29].

SINN, Jacob. Juror to the Oath of Allegiance in March, 1778 [Ref: S-266, but not listed in Ref: C-30]. Also, see "Philip Smith," q.v.

SIPE, Daniel. Non-Enroller who was fined by the Committee of Observation in April, 1776, but he apparently enrolled because the fine was remitted in June, 1776 [Ref: E-248].

SIPERT, George. Juror to the Oath of Allegiance in March, 1778 [Ref: S-266, but not listed in Ref: C-30].

SKAGGS, William. Private who enlisted August 5, 1776, in the Flying Camp under Capt. Philip Meroney [Ref: A-45, N-30:112].

SKILES, Ephraim. Private who enlisted on July 25, 1776 [Ref: A-51].

SKINNER, Peggie. See "James Johnson," q.v.

335

SLACK, Richard. Fifer in Capt. Jacob Good's company of militia on November 29, 1775 [Ref: E-51].

SLAGEL, Charles. Associator in December, 1775 [Ref: E-172]. Juror to the Oath of Allegiance in 1778 [Ref: C-29].

SLAGEL, Henry. Associator in December, 1775 [Ref: E-173]. Juror to the Oath of Allegiance in 1778 [Ref: C-29, and S-266, which latter source spelled the name "Henry Sleagle."].

SLAGEL, John. "John Slagal" was a corporal in Capt. William Luckett, Jr.'s company of militia on November 29, 1775 [Ref: E-55]. Associator in December, 1775 [Ref: E-172]. "John Slagel" was a private who enlisted on July 20, 1776 by Capt. Jacob Good [Ref: A-46]. Juror to the Oath of Allegiance in 1778 [Ref: C-29].

SLATER, Barthw. Private in the 7th Maryland Regiment from July 20, 1778, to December 20, 1778, when reported "deserted." [Ref: A-249].

SLAUGHTER, Jacob. Corporal in the Skipton District Militia under Capt. Thomas Waring on April 16, 1776 [Ref: B-167, D-1814].

SLENDER, Christopher. Private in the German Regiment, 1776, in Capt. Henry Fister's company under the command of Col. Nicholas Hussecker [Ref: A-261].

SLETSOR, George. Associator in December, 1775 [Ref: E-173]. Juror to the Oath of Allegiance in 1778 [Ref: C-29].

SLICK, Jacob. Drafted on June 2, 1783; "agreed to join and pay money in lieu of his service; paid 9.5 pounds." [Ref: B-169].

SLICK, William. Private in the Middle District Militia in 1776 in Capt. Valentine Creager's company [Ref: A-72].

SLIDER, Simon. Petitioned the General Assembly under the Act of July 3, 1780, stating that he had been a non-juror to the Oath of Allegiance and Fidelity in 1778 due to "ignorance" and now desired relief under the Act and to take the Oath [Ref: L-101].

SLOE, Charles. Associator in December, 1775 [Ref: E-172]. Juror to the Oath of Allegiance in 1778 [Ref: C-29].

SLONE, Charles. Private who enlisted on May 13, 1778 [Ref: A-322].

SLUTTERY, Baltis. Associator in December, 1775 [Ref: E-172]. Juror to the Oath of Allegiance in 1778 [Ref: C-29].

SMALLWOOD, Major. See "Robert Miller," q.v.

SMALLWOOD, William (General). See "Thomas Dixon," "John Helmes," "Henry Roberts," and "George Stricker," q.v.

SMATTER, John. "John Smatter" was a private who enlisted on April 24, 1778 [Ref: A-321]. "John Smadern" was a private in the German

Regiment and served in the Battle of White Plains on September 5, 1778, under Lt. Col. Ludwick Weltner [Ref: A-267].

SMELTZER, Adam. Private in the German Regiment in 1776 in Capt. Henry Fister's company under the command of Col. Nicholas Hussecker [Ref: A-261].

SMELTZER, Henry. See "Lawrence Everhart," q.v.

SMERIGRIST, Robert. Associator in December, 1775 [Ref: E-172]. Juror to the Oath of Allegiance in 1778 [Ref: C-29].

SMITH, Acquila. Militia substitute on June 2, 1778 [Ref: A-324]. "Aquilla Smith" was a private in 1st Maryland Regiment, enlisted on June 2, 1778, and served in the Southern Army of the United States under Lt. William Lamar in the late Capt. Beatty's company until he was discharged on June 2, 1781 [Ref: A-391].

SMITH, Adam. 2nd lieutenant in the German Regiment in July, 1776, and on muster roll dated October 23, 1776 [Ref: A-263, X-48]. Adam Smith applied for pension (S40455) on June 11, 1819, in Huntingdon County, Pennsylvania, aged 66, and stated he lived at Hagerstown, Maryland at the time of his enlistment. He was 2nd lieutenant in Capt. William Heyser's Company in Col. Haussegger [Hussecker]'s German Regiment, in May, 1776, and was in the Battles of Trenton, Princeton, and three skirmishes near Maidenhead, New Jersey. He resigned his commission on August 1, 1777. In 1820 he stated his children were all of age (no names given). [Ref: T-3169, K-93].

SMITH, Adam (of Martin). Non-Enroller fined by the Committee of Observation in April, 1776 [Ref: E-248]. An Adam Smith petitioned the General Assembly under the Act of May 12, 1780, stating he had been a non-juror to the Oath of Allegiance and Fidelity in 1778 due to "ignorance" and now desired relief under the Act and to take the Oath [Ref: L-101].

SMITH, Alexander. Private who enlisted on May 20, 1778, and served in the German Regiment at the Battle of White Plains on September 5, 1778, under Lt. Col. Ludwick Weltner [Ref: A-323, A-267].

SMITH, Alexander H. Associator in December, 1775 [Ref: E-173]. Juror to the Oath of Allegiance in 1778 [Ref: C-29].

SMITH, Andrew. See "James Smith," q.v.

SMITH, Baltis. Associator in December, 1775 [Ref: E-172]. Juror to the Oath of Allegiance in 1778 [Ref: C-29].

SMITH, Barbara. See "Adam Kephart," q.v.

SMITH, Caspar (Upper Catoctin). Appointed by the Committee of Correspondence to solicit subscriptions in 1775 to purchase arms and ammunition [Ref: I-85].

SMITH, Christian. Fifer in Capt. Joseph Wood, Jr.'s company of militia on November 29, 1775 [Ref: E-53]. Associator in December, 1775 [Ref: E-172]. Private in the Middle District who enlisted on August 5, 1776 [Ref: A-45, A-72, N-30:112]. Juror to the Oath of Allegiance in 1778 [Ref: C-29]. Served as a 2nd lieutenant in the Catoctin Battalion of militia on August 16, 1781 [Ref: B-122].

SMITH, Christian. Sergeant in Capt. John Carmack's militia company on November 29, 1775 [Ref: E-56, B-122]. 2nd lieutenant in Catoctin Battalion of militia on May 13, 1778 and 1st lieutenant in the 34th Battalion of militia on March 29, 1779 [Ref: B-122, Z-79. Yet, Ref: H-15 stated he was a captain, not a lieutenant, on March 29, 1779].

SMITH, Christopher. Associator in December, 1775 [Ref: E-172]. Juror to the Oath of Allegiance in 1778 [Ref: C-29].

SMITH, Daniel. Private, 1st Maryland Regiment, 1781, and served in the Southern Army of the United States under Lt. William Lamar in the late Capt. Beatty's company [Ref: A-389]. 1st lieutenant in the Catoctin Battalion of militia on May 13, 1778, and a captain in the 34th Battalion of militia on March 29, 1779 [Ref: B-122, and Z-79, although Ref: H-15 stated May 31, 1778]. See "Daniel Smyth," q.v.

SMITH, Edward. Private who enlisted in Frederick on August 21, 1780 and was "not marched [to Annapolis] for want of pay." [Ref: A-344].

SMITH, Eli. Private who enlisted on July 29, 1776 [Ref: A-44].

SMITH, Elias. Defective from the Maryland Line in June, 1780 [Ref: A-414].

SMITH, Everheart. Private in the German Regiment, muster roll dated October 23, 1776 [Ref: A-264].

SMITH, Gaspar. See "John Smith," q.v.

SMITH, George. Gave money in the amount of 2 lbs. 12 sh. 1 p. for arms and ammunition for the militia, 1775 [Ref: E-62]. Associator in December, 1775 [Ref: E-172]. Juror to the Oath of Allegiance in 1778 [Ref: C-29]. One George Smith died testate in 1793, leaving children George, John, Christian, Charlotte, Margaret, Elizabeth, Christiana, Mary, Eva, and Barbara [Ref: M-9:33].

SMITH, Gilbert. Militia substitute from May to December 10, 1781, and "marched to Annapolis." [Ref: A-653].

SMITH, Godfrey. Juror to the Oath of Allegiance in March, 1778 [Ref: S-266, but not listed in Ref: C-30].

SMITH, Henry. Associator in December, 1775 [Ref: E-173]. Private who enlisted on July 1, 1776 in Capt. Peter Mantz's company; marched from Frederick Town to Leonardtown, and from there to Philadelphia, arriving on August 23, 1776 [Ref: A-47].

SMITH, Henry. Private in the German Regiment, enlisted August 5, 1776 [Ref: A-45, A-261, N-30:112]. Juror to the Oath of Allegiance, 1778 [Ref: C-29].

SMITH, Jacob. Associator in December, 1775 [Ref: E-172]. (This name appeared three times on the list of Associators). Subscribed to the Oath of Allegiance in 1778 [Ref: C-29]. One petitioned the General Assembly under the Act of January 14, 1781, stating he had been a non-juror to the Oath of Allegiance and Fidelity in 1778 due to "ignorance" and now desired relief under the Act and to take the Oath [Ref: L-101]. Jacob Smith died testate in 1794, leaving wife Anna Elizabeth and children Jacob, Mary, Susanna, Christina, and Catherine, plus his brother Andrew [Ref: M-9:41]. Also, see "Michael Smith," q.v.

SMITH, James. Served on the Committee of Observation in 1775 [Ref: I-85]. Associator in December, 1775 [Ref: E-172, E-173]. (This name appeared twice on the list of Associators). One was Juror to the Oath of Allegiance in 1778 [Ref: C-29]. One furnished powder and lead for use of the militia in Frederick Town on November 29, 1775 [Ref: E-60, E-61]. One gave money in the amount of 5 lbs. 5 sh. for arms and ammunition for the militia in 1775 [Ref: E-63]. One "James Smith, merchant, one of the wealthiest inhabitants of Frederick County, died on January 3, 1804, aged 66." [Ref: F-470]. "James Smith, of Marsh Hundred" was appointed by the Committee of Correspondence to solicit subscriptions to purchase arms and ammunition in 1775 in Manor Hundred [Ref: I-86].

SMITH, James. "Born in September, 1755, James lived in Frederick County, Maryland, at the time of his enlistment. He applied for a pension on August 9, 1832, in Adair County, Kentucky, and by 1835 had moved to Gibbon [Gibson] County, Indiana. He married Margaret "Peggy" Truax on January 28, 1783, in Loudon County, Virginia. In 1835 he stated that all of his children had moved to Indiana. No children were named, but an Andrew Smith made affidavit in 1835. He (James) died on January 29, 1838, and his widow applied for pension (W9657) on April 9, 1842, aged 87, in Gibson County, Indiana, and a Stephen and Jane Daugherty were witnesses in 1843 (kinship not stated). Also, a John Meane signed the marriage bond with soldier in 1783 in Loudoun County, Virginia." [Ref: T-3193, J-9].

339

SMITH, James. Private qho enlisted on May 20, 1778 [Ref: A-323]. Private, 1st Maryland Regiment, in 1780, and served in the Southern Army of the United States under Lt. William Lamar in the late Capt. Beatty's company. He was a waggoner in July, 1781 [Ref: A-390].

SMITH, James. Private, 2nd Maryland Regiment, who was disabled at the Battle of Camden. His invalid pension commenced on November 29, 1783, and ceased on November 1, 1789 [Ref: A-630, A-631].

SMITH, James. Private in the Middle District Militia in 1776 in Capt. Valentine Creager's company [Ref: A-72]. Private in the German Regiment in 1776 [Ref: A-266]. Served at White Plains on September 5, 1778, under Lt. Col. Ludwick Weltner [Ref: A-267]. Promoted to corporal on August 1, 1779 [Ref: A-264].

SMITH, James (Ironmaster, Pipe Creek). Non-Enroller who was fined by the Committee of Observation in April, 1776 [Ref: E-248].

SMITH, John. Associator in December, 1775 [Ref: E-172]. (This name appeared four times on the list of Associators).

SMITH, John. "Born on July 17, 1760, in Prince George's County, Maryland, he moved at the age of 5 with his father (name not given) to Frederick County, VT (Vermont; an obvious typographical error in the record since this Frederick County is in Maryland). There he enlisted as a private and served for 2 months from January, 1777, in Col. Beatty's Regiment, for two months from August, 1777, as a substitute for his brother Henry Smith in Col. Johnson's Regiment, and again in 1781. He married in Frederick County (date and name of wife not stated) and lived there for 2 years after the war and then moved to Harrison County, Virginia. He applied for pension (S46521) on August 25, 1832, and died prior to January 2, 1840, leaving no widow." [Ref: T-3198, K-94].

SMITH, John. Drafted on June 2, 1783, but "hath not appeared." [Ref: B-169].

SMITH, John. Enlisted in the Maryland Line at Fredericktown. A son, John Smith, Jr., made affidavit on May 16, 1846, in Greene County, Tennessee, aged 51, stating he was the fourth child of the deceased soldier, John Smith, Sr., and that he (John Smith, Jr.) was born in Frederick County, Maryland, in March, 1795. He stated he had left Maryland in 1816 and married and settled in East Tennessee in 1828 at which time he went to Frederick County, Maryland and brought his mother to Sullivan County, Tennessee in November, 1828. He stated that his mother was then living with his brother Gaspar Smith in Sullivan County, Tennessee, and his brother Gaspar made affidavit in

May, 1846, aged 48, and stated he was born December 28, 1797, in Frederick County, Maryland, and his father died February 18, 1821. His widow applied for a pension (W170) on May 13, 1846, aged 80, in Sullivan County, stating her name was Catharine Hohn and she had married John Smith on August 5, 1786, in Frederick County, Maryland and those present were John Ricks and his wife Catharine Ricks, Michael Muller, and Catharine Boyer. The soldier John Smith was a son of Peter Smith who was deceased in 1786. Family data as shown: Chatanah Honin [Hohn?], born November 14, 1765; Christopher Honin [Hohn?], born August 15, 1759; Susanah Honin [Hohn?], born December 29, 1753; Gaspar Smith, born December 28, 1797; David Smith, born January 18, 1801; Daniel Smith, born April 4, 1803. There was also some data in the pension file written in German: Anna Maria Schmid, born August 3, 1787; Barbara Schmid, born September 11, 1789; Wilhelm Schmid, born June 15, 1792; John Smith, our son, born March 12, 1795 (also shown in German as Johannes Schmid). In 1846 Gaspar Smith stated he was the soldier's fifth child. [Ref: T-3198, K-94]. Another source states that "the son of emigrant Johan Schmidt was John Smith (c1753-1802). He was a Revolutionary soldier and on the local Committee of Observation in 1775. John married Elizabeth Keiser as disclosed in the typed genealogy by Dorothy Foreman Still (after 1958) in the files of Calvin E. Schildknecht, of Gettysburg, Pennsylvania." [Ref: O-40].

SMITH, John. Ensign in the Middle District Militia in August, 1776, in Capt. Philip Meroney's company [Ref: A-44, A-46, N-30:111]. "Captain John Smith, of Carroll's Manor, died on August 14, 1804, no age given." [Ref: N-56]. He was a captain in the 6th Maryland Regiment and was involved in and paid for recruiting services on January 11, 1780 [Ref: V-66].

SMITH, John. Juror to the Oath of Allegiance in 1778 [Ref: C-29, S-266].

SMITH, John. Private in the 7th Maryland Regiment who enlisted in Frederick Town between January and April, 1780, and was reported as "gone to Camp" [Ref: A-334].

SMITH, John. Private in the Middle District Militia in 1776 in Capt. Valentine Creager's company [Ref: A-72]. Private in the German Regiment, on muster roll dated October 23, 1776, and was discharged on October 12, 1779 [Ref: A-264, A-265].

SMITH, John. Private who enlisted July 1, 1776 [Ref: A-43]. Another John Smith was a private who enlisted March 28, 1778 [Ref: A-315]. Perhaps one of these men (or others listed herein) was the soldier who moved to Pendleton County, Virginia, and applied for a pension (W6117), aged 73. He lived in Frederick County, Maryland, at the time of his enlistment and in 1781 he moved with his father to Shenandoah County, Virginia, and also enlisted there. "John Smith married Sarah Hawn on October 4, 1778, and had 1 if not 2 children while he was in the service," according to his brother Jacob Smith, aged 74, in June, 1843. Magdalena Ridenour, aged 82 in 1844, also made affidavit in Shenandoah County, Virginia, but no relationship was given. [Ref: T-3199].

SMITH, John. Sergeant in Capt. William Blair's company of militia on November 29, 1775 [Ref: E-55].

SMITH, John (dyer). Private who enlisted on July 1, 1776 in Capt. Peter Mantz's company; marched from Frederick Town to Leonardtown, and from there to Philadelphia, arriving August 23, 1776 [Ref: A-47].

SMITH, Jonathan. Associator in December, 1775 [Ref: E-172]. Juror to the Oath of Allegiance in 1778 [Ref: C-29].

SMITH, Joseph. Served on the Committee of Observation in 1775 [Ref: I-85]. Lieutenant colonel in the 36th Battalion of militia in Frederick County on January 6, 1776, and commissioned colonel on April 20, 1776 [Ref: B-122, W-356]. Reviewed and passed recruits in Frederick County in 1776 [Ref: A-50]. Colonel in Washington County on June 22, 1778 [Ref: B-122, Z-145].

SMITH, Joseph. Private in the Middle District Militia in 1776 in Capt. Valentine Creager's company [Ref: A-72].

SMITH, Leonard (1734-1794). Served on the Committee of Observation in 1775 [Ref: I-85]. Resident of Lower Monocacy Hundred. Appointed by the Committee of Correspondence to solicit subscriptions in 1775 to purchase arms and ammunition [Ref: I-86]. Associator in December, 1775 [Ref: E-172]. Coroner in 1777 [Ref: F-476]. Juror to the Oath of Allegiance in 1778 [Ref: C-29]. He died testate in 1794, leaving wife Elizabeth (died June 27, 1820, and her maiden name was Neale) and their children Raphael, Benjamin, John, Joseph, Charles, Francis, Mary (1764-1834, and married Leonard Jamison), and Jean [Ref: M-9:37, M-9:38, U-990].

SMITH, Levy. Private who enlisted February 27, 1778 [Ref: A-314].

SMITH, Mathias. Private in the German Regiment. Served at White Plains on September 5, 1778, under Lt. Col. Weltner [Ref: A-266].

SMITH, Michael. Private who enlisted on May 20, 1778 [Ref: A-323]. Served in the German Regiment at White Plains on September 5, 1778, under Lt. Col. Weltner [Ref: A-267]. One Michael Smith died testate in

1787, leaving a wife (not named) and children John (oldest son), Christopher, Michael (third son), Catharina, Mary, and "my stepson Philip Lipps." [Ref: M-7:32]. Another "Michael Smith, farmer," died testate in 1781, leaving wife Anna Mary and children Andrew (oldest son), Henry, Jacob, and Anna Mary, and also mentioning his brother Jacob Smith [Ref: M-5:168]. "Michael Smith, nailor," was drafted on June 2, 1783, but "hath not appeared." [Ref: B-168].

SMITH, Peter. Associator in December, 1775 [Ref: E-173]. Juror to the Oath of Allegiance in 1778 [Ref: C-29].

SMITH, Philip. Associator in December, 1775 [Ref: E-172, E-173]. (This name appeared twice on the list of Associators). Subscribed to the Oath of Allegiance in 1778 [Ref: C-29, S-266]. Loaned $800 for the use of the State of Maryland in June, 1780 [Ref: V-520]. One "Philip Smith, farmer," died testate in 1786, leaving wife Elizabeth and children Philip, Henry (the youngest son), Catharine (the oldest daughter), Elizabeth, Margarett, Ann Mary, plus his wife's brother Jacob Sinn [Ref: M-7:31]. "Philip Smith, Sr." died testate in 1790, leaving wife Eva Christiana and children Philip Jr., John, Mary Catharine, William, Mary Christiana, Juliana, and Christopher [Ref: M-8:34].

SMITH, Philip Jr. Associator in December, 1775 [Ref: E-172]. 1st lieutenant in the Middle District Militia on October 3, 1776, in Capt. Valentine Creager's company [Ref: A-72, X-317]. Juror to the Oath of Allegiance in 1778 [Ref: C-29]. Promoted to captain on May 15, 1776, and major in the 37th Battalion of militia on April 27, 1779 [Ref: H-16, B-122, W-427, Z-368]. See "Peter Barrick," q.v.

SMITH, Richard. Served on the Committee of Observation in 1775 [Ref: I-85]. Gave money in the amount of 7 lbs. 5 sh. for arms and ammunition for the militia in 1775 [Ref: E-62]. "R. Smith" was appointed by the Committee of Correspondence in 1775 to solicit subscriptions to purchase arms and ammunition in Sugar Loaf Hundred [Ref: I-86]. Richard Smith was commissioned the captain of a cadet company in the Lower District on March 26, 1776 [Ref: W-287].

SMITH, Richard. Substitute on June 13, 1781, and marched with Capt. Dyer [Ref: D-1814].

SMITH, Robert. Private who enlisted on May 20, 1778 [Ref: A-323]. Served in the German Regiment at White Plains on September 5, 1778, under Lt. Col. Ludwick Weltner [Ref: A-266].

SMITH, Samuel (General). See "John Stricker," q.v.

SMITH, Samuel. Non-Enroller who was fined by the Committee of Observation in April, 1776 [Ref: E-248]. Enlisted as a private on July 19, 1776 [Ref: A-51].
SMITH, Thomas. Private who enlisted on July 1 or 19, 1776 [Ref: A-47, A-51]. Juror to the Oath of Allegiance in 1778 [Ref: C-29]. Militia substitute on June 8, 1778 [Ref: A-325]. One Thomas Smith provided wheat for the military in May, 1782 [Ref: R-515]. "Thomas Smith, of Taney Town Hundred, planter," died testate in 1785, leaving a wife Mary and children Amos, Jacob, and Patience [Ref: M-6:187].
SMITH, Walter (Georgetown). Appointed by the Committee of Correspondence to solicit subscriptions in 1775 to purchase arms and ammunition [Ref: I-85].
SMITH, William. Non-Enroller fined by the Committee of Observation in April, 1776 [Ref: E-248]. One William Smith provided wheat for the military in May, 1782 [Ref: R-515]. One William Smith enrolled as an Associator in December, 1775 [Ref: E-172].
SMITH, William. Sergeant in Capt. Valentine Creager's company of militia on November 29, 1775 [Ref: E-53]. Associator in December, 1775 [Ref: E-173]. Juror to the Oath of Allegiance, 1778 [Ref: C-29].
SMITH, William Jr. 1st lieutenant in the 2nd Battalion of militia on November 29, 1775, under Capt. Joseph Wood [Ref: B-123].
SMITHLY, John. Private in the German Regiment, muster roll dated October 23, 1776 [Ref: A-264]. Discharged on October 12, 1779 [Ref: A-265].
SMITHLY, Matthias. Sergeant in Capt. Philip Rodenbieler's company of militia on November 29, 1775 [Ref: E-51].
SMITHLY, Phillip. Private in the German Regiment, on muster roll dated October 23, 1776 [Ref: A-264]. "Philip Smithly" was discharged on October 12, 1779 [Ref: A-265].
SMYTH, Daniel. Served in the Maryland Line and applied for pension (S35074) on September 29, 1818, in Frederick County, aged 60. Yet, in 1820 he gave his age as 70 and stated he had a wife Aicy (Aixy or Ainy?), aged about 30 [sic] years. [Ref: T-3237, J-25].
SMYTH, Thomas. 1st lieutenant in the militia on February 12, 1776 [Ref: B-123].
SNAKE, Adam. Associator in December, 1775 [Ref: E-172]. Juror to the Oath of Allegiance in 1778 [Ref: C-29].
SNAKE [SNUKE?], John. Juror to the Oath of Allegiance in March, 1778 [Ref: S-266].

SNATZELL [SNATSELL], George. Loaned $2,000 for the use of the State of Maryland in June, 1780 [Ref: V-520]. Served as a private in the horse troops in June, 1781 [Ref: B-168].

SNAVELY, Henry (Salisbury Hundred). Served on the Committee of Observation in 1775. Appointed by the Committee of Correspondence to solicit subscriptions in 1775 to purchase arms and ammunition [Ref: I-85].

SNIDER, Casper. Private stationed at Fort Frederick on June 27, 1778, in Capt. John Kershner's company, and guarding prisoners of war [Ref: A-328].

SNIDER, Jacob. Corporal in Capt. Peter Mantz's company of militia on November 29, 1775 [Ref: E-50].

SNIDER, John. Private in the German Regiment, enlisted on July 1, 1776 [Ref: A-47, A-261]. Corporal, Flying Camp. Disabled at Battle of White Plains (lost his leg) and his invalid pension commenced on December 1, 1776, and ceased on November 1, 1789 (no reason given). [Ref: A-630, A-631, F-476].

SNIDER, Peter. Ensign in Capt. Jacob Snowdenberger's company of militia, 2nd Battalion, on November 29, 1775 [Ref: E-56, B-123]. Ensign in the 37th Battalion on June 22, 1776 [Ref: B-123].

SNIDER, William. Private in the German Regiment, 1776, in Capt. Henry Fister's company under the command of Col. Nicholas Hussecker [Ref: A-261].

SNIDIKER, Christian. Private in the Skipton District Militia under Capt. Thomas Waring on April 16, 1776 [Ref: B-167, D-1814].

SNODIGGLE, John Peter. Associator in December, 1775 [Ref: E-173]. Juror to the Oath of Allegiance in 1778 [Ref: C-29].

SNOWDEGLE, Jacob. Associator in December, 1775 [Ref: E-173]. Juror to the Oath of Allegiance in 1778 [Ref: C-29].

SNOWDEGLE, John. Associator in December, 1775 [Ref: E-173]. Juror to the Oath of Allegiance in 1778 [Ref: C-29].

SNOWDEIGEL [SNOWDENGE], Peter. Private who enlisted on July 1, 1776 in Capt. Peter Mantz's company, and marched from Frederick Town to Leonardtown, and from there to Philadelphia, arriving on August 23, 1776 [Ref: A-47].

SNOWDENBERGER, Jacob. Captain of a company of militia in the 2nd Battalion on November 29, 1775 [Ref: E-56 and B-123, which latter source listed his name as "John Snodenberry" on June 22, 1776].

SNOWFER, Christopher. Juror to the Oath of Allegiance in March, 1778 [Ref: S-266, but not listed in Ref: C-30].

SNOWFER, John. Juror to the Oath of Allegiance in March, 1778 [Ref: S-266, but not listed in Ref: C-30].
SNYDER, Jacob. Non-Enroller who was fined by the Committee of Observation in May, 1776 [Ref: E-248].
SNYDER, Michael. Juror to the Oath of Allegiance in March, 1778 [Ref: S-266, but not listed in Ref: C-30].
SOLAMON, Samuel. Private in the militia in July, 1776 [Ref: A-42].
SOLMAN, Henry. Drafted on June 13, 1781, and provided a substitute [Ref: D-1814].
SOMFNODE, Peter Jr. Associator in December, 1775 [Ref: E-172]. Juror to the Oath of Allegiance in 1778 [Ref: C-29].
SOMFNODE, Peter Sr. Associator in December, 1775 [Ref: E-172]. Juror to the Oath of Allegiance in 1778 [Ref: C-29].
SOUDER, Adam. Associator in December, 1775 [Ref: E-172]. "Draught," from May to December 10, 1781, and "marched to Annapolis." [Ref: A-653]. Signed as Juror to the Oath of Allegiance in 1778 [Ref: C-29].
SOWER, Frederick. Associator in December, 1775 [Ref: E-173]. Juror to the Oath of Allegiance in 1778 [Ref: C-29]. Ann Mary, widow of a "Frederick Sowers," applied for pension (W6144) in Page County, Virginia, in 1836, stating her husband had served in the Virginia Line [Ref: T-3254].
SOWER, Philip. 2nd lieutenant in Capt. Snowdenberger's company of militia in the 2nd Battalion on November 29, 1775. 1st lieutenant in the 37th Battalion of militia on December 28, 1776, under Col. James Johnson [Ref: B-123, E-56, X-555].
SOY, Frederick. Drafted June 13, 1781, with "cert. of his procuring a sub. during the war." [Ref: D-1814].
SPALDING, Catherine. See "Francis Elder," q.v.
SPALDING, Elizabeth. See "Thomas Elder," q.v.
SPARROW, Alexander. Private who enlisted July 24, 1776 [Ref: A-50].
SPEAK, Andrew. Private who enlisted on July 1, 1776 in Capt. Peter Mantz's company; marched from Frederick Town to Leonardtown, and from there to Philadelphia, arriving August 23, 1776 [Ref: A-47].
SPEAKE, Hezekiah. Private who enlisted July 22, 1776 [Ref: A-49].
SPEAKE, Lewis. Private who enlisted on July 22, 1776 [Ref: A-49].
SPEAKE, Nathan. Militia substitute on June 3, 1778 [Ref: A-325].
SPEELMAN, Andrew. Sergeant in Capt. Michael McGuire's company of militia on November 29, 1775 [Ref: E-57].
SPEIGHT, John Conrad. Associator in December, 1775 [Ref: E-173]. Juror to the Oath of Allegiance in 1778 [Ref: C-29].

SPELLMAN, Michael. Associator in December, 1775 [Ref: E-172]. Juror to the Oath of Allegiance in 1778 [Ref: C-29].

SPESSER, Michael. Private stationed at Fort Frederick in June, 1778 [Ref: A-328].

SPIELMAN, Jacob. Associator in December, 1775 [Ref: E-172]. Juror to the Oath of Allegiance in 1778 [Ref: C-29].

SPLISE, Peter. Private who enlisted on July 19, 1776 [Ref: A-51].

SPONSELLER, John (1755-1825). Private in Capt. John Gist's company, in Col. Nathaniel Gist's Regiment of Rangers, attached to the 3rd Maryland Line, commanded by Col. Mordecai Gist in 1778. He married Elizabeth Lambrecht (1761-1807) in 1786 and their son John Jacob Sponseller (1791-1873) married Catherine Shope (1793-1870) in 1814. John was born and died in Frederick County [Ref: U-1745, A-600].

SPOONS, John. Associator in December, 1775 [Ref: E-172]. Juror to the Oath of Allegiance in 1778 [Ref: C-29]. See "John Spuhn," q.v.

SPRAY, John. Private who enlisted on April 24, 1778, and served in the 2nd Maryland Regiment [Ref: A-294, A-321].

SPRICHT, Anthony. Associator in December, 1775 [Ref: E-173]. Juror to the Oath of Allegiance in 1778 [Ref: C-29].

SPRIGG, James. Served on the Committee of Observation in 1775 [Ref: I-85].

SPRIGG, Samuel. Private who enlisted on July 19, 1776 [Ref: A-51].

SPRIGG, Thomas. Captain who died on July 10, 1810 [Ref: F-471].

SPRINGER, Charles. 2nd lieutenant in Capt. Joseph Wood, Jr.'s company of militia, 2nd Battalion, on November 29, 1775 [Ref: E-53, B-124]. Associator in December, 1775 [Ref: E-172]. Juror to the Oath of Allegiance in 1778 [Ref: C-29].

SPRINGER, John. Associator in December, 1775 [Ref: E-172]. Private in the Middle District Militia in 1776 in Capt. Valentine Creager's company [Ref: A-72].

SPUHN, John. Petitioned the General Assembly under the Act of May 12, 1780, stating he had been a non-juror to the Oath of Allegiance and Fidelity in 1778 due to "ignorance" and now desired relief under the Act and to take the Oath [Ref: L-101].

SPUNOGLE, George. Private who was enlisted on July 20, 1776 by Capt. Jacob Good [Ref: A-46].

SPYCER, Samuel. Private who enlisted on July 13, 1776 [Ref: A-43].

SPYKER, Benjamin. Captain in the Lower District Militia in Frederick [now Montgomery] County on August 7, 1776 [Ref: A-42, although Ref: X-187 states he was commissioned on July 26, 1776].

STACKER, Zephaniah. Sergeant in Capt. Abraham Hayter's company of militia on November 29, 1775 [Ref: E-52].

STAGER, Jacob. Associator in December, 1775 [Ref: E-172]. Juror to the Oath of Allegiance in 1778 [Ref: C-29].

STAGER, John. Associator in 1775 [Ref: E-172].

STALEY, Henry (1747-1800). Son of Jacob Stehli and Anna Margaret Rebstock, of Switzerland. "Henry Staly" was 1st Sergeant in Capt. Christopher Stull's company of militia on November 29, 1775 [Ref: E-50]. "Henry Staley" was an Associator in December, 1775 [Ref: E-172], and paid by the Committee of Observation "for carriage of 7 chests of provisional arms" in 1775 [Ref: E-64]. Juror to the Oath of Allegiance in 1778 [Ref: C-29, S-266]. Henry Staley (Stehli) married Catherine ---- and had children Henry, Daniel, Esther, David, Samuel, Mathias, Catherine, Sophia, and Elias [Ref: O-102]. One "Henry Stayley" petitioned the General Assembly under the Act of May 12, 1780, stating that he had been a non-juror to the Oath of Allegiance and Fidelity in 1778 due to "ignorance" and now desired relief under the Act and to take the Oath [Ref: L-101]. "Henry Stealy" was a sergeant in Capt. Michael Troutman's militia company on November 29, 1775 [Ref: E-51].

STALEY, Jacob. There were three men with this name at this time. One was Jacob Staley (or Stehli), son of Jacob Stehli and Anna Margaret Rebstock, of Switzerland, who married (Catharine) Barbara ---- and they had children Joseph, George Peter, John, Jacob, and Susannah. A second was Jacob Staley (1756-1822, son of Johan Jacob Staley), who married Ann Castle and they had children John, Jacob, and Lydia. The third was Jacob Staley (1751-1815, son of Melchoir Staley), who married Anna Barbara ---- and they had children Jacob, John Peter, Charlotte, Anna Maria, Barbara, Jacob H., Frederick, John, and Susanna [Ref: O-102]. Associator in December, 1775 [Ref: E-172]. Juror to the Oath of Allegiance in 1778 [Ref: C-29, S-266]. One Jacob Staley petitioned the General Assembly under the Act of May 12, 1780, stating that he had been a non-juror to the Oath of Allegiance and Fidelity in 1778 due to "ignorance" and now desired relief under the Act and to take the Oath [Ref: L-101].

STALEY, Joseph. Son of Jacob Stehli and Anna Margaret Rebstock, of Switzerland. Associator in December, 1775 [Ref: E-172]. Juror to the Oath of Allegiance in 1778 [Ref: C-29]. Joseph Staley (Stehli) married Maria Juliana Heffner (Hoefner) and they had children Joseph, Anna Maria, John Jacob, Elizabeth, Catherine, George, Solomon, Magdalena, Margaret, Moses, Susanna, and Maria Juliana [Ref: O-102].

STALEY [STAYLEY], Melchor. Loaned $200 for the use of the State of Maryland in June, 1780 [Ref: V-520].

STALLINGS, Abraham. Enlisted on May 20, 1778 [Ref: A-323]. "Abram Stallings" was a fifer in the 1st Maryland Regiment in 1781, and served in the Southern Army of the United States under Lt. William Lamar in the late Capt. Beatty's company [Ref: A-389]. One "Abm. Stallions" was a fifer in the 7th Maryland Regiment, Capt. Beatty's company, in 1779 [Ref: A-310].

STALLINGS, William. Private who enlisted July 18, 1776 [Ref: A-49].

STAMPLE, Frederick. See "Frederick Stembell," q.v.

STANDARD, William. Corporal in Capt. William Duvall's company of militia on November 29, 1775 [Ref: E-54].

STANLEY, Christ. Private who enlisted on July 1, 1776, in Capt. Peter Mantz's company; marched from Frederick Town to Leonardtown, and from there to Philadelphia, arriving on August 23, 1776 [Ref: A-47]. "Chrisr. Stanley" was drafted on June 2, 1783; "absconded." [Ref: B-168].

STANLEY, Thomas. Private who enlisted July 1, 1776 in Capt. Peter Mantz's company; marched from Frederick Town to Leonardtown, and from there to Philadelphia, arriving August 23, 1776 [Ref: A-47].

STANLY, Michael. Private who enlisted on July 29, 1776 [Ref: A-43].

STANNER, Michael. Associator in December, 1775 [Ref: E-173]. Juror to the Oath of Allegiance in 1778 [Ref: C-29].

STANSBURY, Ezekiel. Associator in December, 1775 [Ref: E-173]. Juror to the Oath of Allegiance in 1778 [Ref: C-29].

STANTON, John. Private who enlisted May 7, 1778 [Ref: A-322], and served in the German Regiment at White Plains on September 5, 1778, under Lt. Col. Ludwick Weltner [Ref: A-266]. "John Staunton or Stanton" served in the Maryland Line and applied for a pension (S35086) on June 3, 1818, aged 66, in Frederick County, Maryland. In 1820 he stated he had no family. [Ref: T-3304 and J-25, which latter source stated he was aged 81].

STARFER, Gelles. Associator in December, 1775 [Ref: E-173]. Juror to the Oath of Allegiance in 1778 [Ref: C-29].

STARNS, Thomas and Elizabeth. See "Jacob Brunner," q.v.

STARR, Samuel and Jane. See "Levi Davis," q.v.

STATLER, Henry. Private in the German Regiment, muster roll dated October 23, 1776 [Ref: A-264]. Discharged on October 12, 1779 [Ref: A-265].

STAUB, John. Associator in December, 1775 [Ref: E-173]. Juror to the Oath of Allegiance in 1778 [Ref: C-29].

STAYLEY, Melchor. See "Melchor Staley," q.v.

STAYMAR, Christian. Non-Enroller who was fined by the Committee of Observation in April, 1776 [Ref: E-248].

STEEL, Christopher. Non-Enroller who was fined by the Committee of Observation in April, 1776 [Ref: E-248]. He died testate in 1782, leaving wife Catherine and children Abraham, Susanna, Eve, Salome, and Christopher [Ref: M-6:30].

STEEL, George. Juror to the Oath of Allegiance in March, 1778 [Ref: S-266, but not listed in Ref: C-30].

STEEL, James. Associator in December, 1775 [Ref: E-173]. Juror to the Oath of Allegiance in 1778 [Ref: C-29].

STEEL, John. Private who enlisted on July 18, 1776 [Ref: A-49].

STEHLI, Jacob. See "Jacob Staley," q.v.

STEIGER, John. Associator in December, 1775 [Ref: E-173]. Juror to the Oath of Allegiance in 1778 [Ref: C-29].

STEIN, Frederick. Private who enlisted April 10, 1778 [Ref: A-315].

STEINER, Jacob. Associator in December, 1775 [Ref: E-173]. Juror to the Oath of Allegiance in 1778 [Ref: C-29, S-267].

STEINER [STONER], John (c1735-1798). Captain of a militia company on November 29, 1775 through 1779 [Ref: H-16, E-56, B-126, U-1453]. Associator in December, 1775, and was appointed "to hand about the Association paper in Middle Monocacy Hundred." [Ref: E-172, E-305]. Chosen to serve on the Committee of Observation in 1775 [Ref: E-302, I-85]. Signed as Juror to the Oath of Allegiance in 1778 [Ref: C-29]. "John Stoner (Steiner) married Catharine Elizabeth Ramsburg (1739-1792) and a daughter Catharine Margaret Stoner (1774-1813) married John Derr (1774-1838). [Ref: U-1453]. "Capt. John Steiner or Stoner (c.1757-1798), son of Jacob Steiner (1713-1748), of Germany (and Frederick County), married Catherine Elizabeth Ramsburg (1739-1792) and a son Henry Steiner, Sr. (c1764-1831) married Elizabeth Brengel (1767-1833) on October 14, 1787 [Ref: U-2890, and U-2718, citing *The DAR Patriot Index*, Vol. I, page 653, and *The Genealogy of the Steiner Family*, by Lewis H. and Bernard C. Steiner. It should be noted, however, if Jacob Steiner died in 1748 then John could not have been born circa 1757. He apparently was born circa 1735-1737].

STEINER, Michael. Private in German Regiment, 1776, in Capt. Henry Fister's company under the command of Col. Hussecker [Ref: A-261].

STELLY, Peter. See "Peter Stilly," q.v.

STEM, Elizabeth. See "Philip Angler (Englar)," q.v.

STEMBELL, Frederick. "Frederick Stembell" was an Associator in December, 1775 [Ref: E-173]. and a Juror to the Oath of Allegiance in 1778 [Ref: C-29]. One "Frederick Stample" was 1st lieutenant in Capt. Van Swearingen's company of militia, 33rd Battalion, on January 17, 1777 [Ref: Y-54, B-124, 125, which latter source also spelled his name "Stemple."].

STEPHANS, Peter. Corporal, 1st Maryland Regiment, 1781, and served in the Southern Army of the United States under Lt. William Lamar in the late Capt. Beatty's company [Ref: A-389].

STEPHEN, Jacob. Associator in December, 1775 [Ref: E-173]. Juror to the Oath of Allegiance in 1778 [Ref: C-29].

STEPHEN, William. Provided wheat for the military in July, 1782 [Ref: R-537].

STEPHENS, Charles Crouch. 1st lieutenant in the militia on December 28, 1776, under Capt. William Brashears [Ref: B-125, X-555].

STEPHENS, William. Private who enlisted in 1778 and served in the 2nd Maryland Regiment [Ref: A-294].

STEPHENSON, Charles. 1st lieutenant in the militia on December 28, 1776 [Ref: B-125, X-555, Y-54]. Also, see "Charles Stevenson," q.v.

STEPHENSON, Daniel (Burnt House Woods Hundred). Non-Enroller who was fined by the Committee of Observation in June, 1776 [Ref: E-248]. Provided wheat for the military in June, 1782 [Ref: R-521].

STEPHENSON, Edward (of Richard), Little Pipe Creek Hundred. Non-Enroller who was fined by the Committee of Observation in June, 1776 [Ref: E-248].

STEPHENSON, Henry. Captain in the militia on December 28, 1776 [Ref: B-125, X-555, Y-54]. Also, see "Henry Stevenson," q.v.

STEPHENSON, John Jr. Non-Enroller who was fined by the Committee of Observation in April, 1776 [Ref: E-248].

STEPHENSON, Richard (Little Pipe Creek Hundred). Non-Enroller who was fined by the Committee of Observation, June, 1776 [Ref: E-248].

STEPHENSON, William. Ensign in the militia on December 28, 1776 [Ref: B-125, X-555, Y-54]. Also, see "William Stevenson," q.v.

STERLING, Alexander. Private in the 7th Maryland Regiment who enlisted in Frederick Town some time between January and April, 1780, and was reported as "gone to Camp" [Ref: A-334].

STEUARD, James. Ensign in the Upper District Militia on July 4, 1776, under Capt. Joseph Chapline [Ref: B-125, W-546].

STEVENS, Charles. 1st lieutenant in the Linganore Battalion of Militia on January 17, 1777 [Ref: Y-54. Ed. Note: This may be a reference to "Charles Stevenson" rather than "Charles Stevens."]

STEVENS, Jacob. Private who enlisted on July 1, 1776 in Capt. Peter Mantz's company; marched from Frederick Town to Leonardtown, and from there to Philadelphia, arriving August 23, 1776 [Ref: A-47].

STEVENS, Peter. Non-Enroller who was fined by the Committee of Observation in April, 1776 [Ref: E-248].

STEVENS, William. Private who enlisted May 19, 1778 [Ref: A-324].

STEVENSON, Charles. Associator in December, 1775, who "assisted in handing about the Association paper" in 1776 [Ref: E-172, E-245]. 1st lieutenant in the Linganore Battalion of militia on January 17, 1777 [Ref: B-125]. Juror to the Oath of Allegiance in 1778 [Ref: C-29]. Also, see "Charles Stevens" and "Charles Stephenson," q.v.

STEVENSON, Colonel. See "Moses Rawlings," q.v.

STEVENSON, Henry. Associator in December, 1775 [Ref: E-172]. Juror to the Oath of Allegiance in 1778 [Ref: C-29]. Captain in the Linganore Battalion of militia on January 17, 1777 [Ref: B-125]. One Henry Stevenson petitioned the General Assembly under the Act of July 3, 1780, stating he had been a non-juror to the Oath of Allegiance and Fidelity in 1778 due to "ignorance" and now desired relief under the Act and to take the Oath [Ref: L-101]. See "Henry Stephenson," q.v.

STEVENSON, Steven. Private who enlisted on April 29, 1778 [Ref: A-321].

STEVENSON, William. Associator in December, 1775 [Ref: E-172]. Juror to the Oath of Allegiance in 1778 [Ref: C-29]. See "William Stephenson," q.v.

STEWART, James. Private who enlisted on July 25, 1776 [Ref: A-51].

STEWART, John. Private who enlisted on July 13, 1776 [Ref: A-43].

STEWART, Thomas. Private who enlisted on July 13, 1776 [Ref: A-43].

STICKLEY, Catherine. See "Philip Ramsburg," q.v.

STICKLEY, Valentine. Associator in December, 1775 [Ref: E-173]. "Valentine Stickle" died testate in 1783, and left his entire estate to his wife Sybilla [Ref: M-6:32].

STIDLEY, Jacob. Associator in 1775 [Ref: E-173].

STIDLEY, Valentine. Juror to the Oath of Allegiance in 1778 [Ref: C-29].

STILE [STITE], James. Private who enlisted on May 14, 1778 [Ref: A-322, R-167, which both spelled the name as "Stite"]. "James Stiles" was a private in the German Regiment at White Plains on September 5, 1778, under command of Lt. Col. Ludwick Weltner [Ref: A-266].

STILL, Dorothy Foreman. See "John Smith (Johan Schmidt)," q.v.

STILLY, John. Associator in December, 1775 [Ref: E-172]. Juror to the Oath of Allegiance in 1778 [Ref: C-29].

STILLY [STELLY], Peter. "Peter Stelly" was 1st lieutenant in Capt. John Stoner's company of militia on November 29, 1775 [Ref: E-56, B-125]. "Peter Stilly" was an Associator in December, 1775 [Ref: E-172]. Juror to the Oath of Allegiance in 1778 [Ref: C-29, and S-266, which latter source spelled his name "Peter Stilley."]. Provided wheat for the military in May, 1782 [Ref: R-509].

STIMMEL, Catherine. See "John Carmack," q.v.

STIMMEL [STIMMLE], Peter. Loaned $600 for the use of the State of Maryland in June, 1780 [Ref: V-520]. See "William Albaugh," q.v.

STINE, Henry. Associator in December, 1775 [Ref: E-173]. Juror to the Oath of Allegiance in 1778 [Ref: C-29].

STINSON, John. Associator in December, 1775 [Ref: E-172]. Juror to the Oath of Allegiance in 1778 [Ref: C-29]. Officer [2nd lieutenant] in the militia, 1778-1779 [Ref: H-17, which source misspelled his name "Slinson" and omitted his rank].

STIRNELL, Jacob. Associator in December, 1775 [Ref: E-173]. Juror to the Oath of Allegiance in 1778 [Ref: C-29].

STITE, James. See "James Stile," q.v.

STITELEY, Frederick. Militia substitute from May to December 10, 1781 [Ref: A-652].

STITLEY, John. Corporal in Capt. John Carmack's company of militia on November 29, 1775 [Ref: E-56].

STITTLE, John. Associator in December, 1775 [Ref: E-173]. Juror to the Oath of Allegiance in 1778 [Ref: C-29].

STOAP, Peter. Associator in December, 1775 [Ref: E-173]. Juror to the Oath of Allegiance in 1778 [Ref: C-29].

STOCK, Anthony. Associator in December, 1775 [Ref: E-173]. Juror to the Oath of Allegiance in 1778 [Ref: C-29]. Also, see "Anthony Stoke," q.v.

STOCK, Peter. Associator in December, 1775 [Ref: E-173]. Juror to the Oath of Allegiance in 1778 [Ref: C-29].

STOCKMAN, George. Sergeant in Capt. William Luckett, Jr.'s militia company on November 29, 1775 [Ref: E-55]. Associator in December, 1775 [Ref: E-172]. Juror to the Oath of Allegiance in 1778 [Ref: C-29]. Provided wheat for the military in May, 1782 [Ref: R-515].

STOGDON, Thomas. Private who enlisted on July 18, 1776 [Ref: A-50].

STOKE, Anthony. 1st Corporal in Capt. Philip Thomas' company of militia on November 29, 1775 [Ref: E-50]. Also, see "Anthony Stock," q.v.

STOKES, James. Militia substitute from May to December 10, 1781, and "marched to Annapolis." [Ref: A-653].

STONE, Adam. Drafted on June 13, 1781, and was discharged, noting that he "comes under the law as an indigent person." [Ref: D-1814].

STONE, Charles. Private who enlisted in 1778 and served in the 2nd Maryland Regiment [Ref: A-294].

STONE, Cuthbert. Private in the 1st and 7th Maryland Regiments in 1780, and served in the Southern Army of the United States under Lt. William Lamar in the late Capt. Beatty's company in 1781. He also served in light infantry and was on hospital duty in July, 1781 [Ref: A-250, A-391].

STONE, Jacob. Associator in December, 1775 [Ref: E-172]. Juror to the Oath of Allegiance in 1778 [Ref: C-29].

STONE, John. Associator in December, 1775 [Ref: E-173]. Juror to the Oath of Allegiance in 1778 [Ref: C-29].

STONE, Sylvester. See "Humphrey Beckett," q.v.

STONE, Thomas (Signer). "The fame of Charles Carroll of Carrollton who never lived in Fredericktown has eclipsed that of a second Maryland Signer of the Declaration of Independence who lived in Frederick from 1764 until 1771, namely Thomas Stone (1743-1787). In August, 1765, on the recommendation of Edmund Key, Esquire, he was admitted as a lawyer to practice before the Court of Frederick County. Thomas Stone married Margaret Brown (1751-1787)... and his second wife was Margaret Block (of Frederick County)... Their son Frederick was born in Frederick in 1768 and died in Princeton, N.J. in 1793 of yellow fever." (They also had twin daughters Margaret, 1771-1809, and Mildred, 1771-1836.) "After leaving Frederick lawyer Stone practiced at Port Tobacco and then built a house in Annapolis in 1783... He attained the status of Esquire in 1778. Stone was a leader in the State Conventions preceding the Revolution and in the State Assembly thereafter. He was elected to the Constitutional Congress, 1774-1784, and to the Federal Convention that formed the Constitution. When his wife died suddenly in 1787, his physician recommended a sea voyage to cure him of despondency. He died in Alexandria while awaiting the ship." [Ref: O-33].

STONE, William. Associator in December, 1775 [Ref: E-172]. Juror to the Oath of Allegiance in 1778 [Ref: C-29].

STONEBREAKER, Adam. Private in the German Regiment on muster roll dated October 23, 1776 [Ref: A-264], and a corporal in the German Regiment until discharged July 24 or 26, 1779 [Ref: A-251, A-264].

STONEBREAKER [STONEBRAKER], Bostain. Associator in December, 1775 [Ref: E-173]. Juror to the Oath of Allegiance in 1778 [Ref: C-29].

STONEBREAKER [STONEBREAK], Valen [Valentine]. Private in the 7th Maryland Regiment on May 2, 1778; later "deserted." [Ref: A-249].

STONER, Christian. Loaned $400 for the use of the State of Maryland in June, 1780 [Ref: V-520].

STONER, Christopher. Associator in December, 1775 [Ref: E-173]. Juror to the Oath of Allegiance in 1778 [Ref: C-29].

STONER, David (of Jacob). Non-Enroller who was fined by the Committee of Observation in April, 1776 [Ref: E-248].

STONER, George. Private who enlisted on July 1, 1776 in Capt. Peter Mantz's company; marched from Frederick Town to Leonardtown, and from there to Philadelphia, arriving August 23, 1776 [Ref: A-47].

STONER, Jacob. Non-Enroller who was fined by the Committee of Observation in April, 1776 [Ref: E-248]. (Note: There appears to have been two men with this name on the list of non-enrollers). One Jacob Stoner provided wheat for the military in July, 1782 [Ref: R-533]. One Jacob Stoner (1752-1804) is buried in the Johnsville area [Ref: O-219].

STONER, John (of Jacob). Non-Enroller who was fined by the Committee of Observation in April, 1776 [Ref: E-248]. One John Stoner enlisted as a private on July 19, 1776 [Ref: A-51].

STONER, John (Sam's Creek, Unity Hundred). Non-Enroller who was fined by the Committee of Observation in June, 1776 [Ref: E-248].

STOOR, John. Associator in December, 1775 [Ref: E-173]. Juror to the Oath of Allegiance in 1778 [Ref: C-29].

STOPHEL, Frederick. Enlisted on April 10, 1781 for 3 years; marched with Capt. Lynn [Ref: D-1814].

STOPHEL, John. Enlisted on April 11, 1781 for 3 years; marched with Capt. Lynn [Ref: D-1814].

STORM, Christina. See "John Brunner," q.v.

STORM [STORAM], Jacob (May 12, 1754 - October 4, 1799). Private who enlisted July 19, 1776, and served in the Maryland Regiment [Ref: A-51, A-248, A-306]. Jacob Storm married Juliana Herr, or Herrmann (1760-1791) on April 15, 1784, in Frederick County, and a son Peter (or John Peter) Storm (January 21, 1787 - April 28, 1821) married Mary Magdelen Haller (1784-1862) on January 13, 1811 [Ref: U-2853, and U-2672, citing the *DAR Patriot Index*, Vol. I, page 653].

STORM (STURM), Maria A. and Maria B. See "Jacob Brunner," q.v.

STORM, Vandal. Associator in December, 1775 [Ref: E-173]. Juror to the Oath of Allegiance in 1778 [Ref: C-29].

STOTTLEMEYER [STADELMAYER], David (Jr). Son of David and Mary Magdalena Stottlemyer [Ref: O-55]. Associator in December, 1775 [Ref: E-173]. Juror to the Oath of Allegiance in 1778 [Ref: C-29]. Corporal in the Maryland militia and pensioned April 24, 1816. [Ref: J-9, but was not found in pension abstracts in Ref: T-3364].

STOTTLEMEYER [STADELMAYER], David, Sr. (c1725-1789) "David Stattle Myer" was an Associator in December, 1775 [Ref: E-170], and a juror to the Oath of Allegiance in 1778 [Ref: C-27]. "David Stadelmayer and wife Mary Magdalena, who emigrated in 1750, are said to have operated a mill at the site of Spoolsville on Catoctin or Middle Creek, west of Middletown (north of the National Pike). If David came in fact from Munich, Germany, that is remarkable, since it is so far from the Rhine River, the usual route of emigration for early settlers to Pennsylvania, and Western Maryland. David Stottlemire bought land from Nicholas Fink in Middletown Valley in 1761... The will of David Stottlemeyer gives children: Dewalt, David Jr., George, Jacob, John, Mary Ann Alexander, Eve Magdalena, Catherine, and Elizabeth." [Ref: O-55]. Another source lists them this way: Devault, David, George, Jacob, John, "Mary Ann Alexander Catherine Stottlemeyer," Eve Magdalena, and Catharine Elizabeth Stottlemeyer [Ref: M-8:38].

STOUDER, David. Non-Enroller who was fined by the Committee of Observation in April, 1776 [Ref: E-248].

STOUDER, John. Non-Enroller who was fined by the Committee of Observation in April, 1776 [Ref: E-248].

STOUDER, Philip. Private in the German Regiment in 1776 in Capt. Henry Fister's company under the command of Col. Nicholas Hussecker [Ref: A-261].

STOUFER, Elias. Non-Enroller who was fined by the Committee of Observation in April, 1776 [Ref: E-248].

STOUT, John. Private who enlisted on May 20, 1778 [Ref: A-323].

STOVER, Jacob. Non-Enroller who was fined by the Committee of Observation in April, 1776 [Ref: E-248].

STOVER, John. Non-Enroller who was fined by the Committee of Observation in April, 1776 [Ref: E-248].

STOWFER, Daniel. Associator in December, 1775 [Ref: E-173]. Juror to the Oath of Allegiance in 1778 [Ref: C-29].

STRADFORD, Valentine. Associator in December, 1775 [Ref: E-173]. Juror to the Oath of Allegiance in 1778 [Ref: C-29].

STRAYLY, Wentle. Private in the German Regiment, muster roll dated October 23, 1776 [Ref: A-264].

STRESNER, John. Soldier from Frederick County who was wounded at the Battle of Germantown while serving in the 7th Maryland Regiment [Ref: F-475].

STRICER, John. Private in Capt. Beatty's company, 7th Maryland Regiment, enlisted December 3, 1776 and discharged January 6, 1780 [Ref: A-311].

STRICKER, George (1732-1810). Served on the Committee of Observation in 1775 [Ref: I-85]. Associator in December, 1775 [Ref: E-172]. Gave money in the amount of 5 lbs. 15 sh. 4 p. for arms and ammunition for the militia in 1775 [Ref: E-62]. Chosen to serve on the Committee of Observation on September 12, 1775 [Ref: E-302]. Resident of Catoctin Hundred. Appointed by the Committee of Correspondence to solicit subscriptions in 1775 to purchase arms and ammunition [Ref: I-86]. Captain in the militia on September 2, 1775 [Ref: B-126]. Captain in Gen. William Smallwood's Maryland Regiment, January 14, 1776. Lieutenant Colonel of the German Regiment on July 17, 1776, and resigned on April 29, 1777. Juror to the Oath of Allegiance in 1778 [Ref: C-29]. Provided wheat for the military in June, 1782 [Ref: R-521]. "Col. George Stricker, of the Revolutionary Army, was the descendant of Swiss immigrants who settled in North Carolina at an early period of our colonial history. His mother was a native of one of the French districts of Switzerland. His first wife was named Springer, the mother of all his children; his second wife, it is said, was the mother of John V. L. McMahon, of Baltimore. Colonel Stricker removed to Frederick some time prior to the Revolution, and when the war broke out he raised a company in the neighborhood and repaired to the scene of military operations. He commanded under General Smallwood, and in 1776 was stationed at Annapolis. At Long Island [New York] so great was the havoc in his company that scarcely a single member escaped being wounded or killed. In the mean time, he had been promoted to the lieutenant-colonelcy of the German Battalion, and continued in that position until the death of the colonel, when, considering himself ill treated in the promotion of Baron Hanseigger to the chief command, resigned his commission and left the army. Subsequently, he was elected a member of the Maryland Legislature. He removed to an estate in the vicinity of Wheeling, West Virginia, where he died on November 29,

1810, age 78." [Ref: F-455, F-471, F-479]. Father of Gen. John Stricker of the War of 1812 fame (who was also a soldier in the Revolutionary War). [Ref: E-302].

STRICKER, John. "Born in Frederick on February 15, 1759, and served as a cadet in Capt. George P. Keeport's company, German Battalion, of which his father was lieutenant colonel, until commissioned an officer in Boctar's artillery, in which he rose to the rank of captain. He was at the Battles of Trenton, Princeton, Brandywine, Germantwon, Monmouth, and others, and accompanied Gen. Sullivan on his expedition against the Indians. He was sent from New Jersey with the Hessians captured at Trenton under his charge to Frederick, Maryland. He was present at the execution of Major Andre, within a few paces of the gallows. At the close of the war he married the daughter of Gunning Bedford at Philadelphia. About the same time Commodore Barney married Ann, another daughter of Gunning Bedford. In 1783, Capt. Stricker removed to Baltimore and associated himself in business with Commodore Barney. He took a keen interest in the organization of the militia, and himself formed and trained one of the earliest commands in Baltimore. He was soon made brigadier general and accompanied Gen. Samuel Smith as second in command of Baltimore troops on the expedition for the suppression of the Whisky Insurrection in 1794. In 1801 he was made naval agent for Baltimore and held the position for many years. General Stricker was a Republican, or Anti-Federalist, and was bitterly censured by the friends of Hanson and others for his course as commander of the State militia during the terrible riots which culminated in the death of Gen. Lingan at the Baltimore City jail. During the attack on Baltimore in 1814 by the British troops under the command of Gen. Ross, Gen. Stricker commanded the brigade which was sent forward to check the enemy's advance, and performed this difficult task with rare discretion and success. In November, 1814, Gen. Stricker resigned, owing to the appointment of Robert Goodloe Harper, an inferior in rank, to the major generalship vacated by the resignation of Gen. Smith. He was elected to the State Senate in 1820, but declined, and Reverdy Johnson was chosen in his place. In 1824 he was a member of the committee to receive Gen. Lafayette, and in 1825, on the death of General Harper, the major generalship was tendered him, but was declined on the score of ill health. He died on June 23, 1825." [Ref: F-455, F-456]. He was an Associator in December, 1775 [Ref: E-173], and Juror to the Oath of Allegiance in 1778 [Ref: C-29].

STRINE, Adam. "Draught," May to December 10, 1781, and "marched to Annapolis." [Ref: A-653]. "John Adam Strein and wife Susanna had a son John William Strein baptized at Rocky Hill in 1784. Adam and Peter Strine (over age 45) were the only Strine heads of families in eastern Frederick County in the census of 1800." [Ref: O-262].

STRISER, John. Private who enlisted on July 1, 1776, in Capt. Peter Mantz's company; marched from Frederick Town to Leonardtown, and from there to Philadelphia, arriving August 23, 1776 [Ref: A-47].

STROAM, Henry. Private in the German Regiment, muster roll dated October 23, 1776. "Henry Straam" was a private in the German Regiment; discharged July 17, 1779 [Ref: A-264].

STROUB, Simon. Associator in December, 1775 [Ref: E-172]. Juror to the Oath of Allegiance in 1778 [Ref: C-29].

STRYT, Godfrey. Associator in December, 1775 [Ref: E-173]. Juror to the Oath of Allegiance in 1778 [Ref: C-29]. He died testate in 1782, leaving no heirs, but bequest some of his money to the Rocky Hill Church (and a few named friends). [Ref: M-6:29].

STUART, George. Private stationed at Fort Frederick in June, 1778 [Ref: A-328].

STRUCK, Anthony. Loaned $300 for the use of the State of Maryland in June, 1780 [Ref: V-520].

STUDDLEMIER, George. Private in the German Regiment, 1776, in Capt. Henry Fister's company under the command of Col. Nicholas Hussecker [Ref: A-261].

STUDEBAKER, Christina. See "Peter Grossnickle," q.v.

STUDER, Philip. Associator in December, 1775 [Ref: E-173]. Juror to the Oath of Allegiance in 1778 [Ref: C-29].

STUDEY, Peter. Juror to the Oath of Allegiance in March, 1778 [Ref: S-266, but not listed in Ref: C-30].

STUFFLE, Fettea. Private who was enlisted on July 20, 1776 by Capt. Jacob Good [Ref: A-46].

STULL, Anna Catherine. See "George Devilbiss," q.v.

STULL, Christiana. See "Ninian Beall," q.v.

STULL, Christopher (Middle Monocacy). Appointed by the Committee of Correspondence to solicit subscriptions in 1775 to purchase arms and ammunition [Ref: I-86]. Captain in the 1st Battalion of militia on November 29, 1775, and captain in the 33rd Battalion of militia on March 3, 1777 [Ref: E-50, and Z-368, which states his name was "Christo. Stull" and B-126, which states "Christian Stull" was a captain in the 37th Battalion of militia on April 27, 1779]. He also enrolled as an

Associator in December, 1775 [Ref: E-172], and signed as a Juror to the Oath of Allegiance in 1778 [Ref: C-29]. Christopher Stull died testate in 1790, naming wife Philippina and children Adam, John, Jacob, Catharine and Magdalene. Executors were Philippina Stull and Joseph Staley, her brother [Ref: M-7:188, M-7:189]. Also, one Christopher Stull petitioned the General Assembly under the Act of May 12, 1780, stating that he had been a non-juror to the Oath of Allegiance and Fidelity in 1778 due to "ignorance" and now desired relief under the Act and to take the Oath [Ref: L-101].

STULL, Daniel. 1st lieutenant in the Upper District Militia of Frederick [now Washington] County in 1776 [Ref: A-48]. Captain in the 7th Maryland Regiment from December 10, 1776, until September 13, 1778, when he resigned [Ref: A-248].

STULL, John (Elizabeth Hundred). Appointed by the Committee of Correspondence to solicit subscriptions in 1775 to purchase arms and ammunition [Ref: I-86]. Served on the Committee of Observation in 1775 [Ref: I-85]. Associator in December, 1775 [Ref: E-172]. Gave money in the amount of 19 lbs. 19 sh. 4 p. for arms and ammunition for the militia in 1775 [Ref: E-63]. Colonel of the 32nd Battalion of militia on January 6, 1776 [Ref: B-126]. Served in the House of Delegates from the Upper District in 1776 [Ref: F-476, F-479]. Juror to the Oath of Allegiance in 1778 [Ref: C-29]. One John Stull died testate in 1788, leaving a wife (not named) and children Jacob, Christopher, Laurence, Cathrean, Margarett, Mary, Barbary, Caty, Magdalene, Christina, and Susannah [Ref: M-7:135].

STULL, Laurance [Laurence]. Corporal in Capt. Joseph Wood, Jr.'s company of militia on November 29, 1775 [Ref: E-53]. Private in the Middle District Militia in 1776, Capt. Valentine Creager's company [Ref: A-72]. Petitioned the General Assembly under the Act of May 12, 1780, stating he had been a non-juror to the Oath of Allegiance and Fidelity in 1778 due to "ignorance" and now desired relief under the Act and to take the Oath [Ref: L-101].

SULGAR, George. Drafted on June 2, 1783 [Ref: B-168].

SULLIVAN, Andrew. Associator in December, 1775 [Ref: E-172]. Juror to the Oath of Allegiance in 1778 [Ref: C-29].

SULLIVAN [SULAVAN], Cornelius. Associator in December, 1775 [Ref: E-173]. Juror to the Oath of Allegiance in 1778 [Ref: C-29].

SULLIVAN [SULIVAN, SULIVANE], Philip. Private in the 1st Maryland Regiment in 1781, and served in the Southern Army of the United States under Lt. William Lamar in the late Capt. Beatty's company.

Record indicates he was an orderly in the hospital in July, 1781 [Ref: A-392]. One "Philip Sulivane" was a private who enlisted on July 25, 1776 [Ref: A-49].

SUMMERS, John. Private in the German Regiment in 1776 [Ref: A-266]. "John Summers, taylor" died testate in 1780, leaving wife Ann a lot in Westminster, money to his children John, Jacob, Mary, and land in Baltimore County to his grandson John Summers [Ref: M-5:167].

SUMMERS, Margaret. See "Martin Clabaugh," q.v.

SUMMERS, Thomas. Associator in December, 1775 [Ref: E-172]. Juror to the Oath of Allegiance in 1778 [Ref: C-29]. Private who served in the 2nd Maryland Regiment and was referred to as an "old soldier" in 1778 [Ref: A-294].

SUMMERS, Valentine. Corporal in Capt. Michael Troutman's company of militia on November 29, 1775 [Ref: E-51]. "Valentine Sommer" was paid for services rendered to the military in 1779 [Ref: V-151].

SWAIN, Timothy. Fifer in Capt. Charles Beatty's militia company on November 29, 1775 [Ref: E-51]. Associator, December, 1775 [Ref: E-173]. Juror to the Oath of Allegiance in 1778 [Ref: C-29]. Paid for services rendered to the military in December, 1779 [Ref: V-45].

SWAN, Asa. See "Aeneas Campbell, Jr.," q.v.

SWAN, John (Elizabeth Hundred). Appointed by the Committee of Correspondence to solicit subscriptions in 1775 to purchase arms and ammunition [Ref: I-86].

SWANK, David. Corporal in the Skipton District Militia under Capt. Thomas Waring on April 16, 1776 [Ref: B-167, D-1814].

SWANNICK, Thomas. Militia substitute on June 8, 1778 [Ref: A-325].

SWARTZ, Andrew. Petitioned the General Assembly under the Act of May 12, 1780, stating that he had been a non-juror to the Oath of Allegiance and Fidelity in 1778 due to "ignorance" and now desired relief under the Act and to take the Oath [Ref: L-101].

SWEARINGEN, Charles (Marsh Hundred). Served on the Committee of Observation in 1775 [Ref: I-85]. Appointed by the Committee of Correspondence to solicit subscriptions in 1775 to purchase arms and ammunition [Ref: I-86]. "Charles Swearingan" gave money in the amount of 4 lbs. 1 sh. 9 p. for arms and ammunition for the militia in 1775 [Ref: E-62]. "Charles Swearingen" was 1st major in the 36th Battalion of militia on April 20, 1776 [Ref: B-127, W-356].

SWEARINGEN, Joseph. Associator in December, 1775 [Ref: E-173], and a Juror to the Oath of Allegiance in 1778 [Ref: C-29]. Paid for his recruiting services for the 7th Maryland Regiment on January 11, 1780

[Ref: R-260, V-54]. One "Gen. Joseph Swearingen, late of the Ninth Brigade Militia, died on July 15, 1825." [Ref: F-472].

SWEARINGEN, Joseph. Private in horse troops in 1781 [Ref: B-167].

SWEARINGEN, Samuel. Ensign in Capt. Elias Harden's Company, 29th Battalion, on May 14, 1776. [Ref: D-1814, W-424, and B-127, which latter source notes that the battalion was in Montgomery County and Samuel Swearingen had served in Capt. Harding's company in 1777].

SWEARINGEN, Van Jr. "Van Swearingen, Jr." was an Associator in December, 1775 [Ref: E-173]. "Van Swearingan" gave money in the amount of 15 sh. for arms and ammunition for the militia in 1775 [Ref: E-63]. He assisted the Committee of Observation in "handing about" the Association paper by having it "lodged" [at his place of business in Middle Town] in March, 1776 [Ref: E-244]. Juror to the Oath of Allegiance in 1778 [Ref: C-29]. Captain in the 33rd Battalion of militia on January 17, 1777, and captain in the 34th Battalion on April 19, 1781 [Ref: B-131]. County Coroner in 1777 [Ref: F-476]. "Van Swearingen" provided wheat for the military in May, 1782 [Ref: R-515]. He died testate in 1784, leaving a wife Margaret and ten children: Joseph, Thomas, John, Isaac Stull, Eleanor, Margaret, Mary, Drusilla, Eleanor, and Elizabeth [Ref: M-6:121].

SWEARINGEN, Weltner Van. Served on the Committee of Observation in 1775 [Ref: I-85].

SWEET, George (Lower Manor Hundred). Non-Enroller who was fined by the Committee of Observation in April, 1776 [Ref: E-248].

SWIGART, Mary Ann. See "Peter Leatherman," q.v.

SWINEHEART, Gabriel. Non-Enroller who was fined by the Committee of Observation in April, 1776 [Ref: E-248].

SWINEHEART, Jacob. Non-Enroller who was fined by the Committee of Observation in April, 1776 [Ref: E-248].

SWINEHEART, Peter. Associator in December, 1775 [Ref: E-172]. Juror to the Oath of Allegiance in 1778 [Ref: C-29].

SWINGLEY [SWIMLEY, SWINGLE], George. "George Swingley" gave money in the amount of 1 lb. 14 sh. 1 p. for arms and ammunition for the militia of Frederick County in 1775 [Ref: E-63]. "George Swingle" was a captain in 2nd Battalion of militia of Washington County on June 22, 1778 [Ref: B-127, Z-145]. "George Swimley" was appointed by the Committee of Correspondence to solicit subscriptions to purchase arms and ammunition in Marsh Hundred in 1775 [Ref: I-86].

SWISER, Matthias (Pipe Creek Hundred). Non-Enroller who was fined by the Committee of Observation in May, 1776 [Ref: E-248].

SWISER, Rudolf (Pipe Creek Hundred). Non-Enroller who was fined by the Committee of Observation in April, 1776 [Ref: E-248].

SWISHER, Anthony. See "William Pope," q.v.

SWITZER, Frederick. Private in the German Regiment, on muster roll dated October 23, 1776. "Fredrik. Schwidzer" was a private in the German Regiment and was discharged on July 16, 1779 [Ref: A-264].

SWITZER, Jacob. Drafted on June 2, 1783, and "agreed to join and pay money in lieu of his service; paid 9.5 pounds." [Ref: B-169].

SYBERT, Peter. Private stationed at Fort Frederick on June 27, 1778, in Capt. John Kershner's company, and guarding prisoners of war [Ref: A-328].

SYDER, Frederick. Associator in December, 1775 [Ref: E-172]. Juror to the Oath of Allegiance in 1778 [Ref: C-29].

SYDEY, Adam. Private in Capt. John Kershner's company; guarded prisoners at Fort Frederick, 1777-1778; discharged June 8, 1778 [Ref: A-328].

SYPHERD, John. See "John Ciferd," q.v.

SYPHERD, Matthias. Served in the Maryland Line and applied for a pension (S35092) in Frederick County in 1818, aged 56, stating he had no family. [Ref: T-3410, J-25].

SYPHERS, John. Sergeant in Capt. Benjamin Ogle, Jr.'s company of militia on November 29, 1775 [Ref: E-53].

TABLER, Jacob. Private in the German Regiment, 1776, in Capt. Henry Fister's company under the command of Col. Hussecker [Ref: A-261].

TAGER, George. Associator in December, 1775 [Ref: E-173]. Juror to the Oath of Allegiance in 1778 [Ref: C-29].

TAILER, Matthias. Juror to the Oath of Allegiance in 1778 [Ref: C-29].

TALBOT, Joseph (Linganore Hundred). Non-Enroller who was fined by the Committee of Observation in April, 1776 [Ref: E-248].

TALBOT, Notley. Private who enlisted on July 18, 1776 [Ref: A-49].

TALLAWER, William. Private who enlisted March 2, 1778 [Ref: A-315].

TALLIBOUGH, Samuel. Associator in December, 1775 [Ref: E-173]. Juror to the Oath of Allegiance in 1778 [Ref: C-29].

TANNEHILL, Adamson. "Born in Frederick County, Maryland, in 1752, and served as a captain through the Revolutionary War. He removed to Pennsylvania and settled near Pittsburgh. He was a Justice of the Peace at the breaking out of the Whisky Rebellion [1794] and firmly opposed that outbreak. He served as a brigadier-general in the War of 1812, and was a representative in Congress from 1812 to 1815. He died at Grant's Hill in 1817." [Ref: F-469, and T-3418, which source indicates some discrepancy in his date of birth (May 23, 1750 vs. 1752) and date of death (December 23, 1820 vs. July 7, 1817). One should consult original records for more clarification].

TANNEHILL, Carlton. "Carlton Tannehill" was a 1st lieutenant in the 34th Battalion of militia on May 15, 1776 in Capt. Philip Meroney's company. "Carleton Tanyhill, or Carlton Tannehill" was a captain on December 28, 1776 [Ref: B-127, W-426, X-555]. "Carleton Tannehill" was a Justice of the Peace in 1777 [Ref: F-476].

TANNEHILL, James. Private who enlisted on August 5, 1776, in the Flying Camp under Capt. Philip Meroney [Ref: A-45, and N-30:112, which latter source spelled his surname "Tannenhill"]. A "James Tannehill applied for a pension (S14643) on September 10, 1832, in Daviess County, Kentucky, aged 72, stating he lived in Frederick County, Maryland, at time of enlistment and he moved to Somerset County, Pennsylvania in 1796. Twenty-three years later he moved to Virginia and in 1824 he moved to Kentucky." Also, a "James Tanehill served in the Pennsylvania Line and received a disability pension (S3771) from March 4, 1789. He was in Beaver County, Pennsylvania in 1820." [Ref: T-3418].

TANNER, Edward. Substitute on June 13, 1781, and marched with Capt. Dyer [Ref: D-1814].

TANNER, Thomas. Associator in December, 1775 [Ref: E-174]. Juror to the Oath of Allegiance in 1778 [Ref: C-29]. Enlisted March 26, 1781 for 3 years; marched with Capt. Lynn [Ref: D-1814].

TARMAN, Benjamin. Militia substitute on June 13, 1778 [Ref: A-326].

TARRANCE, William S. Associator in December, 1775 [Ref: E-173]. Juror to the Oath of Allegiance in 1778 [Ref: C-29].

TATE, John. Private in the Skipton District Militia under Capt. Thomas Waring on April 16, 1776 [Ref: B-167, D-1814].

TAWNEY, Frederick. Associator in December, 1775 [Ref: E-174]. Juror to the Oath of Allegiance in 1778 [Ref: C-29]. He is mentioned in Ref: A-253 as being a soldier in the German Regiment, "but not on any musters." Also, see "Frederick Downey," q.v.

TAWNEY, John. 2nd lieutenant in Linganore Battalion of militia in June, 1778 [Ref: H-17, and B-130, which spelled his name "Towney"].

TAWNEY, Michael. Associator in December, 1775 [Ref: E-174]. Juror to the Oath of Allegiance in 1778 [Ref: C-29]. 2nd lieutenant in the Linganore Battalion of militia on June 22, 1778 [Ref: H-17, B-128, Z-145]. One Michael Tawney died testate in 1784, leaving a wife Christina (daughter of Conrad Oringdurf [Orndorff], then living) and four minor children, Christina, Elizabeth, Abraham, and Jacob Tawney [Ref: M-6:124].

TAYLOR, Alexander. Private in the German Regiment until discharged on August 9, 1779 [Ref: A-265].

TAYLOR, Charles Philpott. See "Charles Philpott (taylor)," q.v.

TAYLOR, James. Private in the 7th Maryland Regiment from December 10, 1776, until September 13, 1777, when reported "deserted," but he joined again on September 26, 1777, and was discharged in May, 1778 [Ref: A-252].

TAYLOR, James. Enlisted on April 8, 1781, for 3 years, and marched with Capt. Lynn [Ref: D-1814].

TAYLOR, James. Enlisted on May 16, 1781, for 3 years, and marched with Capt. Lynn [Ref: D-1814].

TAYLOR, John. Private who enlisted on July 13, 1776 [Ref: A-43].

TAYLOR, Joseph. Non-Enroller who was fined by the Committee of Observation in April, 1776 [Ref: E-248].

TAYLOR, Richard. Private in the 1st and 7th Maryland Regiments in 1780, and served in the Southern Army of the United States under Lt. Lamar in the late Capt. Beatty's company [Ref: A-253, A-389].

TAYLOR, Samuel. Private in the militia in July, 1776 [Ref: A-42]. Fifer in the 1st and 7th Maryland Regiments, 1778, and served in the Southern Army of the United States under Lt. Lamar in the late Capt. Beatty's company until his death in June, 1781 [Ref: A-389]. Another Samuel Taylor was a private in the 7th Maryland Regiment from May 20, 1778, until "deserted" on June 2, 1778 [Ref: A-253].

TAYLOR, Thomas. Non-Enroller who was fined by the Committee of Observation in April, 1776 [Ref: E-248]. One Thomas Taylor was a private in the 7th Maryland Regiment from March 13, 1777, until May 3, 1780, when he was discharged [Ref: A-252].

TAYLOR, William. Associator in December, 1775 [Ref: E-173]. Private, 1st Maryland Regiment, who served in the Southern Army of the United States under Lt. William Lamar in the late Capt. Beatty's company in 1780. Record indicates he "deserted" some time in 1781 [Ref: A-391]. Juror to the Oath of Allegiance in 1778 [Ref: C-29].

TEENER, Henry. Private who enlisted on July 1, 1776 in Capt. Peter Mantz's company; marched from Frederick Town to Leonardtown, and from there to Philadelphia, arriving August 23, 1776 [Ref: A-47].

TEETER, Jacob. Private who enlisted on July 25, 1776 [Ref: A-51].

TEETER, John. Private who enlisted on July 25, 1776 [Ref: A-51].

TEMAN, Benjamin. Associator in December, 1775 [Ref: E-173]. Juror to the Oath of Allegiance in 1778 [Ref: C-29]. (Note: Could be the same person as "Benjamin Terman," q.v.)
TEMBLIN, John. Private who enlisted on April 28, 1778 [Ref: A-321].
TENNALY, George. Private who enlisted July 1, 1776 in Capt. Peter Mantz's company; marched from Frederick Town to Leonardtown, and from there to Philadelphia, arriving August 23, 1776 [Ref: A-47].
TENNER, Jacob. Juror to the Oath of Allegiance in 1778 [Ref: C-29].
TERMAN, Benjamin. Associator in December, 1775 [Ref: E-174]. Juror to the Oath of Allegiance in 1778 [Ref: C-29]. (Note: Could be same as "Benjamin Teman," q.v.)
TERTESEBAUGH, Peter. Corporal in Capt. Peter Mantz's company of militia on November 29, 1775 [Ref: E-50].
TEST, John. Private who was enlisted on July 20, 1776, by Capt. Jacob Good [Ref: A-46]. Also, John Test was a private who enlisted August 5, 1776 in the Flying Camp under Capt. Philip Meroney [Ref: A-45, N-30:112].
TESTILL, Joshua (living with George French). Non-Enroller who was fined by the Committee of Observation in April, 1776 [Ref: E-248].
THAD, William Edward. 1st lieutenant in Capt. N. Bruce's company of militia, 3rd Battalion, on November 29, 1775 [Ref: E-54, B-128].
THATCHER, William. See "Matthias Young," q.v.
THESER, John. Associator in December, 1775 [Ref: E-173]. Juror to the Oath of Allegiance in 1778 [Ref: C-29]. Also, see "John Thrasher (Thresher)," q.v.
THOM, Heinrich. See "Henry Tomm," q.v.
THOMAS, Alexander. Non-Enroller who was fined by the Committee of Observation in April, 1776 [Ref: E-248].
THOMAS, Anthony. Private who was enlisted on July 20, 1776 by Capt. Jacob Good [Ref: A-46].
THOMAS, Barbara Shafer. See "Abraham Hargett (Hargis)," q.v.
THOMAS, Benjamin. Lieutenant in Capt. James Mackall's company of militia in the 34th Battalion on June 11, 1776 [Ref: E-239, B-128, W-476]. Benjamin Thomas (1741-1816) was a son of Mark [Ref: O-232].
THOMAS, Betsy and Richard. See "Roger Johnson," q.v.
THOMAS. Francis. He testified regarding prisoner delivery in Frederick County on July 22, 1782 [Ref: R-530].
THOMAS, Gabriel. Juror to the Oath of Allegiance in March, 1778 [Ref: S-266, but not listed in Ref: C-30].

THOMAS, Hugh. Associator in December, 1775 [Ref: E-173]. Juror to the Oath of Allegiance in 1778 [Ref: C-29].

THOMAS, Jacob. Associator in December, 1775 [Ref: E-173]. Juror to the Oath of Allegiance in 1778 [Ref: C-29]. Provided wheat for the military in May, 1782 [Ref: R-515].

THOMAS, John (June 21, 1728, Schifferstadt, Germany - 1801). A son of Michael Thomas and Anna Veronica Lang, and grandson of Christian Thomas, John married Catherine Getzendanner (1734-c1812) in 1753 in Frederick County, and both are buried in Adamstown, Maryland. Their son, Philip Henry Thomas (1765-1828), married Ann Margaret Remsburg (1767-1811) on November 22, 1790 [Ref: T-2087, U-2903]. John Thomas was an ensign in the militia on November 9, 1776, under Capt. James Mackall [Ref: B-128, X-432]. Juror to the Oath of Allegiance in March, 1778 [Ref: S-266, but not listed in Ref: C-30].

THOMAS, Nathan. "Nathan Thomas" was drafted on June 2, 1783 [Ref: B-168]. "Nathan G. Thomas" petitioned to form the horse troops in 1781 [Ref: B-167]. "Nathaniel Thomas" was a private in the horse troops in June, 1781 [Ref: B-168].

THOMAS, P. Henry. Served on the Committee of Observation in 1775 [Ref: I-85].

THOMAS, Philip Dr. (June 11, 1747 - April 25, 1815). Born near Chestertown in Kent County, Dr. Philip Thomas studied medicine in Philadelphia and moved to Frederick County in 1769 [Ref: E-303]. Captain of a militia company on November 29, 1775 [Ref: E-50]. Gave money in the amount of 44 lbs. 14 sh. 7 p. for arms and ammunition for the militia in 1775 and also collected 20 lbs. 18 sh. 9 p. in 1775 [Ref: E-62, E-63]. Resident of Fredericktown Hundred, he was appointed by the Committee of Correspondence to solicit subscriptions in 1775 to purchase arms and ammunition [Ref: I-86]. Chosen to serve on the Committee of Observation in 1775 [Ref: E-302, I-85]. Associator in December, 1775 [Ref: E-173]. (This name appeared twice on the list of Associators). Took the Oath of Allegiance in 1778 [Ref: C-29]. Captain in the 4th Battalion of militia on November 29, 1775, and captain in the 34th Battalion on March 7, 1776 [Ref: B-128]. Colonel of the 4th Battalion in 1776 [Ref: E-58]. County Lieutenant of Frederick County, 1781-1783, and also "marched to Annapolis." [Ref: A-653, B-169]. Was paid for wintering a cow for the military in 1782 [Ref: R-517]. Medical Purveyor for Frederick County from 1781 to 1783. Elector for President George Washington. One of the founders and President of the Medical and Chirurgical Faculty of Maryland, 1801-1815 [Ref: E-303]. Judge of the Orphans' Court in 1779-1780 [Ref: F-480]. "Dr. Philip Thomas, father of Hon. John Hanson Thomas [1776 - May 2, 1815], was born near Chestertown [Kent County] on June 11, 1747, and removed to Frederick, commencing the practice of medicine in that town on August 1, 1769, after having studied for four years under Dr. Vandyke... Dr. Thomas took an active and prominent part in the Revolutionary War. He was the chairman of the Frederick County Committee of Safety, one of the Presidential electors who voted for Gen. Washington at the first election, the first President of the Medical Society of Maryland, and died on April 25, 1815." [Ref: F-459, F-471].

THOMAS, Samuel. Non-Enroller who was fined by the Committee of Observation in April, 1776 [Ref: E-248].

THOMAS, William. He testified regarding prisoner delivery in Frederick County on July 22, 1782 [Ref: R-530].

THOMASON, Ezekiel. Private in the 7th Maryland Regiment from June 3, 1778, until August 16, 1780, when reported missing (after the Battle of Camden, South Carolina). [Ref: A-253].

THOMLONG, Nicholas. Associator in December, 1775 [Ref: E-173]. Juror to the Oath of Allegiance in 1778 [Ref: C-29]. Also, see "Nicholas Tom Long," q.v.

THOMPSON, James. Private who enlisted on July 24, 1776 [Ref: A-50].

THOMPSON, Jeremiah. Private in the 7th Maryland Regiment on August 8, 1777, and "deserted" (no date given), and again from January 20, 1778, until February 8, 1778, when "deserted" again [Ref: A-253].

THOMPSON, John. Associator in December, 1775 [Ref: E-173]. (This name appeared twice on the list of Associators). One subscribed to the Oath of Allegiance in 1778 [Ref: C-29]. One was a private in the 6th Maryland Regiment from June 2, 1777, through January 1, 1780 [Ref: A-252].

THOMPSON, John Baptist. 1st lieutenant in the Middle District Militia in 1776 [Ref: A-44, A-46].

THOMPSON, Lambert. Private who enlisted on January 12, 1778 [Ref: A-314].

THOMPSON, Nathan. Private who enlisted July 22, 1776 [Ref: A-49].

THOMPSON, Richard. Associator in December, 1775 [Ref: E-173]. Juror to the Oath of Allegiance in 1778 [Ref: C-29].

THOMPSON, William. Private who enlisted July 25, 1776 [Ref: A-50].

THOMS, William. Associator in December, 1775 [Ref: E-173]. Juror to the Oath of Allegiance in 1778 [Ref: C-30].

THOMSON, Thomas. In November, 1779, Barbara Thomson, wife of Thomas Thomson, a soldier in the Continental service, petitioned the court of Frederick County for relief for herself and family (number of children not stated), and she was granted 200 lbs. [Ref: Q-6835].

THOPARL, Thomas. Associator in December, 1775 [Ref: E-174]. Juror to the Oath of Allegiance in 1778 [Ref: C-30].

THORNBOURGH, Francis. Private who enlisted on July 24, 1776 [Ref: A-50].

THRASHER, Benjamin. Associator in December, 1775 [Ref: E-173]. Juror to the Oath of Allegiance in 1778 [Ref: C-30].

THRASHER, John. Ensign in Capt. William Luckett, Jr.'s company of militia, 4th Battalion, on November 29, 1775 [Ref: E-55, B-129]. Associator in December, 1775 [Ref: E-174]. Juror to the Oath of Allegiance, 1778 [Ref: C-30, and S-266, which latter source spelled his name "Jno. Thresher."].

THRASHER, Thomas. Associator in December, 1775 [Ref: E-173]. Juror to the Oath of Allegiance in 1778 [Ref: C-30].

THRELKELD, Joseph. Served on the Committee of Observation in 1775 [Ref: I-85].

TICE, Nicholas. Served on the Committee of Observation in 1775 [Ref: I-85]. Associator in December, 1775 [Ref: E-173]. Quartermaster of the 4th (or 34th) Battalion on January 6, 1776 [Ref: E-58, B-129, I-95]. On July 13, 1776, he was noted by Col. Charles Beatty as being "a man of credit and may be depended on." [Ref: A-47]. Juror to the Oath of Allegiance in 1778 [Ref: C-30]. Loaned $600 for the use of the State of Maryland in June, 1780 [Ref: V-520]. Deputy Quartermaster General on September 14, 1779 [Ref: Z-525].

TILENBROCK, Christian. Associator in December, 1775 [Ref: E-174]. Juror to the Oath of Allegiance in 1778 [Ref: C-30].

TIMBERLIN, John (Burnt House Woods Hundred). Non-Enroller who was fined by the Committee of Observation in June, 1776 [Ref: E-248]. "John Timblin" was a private in the German Regiment from April 28, 1778, through August 1, 1780 [Ref: A-253]. "John Timhen" (Timbin?) was a private in the German Regiment and served in Battle of White Plains on September 5, 1778, under Lt. Col. Weltner [Ref: A-267].

TIME, Rolat. Associator in December, 1775 [Ref: E-173]. Juror to the Oath of Allegiance in 1778 [Ref: C-30].

TIMILY, Leonard. Ensign in Capt. James Mackall's company of militia in 1776 [Ref: E-65].

TIMLY, John. Private who enlisted on June 23, 1778, for 3 years [Ref: A-326].

TINER, Elizabeth C. See "Aeneas Campbell, Jr.," q.v.

TINK, John. Associator in December, 1775 [Ref: E-173]. Juror to the Oath of Allegiance in 1778 [Ref: C-30].

TIPER [TIPES?], Jacob. Juror to the Oath of Allegiance in March, 1778 [Ref: S-266, but not listed in Ref: C-30].

TIPTON, Silvester. Private in the Skipton District Militia under Capt. Thomas Waring on April 16, 1776 [Ref: B-167, D-1814].

TNILER [sic], Matthias. Associator in December, 1775 [Ref: E-173].

TOBIRY, Thomas. Private who enlisted on July 1, 1776 in Capt. Peter Mantz's company; marched from Frederick Town to Leonardtown, and from there to Philadelphia, arriving August 23, 1776 [Ref: A-47].

TODD, William. Militia substitute on June 4, 1778 [Ref: A-325].

TOGEL, John. Associator in December, 1775 [Ref: E-173]. Juror to the Oath of Allegiance in 1778 [Ref: C-30].

TOMER, Christian. Associator in December, 1775 [Ref: E-173]. Juror to the Oath of Allegiance in 1778 [Ref: C-30].

TOMKINS, Silus. Private who enlisted on July 18, 1776 [Ref: A-50].

TOMLIN, Grove. Private who enlisted on July 18, 1776 [Ref: A-49].

TOMLINSON, Hugh. Corporal in Capt. John Carmack's company of militia on November 29, 1775 [Ref: E-56]. Associator in December, 1775 [Ref: E-174]. Juror to the Oath of Allegiance, 1778 [Ref: C-30].

TOMLINSON, Thomas. Associator in December, 1775 [Ref: E-173]. Juror to the Oath of Allegiance in 1778 [Ref: C-30].

TOMLINSON, Zadock. Militia substitute on June 8, 1778 [Ref: A-325].

TOMM, Henry. Private in the German Regiment, muster roll dated October 23, 1776 [Ref: A-264]. "Heinrich Thom, born in Germany, received communion at the Lutheran Church in Frederick in 1765." [Ref: O-118].

TOMS, Samuel. Non-Enroller who was fined by the Committee of Observation in April, 1776 [Ref: E-248]. "Samuel Toms (born 1744), the father of Jacob Toms, Sr., may have been in Middletown Valley since a Catherine Toms (died 1770), mother of Samuel, bought a tract called 'Humbert's Delight' in 1759. A tract called 'Tom's Bottom' [is in] the western part of later Middletown... Serving in the Revolution from Washington County [Maryland] are recorded Adam, George, Mathias and Michael Tom (without the 's')." [Ref: O-118].

TOMS, William. Non-Enroller who was fined by the Committee of Observation in April, 1776 [Ref: E-248].

TONGUE, Richard. Private who enlisted on August 5, 1776, in the Flying Camp, under Capt. Philip Meroney [Ref: A-45, and N-30:112, which later source spelled his name "Robert Tounge"].

TOPHAM, Benjamin. See "Benjamin Popham," q.v.

TOSHMAN, Martin. Paid for services rendered to the military in December, 1779 (nature of the services not stated). [Ref: V-44].

TOUGHMAN, John. Private who was enlisted on July 20, 1776, by Capt. Jacob Good [Ref: A-46]. Juror to the Oath of Allegiance in March, 1778 [Ref: S-266, but not listed in Ref: C-30].

TOWNEY, John. See "John Tawney," q.v.

TOWNSEND, William. Private, 1st Maryland Regiment, 1778, who served in the Southern Army of the United States under Lt. William Lamar in the late Capt. Beatty's company until he was discharged on May 2, 1781 [Ref: A-391].

TRACE, William. Private who was enlisted on July 20, 1776, by Capt. Jacob Good [Ref: A-46].

TRACY, Philip. Private who enlisted on July 22, 1776 [Ref: A-49].

TRAIL, Archibald. Private who enlisted July 29, 1776 [Ref: A-43].

TRAIL, Nathan. Private who enlisted on July 29, 1776 [Ref: A-44].

TRAINER, Patrick. Private who enlisted May 20, 1778 [Ref: A-323].

TRAMMEL, Nicholas. Private in the Skipton District Militia under Capt. Thomas Waring on April 16, 1776 [Ref: B-167, D-1814].

TRAMMEL, Philip. Private in the Skipton District Militia under Capt. Thomas Waring on April 16, 1776 [Ref: B-167, D-1814].

TRENDALL, Michael. Private in the 7th Maryland Regiment from April 20, 1778, until August 16, 1780, when reported missing (after the Battle of Camden, South Carolina). [Ref: A-253].

TRESLER, Frederick. Soldier in the Maryland and Pennsylvania Lines who "applied for his pension (R10696) on November 21, 1842, in Chambersburg, Franklin County, Pennsylvania, stating he was born in 1749 in Northampton County, Pennsylvania, and lived in Frederick County, Maryland, at the time of his first enlistment. He moved to York County, Pennsylvania, and also enlisted there." [Ref: T-3537].

TRESSEL, Goodhert. Private in Capt. John Kershner's company who guarded prisoners at Fort Frederick, 1777-1778, and subsequently reported as "deserted" on June 2, 1778 [Ref: A-328].

TRESSNER, Jacob. Juror to the Oath of Allegiance in March, 1778 [Ref: S-266, but not listed in Ref: C-30].

TRIPLER, Michael. Associator in December, 1775 [Ref: E-173]. Juror to the Oath of Allegiance in 1778 [Ref: C-30].

371

TRISNER, John. Private in the 7th Maryland Regiment. Disabled at the Battle of Germantown, his invalid pension commenced on April 12, 1785, and ceased on November 1, 1789 [Ref: A-630, A-631].

TROSS, Nicholas. Associator in December, 1775 [Ref: E-174]. Juror to the Oath of Allegiance in 1778 [Ref: C-30].

TROUT, Edward. Private in the militia in July, 1776 [Ref: A-42].

TROUT, Henry. Drafted on June 13, 1781, and provided a substitute [Ref: D-1814].

TROUT, Jacob. 2nd lieutenant in Capt. Christopher Stull's company of militia, 1st Battalion, on November 29, 1775 [Ref: E-50, B-130]. Captain in the 37th Battalion on April 27, 1779 [Ref: H-16, Z-368].

TROUT, Michael. Juror to the Oath of Allegiance in March, 1778 [Ref: S-266, but not listed in Ref: C-30].

TROUTMAN, Michael. Captain of militia company in the 4th Battalion on November 29, 1775 [Ref: E-51, B-130]. Associator in 1775 who was appointed "to hand about the Association paper" in the Upper Kittockton [Catoctin] Hundred [Ref: E-173, E-305]. Juror to the Oath of Allegiance in 1778 [Ref: C-30]. "Michael Trout, potter" died testate in 1780, leaving wife Catherine, son Henry (in Pennsylvania), son John, and Elizabeth (youngest child and a minor). [Ref: M-5:167].

TROUTMAN, Peter. Corporal in Capt. Robert Wood's company of militia on November 29, 1775 [Ref: E-53].

TROXEL, Abraham. Private who enlisted on July 19, 1776 [Ref: A-51]. "Abraham Troxal, Jr." was a private at Fort Frederick in June, 1778 [Ref: A-328]. "Abraham Troxell of Washington County served in the Revolution." [Ref: O-51].

TROXEL, Jacob. Soldier in the Virginia Line who applied for pension (R10717) in 1832 in Marion County, Tennessee, and died on July 1, 1843, in Dekalb County, Alabama. Part of his application states he was born in 1759 in Frederick County, Maryland, and moved when age 13 to Loudoun County, Virginia. After six years they returned to Maryland for 4 years and then moved to Tennessee (and other states thereafter). His widow Elizabeth was alive in 1853. [Ref: T-3542].

TROXEL, John. "John Troxel" was a private who enlisted on July 19, 1776 [Ref: A-51]. "John Troxall" took the Oath of Allegiance, 1778 [Ref: C-30]. "John Troxall" was an Associator in December, 1775 [Ref: E-173]. One "(John) Peter Troxell (1719-1799) emigrated 1737 to Egypt village near Bethlehem, Pennsylvania, and in 1776 came to Tom's Creek [in Frederick County, Maryland]. He is buried at Tom's Creek Church." [Ref: O-50].

TROXELL, Elizabeth. See "John Zimmerman," q.v.

TRUAX, Margaret. See "James Smith," q.v.

TRUCK, George. Associator in December, 1775 [Ref: E-173]. Juror to Oath of Allegiance in 1778 [Ref: C-30].

TRUCK [TRUCKS, TRUX], John. "John Truck" was a sergeant in the German Regiment until discharged on July 24, 1779 [Ref: A-253]. "On March 1, 1826, the Treasurer of the Western Shore was directed to pay 'John Truck' of Frederick County, the half pay of a sergeant, as a further remuneration for services in the Revolutionary War." On March 9, 1826, "a land warrant for 50 acres for state land in Allegany County was granted for soldiers who served in the Maryland Line during the war, and to which he is entitled." [Ref: G-400]. On March 6, 1832, the Treasurer was directed to pay to "Elizabeth Trux," of Frederick County, widow of "John Trux," a soldier of the Revolutionary War, during widowhood, half yearly, half pay of a sergeant, for the service rendered by her husband during said war. [Ref: G-401]. "John Trucks, or Trux, applied for a pension on July 21, 1825, in Frederick County, aged 69, with a wife Catherine, aged about 40, and these children were living at home: Hetty, aged 20; Harriet, aged 19; John, aged 12; William, aged 10. John had married Catherine E. Flannigan on June 10, 1811, in Frederick County, and had died on November 11, 1831. His widow applied for a pension (W11658) on July 1, 1856, at Philadelphia, Pennsylvania, aged 68. She also applied for his bounty land warrant no. 53666-160-55 in 1856. [Ref: T-3543, J-25].

TRUCK [TRUCKS, TRUX], Peter. Fifer in the Middle District Militia in 1776 in Capt. Valentine Creager's company [Ref: A-72].

TUCKER, Alexander. Private in the militia, July, 1776 [Ref: A-42].

TUCKER, Benjamin. Private in the militia, July, 1776 [Ref: A-42].

TUCKER, John. Private in the militia in July, 1776 [Ref: A-42].

TUCKER, William. Drummer in Capt. Charles Beatty's company of militia on November 29, 1775 [Ref: E-51]. Associator in December, 1775 [Ref: E-173]. Juror to the Oath of Allegiance, 1778 [Ref: C-30].

TUCMAN, John. Corporal in Capt. Jacob Ambrose's company of militia on November 29, 1775 [Ref: E-54].

TUDDEROW, Jacob. See "Jacob Tutterow" and "Jacob Dutterer," q.v.

TUFF, John. Private who enlisted on May 5, 1778 [Ref: A-322].

TULLY, Aquilla. Soldier in the Maryland Militia who pensioned on October 4, 1814. [Ref: J-9, but was not found in Ref: T-3553].

TUMBLESON, Thomas. Private in the Middle District Militia in 1776 in Capt. Valentine Creager's company [Ref: A-72].

373

TURNER, Charles. Juror to the Oath of Allegiance in March, 1778 [Ref: S-266, but not listed in Ref: C-30].

TURNER, James. Associator in December, 1775 [Ref: E-173]. Juror to the Oath of Allegiance in 1778 [Ref: C-30].

TURNER, John. Private who enlisted on July 29, 1776 [Ref: A-43]. Served in the 7th Maryland Regiment from May 8, 1778, until he was reported dead in November, 1778 [Ref: A-253].

TURNER, Philip. Ensign in the Linganore Battalion of militia on December 28, 1776, under Capt. Brashears [Ref: B-130, X-555, Y-55].

TURNER, Soloman. Private who enlisted on March 2, 1778 or May 12, 1778. in the 7th Maryland Regiment, and served in Capt. William Beatty's company in 1779 [Ref: A-253, A-311, A-314]. Private in the 1st Maryland Regiment, 1780, and served in the Southern Army of the United States under Lt. William Lamar in the late Capt. Beatty's company. Reported missing on August 16, 1780 (after the Battle of Camden, South Carolina), he apparently survived the battle as he was transferred to the light infantry on March 12, 1781, and later discharged from the service on May 12, 1781 [Ref: A-253, A-391].

TURNER, Solomon Jr. Militia substitute from May to December 10, 1781, and "marched to Annapolis." [Ref: A-653].

TURNER, William. Petitioned the General Assembly under the Act of July 3, 1780, stating that he had been a non-juror to the Oath of Allegiance and Fidelity in 1778 due to "ignorance" and now desired relief under the Act and to take the Oath [Ref: L-101].

TUTEN, William. Private who enlisted January 29, 1778 [Ref: A-314].

TUTTERER, Baltis. Provided wheat for the military in May, 1782 [Ref: R-512, R-515].

TUTTEROW [TUDDEROW], Jacob. Corporal in the German Regiment, 1776, in Capt. Henry Fister's company under the command of Col. Nicholas Hussecker [Ref: A-261]. Also, see "Jacob Dutterer," q.v.

TUTTRO, John. Fifer in Capt. Christopher Stull's company of militia on November 29, 1775 [Ref: E-50]. Also, see "John Dutterer," q.v.

TUTZBAUGH, George. Associator in December, 1775 [Ref: E-173]. Juror to the Oath of Allegiance in 1778 [Ref: C-30].

TWINER, John. Private who enlisted on July 1, 1776 in Capt. Peter Mantz's company, and marched from Frederick Town to Leonardtown, and from there to Philadelphia, arriving on August 23, 1776 [Ref: A-47]. Also, John Twiner was a private who enlisted on May 6, 1778 [Ref: A-322], and served in the 1st Maryland Regiment with the Southern Army of the United States under Lt. William Lamar in the late Capt. Beatty's company in 1781 [Ref: A-390]. "John Twiner applied for a pension (R10783) on March 20, 1825, Claiborne County, Mississippi, aged 67, stating he married Judith Peck on November 26, 1789. In 1826 his wife Juda or Judith was aged 56 and they had two sons at home, aged 21 and 12 (no names given). John died October 24, 1831, and his widow applied for a pension on September 10, 1840, aged 79, in Claiborne County, stating her husband had enlisted at Frederick Town, Maryland, and their children were: Samuel (born March 10, 1790); Elizabeth Ranserval (born November 1, 1791); Frances Davis (born March 27, 1799); Mary Willson (born February 15, 1801); George (born April 6, 1805); and, James (born November 25, 1809). A daughter Frances Webb was alive in 1852." [Ref: T-3565, T-3566].

TYCE, Henry. Private stationed at Fort Frederick on June 27, 1778, in Capt. John Kershner's company, guarding prisoners of war [Ref: A-328].

TYLER, Grace C. See "Roger Nelson," q.v.

TYLER, Harriet and William. See "George Murdock," q.v.

TYLER, W. Bradley. See "Samuel Beall White," q.v.

TYRRELL, Edward. Associator in December, 1775 [Ref: E-173]. Juror to the Oath of Allegiance in 1778 [Ref: C-30].

TYSHER, Jacob. Private stationed at Fort Frederick on June 27, 1778, in Capt. John Kershner's company, and guarding prisoners of war [Ref: A-328].

ULEGUYER, Susannah. See "James Earel," q.v.

ULREY, Christopher. Ensign in the militia, 1778-1779 [Ref: H-17].

ULRICK, Jacob. Associator in December, 1775 [Ref: E-174]. Juror to the Oath of Allegiance in 1778 [Ref: C-30].

UNGLES, Mary. See "Abraham Lakin," q.v.

UNSELD [UNSILD], John. Along with Henry Yost, he "supplied musquets and bullet moulds for the use of the province" in April, 1776 [Ref: W-308, W-400].

UNSELL, Frederick. "Soldier in the Pennsylvania Line whose widow Jane applied for a pension (W22472) on October 10, 1840, in Clark County, Illinois. Frederick was born August 25, 1765, in Frederick County, Maryland, and moved with his parents (not named) about 1770 to Little Wheeling for a short time and his father died. His mother moved to what became Washington County, Pennsylvania. After living in Virginia, Kentucky, and Indiana, Frederick died in Illinois on September 11, 1835." [Ref: T-2573].

UPPERHOUR, Harman. Drafted on June 2, 1783; "discharged, having been... unable to serve by a long fit of sickness." [Ref: B-168].

375

URNGES, Michael. Ensign in the battalion of militia under Col. James Johnson on December 28, 1776 [Ref: X-555].

VALENTINE, Jacob. Corporal in Capt. Benjamin Ogle, Jr.'s company of militia on November 29, 1775 [Ref: E-54]. A George Valentine died testate in 1783, naming a son Jacob (among others). [Ref: M-6:85].

VALENTINE, Mary. See "Jacob Mikesell," q.v.

VANDALIA COMPANY. Furnished powder and lead for use of the militia in Frederick Town on November 29, 1775 [Ref: E-60, E-61].

VANHORN, Benjamin. Non-Enroller who was fined by the Committee of Observation in April, 1776 [Ref: E-248]. Juror to the Oath of Allegiance in March, 1778 [Ref: S-266, but not listed in Ref: C-30].

VANHORN, Peter. Non-Enroller who was fined by the Committee of Observation in April, 1776, but he apparently enrolled because the fine was remitted in August, 1776 [Ref: E-248].

VAN SWEARINGEN. See "Van Swearingen, Jr." q.v.

VAN SWEARINGEN, Weltner. See "Weltner Van Swearingen," q.v.

VANTIER [VANTIRE], Daniel. Private who enlisted on April 20, 1778, and served in the 2nd Maryland Regiment [Ref: A-294, A-324].

VAUGHAN, Cornelius. Private who enlisted on May 20 or 21, 1778 [Ref: A-323]. Served in the German Regiment at White Plains on September 5, 1778, under Lt. Col. Ludwick Weltner [Ref: A-266]. Still in the 7th Maryland Regiment on August 1, 1780 [Ref: A-254].

VAUGHAN, James. Private who was enlisted on July 20, 1776, by Capt. Jacob Good [Ref: A-46].

VEATCH, Abram [Abraham]. Private in the German Regiment who was recruited by April 1, 1780, and served until reported "deserted" on November 22, 1780 [Ref: A-154, V-126].

VEATCH, Elias. Soldier in the South Carolina Line who applied for a pension (R10926) on September 4, 1832, in White County, Illinois, stating he was born May 5, 1759, in Frederick County, Maryland, and after the war he moved to the Nolichucky River in North Carolina to the part that later became Tennessee. He also lived in Kentucky, and died in Illinois on September 12, 1839 [Ref: T-3611].

VEATCH, Jacob. Private who enlisted on July 13, 1776 [Ref: A-43].

VEATCH, Jeremiah. Soldier in the Maryland Line who "applied for a pension on October 31, 1833, in Jessamine County, Kentucky, aged 74, stating he was born and raised in Frederick County, Maryland, and married Priscilla ---- on July 18, 1782, in Pennsylvania not far from Brownstown. He died on January 13, 1836, and his widow applied for a pension (W8800) on October 24, 1838, in Jessamine County, Kentucky, aged 74. Their six children were as follows: Ann (born August 4, 1783); Nathan (born July 29, 1785); Elizabeth (born February 2, 1788); Dorcas (born March 13, 1790); John W. (born July 22, 1792); and, Francis (born October 19, 1794). The widow died on February 13, 1853." [Ref: T-3612].

VEATCH, William. Private who enlisted on July 18, 1776 [Ref: A-49].

VER HULST, Frederika. See "Lindsey Delashmutt," q.v.

VERNER, Stofle. Petitioned the General Assembly under the Act of July 3, 1780, stating that he had been a non-juror to the Oath of Allegiance and Fidelity in 1778 due to "ignorance" and now desired relief under the Act and to take the Oath [Ref: L-101].

VERNOR, Adam. Petitioned the General Assembly under the Act of July 3, 1780, stating he had been a non-juror to the Oath of Allegiance and Fidelity in 1778 due to "ignorance" and now desired relief under the Act and to take the Oath [Ref: L-101].

VERREFELTZ, Jacob. Non-Enroller who was fined by the Committee of Observation in April, 1776 [Ref: E-248].

VIEILLIARD, Jacob. See "Elias Williard," q.v.

VINCENT, William. Private who enlisted on May 20, 1778, and served in the German Regiment at the Battle of White Plains on September 5, 1778, under Lt. Col. Ludwick Weltner [Ref: A-323, A-266].

VISINGER, Ludwick. Private in the German Regiment, 1776, in Capt. Henry Fister's company under the command of Col. Nicholas Hussecker [Ref: A-261].

VON WINTZ, Margaret. See "John Thomas Schley," q.v.

WACHTEL, John. Private in the German Regiment, 1776, in Capt. Henry Fister's company under the command of Col. Nicholas Hussecker until discharged on July 14, 1781 [Ref: A-261].

WADDLE, George. Soldier in the Maryland Line who "applied for a pension (S9515) on June 10, 1834, in Allegany County, Maryland, stating he was born May 14, 1757, in Frederick County, Maryland, lived there until age 12 when he moved to North Carolina. In 1775 he returned to Frederick County, Maryland, where he lived until 1780 when he moved to Allegany County, Maryland." [Ref: T-3628].

WADE, John. Private who enlisted July 18, 1776 [Ref: A-50]. This or another John Wade enlisted May 5, 1778 [Ref: A-322]. One John Wade was a private in the German Regiment at White Plains on September 5, 1778, and served under Lt. Col. Ludwick Weltner [Ref: A-267].

WAGGONER [WAGONER], Adam. Private in the Middle District Militia in 1776, Capt. Valentine Creager's company [Ref: A-72]. "Adam

Wagon" [sic] was an Associator in December, 1775 [Ref: E-174]. "Adam Wagoner" died testate in 1779, leaving a wife Sophiah and sons William and Christopher, and his brother's daughter Catherine Wagoner (minor). [Ref: M-5:138].

WAGGONER, Christian. Militia substitute from May to December 10, 1781 [Ref: A-652], and drafted on June 2, 1783 [Ref: B-168].

WAGGONER, Christopher. "Christopher Waggener" was a private in the Skipton District Militia with Capt. Thomas Waring on April 16, 1776 [Ref: B-167, D-1814]. "Christopr. Waggoner" or "Chrisr. Waggoner" was a private in the German Regiment until discharged on October 12, 1779 [Ref: A-259, A-265].

WAGGONER [WAGONER], Jacob. Private in the German Regiment until discharged on July 24, 1779 [Ref: A-259].

WAGGONER [WAGONER], John. "John Waggoner" was a sergeant in Capt. Peter Mantz's company of militia on November 29, 1775 [Ref: E-50]. "John Waganar" was an Associator in December, 1775 [Ref: E-174]. "John Waggoner" was a private in the Middle District Militia in 1776, Capt. Valentine Creager's company [Ref: A-72]. "John Wagoner" took the Oath of Allegiance in 1778 [Ref: C-30]. Paid for services rendered to the military in December, 1779 (nature of the services not stated). [Ref: V-44].

WAGGONER [WAGONER], Leonard. Associator in December, 1775 [Ref: E-174]. Juror to the Oath of Allegiance in 1778 [Ref: C-30].

WAGGONER [WAGONER], Michael Jr. Associator in December, 1775 [Ref: E-174]. Juror to the Oath of Allegiance in 1778 [Ref: C-30, S-266].

WAGGONER, Michael Sr. Juror to the Oath of Allegiance in March, 1778 [Ref: S-266, but not listed in Ref: C-30].

WAGGONER [WAGONER], Peter. Private who enlisted on July 1, 1776 in Capt. Mantz's company, marched from Frederick Town to Leonardtown, and then to Philadelphia, arriving on August 23, 1776 [Ref: A-47]. Paid for services rendered to the military in 1779 [Ref: V-151].

WAGNER, Henry. Private in the German Regiment, muster roll dated October 23, 1776 [Ref: A-264].

WAGNER, Stuffle. Private in the German Regiment, muster roll dated October 23, 1776 [Ref: A-264].

WAGON, Adam. See "Adam Waggoner," q.v.

WAKER, Edward. Private who enlisted on August 5, 1776 [Ref: A-44].

WALKER, Arthur. Associator in December, 1775 [Ref: E-174]. Juror to the Oath of Allegiance in 1778 [Ref: C-30].

WALKER, Christopher. Private who enlisted on July 19, 1776 [Ref: A-51].

WALKER, Gideon Jr. Enlisted on June 8, 1781, for 3 years, and later reported as "deserted" (no date given). [Ref: D-1814].
WALKER, John. Private who enlisted on July 20, 1776 [Ref: A-50]. "On February 16, 1820, Treasurer of the Western Shore was directed to pay to John Walker, of Frederick County, half pay of a corporal, as a further compensation for those services rendered by him during the Revolutionary War. On March 8, 1848, the State Treasurer was directed to pay to Mary Walker, widow of John Walker, a soldier of the revolution, quarterly, beginning January 1, 1848, half pay of a corporal, in consideration of her husband's services during the Revolutionary War." [Ref: G-402]. John Walker was pensioned April 4, 1818, aged 76, and died in 1831. [Ref: J-25. Also, see T-3645]. "John Walker, tobacconist, aged 77, a Revolutionary soldier, died on August 17, 1831." [Ref: F-473].
WALKER, Thomas. Associator in December, 1775 [Ref: E-174]. Juror to the Oath of Allegiance in 1778 [Ref: C-30].
WALKER, William. Private who enlisted on July 13 or July 18, 1776 [Ref: A-43, A-50].
WALLACE, Hugh. Associator in December, 1775 [Ref: E-174]. Juror to the Oath of Allegiance in 1778 [Ref: C-30].
WALLER, John. Private who enlisted in 1778 and served in the 2nd Maryland Regiment [Ref: A-294].
WALLING, John. Sergeant in Capt. John Stoner's company of militia on November 29, 1775 [Ref: E-56]. Associator in December, 1775 [Ref: E-174]. Juror to the Oath of Allegiance in 1778 [Ref: C-30].
WALLIS, John (Burnt House Woods Hundred). Non-Enroller who was fined by the Committee of Observation in June, 1776 [Ref: E-248].
WALLIS, Thomas. Associator in December, 1775 [Ref: E-174]. Private in the militia, July, 1776 [Ref: A-42]. Juror to the Oath of Allegiance in 1778 [Ref: C-30]. One "Thomas Wallace" died testate in 1779, naming his minor son William Wallace and his minor daughter Elizabeth Wallace [Ref: M-5:138].
WALLIS, William. Private who enlisted on July 19, 1776 [Ref: A-51].
WALRATH, Albert and Catharine. See "James Yule," q.v.
WALSE, Simon. Associator in December, 1775 [Ref: E-174]. Juror to the Oath of Allegiance in 1778 [Ref: C-30].
WALTENBACK, Teeter. Private who enlisted July 24, 1776 [Ref: A-50].
WALTER, Adam. Soldier in the New York Line who applied for pension (R11099) on September 11, 1832, in Onondaga County, New York, and stated he was born on April or May 15, 1753, in Frederick County,

Maryland, and lived in Montgomery County, New York, at the time of his enlistment [Ref: T-3661, with contains additional information].

WALTER, David. Associator in December, 1775 [Ref: E-174]. Juror to the Oath of Allegiance in 1778 [Ref: C-30].

WALTER, Henry. On December 3, 1776, the Treasurer of the Western Shore was ordered "to pay to Henry Walter for the Committee of Observation for Frederick County 300 pounds on account of the prisoners of war." [Ref: X-502].

WALTER, Jacob. Associator in December, 1775 [Ref: E-174]. Juror to the Oath of Allegiance in 1778 [Ref: C-30].

WALTER, Mathew. Private in the 7th Maryland Regiment from December 27, 1777, until February 8, 1778, when he "deserted." [Ref: A-258].

WALTER, Thomas. Non-Enroller who was fined by the Committee of Observation in April, 1776 [Ref: E-248].

WALTERS, Levi. Private who enlisted on July 18, 1776 [Ref: A-49].

WALTMAN, Michael. Private in the 1st and 7th Maryland Regiments who enlisted on April 15, 1778. Disabled at the Battle of Guilford Court House, his invalid pension commenced on March 29, 1784, and ceased on November 1, 1789 [Ref: A-258, A-390, A-630, A-631. This same source indicates he was still in military service in 1781]. On February 8, 1818, he was pensioned at $40 per annum under the Act of June 7, 1785, from March 4, 1789, and $64 per annum from April 24, 1816; also received the half pay of a private by order dated February 18, 1825. "On March 16, 1840, the Treasurer was directed to pay to Mary Waltman, of Frederick County, the widow of Michael Waltman, a soldier of the revolution, or her order during her life, quarterly, half pay of a private, in consideration of the services of her husband." [Ref: G-403]. Also, "Michael Waltman, or Walckman, received a disability pension from March 4, 1789, and reapplied for a pension in 1818, aged 64, stating he had married Magdalin or Mary ---- [no name given] in April, 1784, in Frederick County. He died on August 24, 1839, in Frederick County and his widow applied for his pension (W25853). She died June 29, 1847, and was buried in the Apples Church Grave Yard. Michael and Magdalin had 11 children and in 1847 the following survived: Christian or Christiana Waltman (a daughter), aged 60; John Waltman, aged 59; Henry Waltman, aged 57; Jacob Waltman, aged 55; Margaret Secrist; Mary Eldridge; Michael Waltman; and, Peter Waltman." [Ref: T-3664, J-9, F-475].

WALTON, John. Private who enlisted on April 25, 1778 [Ref: A-321].

WALTZ, George. On July 27, 1776, the Treasurer of the Western Shore was directed "to pay 500 pounds to George Waltz to be lodged with the Committee of Observation for the Upper District of Frederick County for the purchase of arms and ammunition." [Ref: X-127].

WALTZ, Martin. Associator in December, 1775 [Ref: E-174]. Juror to the Oath of Allegiance in 1778 [Ref: C-30].

WALTZ [WALTS], Peter. Private who enlisted on July 1, 1776 in Capt. Peter Mantz's company; marched from Frederick Town to Leonardtown, and from there to Philadelphia, arriving August 23, 1776 [Ref: A-47]. "Rhinehart Waltz" died testate in 1782, leaving a wife Charity and a son Peter Waltz (among other named children). [Ref: M-6:31].

WANES, Isaac. See "Isaac Wayne," q.v.

WANTZ, Francis. Loaned $300 for the use of the State of Maryland in June, 1780 [Ref: V-520].

WARBLE, John. Associator in December, 1775 [Ref: E-174]. Juror to the Oath of Allegiance in 1778 [Ref: C-30].

WARBLE, Philip. Associator in December, 1775 [Ref: E-174]. Juror to the Oath of Allegiance in 1778 [Ref: C-30, S-267].

WARD, John. Private who enlisted on July 19, 1776 [Ref: A-51].

WARD, Julia. See "Charles Elder," q.v.

WARD, Owen. Associator in December, 1775 [Ref: E-174]. Juror to the Oath of Allegiance in 1778 [Ref: C-30].

WARD, Zachariah. Private who was enlisted on July 20, 1776 by Capt. Jacob Good [Ref: A-46].

WARFIELD, Alexander. Associator in December, 1775 [Ref: E-174]. Juror to the Oath of Allegiance in 1778 [Ref: C-30]. Private in the horse troops in 1781 [Ref: B-168].

WARFIELD, Benjamin. Sergeant in Capt. David Moore's company of militia on November 29, 1775 [Ref: E-56].

WARFIELD, Charles (Burnt Woods Hundred). Appointed by the Committee of Correspondence to solicit subscriptions in 1775 to purchase arms and ammunition [Ref: I-86]. Served on the Committee of Observation in 1775 [Ref: I-85]. Associator in December, 1775, and was appointed "to hand about the Association paper" in the Burnt House Woods Hundred [Ref: E-305]. Quartermaster on November or December 28, 1776, and 1st lieutenant in the Linganore Battalion of militia on January 17, 1777 [Ref: B-133, X-555, Y-54]. Justice of the Peace in 1777 [Ref: F-476].

WARFIELD, Richard. 1st lieutenant in Linganore Battalion of militia on June 22, 1778, under Capt. Beckwith [Ref: H-17, B-133, Z-145].

WARING, Sarah C. See "Roger Nelson," q.v.

WARING [WARRING], Thomas. Captain in the Skipton District Militia on May 15, 1776 [Ref: B-134, B-167, D-1814, W-427].

WARMAN, Stephen. Private who enlisted August 5, 1776 [Ref: A-44].

WARNER, Adam. See "Peter Engel," q.v.

WARNER, George. Associator in December, 1775 [Ref: E-174]. Non-Enroller who was fined by the Committee of Observation in April, 1776 [Ref: E-248]. Juror to the Oath of Allegiance, 1778 [Ref: C-30].

WARNER, John. Non-Enroller fined by the Committee of Observation in April, 1776 [Ref: E-248]. Drafted on June 2, 1783, but reported as "discharged, being a poor invalid, and has a family." [Ref: B-169].

WARNER, John. Corporal in the 7th Maryland Regiment from July 13, 1777, to October 20, 1777, when he was reported dead [Ref: A-257].

WARNER, John Nichlos. See "Peter Engel," q.v.

WARNER, Peter Jr. Associator in December, 1775 [Ref: E-174]. Juror to the Oath of Allegiance in 1778 [Ref: C-30, S-266].

WARNER, Peter Sr. Juror to the Oath of Allegiance in March, 1778 [Ref: S-266, but not listed in Ref: C-30].

WARNER, Samuel. Sergeant in the 7th Maryland Regiment from March 25, 1777, until February, 1778, when "off rolls." [Ref: A-257].

WARNER, Stophel. Non-Enroller who was fined by the Committee of Observation in May, 1776, but he apparently enrolled because the fine was remitted in June, 1776 [Ref: E-248].

WARREN, Thomas. Served on the Committee of Observation in 1775 [Ref: I-85].

WART, John. Private who was enlisted on July 20, 1776, by Capt. Jacob Good [Ref: A-46].

WARTERS, George. Private in militia on March 9, 1776 [Ref: B-166].

WARTONBURGER, Adam. Associator in December, 1775 [Ref: E-174]. Juror to the Oath of Allegiance in 1778 [Ref: C-30].

WASHINGTON, Colonel. See "Lawrence Everhart," q.v.

WASHINGTON, George (General). See "Isaac Shelby," "Peter Fine," "Charles Beatty," "Moses Rawlings," "Otho Holland Williams," and "Benjamin T. Dulany," q.v.

WASKEY, Augustus. Juror to the Oath of Allegiance in March, 1778 [Ref: S-266, but not listed in Ref: C-30].

WASKEY [WHOSKEY], George. Associator in December, 1775 [Ref: E-174]. Juror to the Oath of Allegiance in 1778 [Ref: C-30].

WATERS, Azel (Manor Hundred). Appointed by the Committee of Correspondence to solicit subscriptions in 1775 to purchase arms and ammunition [Ref: I-86]. "Azel Waters" was an Associator in December, 1775, and "Hazel Waters" was appointed "to hand about the Association paper" in the Manor Hundred [Ref: E-174, E-305]. Served on the Committee of Observation in 1775 [Ref: I-85]. "Azel Waters" was quartermaster in the 2nd (or 37th) Battalion of militia in 1776 [Ref: E-58, B-134]. He signed as a Juror to the Oath of Allegiance in 1778 [Ref: C-30].

WATERS, John. Associator in December, 1775 [Ref: E-174]. Juror to the Oath of Allegiance in 1778 [Ref: C-30].

WATERS, Nathan. Private in the militia in July, 1776 [Ref: A-42].

WATERS, Richard. 2nd lieutenant in the Frederick Town Battalion of Militia on September 18, 1780 [Ref: B-134, V-295].

WATERS, Samuel (Linganore Hundred). Non-Enroller who was fined by the Committee of Observation in April, 1776 [Ref: E-248].

WATERS, Wevour. Private in the militia in July, 1776 [Ref: A-42].

WATERS, Z. (Sugar Loaf Hundred). Appointed by the Committee of Correspondence to solicit subscriptions in 1775 to purchase arms and ammunition [Ref: I-86].

WATKINS, Leonard (1754-1828). Enlisted in the 1st Maryland Line and served at the Battle of Long Island in 1776, where he was wounded. He returned to duty on May 23, 1778, and was promoted to sergeant in Capt. Miles' company in the 6th Maryland Line. He participated in the battles of York Island, White Plains, and Monmouth, and was honorably discharged on May 11, 1780. He married Mary Ellen Higdon (1761-1841) in 1781. In 1816 Leonard was elected a member of the Maryland Legislature (House of Delegates) from the Medley District in Montgomery County, Maryland. [Ref: U-1787, A-9, A-172, A-256].

WATKINS, Martin. Private in the German Regiment, 1776, in Capt. Henry Fister's company under the command of Col. Nicholas Hussecker [Ref: A-261].

WATKINS, Peter. Associator in December, 1775 [Ref: E-174]. Juror to the Oath of Allegiance in 1778 [Ref: C-30]. "Peter Wotkins" provided wheat for the military in June, 1782 [Ref: R-522].

WATSON, Patrick. 2nd lieutenant in Capt. Samuel Shaw's company of militia, 3rd Battalion, on November 29, 1775 [Ref: E-51, B-134]. Captain in the 33rd Battalion on January 10, 1777 [Ref: B-134].

WATTS, Robert. Served in the 38th Maryland Regiment. Resided in Frederick County and appears to have died by January 5, 1815. His heirs included Betsy, Rebecca, and Michael Watts [Ref: J-16].

WAYLON, Dennis. Private who enlisted on May 20, 1778 [Ref: A-324].

383

WAYNE, General. See "Peter Fine," q.v.

WAYNE, Isaac. Associator in December, 1775 [Ref: E-174]. Juror to the Oath of Allegiance in 1778 [Ref: C-30]. "Isaac Wanes" provided wheat for the military in May, 1782 [Ref: R-512].

WEAGLE, George. See "George Wigle (Weagle)," q.v.

WEAKLEY [WEEKLEY], Frederick. Soldier in the Maryland Line "who applied for a pension (S3643) on January 19, 1833, in Tyler County, Virginia, stating he lived 10 miles below Fredericktown, Maryland, at the time of his enlistment. He was born about 1754 in Frederick County and after the war lived in Green County, Pennsylvania, for 15 years and then moved to Tyler County, Virginia." [Ref: T-3727].

WEAKLEY, James. "James Weakly" was an Associator in December, 1775 [Ref: E-174]. "James Weakley" was a private who enlisted on August 8, 1776 [Ref: A-49]. "James Weakly" took the Oath of Allegiance in 1778 [Ref: C-30].

WEATHERBECKER, Jacob. Associator in December, 1775 [Ref: E-174]. Juror to the Oath of Allegiance in 1778 [Ref: C-30].

WEATHERFORD, Thomas. Associator in December, 1775 [Ref: E-174]. Juror to the Oath of Allegiance in 1778 [Ref: C-30].

WEATHERHOLT, Adam. Defective from the Maryland Line in 1781 [Ref: A-416].

WEAVER, Anthony. Private who enlisted in 1780 [Ref: A-345].

WEAVER, Christian. Sergeant in Capt. Charles Beatty's company of militia on November 29, 1775 [Ref: E-51]. Associator in December, 1775 [Ref: E-174]. 2nd lieutenant in the Middle District Militia on March 26, 1776, in Capt. Adlum's company [Ref: B-134, W-199, W-287]. Juror to the Oath of Allegiance in 1778 [Ref: C-30].

WEAVER, Conrad. Corporal in Capt. Philip Rodenbieler's company of militia on November 29, 1775 [Ref: E-51]. Juror to the Oath of Allegiance in March, 1778 [Ref: S-266, but not listed in Ref: C-30].

WEAVER, Jacob. Private in the German Regiment, 1776, in Capt. Henry Fister's company under the command of Col. Hussecker [Ref: A-261].

WEAVER, James. Juror to the Oath of Allegiance in March, 1778 [Ref: S-267, but not listed in Ref: C-30].

WEAVER, Magdalena Catherine. See "Thomas Gilbert," q.v.

WEAVER, Michael. Private in German Regiment; roll dated October 23, 1776 [Ref: A-264]. Discharged on July 26, 1779 [Ref: A-259, A-265].

WEAVER, Peter. Private who was enlisted on July 20, 1776, by Capt. Jacob Good [Ref: A-46].

WEAVER, Philip. Non-Enroller who was fined by the Committee of Observation in April, 1776, but apparently enrolled because he was "struck off" on April 29, 1776, and the fine remitted [Ref: E-248].

WEBB, John. Private in the 1st and 7th Maryland Regiments, having enlisted on May 4, 1778, and served in the Southern Army of the United States under Lt. William Lamar in the late Capt. Beatty's company in 1780-1781. Record indicates he was a prisoner of war in February, 1781 [Ref: A-258, A-391].

WEBB, Frances. See "John Twiner," q.v.

WEBSTER, Thomas. Private who served in the 2nd Maryland Regiment and was referred to as an "old soldier" in 1778 [Ref: A-294].

WEDDLE, Peter. Provided wheat for the military in May, 1782 [Ref: R-515].

WEDGE, Samuel. Private in the 7th Maryland Regiment who enlisted in Frederick Town on February 2, 1780; reported as "gone to Camp." He was reported as missing on August 16, 1780 (following the Battle of Camden, South Carolina). [Ref: A-258, A-334].

WEDGE, William. Private who enlisted on either March 14, 1778, or March 28, 1778 or May 2, 1778 (all three dates given in records), and served in Capt. William Beatty's company, 7th Maryland Regiment in 1779 [Ref: A-258 A-311, A-315]. Private in 1st Maryland Regiment in 1781, and served in the Southern Army of the United States under Lt. William Lamar in the late Capt. Beatty's company. The record indicates he was dead in March, 1781 [Ref: A-391].

WEEKLEY, Frederick. See "Frederick Weakley (Weekley)," q.v.

WEEMER, Matthias. Associator in December, 1775 [Ref: E-174]. Juror to the Oath of Allegiance in 1778 [Ref: C-30]. "Matheas Weimert, of Pipe Creek Hundred, farmer" died testate in 1786, leaving a wife Barbara and children Vallentin (older son), Jacob, John, and Adam [Ref: M-7:29].

WEGFIELD, Benjamin. Associator in December, 1775 [Ref: E-174]. Juror to the Oath of Allegiance in 1778 [Ref: C-30].

WEIR, Andrew. Sergeant in Capt. Normand Bruce's company of militia on November 29, 1775 [Ref: E-54].

WEIRICH, Christian. Private who enlisted July 20, 1776 [Ref: A-50].

WEIRICH, Nicholas. Private who enlisted July 20, 1776 [Ref: A-50].

WEISONG, Jacob. Private who enlisted on July 24, 1776 [Ref: A-50].

WELCH, James. Private who enlisted on April 28, 1778, and served in the 2nd Maryland Regiment [Ref: A-294, A-321].

WELDER, John. Drafted on June 2, 1783 [Ref: B-169].

WELLER, Henry. Associator in December, 1775 [Ref: E-174]. Juror to the Oath of Allegiance in 1778 [Ref: C-30, S-267].

WELLER, Jacob. Associator in December, 1775 [Ref: E-174]. Signed as Juror to the Oath of Allegiance in 1778 [Ref: C-30]. See "Philip Weller," q.v.

WELLER, Jacob Jr. Associator in December, 1775 [Ref: E-174]. Juror to the Oath of Allegiance in 1778 [Ref: C-30].

WELLER, Jo. [sic]. Associator in December, 1775 [Ref: E-174]. Juror to the Oath of Allegiance in 1778 [Ref: C-30]. One "Johannes Weller" died testate in 1792, leaving a wife Catharine and children Catharine, John, Philip, Frederick, Mathias, Magdalina, Barbara, and Jacob [Ref: M-8:137].

WELLER, John. Associator in December, 1775 [Ref: E-174]. (This name appeared three times on the list of Associators). Subscribed to the Oath of Allegiance in 1778 [Ref: C-30, S-267].

WELLER, John Jr. Juror to the Oath of Allegiance in March, 1778 [Ref: S-267, but not listed in Ref: C-30].

WELLER, Philip. Fifer in Capt. Jacob Ambrose's company of militia on November 29, 1775 [Ref: E-54]. Associator in December, 1775 [Ref: E-174]. Juror to the Oath of Allegiance in 1778 [Ref: C-30, S-267]. One Philip Weller died testate in 1779, leaving wife Juliana, sons Jacob and Daniel, daughters Elizabeth and Barbara (all minors), and brother Jacob Weller, executor. [Ref: M-5:138].

WELLS, Duckett. Associator in December, 1775 [Ref: E-174]. Juror to the Oath of Allegiance in 1778 [Ref: C-30]. Drafted on June 13, 1781 and provided a substitute [Ref: D-1814].

WELLS, James. Associator in December, 1775, and was appointed "to hand about the Association paper" in the Burnt House Woods Hundred [Ref: E-174, E-305]. Lieutenant colonel of militia on November or December 28, 1776 [Ref: B-135, X-555]. Colonel of the Linganore Battalion of militia from January 17, 1777, through 1781 [Ref: H-16, B-135, Y-54]. Signed as Juror to the Oath of Allegiance in March, 1778 [Ref: C-30].

WELLS, John. Private who enlisted in Frederick on August 10, 1780, and later marched to Annapolis under Capt. Beatty [Ref: A-344].

WELLS, Joseph. Associator in December, 1775 [Ref: E-174]. Signed as Juror to the Oath of Allegiance in 1778 [Ref: C-30]. Election Judge in November, 1776. Justice of the Orphans' Court in 1777 [Ref: F-476, F-480].

WELLS, Peter. Soldier in the Maryland Line who "applied for pension (R11317) on July 3, 1834, in Warren County, Indiana, stating he was born in 1759 in Bucks County, Pennsylvania, and lived in Frederick County, Maryland, at the time of his enlistment. After the war he lived in Maryland and then moved to Ross County, Ohio, and in 1831 he moved to Warren County, Indiana." [Ref: T-3743].

WELLS, Richard. Private who enlisted on August 5, 1776, in the Flying Camp under Capt. Philip Meroney [Ref: A-45, N-30:112].

WELLS, Robert. Private who enlisted on July 20, 1776 [Ref: A-50].

WELLS, Thomas. Associator in December, 1775 [Ref: E-174]. (This name appeared twice on the list of Associators). One subscribed to the Oath of Allegiance in 1778 [Ref: C-30].

WELLS, Valentine. Private in the 7th Maryland Regiment from March 27, 1777, until April, 1778, when "off rolls." [Ref: A-257].

WELLS, William. Associator in December, 1775 [Ref: E-174]. Juror to the Oath of Allegiance in 1778 [Ref: C-30].

WELSH, John. Private who enlisted on July 19, 1776 [Ref: A-51].

WELSH, John Pierce. Private who enlisted July 25, 1776 [Ref: A-51].

WELSH, Mark. Associator in December, 1775 [Ref: E-174]. Juror to the Oath of Allegiance in 1778 [Ref: C-30].

WELSH, Thomas. Associator in December, 1775 [Ref: E-174]. Juror to the Oath of Allegiance in 1778 [Ref: C-30].

WELTNER, Jacob. Associator in December, 1775 [Ref: E-174].

WELTNER, Lodwick. "Ludwick Weltner" was an Associator in December, 1775 [Ref: E-174]. "Ludwig Weltner" was appointed by the Committee of Correspondence to solicit subscriptions to purchase arms and ammunition in Fredericktown Hundred in 1775 [Ref: I-86]. Furnished lead for use of the militia in Frederick Town in 1775 and collected 27 lbs. 13 sh. 6 p. to buy arms and ammunition [Ref: E-61, E-63]. "Ludowick Weltner" was 1st major in the 4th (or 33rd) Battalion of militia on January 6, 1776 [Ref: E-58, B-135]. "Lodwick Weltner" was lieutenant colonel from April 9, 1777, until declared supernumerary on January 1, 1781 [Ref: A-365]. "Ludwick Weltner" took the Oath of Allegiance in 1778 [Ref: C-30]. "Lodowick Weltner" died testate in early 1782, leaving a wife Mary, and daughter Mary Heanop (wife of Frederick) and her son Frederick Heanop [Ref: M-5:170]. Also, see "Frederick Henep," "David Levy," "Thomas Pollhouse," "Casmer Hill," "Thomas Halfpenny" and "John Zimmerman," q.v.

WELTY, John. 1st lieutenant in Capt. Robert Beatty's company of militia, 3rd Battalion, on November 29, 1775 [Ref: E-55, B-135].

WELTY, John. Private in the German Regiment in 1776 [Ref: A-266]. One John Welty "applied for a pension (S39882) on January 26, 1831, in Greene County, Tennessee, stating he had enlisted in Maryland. Living with him was his wife Mary, aged 81, and daughter Ruahamy [sic], aged 22, and her infant child aged 6 or 7 months. In 1856 a Barbara Hauff, of Greene County, was one of his surviving children (others not named). Also mentioned in 1856 was a Peter Hauff (no relationship stated)." [Ref: T-3746]. A John Welty also enlisted in the German Regiment on July 17, 1778, serving to 1780 [Ref: A-258].

WERK, John. Juror to the Oath of Allegiance in 1778 [Ref: S-267; not listed in Ref: C-30].

WERNER [WERMER], Henry (Burnt House Woods Hundred). Non-Enroller who was fined by the Committee of Observation in April, 1776 [Ref: E-248]. Son of Christofell Werner who died in 1789 [Ref: M-7:185].

WERNER [WERMER], Jacob (Burnt House Woods Hundred). Non-Enroller who was fined by the Committee of Observation in April, 1776 [Ref: E-248]. Son of Christofell Werner who died in 1789 [Ref: M-7:185].

WERN, James. Associator in December, 1775 [Ref: E-174]. Juror to the Oath of Allegiance in 1778 [Ref: C-30].

WERT, Jacob. Associator in December, 1775 [Ref: E-174]. Juror to the Oath of Allegiance in 1778 [Ref: C-30].

WERT, John. Associator in December, 1775 [Ref: E-174]. (This name appeared twice on the list of Associators). One subscribed to the Oath of Allegiance in 1778 [Ref: C-30].

WERTENBAKER, Adam. Juror to the Oath of Allegiance in March, 1778 [Ref: S-267, but not listed in Ref: C-30].

WESDENHAVER, Christopher. Non-Enroller who was fined by the Committee of Observation in April, 1776 [Ref: E-248].

WEST, Joseph. Petitioned the General Assembly under the Act of May 12, 1780, stating he had been a non-juror to the Oath of Allegiance and Fidelity in 1778 due to "ignorance" and now desired relief under the Act and to take the Oath [Ref: L-101]. Provided wheat for the military in June, 1782 [Ref: R-520].

WEST, Osborn. Private who enlisted on July 29, 1776 [Ref: A-44].

WEST, Samuel (upper part of Potomac Hundred). Appointed by the Committee of Correspondence to solicit subscriptions in 1775 to purchase arms and ammunition [Ref: I-86].

WEST, Shadrick. Militia substitute from May to December 10, 1781, and "marched to Annapolis." [Ref: A-653].

WEST, Stephen. Private who enlisted on July 22 or July 25, 1776 [Ref: A-49, A-50]. Also, furnished lead for use of the militia in Frederick Town on November 29, 1775 [Ref: E-61].

WEST, Thomas. Private who enlisted on July 19, 1776 [Ref: A-51].

WETLER, Daniel. See "Frederick Wilhite (Willhide)," q.v.

WETLER, John. Ensign in the 2nd Battalion of militia on November 29, 1775, under Capt. Jacob Ambrose [Ref: E-54, B-135].

WETSELL, Jacob. Associator in December, 1775 [Ref: E-174]. Juror to the Oath of Allegiance in 1778 [Ref: C-30, S-267].

WETSELL [WETSILL, WETSEL], Peter. Non-Enroller who was fined by the Committee of Observation in April, 1776, but he apparently enrolled because the fine was remitted in June, 1776 [Ref: E-248]. Served as a 1st lieutenant in the 35th Battalion of militia on November or December 28, 1776, under Capt. Peppel [Ref: B-135, X-555].

WEYANT, Jacob. Associator in December, 1775 [Ref: E-174]. Juror to the Oath of Allegiance in 1778 [Ref: C-30]. Private in the Middle District Militia in 1776 in Capt. Valentine Creager's company [Ref: A-72].

WEYKE, Henry. Associator in December, 1775 [Ref: E-174]. Juror to the Oath of Allegiance in 1778 [Ref: C-30].

WEYMAR, Barnet. Juror to the Oath of Allegiance in March, 1778 [Ref: S-266, but not listed in Ref: C-30].

WHALEY [WHELEY], Zadock. Private in the 1st and 7th Maryland Regiments, having enlisted as a fifer on October 20, 1778, and became a private in March 1, 1779. Served in the Southern Army of the United States under Lt. Wm. Lamar in the late Capt. Beatty's company in 1780. Later reported "off the rolls" and he rejoined in 1782 [Ref: A-258, A-389].

WHALIN [WHALING], Lawrence. Private in the 7th Maryland Regiment who enlisted on May 13 or May 14, 1778, and was reported "deserted" on September 1, 1778 [Ref: A-258, A-322].

WHARTON, William. Private in the 7th Maryland Regiment from May 28, 1778, until August 16, 1780, when reported missing (following the Battle of Camden, South Carolina). [Ref: A-258].

WHEELEN, Christopher. "Christopher Wheelan" was a private in Capt. James Johnson's company of militia on November 29, 1775 [Ref: E-52]. "Christopher Wheelen" was a private who enlisted on August 5, 1776, in Capt. Philip Meroney's Flying Camp [Ref: A-45, N-30:112].

WHEELER, Ann. See "William Elder, Jr.," "William Elder, Sr.," "Guy Elder," and "Charles Elder," q.v.

WHEELER [WHALOR], Ignatius. "Ignatius Wheeler" was a sergeant in the 1st Maryland Regiment in 1780-1781, and served in the Southern Army of the United States under Lt. William Lamar in the late Capt. Beatty's company. He was "recruiting in Maryland from January to July, 1781." [Ref: A-389]. "Ignatius Mitchell Whalor" enlisted as a sergeant on February 25, 1778, and served in the 7th Maryland Regiment to at least November 1, 1780 [Ref: A-257].

WHEELER, John Hanson. Private in militia in July, 1776 [Ref: A-42].

WHEELER, Richard (Burnt House Woods Hundred). Non-Enroller who was fined by the Committee of Observation in June, 1776 [Ref: E-248]. One Richard Wheeler was a sergeant who was paid for his recruiting services for the Extra Regiment on August 17, 1780 [Ref: V-257].

WHEELER, Samuel. Private in the militia in July, 1776 [Ref: A-42]. Also, Samuel Wheeler enlisted as a private on August 5, 1776, in the Flying Camp under Capt. Philip Meroney [Ref: A-45, N-30:112].

WHEELER [WHEALER], Thomas. Sergeant in Capt. Basil Dorsey's company of militia on November 29, 1775 [Ref: E-52].

WHELAND, William. Enlisted on May 12, 1781 for 3 years; marched with Capt. Lynn [Ref: D-1814].

WHIP, Martin Jr. (Lower Monocacy Hundred). Son of Martin Whip who died testate in 1781 [Ref: M-5:169]. Non-Enroller who was fined by the Committee of Observation in June, 1776 [Ref: E-248]. "Martin Whip" provided wheat for the military in July, 1782 [Ref: R-534].

WHIP, Tobias. Son of Martin Whip who died testate in 1781 [Ref: M-5:169]. Non-Enroller who was fined by the Committee of Observation in June, 1776 [Ref: E-248].

WHITAKER [WHITTAKER], Alexander (Sugarland Hundred). Appointed by the Committee of Correspondence to solicit subscriptions in 1775 to purchase arms and ammunition [Ref: I-86]. Gave money in the amount of 1 lb. 17 sh. 6 p. for arms and ammunition for the militia in 1775 [Ref: E-62].

WHITE, Abraham. Ensign in Capt. Samuel Shaw's company in the 3rd Battalion on November 29, 1775 [Ref: E-51, B-136]. 1st lieutenant in the 33rd Battalion on January 10, 1777 [Ref: B-136]. "Abraham White, in the 88th year of his age, died June 10, 1833. A native of Pennsylvania, he emigrated to Frederick County, Maryland some time prior to the Revolutionary War, and was among the first to enter the Revolutionary Army. He was active in recruiting troops and by his exertions in a short time organized a company, of which he became captain, and which was attached to Capt. Bruce's battalion. He remained in command until

1780, when appointed by the commander of the French forces, then at Williamsburg, first conductor of the First Brigade of Artillery, with a major's commission, in which capacity he acted until the general disbandment. In 1802 he removed to Baltimore, where he resided for many years." [Ref: F-473]. He "applied for his pension (R11400) on May 18, 1833, aged 87, in Baltimore, Maryland, stating he had enlisted in Frederick County, Maryland and served in the Maryland and Virginia Lines. He was born in 1745 in York County, Pennsylvania. A son John lived in Baltimore in 1833. Abraham signed his name Abraham White, Sr." [Ref: T-3783].

WHITE, Benjamin. Enlisted on May 10, 1781, for 3 years, and later reported "deserted" (no date was given). [Ref: D-1814].

WHITE, Charles. Private who enlisted on July 19, 1776 [Ref: A-51].

WHITE, Henry. Militia substitute from May to December 10, 1781, and "marched to Annapolis." [Ref: A-653].

WHITE, James. Private in the 1st Maryland Regiment in 1781 who served in the Southern Army of the United States under Lt. William Lamar in the late Capt. Beatty's company [Ref: A-390].

WHITE, John. Private in the Middle District Militia, July 25, 1776 [Ref: A-50, A-72]. Also, John White was a private who enlisted in Frederick on August 15, 1780, but "not marched for want of pay." [Ref: A-344].

WHITE, Lewis. Substitute on June 13, 1781, for the duration of the war, and marched with Capt. Lynn [Ref: D-1814].

WHITE, Nicholas. Ensign in Capt. Peter Mantz's militia company in the 1st Battalion on November 29, 1775 [Ref: E-50, B-136, W-287]. Associator in December, 1775 [Ref: E-174]. Attested to the enrollment of Capt. Peter Mantz's company on July 13, 1776, and was noted by Col. Charles Beatty to be "a man of credit and who may be depended on." [Ref: A-47]. Captain in the 33rd Battalion of militia on January 10, 1777 [Ref: H-15, B-136].

WHITE, Patrick. Private who was enlisted on July 20, 1776, by Capt. Jacob Good [Ref: A-46].

WHITE, Philip. Associator in December, 1775 [Ref: E-174]. Juror to the Oath of Allegiance in 1778 [Ref: C-30].

WHITE, Samuel Beall. Private in the militia in July, 1776 [Ref: A-42]. Soldier in the Maryland Line who "received a pension (S25482) and in 1790 was living in Montgomery County, Maryland. Was referred to as an invalid pensioner in 1819 and his physicians (Jacob Baer and W. Bradley Tyler, of Frederick County) confirmed his disability on October 4, 1823." [Ref: T-3796].

WHITE, Thomas. Private who was enlisted on July 20, 1776, by Capt. Jacob Good [Ref: A-46].

WHITE, Walter. Commissioned 1st lieutenant of a cadet company in the Lower District on March 26, 1776 [Ref: W-287].

WHITE, William. Enlisted on February 27, 1781, for the duration of the war, but subsequently reported as "deserted." [Ref: D-1814].

WHITE, William. Private who enlisted on May 5, 1778 [Ref: A-322].

WHITEHEAD, Joseph. Associator in December, 1775 [Ref: E-174]. Juror to the Oath of Allegiance in 1778 [Ref: C-30].

WHITMORE, Abraham. Non-Enroller who was fined by the Committee of Observation in May, 1776 [Ref: E-248].

WHITMORE, Benjamin. Associator in December, 1775 [Ref: E-174]. Non-Enroller who was fined by the Committee of Observation in April, 1776 [Ref: E-248]. Juror to the Oath of Allegiance in 1778 [Ref: C-30].

WHITMORE, Benjamin Sr. Associator in December, 1775 [Ref: E-174]. Juror to the Oath of Allegiance in 1778 [Ref: C-30].

WHITMORE, David. Non-Enroller who was fined by the Committee of Observation in April, 1776 [Ref: E-248].

WHITMORE, Henry. Non-Enroller who was fined by the Committee of Observation in May, 1776 [Ref: E-248].

WHITMORE, John Jr. Associator in December, 1775 [Ref: E-174]. Juror to the Oath of Allegiance in 1778 [Ref: C-30].

WHITMORE, John Sr. Associator in December, 1775 [Ref: E-174]. Juror to the Oath of Allegiance in 1778 [Ref: C-30].

WHOSKEY, George. See "George Waskey," q.v.

WICKHAM, Eleanor. See "Guy Elder," q.v.

WICKHAM, Rebecca. See "Joseph Wood," q.v.

WICKHAM, Sabina. See "William Elder, Jr." q.v.

WICKLE, Bostian. See "Sebastian Wigle," q.v.

WICKMAN [WHICKMAN], Frederick. Associator in 1775 [Ref: E-174], and signed as a Juror to the Oath of Allegiance in 1778 [Ref: C-30].

WICKMAN, Michael. Soldier in the Maryland Line who pensioned on May 13, 1818, aged 76. [Ref: J-25, but was not found in Ref: T-3820].

WICKOUT, Malchor. Corporal in Capt. Jacob Good's company of militia on November 29, 1775 [Ref: E-51].

WICKS, Daniel. Private who enlisted on July 19, 1776 [Ref: A-51].

WIGGINS, William. Associator in December, 1775 [Ref: E-174]. Juror to the Oath of Allegiance in 1778 [Ref: C-30].

WIGLE, Francis. Non-Enroller who was fined by the Committee of Observation in April, 1776 [Ref: E-248].

WIGLE [WEAGLE], George. Private in the 7th Maryland Regiment from January 9, 1778, until March 9, 1779, when discharged [Ref: A-258].

WIGLE [WEIGLE], Joseph. Private who enlisted April 25, 1778 [Ref: A-321].

WIGLE, Sebastian. "Bostian Wickle" was an Associator in December, 1775 [Ref: E-174], and Juror to the Oath of Allegiance in 1778 [Ref: C-30]. One "Sebastian Wigle" died testate in 1784, apparently unmarried, as he left his property to the children of his brother John Wigle [Ref: M-6:123].

WIGLE, William. Non-Enroller who was fined by the Committee of Observation in April, 1776 [Ref: E-248].

WILCOX, Jacob and Catharine Ann. See "John Shellman, Jr.," q.v.

WILCOXEN, John. Private in the militia in July, 1776 [Ref: A-42].

WILCOXON, Jesse. Associator in Frederick County, 1775 [Ref: E-174]. Juror to Oath of Allegiance in 1778 [Ref: C-30]. "Jesse Willcoxen" was a 1st lieutenant on September 12, 1777, in the 29th Battalion of militia, and captain in the Montgomery County militia, Lower Battalion, on August 4, 1780 [Ref: B-137].

WILD, Thomas. Drafted on May 1, 1781, and provided a substitute [Ref: D-1814].

WILEY, James. Captain in the 35th Battalion of militia on October 4, 1779 [Ref: B-136]. Provided wheat for the military in June, 1782 [Ref: R-518].

WILEY, Margaret or Peggy. See "James Yule," q.v.

WILHELM, George. Private in the German Regiment, on muster roll dated October 23, 1776. Discharged July 17, 1779 [Ref: A-264].

WILHITE [WILLHIDE], Frederick. Corporal in the German Regiment, 1776, in Capt. Henry Fister's company under the command of Col. Nicholas Hussecker [Ref: A-261]. "Frederick Wilhide or Wilheid" applied for a pension (S35138) on April 8, 1818, in Frederick County, aged 65; however, in 1820 he again gave his age as 65, with a wife Catherine, aged about 65, and living with them was a child, Barbara, aged 24, and a grandson John, aged about 7. [Ref: T-3836, J-25]. "Major Frederick Willhide, a soldier of the Revolution, died at the residence of his son-in-law Daniel Wetler, near Creagerstown in Frederick County, in the 85th year of his age. Major Willhide on the 2nd of November, 1776, enlisted in the German Regiment of this State for 3 years, during which period he was promoted to orderly sergeant in the company to which he was attached, and faithfully served out the term of enlistment. He afterwards acted as volunteer until the close of the war. During the period of his service he was engaged in some of the hardest fought battles of the Revolution, having been present at Brandywine, Germantown, Trenton, and Monmouth, and witnessed the closing struggle at Yorktown. Major Willhide afterwards commanded a company of volunteers, and was subsequently commissioned a major in the old Maryland line, though he was never in any active service after the war." [Ref: F-473]. It should also be noted that one "Frederick Wilhide, Jr. (1723-1792) emigrated to near what later became Thurmont." [Ref: O-48].

WILHITE [WILLHIDE], George. Served in the militia during the Revolutionary War (no dates given). [Ref: O-49].

WILHITE [WILHYDE, WILLHIDE, WOOLHIDE], Henry. "Henry Wilhyde" was a sergeant in Capt. James Johnson's militia company on November 29, 1775 [Ref: E-52, O-49]. "Henry Woolhide" was an ensign in the 37th Battalion of militia on February 1, 1777 [Ref: B-139].

WILHITE [WILLHIDE], Jacob. Served in the militia during the Revolutionary War (no dates were given). [Ref: O-49].

WILHITE, John. Militia substitute from May to December 10, 1781; "marched to Annapolis." [Ref: A-653; not mentioned in Ref: O-49].

WILKES, John. See "William Blair (Captain)," q.v.

WILKINS, Thomas. Private who enlisted on July 20, 1776 [Ref: A-50].

WILL, George. Drafted on June 13, 1781, but was noted to be a "non-resident." [Ref: D-1814].

WILLETS, John (Unity Hundred). Non-Enroller who was fined by the Committee of Observation in June, 1776 [Ref: E-248].

WILLIAHR, Elias and Theobold. See "Elias and Theobold Williard."

WILLIAM, Thomas. See "Thomas Williams," q.v.

WILLIAMS, Basil. Private who enlisted on July 25, 1776 in Frederick County [Ref: A-51]. One Basil Williams was the captain of a militia company in Washington County in 1777 [Ref: B-244].

WILLIAMS, Benjamin. Private in the 7th Maryland Regiment on June 9, 1778, and fifer on February 11, 1779. Served to April 15, 1780, and was discharged. Substitute on June 13, 1781, and marched with Capt. Boyer. Joined 7th Maryland Regiment in 1782 [Ref: A-258, D-1814].

WILLIAMS, Charles. Soldier from Frederick County who died while serving in the Revolutionary War (no details given). [Ref: F-475].

WILLIAMS, Eli (Marsh Hundred). Appointed by the Committee of Correspondence to solicit subscriptions in 1775 to purchase arms and ammunition [Ref: I-86]. "Eli Williams" served on the Committee of Observation in 1775 [Ref: I-85]. "Elie Williams" was a quartermaster in the 32nd Battalion of militia on January 6, 1776 [Ref: B-137]. Election Judge in the Upper District on July 2, 1776 [Ref: F-476]. "Col. Elie Williams, brother of Gen. Otho Holland Williams, was born in Prince George's County and raised in Frederick County. He died in 1823." [Ref: U-1189].

WILLIAMS, Elisha. Ensign in the Lower District Militia [now in Montgomery County] under Capt. Edward Burgess on August 7, 1776 [Ref: A-42]. Served in the House of Delegates on August 14, 1776 [Ref: F-476, F-480]. Soldier in the Maryland Line who "was born in Frederick County, Maryland, the part that became Montgomery County, and he lived there at enlistment. He married Harriet Beale on May 6, 1784, and both were of Georgetown in the District of Columbia, where he died on December 14, 1805. His widow applied for a pension (W26019) on September 1, 1838, aged 69, and died on March 23, 1843. The only child mentioned was daughter Margaret A. Johns. Harriet's sister, Catharine Marshall, made affidavit in 1838 in Georgetown, D. C. (as did Margaret). Also mentioned was one Brooke Marshall, a Justice of the Peace (no relationship was stated)." [Ref: T-3852].

WILLIAMS, Francis. Private in the 7th Maryland Regiment, 1780, who enlisted in Frederick Town between January and April, 1780, and was subsequently reported "deserted" (no date was given). [Ref: A-334].

WILLIAMS, Gabriel. Sergeant, 1st Maryland Regiment, who enlisted on February 6, 1780, served in the Southern Army of the United States under Lt. William Lamar in the late Capt. Beatty's company, and was "recruiting in Maryland from January to July, 1781." [Ref: A-389].

WILLIAMS, Henry. Second lieutenant in Capt. William Blair's company of militia, 3rd Battalion, on November 29, 1775 [Ref: E-55, B-137]. Associator in December, 1775 [Ref: E-174]. Served as a 1st lieutenant in 35th Battalion of militia on December 28, 1776 [Ref: B-137, X-555]. Juror to the Oath of Allegiance in 1778 [Ref: C-30]. Provided wheat for the military in 1782 [Ref: R-510]. "Capt. Henry Williams, of Revolutionary fame, was the son of John and Mary Williams, who had emigrated from Chester County, Pennsylvania to Frederick County about the year 1753 and settled in the valley of Flat Run below Emmittsburg. Capt. Williams first wife was Miss McDonald (of Adams County, Pennsylvania), and his second wife was a Mrs. Cooper (whose maiden name was Witherow). Upon the outbreak of the Revolutionary War, Williams was elected 2nd lieutenant of Capt. William Blair's company, belonging to the regiment commanded by Col. John Eager Howard. When Capt. Blair fell mortally wounded at Brooklyn Heights,

Long Island, Williams took charge of the 'Game Cock' company. First lieutenant Hockersmith yielded the palm to [2nd] Lieut. Williams on account of his great popularity with the non-commissioned officers and privates of the company... The company participated in many hard fought battles [including Yorktown]... When the war was over he returned home to his estate near Emmittsburg, where, until his death, he followed the quiet pursuits of a farmer. He also took an active part in the politics of the county, the state, and nation from 1786 to 1816, but seldom appeared as a candidate for office, although frequently solicited to stand for the House of Delegates, which he invariably declined... Capt. Williams frequently filled the position of a member of the Levy Court and County Magistrate, and at the time of his death in 1821 was a Justice of the Peace... He was a firm and consistent member of the Presbyterian Church." [Ref: F-457]. See "William Elder, of Guy" and "John Ross Key," q.v.

WILLIAMS, James. Associator in December, 1775 [Ref: E-174]. Juror to the Oath of Allegiance in 1778 [Ref: C-30]. One James Williams was a private who enlisted on July 18, 1776 [Ref: A-49].

WILLIAMS, John. Private who enlisted on July 18, 1776 [Ref: A-49]. Private in the 7th Maryland Regiment who enlisted in Frederick Town between January and April, 1780 [Ref: A-334]. One John Williams petitioned the General Assembly under the Act of May 12, 1780, stating that he had been a non-juror to the Oath of Allegiance and Fidelity in 1778 due to "ignorance" and now desired relief under the Act and to take the Oath [Ref: L-101].

WILLIAMS, Joseph. Associator in December, 1775 [Ref: E-174]. Private who enlisted on July 1, 1776 in Capt. Peter Mantz's company; marched from Frederick Town to Leonardtown, and from there to Philadelphia, arriving on August 23, 1776 [Ref: A-47]. Juror to the Oath of Allegiance in 1778 [Ref: C-30].

WILLIAMS, Laurance. Private who enlisted July 25, 1776 [Ref: A-51].

WILLIAMS, Lot. Served in the Dragoons. Resided in Frederick County and died November 24, 1814. Heir was William Williams [Ref: J-16].

WILLIAMS, Matthew. Private stationed at Fort Frederick in June, 1778 [Ref: A-328].

WILLIAMS, Nathan. Ensign in the Upper District Militia of Frederick [now Washington] County, July, 1776 [Ref: A-48; not in Ref: B-137].

WILLIAMS, Otho Holland (Elizabeth Hundred). Appointed by the Committee of Correspondence to solicit subscriptions in 1775 to purchase arms and ammunition [Ref: I-86]. Colonel in the Frederick

County militia on July 23, 1776 [Ref: B-137, X-104, X-105, X-140]. Colonel of the 6th Maryland Regiment from December 10, 1776, to the end of the war, after which he was appointed Collector of the Port of Baltimore by President George Washington. He founded the town of Williamsport, Maryland, where he died in 1794 [Ref: U-1189, A-255]. Also, see "Moses Rawlings," q.v.

WILLIAMS, Thomas. Associator in December, 1775 [Ref: E-174]. Juror to the Oath of Allegiance, 1778 [Ref: C-30, S-266]. Militia substitute on June 2, 1778, and served in the 7th Maryland Regiment from July 1, 1778, to February, 1779 [Ref: A-256, A-324]. A "Thomas William" provided wheat for the military in May, 1782 [Ref: R-515].

WILLIAMS, William. Sergeant in Capt. Jacob Good's militia company on November 29, 1775 [Ref: E-51]. Juror to the Oath of Allegiance in March, 1778 [Ref: S-266, but not listed in Ref: C-30]. One William Williams "applied for a pension (S11627) in 1835 in Clermont County, Ohio, having served in Washington [then Frederick] County, Maryland." Another William Williams "who was born in Anne Arundel County, moved to Frederick County after the war, then moved to Loudon County, Virginia, and west to Pike County, Ohio, where he applied for a pension (S3587) in 1833." [For more information on these William Williams families, see Ref: T-3870].

WILLIARD, Andrew. Non-Enroller who was fined by the Committee of Observation in April, 1776 [Ref: E-248]. One "Andrew Williar (1758-1827), son of Peter Williar (1714-1794) and Elizabeth Schlim (1722-1792), married Margaret Harbaugh (1761-1819)." [Ref: O-155, O-156].

WILLIARD, Elias (1734-1819). Son of Dewalt Williard (1711-1782) and Anna Katherine Kirch (died 1813), and grandson of Jacob Vieilliard (1667-1717) and Maria Elizabeth Gordier (1682-1770), of France. Elias Williard married Rosina Gumpf (1743-1819). [Ref: O-155]. He was an Associator in December, 1775 [Ref: E-174]. "Elias Williahr" was a 2nd lieutenant in the 34th Battalion of militia on June 11, 1776, under Capt. George Poe [Ref: B-137, W-476].

WILLIARD, Henry. Associator in December, 1775 [Ref: E-174]. Juror to the Oath of Allegiance in 1778 [Ref: C-30].

WILLIARD, John. Non-Enroller who was fined by the Committee of Observation in April, 1776 [Ref: E-248].

WILLIARD, Philip. Associator in December, 1775 [Ref: E-174]. Juror to the Oath of Allegiance in 1778 [Ref: C-30].

WILLIARD [WILLIAHR], Theobold. Ensign in the 34th Battalion of militia on June 11, 1776, under Capt. G. Poe [Ref: B-137, W-476].

WILLSON, Mathew. Juror to the Oath of Allegiance in March, 1778 [Ref: S-267, but not listed in Ref: C-30].

WILLSON, Obed. Private in the militia in July, 1776 [Ref: A-42].

WILLSON, William. Ensign in the 34th Battalion of militia on May 15, 1776 [Ref: B-138, W-426].

WILSON, Edward. 2nd lieutenant in Capt. William Duvall's company of militia, 4th Battalion, on November 29, 1775 [Ref: E-54, B-138].

WILSON, James. Enlisted on March 28, 1781, for 3 years, and marched with Capt. Lynn [Ref: D-1814].

WILSON, James. Private who enlisted on July 29, 1776 [Ref: A-43].

WILSON, John. Non-Enroller who was fined by the Committee of Observation in May, 1776, but he apparently enrolled because the fine was remitted in June, 1776 [Ref: E-248]. Private who enlisted on July 29, 1776 [Ref: A-43].

WILSON, Jonathan. Served on the Committee of Observation in 1775 [Ref: I-85]. Gave money in the amount of 9 lbs 3 sh. 4 p. for arms and ammunition for the militia in 1775 [Ref: E-62]. Served as an Election Judge in the Lower District on July 2, 1776, and in the House of Delegates on August 14, 1776 [Ref: F-476, F-479].

WILSON, Nathan. Private who enlisted on July 13, 1776 [Ref: A-43].

WILSON, Richard. Private in the Skipton District Militia under Capt. Thomas Waring on April 16, 1776 [Ref: B-167, D-1814].

WILSON, Robert. Private who enlisted on July 13, 1776 [Ref: A-43].

WILSON, Samuel. 2nd lieutenant in Capt. Jacob Good's company of militia on November 29, 1775 [Ref: E-51, B-138].

WILSON, Thomas. 2nd lieutenant in Capt. Normand Bruce's company of militia, 3rd Battalion, on November 29, 1775 [Ref: E-54, B-138]. Associator in December, 1775 [Ref: E-174]. Juror to the Oath of Allegiance, 1778 [Ref: C-30].

WILSON, Thomas. Non-Enroller who was fined by the Committee of Observation in April, 1776 [Ref: E-248]. Petitioned the General Assembly under the Act of May 12, 1780, stating that he had been a non-juror to the Oath of Allegiance and Fidelity in 1778 due to "ignorance" and now desired relief under the Act and to take the Oath [Ref: L-101].

WILSON, Tobias. Substitute on June 13, 1781; marched with Capt. Dyer [Ref: D-1814].

WIMER, John. Private who was enlisted on July 20, 1776, by Capt. Jacob Good [Ref: A-46].

WINCHESTER, George. Associator in December, 1775 [Ref: E-174]. Juror to the Oath of Allegiance in 1778 [Ref: C-30].
WINCHESTER, James. Associator who was appointed "to hand about the Association paper" in Pipe Creek Hundred in 1775 and "assisted in handing about the Association paper" in 1776 [Ref: E-245, E-305]. 1st lieutenant in the Linganore Battalion of militia on January 17, 1777 [Ref: B-139].
WINCHESTER, John. Associator in December, 1775 [Ref: E-174]. Juror to the Oath of Allegiance in 1778 [Ref: C-30].
WINCHESTER, Richard. Associator in December, 1775 [Ref: E-174]. Juror to the Oath of Allegiance in 1778 [Ref: C-30].
WINCHESTER, William (Pipe Creek Hundred). Appointed by the Committee of Correspondence to solicit subscriptions in 1775 to purchase arms and ammunition [Ref: I-86]. Served on the Committee of Observation in 1775 [Ref: I-85]. Associator in December, 1775 [Ref: E-174]. (This name appeared twice on the list of Associators). Took the Oath of Allegiance in 1778 [Ref: C-30]. Captain in the Linganore Battalion of militia from January 17, 1777 through December 12, 1781 [Ref: H-17, B-138, B-139, Y-54]. "William Winchester, Sr." died testate in 1790, leaving wife Lydia and children Catherine, Mary, Elizabeth, Lydia, David, Richard, Stephen, William, and George [Ref: M-8:35].
WINDHAM, William. Private who enlisted July 22, 1776 [Ref: A-49].
WINE, Michael. Non-Enroller who was fined by the Committee of Observation in April, 1776 [Ref: E-248].
WINEHOLT, Conrad. Associator in December, 1775 [Ref: E-174]. Juror to the Oath of Allegiance in 1778 [Ref: C-30].
WINEMILLER, Henry. Associator in December, 1775 [Ref: E-174]. Juror to the Oath of Allegiance in 1778 [Ref: C-30]. One Henry Winemiller, of Frederick Town, was an heir (son) in the will of John Winemiller in 1784 [Ref: M-6:124].
WINGATE, Thomas. Drummer or fifer, 1st Maryland Regiment, enlisted on October 26, 1780, and served in the Southern Army of the United States under Lt. William Lamar in the late Capt. Beatty's company. Reported to be a prisoner of war on April 25, 1781 [Ref: A-389].
WINROE, Jacob. Associator in December, 1775 [Ref: E-174]. Juror to the Oath of Allegiance in 1778 [Ref: C-30].
WINTBOCK, Francis. Associator in December, 1775 [Ref: E-174]. Juror to the Oath of Allegiance in 1778 [Ref: C-30].
WINTZ, George. Associator in December, 1775 [Ref: E-174]. Sergeant in the German Regiment in 1776, Capt. Henry Fister's company under the

command of Col. Hussecker [Ref: A-261]. Juror to the Oath of Allegiance, 1778 [Ref: C-30]. One George Wintz died testate in 1789, leaving a wife Catherine, son John George, and his "youngest children" Jacob, Margareth, and Mary Ann [Ref: M-7:185].

WIRLEY, David. Private in Capt. John Kershner's company who guarded prisoners at Fort Frederick, 1777-1778. and was discharged June 5, 1778 [Ref: A-328].

WISE, Amelia. See "William Crom," q.v.

WISE, Davis. Paid for the services he rendered to the military in December, 1779 (nature of the services not stated). [Ref: V-44].

WISE, George. Sergeant in Capt. John Haass' company of militia on November 29, 1775 [Ref: E-53]. Associator in December, 1775 [Ref: E-174]. Another George Wise was a private in the German Regiment, muster roll dated October 23, 1776 [Ref: A-264]. Juror to Oath of Allegiance in 1778 [Ref: C-30].

WISE, Jacob. See "Philip Rodenpieller," q.v.

WISE, Thomas. Private who enlisted on August 5, 1776 [Ref: A-44].

WISCHAIR, John George. "John George Wisehaar" was an Associator in December, 1775 [Ref: E-174]. Juror to the Oath of Allegiance in 1778 [Ref: C-30]. "John George Wischair, blue dyer," died testate in 1784, leaving his wife Maria Apolonia and children John Christian, Eve Elizabeth, Cathrine [sic], Susanna, Dorothea, Anna Maria, and Anna Cathrine [Ref: M-6:121].

WISMAN, Mary Magdalene. See "Adam Kephart," q.v.

WISTMAN, Jacob. Associator in December, 1775 [Ref: E-174]. Juror to the Oath of Allegiance in 1778 [Ref: C-30].

WITHEROW, John. Associator in December, 1775 [Ref: E-174]. Juror to the Oath of Allegiance in 1778 [Ref: C-30].

WITNELL, William. Corporal in Capt. William Beatty's company of militia on November 29, 1775 [Ref: E-55].

WITSINGER, Ludwick. Private in the German Regiment until discharged on July 20, 1779 [Ref: A-259].

WITTEN, Thomas. Drafted on June 2, 1783; "discharged, being poor, having a large family, and was ill 2 months after." [Ref: B-168].

WOLER, John. Private who enlisted on May 20, 1778 [Ref: A-323].

WOLF, Andrew. "Andrew Wolfe" was an Associator in December, 1775 [Ref: E-174]. "Andrew Woolf" was a non-enroller fined by the Committee of Observation in May, 1776 [Ref: E-248]. "Andrew Wolf" was a private who enlisted on July 1, 1776, in Capt. Peter Mantz's company, and marched from Frederick Town to Leonardtown, and from there to

Philadelphia, arriving on August 23, 1776 [Ref: A-47]. "Andrew Wolf" subscribed to the Oath of Allegiance in 1778 [Ref: C-30].

WOLF, Anna Elizabeth. See "Valentine Schriner (Shriner)," q.v.

WOLF [WOOLF], George. Juror to the Oath of Allegiance in March, 1778 [Ref: S-267, but not listed in Ref: C-30].

WOLF [WOLFE], Henry. "Henry Wolfe" provided wheat for the military in May, 1782 [Ref: R-515].

WOLF, Jacob. Associator in December, 1775 [Ref: E-174]. Juror to the Oath of Allegiance in 1778 [Ref: C-30].

WOLF [WOOLF], John (1744 - June 10, 1818). "John Wolf" was enrolled as an Associator in December, 1775 [Ref: E-174]. "John Woolf" was recommended to be an ensign on October 13, 1777 [Ref: H-26, G-410]. "John Wolf" took the Oath of Allegiance in 1778 [Ref: C-30]. "John Woolf (1744-1818) married Margaret ---- in 1766 and lived at Sabillasville, Maryland. Their daughter Amelia (Emelia) Woolf (1776-1818) married Jacob Flautt (1777-1863) in 1797 at Emmitsburg." [Ref: U-2719, U-2889].

WOLF [WOOLF], Jonas. Juror to the Oath of Allegiance in March, 1778 [Ref: S-267, but not listed in Ref: C-30].

WOLF, Mary. See "Even Carmack," q.v.

WOLF, Mathias. Private who enlisted on July 20, 1776 [Ref: A-50].

WOLF [WOOLF], Peter. "Peter Woolf" was adjutant in Capt. William Duvall's company of militia on November 29, 1775 [Ref: E-54]. Juror to the Oath of Allegiance in March, 1778 [Ref: S-267, but not listed in Ref: C-30]. "Peter Wolf" was a private in the 6th Maryland Regiment from June 3, 1778, until discharged on April 1, 1779 [Ref: A-256].

WOLFE, Sarah. See "John Carmack," q.v.

WOLFORD [WOOLFORD], Conrad. "Conrad Woolford" was a corporal in Capt. William Luckett, Jr.'s company of militia on November 29, 1775 [Ref: E-55]. "Conrad Wolford" was an Associator in December, 1775 [Ref: E-174]. Juror to the Oath of Allegiance in 1778 [Ref: C-30].

WOLFRED, Thomas. Private who enlisted on May 15, 1778 [Ref: A-322].

WOLGAMOT, David. Sergeant at Fort Frederick in 1778 with Capt. John Kershner's company, guarding prisoners of war [Ref: A-328].

WOLLENSCHLAEGER, Elizabeth. See "Adam Horine," q.v.

WOLLERT, Ludwick. "Ludwick Wollert" was an Associator in December, 1775 [Ref: E-174]. "Lodwick Woller" was a private in the Middle District Militia in 1776, with Capt. Valentine Creager's company [Ref: A-72]. "Ludwick Wollert" subscribed to the Oath of Allegiance in 1778 [Ref: C-30].

WOLTZ, George. 2nd major in the 33rd Battalion of militia on January 6, 1776 [Ref: B-139].
WOOBRY, Stephen. Associator in December, 1775 [Ref: E-174]. Juror to the Oath of Allegiance in 1778 [Ref: C-30].
WOOD, Aaron. Private who enlisted on July 29, 1776 [Ref: A-44].
WOOD, Ann. See "Lindsey Delashmutt" and "Ralph Briscoe," q.v.
WOOD, Basil. Sergeant in Capt. David Moore's company of militia on November 29, 1775 [Ref: E-56]. Paid for recruiting services for the 7th Maryland Regiment on January 11, 1780 [Ref: R-260, V-54]. One Basil Wood was a private in the horse troops in 1781 [Ref: B-168].
WOOD, Benjamin. Sergeant in Capt. David Moore's company of militia on November 29, 1775 [Ref: E-56].
WOOD, Edward. Private in the Skipton District Militia under Capt. Thomas Waring on April 16, 1776 [Ref: B-167, D-1814].
WOOD, James. Corporal in Capt. David Moore's company of militia on November 29, 1775 [Ref: E-56]. Associator in December, 1775 [Ref: E-174]. Juror to the Oath of Allegiance in 1778 [Ref: C-30].
WOOD, John. Ensign in the 37th Battalion of militia on April 27, 1779 [Ref: H-16, B-139, Z-368]. Soldier in the Maryland Line who "was born on November 20, 1754, in Frederick County, Maryland, and lived there until the spring of 1783 when he moved to Berkeley County, Virginia, for 10 years. He returned to Frederick County for 2 years and then moved to Lexington, Kentucky, for three years and then moved to Warren County, Kentucky, for 14 years. In 1809 he moved to Wabash County, Illinois, where he applied for a pension on December 3, 1832. His son, John Wood, signed power of attorney on June 7, 1851, in Wabash County, stating his father, John Wood, Sr., had served as an ensign and died on November 11 or 14, 1832, in Wabash County. Soldier's widow applied for a pension (W2311) on April 21, 1853, in Edwards County, Illinois, and was still living there in 1868. Soldier had married Rachel (Greathouse) Bratton, the widow of James Bratton, on February 7, 1824, as stated by the widow, or January 27, 1824, as shown in the Edwards County records. Soldier's widow had first married to James Bratton on June 11, 1805 in Warren County, Kentucky, and he (James) later served in the War of 1812. On his return from his War of 1812 service he died on April 6, 1815, in Fort Deposit, Tennessee." [Ref: T-3931]. Also, see "Alexander Ogle," q.v.
WOOD, Jonathan. Ensign in the Linganore Battalion of militia on June 22, 1778, under Capt. G. Beckwith [Ref: H-17, B-139, Z-145]. Soldier in the Maryland Line who "applied for a pension (S11899) on September

3, 1832, in Nelson County, Kentucky, aged 85, stating he enlisted at Fredericktown, Maryland." [Ref: T-3932].

WOOD, Joseph. Associator in December, 1775 [Ref: E-174]. Juror to the Oath of Allegiance in 1778 [Ref: C-30]. One "Joseph Wood arrived in the Linganore area, coming westward by the Annapolis Road before 1748... and served on the Grand Jury of Frederick County in 1750." [Ref: O-43]. Joseph Wood died testate in 1782, leaving his wife Catherine and children Joseph Wood Jr., Sarah Wickham, Mary Hedges, Catherine Reynolds, Rachel Bernhart, Rebecca Bentley, Ruth Bentley, Robert Wood, Abraham Wood, and John Wood [Ref: M-6:30].

WOOD, Joseph Jr. (born September 17, 1743). Captain of a company of militia in the 2nd Battalion on November 29, 1775 [Ref: E-53, B-139]. Resident of Manor Hundred. Appointed by the Committee of Correspondence to solicit subscriptions in 1775 to purchase arms and ammunition [Ref: I-86]. Chosen to serve on the Committee of Observation on September 12, 1775. Associator in December, 1775 [Ref: E-174, E-302]. (This name appeared twice on the list of Associators in 1775). Lieutenant colonel in the 2nd Battalion in 1776 [Ref: E-58, H-16, I-95]. Colonel who reviewed and passed recruits in 1776 [Ref: A-45]. Court Justice on November 21, 1778 [Ref: E-303], and Justice of the Peace in 1777 [Ref: F-476]. Judge of the Court of Appeals for Frederick County on May 23, 1778 [Ref: Z-109]. Juror to the Oath of Allegiance, 1778 [Ref: C-30]. "Son of Judge Joseph Wood who lived at Woodsboro and was constable of Pipe Creek Hundred in 1749, and not to be confused with Joseph Wood of Linganore." [Ref: O-43]. "Joseph Wood, Jr. married Ann Reed on April 9, 1769, in Frederick County, and son Joseph Wood III (1781-1849) married Nancy Graybill (born 1786) on December 24, 1804, in Woodsboro." [Ref: U-2912].

WOOD, Joseph Sr. Associator in December, 1775 [Ref: E-174]. Juror to the Oath of Allegiance in 1778 [Ref: C-30]. Loaned $2,000 for the use of the State of Maryland in June, 1780 [Ref: V-520]. Also, see comment above under "Joseph Wood, Jr."

WOOD, Leonard. Private in the militia in July, 1776 [Ref: A-42].

WOOD, Martha and John. See "Alexander Ogle," q.v.

WOOD, Richard. Associator in December, 1775 [Ref: E-174]. Juror to the Oath of Allegiance in 1778 [Ref: C-30].

WOOD, Robert. Served on the Committee of Observation in 1775 [Ref: I-85]. Captain of a company of militia on November 29, 1775 [Ref: E-53]. Associator in December, 1775, and appointed "to hand about the Association paper in Upper Monocacy Hundred." [Ref: E-174, E-305].

Juror to the Oath of Allegiance in 1778 [Ref: C-30]. Loaned $1,000 for the use of the State of Maryland in June, 1780 [Ref: V-520].

WOOD, Thomas. Private in the militia in July, 1776 [Ref: A-42].

WOOD, William. Provided wheat for the military in July, 1782 [Ref: R-535].

WOODEN, John. Private who enlisted some time in 1780 [Ref: A-345].

WOODWARD, Jessee. Private who enlisted July 13, 1776 [Ref: A-43].

WOOLFORD, James. Private in the German Regiment; at White Plains on September 5, 1778, under Lt. Col. Ludwick Weltner [Ref: A-266].

WOOLHIDE, Henry. See "Henry Wilhite (Willhide)," q.v.

WOOLLICK, Henry. Ensign in the 37th Battalion of militia on January 17, 1777, under Col. James Johnson [Ref: B-139, Y-54].

WOOLRINGER, Daniel. Substitute on June 13, 1781; marched with Capt. Boyer [Ref: D-1814].

WOOLVERTON, Charles. Private in the militia on March 9, 1776 [Ref: B-166]. Juror to the Oath of Allegiance in March, 1778 [Ref: S-266, but not listed in Ref: C-30].

WOOLVERTON, Isaac. Associator in December, 1775 [Ref: E-174]. Juror to the Oath of Allegiance in 1778 [Ref: C-30, S-266].

WOOTTON, Thomas Sprigg. Collected 33 lbs. 10 sh. 4 p. for arms and ammunition for the militia in 1775 [Ref: E-62]. Served in the House of Delegates from 1773 to at least 1776 [Ref: F-476, F-479]. Served on the Committee of Observation in 1775 [Ref: I-85].

WORIEW, Daniel. Private who enlisted on May 5, 1778 [Ref: A-322].

WORLEY, David. Soldier in the Maryland Line who "applied for a pension (R11870) on April 5, 1833, in Union County, Ohio, stating he was born in 1759 in Frederick County, Maryland, and enlisted at Fort Frederick in Washington County, Maryland. He also served as a substitute for Thomas Worley (no kinship stated)." [Ref: T-3961].

WORLEY, Francis. Private in militia on March 9, 1776 [Ref: B-166].

WORT, Barbara. See "Henry Cronise," q.v.

WORTHINGTON, Nicholas and Kitty. See "Baker Johnson," q.v.

WORTSETTER, Nicholas. Associator in December, 1775 [Ref: E-174]. Juror to the Oath of Allegiance in 1778 [Ref: C-30].

WOTKINS, Peter. See "Peter Watkins," q.v.

WRIGHT, Amos. Sergeant in Capt. Basil Dorsey's company of militia on November 29, 1775 [Ref: E-52].

WRIGHT, Edward. Private who enlisted on April 20, 1777, and served in Capt. William Beatty's company, 7th Maryland Regiment, in 1779 [Ref: A-311].

WRIGHT, F. Edward. See "Peter Zollinger," q.v.

WRIGHT, Henry. Provided wheat for the military in July, 1782 [Ref: R-533].

WRIGHT, Joel. Non-Enroller who was fined by the Committee of Observation in April, 1776 [Ref: E-248].

WRIGHT, John. Private who served in the 2nd Maryland Regiment and was referred to as an "old soldier" in 1778 [Ref: A-294]. Drafted on June 13, 1781, and discharged (no reason or date was given). [Ref: D-1814].

WRIGHT, Jonathan. Non-Enroller who was fined by the Committee of Observation in April, 1776 [Ref: E-248].

WRIGHT, Joseph (Pipe Creek Hundred). Non-Enroller who was fined by the Committee of Observation in April, 1776 [Ref: E-248].

WRIGHT, Joshua. Associator in December, 1775 [Ref: E-174]. Juror to the Oath of Allegiance in 1778 [Ref: C-30].

WRIGHT, Philburd. Associator in December, 1775 [Ref: E-174]. Juror to the Oath of Allegiance in 1778 [Ref: C-30].

WRYON, Patrick. Private who enlisted April 22, 1778 [Ref: A-320].

WYCHALL, Bostian. Loaned $200 for the use of the State of Maryland in June, 1780 [Ref: V-520].

WYER, Peter. Associator in December, 1775 [Ref: E-174]. Juror to the Oath of Allegiance in 1778 [Ref: C-30].

WYLE, Elizabeth. See "Jacob Yoast (Yeast)," q.v.

WYSONGE, Philip. Private who enlisted on July 24, 1776 [Ref: A-50].

YANG, Francis. Associator in December, 1775 [Ref: E-175]. Juror to the Oath of Allegiance in 1778 [Ref: C-30].

YANTERS, Jacob. Associator in December, 1775 [Ref: E-175]. Juror to the Oath of Allegiance in 1778 [Ref: C-30].

YART, Jacob. Associator in December, 1775 [Ref: E-175]. This name appeared twice on the list of Associators. Perhaps one of them was "Jacob Yatt," q.v.

YATES [YEATES], Benjamin. Militia substitute from May to December 10, 1781, and "marched to Annapolis." [Ref: A-653]. "Benjamin Yeats (or Yeates) applied for a pension on March 10, 1834, in Highland County, Ohio, stating he was born in Baltimore County, Maryland, on April 3, 1745, and he lived in Frederick County, Maryland, when he enlisted. After the war he moved to Westmoreland County, Pennsylvania for 15 years, then moved to Adams County, Ohio for 14 years, and then moved to Highland County, Ohio. He had married Sarah Ann Robinson on July 16, 1835, at Hillsborough in Highland County, Ohio (referred to as Benjamin Yeats, Sr. in 1834). He died on January 30, 1849, at Manchester in Adams County, Ohio. His widow applied for a pension (W8202) on May 8, 1834, at Fulton in Hamilton County, Ohio. In 1855 she applied for bounty land warrant no. 3134-160-55 at Cincinnati, Ohio, aged 50 years and upwards." [Ref: T-3988].

YATES, John. Private who enlisted on July 13, 1776 [Ref: A-43]. Corporal in the 7th Maryland Regiment on April 15, 1777, sergeant on June 7, 1777, and quartermaster sergeant on August 1, 1777. Served until discharged on April 16, 1780 [Ref: A-259].

YATES [YEATS], Robert. Sergeant in Capt. William Beatty's company, 7th Maryland Regiment. Enlisted on January 8, 1777 and discharged January 6, 1780 [Ref: A-310].

YATES, Thomas. Juror to the Oath of Allegiance in March, 1778 [Ref: S-267, but not listed in Ref: C-30].

YATT, Jacob. Associator in December, 1775 [Ref: E-174]. Juror to the Oath of Allegiance in 1778 [Ref: C-30]. Also, see "Jacob Yart," q.v.

YAULET, Samuel. Private who enlisted on July 1, 1776 in Capt. Peter Mantz's company; marched from Frederick Town to Leonardtown, and from there to Philadelphia, arriving August 23, 1776 [Ref: A-47].

YEAKLY, Michael. Private in the German Regiment, muster roll dated October 23, 1776 [Ref: A-264].

YEAST, Jacob and David. See "Jacob and David Yost (Yeast)," q.v.

YESTERDAY, Christian Jr. Associator in December, 1775 [Ref: E-175]. Juror to the Oath of Allegiance in 1778 [Ref: C-30, S-267].

YESTERDAY, Christian Sr. Associator in December, 1775 [Ref: E-175]. Juror to the Oath of Allegiance in 1778 [Ref: C-30, S-267].

YESTERDAY, Martin. Juror to the Oath of Allegiance in March, 1778 [Ref: S-267, but not listed in Ref: C-30].

YINGLING, Abraham. See "Peter Engel," q.v.

YINGLING, John. "John Yingelling" was an Associator in December, 1775 [Ref: E-175], and a Juror to the Oath of Allegiance in 1778 [Ref: C-30].

YOCKLEY [YAKELY], Michael. Private in the German Regiment until discharged on July 17, 1779 [Ref: A-260, A-265].

YONTZ, George. Associator in December, 1775 [Ref: E-174]. Juror to the Oath of Allegiance in 1778 [Ref: C-30].

YORDON, Mary or Polly. See "James Yule," q.v.

YORK, William. Private in the 7th Maryland Regiment from July 12, 1778, until reported dead on September 14, 1778 [Ref: A-259].

YOST [YOAST], George. "George Yoast" enrolled as an Associator in December, 1775 [Ref: E-175], and signed as a Juror to the Oath of Allegiance in 1778 [Ref: C-30]. "George Yost" was a drummer in the 7th

Maryland Regiment from May 4, 1777, until he was discharged on May 20, 1780 [Ref: A-259].

YOST, Henry. Along with John Unseld, he "supplied musquets and bullet moulds for the use of the province" in April, 1776 [Ref: W-308, W-400].

YOST [YOAST], Herman. "Herman Yost" was captain of a company of militia on November 29, 1775, in the 1st Battalion [Ref: E-52, B-140]. "Harman Yost" was an Associator who was appointed "to hand about the Association paper" in Lower Kittockton [Catoctin] Hundred on November 29, 1775 [Ref: E-305].

YOST [YOAST, YEAST], Jacob. Fifer in Capt. Peter Mantz's militia company on November 29, 1775 [Ref: E-50]. Associator in December, 1775 [Ref: E-174]. Juror to the Oath of Allegiance in 1778 [Ref: C-30]. "Catherine Peveler, a daughter of Jacob Yeast, a soldier in the Maryland Line, applied for a pension (R11934) in August, 1853, in Mercer County, Kentucky, stating her father, Jacob Yeast, had enlisted in Frederick County, Maryland, and had married Elizabeth Wyle as early as 1774 as their oldest child was born in October, 1775. They were married in Frederick County and the soldier died on April 15, 1829, and his widow died on February 17, 1838, in Mercer County, Kentucky, leaving children Catharine Peveler and Leonard Yeast. Leonard made affidavit on March 31, 1853, in Mercer County, stating that at his mother's death she left 3 children: Leonard Yeast, Catharine Peveler, and Elizabeth Borders, and that the said Elizabeth (the eldest daughter) had since died. On April 22, 1854, Lewis Peveler, or Peaveler, made affidavit in Mercer County, aged 77, stating he was the brother-in-law of the soldier's daughter Catharine, and the soldier's younger son Jacob Yeast had died some years earlier, and he referred to soldier's and widow's 2nd child and their 4th and 5th children having died in infancy. It was also stated that the soldier's son Jacob Yeast, Jr. served in the War of 1812. Leonard Yeast stated he was aged 68 in 1854 and he was the 7th child of his parents." [Ref: T-3987].

YOST [YOAST], John Harman [Hammand]. Associator in December, 1775 [Ref: E-175]. Juror to the Oath of Allegiance in 1778 [Ref: C-30, and S-267, which latter source listed his name as "Jno. Hd. Yost."]. One "John Hd. Yost" was a captain in the 33rd Battalion of militia on March 3, 1777, in the Minuteman Company [Ref: B-140].

YOST [YOAST, YEAST], Philip. Juror to the Oath of Allegiance in March, 1778 [Ref: S-267, but not listed in Ref: C-30]. "Philip Yeast, a soldier in the Maryland Line, applied for a pension (S7986) on March 8, 1833, in Frederick County, Maryland, aged upwards of 90 years, stating he was born in Germany and had lived in America over 60 years. He enlisted in the Revolution in Frederick County." [Ref: T-3987].

YOUNG, Andrew. Associator in December, 1775 [Ref: E-174]. Non-Enroller who was fined by the Committee of Observation in May, 1776 [Ref: E-248]. Juror to the Oath of Allegiance in 1778 [Ref: C-30].

YOUNG, Barbara. See "Henry Crowell," q.v.

YOUNG, Casper. Juror to the Oath of Allegiance in March, 1778 [Ref: S-267, but not listed in Ref: C-30].

YOUNG, Daniel. Associator in December, 1775 [Ref: E-175]. Juror to the Oath of Allegiance in 1778 [Ref: C-30].

YOUNG, Gasper. Sergeant in Capt. Jacob Ambrose's company of militia on November 29, 1775 [Ref: E-54].

YOUNG, George. Associator in December, 1775 [Ref: E-175]. Juror to the Oath of Allegiance in 1778 [Ref: C-30].

YOUNG, Godfrey. Private in the German Regiment, muster roll dated October 23, 1776 [Ref: A-264].

YOUNG, Henry. Associator in December, 1775 [Ref: E-175]. Juror to the Oath of Allegiance in 1778 [Ref: C-30]. Militia substitute on June 2, 1778 [Ref: A-324]. Private in the 7th Maryland Regiment from July 1, 1778, through February, 1779 [Ref: A-259]. Militia substitute from May to December 10, 1781; "marched to Annapolis." [Ref: A-653]. One Henry Young died testate in 1791, leaving a wife Elizabeth (no children were mentioned in his will). [Ref: M-8:89].

YOUNG, Henry. Petitioned the General Assembly under the Act of May 12, 1780, stating he had been a non-juror to the Oath of Allegiance and Fidelity in 1778 due to "ignorance" and now desired relief under the Act and to take the Oath [Ref: L-101].

YOUNG, Jacob. Associator in December, 1775 [Ref: E-174, E-715]. (This name appeared twice on the list of Associators). Subscribed to the Oath of Allegiance in 1778 [Ref: C-30]. Justice of the Peace in 1777 and served in the House of Delegates, 1777-1778 [Ref: F-476, F-479].

YOUNG, James. Associator in December, 1775 [Ref: E-174]. Juror to the Oath of Allegiance in 1778 [Ref: C-30, S-267].

YOUNG, John. Drummer in Capt. John Carmack's company of militia on November 29, 1775 [Ref: E-56]. Associator in December, 1775 [Ref: E-174, 175]. (The name appeared twice on the list of Associators). Took the Oath of Allegiance in March, 1778 [Ref: C-30, S-267].

YOUNG, John Jr. Juror to the Oath of Allegiance in March, 1778 [Ref: S-267, but not listed in Ref: C-30]. Drafted on June 2, 1783 [Ref: B-169].

YOUNG, John Sr. Associator in December, 1775 [Ref: E-174]. Juror to the Oath of Allegiance in 1778 [Ref: C-30].

YOUNG, John Casper. Associator in December, 1775 [Ref: E-174]. Juror to the Oath of Allegiance in 1778 [Ref: C-30].

YOUNG, Mary Ann. See "George Scott," q.v.

YOUNG, Matthias. Soldier in the Maryland Line who "applied for a pension (R11949) on March 25, 1834, in Clinton County, Indiana, aged 74, stating he was born in 1760 in Frederick County, Maryland and lived there when he enlisted in the Revolutionary War. After the war he moved to Warren County, Ohio, and in 1829 he moved to Clinton County, Indiana. He had married Anna Barbara Christ on November 2, 1783, at Fredericktown, Maryland, and their children were: John (lived in Ohio in 1852); Matthias, Jr. (married Hannah Aughe and was deceased by 1852; their children were John, Abraham, Barbara, Matthias, Margaret, Joseph, Peter, Hannah, Catherine, and Jackson, all of Howard County, Indiana); Daniel (married Peggy Creiger and was deceased by 1852; their children were Peggy, Eliza, Samuel, John, and Mary); Polly (married Edward Ryan and lived in Tippecanoe County, Indiana, in 1852); Catherine (married John B. Coleman and both were deceased by 1852; their children were Thomas, Elizabeth, Barbara Ann, Catherine, John, James); Susanna (married Henry Kriser; she was deceased by 1852; he was living near Potosi, Wisconsin; their children were Louvisa and Mary); Henry (married Sally Keiser and he was deceased by 1852; she was living in Clinton County, Indiana; their children were Minerva, Sarah, Elizabeth, Henry, Keziah, Mary Ann, John, and Perry); David (aged 52 in 1852 and living in Ohio); Solomon (living in Indiana in 1852); Samuel (married Debora Ann Hevlin and died by 1852; their children were Jacob, Martha, Amos, Mary, and Albert; widow then married William Thatcher); and, Elizabeth (married John McCain; he was deceased by 1852; she was living in Clinton County, Indiana)." [Ref: T-4000].

YOUNG, Peter. Associator in December, 1775 [Ref: E-174]. Juror to the Oath of Allegiance in 1778 [Ref: C-30, S-267].

YOUNG, William. Private in the 1st Maryland Regiment in 1781 who served in the Southern Army of the United States under Lt. William Lamar in the late Capt. Beatty's company [Ref: A-390].

YOUNGER, George. Private in the Middle District Militia in 1776 in Capt. Valentine Creager's company [Ref: A-72]. Private in the 7th Maryland Regiment, having enlisted on March 8, 1777 [Ref: A-259].

YOUNGER, Kenard. Soldier in the Maryland Line who "applied for a pension (S32620) on September 21, 1833, in Henry County, Kentucky, stating he was born in 1760 in Frederick County, Maryland, and he lived there at time of his enlistment. In February, 1783, he moved to Fort Pitt, which later became Pittsburgh, Pennsylvania, and he also enlisted there. After the war he moved to what later became Louisville, Kentucky. By May, 1850, he had moved to Ripley County, Indiana, and he was living in the family of Joshua King, his step son-in-law. Kenard died on August 2, 1851." [Ref: T-4003, T-4004].

YOUNS, David. 2nd lieutenant in the Upper District Militia, 31st Battalion, on May 15, 1776 [Ref: B-141, W-426].

YOUTSE, Peter. Provided wheat for the military in May, 1782 [Ref: R-515].

YUDY, Philip. "Philip Yudi" was an ensign in Capt. Herman Yost's company of militia on November 29, 1775 [Ref: E-52, B-141]. "Philip Yudy" was an Associator in December, 1775 [Ref: E-175]. Juror to the Oath of Allegiance in 1778 [Ref: C-30].

YULE, James. Soldier in both the Maryland and Massachusetts Lines who "applied for a pension on April 8, 1818, at German Fields in Herkimer County, New York, stating he was born September 13, 1755, in County Antrim in Ireland, and he landed at Baltimore, Maryland, about January 1, 1774. He enlisted at Fredericktown, Maryland, in the Revolutionary War. He married Margaret Christman, daughter of Nicholas, on September 12, 1779. She was born December 27, 1758, or December 28, 1759 (both dates shown in record) in Herkimer County, New York. Soldier died on March 30, 1832, at the home of his son-in-law Albert Walrath in Danube, Herkimer County, New York, and his widow (who applied for pension W20152) died there on February 17, 1836, or between February 20 and 25, 1837 (both dates shown in record). Their children were: James (born September 12, 1780, and died August 20, 1811); Margaret or Peggy (born September 5, 1782, married a Wiley, and lived in Oppenheim, Fulton County, New York, in 1853); Nicholas (born November 5, 1784); John (born August 9, 1787, and moved to Wisconsin); George (born June 28, 1789); Catharine (born October 2, 1791, and married Albert Walrath; she died September 12, 1847); Jacob (born October 3, 1793); Mary or Polly (born April 18, 1796, married a Yordon); and, Elizabeth or Betsey (born August 31, 1800, married a House)." [Ref: T-4005].

ZACHARIUS, Daniel. Juror to the Oath of Allegiance in March, 1778 [Ref: S-267, but not listed in Ref: C-30].

ZACHARIUS, Frederick. Private in the 7th Maryland Regiment from June 4, 1778, until discharged on March 30, 1779 [Ref: A-260].

ZACHARIUS [ZACHARIAS], Jacob. Associator in 1775 [Ref: E-175]. Juror to the Oath of Allegiance in 1778 [Ref: C-30].

ZEALISON, James. Sergeant in the Skipton District Militia under Capt. Thomas Waring on April 16, 1776 [Ref: B-167, D-1814].

ZEALOR, Anna Mary. See "John Godlieb Boyer," q.v.

ZEIGLER, John. Corporal in Capt. Bayer's company in the German Regiment, served 3 years, and was discharged on July 21, 1779 at Camp Wyoming [Ref: A-270].

ZERRICK [ZERECK], Anthony. Non-Enroller fined by the Committee of Observation in April, 1776 [Ref: E-248]. "Anthony Zereck, weaver" died testate in 1782, leaving his children Daniel (the oldest son), Jacob (the second son), John, Catharine (the oldest daughter), and Betsy (the youngest daughter). [Ref: M-6:31].

ZIEGLER, Henry. Private in the German Regiment in 1776, with Capt. Henry Fister's company under the command of Col. Nicholas Hussecker [Ref: A-261].

ZIMMERMAN, George. Corporal in Capt. Ludowick Kemp's company of militia on November 29, 1775 [Ref: E-52]. Associator in December, 1775 [Ref: E-175]. Juror to the Oath of Allegiance in 1778 [Ref: C-30]. One "(John) George Zimmerman, Jr. (born 1745) was a son of (Johan) Georg (1714-1795) Zimmerman who married Ann Catharina Seidel (1724-1804) in 1742 in Pennsylvania; both buried at Frederick Lutheran Church. A son George Jr. married Margaret ----, to N. Y. City." [Ref: O-123]. Another George Zimmerman (1755-1820) was a son of (John) Michael Zimmerman (1732-1762) and he married Elizabeth Weiss (1760-1823). Both are buried at Woodsboro Reformed Cemetery. [Ref: O-39, O-112]. "George Zimmerman, a soldier in the Maryland Line, applied for his pension (R11991) on October 31, 1832, in Ontario County, New York, aged 87, stating he was born in Philadelphia County, Pennsylvania, in 1745, lived in Frederick County, Maryland, at the time of his enlistment, and he moved from there to Phelps, New York, in 1802. A daughter, Margaret Learn, made affidavit in Wayne County, New York, on May 26, 1853, aged 64. A son, George Zimmerman, signed power of attorney on December 6, 1852, in Ontario County, New York." [Ref: T-4007].

ZIMMERMAN, Jacob. Associator in December, 1775 [Ref: E-175]. Juror to the Oath of Allegiance in 1778 [Ref: C-30].

ZIMMERMAN, John. Private in the German Regiment in 1776, with Capt. Henry Fister's company under the command of Col. Nicholas

Hussecker until discharged on October 12, 1779 [Ref: A-260, A-261]. One "John Nicholas Zimmerman (1756-1826) was son of (Johan) Georg (1714-1795) Zimmerman who married Ann Catharine Seidel (1724-1804) in 1742 in Pennsylvania. John Nicholas Zimmerman married Elizabeth Troxell (born 1769), at Rocky Hill Church near Woodsboro; ran paper mill." [Ref: O-123]. On April 15, 1779, Col. Ludwick Weltner petitioned the Frederick County Court in behalf of John Zimmerman, a soldier in his regiment, and his needy family. Mrs. Zimmerman was granted 20 lbs. for herself and their two children [Ref: Q-6835]. A "John Zimmerman" was sergeant in Capt. Ludowick Kemp's militia company on November 29, 1775 [Ref: E-52]. One "(George) John Zimmerman (1755-1813) was a son of (Johan) Georg (1714-1795) Zimmerman who married Ann Catharine Seidel (1724-1804) in 1742 in Pennsylvania. A John Zimmerman married Eleanora Holtz (born 1756), at Frederick Reformed Church." [Ref: O-123]. One John Zimmerman was paid for the services he rendered to the military in December, 1779 [Ref: V-151].

ZINDORF, George. Associator in December, 1775 [Ref: E-175]. Juror to the Oath of Allegiance in 1778 [Ref: C-30].

ZIRK, Anthony. Associator in December, 1775 [Ref: E-175]. Juror to the Oath of Allegiance in 1778 [Ref: C-30].

ZISLAR, Henry. Associator in December, 1775 [Ref: E-175]. Juror to the Oath of Allegiance in 1778 [Ref: C-30].

ZOLLINGER, Peter. Captain in the militia who appeared on the 1840 list of pensioners in the 10th District of Frederick County, age 84 [Ref: J-33, J-37]. Peter Zollinger was born December 22, 1756, in Germantown, Pennsylvania, and lived in York County, Pennsylvania at the time of his enlistment. He applied for a pension (S8005) on May 23, 1833, in Frederick County, Maryland. His wife died (not named) prior to October, 1833, at which time Peter moved to Adams County, Pennsylvania, to live with his son-in-law, Zephaniah Herbert. In November, 1835, Peter returned to Frederick County, having married a woman of Maryland (name not given). He died on November 4, 1842, at the home of his daughter Barbara Carlley in McKessontown, Adams County, Pennsylvania, leaving no widow, but the following children: Elizabeth Crabbs, a widow; Barbara Carlley, the widow of Reuben R. Carlley; Mary Herbert, wife of Zephaniah Herbert; George Zollinger; and, John Zollinger, who died prior to 1851 and left a widow Ellen and 9 children [Ref: T-4007, J-37]. Elizabeth Zollinger, a daughter of Peter and Barbara Zollinger, was born on September 12, 1782, and was baptized on October 13, 1782, at the Lower Bermudian Church in Adams County,

Pennsylvania. George Zollinger, a son of Peter and Barbara Zollinger, was born on August 17, 1791, and was baptized on November 7, 1791, at Abbottstown Reformed Church in Adams County, Pennsylvania. [Ref: F. Edward Wright's *Adams County Church Records of the 18th Century*, pp. 34, 97].

ZOOK, Abraham. Associator in December, 1775 [Ref: E-175]. Juror to the Oath of Allegiance in 1778 [Ref: C-30].

Other books by the author:

A Closer Look at St. John's Parish Registers [Baltimore County, Maryland], 1701-1801
A Collection of Maryland Church Records
A Guide to Genealogical Research in Maryland: 5th Edition, Revised and Enlarged
Abstracts of the Ledgers and Accounts of the Bush Store and Rock Run Store, 1759-1771
Abstracts of the Orphans Court Proceedings of Harford County, 1778-1800
Abstracts of Wills, Harford County, Maryland, 1800-1805
Baltimore City [Maryland] Deaths and Burials, 1834-1840
Baltimore County, Maryland, Overseers of Roads, 1693-1793
Bastardy Cases in Baltimore County, Maryland, 1673-1783
Bastardy Cases in Harford County, Maryland, 1774-1844
Bible and Family Records of Harford County, Maryland Families: Volume V
Children of Harford County: Indentures and Guardianships, 1801-1830
Colonial Delaware Soldiers and Sailors, 1638-1776
Colonial Families of the Eastern Shore of Maryland
Volumes 5, 6, 7, 8, 9, 11, 12, 13, 14, and 16
Colonial Maryland Soldiers and Sailors, 1634-1734
Dr. John Archer's First Medical Ledger, 1767-1769, Annotated Abstracts
Early Anglican Records of Cecil County
Early Harford Countians, Individuals Living in Harford County, Maryland in Its Formative Years
Volume 1: A to K, Volume 2: L to Z, and Volume 3: Supplement
Harford County Taxpayers in 1870, 1872 and 1883
Harford County, Maryland Divorce Cases, 1827-1912: An Annotated Index
Heirs and Legatees of Harford County, Maryland, 1774-1802
Heirs and Legatees of Harford County, Maryland, 1802-1846
Inhabitants of Baltimore County, Maryland, 1763-1774
Inhabitants of Cecil County, Maryland, 1649-1774
Inhabitants of Harford County, Maryland, 1791-1800
Inhabitants of Kent County, Maryland, 1637-1787
Joseph A. Pennington & Co., Havre De Grace, Maryland Funeral Home Records:
Volume II, 1877-1882, 1893-1900
Maryland Bible Records, Volume 1: Baltimore and Harford Counties
Maryland Bible Records, Volume 2: Baltimore and Harford Counties
Maryland Bible Records, Volume 3: Carroll County
Maryland Bible Records, Volume 4: Eastern Shore
Maryland Deponents, 1634-1799
Maryland Deponents: Volume 3, 1634-1776
Maryland Public Service Records, 1775-1783: A Compendium of Men and Women of
Maryland Who Rendered Aid in Support of the American Cause against
Great Britain during the Revolutionary War
Marylanders to Carolina: Migration of Marylanders to
North Carolina and South Carolina prior to 1800

Marylanders to Kentucky, 1775-1825
Methodist Records of Baltimore City, Maryland: Volume 1, 1799-1829
Methodist Records of Baltimore City, Maryland: Volume 2, 1830-1839
*Methodist Records of Baltimore City, Maryland: Volume 3, 1840-1850
(East City Station)*
More Maryland Deponents, 1716-1799
*More Marylanders to Carolina: Migration of Marylanders to
North Carolina and South Carolina prior to 1800*
More Marylanders to Kentucky, 1778-1828
Outpensioners of Harford County, Maryland, 1856-1896
Presbyterian Records of Baltimore City, Maryland, 1765-1840
Quaker Records of Baltimore and Harford Counties, Maryland, 1801-1825
Quaker Records of Northern Maryland, 1716-1800
Quaker Records of Southern Maryland, 1658-1800
Revolutionary Patriots of Anne Arundel County, Maryland
Revolutionary Patriots of Baltimore Town and Baltimore County, 1775-1783
Revolutionary Patriots of Calvert and St. Mary's Counties, Maryland, 1775-1783
Revolutionary Patriots of Caroline County, Maryland, 1775-1783
Revolutionary Patriots of Cecil County, Maryland
Revolutionary Patriots of Delaware, 1775-1783
Revolutionary Patriots of Dorchester County, Maryland, 1775-1783
Revolutionary Patriots of Frederick County, Maryland, 1775-1783
Revolutionary Patriots of Harford County, Maryland, 1775-1783
Revolutionary Patriots of Kent and Queen Anne's Counties
Revolutionary Patriots of Lancaster County, Pennsylvania
Revolutionary Patriots of Maryland, 1775-1783: A Supplement
Revolutionary Patriots of Maryland, 1775-1783: Second Supplement
Revolutionary Patriots of Montgomery County, Maryland, 1776-1783
Revolutionary Patriots of Prince George's County, Maryland, 1775-1783
Revolutionary Patriots of Talbot County, Maryland, 1775-1783
Revolutionary Patriots of Worcester and Somerset Counties, Maryland, 1775-1783
Revolutionary Patriots of Washington County, Maryland, 1776-1783
*St. George's (Old Spesutia) Parish, Harford County, Maryland:
Church and Cemetery Records, 1820-1920*
St. John's and St. George's Parish Registers, 1696-1851
Survey Field Book of David and William Clark in Harford County, Maryland, 1770-1812
The Crenshaws of Kentucky, 1800-1995
The Delaware Militia in the War of 1812
*Union Chapel United Methodist Church Cemetery Tombstone Inscriptions,
Wilna, Harford County, Maryland*

www.ingramcontent.com/pod-product-compliance
Lightning Source LLC
Chambersburg PA
CBHW050327230426
43663CB00010B/1770